2004

The New School Leader for the 21st Century: The Principal

Edward H. Seifert
James A. Vornberg

A SCARECROWEDUCATION BOOK

The Scarecrow Press, Inc.
Lanham, Maryland, and Oxford
2002

A SCARECROWEDUCATION BOOK

Published in the United States of America
by Scarecrow Press, Inc.
A Member of the Rowman & Littlefield Publishing Group
4720 Boston Way, Lanham, Maryland 20706
www.scaroweducation.com

PO Box 317
Oxford
OX2 9RU, UK

British Library Cataloguing in Publication Information Available

Library of Congress Cataloging-in-Publication Data

Seifert, Edward H.
  The new school leader for the 21st century, the principal / Edward H.
Seifert, James A. Vornberg.
       p. cm.
"A ScarecrowEducation book."
Includes bibliographical references (p.) and index.
  ISBN 0-8108-4394-3 (alk. paper)—ISBN 0-8108-4393-5 (pbk. : alk. paper)
  1. School principals—United States—Case Studies. 2. Educational leadership—
United States—Case Studies. 3. School management and organization—United
States—Case studies. I. Vornberg, James A., 1943– II. Title.
  LB2831.92 .S44 2002
  371.2'102—dc21   2002005569

∞™ The paper used in this publication meets the minimum requirements of
American National Standard for Information Sciences—Permanence of Paper
for Printed Library Materials, ANSI/NISO Z39.48-1992.
Manufactured in the United States of America.

We dedicate this book to our families: Judy, Audra, Becky, and Beth; and Caroline, Scott, Lauri, Mark, Dierdre, and Jennifer. We also dedicate this book to all of those hardworking principals who are attempting to improve teaching and learning for all children.

Contents

Section V: Organizational Management and Operations

Section VI: The Politics of the Educational Environment

Preface

The structure of this book has been developed around the six standards outlined in the Interstate School Leaders Licensure Consortium: Standards for School Leaders (ISLLC) adopted in 1996. This set of standards was developed under the guidance of the Council of Chief State School Officers with a grant supported by the Pew Charitable Trusts. The chapters in this book are divided utilizing the ISLLC standards as the section dividers. Chapters begin with a short situation that emanates from chapter 1, which describes the Fort Spirit School District. In addition, each chapter includes an ethical discussion related to the chapter topic followed by a chapter summary that identifies the important information contained in the chapter. Chapter activities and questions for inquiry provide the reader with the opportunity to check their understanding of the concepts and skills discussed in the chapter. Activities and questions address each of the case studies found at the beginning of each chapter.

Section I addresses the administrator's knowledge and understanding contained in ISLLC Standard 1. Chapter 1 sets the stage for the entire discussion of the principalship by establishing a simulated school district from which to address issues and activities found at the end of each chapter.

Chapters 2 and 3 address the ISLLC Standard 1 with discussions about the changing view of school and community leadership. The principal as a leader of leaders, along with the moral and ethical leadership models, provides the foundation for the effective principal. School improvement supports the principal by providing strategies for planning and designing school improvement. Evaluating models of a changing school environment provide contrast to the traditional government run educational institutions.

Chapters 4, 5, 6, and 7 address the principal's responsibility for the school culture, accountability, curriculum, instruction, and student services aspects of the school operation in section II. The principal's role in changing the school culture is discussed with a focus on the role the principal plays in raising test scores.

Section III gives the principal help in understanding the use of marketing strategies for his or her campus. The development of a strong marketing plan provides structure for communication and customer awareness. This can be accomplished through media relations, grant procurement, fund-raising, and the creation of development and gift programs. Site-based decision making provides the principal with several tools that help all stakeholders become an active part of the school organization. The site-based models outlined in this section provide direction for continuous school improvement.

Section IV addresses the subject of ethical behavior of principals. The topic of ethical conduct of principals, along with a discussion of core values and ethical decision making, provides the principal with a framework for ethical decision making. Ethical leadership demands that principals model a set of core values that is supported by the community stakeholders.

Budgeting, human resources, safe schools, and facilities are the topics covered in section V. Several budget development models and budgeting tools provide the principal with strategies that make utilizing the budgeted resources more efficient. Recruitment, selection, and retention of teachers is discussed with a focus on helping teachers be the very best instructors they can become. Safe schools planning and implementation provide principals with ideas about creating school environments that are safe and secure. In addition, principals will learn concepts that will enable them to make the most out of a bad situation. Practicing the safe schools plan is the key to keeping the students safe when a violent event occurs. Facilities play an important part in the safe schools plan as well as creating a learning environment that is conducive to learning. Maintenance of school facilities and equipment is a requirement if the school is to be a safe place for students.

Section VI addresses the economic and policy implications for the principal from the prospective of schools as an investment for the community, the school's obligation for preparing students to participate in the community as workers, and how the school schedule impacts the economy. The basic concepts of educational politics is discussed from the principal's perspective. Working with special interest groups and communicating in the political arena are tools that the principal needs to have in his or her personal "tool kit."

The purpose of this book is to provide the reader with concepts that have been identified as necessary knowledge and skills by the ISLLC by tying them together with situations that require application of the information to a specific setting. Each of the chapters provides the reader with the opportunity to transfer the knowledge and skills through practical application of this knowledge and skills.

Section I

Vision for a Community of Learning

ISLLC Standard 1

A school administrator is an educational leader who promotes the success of all students by facilitating the development, articulation, implementation, and stewardship of a vision of learning that is shared and supported by the school community. The administrator has knowledge and understanding of:

- Learning goals in a pluralistic society
- The principles of developing and implementing strategic plans
- Information sources, data collecting, and data analysis strategies
- Effective communication
- Effective consensus building and negotiation skills

Chapter One

Fort Spirit School District

FORT SPIRIT SCHOOL DISTRICT
WHERE "EXCELLENCE IS OUR GOAL"

The Fort Spirit School District (FSSD) is located in the central part of the state and is composed of two communities of distinctly different populations and cultural backgrounds. The largest incorporated community is Cameron with a population of 75,000. Approximately three miles to the east of Cameron is the community of Bethany with a population of 12,500.

The FSSD provides comprehensive educational services for K–12 students and adults in safe and well-maintained schools staffed by quality teachers and support staff meeting the highest professional standards. Adult education, English language development programs, fine arts education, Gifted and Talented Education, and special education are among the many support programs provided by the district.

All schools in the district focus on a core curriculum of basic skills development in reading, writing, science, and mathematics, while recognizing the importance of offering varied educational experiences through comprehensive music and visual arts instruction, electives, athletics, and leadership development.

Computers and other technologies in classrooms, school libraries, and dedicated laboratories complement the delivery of the basic curriculum. All sites are connected to a wide area network, enabling classrooms, schools, and offices to exchange information electronically and have access to the Internet. The FSSD is recognized for its efficiency and conservative fiscal policies, and for operating on a very lean management structure in which only a small percentage of the budget is directed to overhead and administration.

3

COMMUNITIES

Twenty-two years ago Bethany was a small rural community of 1,340 farming and working-class people who commuted to Cameron to work in the city's various business and manufacturing jobs. Since that time, Bethany has steadily increased in population because of the development of two industrial parks and three major business campuses. These business campuses have been developed by companies involved in technology, communication equipment, and worldwide airline reservations. These industry and business developments employ more than 10,000 workers in management, technical, and service positions.

Following the influx of the business and industry jobs, Bethany has experienced an astronomical growth in medium to expensive housing on six plots of land that were formerly part of several farms that surrounded the small community. As home building boomed, so did the need for more schools. Bethany will continue to grow with a total build out population of between 25,000 and 30,000 inhabitants. The Bethany population will grow on an average of 12.5 percent per year, reaching a build-out growth in about ten years. The ethnic breakdown for this community is currently 93 percent white, 4 percent African American, 2 percent Hispanic, and 1 percent Asian. The average cost for a house in Bethany is $174,354 and no apartments are located in the community. According to the 2000 U.S. Census, the median family income for residents of Bethany is $56,234.

The community of Bethany has been experiencing increased gang activity over the past year. The mayor and police chief have put together a community task force to address the problem. They have asked the school district to implement a schoolwide gang awareness program for teachers and administrators.

The community of Cameron has had a stable population of between 70,000 and 75,000 for the past twenty years. The major industry in the community manufactures heavy earth moving equipment and employs around 4,000 workers. Various other small businesses offer the community with an economic prosperity that has provided the population with enough jobs to have a limited number of economically disadvantaged. The ethnic picture for Cameron shows a white population of 56 percent, Hispanic 23 percent, and African American 21 percent. According to the 2000 U.S. Census, the median family income for the city of Cameron is

$23,417. The population will remain very stable with a projected 1.5 percent growth for the next ten years. Most of the growth in Cameron stems from the inmigration of workers to the heavy equipment plant, the hospital, and the gated senior citizens complex.

Four years ago the community passed a bond issue to build a state-of-the-art hospital with an attached doctors' office building that would serve both Cameron and Bethany. The hospital and doctors' offices came on line in the past two years. Since the completion of the construction, the community has experienced a 2 percent increase in senior citizens. These seniors are attracted to the area by the mild climate, the inexpensive golf course, and the recreational opportunities afforded by two Corps of Engineer lakes in the Cameron–Bethany area and the state-of-the-art medical facilities. A local land developer has begun developing a gated housing community for seniors on the Cameron–Bethany city limits line. This development will build 980 houses and condominiums with an average selling prince of $180,000. The average cost for a house in Cameron is $75,123. Several apartment complexes are available in the community at an average cost of $475 per month. In addition, the city has two low-income housing developments for those individuals who qualify.

THE SCHOOL DISTRICT

In 1977, after a bitter political battle, the two communities consolidated their individual school districts into the Fort Spirit School District. Since the consolidation, the two communities have battled over school issues including such things as school board representation, where new buildings need to be built, school taxes, and other issues related to the daily operation of the school district. These battleground issues have created a revolving door superintendency with six superintendents in the past twelve years. The FSSD strives for excellence in all aspects of the community–school partnership. The FSSD is the third largest public school district in the county and ranks thirty-ninth in size among the school districts in the state with a student population of 20,838. The district employs more than 1,200 certified and 200 classified staff and operates 28 schools — 14 elementary schools (prekindergarten through grade 3), 5 intermediate schools (grades 4–6), 4 middle schools (grades 7–8), 3 high schools (grades 9–12), one alternative placement school enrolling students in grades 1–12, and an opportunity high school for working students in grades 9–12.

Each year the FSSD provides the patrons of the district with a report card covering many facets of district operation. This report entitled "Snapshot" is made available to all patrons and is posted on the district's website.

SNAPSHOT OF THE FORT SPIRIT SCHOOL DISTRICT, 200X–200X

Superintendent—J. B. Tucker
Central Administrative Staff
Assistant Superintendent for Finance –William Walls
Assistant Superintendent for Curriculum—M. Judith Boswell
Director of Instructional Support Services—Nancy McNew
Executive Director for Personnel Services—Jane Thomas
7 Program Directors
26 Instructional Support Staff

Elementary Schools PreK–3 in Cameron

Logan Elementary—Don Dimple, Principal
19 teachers
395 students 21:1 teacher/student ratio

Forsythe Elementary—Mary J. Mills Principal
22 teachers
455 students 21:1 teacher/student ratio

Walk-up Road Elementary—Wanda Nugent, Principal
20 teachers
420 students 21:1 teacher/student ratio

Cameron Elementary—Wiley Wilson, Principal
25 teachers
500 students 21:1 teacher/student ratio

Old Cameron Road Elementary—Audra Hall, Principal
18 teachers
378 students 21:1 teacher/student ratio

Tractor Plant Road Elementary—Dale Smith, Principal
19 teachers
387 students 21:1 teacher/student ratio

Falcon Elementary—Donna Dingle, Principal
17 teachers
357 students 21:1 teacher/student ratio

East Elementary—Darva Morgan, Principal
18 teachers
345 students 21:1 teacher/student ratio

Northwest Elementary—Robert C. Snow, Principal
16 teachers
336 students 21:1 teacher/student ratio

Elementary Schools PreK–3 in Bethany

Bethany Elementary—Phyllis Taylor, Principal
43 teachers—3 assistant principals
903 students 21:1 teacher/student ratio

New Area Road Elementary—Kailey Fischbeck, Principal
30 teachers—1 assistant principal
630 students 21:1 teacher/student ratio

High Tech Avenue Elementary—Zelda Zimmerman, Principal
37 teachers—2 assistant principals
756 students 21:1 teacher/student ratio

City Line Road Elementary—Farley Weeks, Principal
25 teachers
525 students 21:1 teacher/student ratio

Bethany Springs Elementary—Martha Smith, Principal
38 teachers—2 assistant principals
798 students 21:1 teacher/student ratio

Students by Grade	Count
Early Childhood Education	154
Prekindergarten	187
Kindergarten	1,571
Grade 1	1,789
Grade 2	1,705
Grade 3	<u>1,779</u>
Total	7,185

Intermediate Schools Grades 4–6 in Cameron

Moss Intermediate School—Harley Tires, Principal
27 teachers—1 assistant principal
650 students 25:1 teacher/student ratio

Deleon Intermediate School—Hector Sierra, Principal
32 teachers—1 assistant principal
789 students 25:1 teacher/student ratio

Waldorf Intermediate School—Micah Maldanado, Principal
37 teachers—3 assistant principals
903 students 25:1 teacher/student ratio

Intermediate Schools Grades 4–6 in Bethany

Reagan Intermediate School—Betty Bones, Principal
48 teachers—3 assistant principals
1,199 students 25:1 teacher/student ratio

Kennedy Intermediate School—Harley Fugua, Principal
52 teachers—3 assistant principals
1,306 students 25:1 teacher/student ratio

Students by Grade	Count
Grade 4	1,631
Grade 5	1,593
Grade 6	<u>1,623</u>
Total	4,847

Middle Schools Grades 7–8 in Cameron

Foster Middle School—Brad Barnes, Principal
28 teachers—1 assistant principals
710 students 25:1 teacher/student ratio

Sierra Middle School—William West, Principal
31 teachers—1 assistant principals
820 students 26:1 teacher/student ratio

South Park Middle School—Velma Dietters, Principal
27 teachers—1 assistant principal
701 students 26:1 teacher/student ratio

Middle School Grades 7–8 in Bethany

High Tech Avenue Middle School—Jerry Johnson, Principal
 47 teachers—2 assistant principals
1,352 students 28:1 teacher/student ratio

Students by Grade	Count
Grade 7	1,716
Grade 8	<u>1,866</u>
Total	3,582

High Schools in Cameron (Grades 9–12)

Cameron High School—Manny Flores, Principal
97 teachers—2 assistant principals
1,660 students 17:1 teacher/student ratio
15 FTE coaches who receive 1 additional planning period per day.

> *Cameron High School has the following unique programs for the district: Vocational nursing, computer maintenance, building construction and trades, and art design.*

South Cameron High School—Valrie Watson, Principal
89 teachers—2 assistant principals
1,513 students 17:1 teacher/student ratio
13 FTE coaches who receive 1 additional planning period per day

> *South Cameron High School has the following unique programs for the district: In addition to the general offerings, this school houses the district's charter Math and Science Academy created from grant monies secured from the state and Aero Industries of America. This grant totaling $14.5 million a year for equipment and materials is the district's show piece program. The faculty for this program is included in the teacher count for this campus. This math and science program is for students in grades 9–12 and only accepts twenty-five students per class per year and these slots are highly competitive.*

High Schools in Bethany (Grades 9–12)

Bethany High School—Riley James, Principal
120 teachers—3 assistant principals
2,051 students 17:1 teacher/student ratio
22 FTE coaches who receive 1 additional planning period per day.

> *Bethany High School has the following unique programs for the district: An advanced computer and software design program associated with two of the communities' computer development businesses, vocational agriculture, marketing, computer animation, and a discovery lab where students explore wind tunnel technology, global positioning systems, and laser technology.*

New Directions High School—Sarah Snodgrass, Principal
12 teachers
120 students 10:1 teacher/student ratio
2 psychologists on call

> *New Directions High School is an alternative placement center for students. They may be sent to this campus for a variety of infractions such as student-on-student violence, abuse of teachers and other school personnel, and other discipline problems.*

Mary Motley Extended Day High School—Harry Boggess, Principal
8 teachers
75 students currently attending

> *Mary Motley High School educates students who must get their education in an alternative manner. Most of the students are required to work and they attend at times when they are not working. The school operates from 8:00 A.M. to 10:00 P.M. Monday through Friday.*

Students by Grade	Count	Teachers by Level	
Grade 9	1,606	High School	306
Grade 10	1,528	Middle School	133
Grade 11	1,145	Inter. School	196
Grade 12	945	Elem. School	347
Total	5,224	Other Cert. Staff	310
Total Students All Grades 20,838			

Students Passing the Accountability Examination

Each student in grades 3 through 8 takes the state accountability examination in reading, writing, and mathematics. Each student must score 70 percent or higher in order to advance to the next grade. Students in grade 12 must pass the exit-level examination in order to receive their high school diploma. The following are the district's scores for the test that has been just completed.

State Accountability Examination Results By District				
	Reading	Writing	Math	All Scores
African American	84.0%	80.9%	76.6%	70.6%
Hispanic	86.9%	79.6%	82.3%	76.1%
White	93.4%	92.0%	91.5%	87.0%
Asian/Pac. Is.	88.9%	90.6%	82.9%	82.9%
Male	90.5%	87.8%	83.3%	83.3%
Female	94.5%	93.9%	90.9%	87.8%
Econ. Disadvantaged	82.5%	80.3%	81.9%	72.8%

Other Student Indicators for the District		
Academic	*Mean SAT Score*	*Mean ACT Score*
African American	855	17.1
Hispanic	1037	20.5
White	1050	21.3
Asian/Pac. Is.	1011	21.9
Male	1055	21.9
Female	1025	20.6
Average All Tests	1040	21.2

High School and Alternative Education Data			
	Graduation Rate	*GED*	*Continuing*
African American	80.8%	11.5%	7.7%
Hispanic	69.2%	5.1%	12.8%
White	82.5%	7.3%	5.1%
Asian/Pac. Is.	77.1%	8.6%	11.4%
Male	78.4%	9.6%	6.3%
Female	85.0%	4.9%	5.5%
Econ. Disadvantaged	62.3%	9.8%	16.4%

Other Staff Information

Total certified staff	1,292
Average central admin. salary	$73,420
Average campus admin. salary	$53,485
Average prof. support staff salary	$37,248
Average teacher salary	$33,532
Minority certified staff	8%
Average years of experience	9.4 years
Average years tenure in district	5.1 years
Teacher turnover rate	16.1%

Budget information

Revenue

Taxable value per pupil	$161,134
Total revenue	$103,541,723
Total revenue per pupil	$4,989
State	43%

Local	56%
Federal	1%
Fund balance	$20,952,711

Expenditures	
Total instructional expenditures	$45,468,283
Total instructional expend/pupil	$2,404
Regular education	81%
Special education	10%
Bilingual education	1%
Career and technology education	3%
Talented and gifted education	1%

FORT SPIRIT SCHOOL DISTRICT
BOARD OF EDUCATION PROFILES

Arley Cool, Board Member

Mr. Cool is a member of one of the most influential families in the community. He is an insurance salesman by profession, but devotes a great deal of time promoting his ideas in the community. He has been a board member for four years. Mr. Cool has two children, a girl in the eleventh grade and a son who will be an incoming freshman. Mr. Cool is very interested in supporting his children since his recent divorce. His daughter has become a problem and he continuously tries to make her problems someone else's.

Bradford Phillips, Board Member

Mr. Phillips has been a member of the board of education for six years. He operates a local hardware store where community gossip is traded more than some of Mr. Phillips's products. He is well known for his very fundamental religious beliefs and friendly demeanor and is popular in the community. Mr. Phillips has no children in the local schools at the present time, but had two children graduate from Cameron High School. Mr. Phillips's brother is the vocal music director at Cameron High School.

Ysabel Contanada, Board Vice President

Ms. Contanada has been a board member for seven years. She has three children in the FSSD, a girl who will be a senior at Cameron High School, a boy in the tenth grade, and a girl in the third grade. Ms. Contanada is politically active in the community and in the state. She has been involved in two equal rights investigations and fully supports equal funding for all children.

Darla Smiley, Board Member

Ms. Smiley was a second grade teacher in the years before starting a family. Her children have all graduated from South Cameron High School and are no longer living at home. Ms. Smiley is an active member of her church and volunteers in many areas in the community, especially at a local literacy project, and helps operate a local food pantry. She has been a board member for two years.

Barclay Fark, Board President

Mr. Fark moved into the community more than twenty years ago. He is an attorney by profession and spends a great deal of time working in the community. He has been a board member for nine years and his youngest son is a senior at Bethany High School. Mr. Fark is alarmed by the alcohol and drug problems that have entered the community over the past twenty years. He believes all of this change is damaging the way of life in the Cameron–Bethany area.

Fernando Cristobal, Treasurer

Mr. Cristobal is the newest member of the board of education, having been elected at the last election. He was transferred to the community, where he manages the Silicon Water manufacturing facility. He has one child attending second grade at High Tech Avenue Elementary and another attending Kennedy Intermediate School. He has helped his company become successful and is very skilled in understandings management problems.

Betty Sue South, Board Secretary

Ms. South is a highly successful real estate agent who is well known in the community. She has one child at Bethany High School and has been a board member for three years. She ran for the board because she was concerned about the quality of her daughter's education. Ms. South is a life-long member of the community and is married to the pastor of the communities' First Church.

Chapter Two

Leadership in the Community

Brad Barnes sat at his desk. In three weeks he would be opening the school year as the new principal of Foster Middle School. He had been preparing for this first principalship for several years, two and a half as a graduate student at State University, half a year as an administrative intern, and two years as an assistant principal in a middle school across the state. Prior to that he had been a teacher in a high school and a middle school for a total of eight years. His mind raced over the challenges that the year had in store for both him and the twenty-eight teachers and twenty other professional personnel that worked at the school. There had been some difficult periods recently for the last principal who had retired after many years in the district. The academic standing of the students had been less than desired by both parents and the superintendent, Dr. J. B. Tucker. Teachers at the school had been asking for transfers and five of them had left, which made an opportunity to hire some new personnel. From what Mr. Barnes could determine, there was less than adequate cooperation and teamwork among the teachers in recent years. As a result of these difficulties, school climate was sagging and instructional enthusiasm was down. Many teachers had drawn themselves into a defensive stance and became somewhat isolated as they worked with students. Ron Johnson, the assistant principal, seemed competent enough in his role, but it mostly involved dealing with student difficulties in classroom management and out of class decorum.

Mr. Barnes knew this was an opportunity to make some changes in Foster Middle School. He had invited the counselors and department heads of the disciplines to meet in two days to start laying the groundwork for what he hoped would be a new era at the school. He had many ideas to jump-start the school year but he knew that there must be more substance behind the changes he hoped would happen. It was going to take involvement and teamwork from everyone on the faculty and staff as well as student and parent support to make the changes he thought would be required to meet the goals that Dr. Tucker and the board of education were requiring. And to make those changes happen, he knew that his leadership would be required to make a difference from the past. He continued thinking about the leader he wanted to be and what he would say to the group of key educators from his school with whom he would meet.

THE CHANGING SCHOOL: THE NEW VIEW

The American school has developed over two centuries of change in the technological and cultural aspects affecting society. Schools were once the center of the community, especially in the rural setting, but also in urban centers where children and families came to know one another because of their proximity to each other and their attendance at a common educational institution. These institutions, along with religious institutions, often established the tone of the community because of the expectations of the citizens and the homogeneity of the value systems that permeated the social climate and culture of the population. As more technological and industrial development materialized and the communities' populations became increasingly diversified in ethnic, religious, and cultural backgrounds, the work of the school as the foundation to the community has become more highly criticized. Leaders of these institutions have realized that there are many, many conflicting views of what should be taught and what the role of the school should be in educating children.

So the nation and the world have changed a great deal, and those changes have had a direct impact on the school. These not only include the liberalization of beliefs and actions from outside the institution such as family values and the tremendous impact on students of mass media's messages in the form of entertainment, they also include the changes that are brought into the school by the participants—the teachers, the students, the parents, and the principal. These are the changes in the codes by which the actors live and participate in society, the changes in their morals, their values, and their beliefs. So how to begin the discussion of leadership in the school is a difficult decision.

To start, one must understand the concept that the school is part of a tremendously large system and it is also a system within itself. That which impacts the school includes all of the outside institutions and all of the participants inside the institution. The school is part of a greater milieu, and it creates a milieu where the students, teachers, and parents interact and go about the educational process. The school, then, is a community of learners and it is a community for learners. Although everyone in the community has what is seen as a designated role, that is, student, teacher, parent, and so on, everyone is also a learner in the community. No one is immune to learning. The more that is learned by each member of that community, the better the community becomes, because each bit of knowledge helps to strengthen the community.

No discussion of leadership can progress without considering the culture where the leadership activity takes place. This is usually referred to as the organization's culture or the school's culture. This culture is made up of the beliefs and values that those participating in the school hold to be meaningful in the actual operation of the system. These values are manifested in things such as rituals, roles, mores, traditions, and significant artifacts that represent these values. Examples include everything from the morning announcements to the athletic activities to the artistic and social events that take place during and after the normal school day. Other beliefs, such as the teachers' need to direct students' actions, influence heavily the activities that are used in the classroom by teachers and students in the learning process. This culture plays a major influence in the leadership that is provided by the principal because the beliefs that are present in the school's culture, actions of the principal, teachers, and students are somewhat circumscribed by expectations for the goal of the school. The actions are also impacted by the needs of the participants and the roles that are being carried out (Getzels and Guba 1957). Gardner (1986) reminds students of leadership that "leaders are almost never as much in charge as they are pictured to be, followers almost never as submissive as one might imagine" (2).

THE PRINCIPAL AS STEWARD

The principal, as the formal leader, becomes a steward of the system and the mission of the school as well as those individuals who are part of the school (Senge 1990). He or she protects the system from being undermined by outside forces that will injure the community and its purpose. But likewise the principal is expected to examine the beliefs and values of the system, weighing them carefully for their impact on the purpose of the school, and then determining those that need to be changed to best meet the challenges of the larger community in which the school participates. This is a difficult task, for the participants in the learning community sometimes do not see or understand how the big picture changes and how the school must accommodate itself to such shifts in the larger world. Sergiovanni (1992) refers to this difficult situation as the leader, due to enthusiasm and commitment, defining the needs of those who are being served. The school does contribute to the development of society by extending the education of its participants. But the school is very much an institution that is itself a participant in a larger environment—that of social institutions. As such, it is impacted and changed by all of the other institutions that participate in this society; these are the political, the religious, the economic, and the social institutions that have developed over the centuries.

The community member's expectation for the leadership of the principal has gone through a metamorphosis over the past century. Where originally the principal teacher of a school was a director of other teachers and a coordinator of educational resources, today the principal's role is expected to meet all challenges in everyday operations and to also move the entire school toward accomplishment of the established mission. Where this was once done in a somewhat authoritarian and often charismatic manner by directing all the players, today this is accomplished through collaborative efforts of many stakeholders. The principal is to encourage and empower all of the participants to analyze their situations and improve their actions to meet goals that are established by the stakeholders as a group. Yet, the principal must also step into a more directive role when the situation calls for immediate action and ensure that measures are accomplished to protect the educational participants and the overall mission of the school. The charismatic leader generally appears at times of stress and "the state of mind of followers is a powerful ingredient in explaining this emergence" (Gardner 1986, 2). The risk of a school following the charismatic leader is to depend on one individual to have all of the ideas and to deal with all threats. Today's world of high-speed communications, mass media, and multiple stimuli does not allow such focus in organizations.

In the environment of the twenty-first century, no longer is the leader the individual who thinks the organization's way through the problems and assigns tasks to those on the front lines in the classrooms. Senge (1990) refers to the new model that incorporates integrating thinking and acting at all levels as learning organizations. This requires not only "adaptive learning" in schools to cope with new challenges, but also ones that focus on "generative learning"—which is about creating new strategies for unknown contingencies and ensuring that processes exist that continually improve those strategies. Senge goes on to explain how leaders in learning organizations influence their colleagues to focus not on events that occurred (which is reactive), but to the systemic structure of what is occurring (which is generative).

The notion of the school as a community has not been adopted as readily by the public as some other popular ideas such as standards or school choice. Schaps (2000) indicates that three reasons exist reinforcing this avoidance: the public's unfamiliarity with this concept as a viable school model; policy makers overlooking this as a solution to many problems such as misbehavior, lack of student motivation, and raising aspirations; and the dominant one of regarding the school's purpose to be that of academic achievement as measured by high-stakes testing. Unfortunately, this latter one stems back to a philosophical and political notion that competition is the driving force that is preferred over cooperation in achieving the aims of schools and education.

Many of the educational researchers of the past fifteen to twenty years have focused their efforts on determining what makes a successful school, primarily in terms of characteristics of those schools considered to be a success. Success has most recently been defined as improvement of student achievement, usually based on some type of norm-referenced or standardized test. As a result, those outside the system and many that are part of the system usually measure success in all schools with the same yardstick. And so the formula to make a better school is to emulate the desired behaviors of teachers of the successful schools so all other schools become "high achieving" schools (Barth 1990). The assumption now is that those inside the schools are usually incapable of determining what actions should be taken to make the schools better, so those outside are better able to develop such a formula. These assumptions sound characteristic of the "Theory X" assumptions of McGregor's Theory X and Y (McGregor

1960), which were only focused toward the school instead of individuals. People outside of the institutions of education can understand these formula lists to improve the schools and support them in hearings before policy bodies such as lawmakers. Somehow, these lists find their way into the platforms of political candidates at all levels of government. What must be realized is that one yardstick cannot measure everyone and there is no one formula to guarantee success to all schools.

Rather than determining the formula of a successful school, the real question a community of learners seeks to answer is perhaps best stated by Barth (1990): "Under what conditions will principal and student and teacher become serious, committed, sustained, lifelong, cooperative learners?" (45). Barth continues to describe those assumptions, which help to alter this formula:

- Schools have the capacity to improve themselves, if the conditions are right. A major responsibility of those outside the schools is to help provide and support these conditions for those inside.
- When the need and the purpose is there and when the conditions are right, adults and students alike learn while energizing and contributing to the learning of each other.
- What needs to be improved about schools is their culture, the quality of interpersonal relationships, and the nature and quality of learning experiences.
- School improvement is an effort to determine and provide, from actions inside and outside the school, conditions under which the adults and youngsters who inhabit schools will promote and sustain learning among themselves.

Principals in the schools of today must somehow ensure that relationships that develop in the school are healthy ones (Barth 1990). These relationships work together to foster growth in all participants, interdependence among efforts to accomplish all the goals, and independence in the reflection and thinking of the students. Each of the participants—teachers, students, principals, and parents—develops a relationship with each of the other participants. That relationship must be built on trust if it is healthy and productive in nature. And trust must be part of the climate of the system or group that is working toward some purpose (Gardner 1986). Trust means that there is a feeling of predictability in how each acts with the others in situations requiring decisions. The relationships and roles between the principal and teacher, the teacher and student, and the parent and educator should be those of mutual support and not that of suspicion in motives for decisions and actions. This is not to purport that conflict and differences will not surface as the educational process progresses, but there should be some philosophy that undergirds the decisions and actions that all stakeholders can understand. All must somehow remember that the school is the institution that provides, ultimately, service to students. The principal must assume the greatest part of the burden to protect the teachers and free them to use their knowledge and energies to deliver learning opportunities for student growth. This protection will go the distance to strengthen the relationships between and among all of the stakeholders in the school.

THE TEACHER AS LEADER

The successful school then depends on many to help lead. Unfortunately, society does not now view teachers particularly as leaders, nor do teachers traditionally view themselves as leaders. Hampel, who spent four years studying schools within the Coalition of Essential Schools, found that different factions of teachers developed or emerged in each school (as cited in Barth 1999). One of these was the teacher leaders' group, but even in reform-minded schools, he never found this group to be larger than 25 percent of the faculty. An exhaustive analysis of more than 250 major reform studies reported that the most prevalent recommendation in improving schools is that teachers should take on and share more of the leadership in their schools. This is the action that will best help the transformational process in the search to improve schools (Barth 1999).

Teachers perform leadership functions of various types, and since they are the closest to the instructional process for students they make many decisions of a leadership nature that influence their learning as well as the health of the school (Barth 1999):

- Selecting texts and instructional materials
- Shaping the curriculum

- Setting standards for student behavior
- Deciding tracking assignments into special classes
- Designing staff development needs and in-service programs
- Setting promotion and retention policies
- Deciding school budgets
- Evaluating teacher performance
- Selecting new teachers
- Selecting new administrators

Of course, the principal or others can provide these decisions and functions in the central administration of a school district. But those closest to the students' learning have the capacity to change how instruction will proceed if they can influence decisions that support such changes. A dialogue must develop between teachers who work together to discuss their plans in order to coordinate and integrate the experiences they develop for their students. The principal is the individual who must encourage this discussion and interaction. Teachers must be trusted. Once an environment for dialogue has been established, teachers can share their ideas and successes with their colleagues. With such sharing, new growth in the thinking of teachers will emerge, while curriculum approaches and instructional creativity expand with the pontooning of ideas off of one another. "Pontooning" refers to building better and more integrated plans using many people's ideas in structuring a better approach. Teams may develop in informal ways that have not previously been operating and ultimately more formal connections can establish interdependence on one another. Although principals can take the lead in starting such development, empowering individual teachers to continue such connections will enhance creativity among the teacher leaders.

Teachers play other subtle roles in their exercise of leadership. Individual teachers may influence their colleagues through their knowledge of instructional skills, charisma, experience, political clout, and other power resources. The experienced teacher who is respected by colleagues can, through the use of interpersonal skills, bring fellow teachers along on the path to implementing new ideas and taking risks they otherwise might not be anxious to attempt. Likewise, the respected teacher influences the principal to encourage certain changes and to modify other practices in the search to reform or restructure efforts (Crow, Matthews, and McCleary 1996).

THE PRINCIPAL AS LEADER OF LEADERS

Principals often will not begin their tenure functioning as "leader of teacher leaders." This notion takes maturation on the part of the principal in his or her role. A point will come in this journey that the principal realizes the old approach of directing the "ship's journey in the educational sea" will become overwhelming. The captain of any vessel cannot stand the watch all of the time. Others must be trusted at the helm. This maturation process as a leader will bring on honest and open communications, trusting the decisions of others, and instilling the vision of what could be accomplished in the empowerment of other leaders.

Childs-Bowen, Moller, and Scrivner (2000) suggest the following four strategies be used to create teacher-leaders:

- The principal must create opportunities for teachers to lead.
- Encouraging autonomy and reducing restrictions opens many possibilities.
- Teachers must have the flexibility to implement curriculum and instruction without using scripted programs but to develop their own approaches with their peers through teaming.
- Teachers can create action research involving data collection and analysis to validate their innovations and evaluate the results of their efforts.

They should also receive encouragement to participate in external professional networks and organizations that will provide many ideas and stimulate their creative power in innovative practice. When the school authorities make all of the decisions concerning new efforts at improvement, even professionals feel they have become mindless implementers.

Schools must become professional learning communities. This means that the workplace is more than a place for teachers to share friendships and develop camaraderie. Continuous inquiry and improvement of work with open communications established through trust and rapport are required. Hord (1992) describes five dimensions of such communities:

1. Supportive and shared leadership
2. Shared values and vision
3. Collective learning and application of learning

4. Supportive conditions
5. Shared professional practice

Quality professional development opportunities must be provided and encouraged. The frontline players in the school must be considered candidates for these opportunities. Building-level staff development decisions are made by the teachers after they have examined school improvement data, made decisions about needed changes, and selected appropriate content for making changes for the faculty and staff. The principal must understand the knowledge base for adult learning principles as well as professional development standards. Then the principal can encourage the faculty in selecting options and providing the development support for making changes happen in the school's program.

Celebrating innovation and the impact that teachers have on successful accomplishment of program goals should be an important part of the school's culture. Genuine praise for all faculty members is powerful when it is warranted. Celebrating successes of the group may be even more important, however. Team achievement of program implementation or outside recognition must be credited to the team. And teachers who are paving the road to make this happen should be recognized also, but not at the expense of the climate of the school. Teaching culture usually formulates that all teachers are equal, so care must always be taken when celebrating success to remember that everyone's efforts are involved. Teachers are more and more being recognized as leaders in such efforts, so with such acceptance recognition is appropriate.

Creating opportunities for teachers to lead within the school should be a welcome process for principals in this era of constant change. One individual cannot effectively coordinate and guide all of the changes that are entering the school's environment. Teachers are the obvious solution to this difficult task. Yet everyone is not suited to guide every challenge. So the principal needs to get to know individual faculty members at the beginning of his or her tenure. Kahrs (1996) indicates that this means understanding their motivation, what they like to do, what skills they possess, and their strengths and weaknesses. Talking to them and observing their successes as well as working with them on projects can enable the principal to learn how teachers can best give leadership. Then the process of empowerment takes place as teachers are asked to take the lead on specific functions or problems. Oftentimes, an outstanding teacher will be found to be dealing with such a problem, working with colleagues in informal ways, or by initiating improvements in teacher team or department operations. These initiatives provide examples of leadership being accomplished without encouragement of the formal leader and are evidence that the faculty member is capable of taking charge of school-related issues.

Time is a resource of which educators always seem to be in short supply. When teaching, there is always a need for additional time to plan, evaluate work of students, and prepare materials for presentations or demonstrations and to participate in the lives of their personal families. When teachers take part as leaders and shared decision makers for improving the school, more time is needed. Shared decisions require conversation with colleagues to solve problems and consider options. This means that principals must enable teachers to have time together to meet and discuss (Kahrs 1996). Department chairpersons and team leaders must have schedules that accommodate this activity during the school day. Barth (1990) indicates that by sharing leadership teachers will have more ownership and support decisions. He states "that research suggests that the greater the participation in decision making, the greater the productivity, job satisfaction, and organizational commitment" (130).

MAKING THE EQUATION WORK

In most schools, moving toward a shared, collaborative leadership environment requires a shift in the culture of the school. Teachers begin their teaching careers much the same way a principal begins his or her career as a principal—focused on survival from a day-to-day situation. As individuals master these roles, they are able to contend with the regular day-to-day demands of the setting and they see opportunity to make changes in the situation to be more productive. In many cases, they see the problems that need to be addressed but individually both teachers and principals are somewhat constrained from being able to address these problems. These constraints are usually a function of the culture of the school. The beliefs, mores, and values of those in stable positions tend to maintain the process as it is. Only by changing some of those beliefs and values will progress be made. To change these, the informal power figures in the school must feel they are part of the process of change, and this is how the shared, collaborative leadership style perhaps makes its most important contribution.

Unfortunately, change toward a collaborative style of decision making is often mistrusted because it has not been modeled in the past by previous principals. Shared decision making is a learned behavior. Consequently, the transition must begin with small steps toward an impact in the total picture. To begin, faculty members may contribute to identification and prioritization of problems. Often, this requires carefully setting the stage when starting this process and having a structured way for all to contribute without being overwhelmed by the power brokers among the faculty. Individual faculty members need to be heard also. Some will not be ready to risk embarrassment in front of friends and colleagues, and others will attempt to control the process unless there are mechanisms in place to allow all to be heard and participate with their input and vote. This is where the principal's facilitator skills emerge. As successful resolution of issues are accomplished, then members will build trust for such process while beliefs and values of the culture will start undergoing modification. Eventually, the expectation for solutions will come from group settings.

The role of the leader as a facilitator becomes critical in this type of a setting. Schools, as most of the social structures and institutions today, are in a state of change. Principals must provide leadership as this change is developing. Judgment in action is the first characteristic of a leader in this type of situation, according to Gardner (1991). He clarifies this by elaborating on such a situation—"by judgment in action I mean judgment while people are shouting at you," especially when the deadlines are short and the stakes are high. Principals must have the capacity to function under cross-pressures (3). Principals do this by communicating persuasively with various constituencies, demonstrating their willingness to accept responsibility, confidently taking risks, and showing reliance in the school and its teachers and staff.

By demonstrating this confidence in the staff, the principal entrusts faculty with issues that are important to them. The types of issues on which faculty members wish to be included are those for which they have some expertise and that have an impact on their roles as teachers. Bridges (1967) theorizes that although other issues may have an importance in the school, teachers generally want to be involved primarily when they are concerned with the issue and have something to contribute in a constructive way because of their knowledge and skill in the topic being considered.

Sustaining such a learning community requires dedication and development of values that eventually must be part of the belief system of the school culture. Ackerman, Donaldson, and van der Bogert (1996) refer to this as trusting in the community. This means that the school can thrive despite differences in philosophy, interests, and personalities. These differences create tensions, of course, but these tensions of diversity can actually serve to strengthen the school when the principal turns responsibility for a collaborative solution to faculty members and the competing parties. In these cases, tensions can help to make school partners creative. Ackerman, Donaldson, and van der Bogert (1996) go on to describe some basic values that support the view that trust in the community is a valid path for the principal to follow. These values include modeling democracy in the school, creating a synergy that can create outcomes that exceed expectations, reducing isolation, building relationships that give support among students and teachers, and providing broad-based support for the decisions made. By modeling such a democracy in the school, the participants teach students to resolve conflict in an open and participatory manner. And a community is created that includes the rights and responsibilities that are expectations in a democratic society. The synergy that can be created in this type of environment enables the group to struggle through new practices and helps to reduce the isolation that sometimes develops in faculty members. Thus, through trust and group value development, a school can build healthier relationships among students and faculty demonstrating a true community where individuals reach out to help other individuals.

LEADERSHIP ACTIONS

To discuss actions or behaviors as those of a leader is to define just what leadership is. Certainly, there are many definitions of leadership and those definitions vary oftentimes with the fields of focus. The use of the word "leadership" in military environments certainly conjures up a completely different connotation in contrast to working in a nonprofit organization, which depends on volunteers to accomplish many of the tasks. The amount of training, education, and experience also tends to change the way the word is defined because it changes the relationships between individuals. In the education field, where most of the participants are professionals with licenses to practice and often advanced degrees, the knowledge differences between various levels of formal authority may be negligible. Roost (1991) points out in his research that of 587 works on leadership between 1900 and 1990, only 221 of these works even defined leadership. But leadership is still thought of in numerous ways: doing the leader's wishes, achieving group or organizational goals, as management, as influence, as traits of the individual, and as transformation of the organization. Roost goes on to construct a definition of "leadership" that is helpful in capturing the meaning for the education setting: "Leadership is an influence relationship among leaders and followers who intend real changes that reflect their mutual purposes" (102). And he discusses four essential elements that need to exist for leadership to be present:

- a relationship that is based on influence that is multidirectional and non-coercive
- there are numerous active people involved, which usually construes a difference of levels of authority—whether earned or formal
- these leaders and followers intend real changes to occur
- those changes are the reflection of common purposes

The most often written and spoken of function of leadership is "vision." Providing a group or organization with an idea of what it is about, what it can create, what it could produce, how this can occur, what it will look like when complete, and what the group is capable of is what "visioning" is all about. This relates very closely to the last of essential elements that Roost includes in his definition: that of purpose. Leaders help the group understand what can be done and how the group can accomplish it. In some instances, leaders work with internally divided groups to define overarching goals and unify the constituencies to provide focus for the mission.

Groups are usually most successful, according to Bennis and Biederman (1997), when they are undertaking tangible products. Frequently, the project brings them together and they produce their collective best. When finished, the group comes apart. This attribute is, in many cases, not present in educational settings. Learning, in and of itself, is usually intangible. It is difficult to see success in many ways in learning situations. The skill in learning to read is somewhat intangible—although it can be measured to a degree by using a test. Many of the purposes of education are more difficult to observe. Attitudes, mores, values, and beliefs as well as things like creativity, insight, character, and even leadership are concepts that are very much a part of educational purposes. Although these are not easily seen as tangible, educational leaders must create environments where these are taught and encouraged.

Visioning in schools by leaders may begin with the principal as formal leader, but visioning must be encouraged as a task for all participants to be involved. Every participant in the educational setting tends to create a vision for what he or she does, so if the greater vision is to be realized all participants and stakeholders are best to contribute to that concept of what will be achieved and how it might be done. It is possible, even in large groups, to share visioning ideas and to develop a consensus about things that everyone can support. This can be started by using brainstorming and continued with nominal group techniques to develop individual visions while moving them toward consensus. But to start this process the leader must ask the deeper questions. The leader does not take the system as it is without examining it for changes that are needed. Gardner (1999) states that the leader is asking constantly: "Is the system doing what it is supposed to do? Have we reexamined the goals of the system?" (2). The evolution of the system must be reexamined when renewal is necessary.

While examining the tasks of leadership, one quickly identifies relationships as a critical part of the picture—for whenever individuals work together their relationships develop. Roost indicates that these relationships have a range of formal levels, which are present in most groups. This, of course, is true in a school where one individual is referred to as the principal; however, in effective groups the role of leader is taken on by many or everyone at various points in time. Creative energy can come from anyone involved by providing thought and direction for accomplishment of goals and can be shared by all. The principal or formal building leader, however, can set the stage by encouraging individuals to take on this role when someone is reticent to act yet is clearly capable of guiding others to accomplish that which is the common agenda.

The task of facilitation is perhaps one frequently not outwardly acknowledged in much of the research and writing on leadership. Yet the meaning is captured in the first point of Roost's previously mentioned list of elements—that of influence, which is multidimensional and noncoercive. Leaders guide their colleagues in solving difficult or easy problems through the facilitation process: they guide the process of community building by asking questions and getting all participants to acknowledge the value of each individual. This helps ambiguity to be resolved. Principals and other teacher leaders need the skills to facilitate discussion among group members when conflict arises, to sustain attention on the group's work to resolve those problems, and to keep members' focus on the benefits that will result for the students (Ackerman, Donaldson, and van der Bogert 1996).

Facilitation has the possibility to empower the people within the school setting. Empowerment is team building in its best sense. Inside the word "empowerment" is the word "power." Too often leadership is equated with power. Gardner (1991) warns that there are "power holders for whom there is no end other than power itself. The sheer pleasure of dominating is the object of the exercise. We have learned neither to admire nor trust such people" (18). What principals need to develop in their schools is the knack of letting the power extend to others if the significant strides are to be realized in a school setting. Bolman and Deal (1995) talk about the leader being able to offer the essence of leadership by "offering oneself and one's spirit" (102). To move a group to develop a transformational character is a reciprocal process. The important things a leader has to offer are: *love and caring* for those involved; the opportunity for members of the group to grow through their *authorship* of their craft and creativity; the liberation of energy of the members through their *empowerment*; and the chance for members to find meaning in their work, confidence in themselves, and value in their lives by building *significance* through many expressions that demonstrate their contributions to the community (Bolman and Deal 1995).

Understanding and sharing cultural ties is an important facet of leadership (Gardner 1986). The feeling of a close, spirited link between the leader and constituents is supportive of the relationship that develops and cements the school as a community to achieve learning. The principal must concern him- or herself with the affirmation of values verbally, in policy decisions, in the kinds of people with which they surround themselves, and in their personal and organizational conduct (Gardner 1991). The link of shared beliefs and values promotes communication of a two-way nature between all of the stakeholders in the community. As schools get larger, the communication link becomes more difficult, especially when face-to-face exchange is the most productive. This communication must also include dissent and healthy disagreement between those in the community in order to promote change and growth. The difficulty, which can develop, is when the leader(s) fails to recognize that renewal is needed and the entire group settles for much less than the school is capable of achieving.

A principal is a representative of the school and the faculty to outside groups and jurisdictions. In this role the principal must rise above jurisdictions to help bind greater constituencies to work together to solve a problem (Gardner 1991). This occurs as a school works within a school district to solve instructional problems or as the school works within a state's educational system to change policy and parameters of a larger governance system as it deals with educational issues. Leaders, such as principals, must be concerned with weaving the society together and thus must be able to deal with dispute resolution, with trade-offs, and with brokering and mediation (Gardner 1981). This means that the principal must have political skills to cope with groups outside the school that enact requirements under which the school must operate. In these situations principals must have the courage to risk again and again, and function under stress, and survive defeat yet keep the faculty and staff motivated in their daily work with students.

MORAL LEADERSHIP

Leadership can be envisioned from many angles and in many different models. Researchers have often indicated that the situation in which the leader finds the group helps to determine what sort of style of leadership should be practiced. "Style of leadership" might also be defined as the philosophy of leadership that the practitioner chooses to embrace for the situation at hand. In a democratic society, the notion that leadership is granted by the led is somewhat appropriate. This is often referred to as earned leadership, when those being led choose to follow a leader and grant legitimacy to that leader's actions. This concept is also referred to as moral authority, which Sergiovanni (1992) calls servant leadership. Servant leaders have the skills of the leader discussed earlier. These leaders institute a purpose that is acceptable to those being led who are unable to establish it for themselves. They establish trust and confidence, built through the belief that judgments are made with competence and values that do not serve the leader's personal interests. Barth (1990) states that the "crucial role of the principal is as head learner, engaging in the most important enterprise of the schoolhouse—experiencing, displaying, modeling, and celebrating what it is hoped and expected that teachers and pupils will do" (46).

Greenleaf (1970) writes of the idea of the servant leader:

> The servant-leader is servant first. . . . It begins with the natural feeling that one wants to serve, to serve first. Then conscious choice brings one to aspire to lead. . . . The difference manifests itself in the care taken by the servant—first to make sure that other people's highest priority needs are being served. The best test, and the most difficult to administer, is: Do those served grow as persons? Do they, while being served, become healthier, wiser, freer, more autonomous, more likely themselves to become servants? And, what is the effect on the least privileged in society; will they benefit or, at least, not be further deprived? (7)

A servant leader has many basic ingredients of real leadership, which are discussed by Bennis (1990). These include integrity, dedication, magnanimity, humility, openness, and creativity. Integrity is the standard of moral and intellectual honesty and leaders conduct themselves based on this expectation of honesty. Every school leader must assert such integrity in order for the real business of schools to be achieved. Each decision must be predicated on the notion that the correct path to take will be the one in the best interest for the child. To be dedicated, the leader of the school must have an "intense and abiding commitment" to the task of betterment of the child.

As a dedicated leader, the servant leader is committed to the work of education, believing that the key to a strong healthy community and society is an educated populace. The basis for this level of understanding begins in the school, where the seeds of knowledge are sown to develop lifelong learning skills and attitudes, which will put a continuing discussion of issues in the understanding of all citizens. To make this happen the servant leader principal makes his or her level of involvement more than a job; it becomes his or her passion.

Magnanimous leaders have healthy egos and take pride in leading educators to accomplish their mission because this is what is right for children, not because it promotes their self-importance. These leaders are humble individuals and when praise and recognition comes in their direction, they focus it on the teachers, staff, and students within the school.

Openness in leaders connotes a willingness to try new things, even when these ideas may be outside the confines of personal comfort. When leaders in schools are serving populations of students who come from backgrounds different from their own, it is easy not to be comfortable with some ideas that may be set forth by those with different cultural expectations. These leaders are willing to try ideas that may not be congruent with their own values; they become, as Bennis (1990) states, "adventurous and creative" (119). To be creative is to restore the sense of wonder that one is born with, but that one somehow often loses in the process of becoming a responsible leader. These principals break though preconceptions and view things as new and fresh, making the "familiar strange and making the strange familiar" (Bennis 1990, 119).

To be able to capture the servant-leadership style as a workable philosophy for a principal, the leader must understand "that serving others is important but that the most important thing is to serve the values and ideas that help shape the school as a covenantal community. In this sense, all of the members of a community share the burden of servant leadership" (Sergiovanni 1992, 125). This is also captured in the words of Lao-Tae, 656 B.C.: "A leader is . . . best when people barely know he exists. Not so good when people obey and proclaim him. But of a good leader who talks little when his work is done, his aim fulfilled, they will say 'We did it ourselves'" (Legend, Inc., 2002).

ETHICAL DISCUSSION

- If democracy requires that the leader be granted leadership power by those being led in order to be effective, how does the principal decide when to be assertive in leadership and when to be more democratic in actions?
- Does the high-stakes testing environment that presently exists in most schools and districts require that the principal use a different type of leadership to attain the results necessary within the school?
- Should all stakeholders in the school community have equal influence on what occurs or should those who are closest to the action—the teachers and administrators—have a greater influence?
- Should the competitive model of achievement be the model adopted by the school to motivate students and faculty members or would a cooperative model be more effective?

CHAPTER SUMMARY

The American school has changed in its role and relationship to the rest of the community's institutions as the industrial, technological, and sociological changes have occurred in society. The school is one of several fundamental institutions in the community and as such it responds to the needs and changes of the community. As these changes have evolved, the school has become a community of learners, with the teachers, staff, and parents joining the students as learners in this community of learners. The principal, as leader of this institution, has seen his or her role also change from one of more directive or authoritarian in moving the school toward its goal of educating children to one who accomplishes goals through the collaborative work of all stakeholders. With this philosophical change to a community of learners, the school becomes an institution that promotes and sustains learning among all who are involved.

Teachers then, with the pressure to meet all demands of society and commerce, take on a more involved role as leaders in the school, helping to develop and manage the systems of learning in the transformational process of improving schools. A new environment has had to develop within the schools. This environment is one that values teaming, cooperation, collaboration, and sharing of ideas. To sustain this type of setting, the principal must encourage the teachers as leaders of continuous improvement for their ability to analyze difficult learning situations. Organizational commitment is developed through participation in decision making and job satisfaction. Modeling democracy and creating synergy help to build relationships among the stakeholders, which also spans differences and reduces isolation among them.

Leadership is an influence relationship among individuals who intend to make changes that reflect mutual purposes. Although researchers have enumerated many tasks of leadership, almost all include visioning or establishing an idea of what could be achieved. Other functions of leaders include facilitation, empowerment, sharing or developing organizational cultural ties, and providing links and representation with other groups or jurisdictions.

Accomplished leaders usually embrace a philosophy or principles in the way that they practice leadership. In a democracy, individuals frequently are granted their leadership position due to their actions and recognition by those who benefit from their leadership. This is often referred to as earned leadership. When those who are granted such legitimacy establish themselves in a way that depicts moral authority, they may be considered servant leaders. They establish trust and confidence by instituting a purpose that is acceptable to those being led, but who cannot accomplish that purpose by themselves. These servant leaders have integrity, dedication, and humility yet still serve others and not their own personal interests. In the case of the principal, the leader has an intense and abiding commitment to the education and betterment of the student by serving the values and ideas that shape such a community of learners.

CHAPTER ACTIVITIES AND QUESTIONS

1. When defining leadership, what are the generic components or behaviors of leadership?
2. Create an assessment instrument to measure the school's culture that can be used in determining leadership actions that might be most productive for the school.
3. What is meant by the school is a subsystem of a greater system? Identify and describe components of both the subsystems and the larger systems.
4. Describe leadership in terms of being authoritarian, charismatic, democratic, or a steward. Analyze yourself by describing the advantages and disadvantages of each of these types/descriptions.
5. What does the phrase "school as a learning community" imply? What roles do competition and cooperation play in such a picture?
6. Outline the elements of shared leadership that make it the preferred method to solve problems facing schools. Identify ways that teachers and other staff can demonstrate such leadership in the school. Give examples of topics where teacher/staff leadership is very appropriate. How does the principal promote shared leadership?
7. Compare your leadership style with the concept of moral leadership. What motivates the moral leader?

CASE STUDY ACTIVITIES AND QUESTIONS

1. Create an outline of topics that Mr. Barnes would use in approaching the counselors and department heads in his first meeting with this group in order to enlist its support and involvement.

2. List the concepts that Mr. Barnes should focus on to initiate the types of changes necessary. Should he immediately attack the problem of test scores or should he first work on the school culture as a community of learners?

3. Should Mr. Barnes be directive and make the changes that are needed or should he work to enlist all faculty and staff members in generating a direction and goals? Discuss what should occur in either case.

4. What strategies should Mr. Barnes use to make the faculty a team instead of using the isolation defensive tactic he has identified in many of the teachers?

5. Develop a list of changes that Mr. Barnes should make to Mr. Johnson's role as the assistant principal to better support the changes Mr. Barnes feels are necessary.

6. Write a speech that Mr. Barnes would deliver to the teachers and staff on the first day back that will set the tone for the new year and begin changes that are needed.

7. Outline the roles of the school board, Superintendent Tucker, and the district in creating change at Foster Middle School.

REFERENCES

Ackerman, R. H., Donaldson, G. A., Jr., and van der Bogert, R. (1996). *Making sense as a school leader*. San Francisco: Jossey-Bass.

Barth, R. S. (1999). *The teacher leader*. Providence, RI: The Rhode Island Foundation.

——. (1990). *Improving schools from within*. San Francisco: Jossey-Bass.

Bennis, W. (1990). *Why leaders can't lead*. San Francisco: Jossey-Bass.

Bennis, W., and Biederman, P. W. (1997). *Organizing genius: The secrets of creative collaboration*. Reading, MA: Addison-Wesley.

Bolman, L. G., and Deal, T. E. (1995). *Leading with soul*. San Francisco: Jossey-Bass.

Bridges, E. M. (1967). "A model for shared decision making in the school principalship." *Educational Administration Quarterly* 3: 49–61.

Childs-Bowen, D., Moller, G., and Scrivner, J. (2000). "Principals: Leaders of leaders." *NASSP Bulletin* 84 (616): 27–34.

Crow, G. M., Matthews, L. J., and McCleary, L. E. (1996). *Leadership*. Larchmount, NY: Eye on Education.

Gardner, J. W. (1991). *John W. Gardner on leadership*. Reston, VA: National Association of Secondary School Principals.

——. (1986). *The heart of the matter: Leader-constituent interaction.* Leadership papers no. 3. Washington, DC: Independent Sector.

——. (1981). *Leadership.* Minneapolis: Hubert H. Humphrey Institute of Public Affairs.

Getzels, J. W., and Guba, E. G. (1957). "Social behavior and the administrative process." *School Review* 65: 423–441.

Greenleaf, R. K. (1970). *The servant as leader.* Indianapolis, IN: Robert K. Greenleaf Center for Servant-Leadership.

Hord, S. M. (1992). *Facilitative leadership: The imperative for change.* Austin, TX: Southwest Educational Development Laboratory.

Kahrs, J. R. (1996). "Principals who support teacher leadership." In *Every teacher as a leader: Realizing the potential of teacher leadership—New directions for school leadership*, ed. G. Moller and M. Katzenmeyer. San Francisco: Jossey-Bass.

Legend, Inc. (2002). *Quote of the Day Archives: Leadership*, at www.legendinc.com /pages/ArchivesCentral/QuoteArchives/Leadership.html (accessed May 22, 2002).

McGregor, D. (1960). *The human side of enterprise.* New York: McGraw-Hill.

Moller, G., and Katzenmeyer, M., eds. 1996. *Every teacher as a leader: Realizing the potential of teacher leadership—New directions for school leadership.* San Francisco: Jossey-Bass.

Roost, J. C. (1991). *Leadership for the twenty-first century.* Westport, CT: Praeger.

Schaps, E. (2000). "Building community from within." *Principal* 80 (1): 18–20.

Senge, P. M. (1990). "The leader's work: Building learning organizations." *Sloan Management Review* (Fall): 7–22.

Sergiovanni, T. J. (1992). *Moral leadership.* San Francisco: Jossey-Bass.

Chapter Three

School Improvement

It was only two weeks until the new school year began for Wiley Wilson, the principal at Cameron Elementary School. As he sat in his office this hot August day, he contemplated how he would address the faculty at the first meeting of the new year. He thought about how he might break the news to this crew of mostly experienced teachers that the accountability scores for students at Cameron Elementary had declined sharply from the previous year. Mr. Wilson was given assurance from Dr. J. B. Tucker that the district would not release the test scores to the media before he had a chance to talk with the faculty.

The students at Cameron Elementary had never scored the highest among all district elementary schools but neither had they scored the lowest of the fourteen elementary schools in the Fort Spirit School District. The landscape was about to change as Mr. Wilson had gotten the results of the reading, writing, and math scores from the state's accountability examination. The school's average reading scores had declined by ten points from 80 percent to 70 percent, the writing declined by four points from 86 percent to 82 percent pass rate, but the real shocker for Mr. Wilson was the sixteen-point decline in mathematics from a 76 percent pass rate to a 60 percent pass rate. Even more disturbing was the number of students who had failed to pass all parts of the examination. Last year, the overall examination pass rate was 78 percent but this year's rate was 61 percent, a 17 percent decline in the student pass rate.

Mr. Wilson knew the pressure would be on the faculty and himself to remedy this situation soon. As soon as the media had this information, parents, community leaders, and the school board would be placing Cameron Elementary under the school improvement microscope. The questions became clear as he sat at his desk. How do I facilitate the improvement of school achievement? How can I engage the parents with children at Cameron Elementary to participate in this improvement? Finally, how do I tell this faculty that change is necessary and provide direction for that change?

SCHOOL IMPROVEMENT REQUIRES CHANGE

The view of public education has changed over the past two decades and society no longer holds public education in high regard. Carl Glickman (1998) supports this view when he stated that public schools "are being attacked continuously, with some calling to replace public schools with privatization, tuition vouchers, and unbridled free choice" (1). The question in the minds of many critics of public education is "can the schools serve student needs in a fast-paced society?" Wagner (1998) answers that question with a resounding "no" when he says that many others have attacked the system as obsolete. In the future, the only competitive advantage that students will have is what they have learned, so it seems appropriate that school improvement may be an essential priority for all principals.

As Mr. Wilson, in the aforementioned situation, knows too well, the change process will create faculty unrest, fear, and hostility. Change is never an easy undertaking by any organization and schools may be the most difficult of all organizations to change. The uncertainty of direction and the fear of the unknown appear to be the major players in this concern about change. Fullan and Miles (1992) suggest that the maps for change are unclear or incorrect and thus the ability to understand and overcome the fear of change is made more difficult. The fear of change may be inherent in the fact that every person in the school organization has a personal map of how change proceeds. Principals involved in the change process often hear teachers, parents, and other colleagues express their concern or contempt for change by stating, "people resist change, it is inevitable" or "you will have to enforce and mandate change, otherwise they won't do it."

Louis and Miles (1990) believe that knowledge, will, and skill are the essential elements that cause change to be successful. They go on to outline these five factors for successful implementation of change.

- Clarity for all parts of the change process must be clearly communicated to all stakeholders

- Relevance for change must be meaningful and connected to all the stakeholders
- Action images for change must be expressed in specific terms and clearly understood by all of the stakeholders
- Will to accomplish the change must include the motivation and interest of all of the stakeholders to complete the task
- Skill to accomplish the change is needed by the stakeholders in terms of the individual's ability to accomplish the envisioned tasks

It is essential in any change operation that stakeholders understand that change is a journey over time, should be systemic, and be implemented locally. Failure to consider these three factors will direct the process toward certain doom. The more the stakeholders know about the reason for the change the more likely they are to support and participate in the change.

O'Grady (1994) suggests that hardening of the attitudes stops change more often than resistance. People make up their minds to oppose the different ideas that change instruction, curriculum, or day-to-day operation of the school organization. The individuals with hardened attitudes are unwilling or unable to view any good in the change, thus they oppose the change without ever considering its usefulness in making the school operate in a more effective and/or efficient manner. In the case of instructional change, the "hardening of the attitudes" means students lose any benefit from new instructional strategies and a more aligned curriculum. According to O'Grady (1999) one's willingness to change is tied to one or a combination of the following:

- Fear of the unknown—losing control is the major concern for most individuals.
- Fear of failure—what happens if this change does not work?
- Fear of commitment—requires a commitment to one solution for the change.
- Fear of disapproval—forces new relationships, sometimes at a cost to old relationships.
- Fear of success—what else will I have to do if I change? With each success comes a requirement for more success.

Resistance to change happens because of fear as O'Grady points out in the aforementioned paragraph. People manifest their fear in many ways and educators are no different. The National School Boards Association's Institute for Transfer of Technology to Education (1999) classifies resistance to change in the following way:

- Positive resister—agrees with the change, but never puts the change into practice
- Not-for-me resister—agrees that change is needed for everyone else but not for him- or herself
- Been-here-longer-than-you resister—believes if he or she holds out long enough the change will go away
- More-time-to study resister—knows it is hard to object to this type of resistance
- States-rights resister—changes are of no value unless they come from within the school
- Stacking change resister—supports the change as long it adds to the current structure

Resistance to change is a normal process that all of us must address. You may recognize yourself or someone you know on the National School Boards list. As principal, knowing what people's attitudes are about the change process provides you with a tool for addressing each person's concerns. Classification of individuals into various groups allows the principal to prepare an individualized strategy for bringing the resister on board with the change process.

Teachers and principals fail the community when they decide that change is either too difficult, unwarranted even though the data suggests otherwise, or use the traditional "yes but" response to new ways of accomplishing school improvement. Schools need to engage the community in the school change process even though this might not be the most efficient manner in which to make organizational change. In this case, efficiency is sacrificed for community input, advice, and understanding from these stakeholders. It must be understood that change is equally difficult for the community as it is for those that are directly affected by the change.

According to Sparks (1993), the first step in managing the complex and difficult change process is educating the leaders of change, which in the area of school improvement are all stakeholders. Sparks goes on to outline additional steps in this process.

- Stakeholders from all constituencies must be included directly in the school improvement process.
- Stakeholders need to understand that they are no longer individuals operating alone but that they are an integral part of a team.
- Stakeholders need to understand that plans are loosely coupled and fluid documents will change as necessary.
- Stakeholders must be educated in how the change process works.
- Stakeholders must recognize that change will happen only if they cause it to happen. Knowing that resistance is inevitable and working with it is mandatory.
- Stakeholders must understand that the desired improvement may take some time to be realized and in some cases things may get worse before improvement is realized.
- Stakeholders must have an intellectual understanding of the changes being implemented. Understanding the purpose and function of school improvement is most important.
- Stakeholders must realize that school improvement takes time and forcing change can have catastrophic effects on school improvement.

All change is not the same and in fact change processes differ significantly. Organizations face change differently, not because they are different but because they approach the process of change in distinctly different ways. Slavin (1997) argues that principals need to match the willingness of the school faculty for change with detailed change models. He goes on to say that principals need to ascertain exactly which faculty need to be guided toward success, which can understand and execute the model, and which are not capable of change. Nadler and Tushman (1995) make the case that change models have a "language system" of their own and in order to effectively manage change the stakeholders must understand the "language system." Each type of change requires unique managerial strategies and techniques.

Fullan (1993) suggests eight ideas that must be learned about change and school improvement. He says that change and school improvement requires that those leading the process possess the ability to work along a continuum of opposites. The following ideas provide leaders with pitfalls to avoid when working toward school improvement.

- Leaders can't force change, the more complicated the change the less likely force will work.
- Change is a trip full of excitement and uncertainty.
- Problems are part of the process and you can't be successful without them.
- Early vision and planning may cloud the targeted improvement.
- Individual and group think must have equal consideration.
- Strategies should come from the top-down and the bottom-up.
- Successful change gathers ideas externally as well as internally.
- All organizational stakeholders are change agents.

DESIGNING SCHOOL IMPROVEMENT

School improvement is a targeted change process involving parents, students, teachers, community members, and other stakeholders. The structure of the improvement process is critical to the success or failure of the improvement sought. This process begins by looking at the various aspects of time, cost, and value to the organization. How much time are the improvements going to require, not only in terms of calendar days, but in person-hours the various individuals are going to devote to the improvement? Cost must be measured in more than dollars. What political capital will be needed to make the desired school improvements and is that capital available to be spent on the project? Adding value to the school organization must be assessed through student achievement, teacher implementation, and community acceptance. All three of the aforementioned aspects of the school improvement process must be answered before any substantive school improvement process can be put in place.

Given the necessity of working in a complex and rapidly paced school organization, it is important to decide which change model to utilize: an incremental or systemic improvement model. Incremental improvement is characterized by step-by-step adjustments in which schools routinely engage. Nadler and Tushman (1995) define incremental school improvement as a compilation of initiatives, with each one building on the work that has been previously completed and improves the operation of the organization in small increments. Quinn (1996) supports Nadler and Tushman when he writes that incremental change is "limited in scope, is often reversible, is not disruptive to the organization's past patterns, and is an extension of the past" (3). Incremental improvement is what normally occurs in any effective organization. In the school organization, the incremental improvement process produces a better means of working with parents for the purpose of their children's education, improving teachers' working relationships, and adopting strategies that will allow teachers across the curriculum to communicate. The foundation on which incremental improvement is founded is the improvement of the organization, constantly improving the relationship among all parts of the school. The negative aspects of incremental change are time stretched over months and years with insignificant changes occurring in the operation or effectiveness of the school. The "Band-Aid" analogy as it is applied to incrementalism suggests that as the organization discovers new problems it attacks those problems. Incrementalism is more of a see-and-react attempt to change the organization and is not systemic in any way.

Systemic improvement is a model that requires a profound shift in paradigms and fundamental ways of thinking. This process alters the identity of the school and transforms the organization. Systemic improvement is analogous to the demolition of a structure. The structure is completely dismantled until it is unrecognizable. Quinn (1996) believes that systemic change takes a greater commitment from those in the organization and is much more difficult to implement. This change model creates irreversible actions and involves risk taking. An example of a systemic change in schools is the implementation of curriculum alignment across the K–12 spectrum. In most cases, all of the teachers must work with colleagues one grade below and one grade above to make the alignment meaningful. Teachers will be called on to examine what they teach students and why. All teachers will be required to drastically alter their current curriculum, a dramatic change from the past. Curriculum alignment, in most cases, will create a new curriculum, and it will be necessary for teachers to restructure their lessons.

Systemic improvement brings with it the concern that completely destroying the organization will disrupt the organization's ability to function during the rebuilding period. Most organizations would not risk the dysfunction that attaches itself to fundamental change. The product that emerges from systemic change may not look or function much differently than what was in place prior to the change, but it must be aligned with the vision for the organization.

Systemic school improvement provides the organization an opportunity to go beyond individuals, single problems, and single solutions. When thinking about systemic improvement, the principal must realize that all parts of the organization and their relationships with one another are open to scrutiny. In the school context, the fundamental improvement process for the principal is more about reflection, reevaluation, and organizational structure than it is about a detailed blueprint. Systemic school improvement is mostly about school context and stakeholders across the total school spectrum. When using a systemic school improvement model, the principal is responsible for working with the stakeholders.

When comparing incremental change with systemic change, it is important to understand that systemic change is not better than incremental change or vice versa. The key to utilizing a particular model is founded in the purpose for the change. Incremental change works well in situations involving faculty relationships, school–community relationships, and organizational effectiveness. For example, creating and adopting a discipline policy for students that is easier to understand results in a number of benefits that include an enhanced communication among parents, students, teachers, and principals. However, in some situations, schools would vastly improve their productivity if they would demolish the entire organizational structure and build it back from the ground up. To suggest the total dismantling of any organization takes courage of the highest order because of the all-or-nothing outcomes generated by the systemic model of school improvement.

Principal Wilson at Cameron Middle School must change the academic atmosphere in order to meet the expectations of the school, the district administration, and the community stakeholders. He could choose to implement the incremental model of change by finding out where the teachers failed to teach students and specifically address those problems. The finger in the dike approach may solve the immediate needs of the school and might work over the short run. Principal Wilson could implement the systemic change model, which would probably require a total transformation of the school organization. If you were in Principal Wilson's position, which model would you choose to solve the accountability problem?

PLANNING FOR SCHOOL IMPROVEMENT

Planning views the organization from a cultural, environmental, and values perspective, and relates those factors to some desired outcomes in specific time frames, usually in two- to five-year increments. Planning for improvement is the process of reviewing the results of an organization's assessment of its internal and external environments, its daily operation, and its future. Planning maximizes the organization's strengths and minimizes weaknesses, defends against threats, and allows opportunities to become a reality. Planning in essence is an ongoing fluid process and is about choice and daily direction. Cook (1998) writes that school improvement planning is directed toward a complete concentration of the school's resources on predetermined measurable goals. An effective plan provides a context for change solely for the purpose of improving the organization's performance.

Planning has many benefits, but perhaps its most important contribution to school improvement is in the area of assessment. The school cannot know how well it is doing in academic, community relations, stakeholder confidence, and a myriad of other areas unless it establishes and monitors its goals. Planning for improvement provides the road map to the future and gives the school direction. Several factors that will affect schools in the future are: an aging population, fewer children being born, an increased presence of special interest groups, and an increasing minority population. These factors must be addressed in the most effective way possible and can only be achieved by planning for school improvement.

A number of planning models have surfaced over time and in almost all cases the models schools have used come from the world of business. Sergiovanni (1996) argues that successful business models applied to schooling are inappropriate. He goes on to say that positive leadership in the corporate community may not fit the needs of schools because schools have moral obligations not found in other organizations in society. Sergiovanni further states that educators need to begin to create their "own practice" and until they do, significant school improvement is not likely to occur. Nevertheless, fundamental improvement in schools can be generated from the planning models used in business and other institutions. Schools are unique entities and it would be a mistake to suggest that all planning insights garnered from fields outside of education will be useful.

Planning for school improvement generally begins with one or more of the stakeholders suggesting that the institution needs to examine its practices. Low test scores on statewide accountability examinations, parents concerned about the quality of their child's instruction, concern about rising taxes, and the value-added requirements of the business community are some of the triggers that cause schools to examine, assess, and plan for the future. The question that needs to be answered before any planning process begins is "should we develop a school improvement plan?" because this process will involve questioning the school's current status and attitudes of the leadership. If this question is not answered in the most honest of terms, the process is doomed to failure. Stakeholder leadership must unabashedly support the process. Questions that invariably surface when discussions of a school improvement plan surface revolve around such things as:

- Will we use the plan?
- Can we do this?
- Will this process create a better school?
- How much will it cost and is it worth the expenditures?
- Will the school leadership support the planning process?

The caution for the principal is: Don't begin the planning process unless you are willing to take the process to completion and implement the plan. The answers to these questions and others must be in the affirmative before a commitment to school improvement planning commences.

Creation of the planning committee is as important as is the planning process itself. It is most important to recruit members for the committee from a wide variety of groups. Diversity of opinion is of the utmost importance if "buy in" and implementation of the final product is desired. To do otherwise would be political and moral genocide. A manageable committee in terms of size is important to consider. A large committee composed of twenty-five to thirty members may be appropriate depending on the population of your school community. It is also important to establish a steering committee composed of eight to ten members making sure that each group, if possible, has one representative. The steering committee manages the process, provides guidance to the subcommittees, and is responsible for putting together the final report. You may want to partition the committee of the whole into subcommittees for the purpose of efficiency of work. It is important that each subcommittee receive from the steering committee specific directions about what it is to accomplish and a time line in which to accomplish it. Committee members must be nominated and selected from groups such as ethnic, religious, school supporters, school detractors, teachers, administrators, parents, business owners, patrons without children, and other groups that are appropriate for your context.

The model that a school uses in the planning process is not as important as is the commitment to following the process. Most planning models contain similar elements with varying amounts of emphasis being placed on specific steps in the model. The elements of a generic planning model for school improvement are outlined in the following seven steps:

1. Needs assessment and data collection
2. Assessment the internal and external environment
3. Creation of a vision for the future
4. Creation of the road map to the future through development of goals and objectives
5. Plan implementation
6. Evaluation of the plan
7. Reflection on the plan and a return to the road map

Assessing the internal and external environments can be accomplished in several different ways. Trend analysis is a technique that examines change over time as a means of predicting future events. Analysis of the economy, demographics, social issues, and political climate provide data that will allow the identification of patterns that have implications for school improvement.

A SWOTs analysis assesses the internal and external environments by analyzing strengths, weaknesses, opportunities, and threats for the school. Strengths address issues that have provided the school with its successes. Weaknesses are those problem areas that are known or have surfaced during a needs assessment of the school. Opportunities are issues that provide the school with possibilities such as grants dollars, new programs, and a unified approach to instruction. Threats address those issues that cause concern for the organization such as new legislation, tax code revision, local tax groups, legal decisions, and state education agency policies and procedures. These threats are usually external to the school. A SWOTs analysis for a school might look like table 3.1

Table 3.1   Example of a SWOTs Analysis for a school

Strengths	*Weaknesses*
1. Strong curriculum developed	1. Facilities are inadequate for enrollment
2. Experienced faculty	2. Parental involvement
3. Very focused administrative leadership	3. Financial resources are limited
4. Located on large acreage	4. Faculty fights change
5. Few discipline problems	5. Student attendance is low

Opportunities	*Threats*
1. Qualified for inclusion grant	1. Increased class size
2. Involve parents in volunteer program	2. School Board changing student/teacher ratio
3. Develop a school/business partnership	3. Increased salary costs
4. Improve student test scores	4. Change in teacher certification requirements
5. Recruitment of new faculty	5. Retirement of most experienced faculty

Step three in the planning for improvement model incorporates the use of the current data and information with future projections, provides the foundation for creating the future, and is expressed as a vision for the school. Approaches vary on how the vision is created. One means of creating a vision is to come to a consensus in the committee concerning the philosophical and practical direction of the school of the future. Several scenarios can be developed and presented to the planning committee. By consensus, the committee will select the scenario that best fits the community and school. With vision for the school improvement in place, the committee will create goals and objectives that support the vision. Questions that may guide vision creation are:

- What will the school look like in five years?
- What will the financial resource level be in five years?
- What challenges will our community face in five years?
- What will be our strengths and weaknesses in five years?
- What will the needs of students be in five years?

Goals and objectives create the road maps for plan implementation. They provide direction, time, and cost for the plan. Goals are more global than objectives by providing an overview of the direction the school is going to take. Objectives are very specific and assign tasks to specific members or groups in the school. Objectives should carry time lines, cost implementation estimates, and the person responsible for operationalizing the objective. In addition, budget impact statements should be created for each objective.

Implementing the plan sharply defines and changes the direction from planning to action. This implementation phase puts all segments of the organization on notice that they are now responsible for accomplishing the goals and objectives for the future state of the organization. If the planning committee has done an outstanding job of developing the document through an open and honest self-examination and stakeholder involvement, then the implementation phase of this process should move forward with few concerns. Implementation is in reality an assessment of the visioning process, goal and objective creation, as well as the test of the school's capacity to achieve the goals. Implementation defines the short-term actions that direct the organization toward goal achievement. This phase of the planning process lends itself to providing direction for professional development and assessment.

Evaluation of the goals and objectives begins at the very instant the plan is officially adopted. Being the cornerstone of the planning process, evaluation requires a systematic approach to collecting information and data. The information and data retrieval system needs to be effective and efficient and at the same time it must not be burdensome for those supplying the data and information. The creation of an electronic system for receiving and sorting data coming in from the various segments of the school must be easily catalogued and retrieved. The results of the various objectives must be catalogued so that all stakeholders can access, review, and understand the results. In this type of access, when data is not available the school may find itself being accused of not being forthright. This piece of the planning process will require technology and communication support from the school district. If that support is not available, then contracting and securing that support is of the utmost importance.

Reflection and returning to the road map is perhaps the one part of the planning for school improvement process that is most often neglected but in reality is the most important. Reflection requires the stakeholders to review, understand, and analyze the process that they have created. The environment in which the planning took place is fluid and decisions made six months ago may no longer be accurate. Reflection allows the stake-holders to address the continuously changing environments by returning to the goals and objectives road map for minor or major adjustments. In addition, reflection fosters the true spirit of planning for school improvement by allowing stakeholder assessment of the process itself. Improved planning is a part of the overall process of assessing the school. Reflection provides each organization the opportunity to consider the planning in conjunction with the results of the process.

Planning is a time-consuming and tedious process that will pay huge dividends if completed and implemented in a timely fashion. You may be among the schools with a powerful and well-executed school improvement plan but you can very easily fall prey to some ordinary pitfalls. According to Schinnerer (1998), in order to avoid these pitfalls you need to ask yourself: Does the plan

- produce a "real world" plan or have we created an academic document for the bookshelf?
- produce a document for the future or an operational guide?
- include fresh views from individuals outside of the school or was it internally created?
- live for the school and drive behavior or does it serve as a public relations document?
- assign specific duties to individuals with deadlines or is it a Christmas list?
- reward and sanction the responsible individuals or is implementation left to chance?
- require the stakeholders to view the "big picture" or focus on the unique parts?

EVOLVING MODELS OF SCHOOLING

Models for educating children have evolved over time starting with home schooling in the earliest stages of U.S. history and resurfacing on the educational scene in most states recently as an option for school choice. Education is the role of the fifty states and in essence the United States has fifty unique and different models for schooling. A similarity among the state models does exist and in many cases the differences are minute, yet they are different.

During the past several years, the educational debate has focused on the balance between family rights and the legal obligation of the community. Known as school choice, this debate has questioned the most basic principles about public school education since the inception of the government-supported schools of the 1800s. For some people, school choice is manifested by parents' choice of school, school improvement, and values they want for their children. For others, school choice is made as they elect school board members that establish school policy by voting on tax levies to fund school budgets and construction of new school facilities in the form of bond issues. Students exercise their school choice by selecting levels and types of courses in which they enroll. Tyack (1999) makes the observation that the school choice debate should focus on the type of choice rather than taking the position for or against the concept of choice. Critics of public school education have gone about the business of trying to empower every group except elected boards of education. Items such as national tests, national standards, state mandated curriculum, and school vouchers have all received support in lieu of local control of schools.

There are several choice options and considerable disagreement concerning which option is best. These choice plans can be divided into interschool, intraschool, year-round, and home schooling models for educating today's youth. Intraschool choice plans include charter, year-round, magnet, and contracted schools with vouchers representing the interschool choice plan. Home schooling is a choice option outside government-supported public education and is guided by a disapproval of the culture of public schools. The proponents of school choice equate choice with excellence because of the market dynamics of the economy. They go on to state that with choice comes parental involvement and higher expectations by allowing parents to decide how their child will be educated. Supporters of choice programs want to provide parents with dollars from state and local tax resources to help fund parents' right to send their child to a school of their choosing. These supporters are pursuing the fiscal authority to send their child to a school that suits the child or parent, regardless of the school's religious, private, charter, or magnet orientation. One reason Americans believe their children do not compare positively with international students is the story told by the dominant media culture and the politics of education. Both the Reagan and Bush administrations directed hostile agendas toward public schools by promoting bad publicity about U.S. schools in far greater numbers than they did the positive results of what was happening in schools and on the testing front.

When school choice is discussed, it generally refers to programs that are tied directly to the tuition voucher providing parents with part or all of the cost of educating their child in a school requiring tuition. Parents have the belief that school choice means a better educational opportunity for their children. In most cases, parents have bought in to the "competitiveness" concept generated by the state of the economy and media reports of how poorly U.S. students have performed on international tests in mathematics, reading, and science. The idea is that choice creates healthy competition among schools and therefore gives the schools an incentive to improve. The bottom line for this form of choice is any school that cannot attract enough students will go out of business. Bracey (1999) argues that the results generated by global comparison of U.S. students on international tests is not what critics would like us to believe and has nothing to do with the U.S. economic competitiveness on the world economic stage. Bracey goes on to say that U.S. schools do need improvement, but that a full two-thirds of the public schools do a good job of educating children. In reality, public schools have very little, if anything, to do with the world economy. Most of those that make the stretch from education to the economy do so from the point of view that educated children grow into the business leaders of tomorrow and thus the economy of the United States is dependent on the entrepreneurship of these students to keep the country as a world leader in business.

SCHOOL VOUCHERS

Vouchers for public school students were originally conceptualized by Nobel Prize winner Dr. Milton Friedman in a 1955 essay proposing an end to the "socialist model" of educating America's children. Friedman's (1962) concept was that government would provide a minimum education grant or voucher that would allow parents to send their children to any secular or religious school of their choice. This minimum grant would provide enough money to pursue a basic education with parents paying the difference between the school's tuition and the amount of the voucher.

Friedman believed that the voucher system would force the public schools to improve the quality of education offered to students. According to Molnar (1996), Friedman's ideas drew little attention or support. Realizing that there would be a greater demand for vouchers than private or secular schools to accommodate these students, the voucher advocates argue that an educationally free market will entice entrepreneurs to create private schools to meet the demand. Advocates also believe that students are being held captive in low performing and dangerous schools.

President Lyndon B. Johnson requested that the Office of Economic Opportunity develop a voucher system. This system was rejected by all communities except Alum Rock, California, where it was implemented and eventually abandoned. The Nixon administration took up the cause of vouchers in 1971 through the Panel on Non-public Education of the Presidential Commission on School Finance. The commission expressed a desire to fund religious schools with public school tax dollars. In 1983, 1985, and in 1986, the Reagan administration attempted to convince Congress to pass voucher legislation. Not able to get the legislation he wanted, President Reagan changed the tone of the voucher argument by talking about school choice. Choice became the political strategy for reforming public schools and Reagan began tying this concept to academic excellence and racial equity. In 1988, the Minnesota legislature passed the first school choice law. The 1997 Phi Delta Kappa/Gallup Poll asked their opinion responders about allowing students to attend private school at public expense, 52 percent opposed and 48 percent supported the idea. The opposition to public use of taxpayer dollars for private education has decreased from 74 percent opposed in 1993 to a country that is about equally divided on the topic of vouchers.

In 1990, the Milwaukee Parental Choice Program allowing tax dollars to be used for students who wanted to attend nonsectarian schools was enacted. This program allowed 1 percent of the Milwaukee public school students to participate in the choice program. Initially, the legislature limited the Milwaukee project to 49 percent of the total school enrollment but in 1995 it raised the limit to 65 percent and allowed religious schools to participate in the program, thereby allowing students in kindergarten through grade 3 who were already attending private school to enter the program; at the same time, the legislature eliminated funding for data collection. It directed the Legislative Audit Bureau to file a yearly report on the projects beginning in 2000. Murphy and Rosenberg (1997) argue that the promise made to parents concerning improved student achievement has not materialized when gender, prior achievement, ethnicity, family structure, and family income are considered. By the end of 1995, 25 percent of the eighteen schools involved in the program were closed amid charges of fraud and mismanagement. In the same year, approximately 33 percent of the voucher students dropped out of the program (Murphy and Rosenberg 1997). Questions remain about how the voucher schools admitted their students. Accusations charged that seventeen of the eighteen voucher schools had violated state law by not randomly admitting students. According to Pardina (1999), the Milwaukee choice program schools do not

- have to obey the state's open meetings law.
- have to employ licensed teachers.
- have to release employee salary information.
- have to administer the state accountability examination.
- have to inform the public of the school's attendance or drop-out rates.

Gunn (1999) reports that surveys conducted on the impact of vouchers in the Milwaukee choice program indicated that Milwaukee public school students performed at about the same level as the choice students. Parents of choice students expressed a higher degree of satisfaction toward the school than did the parents of Milwaukee public school parents. Archer (2000) questions the academic achievement of this school choice program because uniform testing is not required and data is not available for comparisons with public school students.

The Cleveland Scholarship and Tutoring Program was established in March 1995 providing $2,250 toward the cost of attending a private school of the parents' choice. The cost for educating students in Cleveland was $4,000 at the time and it was impossible to operate a school using the tuition voucher of $2,250 as evidenced by the 41 percent budget deficit in the voucher program (Feldman 1998, 9). It took a $2.9 million bailout from the state to salvage the program, all of it coming from dollars intended for the Ohio public schools. The program began in 1996 with about 2,000 students in grades kindergarten through grade 5 and in 1997–1998 approximately 4,000 students were enrolled. Budget concerns and charges of unlicensed teachers, poor facilities, and secular videos has caused the Ohio Department of Education to intervene.

Two studies of the first-year program have been conducted with opposite conclusions. Greene, Howell, and Peterson (1997) found high levels of parental satisfaction and test data that indicated a significant gain in all four grades studied. Using the same data, an Indiana University study found no programmatic effect on test results when comparing choice students with nonchoice students, except for one instance. Most experts believe that the voucher debate will eventually end up in the hands of the U.S. Supreme Court after a federal judge struck down the Cleveland plan for violating the separation of church and state (Wildavsky 2000).

Despite inconclusive data, the voucher wars continue in the state of Florida where the governor initiated the nation's first state program granting vouchers to students whose schools failed to meet the state standard on the accountability examination. As with other voucher programs that funnel state tax dollars into private schools, Florida's program found itself being argued in the courts. In April 2000, Circuit Judge L. Ralph Smith Jr. ruled that Florida can move forward using taxpayer-funded school vouchers while the legal question of voucher constitutionality is argued. Those who support vouchers believe they provide the following:

- Public schools are academically inadequate and will not prepare graduates with the skills necessary for a twenty-first-century economy.
- Voucher schools will foster innovation and improvement.
- Competition from private education will improve public education.
- The market place model suggests that the market will control schools not the government.
- Parents are encouraged to participate in their child's education.
- Voucher-supported schools are more responsive to parent and student needs.
- Vouchers will provide adequate workforce skills.
- Parents of poor children view the voucher plan as a way out of poverty.
- Vouchers will place the United States back in competition for international supremacy academically and economically.

Ramirez (1998) states that voucher proponents believe that schools will be more efficient and business like, will more effectively complete their mission, will be more accountable to the schools' stakeholders, will be less bureaucratic, and will be free of teacher union domination.

The United States as a nation believes that improving education should be a priority for the local government. School boards, education professionals, and community organizations are interested in making sure children are successful in school and in life. The question is how do all of us accomplish the task of educating a student population that appears to be less interested in learning and more interested in money and fame? On the surface, the voucher solution seems to address the aforementioned question with the motivation for success harbored in competition. Using public dollars for private education undermines one hundred years of public education in America. Stanford professor Henry Levin estimates it would cost an additional $73 billion per year to support a national voucher system (Feldman 1998, 9).

McCarthy (2000) suggests that school vouchers would have a destructive effect on the nation's educational system because public schools have traditionally served as the nation's cultural melting pot and the foundation for democratic values. Those who oppose vouchers believe that:

- societal values will be diminished.
- accountability standards will not be equal.
- the First Amendment of the U.S. Constitution, which supports the Establishment Clause respecting establishment of a religion and supports the mandate of church/state separation, will be compromised.
- vouchers will promote economic, ideological, and racial segregation.
- the fundamental values of democracy will be destroyed.
- the student creaming of public schools is inevitable.

Facts concerning the inherent good or evil of vouchers is surely in the eye of the beholder. The special interest group Americans United for Separation of Church and State (1999) has published five myths about vouchers that appear to sum up the argument against vouchers.

Myth 1—The U.S. Public School System Is Failing Our Children

Bracey and others have demonstrated with data that U.S. students are among the best in the world. Looking at graduation rates, college admissions, and other postsecondary education supports the concept that U.S.

students are being successful. Furthermore, a Money Magazine study indicated that private schools ranked no better than public schools when comparing Scholastic Achievement Test results. In a 1996 research paper written by the Wisconsin Education Association, abandoning public schools and turning to marketplace solutions is rhetoric driven by crisis. The failing public school debate may have eroded public confidence in the institution that has formed the foundation of our democracy. Distorted data and the education in crisis drumbeat rests not on fact but on the relationship between education critics and other social problems such as crime, drug use, family instability, and economic uncertainty (Americans United 1999).

Myth 2—Vouchers Are a Constitutional Way to Assist Parochial and Other Private Schools

Continued accusations state that public schools are a monopoly and the only way to defeat this evil is to subject it to market forces. About 85 percent of the private schools in the United States are sectarian. The curriculum in these schools serves religious values and doctrine to the students and would do so using taxpayer dollars. Over fifty years ago, the U.S. Supreme Court issued a decision on the Establishment Clause of the First Amendment to the Constitution by stating that "no tax large or small . . . be levied to support any religious activities." In 1997, the court reaffirmed its stance on the issue of separation of church and state (Anti-Defamation League 1999). Voters in nineteen states have voted down sectarian use of taxpayer dollars and only two states have implemented voucher plans (Americans United 1999). A 1998 poll conducted by the Joint Center for Political and Economic Studies revealed that support for vouchers had declined from 57.3 percent to 48.1 percent among African Americans and from 47 percent to 41.3 percent among Caucasians. This same poll indicated that 50.2 percent of Americans opposed vouchers, while 42 percent supported them (Anti-Defamation League 1999).

Myth 3—Vouchers Will Make Public Schools Better by Promoting Competition in Education

There is no data that supports this concept and to date this is the most discussed of the concepts espoused by those supporting vouchers. Sikes

(1996) argues that competition should be played on a level playing field using the same rules, something that is not a possibility in the public and private school debate. Selection of students by the private schools and hiring practices that do not meet the same standards as in the public schools are but two of the issues of private and public equality.

Myth 4—Vouchers Will Ensure Parental Choice in Education

Parental choice is meaningless when discussing private schools because the choice is with the schools not the parents. The school may reject students for a variety of reasons, some of which are parental income, religious incompatibility, and parental status in the community. The enrollment numbers and the school's curriculum are also the school's choice. The reality is that supporters of vouchers really don't want poor children going to the same school with their children. These schools provide a safe way to segregate children without actually making the school setting a political issue. Chase (1998) of the National Education Association asserts that no tuition voucher will cover the entire cost of private education and he goes on to state that sectarian schools reject two of every three applicants.

Myth 5—Vouchers Will Correct the Injustice of "Double Taxation" for Private School Parents Who Pay for a System They Don't Use

The fallacy in this argument is that tuition is not a tax, it is a personal choice that parents make, mostly for religious training. Vouchers appear to subject all citizens to a double taxation as evidenced by increased school taxes in the voucher schools of Cleveland and Milwaukee. When comparing the cost of education across the fifty states, public schools average about $5,200 per student, sectarian schools average about $4,200 per student, and private schools cost an average of about $8,500 per student (Issues 2000 2000).

As an empirical matter, the reports and data on school vouchers are mixed at best. Anecdotal reports of successes and failures only cloud the picture of reality. Some studies of vouchers report positive academic results, yet, there is sparse evidence that the quality of public education will improve with the implementation of vouchers. Rangazas (1997) finds that the effects of vouchers could raise the costs of public education by 25 percent or more. The debate continues to rage on with emotional triads from both sides of the issue. If the question is about school choice, then parents have many options from which to choose: charter schools, magnet schools, home schooling, and districts that allow students to attend any school in the district. However, if the choice comes to use of taxpayer dollars for private and sectarian schools the question has yet to be answered. And so the voucher question goes on and the courts once again will be the final authority in a politically charged debate.

CHARTER SCHOOLS

Charter schools are public schools. When a child leaves his or her public school for a charter, the state and local financial support follows the child. Over the past ten years, the charter school movement has slowly been implemented with thirty-six states passing legislation that allows for the implementation of charter schools of various types. According to the "Fourth Year Report" by the State of Charter Schools 2000 (2000), there are more than 1,400 charter schools in operation in the fifty states. In the year 1998–1999, more than 420 new charter schools were opened, with Texas and California opening sixty-four and fifty-six schools, respectively. Four states—Arizona, California, Michigan, and Texas—have approximately one-half of the charter schools in operation.

The basic concept that identifies charter schools is "autonomy of accountability." States differ in how they approach the topic of accountability, some use a "centralized" state agency model, others a "market-driven" model, and others a "district-based model that relies on local accountability. These schools become schools of choice for those who attend. In return for this autonomy the schools are held accountable for the achievement of the students and thus can face closure should the students not meet the state standards" (Northwest Regional Education Laboratory 2000). The Center for Education Reform (2000) states that charter schools are independent public schools, operated by educators, parents, community leaders, and others that are sponsored by local and state organizations for the purpose of reducing the control of local and state bureaucracy. Outside the controls of many state regulations, these charter schools can be tailored to meet the needs of students and the community. This alternative vision of schooling could be accomplished in the traditional public school system. Alternative curriculum and instructional models were much easier to implement where a vision for a change in school climate was to be created. Public schools moved to the charter concept in hopes of gaining an increased autonomy and private schools saw the opportunity to stabilize their funding and increase student population. More and more, the charter school concept is being implemented for special populations, especially the at-risk student. The "Fourth Year Report" by the State of Charter Schools 2000 (2000) indicates that 58 percent of all charter schools were founded to realize a vision for schooling, about 23 percent of the schools were created to serve special populations, 9 percent were founded to gain autonomy, and 3 percent were developed because of parent involvement.

Three types of charter schools have emerged since several state legislatures passed the enabling legislation. Parents or community groups with specific educational agendas create about 56 percent of the charter schools nationwide. The second type of charter comes from preexisting schools. This group makes up about 43 percent of the charters and is created by converting public and private schools to charter schools. The third type of charter school is the for-profit charter and about 5 percent of all charters fall into this category (Northwest Regional Education Laboratory 2000). Perhaps the most well known nationally of this type of charter is the Edison Project and the Excel Academies found in Arizona and Michigan, respectively. Generally, all three types of charter schools have a specific curriculum focus aimed at providing students with the highest level of academic accomplishment.

Charter schools are public schools and are funded using each state's system of funding public schools. This funding is most often based on enrollment or average daily attendance. In several states, charter schools receive less funding than do the regular public schools. For example, in Minnesota charter schools receive 75 percent of the state allotment provided public schools, and in Colorado and New Jersey charters receive less than 100 percent of the state financial subsidy (Center for Education Reform 2000). Some differences of funding between regular and charter schools is evident. Charter schools generally do not receive money to build, lease, or rent facilities. Some states may provide start-up dollars for the purpose of securing buildings and in most cases charters use existing school district facilities where available, but the facility funding issue is still a major problem for charter schools. Implementing a charter school is a challenging process with many obstacles to overcome. Resource limitation is perhaps the most difficult of the challenges to overcome, especially for start-up programs. Policies and procedures posed by state and local school boards provide some barriers for start-up implementation and create barriers for the operation of charter schools. Teacher unions and collective bargaining have created difficulty for some charters in heavily unionized states in terms of teacher salary and benefits. Teacher unions recognize that the charters are not bound by required collective bargaining and thus oppose the charters and urge their members to avoid working for charter schools.

How do charter schools compare academically with traditional public schools? Academic rigor is the mantra sounded by most charter schools. The data on the academic success of charter schools is mixed at best. Some anecdotal evidence indicates that students are learning but little empirical evidence is available to support the feelings of the participants. Since many of the charter schools serve special populations and a large number of the charters provide educational opportunities for at-risk students, it is difficult to make comparisons with traditional schools. In the area of student, parent, and teacher satisfaction, charter schools rate at the top of the scale. Students with bad educational experiences at traditional public schools appear to be progressing at an average or better pace in the charter situation. Teachers working in charter schools seem to find personal and professional reward, in addition to the empowerment they feel with the autonomy they have in teaching (Center for Education Reform 2000).

Each state that has charter-enabling legislation uses a different application process. The process generally requires a charter proposal that includes the following:

- A written proposal by the requesting group to the authority that grants the charters and the proposal must contain a
    detailed rationale outlining the need for the charter.
    clear mission statement and appropriate goals.
    financing, administrative, and facility plan.
    detailed curriculum plan.
    comprehensive plan assessing student and teacher achievement.

Groups that can hold school charters, depending on the state, include:

- Community groups
- Parents, teachers, and administrators
- For-profit companies
- Higher education

Charter granting groups, depending on the state include:

- State boards of education
- State legislatures
- Local boards of education
- State education agencies

Once the granting authority approves the charter, the charter founders will generally design specific standards for measuring student success. In addition, any accountability examination administered by the state will be included in measuring student success. In most states, the charter is reviewed periodically and may be renewed or revoked. The granting group is generally responsible for program oversight, basing its renewal decision on the level of student achievement as measured against the charters goals.

Charter schools provide the choice that some parents want for their children's education. The perception is that charter schools are academically more rigorous than the traditional public schools. Charter schools avoid the rancor that perpetuates the voucher debate and at the same time they provide the academic flexibility parents want. Whether charters meet the academic rigor that their supporters claim is still in question. The financial expenditures that charters require is based on the state or district's per pupil costs and appears to be no added cost to the district. The problem faced by most charter schools is finding facilities that meet school needs and are affordable. Are charter schools a value-added enterprise? Only time will tell.

YEAR-ROUND SCHOOLS

Year-round schools began in 1904 in Bluffton, Indiana, with a four-quarter calendar, and the multitrack calendar surfaced in 1969 in the Francis Howell School District in St. Charles, Missouri (National Association for Year-Round Education 2000). About 2,000 year-round schools exist in the United States and this amounts to less than 3 percent of the schools nationwide in some type of year-round configuration. Year-round education means different things to different people, with the National Association for Year-Round Education (2000) defining year-round education as continuous learning by reducing the summer vacation into shorter more periodic vacations. Typically, year-round education does not expand the school year it only lengthens it, by placing the same number of attendance days over a longer calendar. Depending on your point of view, year-round schools may be an extension of the traditional 9-month 185-day calendar with strategically placed vacations throughout the twelve-month academic calendar that is referred to as the reorganized year calendar. The concept of extending the total number of days students attend school from 185 to 240 days is generally referred to as the extended year calendar. This concept of year-round education increases teacher–student contact and purports to provide more learning time for students. The major difference between the extended and reorganized models of year-round education is the length of student vacations. Year-round schools are formatted in a variety of multitrack and single-track calendars. The multitrack calendar is generally associated with growing school districts for the purpose of reducing overcrowded facilities, while the single-track format is most often implemented for academic reasons (Kneese 2000).

Multitrack format year-round schools come in several different configurations. The forty-five/fifteen and the sixty/twenty formats are the most commonly used configurations. The forty-five/fifteen format is the most popular of the year-round calendars indicating that students will have forty-five contact days with the teacher and then fifteen days of vacation and will repeat this scenario four times during the calendar year. School districts utilize the forty-five/fifteen model in order to decrease the number of students using the facility at any one time. Placing students in manageable groups based on the capacity of the facility allows the school district to increase the enrollment on a campus by one-third. The student body is divided into four equal groups and each group is given a designation such as track A, B, C, or D. While tracks A, B, and C are in school track D is on vacation. Each track has its own calendar of forty-five days in school followed by fifteen days of vacation for the entire twelve months. The three-week vacation is referred to as an intercession and may be used for a multitude of student activities such as tutorials, academic exploration, recreation activities, and field trips. The sixty/twenty multitrack calendar requires that students attend classes for sixty days followed by twenty days of vacation. Students will complete a total of three or four terms of 60 days, meaning this could be a 180- or a 240-day school year depending on the wishes of the community. Students are in class three of the four terms and are tracked in a similar manner to the forty-five/fifteen plan. This sixty/twenty calendar also provides for overcrowding conditions. When students attend three of the terms, this model increases building utilization by 33 percent.

Figure 3.1 demonstrates 45/15 and 60/20 single-track plans in relation to the traditional school calendar. Traditionally the 45/15 single-track plan is the most popular of the year-round calendars with the school year partitioned into terms of nine-weeks followed by 15 days of vacation. Four rotations of 45 days amounts to 180 days of total attendance for students extended over the calendar year. The 60/20 single-track plan calls for students to attend three 60-day terms interlaced with 20 day vacation periods extended over the calendar years. In both the 45/15 and the 60/20 single track plans additional holidays are scheduled such as a winter break, a spring break and other state and national holidays (NAYRE, 2000) (see fig. 3.1).

The Concept 6 plan is a multitrack plan that has two-thirds of the students body in school at any one time. This plan is specifically designed to be used with overcrowded schools because it allows for up to a 50 percent increase in space available. This plan is composed of six terms of about forty-three days each. Students must attend four of the six terms and must attend two terms in succession. Beginning in July for a forty-three-day term is group 1. Group 2 begins its first forty-three days while group 1 is in its second forty-three-day term, and when group 3 begins its first term, group 1 goes on vacation. This plan is similar to both of the aforementioned multitrack plans (National Association for Year-Round Education 2000).

When investigating the effectiveness of year-round education, it is clear that the results are mixed. The research that has been completed on year-round education discussed both advantages and disadvantages. According to Stenvall (1997), some of the believed advantages of year-round education include:

- Increased achievement
- Fewer lost days for attendance by both students and teachers

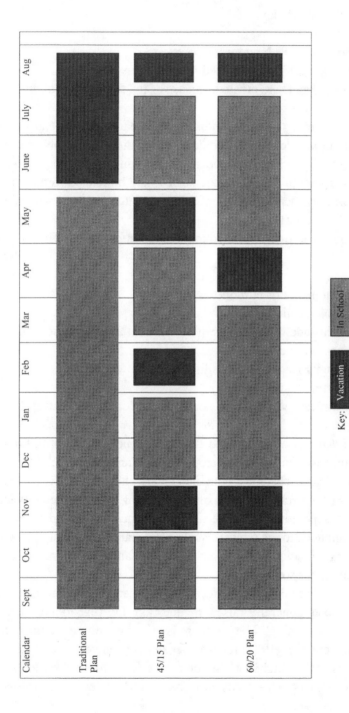

Figure 3.1. Calendars for Year-Round Education

- Fewer discipline problems
- Less teacher stress
- A more motivated teaching force
- A greater opportunity for extended learning activities
- More active students are created because of the frequent vacations

All of these factors seem to indicate that year-round education improves teaching and learning. Certainly, fewer discipline problems and less stress by both teachers and students is an admirable change from the traditional nine-month calendar. Attendance may be related to the stress issue and certainly increased student achievement is always a rewarding attribute for any school calendar.

On the other side of the year-round education debate we find disadvantages:

- Increased administrator burnout
- Family/school vacation conflicts
- Families with students on two or more different attendance schedules
- Increased operating costs
- Parental communication is more difficult
- Constant starting and stopping
- Activity and athletic schedules do not fit the term calendar (Stenvall 1997)

The disadvantages of year-round education appear to focus on family life, operating costs, and administrator burnout. Families with children on different attendance schedules, with elementary children on a year-round schedule and a high school student on a traditional schedule creates vacation conflicts. Operating costs are always a concern for taxpayers and parental communication is a must. While not debated vigorously, activity and athletic participation is important to students and parents and is a major disadvantage for some families.

When comparing year-round education calendars with traditional calendars, the debate generally raises the question: Do year-round schools improve student learning? The literature is mixed at best concerning student achievement. Six (1993) reports that students on year-round education calendars scored higher when comparing tests than did students on traditional calendars. This analysis is based on the review of thirteen studies, ten of which supported the idea that year-round students performed better on comparable tests. Palmer and Bemis (2000) reviewed research for the past thirty years on year-round education and reported that twenty-seven of thirty-three comparisons indicated that year-round education had significant positive effects. They conclude that students enrolled in year-round education calendars achieved equal to or better than students enrolled in traditional calendars. The lynchpin surrounding year-round education is the "summer effect" on students. Worsnop (1996) reports that achievement scores in math and spelling regressed over the summer vacation but reading scores tended to rise. These are but two of several studies that present evidence that year-round education is academically productive.

However, by far the vast majority of studies comparing year-round education with traditional calendars suggest there is no significant academic advantage to one calendar over the other. Kreitzer and Glass (1990) conclude that year-round calendars do no harm to student achievement but neither do they increase it. Schmieder and Townely (1992) state they find no evidence that establishes effectiveness or ineffectiveness concerning year-round education. The Virginia State Department of Education (1992) studied instructional and calendar time and the data from that research indicated that the year-round calendar had no impact on student achievement. Webster and Nyberg (1992) report on one of the few studies focusing on high schools and they find evidence that year-round calendars have little or no influence on achievement scores.

In addition to achievement, another area of concern and debate surrounds the financial savings or expenses created by the year-round education calendar. Before considering a year-round calendar, a school district must detail the costs of operation. Items such as added operating costs, maintenance time, teacher and administrator salary, staff salary and benefits, expenditures for program implementation, student transportation, increased custodial staff, overtime pay increases for maintenance, and utility increases for electricity, water, heat, and air conditioning are expenditure areas that need to be considered in calculating the cost of operation. Cost savings would be realized when considering the capital costs of additional building construction and possible reduction in vandalism. The bottom line of increased operation costs versus the construction of new buildings must be considered and limited evidence exists on both sides of the debate.

Context is the issue and each district must figure its own balance sheet in order to make an informed decision for the community.

Both sides of the year-round education debate cite studies that support their position on the issue. A fundamental reason given by supporters of year-round education is increased student achievement while detractors say there appears to be no statistical evidence that increases occur. The answer to this discussion is that there is no definitive proof on either side of the issue. Financial savings may have merit for the supporters of year-round education but it is a district-by-district savings and cannot be generalized to all districts. Perhaps both sides of the debate have missed the fundamental issues surrounding student achievement when neither side discusses instruction, curriculum, and impact on the family. The bottom line for year-round education and perhaps any other educational change is the community. Without community support any change is likely to fail.

MAGNET SCHOOLS

As an interschool plan, magnet schools provide students program and academic choices within their current school district. Each magnet has a particular educational function, some focus on a specific curriculum and others on a specific instructional philosophy. Magnet schools recruit students by the courses and programs they offer and by providing students with advanced skills in those programs. The first magnet schools were opened in Milwaukee and Cincinnati in the 1970s (Elmore and Fuller 1996). One of the goals for magnet schools was desegregation and the creation of diversity by encouraging students from all parts of the school district to attend. Over time, the focus has moved toward the creation of schools with "high interest, motivation, learning for students, and satisfaction for parents" (Black 1996, 36).

What has research to say about magnet schools? Gamoran (1996) concludes that magnet schools produced students that were better prepared academically than their counterparts in traditional, Catholic, and secular private high schools. He goes on to say that magnet school students increased their scores in "reading, social studies, and science" and traditional high school students "had the lowest scores in these subjects and math" (43). West (1994) asserts that magnet schools fail by not requiring a higher level of ethnic diversity. Even when the schools are diverse the classes are not.

Hausman, Goldring, Moirs (1997) studied teachers from magnet and non-magnet schools in St. Louis and Cincinnati and came to the conclusion that magnet schools have had a minor effect on changing school districts academically or organizationally. He attributes this problem to financial control by central office administrators. Little research has been done on magnet schools and the results of this have once again generated mixed outcomes.

CONTRACT SCHOOLS

Contracting for services by districts is not a new strategy. In the early 1970s, more than 150 school districts used this method to provide instructional services in the subjects of reading, mathematics, and other areas of need with a poor record of success (Ascher 1996). Schools have increasingly contracted with private businesses to supply specific services for school districts such as transportation, custodial, food, and accounting. These services have even found their way into the instructional aspects of the school through the utilization of for-profit language and phonics programs. In addition, districts have contracted with management organizations to operate individual or in some cases all of the district's schools. The concept of contracted school operation is defined as publicly funded schools operated by a private group under the auspices of a legally drawn contract with a public agency. The contract defines the operational style, instructional strategies, curricular content to be implemented, and the level of accountability to which the contractor will be held. Contractors can come from a large spectrum of possibilities including private entrepreneurs, nonprofit groups, parent associations, religious groups, and others with interests in student achievement and profit for their enterprises. Contracting is an extension of the charter schools movement while focusing on alignment and oversight with public schools.

The results generated by contracted schools continue to be mixed at best. Management strategies by various contracting groups have in some cases increased student attendance, parent and school cooperation, community involvement, and staff attitude (Edwards 1997). In most cases, the contractors met the spirit of, if not the letter of, the contract. The most important area to assess is that of increased student achievement. The literature in this area indicates that contractors are not being successful in increasing student test

scores and attendance rates are static. Losses have come in special education, art, physical education, and music (Leak and Williams 1997).

The two most widely known of the national contracting corporations
are the Edison Project and Educational Alternatives, Inc (EAI). The first
corporation to manage an entire school district was Public Strategies
Group, Inc., the contractor for Milwaukee Public Schools. Both the Edison Project and EAI have experienced significant failures and limited successes operating public schools. Competition is nonexistent for contracts,
initiatives are lacking for gathering data, contracts are not profitable, and
claims of instructional gains are unfounded.

HOME SCHOOLING

Home schooling is another choice option for parents, albeit not an option
of which many parents can take advantage. The choice concept allows parents to educate their children at home rather than sending them to a public
or private school. Twenty years ago, laws in all fifty states prevented parents from educating their children at home, but since 1993 it has been legal in all states. Over the past fifteen years home schooling has become one
of the fastest growing educational enterprises. Publicity surrounding violence in public schools has caused some parents to home school but by far
the largest majority of home school parents do so for religious reasons. It
is difficult to determine the number of students being home schooled, but
it is estimated to be between 700,000 and 1.23 million. Based on statistics
generated by the National Center for Education Statistics (1998), only
about 2.7 percent of the school-aged population is being home schooled.

As is the case with all of the other school choice programs, home schooling supporters and detractors disagree on the academic advantages, as well
as argue about the social advantages or disadvantages of home schooling
children. The small amount of data that is available appears to indicate that
home schooled children score equal to or better than traditionally educated
public school students (Lines 1996). Viadero (1997) cites a research study
that stated that home schooled students outscored traditionally educated
students by thirty-seven points on the Iowa Test of Basic Skills and by
thirty points on the Stanford Achievement Test. She goes on to report that
home schooled students with parents that had no teacher certification
scored slightly below students that had parents with teacher certification.

The relationship between home school advocates and public school districts has begun to be one of mutual respect. School districts have begun working with groups representing home schooling that reside in their jurisdiction. Perhaps the reason behind this cooperation is the realization by both groups that most of the home schooled students attend public schools at some time in their K–12 experience. School districts have provided home schooling parents with materials and curricular direction as a means for developing home school–public school partnerships. These collaborative efforts benefit both sides of the debate and help establish lines of communication and trust.

ETHICAL DISCUSSION

Is School Choice an Appropriate Mechanism for Increasing Student Achievement?

One of the more passionate and emotional debates in the past several years has been the argument about parents' rights to choose the type and place for schooling their children. Advocates on both sides believe the issue is of such great importance that it has surfaced at the highest levels of politics. The quality of public school education, especially in America's urban areas, is under siege by the advocates for school choice. On the other side of the debate, advocates claim school choice already exists in many school districts and has existed for some time in the form of magnet, charter, and in some areas contracted schools.

The questions that need to be answered concerning this issue are:

- Does school choice create a creaming effect in schools?
- Will school choice destroy the public school systems and if so how?
- Is the concept of taxpayer dollars for private, secular, or contracted schools a constitutional violation?
- Will school choice restore confidence in the U.S. educational system?
- Would school choice create a two-tiered system that would further divide the United States along racial, economic, and religious lines?
- Ethical dilemmas are right-versus-right issues. Which side of right do you support on the issue of school choice and why?

CHAPTER SUMMARY

It is essential to any change process that stakeholders understand that change is a journey over time, should be systemic, and be implemented school by school. All stakeholders fail students and the community when they decide that change is too difficult or unwarranted even though all indicators suggest otherwise. Organizations face change differently, not because they are different but because change is approached in distinctly different ways.

Designing change for school improvement can be either incremental or systemic. Incremental change is a step-by-step process that occurs in most organizations, while systemic change requires a profound shift in paradigms and fundamental change in operation and structure. Organizations involved in incremental change produce a better means of working with parents for the purpose of their children's education and improve teachers' working relationships and adoption of strategies that will allow teachers across the curriculum to communicate. Improvement of the organization is the key to improving all the relationships among all parts of the school. Systemic improvement requires that the organization implode and build itself up from the foundation, a process most organizations would hesitate to do.

Planning for improvement is a multifaceted approach to mapping the organization's future. The direction the organization takes is dependent on the results of a needs assessment and the vision created by the planning committee and stakeholders. Planning requires each organization to assess its strengths, weaknesses, opportunities, and threats prior to creating its vision and direction for the future. This review of internal and external environments forms the foundation for the planning process.

The school choice debate has questioned the most basic principles of public school education. School choice may be manifested by parents selecting schools for their children, the election of school board members, or a bond issue for the construction of a new school. Interschool choice allows students to attend schools that are financially supported by taxpayers. Examples of interschool choice are charter schools, magnet schools, year-round schools, and contract schools. Intraschool choice requires that taxpayer resources — which are typically called vouchers — follow the students regardless of where they go for their education, private or secular. The third type of choice is home schooling. This model of education is specifically designed for the parents who want to control their children's religious education, moral education, and curriculum. The collaboration between home schooling parents and public schools is a relationship that is beneficial to both groups. Elmore and Fuller (1996) sum up policy implications for school choice in four propositions.

- Proposition 1—The more school choice there is for students, the more likely the disconnection among students by ethnicity, social strata, and culture.
- Proposition 2—Without increased pressure for school improvement, school choice is not going to expand the curriculum or school achievement.
- Proposition 3—The devil is in the details as well as in creating and implementing choice programs.
- Proposition 4—Social context makes a difference in creating and implementing choice programs.

CHAPTER ACTIVITIES AND QUESTIONS

1. According to O'Grady, fear of change makes it difficult to change an organization. Create a list of strategies that you as a principal would use to address these faculty fears.
2. As a principal, list the steps you would employ in managing the change process.
3. According to Fullan, when considering the school improvement process what must a principal remember?
4. Design a school incremental and systemic improvement model that directs the improvement.
5. As a principal, which improvement model would you suggest be implemented by your planning team and why?
6. As a principal, create a SWOTs analysis of your school.
7. In the planning process, the principal must join the group as a participant. How would you guide the planning committee and at the same time remain a working member of the group?
8. Evolving models of education have implications for schools. What are your thoughts about school choice from an educational perspective?
9. As a principal, list the attributes of one of the interschool choice models, defining its positive and negative concepts.

10. As a principal, discuss the intraschool choice model aligned most
    closely with school choice normally called school vouchers, defining
•   its positive and negative attributes.
11. Investigate the positive and negative attributes of the year-round edu-
    cation calendar.

CASE STUDY ACTIVITIES AND QUESTIONS

1. If you were Mr. Wilson, how would you have approached your griev-
   ance with Dr. Tucker over the release of the accountability test scores?
2. What strategies should Mr. Wilson use to facilitate the improvement of
   school achievement?
3. List the strategies Mr. Wilson should use to engage parents in the
   school improvement process.
4. Write Mr. Wilson's speech to the faculty for the poor showing of the
   students on the state's accountability examination.
5. Describe the change process Mr. Wilson needs to employ, incremental
   or systemic.
6. When planning for change, what would be the first step Mr. Wilson
   should take to ensure success for Cameron Elementary?

REFERENCES

Americans United for Separation of Church and State. (1999). "Private school
    vouchers: Myth vs. fact." At www.au.org/vouchers.htm (accessed May 13, 2002).
Anti-Defamation League. (1999). "School vouchers the wrong choice for public
    education." At www.adl.org (accessed May 3, 2001).
Archer, J. (2000). "Positive voucher audit still raises question." *Education Week*,
    at www.edweek.org/ew/ew_printstory.cfm?slug=23milwauk.h19 (accessed
    June 3, 2001).
Ascher, C. (1996). "Performance contracting: A forgotten experiment in school
    privatization." *Phi Delta Kappan* 77 (9): 615–621.
Black, S. (1996). "The pull of magnets." *The American School Board Journal* 183
    (9): 34–36.
Bracey, G. W. (1999). "Are U.S. students behind?" The American Prospect no.
    37, at www.prospect.org/archives/37/3bracfs.html (accessed May 3, 2000).

Center for Education Reform. (2000). "Answers to frequently asked questions about charter schools." At edreform.com/school_reform_faq/charter_schools.htm (accessed June 1, 2001).

Chase, B. (1998). "Save urban schools by bleeding them?" *Brookings Quarterly*, at www.nea.org/issues/vouchers/bleeding.html (accessed May 3, 2001).

Cook, W. (1998). *Bill Cooke's strategic planning for America's schools*. Arlington, VA: American Association of School Administrators, National Clearinghouse on Educational Management (ERIC Document Reproduction Services no. ED 303 870).

Edwards, D. L. (1997). *The private management of public schools: The Dade county, Florida experience*. Arlington, VA: American Association of School Administrators, National Clearinghouse on Educational Management (ERIC Document Reproduction Services no. ED 407 740).

Elmore, R. F., and Fuller, B. (1996). *Who chooses? Who loses?* New York: Teachers College Press.

Feldman, S. (1998). "No bargain: Evidence shows voucher schools don't cost less—or work better." *New Republic* (218): 9.

Friedman, M. (1962). *Capitalism and freedom*. Chicago: University of Chicago Press.

Fullan, M. G. (1993). *Probing the depths of educational reform*. Bristol, PA: Falmer.

Fullan, M. G., and Miles, M. B. (1992). "Getting the reform right: What works and what doesn't." *Phi Delta Kappan* 73 (10): 745–752.

Gamoran, A. (1996). "Do magnet schools boost achievement?" *Educational Leadership* 54 (2): 42–46.

Glickman, C. D. (1998). *Revolutionizing America's Schools*. San Francisco: Josey-Bass.

Green, J. P., Howell, W. G., and Peterson, P. E. (1997). "Lessons from the Cleveland Scholarship Program." At data.fas.harvard.edu/edu (accessed May 3, 2000).

Gunn, E. (1999). "Vouchers and public accountability." *Rethinking Schools*, at www.rethinkingschools.org/Archives/14_01vouch141.htm (accessed July 1, 2001).

Hausman, C. S., Goldring, E. B., and Moirs, K. A. (1997). "Organizational capacity for school improvement: Teacher reports in magnet and nonmagnet schools." Paper presented at the American Educational Research Association, Chicago (ERIC Document Reproduction Service no. ED 407 709).

Issues 2000. (2000). "Background on school choice." At www.issues2000.org/School_Choice.htm (accessed May 7, 2001).

Kneese, C. (2000). "Year-round education: An evaluation." *Catalyst for Change* 29 (2): 15–23.

Kreitzer, A., and Glass, G. V. (1990). "Policy considerations in conversion to year-round schools." *New Brunswick Educational Administrator* 19 (4): 1–5.

Leak, L. E., and Williams, L. C. (1997). *Private management of public schools: The Baltimore Experience*. Arlington, VA: American Association of School Administrators, National Clearinghouse on Educational Management (ERIC Document Reproduction Services no. ED 407 731).

Lines, P. M. (1996). "Home schooling comes of age." *Educational Leadership* 54 (2): 63–67.

Louis, K. B., and Miles, M. B. (1990). "Mustering the will for change." *Educational Leadership* (4): 57–61.

McCarthy, M. (2000). "What is the verdict on school vouchers?" *Phi Delta Kappan* 91 (5): 371–378.

Molnar, A. (1996). "School choice." *Education Resources*, at www.weac.org/resources/nov96/vouchers.htm (accessed August 2, 2001).

Murphy, D., and Rosenberg, B. (1997). "Milwaukee voucher program a poor investment, say AFT." At www.aft.org/research/vouchers.milw972.htm (accessed November 5, 2001).

Nadler, D. A., and Tushman, M. L. (1995). "Types of organizational change: From incremental improvement to discontinuous transformation." In *Discontinuous change: Leading organizational transformation*, ed. D. A. Nadler, R. B. Shaw, and A. E. Walton. San Francisco: Jossey-Bass.

National Association for Year-Round Education. (2000). "What is year-round education?" At www.nayre.org (accessed September 8, 2001).

National Center for Education Statistics. (1998). *School choice: Indicator of the month*. Arlington, VA: American Association of School Administrators, National Clearinghouse on Educational Management (ERIC Document Reproduction Services no. ED 411 570).

National School Boards Association's Institute for the Transfer of Technology to Education. (1999). "Types of resistors to change." At www.nsba.org (accessed May 3, 2000).

Northwest Regional Educational Laboratory. (2000). "Charter schools-definition and specifics." At www.nwrel.org/charter/specifics.html (accessed July 8, 2001).

O'Grady, D. (1999). "Overcoming obstacles to change." At www.nsba.org (accessed May 3, 2000).

———. (1994). "Change happens." At www.changehappens.com (accessed May 3, 2000).

Palmer, E. A., and Bemis, A. E. (2000). "Year-round education." At www.extension.umn.edu (accessed November 7, 2001).

Pardina, P. (1999). "Church/state complexities." *Rethinking Schools*, at www.rethinkingschools.org (accessed May 3, 2000).

Quinn, R. E. (1996). *Deep change*. San Francisco: Jossey-Bass.

Ramirez, A. (1998). "Vouchers and voodoo economics." *Educational Leadership*, at www.ascd.org/readingroom/edlead/9810/externalramirez.html (accessed May 3, 2000).

Rangazas, P. (1997). "Competition and private school vouchers." *Education Economics* 5 (3): 245–263.

Schinnerer, V. O. (1998). "Eight problems with your strategic plan." *The Consultant* 1 (1): 1–2.

Schmieder, J. H., and Townley, A. J. (1992). "Making a smooth transition." *Thrust for Educational Leadership* 21 (6): 26–27, 30–31.

Sergiovanni, T. (1996). *Leadership for the schoolhouse: How is it different? Why is it important?* San Francisco: Jossey-Bass.

Sikes, M. E. (1996). "What's so bad about vouchers?" At www.softdisk .com/comp/shume/politics/vouchers.htm (accessed June 10, 2002).

Six, L. (1993). "A review of recent studies relating to the achievement of students enrolled in year-round education programs." At www.bctf.ca/Research Reports/95ei03 (accessed May 3, 2000).

Slavin, R. E. (1997). "Sand, bricks, and seeds: Several change strategies and readiness for reform." *Center for Research on the Education of Students Placed at Risk*. Baltimore, MD: Johns Hopkins University Press.

Sparks, D. (1993). "Thirteen tips for managing change." *Wisconsin School News* 6 (4) (November): 4.

State of Charter Schools 2000. (2000). "Fourth year report." (January), at www.ed.gov/pubs/charter4thyear/es.html (accessed October 15, 2001).

Stenvall, M. (1997). "A checklist for success." San Diego, CA: National Association for Year-round Education, at www.extension.UMN.edu/distribution/familydevelopment/components/7286-09.html (accessed May 17, 2000).

Tyack, D. (1999). "Choice options: School choice, Yes—but what kind?" *The American Prospect* (42), at www.prospect.org/archives/42/42tvack.html (accessed May 3, 2000).

Viadero, D. (1997). "Curriculum beats scores, survey finds." *Education Week*, at www.educationweek.com (accessed May 4, 2000).

Virginia State Department of Education. (1992). *Instructional time and student learning: A study of school calendar and instructional time*. Arlington, VA: American Association of School Administrators, National Clearinghouse on Educational Management (ERIC Document Reproduction Services no. ED 335 283).

Wagner, T. (1998). "Change as collaborative inquiry: A constructivist methodology for reinventing schools." *Phi Delta Kappan* 79 (7): 512–517.

Webster, W. E., and Nyberg, K. L. (1992). "Converting a high school to YRE." *Thrust for Educational Leadership* 21 (6): 22–25.

West, K. C. (1994). "A desegregation tool that backfired: Magnet schools and classroom segregation." *Yale Law Review* (June): 2567–2592.

Wildavsky, B. (2000). "Vouchers lose in court." *U.S. News*, at www.usnews.com/ usnews/issue/000327/voucher.htm (accessed November 7, 2001).

Worsnop, R. L. (1996). "Year-round schools: Do they improve academic performance?" *CQ Researcher*, at www.capitolresource.org/b_yre.htm (accessed May 21, 2000).

Section II

Instruction and School Culture

ISLLC Standard 2

A school administrator is an educational leader who promotes the success of all students by advocating, nurturing, and sustaining a school culture and instructional program conducive to student learning and staff professional growth. The administrator has knowledge and understanding of:

- Curriculum design, implementation, and evaluation
- Principles of effective instruction
- Measurement, evaluation, and assessment strategies
- Adult learning and professional development
- Technology in promoting student learning
- School cultures

Chapter Four

School Culture and Accountablity

Mr. Riley James was beginning his first year as principal of Bethany High School (BHS) after seven years as principal of a smaller high school down state. He took the BHS position knowing that some problems existed at the school. During the interview process, Mr. James questioned faculty, students, parents, and other administrators in an attempt to discover the magnitude of the problems. In addition, he was attempting to discover what some of the school's problems seemed to be. He was unsuccessful in discovering much substance about either of the questions he asked, but he did feel an undercurrent of dissatisfaction with student behavior from teachers, parents, and Dr. J. B. Tucker. Students seemed to have the feeling that the faculty treated them with little or no respect. Parents were concerned about an unspoken threat of harassment for freshmen by upperclassmen. These subtle comments seemed to surprise Mr. James because all he had heard was that BHS was a model school that had the potential to become a National Blue Ribbon School. Dr. Tucker had indicated to Mr. James that he wanted BHS to make an application for the U.S. Department of Education's Blue Ribbon Award and to achieve that status. Mr. James agreed to become the third principal of BHS.

At the initial meeting of the BHS faculty prior to the first day of school, Mr. James discussed his ideas for making BHS the premier school in the area. He charged the faculty to make magic with the students and to provide them with all the help possible in the learning process. He went on to suggest that this school year would be different, a much more enjoyable experience for all concerned. In concluding his remarks, he asked if anyone had any questions. Mr. Williams, a sixth-year science teacher, stood up and began to question Mr. James's understanding of the role of the teacher at BHS. Mr. Williams discussed the rationale for attempting to be-come a blue ribbon school, in an environment where teachers, students, and parents almost always disagreed about the purpose of school. Mr. James did not respond to Mr. Williams except to say "come and see me at your convenience and we will discuss this further." Riley thought to him-self "what have I gotten myself into?" He went back to his office to reflect on this first conversation and began to think about how he was going make BHS a school for all students, teachers, and parents.

"School culture" has been and can be defined in a number of ways. Schools and education in general do not have a precise definition of school culture and in some cases school culture has been described as "school climate," "ethos," or "saga" (Deal 1993). The noted anthropologist Geertz (1973) defines culture as the "historically transmitted patterns of meaning" with symbols and beliefs fleshing out these concepts, giving them meaning for each of us, and providing the stimulus for our actions. In this chapter, "school culture" refers to the interaction among the following factors: attitudes and beliefs held by stakeholders inside and outside the organization; cultural norms of the school; and relationships among individuals in the school. School culture is composed of traditions, values, and beliefs that are held in common by students, teachers, and principals (Southwest Educational Development Laboratory 1999). As with other forms of educational belief systems, the concept of culture comes primarily from the business world and to some degree from the greater society.

Schools are a direct reflection of the society from which the students matriculate. As principals are fully aware, many of the conflicts, problems, and concerns that find their way into the school are rooted deeply in the community. Students bring to school the conflicts that are occurring where they reside, whether that be with parents, siblings, or another student. Many times these conflicts are manifested outside the school doors only to be brought inside the school in terms of arguments, fights, harassment, and violence. In order to create a school culture that is conducive to student learning, instruction, and self-discipline, principals need to have an understanding of the social and economic context of where the school is located. The issues surrounding this context are poverty, ethnic diversity, linguistic diversity, changing family patterns, and school safety.

While all of these issues are not found in all schools, most schools will find at least one of these issues.

THE CHANGING NATURE OF SCHOOL AND SOCIETY

Most schools have children that live in economic poverty. According to the Children's Defense Fund (2002) every forty seconds a child is born to parents who live in poverty and every day twenty-seven children die from poverty causes. It goes on to tell us that U.S. children have a two to nine times better chance of living in poverty than in other industrialized nations. Thirty-nine percent of the poor are children and they make up 26 percent of the total population (Weinberg 1999). The vast majority of people in the United States who fall under the poverty guidelines are not the shiftless do-nothings but the working poor. Rural and suburban areas are where you would find the greatest concentration of poor children, not in the inner city as most would expect (Colker 1992). The probability increases by 2 percent that children living in poverty will perform below grade for each year they continue to live in poverty. The more poverty-level students a school has the more likely a child is to fail because poverty level appears to be the best predictor of student achievement (Reeves 1988). The economic status of a child has more to do with his or her academic success than any other single factor. Teacher expectations for students living in poverty may play a role in how the student feels about his or her academic well-being. It is inherent that students, regardless of their financial circumstances, expect the highest-quality instruction from all teachers.

Being aware of the schools' ethnic mixture is of utmost importance to principals as they prepare to educate children. The mix of African American, Hispanic, Asian, and Caucasian students has been changing for the past twenty years. Hodgkinson (1992) states that from 1980 to 1990 the Caucasian population increased by 8 percent, African American by 16 percent, Hispanic by 44 percent, and others by 65 percent. In the period between 1998 and 2003, elementary age students will increase by 2 percent. In that same time period, school age Caucasian children will decrease by 3 percent, African American children will increase by 3 percent, and Hispanic children will increase by 15 percent (Synder 1998). The issue for principals is to make sure materials for instruction are made available to all students regardless of their ethnicity. Children who are part of a minority and living in poverty make up a larger percentage of students enrolled in special, vocational, and general education than would normally be expected. Ethnicity should not be an excuse to change the academic expectations of either the teacher or the school. Ethnic diversity provides an opportunity for teachers and children to celebrate their cultural differences and similarities.

With ethnic diversity comes linguistic diversity. More than 1.25 million limited-English-proficient students were in school in the fifty states in 1979; in 1995 there were 2.4 million according to the National Center for Education Statistics (1997). Programs for non-English speakers come in the form of bilingual education and English as a Second Language (ESL). In reviewing the literature, it is clear that bilingual and ESL programs have had limited success in changing the language habits of students enrolled in these programs. It is the role of the principal to make sure that all children have multicultural opportunities and that teachers academically challenge these students.

One of the most dramatic changes in society that has impacted the school is changing family patterns. What used to be considered the atypical family, a single-parent family has over the past thirty years become the norm. More than 27 percent of all families with children have a single parent as head of the household, which is up from 24 percent in 1990 and 11 percent in 1970. The traditional family with a father, mother, and children has continued to decline and single-mother families continue to rise. The ratio of children living in single-parent families is twice as large as it was in 1970 (Casper and Bryson 1998). According the U.S. Census Bureau, there were 2.1 million father–child households and 9.8 million mother–child households in 1998 and 42.2 percent of these women had never been married. Single-parent families have a greater tendency to live in poverty and the children are less successful in school. In 1999, 70 percent of the children living in single-parent families headed by mothers lived in poverty (Casper and Bryson 1998). The fact that 25 percent of all married couples with children were eighteen years of age or under is a factor that affects schools. It is important to note that children raising children has and will continue to be a major concern for schools. Teenage parents tend to be less interested in their children because they have yet to fulfill their personal needs socially, academically, or in their work life. Children living in single-parent families are more likely than not to be unsuccessful in school and are more likely to be living in poverty. This all translates into lunch, breakfast, after school day care, tutoring, and recreation programs for the school to supervise and operate. In many ways, principals and teachers have become surrogate parents to many of these children. As a nation and a society, much has been said, fault has been assigned, and laws have been enacted, yet the traditional family continues to disintegrate. The family structure is in flux and the future of families is uncertain, but the tragedy in society is compounded on the children. For principals the question becomes: What can we do as a school to ameliorate the impact of single parents on the child's educational experience? The answer to this question is one of conscience and effort, not one of citing the cause and continuing to do the same things.

Society continues to become more multifaceted and families more varied with schools assuming more of the responsibilities that used to be the role of the home. The roles that parents and teachers play in the lives of children have become blurred as schools perform many of these roles. Dodd and Konzal (2000) argue that educators many times view parents as problems, to be kept out of the teacher's purview. Keeping parents outside of the schoolhouse may cause an increased hostility by parents. If principals do not manage parent involvement, it can lead to conflict with the school. Which group knows the best: teachers, principals, or parents? Dodd and Konzal (2000) list three principles that need to be utilized by principals wanting to develop healthy school–parent relationships: (1) both parents and teachers have ideas about what constitutes quality schools; (2) the discussion must change from talking about sharing power to sharing perspectives; and (3) the best schools are found where all students learn and care about one another.

The societal issue that has received the most attention in the current past is the safety and security of students, teachers, and administrators that will be covered in more detail in chapter 14. The National Center for Educational Statistics (1997) reported that 47 percent of the survey respondents indicated that they had experienced some type of child-directed violence in their school. The types of student-on-student violence that were reported included intimidation, verbal and written threats, theft, vandalism, fights, and assaults with weapons. About 10 percent of the principals reported assaults against persons in the form of rape, robbery, and attacks involving weapons. Student suicide, while not considered an act of violence against another person, is a concern for mental health workers and needs school attention. There have been about twenty major gun-related incidents in schools across the United States since 1996 that have resulted in student death or students being wounded. The societal question is: Why have these tragedies occurred and what can schools do to stop these activities? The dichotomy of the question implies that this is a societal problem and is to be solved by the school. Schools do have a role in solving the violence issue but so do the community and the greater society. What students bring to school they almost always get from parents, peers, and the community. They do not get taught violence at school. The principal's role in this societal issue is to provide a safe and caring learning environment for students and teachers. Principals need to plan, implement, and most of all practice the school's crisis management plan. Most principals will never have to endure students shooting students in school, but almost all principals will endure the death of a student or teacher. Preparation is the key for principals to make the school as safe as possible for everyone.

Schools are and have been a major player on the societal stage. In the past twenty-five to thirty years, the societal issues discussed in the aforementioned paragraphs have become the school's responsibility to correct. The school can't be totally responsible for correcting these issues but is considered a major player in creating the problem remedies. Is the school setting the best place to solve issues such as poverty, single-parent families, violence, and diversity? Do teachers and principals have the education and training to help children solve these societal issues? The role of schooling has expanded throughout the history of public school education and will no doubt continue to expand. These questions remain and principals will continue to attempt to solve these societal ills.

SCHOOL CULTURE

Successful schools emerge from the direction of principals who see the school organization from a holistic point of view. Seeing the big picture is what principals do when they understand and are able to communicate and shape the values, beliefs, and attitudes of faculty and students. This allows them to give guidance to the future of the organization. They see and understand complex problems from a much different perspective than they would if they treated the problem in isolation. Culture can affect what teachers discuss in their classroom, in the teachers' lounge, and in the instruction that takes place in the classroom. In most ways, the school's culture is a direct reflection of the community culture. If the community is supportive of the local school system and takes pride in what the district accomplishes, then students will reflect that same pride in their academic and extracurricular pursuits. If not, the district's culture will suffer dramatically as will the community. Community values influence the direction and culture of the school. Deal (1985) outlines four community influences that have negatively affected the school's culture: (1) the belief that education is the pathway to life's success; (2) research has replaced tradition and experience of local teachers and principals; (3) effect of accountability examinations on instruction; and (4) professional educators associations are negatively vocal and have taken on the essence of labor unions. When the school focuses on values, beliefs, and attitudes, both the school and the community can be rewarded. Unfortunately, some schools have been allowed to deteriorate to the point where faculty do not serve students, where negativity reigns and hopelessness is the norm.

According to Patterson, Purkey, and Parker (1986), school culture has the following positive and negative attributes. The following school culture attributes may produce positive effects for the school, and these attributes:

- affect student achievement
- are created and controlled by people in the school
- are different for each school
- are the glue that holds the school together

They go on to elaborate about the negative attributes of school culture and how it can:

- be a roadblock to organizational success
- seem cruel to some subgroups in a school
- take a long time to change the organization

Developing or changing the existing school culture may be an honorable goal and perhaps needs to be done in the worst way, but keep in mind that the mental images held by both internal and external stakeholders is very powerful and limits the way the stakeholders think. Changing these images will take time and the will of the change agent may be in direct conflict with the will of the majority of the stakeholders. The culture of the school was not created overnight and it will not be changed overnight. Principals can send powerful messages by what they say and model. According to Peterson (1999), the principal needs to strengthen the psyche and heart of the school by:

- public displays of student and teacher achievement
- using the school's history to strengthen positive values
- providing the structure to classify the school's core values and to operationalize these values

In many situations, the school culture is grounded in negativity created by the students, teachers, and principals who never attempt to promote the positive things the organization accomplishes. These kind of schools are truly an example of a self-fulfilling prophecy, what can go wrong will. The development of new traditions, symbols, and the selection of faculty and staff that are willing to help develop a positive attitude among the students about the school and what it intends to accomplish is essential.

Attitudes and beliefs of the stakeholders in the school form the foundation on which the school culture is built. These attitudes and beliefs come from a variety of individuals inside and outside of the school. Parents, teachers, peers, and friends all play a part in student attitudes and beliefs about learning. If the students can be convinced that the school will provide them with opportunities to be successful, then attitudes and beliefs about the school will change to meet the demands of today's society. It is a must that students believe they are respected as individuals and are a meaningful part of the school. The most important of these attitudes and beliefs is the concept that all students can and will succeed. Without this belief, the school will be mired in the toxic waste of cultural impotence. In order to create the opportunity for each student to bond with his or her school, the following actions are required:

- Students are rewarded for their positive social behavior. The principal is responsible for acknowledging cooperative student and teacher behaviors.
- Students understand the type of conduct that is expected of them. The principal is responsible for making sure that students and teachers understand the school's policies and procedures concerning school conduct and the sanctions that are attached to those conduct policies. As often as possible, these conduct policies and procedures should be

stated in positive rather than negative ways. For example, "students will be rewarded for getting to class on time," rather than "students will serve one hour of Saturday school for each three times they are tardy for a class." Consistency of application of policies and procedures across the spectrum of school activities is essential. Positive student behavior should be rewarded with attention and concrete rewards from the principal with activities that are consistent with the context of the school.

- Students have the opportunity to make decisions about their daily school life. The principal solicits input about school policies and procedures that will cause most students to comply with these expectations because they have had some opportunity to influence the direction of the policy or procedure. The level of student involvement in decision making is dependent on the student's level of maturity.
- Students learn a common vocabulary in describing positive interactions. The principal and teachers agree on a common vocabulary on which standard phrases are created. These phrases are utilized to reinforce the type of behavior the school wants to promote. These phrases are used by all faculty and staff to indicate positive student action. For example, if the school's goal is to teach caring and sharing, the key phrase might be "collaborative caretakers" to describe student actions that demonstrate students helping students.
- Students learn to be receptive to new ideas. The principal is responsible for creating the norm that new ideas are the lifeblood of the school. New ideas should be rewarded and promoted among the students, faculty, and the staff. Experimentation is the basis for cultural change in any organization and so too it is with schools. Innovative student and academic programs give life to what will become school tradition and beliefs. Time to reflect and celebrate student and faculty achievement is a must.
- Students learn that individual differences are to be celebrated. The principal constantly reinforces the concept that no single group in the school is more important than any other group. Ethnicity, religion, and gender must be honored in order for all groups to see themselves as successful. (Bosworth 1999)

Cultural beliefs and attitudes impact school improvement to the point that teachers and students internalize those beliefs and make them personal values. People new to the school must learn the culture or face sanctions employed by the school. Likewise, students and teachers must not become totally socialized to the culture or the organization will run the risk of stagnation. A deterrent to a positive school culture is teacher and principal mobility. The loss of key members of any organization always impacts the improvement of the organization and that applies to schools as well. School improvement based on the change of a culture mandates teacher and principal leadership. Fullan (1992) argues that highly charismatic principals that radically change the school's culture over a short time frame have a profound effect on the culture when they leave. It is the principal's responsibility to provide direction so that the school culture becomes a positive force in allowing the school to become the best it can be.

Principals interested in modifying or changing their school's culture must identify and understand the current culture. This must be done carefully and with some hesitation. As is with all other change, principals will want to model the type of change they want students, teachers, and all other stakeholders to achieve. A caring principal who puts people first sends the message to students and teachers about what the principal believes is important. Investigating routines and traditions can provide the principal with information prior to change that will provide him or her with insights about the significance of a proposed change. The principal may want to invest in the National Association of Secondary School Principal's Comprehensive Assessment of School Environments–Information System Management (CASE–ISM) to analyze the school's culture prior to approaching the question of cultural change. Keefe (1993) states that CASE-ISM provides a diagnostic analysis of school leadership, structure, values, and satisfaction.

Before the principal can exert any influence over the school culture, he or she must work to ameliorate the long-standing saga regarding schools and schooling. Some of the closest held beliefs that fail to meet the scrutiny of time are:

- *Principals and teachers are adversaries.* Individuals who promote that kind of thinking are dedicated to school destruction and need to be eliminated from the organization. Principals and teachers are in the business of educating children, not destroying each other.
- *Principals and teachers believe parents and other stakeholders are the enemy.* Principals and teachers complain about parents and other stake-

holders but do not see them as the enemy. If this were true, why would schools constantly solicit parental input?

- *Principals and teachers believe that students innately lack intelligence.* All educators understand that students generally meet the expectations presented to them. Learning is a result of attitude and perseverance, not intelligence.
- *Principals and teachers believe that the direct-teach model is the only instructional strategy to use with children.* While it is true that the vast majority of teachers use the direct-teach model for instruction, it is not the only model being employed. Principals and teachers must pursue other models of instruction to meet the needs of all students and in turn they change with the culture of the organization.

Principals must understand that actions support deeply held beliefs. It is important that principals wanting to improve schools must address the beliefs of all the stakeholders if school improvement is to occur. As part of this process, principals must be open to constructive criticism and the willingness to confront their own beliefs. A continuous reflection is required in order to meet the needs of all school stakeholders. Changing the school culture for school improvement must be the target, not change for change's sake, because most of the time it will not work. As Senge (1990b) notes in his article "The leader's new work: Building learning organizations," at any point in time the image of the future will evolve and the principal that can adapt to internal and/or external threats is the person capable of creating a dynamic school culture.

As a principal, how do you achieve the desired school culture? Depending on your school's context, you may want to employ one or all of the following strategies for changing the school culture.

- Establish a program of rewards for positive behavior.
- Communicate core values by modeling appropriate behavior.
- Celebrate staff, student, and community accomplishments.
- Use staff development for teachers and students that allows for giving and receiving praise.
- Assure that teachers and students learn to optimize the opportunities to demonstrate respectful behavior.
- Communicate expectations in a clear and concise manner.

• Provide development in conflict and negotiation skills. (Bosworth 1999)

Cavanaugh and Dellar (1997) create a model for developing school culture and school improvement. They state that the nucleus of the model is composed of the values and norms held by individual teachers. These values and norms form the elements of school culture as they are exchanged among all the faculty members. Should this fail to occur, there will be an absence of school culture. Teachers working in isolation have no way of collectively solving school-related problems.

Cavanaugh and Dellar (1997) state that the cultural elements of teacher efficacy, collegiality, collaboration, shared planning, transformational leadership, and emphasis on learning are the forces that cause schools to improve academically and culturally. Teacher efficacy is about the value teachers place on schooling and the level to which they will work to accomplish the goals of the organization. The teachers' values are given credence by their participation in the school community. Collegiality is concerned with and among teachers' interpersonal relationships and their need for empowerment. With collegiality comes support from principals and other teachers which in turn provides educational confidence in the teaching and learning process. With this confidence, teachers become willing participants in classroom research and innovation. Most of all they trust each other and the principal to help with problems and listen when mistakes occur.

Collaboration focuses on teacher-to-teacher discourse in the formal setting of the school organization. This aspect of school culture provides the consistency in instruction that students must have to be successful. Moving from class-to-class and teacher-to-teacher, students' learning experiences are enhanced by a unified curriculum and a variety of instructional strategies.

Shared planning assumes teachers know and understand the school vision and their willingness to participate and implement the school's targets. This type of planning provides a unity of purpose for all stakeholders in the school. Teacher participation in decision making mandates that teachers know and understand school policies, procedures, and most of all the school's future direction. Being equal partners in decision making provides the motivation for teachers to pull their share of the load.

Transformational leadership focuses on the principal's willingness and capacity to support teachers and programs. Principals must be willing to divest themselves of some leadership responsibilities to focus on the school and community. This does not mean an abdication of responsibility by the principal, but it does mean a sharing of that responsibility with the entire school community. Sharing of responsibility should cause individuals in the school to develop leadership skills by capturing the energy and expertise of the professionals in the organization.

The School Improvement Model of School Culture as developed by Cavanaugh and Dellar (1997) focuses on the values and norms of teachers as captured by their interpersonal relationships. This model is a drastic change from the traditional organizational structure of schools and school systems.

Principal Riley James soon finds out that all is not well on the BHS campus and he knows he will need to change the culture of the school if Bethany is to ever achieve blue ribbon status. How is Mr. James going to transform the values, traditions, and perceptions of the teachers on the faculty? Will collaboration and shared decision making be the key elements in creating a vision for BHS? What strategies would you utilize if you were in his position?

PRINCIPAL'S ROLE IN CREATING A VISION

Principals find themselves trying to create a vision when in most cases they are hesitant about the starting point. The "V" word has and will continue to be the topic of all organizations that find themselves in a dilemma. Each principal is, without exception, encouraged to have a vision without a clue as to what one looks like or where it comes from. Lashway (1997) in his book *Leading with Vision* describes the role, purpose, and structure of a vision. He goes on to argue that visions reflect the values of the group creating the vision. Vision is contextual by its very nature and cannot be generalized to another organization. Lashway (1997) argues that there are four concepts associated with visions:

- Visions should be concerned with student learning, the whats and whys.
- Visions should be concerned with student social responsibility.
- Visions should be concerned with the school environment.
- Visions should be concerned with the relationship between external and internal environments.

The principal is a major player in leading the process of creating a vision. Far too much of the time principals seem to revert to "do as I say" instead of "do as I do." They provide lip service for ideas but never follow up with action. It doesn't take long for students and faculty to determine the real values cherished by the person in the principal's role. The vision should be the map that takes the school to its target. The vision is the force that unites all stakeholders to proceed in a similar direction and provides a schema with which to evaluate new programs. Nagel (2000) suggests several questions to ask when creating a vision:

- What does the school want to do in the worst way?
- What is currently being done that is a difference maker?
- What does vision creation mean to each individual?
- Where should the school be in three years?
- What does the school need more or less of?

When thinking about the attributes of a vision, it is important to keep the end in mind. Creating and implementing a vision is critical for the school organization because of the radical changes occurring in twenty-first-century society. The vision for the school takes on a greater significance when one considers the purpose of schooling. Unfortunately for many principals, a vision is nothing more than an exercise in community public relations, a document to serve as a paperweight or as a mystical experience in the same mode as psychic phenomena. According to Bosworth (1999), the characteristics that make up a vision include:

- A shared ideal of the school culture. All stakeholders in the school and the community should be involved in sharing the vision. Avoid the power struggles that can become part of the vision development.
- All segments of the community are directly involved in the decision-making process.
- The vision should be consistent with the culture of the community.
- All stakeholders must participate by examining the vision from their personal perspective.

The vision needs to be developed and acted on utilizing a consensus method of agreement. It makes little sense to have a planning committee vote on ideas for the vision, because a one-vote margin means that at least 49 percent of the committee members oppose the idea. Consensus has never meant that all of the committee members agree 100 percent of the time on any idea, but it does mean that those who do not agree will support the idea. They are willing to suspend their personal wishes for the good of the whole. Consensus then is about agreement to support the idea from a holistic perspective. Using a consensus model of agreement is more time-consuming and in some ways much more frustrating than taking a vote, but it does assure the planning group that all members are on board with the ideas in the vision.

According to Pankake (1998), the implementation of a vision begins with the assessment of the distance between where we are and where we want to be. Senge (1990a) in his book entitled *The Fifth Discipline* refers to this distance as "creative tension." This divergence becomes the boundary line for the implementation field. Principals must know the boundaries because they help:

- Know the direction for progress toward the vision. Knowing where you want to end up can only be determined by where you begin. You would never begin a cross country trip without a road map and even when you arrive at your destination you need directions to specific attractions.
- Know what the human and financial costs will be for vision implementation. These costs may come in the form of time, personnel, and supplies. The question of human and financial cost should have been part of the discussion when the vision was created. Nonetheless, people and supplies are needed to implement the vision and a commitment from the district is most important.
- Know the benchmark data for the purposes of monitoring and assessment. If you do not benchmark the beginning of the implementation process, you have no gauge from which to measure progress. It is critical that you select questions to benchmark based on the vision you have created.
- Know the individuals and groups that are not 100 percent on board with the vision. You need to pay special attention to those who agreed to support the vision through the consensus-building process but had some reservations about the idea contained in the vision. These individuals may slide off of the team if they do not receive the principal's attention and support.
- Know how to practice for the work of the vision. Practice with all the stakeholders the skills necessary to implement a successful vision. Practice, practice, practice, and model, model, model the type of behavior you want others to demonstrate.
- Know where and when the tasks required by the vision are to begin and end. Each task generated by the vision must be attached to an individual with a specific time for completion. Accountability and implementation

strategies are incomplete without specific task assignments. Without these assignments the vision runs the risk of an undetermined failure. (Pankake 1998)

A model for creating a vision for a school does not need to be complex, but it does need to be thorough and to include all stakeholder groups. Implementation can come in various forms, but it is important for the principal to be a participant apart from the format. The principal cannot be the leader of the process and at the same time be a participant, it just doesn't allow a free flow of ideas. Employ a consultant who has had experience in helping schools create a vision. This consultant may have a suggested model or prefer to use a model created by the stakeholders. Either way, a consultant can say and do things the principal cannot or will not. The cost of the consultant will pay dividends several times over.

When thinking about implementing the visioning process, you might start by asking the individuals on the planning committee to describe their ideal school. What would the children, teachers, principals, and parents be doing in this school? The answers to the aforementioned question will vary from person to person, but these results will give you direction for the school's vision. There are certainly more complex models for the beginning steps in creating a vision and as the principal you might choose to ask committee members to respond to a number of specific questions about the current organization. Regardless of the structure of your vision, the target must be a coherent, positive, and simply stated view into the future. For example, at BHS Principal James might produce a vision that says, "At Bethany High School, members of the school community will engage in caring and sharing for each other." This vision will require that all participants—students, teachers, and parents—practice helping one another achieve each individual's goal. The implementation process of the Bethany vision requires Principal James to model the actions he wants to convey to all other stakeholders. As a principal, if you are not willing to model the desired behavior, stay out of the vision arena, because failure is right around the corner.

Implementation of the vision might be aided by reducing all of the ideas and concepts into an implementation grid. This grid addresses the task, the responsible person, the date for implementation completion, the cost, and the expected outcomes. Exhibit 4.1 provides a visual display of a typical implementation grid.

Target or Goal to be Accomplished				
Activity	**Responsible Person**	**Target Date**	**Costs**	**Expectation**
Implementation of a phonics program in reading	Mary Jane Jones, Matilda Smith, and all third-grade teachers	September 1, 2001	$13.50 per student	Better scores on the state accountability test

Exhibit 4.1. **Implementation Grid**

SCHOOL ACCOUNTABILITY

In the current debate concerning student, teacher, principal, and school accountability, it is always helpful to reflect on the history that has led to this discussion. The birth of the big "A" word accountability began in the 1950s with the writing of James B. Conant sounding the warning toll for the need of comprehensive elementary and secondary education programs and an extremely selective system of higher education. Tests were thought to be an answer to Conant's need for a selective and rigorous education. Cremin (1989) notes that Conant thought U.S. education was lacking high-quality schooling for academically talented children. Conant's beliefs were further enhanced when Russia launched the space craft *Sputnik* and the race for space began. Congress immediately passed the National Defense Education Act, which provided grant resources to public schools for science and mathematics education. From Conant's ideas came academic tracking and ability grouping. This is not so different from what is currently practiced in schools across this nation. Course names and designations have been changed to honors, college prep, advanced placement, gifted, remedial, and average. These designations are exactly what Conant was arguing but the results are not. With these course designations comes a wide variance in content and student expectations.

In the mid-1960s, President Lyndon B. Johnson persuaded Congress to pass legislation that would address the differences in achievement students were bringing to school as first graders. In addressing this issue, Congress passed the Elementary and Secondary Education Act (ESEA) of 1965 that focused on compensatory education. This act has become the biggest and most influential of the federal efforts that intervene in public school education. The ESEA legislation is the foundation for accountability and the springboard for the testing industry. Congress provided the resources to improve student achievement and in turn it wanted more oversight concerning how these resources were working. As a result of these congressional demands, Title I of ESEA became the standard barer for accountability for all federally funded educational programs. Testing requirements for Title I were so demanding that a separate program entitled Title I Evaluation and Reporting System (TIERS) was created. In order to do a more comprehensive job of evaluating and reporting, TIERS encouraged and then required participating schools to test two times a year, once in the fall and again in the spring, in order to measure student progress. As you might expect, mixed results came about when schools used various testing instruments to measure student gain. Linn (2000) suggests two cautions for the current accountability phenomenon learned from the TIERS experience: (1) comparing test results from various testing dates distorts the comparison; and (2) continued use of a single test can alter instruction and lead toward distorted academic increases in student achievement.

The 1970s and 1980s brought forth the concept of minimum competency testing. During those two decades, the requirement for minimum competency testing jumped from two to thirty-four states. Basic skills now became the target of attention for state legislatures demanding that schools focus on minimum skills for high school graduation. These minimum academic requirements had little impact on most students and any achievement gains noted because of these tests were found at the lower end of the continuum (Linn 2000). The benchmark federal district court decisions in *Debra P. v. Turlington* (1981) still provides the legal tests for high-stakes testing. Detractors of this decision continue to discuss who is responsible for student success or failure on these high-stakes tests. Students, teachers, parents, curriculum, instruction, or perhaps the test have been cited as the culprit for student failures. This debate will continue to be tested in the courts and in the court of public opinion, but it is clear that high-stakes testing will continue in states that currently use them for student promotion and high school graduation.

In the 1990s, the issue of school accountability continued to revolve around high-stakes testing with the added concept of school choice as the solution to poor public school test results. President George Bush, hearing the cries of certain economic failure for the country because of poor public school systems, commissioned, through the Department of Energy, a study of U.S. student achievement. Secretary of Energy James Watkins was charged with generating the report and enlisted a research team from the Sandia National Laboratory, a federal research facility with impeccable credentials, to study the state of public school education in the United States. The research team found both positive and negative aspects of schooling in the United States. Schrag (1997) reports that the research study discovered that this country's educational system is far more complex and is doing a better job than the rhetoric of alarm had contended. He submitted the report to Energy Secretary Watkins and the secretary declared that the Sandia Report was "dead wrong" and would send the wrong message to the public. The Bush administration never released the Sandia Report, even after attempting to get the research team to alter some of its findings; regardless, some copies were circulated underground. The Sandia Report concludes that about 90 percent of the high school students graduated; graduation rates for higher education are at an all time high; one in four adults has a college degree; the United States has the largest percentage of twenty-two year olds receiving math, science, or engineering degrees in the world; and the researchers estimated that between 1960 and 1988 per pupil expenditures increased by 39 percent for regular students and 150 percent for all students. Over this eighteen-year period, spending increased 111 percent, mostly for special education students, who have little or no impact on the results of standardized tests (Schrag 1997). The Sandia Report was officially released by the Clinton administration with little fanfare and garnering little media attention. The newest iteration of this debate comes in the form of standards-based accountability systems. Schools are struggling to define who they are and what they stand for by aligning curriculum, creating instruments to measure district and state developed tests, and developing curriculums that are designed to take their students to the top of the tested pool of students.

For more than fifty years, schooling has been the chosen battleground for both the liberal and conservative political ideologues. Both sides in this debate have created a sense of crisis in order to further their political interests. In the case of the liberals, more money for education is the issue and for the conservatives the issues are school choice and government-operated schools. In each of the five preceding decades, schooling has come under fire from politically motivated groups trying to press their own agenda. In the 1950s, the political agenda was sparked by *Sputnik,* and the ESEA was the political answer to school problems. The political agenda of the 1980s was marked by the fictional report *A Nation at Risk* and the Bush administration's Goals 2000 program. The 1990s was punctuated by the call for national tests and school choice. One would have to conclude the the accountability movement in education has been successful with forty-eight states now testing their students, forty states issuing school and district "report cards," and nineteen states comparing schools against schools. In more than twenty states, academic bankruptcy and reconstitution of schools allow the state to takeover the individual school and an entire district if it continues to be low performing (Olson 1999). When will the debate end? Perhaps never, because of mixed testing results and because of politicians', educational critics', and educational think tanks' willingness to press their agenda by spinning the data. Without a doubt, schools can and should be involved in a process of continuous improvement, but schools are not gasping for the last breaths of academic failure as some have indicated.

PRINCIPAL'S ROLE IN SCHOOL ACCOUNTABILITY

As a principal, what are the strategies to be employed in order to place a school on the road to developing a program of educational accountability? Several models exist that could help provide the answer to this question, but it is clear that regardless of the model of improvement employed, the principal must develop the process that matches the context of the school. The accountability model utilized must be systematic and links standards, tests, staff development, and consequences as one continuous strand. Watts, Gaines, and Creech (1998) emphasize that testing will have little or no effect if the other three aspects of the accountability system are not in place. They argue that standards must be developed in a collaborative manner with all constituent stakeholders having input into the development process. The systemic effect is more powerful than each of the parts individually, so it is imperative principals understand that a system consists of a set of interrelated parts that are self-correcting. The analogy of the human heart and an organizational system are synonymous. The faster you walk, the harder your heart pumps blood, the higher the blood pressure, and the more oxygen the body consumes and needs; likewise, the slower you walk, the lower the blood pressure, and the less oxygen the body needs. The human circulatory system works in the same way as does school accountability. Each part of the school accountability system must work in unison with all the parts of the system or the school has a fatal heart attack. In order for any system to function properly, all parts must be in good working condition.

For principals, meeting the demands of an accountability system means constant attention to improvement and at the same time meeting the demands a school requires on a daily basis. The principal who provides this type of leadership must be able to multitask and keep several balls in the air at any one time. This amounts to using data to give direction to the system and with a plethora of data at the principal's disposal, it is vital that the principal understand what he or she is trying to find out. Thoughtful examination of the data makes sure that misrepresentation of the data does not occur. Of what value is knowing the average daily attendance rate unless you find out which specific students are absent and how those absences have affected the students' academic progress. Having an average attendance rate of 97 percent is of little value when applied to the accountability model, but when applied to the funding formula it has a huge effect on the school's resources.

Lake et al. (1999) studied forty schools with thirty schools significantly raising test scores on a fourth-grade test. What these researchers discovered was that schools improved when they focused on the "big picture" aspects of school improvement. This meant that making minor changes in curriculum, textbooks, and schedules was not the answer. The answer came in changes in philosophical thinking and unique approaches to instruction. Teachers worked together and spent their intellectual capital on instructional goals and parental involvement. The directive to principals from this study indicated that positive accountability results can be developed by identifying performance deficiencies, by creating a school-wide improvement process, and by seeking help when expertise is lacking. All of this must be done and at the same time teacher morale, educational equity, and avoidance of unintended consequences must be addressed by the principal. The accountability process may have been an easier pill to swallow for educators had it been framed around professional growth rather than changing behavior. Principals need to be aware that one of their roles in the accountability arena is to provide a desire for professional growth (Sammon 2000). Principals need to be risk takers and support teachers and students who are willing to do the same. Risk taking is the highest form of trust. After all, that's what being a principal is all about. The greater society looks toward the principal for continuous improvement and measured student gain.

Principals must do everything in their power to make sure they focus on the individual needs of students as the most important aspect of the accountability program. This type of system establishes a commitment to collective problem solving and student assessment. Darling-Hammond and Ascher (1991) argue that the following questions define the accountability issues that structure students' learning experiences.

- What experiences do children need to succeed?
- Will children have an advocate at school?
- How is time on task evaluated and utilized?
- How are benchmarks established for evaluating progress?

Principals must find the courage to attach meaning to the results of the academic measures they have available to them. In order to apply meaning to these measures, the principal must undertake the process of matching student success to teacher assessment. Reviewing the test results of students provides the principal with information concerning the objectives the students are mastering and those they are not. With this information, the next step needs to involve teachers reviewing the objectives their students mastered and those they did not. Taken over a four- or five-year period, it becomes rather clear what objectives the teacher taught well and what objectives were not taught well. It is the principal's responsibility to disaggregate the test data so that teachers can see their instructional strengths and weaknesses. As stated before, accountability is about school improvement and this can only happen if student instruction improves. Nothing the principal does will impact the school more than improved instruction. Nothing else a principal does comes close to changing the landscape of school leadership than tying student scores on accountability examinations to teacher assessment.

The real challenge for principals advocating this model of teacher assessment comes in marketing the concept of student testing as a means of teacher assessment. There is little doubt that some teacher groups and individual teachers will oppose the concept as being unfair. The teacher argument seems to stem from their belief that their assessments should not be tied to student scores. Some teachers believe that students lack the academic discipline to be learners while others argue the impact of mainstreaming special education students will impact their personal assessment negatively. While the teacher arguments need to be addressed, the principal needs to remember that assessing teachers is really about what students accomplish in the classroom, not about the performance of the teacher. One, two, or three formal observations coupled with periodic classroom walk-throughs only give the observer a small snapshot of what happens in that class on a daily basis. The accountability examination provides both the teacher and the principal with a panoramic view of what the teacher taught and the level of student understanding for any specific measured objective. This concept of teacher assessment of tested objectives should not be punitive but rather designed for instructional improvement and teacher growth. After all, aren't teachers supposed to be lifelong learners both in their knowledge and in the craft of instruction?

When states compare schools to schools and districts to districts, they are trying to motivate teachers and principals to do a better job of instruction. This type of motivation plays on the fears of people, especially building-level principals as they compete with their colleagues across the state. The fear factor has changed the way all stakeholders see the local schools both in a positive and negative manner. More and more pressure is brought to bear on teachers and principals to move the school to the top of the testing pyramid. The question remains: At what point do students begin to lose the opportunity to learn a variety of information, if they are continuously focused on the accountability examination content?

MODELS FOR RAISING TEST SCORES

Of the forty-eight states with mandated accountability examinations, forty require the publishing of a "report card" to the public. The indicators that are used by states most often in their report cards are:

- Assessment score (forty states)
- Dropout rate (thirty-three states)
- Student attendance (twenty-nine states)
- Per pupil expenditure (twenty-seven states)
- Graduation rate (seven states)
- Postsecondary education or employment (sixteen states) (Education Commission of the States [ECS] 1999b)

Other indicator areas are curriculum, culture, and expenditures. While these areas are not directly attached to student achievement, most stakeholders would agree they influence student success.

All of these indicators address students and not the professional staff. However, some states do factor in indicators for the professional staff. Those indicators used most often by states include faculty:

- Attendance (four states)
- Diversity (three states)
- Evaluation (three states)
- Experience (seven states) (ECS 1999b)

A word of caution is needed when discussing student and teacher indicators as a basis of comparison for all districts in any state. That caution is manifested in the fact that educational research is extremely hard to do and is very complex. When looking at cause and effect relationships, it is almost impossible to create controls that avoid contaminating the collected data. However, some models appear to have created school improvements.

The Education Commission of the States (ECS) publication entitled *The Progress of Education Reform 1999–2001* discusses the results of a 1998 study by Steve Ross of the Center for Research in Education Policy. Ross's research examined the effect of eight models of school reform as measured by the Tennessee Comprehensive Assessment Program, the state accountability examination for Tennessee school children. This research ended with two conclusions: (1) schools that adopted a comprehensive school improvement model had higher student achievement gains than did students where no school improvement model was being implemented; and (2) students in the schools utilizing school improvement models, in all grades and subjects, were achieving at a faster pace than the national average (ECS 1999a). In a June 1999 update, Ross discovered the following:

- The Accelerated Schools, Roots and Wings, and Co-NECT models impacted student achievement to the greatest extent
- The Co-NECT model demonstrated the only significant achievement effects across the curriculum
- Schools with high levels of poverty demonstrated the greatest levels of academic gain in comparison with demographically similar schools not focused on school improvement (ECS 1999a)

The Co-NECT model was created by the Educational Technologies Group at BNN Corporation in 1992 and is now used in sixty-five schools in ten states. This model of school improvement is predicated on the following four premises:

- Re-creation of the curriculum for world-class learning—High expectations and total school accountability using multiple assessments
- Creation of technology links so that students can participate in a global society—Learning by doing using the best technology available
- Creation of conditions for individual diversity to enhance lifelong learning—A school divided into learning communities
- Creation of strategies to begin and maintain changes—The development of community resources for continuous school improvement (Goldberg and Richard 1996)

The unique feature of the Co-NECT model revolves around teamwork, project-based teaching, assessment for continuous improvement, and use of technology. Before implementation of phase one can begin, 75 percent of the faculty must agree with the previously outlined concepts. The principal must be committed to supporting the program and be willing to allow a full-time program facilitator to become part of the faculty team and assist with the school accountability process. In addition, the principal must find the resources to send teachers to Co-NECT's national conference and provide Internet connections for all teachers. Phase two, taking two to five years, addresses assessment of student work and creating a sense of community and phase three is directed at institutionalizing the model. The costs of the Co-NECT program run about $65,000 per year for a three-year period (ECS 2000).

Roots and Wings was developed as part of the New American Schools program in 1993 to supplement the program Success for All. This program is designed for children in kindergarten through grade 6 focusing on (1) student achievement based on world-class standards, and (2) developing problem-solving skills in learners (Traub 1999). The philosophy undergirding this program is one of relevancy, age appropriateness, active learning, and critical thinking skills (Office of Educational Research and Improvement 1998).

The unique feature of the Roots and Wings program is the integrated curriculum found in the math and social science areas, the use of phonics in reading, and the integration of reading and writing. In addition, this program prescribes the use of a family support team that promotes parent involvement in school. Staff development for teachers consists of a three-day workshop at the beginning, while trainers provide coaching and other specific staff development activities during the school year. The evaluation of the program revealed increased student achievement in all areas tested and schools that achieved lower scores prior to program utilization scored higher than their comparison group after two years. Implementation costs for Roots and Wings are about $75,000 for the first year, $66,000 for the second year, and $42,00 for the third year (ECS 1999a). As with any program, the major concern is does it work or can it be modified to work? The essential element in this success is found in the willingness of the school to continue to implement the program as it was designed. For too long schools have looked for the "quick fix" to solve student academic problems and have been unable or unwilling to work a program for an extended period of time. This certainly does not mean that schools should become involved with the dead horse syndrome, that is, riding a dead horse takes you nowhere. The key is to implement and adjust.

The third program that appears to allow the school to become more accountable is the Accelerated Schools Project developed by Henry Levin and implemented in 1986. This program focuses on at-risk students, with the underlying assumption that at-risk students have the same ability to learn as do any other students. Lofty expectations, a demanding curriculum, and instructional strategies usually reserved for the gifted and talented students are employed. Accelerated Schools focus on the following:

- A unified purpose—all stakeholders in the organization agree to pursue the same educational targets
- Decision focus and sanctions—all stakeholders agree to assume responsibility for the group's decisions
- Strength development—combining all stakeholder resources for the education of the children (Levin 1994)

The impact of the Accelerated Schools Project on student achievement and school accountability has been marginal at best according to research completed by Traub (1999). Traub cites research studies of schools in Louisiana, Missouri, and Tennessee that indicated that rigorous academic programs were implemented and produced positive, but limited, effects on student achievement. He goes on to state that the program developer provided implementation support on-site and other support. First-year implementation costs for this model were about $27,000 per school as opposed to the $150,000 average cost of all of the models studied (1999).

Traub (1999) cites ten models that are representative samples of the many school improvement strategies that exist in the market place. They do represent the most widely studied models and the data provided gives principals some insight into the types of strategies that work to improve schools and raise accountability scores. The models included in his schoolwide reform approaches are: Accelerated Schools, America's Choice, Coalition of Essential Schools, Success for All, Edison Project, Core Knowledge, and Direct Instruction.

The two accountability models that provide the highest levels of student achievement are the Success for All and Direct Instruction models and cost the most to implement. The Coalition of Essential Schools and Accelerated Schools models appear to have the least effect on student achievement and appear to cost the least to implement. This evidence collected by Traub (1999) concerning the Accelerated Schools Project runs counter to the data collected by Ross in 1999, whose research revealed that the Accelerated Schools Project was one of three models that had the greatest impact on students.

For principals and teachers attempting to raise student achievement scores, the specific model used to reach the target is not as important as are the steps involved in reaching the target. Studying each of the models discussed in exhibit 4.2 provides a process for increasing student success on accountability tests. Using the component parts of each of the models, a principal could develop a strategy for addressing the accountability question and raise the school's percentage of students mastering the accountability examination. The following component parts appear in each of the models in exhibit 4.2:

- A philosophy describing the beliefs supporting the model
- Program targets that provide direction for student achievement
- Program components directed at specific learning strategies
- A systematic value-added evaluation process that is ongoing and longitudinal
- Program costs assessed from the value-added prospective

Ten Schoolwide Reform Approaches at a Glance	Evidence of positive effects on student achievement	School support provided by developer	Installation cost (1st year)	Year introduced in schools	Number of schools	Grade levels
Accelerated Schools	M	P	$27	'86	1,220	K–8
America's Choice	?	S	$190	'98	92	K–12
Coalition of Essential Schools	W	M	$NA	'84	1,200	K–12
Core Knowledge	P	P	$56	'90	968	K–8
Direct Instruction	S	P	$244	'60s	300	K–6
Edison Project	NA	NA	NA	'95	79	K–10
Expeditionary Learning Outward Bound	P	S	$81	'92	60	K–12
Multiple Intelligences	NA	NA	NA	NA	NA	NA
School Development Program	P	P	$45	'68	721	K–12
Success for All	S	S	$270	'87	1,500	K–6

S=strong, P=promising, M=marginal, W=weak, ?=no research, NA=not available

Exhibit 4.2. Schoolwide Reform Approaches
Source: J Traub. (1999). *Better by design: A consumer's guide to schoolwide reform.* New York: Thomas B. Fordham Foundation. Printed by permission.

Using these program parts will allow the principal to create an accountability process that fits the context of the school without having to reinvent the entire process. What teachers and principals do in the school may make a difference in the level of student achievement. Some observers would argue that schools neither have the capacity nor the will to make the necessary improvements to the teaching and learning process to raise student achievement scores. According to Lake et al. (1999), schools can make a difference if they are willing to:

- Focus on expanding the teacher's use of varied models of instruction and materials throughout the school.
- Function as a team from grade-to-grade and course-to-course.
- Provide staff development in the context of developing the school.
- Apply creative tension to the school without teacher fear.
- Pursue accountability improvement by seeking help immediately.
- Use human and financial assets wisely.
- Communicate with parents in an open and honest manner.

As a principal, there is reason to be optimistic about improved student achievement scores as measured by accountability examinations. That reason is found in the ability of the principal to create improvement models that allow teachers to focus their instruction of students on the objectives promulgated by the testing entity and then to expect that it will be accomplished. Every constituent stakeholder group has something to contribute to the success or failure of schools and students when evaluating the results of the accountability protocol.

Principals must establish a process to evaluate school deficiencies. They must provide leadership for teachers, parents, and all stakeholders in the development of an improvement plan. Leaders secure help for improvement strategies that they or other members of the faculty do not possess. Human and financial resources are the principal's responsibility to locate and secure. Perhaps the most important function for the principal, which is often ignored, is productive professional development. This must be staff development that addresses the teacher's need for instructional help with those concepts students fail to master on the accountability examination.

Teachers must be willing and able to be active members of the accountability improvement process and be willing to participate in learning new instructional models. In addition, teachers are to use these instructional strategies to help students meet the demands of the accountability examination. They are also responsible for and helping making sure their colleagues participate fully in the improvement process. Teachers need to make sure that they know and understand the standards and objectives that are being measured by the accountability protocol.

Stakeholders must be willing to accept new instructional strategies and support teachers and principals as they make these commitments to change. Financial resources need to be secured to help students meet the standards for which they are being held accountable. These resources come in many forms—tax dollars, volunteer time, instructional support, and home support—and the stakeholder group must provide oversight to make sure these resources are benefiting the instructional improvement process.

DATA-DRIVEN SCHOOL IMPROVEMENT

As principals, teachers, and students prepare themselves to enter into the twenty-first century's global information age, it becomes apparent that schools must meet the changes much more rapidly than they have in the past. Increased speed in technology and communication make it abundantly clear that educating children can no longer be a process of read and react to the situation. With society, business, and industry moving at warp speed, children are by necessity, going to have to be prepared to work and function in a way that is completely foreign to many of the teachers and principals now serving in today's classrooms. The question becomes: How do schools that are traditionally slow to change meet the educational needs of children destined for rapid change?

Schools, teachers, and principals must meet the challenges of a fluid society by making effective decisions based on accurate information. If indeed education is the one element that gives individuals the competitive edge, then it is mandatory that principals and teachers have the capacity to diagnose student abilities, skills, attitudes, and learning styles. Along with this diagnosis comes the need for educators to be able to write educational prescriptions for students to follow in order to alleviate learning deficits. McLean (1995) wonders whether schools seek to answer the question: Is the quality and appropriateness of today's curriculum for children first-rate because it's been in place for a long time or is it of high quality because it's been assessed and found to be worthy of being labeled first rate? McLean concludes that in most cases the first-rate curriculum label is based on tradition rather than assessment. Collection of data concerning student achievement is arguably the most important aspect that principals and teachers have if students and schools are to improve academically. Serving students and the community in a more purposeful manner means using available data, mostly from test scores, to design more efficient methods of instruction and curriculum development. The key to student and school improvement is not giving students more tests to take, but rather what is done with the test data that is generated. In general, there has been very little effort made by schools to disaggregate the data by test objectives or to determine exactly what students have mastered and then to write a prescription of how to fix what the children have not mastered.

It is impossible to help children achieve at higher levels unless principals take the initiative to interpret the data in a way that is meaningful. Teachers will not or cannot make the necessary adjustments in instructional strategies unless they understand where the individual student needs help. The principal is responsible for making sure teachers meet students' needs and this activity is the lynchpin that makes the entire school improvement process function in a systemic manner. Most schools collect more data on students than they ever use, thus the issue of data collection becomes one of efficiency in data collection. For principals, the challenge becomes collecting and archiving data in a format that can be easily retrieved and manipulated. Archived data becomes the baseline from which comparisons of student and school achievement gains are computed.

Data may be used to assess student accomplishment, diagnose deficiencies, and evaluate solutions. Principals need to share this data with all stakeholders and use it in a judicious manner. According to Calhoun (1994), the concept of school improvement should be stressed by focusing on information about the progress toward the school's academic target and used in making current and future decisions about what actions should be employed. Analyzing the data provides the opportunity for teachers and principals to see previously unnoticed opportunities for improvement. One of the unique ways to foster the concept of data collection by teachers is to designate a "data in a day" program. This program requires teachers to focus on one specific activity early in the day, to collect data, and to submit their findings later the same day. The fast turnaround of information provides students with immediate feedback and reinforcement for the activity assessed (Johnson 1997).

Another data-driven school improvement strategy that has the potential to catapult the organization and students toward world-class status is benchmarking. Benchmarking by definition is used as a reference point by which items can be measured or judged. This process of measuring, in the case of students, achievement gain over a specific time frame allows teachers and principals to learn which instructional innovations give students a competitive edge in mastering state and local accountability examinations. The benchmarking process may utilize the results of criterion-referenced tests to compare student achievement gain over the course of a selected period of time and may be the link to school improvement. The mastery of specific objectives, as measured by the test, can be compared from one testing date to another to determine student progress. The specificity of these results prescribes the instructional focus, which in turn, allows the student to master the previously failed learning objectives. Benchmarking provides education professionals with the capability to research and understand their own instructional strategies and to improve their practice. This practice will provide principals and teachers with the capacity to use the reflection-action-reflection-action cycle in the day-to-day instruction of students (Tucker 1996).

Benchmarking in schools began as a concept when the Baldrige Quality Award for Education was announced in 1995. Both the Association for Supervision and Curriculum Development and the American Association for School Administrators played an important role in the development and promotion of the award. Educational leaders predicted that benchmarking would become the tool of choice for assessing student achievement (Tucker 1996). To date that predication has not been fulfilled with few schools using the tool to measure student progress. Benchmarking has great potential for managing and improving student test scores but it will not change current practice because it lacks support among practicing educators.

Data-driven school and student improvement can be measured in terms of gain or against a specific artificially created standard. While most high-stakes testing claims to compare individual student results with specific criteria, the fact remains that composite school scores are used to assess school quality. Astin et al. (1993) caution educators concerning the use of assessment tools when they opine that assessment of student achievement commences with educational values. They argue that values drive the essence of what and how assessment is performed. Astin et al. (1993)

enumerate eight assessment guidelines for principals to consider as they approach the data-driven school improvement process:

- Assessment should reflect the student's ability to utilize information over time by actually performing complex tasks.
- Assessment is most productive when comparing educational performance and purpose.
- Assessment must address student experiences as well as outcomes. Results are important but student learning is more about attitude, effort, and learning style.
- Assessment is best when it is continuous and measurements are made over time with an array of modalities.
- Assessment is a school activity and should not be isolated to specific grades or courses.
- Assessment should be used to guide and address continuous improvement.
- Assessment should be used to improve teachers, principals, students, and the community.
- Assessment works best when it is part of holistic change.

One the major factors that principals must face and be prepared to deal with in the high-stakes testing environment is teacher knowledge and understanding of externally mandated examinations. The relationship among teacher assessment, instructional practice, and the method of high-stakes testing is critical to the school's performance on these examinations. Most high-stakes testing is done with paper-and-pencil objective examinations utilizing multiple-choice items with some use of performance-based questions. The question for principals to address is: Do teachers utilize both testing formats in the assessment and instruction processes? Vitali (1994) conducted an empirical study to measure teacher utilization of testing formats. He found that teachers in grades K–3 were negatively disposed to objective tests and were positively disposed toward performance-based tests, while fourth- to twelfth-grade teachers favored objective tests and were neutral about performance-based tests. He stated that teachers' instructional methods were aligned with their opinion about their preferred methods of testing.

The dilemma for principals is not deciding whether instructional practice influences testing practice, but rather, encouraging teachers to utilize both testing protocols as they prepare students to take mandated accountability examinations. Principals need to question their teachers on the subject of differing testing protocols as a means of determining teacher understanding. In addition, Vitali (1994) argued that the teachers' knowledge of testing protocols was limited to multiple-choice formats, and thus they needed help in understanding and implementing performance-based examination strategies. Regardless of the cause, the effect of not knowing how to align instruction with testing protocols is a major factor in student success on high-stakes accountability examinations.

ETHICAL DISCUSSION

Should the use of high-stakes testing be continued or decreased?

High-stakes testing for the purpose of school accountability has become a national political issue in almost all fifty states. Both sides of this ethical dilemma have attempted to influence legislative policy makers to adopt their point of view with varying degrees of success.

The questions that need to be answered concerning this are:

- If testing is the answer, what was the question?
- Have the advocates of high-stakes testing misrepresented the results of nationally normed tests?
- High-stakes testing should drive the curriculum. If this statement is true, then how do educators get students to think and to provide reasons for the choices they make?
- Does high-stakes testing measure the scientific base of instruction? What models of instruction does it measure?
- Student assessment of learning is filled with problems. How has the high-stakes testing movement removed testing problems?
- Ethical dilemmas are right-versus-right issues. Which side of the high-stakes testing debate do you support and why?

CHAPTER SUMMARY

Culture is defined in the school setting in a number of ways, but it has been most closely identified with school climate. Attitudes and beliefs of stakeholders inside and outside of the organization and the cultural norms define the culture of school. School populations are a direct reflection of the society from which the students come. Society is changing schools as demonstrated by the increased birth rates of ethnic minorities, changing family patterns, and the safety issues surrounding all stakeholders. Schools have been given the task of correcting many of the societal problems emerging over the past forty years. Whether schools, principals, or teachers are trained to solve these problems is questionable.

Successful schools are products of principals that view the organization holistically. Seeing the big picture is a must for principals if they are to shape the vision, values, and beliefs of the organization. The attributes of school culture affect schools positively in the areas of student achievement and organizational structure. Principals need to recognize that the concept of changing the school culture brings with it negative attributes in the form of roadblocks to school success, attention to selected school subgroups, and the time frame for change. The attitudes of all stakeholders form the foundation on which any school change is based, especially changing the school culture.

Students must understand their role in changing the school culture and be rewarded for that understanding. Principals must recognize that students must be allowed to have some discretion about the day-to-day operation of the school as it affects the student group. Both teachers and students must be receptive to new ideas and be willing to accept these changes as part of the organization's continual growth.

Developing a vision for the school is a necessary tool for school improvement. For far too long principals have taken the position that control is the most important aspect of leading schools. Creating the vision in a collaborative manner allows the principal to participate in a process larger than the role of principal. When thinking about the vision, it is important to keep the end in mind. The creation of a vision requires that all stakeholders understand the direction and purpose for the organization. The consensus method of agreement during the process is of the utmost importance if success of the vision is to be expected.

The current debate over school and student accountability is not new. It began in the late 1950s with the launching of *Sputnik* and has continued until today with the development of high-stakes testing. For more than fifty years, liberals and conservative politicians have argued the relative merits of the public schools. It is safe to say that student accountability is at the pinnacle of its fifty-year existence with forty-eight states now testing students and thirty-five states issuing report cards on each school.

The principal's role in school and student accountability has taken on attributes of major proportion. Principals are expected to lead their school and student achievement scores to the top of the testing mountain. They must understand the process and have the skills to rally all the stakeholders toward that mountaintop. Problem solving, student assessment, and benchmarking are some of the skills school leaders must possess in the twenty-first-century school. Selecting or creating a model for school improvement is as important as hiring outstanding teachers. The model selected must maximize the skills of the current school staff and bring it to its full potential.

Improving student achievement is the goal for all stakeholders and the use of data supports that goal. Information will be the principal's greatest ally in the school of the twenty-first century. Knowing where and how to get information in a manner that is easily understood by all stakeholders will be the challenge for most educational leaders. It will be the principal's responsibility to gather data that will allow teachers to alter instruction so that students will be successful.

CHAPTER ACTIVITIES AND QUESTIONS

1. Define "school culture" and analyze your school to see if your school's culture matches your definition.
2. List the attributes of school culture and how they are different than the attributes of school climate.
3. Analyze the changing nature of society and how it affects your school, teachers, and you as the principal.
4. Create activities necessary for students to connect to your school.
5. List the models and their attributes that were discussed in this chapter concerning student and school accountability.
6. Describe the principal's role in developing the school's vision.
7. List the attributes of a vision.
8. Outline the process for implementing a vision.
9. Write a speech that you as a principal would deliver describing your role in school and student accountability.

10. Compare and contrast the models for raising student test scores discussed in this chapter

CASE STUDY ACTIVITIES AND QUESTIONS

1. List several strategies that Mr. James could use to discover the truth about the problems at BHS prior to accepting the position as principal.
2. Create a plan Mr. James could use to make the current school year enjoyable for the entire faculty.
3. What would you advise Mr. James to tell Mr. Williams about how all stakeholders could learn to work together?
4. Should BHS pursue the Blue Ribbon Award in Mr. James's first year? If yes, why would you support this project? If not, why?
5. Write what Mr. James should tell Superintendent Tucker if he decides to postpone submitting the application for the Blue Ribbon Award.
6. Outline the strategies you would use to address the concerns of the students' view of teacher respect.
7. Did Mr. James make a mistake by outlining his vision for BHS at the first faculty meeting? What could he have done to avoid Mr. Williams and his statements?
8. How should Mr. James proceed in finding out about the parental concerns that underlie the problems at BHS?

REFERENCES

Astin, A. W., Banta, T. W., Cross, K. P., El-Khawas, E., Ewell, P. T., Hutchings, P., Marchese, T. J., McClennery, K. M., Mentkowski, M., Miller, M. A., Moran, E. T., and Wright, B. D. (1993). *Principles of good practice for assessing student learning.* League for Innovation in the Community College (ERIC Document Reproduction Services no. ED 367 427).

Bosworth, Kris. (1999). "Build a healthy school culture so students bond to their school." *Smith Initiatives for Prevention and Education*, at smith.ed.arizona/drug-info/vision/;2.html (accessed May 24, 2000).

Calhoun, E. F. (1994). "How to use action research in the self-renewing school." Alexandria, VA: Association for Supervision and Curriculum Development (ERIC Reproduction Service no. ED 359 646).

Casper, L. M., and Bryson, K. (1998). *Household and family characteristics: March, 1998 Update*. Washington, DC: U.S. Census Bureau.

Cavanaugh, R. F., and Dellar, G. B. (1997). "Toward a model of school culture." Paper presented at the annual meeting of the American Educational Research Association (ERIC Document Reproduction Services no. ED 408 687).

Children's Defense Fund. (2002). "Child poverty: Poverty status of persons younger than 18: 1959–2000." At www.childrensdefense.org/data.php (accessed May 13, 2002).

Colker, L. J., ed. (1992). *Beyond reading, writing, and arithmetic: A retrospective look at how schools have responded to changing societal needs*. 2nd ed. Center for the Study of Social Policy. Springfield, VA: DynEDRS, Inc.

Cremin, L. A. (1989). *Popular education and its discontents*. New York: Harper and Row.

Darling-Hammond, L., and Ascher, C. (1991). "Accountability mechanisms in big school systems." *ERIC/CUE Digest No. 71* (ERIC Reproduction Service no. ED 334 311).

Deal, T. E. (1993). "The culture of schools." In *Educational leadership and school culture*, ed. M. Sashkin and H. J. Walberg. Berkeley, CA: McCutchan.

———. (1985). "The symbolism of effective schools." *The Elementary School Journal* 85 (5): 601–620.

Debra P. v. Turlington, 644 F.2d 397, 6775 (5th Cir. 1981).

Dodd, A. W., and Konzal, J. L. (2000). "Parents and educators as partners." *High School Magazine* 7 (5): 8–13.

Education Commission of the States. (2000). "Co-NECT." At www.ecs.org (accessed July 3, 2001).

———. (1999a). "The progress of education reform 1999-2001: Comprehensive reform." At: www.ecs.org (accessed July 3, 2001).

———. (1999b). "State performance indicators—1999." At www.ecs.org (accessed July 3, 2001).

Fullan, M. G. (1992). "Visions that blind." *Educational Leadership* 49 (5): 19–20.

Geertz, Clifford. (1973). *The Interpretation of Cultures*. New York: Basic Books.

Goldberg, B., and Richard, J. (1996). "The Co-NECT design for school change." In *Bold plans for school restructuring: The new American school designs*, ed. S. Stringfield, S. Ross, and L. Smith. Mahwah, NJ: Erlbaum.

Hodgkinson, H. L. (1992). *A demographic look at tomorrow*. Washington, DC: Institute for Educational Leadership.

Johnson, J. H. (1997). *Data-driven school improvement*. Arlington, VA: American Association of School Administrators, Clearinghouse on Educational Management (ERIC Document Reproduction Services no. ED 401 595).

Keefe, J. W. (1993). "Leadership for school restructuring-redesigning your school." *High School Magazine* 1 (2): 4–9.

Lake, R. J., Hill, P. T., O'Toole, L., and Celio, M. B. (1999). *Making standards work: Active voices, focused learning*. Seattle, WA: Center on Reinventing Public Education.

Lashway, L. (1997). *Leading with vision*. Arlington, VA: American Association of School Administrators, Clearinghouse on Educational Management (ERIC Document Reproduction Services no. ED 412 592).

Levin, H. M. (1994). *Accelerated schools after eight years*. Stanford, CA: Stanford University Press.

Linn, R. L. (2000). "Assessments and accountability." *Educational Researcher* 29 (2): 4–16.

McLean, J. E. (1995). "Improving education through action research: A guide for administrators and teachers." In *The practicing administrator's leadership series: Roadmaps to Success*. Thousand Oaks, CA: Corwin.

Nagel, J. (2000). "Ten questions to ask when creating your vision." At www. digital-women.com/howto04e.htm (accessed July 17, 2001).

National Center for Education Statistics. (1997). "The condition of education 1997." Washington, DC: U.S. Department of Education, at www.nces.ed.gov/ index.html (accessed May 13, 2002).

Office of Educational Research and Improvement. (1998). "Tools for schools: School reform models supported by the National Institute on Elementary Education of At-Risk Students." Washington, DC: U.S. Department of Education.

Olson, L. (1999). "Shining a spotlight on results: Quality counts '99." *Education Week* 18 (17): 8–10.

Pankake, A. M. (1998). *Implementation: Making things happen*. Larchmont, NY: Eye on Education.

Patterson, J. L., Purkey, S. C., and Parker, J. V. (1986). "Productive school systems for a nonrational world." Alexandria, VA: Association for Supervision and Curriculum Development.

Peterson, K (1999). "UW researcher says school culture can be-toxin or tonic." News UW–Madison Office of News and Public Affairs, at www.news.wisc. edu/thisweek/Research/SS/y99/schoolculture.html (accessed May 24, 2000).

Reeves, M. S. (1988). "Self-interest and the common weal: Focusing on the bottom half." *Education Week*, 27 April, 31.

Sammon, G. (2000). "The challenge of change." *High School Magazine* 7 (9): 32–36.

Schrag, P. (1997). "The near-myth of our failing schools." *Atlantic Monthly* (October), at www.theatlantic.com (accessed June 25, 2001).

Senge, P. M. (1990a). *The fifth discipline*. New York: Doubleday/Currency.

———. (1990b). "The leader's new work: Building learning organizations." *Sloan Management Review* (Fall 1990): 11–17.

Southwest Educational Development Laboratory. (1999). "School context-school culture." At www.sedl.org/change/school/culture.html (accessed June 25, 2001).

Synder, T. (1998). "Trends in education." *Principal* 78 (1): 40–42, 44, 46–48.

Traub, J. (1999). *Better by design*. New York: Thomas B. Fordham Foundation, at www.edexcellence.net (accessed June 17, 2001).

Tucker, S. (1996). *Benchmarking: A guide for educators*. Thousand Oaks, CA: Corwin.

Vitali, G. J. (1994). "Factors influencing teachers' practices in an assessment driven reform." (ERIC Document Reproduction Services No. ED 373 053).

Watts, J. A., Gaines, G. F., and Creech, J. D. (1998). "Getting results: A fresh look at school accountability." Atlanta, GA: Southern Regional Education Board.

Weinberg, D. H. (1999). *Income and poverty 1998*. Washington, DC: U.S. Census Bureau.

Chapter Five

Curriculum Development

Principal Kailey Fischbeck felt the need to challenge the students and teachers of New Area Road Elementary to become the best they could become academically. After reviewing the results of the state's high stakes accountability test, Principal Fischbeck knew that the faculty at New Area Road had done a great job of teaching the objectives measured by the test, but she felt there must be more for students than what was currently being tested. Ms. Fischbeck raised this issue with teachers at the last faculty meeting of the year and had received mixed reviews of her proposal from several of the more senior teachers. Ms. Fischbeck acknowledged, at the meeting, that students had been very successful on the state mandated tests and praised the teachers for their hard work and determined effort with the children. She told the faculty that it could not be satisfied and must continue to strive to educate children for the highest levels of academic success. She asked the teachers to reflect on the issue of striving to meet academically higher standards for children and the community over the summer. In addition, Ms. Fischbeck indicated that she had approached the superintendent with her ideas and soon would be discussing her idea with the executive committee of the New Area Road Parent–Teachers Association.

After the faculty meeting, Ms. Fischbeck went back to her office to reflect on the negative comments she had received from several faculty members concerning increased academic standards for children. She wondered why the most concerns came from the most senior teachers, those who had been working at the school for more than eight years, and those who she had handpicked when she had taken on the role of principal. They seemed to be satisfied with the current levels of student achievement. As she pondered her thoughts, she had never considered that this faculty would become complacent.

Several days later, Ms. Sally Most stopped by to visit with Ms. Fischbeck about her teaching assignment for the coming year. Ms. Most was a wonderful teacher, a valued colleague, and one of the teachers questioning the need to raise the academic standards. After the discussion about the teaching assignment, the conversation turned to the standards issue. Ms. Fischbeck asked Ms. Most to provide her with the rationale for not raising the standards. Ms. Most felt that meeting the state standards was about all any principal could ask of the faculty. Going beyond the state standards would be asking teachers to go beyond the needs of students. As the conversation continued on a very friendly and professional basis, Ms. Fischbeck began exploring some other ideas surrounding the issue of academic standards. They discussed curriculum alignment, standards-based instruction, and curriculum development. Ms. Most said she thought that one answer to the question of increased academic standards might be answered by reviewing the curriculum.

Ms. Fischbeck thought about her conversation with Ms. Most and realized that they were talking about doing the same thing in a different way. After a couple of days thinking about what she had learned from her discussion, she decided to change the curriculum and she knew the process would be key to the success of this venture of increasing academic achievement for students. She called Ms. Most and asked her to serve as the chair of a schoolwide curriculum development committee and Ms. Most agreed. Ms. Fischbeck thought about the structure of this committee and who should be on the committee. Parents? Teachers? Principals? Who else? She knew she had to do some preliminary work with the central administration, the community stakeholders, and some of the key business leaders in her attendance zone. In addition, she thought it would be useful to provide some training and expertise for the committee. Maybe this was a bigger task than it was worth but Ms. Fischbeck knew otherwise as she prepared for next year's curriculum development process.

As Ms. Fischbeck began to operationalize the curriculum development process at New Area Road Elementary, she needed to define the term. Over the past several years, the word "curriculum" has been defined in many ways. Some authors and experts have defined it as organized knowledge, guided experiences, content, or instruction. *Webster's New World Dictionary* (1999) provides the following meaning: "[A] course of study in a school." While an argument could be made that all of these definitions contain similar "what" characteristics, some experts believe that instruction is a completely separate activity involving "how" the curriculum is delivered to the students. In this text, "curriculum" is defined as the "intended learning outcomes taught to students." It is completely feasible and more likely than not that students learn and gather useful information at school that is not part of the "intended learning outcomes" and is not part of the school's curriculum. Sowell (2000, 3) in her text *Curriculum: An Integrative Introduction* defines "curriculum" as "what is taught to students." She includes the intended and unintended learning activities in her definition. If you believe that the curriculum describes the knowledge and skills that students should know and be able to do, then it seems that unintended learning cannot be part of the curriculum. This debate might rage on for eternity, but for the purposes of this text, "curriculum" is defined as the "intended learning outcomes" created by teachers, principals, textbooks, and testing programs. All of these elements contribute to and influence the written curriculum. Perhaps the most influential aspect of the curriculum is the implementation of the curriculum. This occurs when the individual teacher decides what he or she is going to teach the students and this is the most compelling reason for defining curriculum as "intended learning outcomes."

CURRICULUM LEADERSHIP

Curriculum leadership is a specific function within the general concept of educational leadership. Principals, in general, have had the opportunity to experience the concept of leadership in their daily work life or in a principal preparation program. Regardless of where the principal garnered exposure to his or her concept of leadership, curriculum leadership requires the principal to have a clear vision of curriculum development. Of all the functions that principals are held accountable for, curriculum leadership is near the bottom of the list. Far too many principals have little or no knowledge about curriculum development, implementation, alignment, and standards to provide much leadership. Doll (1992) asserts that principals "are afraid to make commitments according to what they believe, lest they be blamed for failure" (465). He states that effective curriculum leaders create concepts for their schools and are courageous enough to implement them. Being a courageous leader is not about intestinal fortitude but is mostly about the willingness to stay-the-course over an extended time frame.

If curriculum leadership is about enhancing the subject matter to be learned, and it is, the curriculum leader must posses skills that will create positive results for curriculum improvement. These skills become the tools that leaders use to bring teachers, parents, and students together for the purpose of improving the school's intended learning outcomes. A curriculum development tool that is used most often by curriculum leaders is a planning process that originates in the school district's central administration. Using this tool, the leader initiates the curriculum planning process for the entire district. This is a top-down tool that allows the central administration to make all of the critical decisions in the curriculum development process. Using the top-down tool eliminates teacher, parent, and principal input and feedback concerning curriculum content, alignment, and standards. The advantages of the top-down tool are:

- Efficiency of curriculum development
- Control of the curriculum content by subject matter specialists
- One curriculum for the entire school district suggests continuity
- Central administration supports all of the subject matter concepts incorporated in the curriculum

Certainly, the top-down tool has disadvantages and one of them is that campus personnel, teachers and principals, have limited input and feedback opportunities. In addition, the people responsible for implementing the curriculum have little or no say in developing the "intended learning outcomes."

A second tool curriculum leaders could use to develop and improve the curriculum can be the teacher-to-the-top tool. This tool functions on the assumption that teachers are the professionals that utilize the intended curriculum and thus must actively participate in the curriculum development process. Curriculum cannot progress if teachers do not improve their personal understandings, skills, and attitudes. The leader's role in the teacher-to-the-top tool provides structure, guidance, and resources for the process.

Advantages of the teacher-to-the-top tool are:

- Those implementing the curriculum are directly involved in its development
- Teacher participation in the process is required
- Teacher buy-in is guaranteed
- Teacher acceptance of the curriculum is embedded in this tool

The disadvantage of the teacher-to-the-top tool is the amount of time it takes to work through the process. Many hours of teacher time are required and in some cases teachers resent the additional duties that this tool requires. Additionally, it may be possible for a strong teacher or group of teachers to dominate the curricular content. In some cases, these teachers are well intentioned, but are limited in their knowledge and/or skills.

A third curriculum leadership tool combining the top-down and teacher-to-the-top tools is the integrated tool. Using this tool, the central administration and teachers share the responsibility and work of creating the curriculum. Time is the critical factor in any process and when working with the entire group, time further exacerbates the problems associated with medium to large groups. Dividing the large team into subcommittees is one strategy for working more efficiently. This tool requires that both the central administrators and teachers leave their agendas at the door of the meeting room. Combining the talents of both groups requires that everyone's opinions and ideas are valued and that the group functions utilizing consensus as the decision maker. In this situation, consensus is established when all or some of the leadership team members agree on a curricular issue and others agree to suspend their opposition and are willing to support the issue. Voting on an issue guarantees that perhaps as many as 49 percent of the group might oppose the content and in essence doom the content to failure should it become part of the curriculum. The advantages of the integrated leadership tool are:

- Central administrators, campus administrators, and teachers make up the leadership team.
- The workload is spread among several groups.
- All members of the group agree to collaborate by discarding their personal agendas.

The major disadvantage in using the integrated tool is time. Arranging a time when members of the curriculum development team can meet as a decision-making body is very difficult. It is also very difficult for curriculum administrators, principals, and teachers to suppress their personal agendas on issues of subject matter content.

Curriculum leadership comes from various personnel in the school organization, but the central figure is the principal. Principals are in a position to make sure that all aspects of the curriculum development process are addressed. They have role authority, personal power, and position status to influence teachers' beliefs and attitudes toward subject matter. Historically, the role of principal has focused on supervision of instruction and instructional leadership and not much in the area of curriculum development. With the advent of local, state, and national standards, principals have an opportunity to influence what the curriculum addresses and how it is developed. Principals must know curriculum design, curriculum alignment, and assessment strategies in order to give direction to the organization and structure of the intended learning outcomes. Curriculum leadership from the principal's perspective is more than developing and implementing subject matter content. It is about receiving feedback and marketing to the community curriculum that has been created. This task is accomplished in many ways, foremost of which is communication with all of the school's constituencies. Principals do their work closest to the individuals that benefit from the curriculum leadership: teachers and students. Rutherford (1985) states that curriculum leaders:

- Have visions or targets for student achievement
- Create goals and objectives from the vision
- Create a positive school culture
- Monitor student achievement
- Support teachers and correct problems as they occur

Principals who engage in knowing and understanding curriculum design have a much better opportunity to change not only what is taught, but also how it is taught. It is important that principals know the process of designing, assessing, and implementing intended learning outcomes, but it is equally important that they know how to change subject matter content from an abstract thought to reality. Several states have created standards-based assessments that help define, if not dictate, the school's curriculum. However, the principal wearing his or her curriculum leader's hat can and should guide teachers in moving the intended learning outcomes beyond the local or state curriculum. Continuously raising the standards energizes instruction and student learning.

Evers and Lakomski (1996) come to the conclusion that the traditional view of leadership, where leadership is viewed as a role for principals, does not fit the context of many contemporary schools. They argue that principals need to extend leadership opportunities to others in the school organization, specifically the teacher corp. Brooker et al. (1997), in a survey of 1,500 teachers and administrators, reported that 85 percent of the principals stated that they had been significantly involved in curriculum leadership activities, while only 29 percent of teachers indicated they had been actively involved at the same level. A problem that surfaces when principals attempt to engage teachers in curriculum leadership is the lack of self-confidence in teachers' leadership abilities outside of the classroom. If principals want teachers to be willing participants in curriculum leadership, they are going to have to do more than provide professional development activities. Elliott et al. (1996) argue that teachers must be given opportunities to develop candidness, dedication, trust, and a sense of responsibility if they are to ever view themselves as curriculum leaders. The key to developing teachers into leaders in the current school context is done in an atmosphere where individual character can be enhanced. Teachers need to feel they are leaders and this can only occur when they see themselves in that role (Calderhead and Sharrock 1977).

The fast-paced world in which principals function is the most compelling reason they need to be knowledgeable and skillful in leading the school organization in curriculum development. No longer is the curriculum stagnant, rather, it is a fluid document that needs to be updated continuously. Principals who understand curriculum design, alignment, and standards have the best opportunity to influence teachers, central administrators, and community members about what children need to know.

CURRICULUM DESIGN MODELS

Designing curriculum is a process that is influenced by the beliefs and values of the designers themselves. Curriculum design is essential for several reasons: (1) a holistic view is needed in order to make decisions about what comes first or last in the development process; (2) the curriculum must be organized in a structured manner; (3) the curriculum must be designed with the entire society in mind; and (4) all subjects are enhanced when the relationship among the various content areas is considered (Amuah 1988). The philosophy of the curriculum designers affects the content that becomes student learning. Doll (1992) argues that the first activity that any committee must accomplish prior to changing a curriculum is discussing and deciding on a point of view. He discusses four points of view:

- Science—the scientific method is used for developing and creating the curriculum.
- Society—students must study the many aspects of society.
- Eternal verities from the human past—this model springs from philosophy and the great literature of history.
- Divine will—religious beliefs are used as the basis for the curriculum.

Each of these points of view has merit and built-in liabilities when considering its use in creating a curriculum. Perhaps choosing the best parts of each point of view is the most reasonable approach to creating one common point of view for designing a curriculum. Trying to use any of the four points of view exclusively is not without its problems and perhaps would destroy any attempt to improve or change the curriculum.

When considering curriculum design, history leads us to Tyler's (1949) model. In his model, Tyler identifies four elements that guide curriculum design. These elements consist of objectives, activities, organization of the activities, and evaluation. Most of the negative debate about Tyler's model come from critics who do not like the idea of behavioral objectives because, as the argument goes, these types of objectives stifle teacher creativity. Tyler believes that talented educators should consider the nature of the society, the nature of the learners, and the nature of the profession when creating a curriculum (Simpson 1999). Over the years, Tyler's model has undergone revision but has withstood the test of time and is still a viable model to utilize when designing curriculum. If you are beginning the process of curriculum development, similar to the aforementioned scenario, then you might want to provide the planning committee with the following model, which is based on Tyler's work.

1. Discuss the need for reviewing the curriculum and using the point of view agreed on by the committee to define the role of the committee.
2. Create objectives for the design making sure each objective describes what is to be done and how the committee will know when it has been completed.
3. What subject matter content will be addressed in the teaching and learning process? The initial step in this model requires getting teachers to share the curriculum they teach with other colleagues.
4. Describe what learning experiences students will encounter. This step involves the use of curriculum mapping as a means of determining what composes the specific content for each subject and grade. In addition, curriculum webbing provides the framework for looking at the curriculum across content areas.
5. Develop an evaluation strategy for measuring the teaching and learning process. (Doll 1992)

Tyler's model is devised so that each step informs the next step and allows decision making to proceed. This is a major strength of his model and provides curriculum designers the opportunity to structure the curriculum in a manner that meets the needs of students, community, and the content of each subject. Amuah (1988) argues that Tyler's model fails to tell us who the decision makers would be, a minor flaw albeit, a flaw.

For example, in item three from the previous list, teachers share the curriculum they teach in order to determine the gaps and repetitions in the content. At this point in the process of curriculum development, teachers begin to discuss grade-level and course content responsibilities. Curricular terms and clear definitions are agreed on so that all parties understand and are able to articulate course and grade-level expectations. The goal of this experience is to allow all teachers to understand the complete curriculum.

Curriculum maps provide all of the stakeholders with goals, objectives, and topics that are being taught throughout the school year. This part of the process requires the planning committee and the teachers to examine the grade level, the course sequence, and the amount of instructional time being spent on specific subject matter content. For example, a third-grade teacher might realize that she is focusing five months of the school year on Christopher Columbus's discovery of America and almost no time on the development of the American colonies. If you ask this teacher why she spends so much time on Columbus, she might tell you that the children really like the activities she provides for them when studying the discovery of America. But what you might find if you investigated further is that the teacher really likes that period of U.S. history. Perhaps, if she looks at her curriculum map she would see an imbalance of content and be able to adjust the amount of time she is spending on each of the U.S. history topics. This teacher might discover that the U.S. history topic she so dearly loves has been taught two times before and that she is teaching the children what they already know. According to Fitzharris (1999), curriculum maps can be used in a variety ways:

- The curriculum map should be given to parents in order to inform them about the content of a course or subject at a specific grade level.
- The map could be used in the school's newsletter to highlight topics for the coming month or year.
- The map provides a clear direction and an avenue for dialogue for teachers, students, parents, and principals.
- The map provides a clear analysis of how instructional time is being utilized, a most appropriate use in this era of high-stakes testing.

A second model of curriculum design is the conflicting concepts model. Developed by Eisner and Vallance (1974), this model addresses five sets of issues that form the foundation of the decision-making and curriculum design process:

- Curriculum is primarily designed to focus on cognitive skills of children.
- Curriculum is designed to self-actualize children for the purpose of reaching their ultimate potential.
- Curriculum is designed to create social change.
- Curriculum is designed to perpetuate the nation's culture and political system.
- Curriculum is designed as a means to an end.

This model provides for a plethora of options on which to base the curriculum. From the cognitive aspects of learning to the perpetuation of the culture and political system, this model allows the curriculum designers to mold the curriculum to meet to the needs of students, society, and the content of each academic discipline. Depending on the direction the curriculum designers want to explore, any of the five design techniques can work.

For example, if the target is to create social change the designers would focus on those attributes that create social change. The curriculum would include the teaching of ethics to all students in kindergarten through grade 12. This curriculum content at the secondary level would include reading articles, textbooks, writing papers, and conducting individual research through an interdisciplinary studies approach. In the science area, the curriculum might include the study of human organ donation and transplantation. The study of ethics focuses the right-versus-right dilemmas, not the right-versus-wrong dilemmas, which in reality are moral dilemmas that address the individual's values and beliefs. The entire process of an ethics curriculum allows the biology, the literature, and the social science teachers the opportunity to challenge students to understand the ethical dilemmas faced by society from many points of view.

A third model of curriculum design is the balanced curriculum model developed by the School Development Program founded by Dr. James Comer. The process of creating a balanced curriculum is divided into three parts.

- Describing the curriculum
- Aligning the curriculum
- Assessing student mastery of the system (Squires 1998)

Perhaps the most efficient way to describe the curriculum is by having all of the teachers write down what they taught during the past school year and the amount of time they devoted to the topic. Utilizing this method, the curriculum planners would know what was being emphasized during the instructional process as well as the time each teacher was spending on specific content areas. For example, fourth-grade teachers might indicate that they taught a social studies unit on U.S. heroes that took about fifteen days to completely teach and included the following activities:

1. Read several books about U.S. heroes in class and self-selected
2. Discussed the details of what makes a hero and how these individuals had the attributes of being a hero

3. Discussed how different points of view determine a person's status as a hero
4. Wrote an essay describing the student's favorite hero and how this hero affected his or her life

The unit format is the teacher's shorthand for communicating with other teachers on the same grade level and across the academic spectrum (Squires 1998).

Aligning the curriculum utilizes the work described in the aforementioned paragraph by comparing the content that is taught to national, state, and local standards. Utilizing a gap analysis allows the curriculum designers to find the areas of duplication and missing content when the various comparisons are made. If the designers will place the local, state, national, and professional association standards on a grid, they will easily be able to see where the problems lie. For example, using the U.S. heroes unit the curriculum designers might discover that the unit meets the local and state standards but does not meet the National Teachers of Social Studies standard for understanding U.S. leaders. In this case, the school would need to change the curriculum to meet the national standards by adding additional social studies content. However, the school might choose to only meet state and local standards and in this scenario it would have accomplished its purpose. The key factor in aligning the curriculum is measuring the current curriculum against some form of standard and adding or deleting content to meet the intent of the standard. In most curriculum alignment projects more content will be deleted than added.

According to Squires (1998), student mastery of the curriculum is assessed in two ways: (1) student performance should be designed to measure the conceptual understanding of the content, and (2) students should understand and have practiced the structure and format of how the curriculum is aligned with local and state standards. Each activity in the curriculum needs to combine both performance and format measurements. Cohen (1987) states that students will be more successful when the curriculum is aligned with instruction and the instruction measures the curriculum. Perhaps the problem with the U.S. educational system is not poor instruction, but rather a misalignment of what is taught, intended to be taught, and assessed as having been taught.

A much different approach to curriculum design than those previously discussed is the curriculum web design strategy developed by Cunningham (1999). He begins designing the curriculum by utilizing the following question as his point of departure: What do we want students to learn? While this question seems simplistic, it may be the best way to begin designing a school curriculum. Focusing on the student is the beginning for a process of student-centered instruction. This question should be the driving force regardless of the curriculum design model utilized. Other questions may come to mind that need to be answered as you go about answering what students need to learn, such as: What does your context tell you students need? or What knowledge and skills do students need? Curriculum need not focus on who the learners are, instead it should focus on the types of attitudes, skills, and knowledge they need to possess.

The beginning piece of Cunningham's (1999) curriculum web model looks at the purpose of the curriculum web that he calls an "aim." An aim is very similar to what others have called a goal: general in nature, holistic in content, and clear in direction. Aims may stem from a teacher's experience and internal feeling that this is the right direction to take student learning. Aims are supported by rationales that justify the worthiness of the specific aim.

The next step in the curriculum web model is concerned with subject matter. The curriculum may be subject-centered, learner-centered, or problem-centered. The subject-centered curriculum is driven by specific topics within a content area. This type of curriculum may be organized around specific themes, principles, or processes. Teaching students in an interdisciplinary manner works well when using the subject-centered curriculum.

The learner-centered curriculum uses the students to form the basis for the curriculum. Student experiences and contact with their own environment focuses the curriculum content for this strategy. Students may participate in the development of the curriculum by suggesting to the curriculum designers the important concepts that they feel need to be learned. The learner-centered curriculum makes sure the attitudes, beliefs, and values of students is paramount in answering the question: What do students want to learn (Cunningham 1999)?

Curriculum webbing is the process of determining logical connections across areas of subject matter content. Creating these connections helps provide the student with a high level of continuity from course to course and from grade to grade. Without these connections, students get fragmented information with no means of transferring learning from one class to another. For example, a high school instructor teaching U.S. literature should recognize that U.S. history could bring the literature and history to life for students. In addition, music, art, and science teachers could contribute to the entire webbing process by teaching art, music, and science of the historical period being taught. The webbing process links curriculum to instruction.

The problem-centered curriculum is developed around real-world problems. The question for this curriculum design strategy is: What are the important problems facing society? Teachers, students, and the community define problems. From an instructional point of view, this strategy fits well with cooperative learning, but all content areas may use the problem-centered curriculum design strategy. This model requires students to be academically disciplined to accept the fact that there is more than one strategy for solving any problem. Creativity and individual determination are but two of the attributes that students must enjoy if teachers are to be successful using this curriculum strategy.

The Tyler, conflicting concepts, balanced, and web curriculum models all contain similar parts for designing curriculum. In some form, each addresses the needs of students, goals, objectives, and specific subject matter content. Each design model has strengths and weaknesses and it is up to the individual curriculum design team to adapt, adopt, or create a design model that fits its needs best. Curriculum design is the key to the instructional phase of student achievement. Without a world-class curriculum map, there will not be a world-class student nor will there be world-class instruction. Curriculum design is the foundation for all student achievement.

DEVELOPING CURRICULUM STANDARDS

The fictional report *A Nation at Risk* is credited by many as the defining moment of the modern standards movement. Even though the report was based on opinion and not research Shepard (1993) believes that the report changed the school reform movement dramatically by linking the educational system to the nation's international economic competitiveness. One of the most influential supporters and designers of the curriculum standards movement was Ravitch. Ravitch, a former assistant secretary of education, writes that Americans expect stringent standards in highway construction, food inspection, and air quality. She believes that standards improve the quality of life and in schooling standards improve student achievement by defining the subject matter and the level of achievement expected (1995). Standards are always based on a comparison against recognized aims created by states or professional organizations. Most academic areas are supported by professional organizations at both the state and national levels. These professional organizations have over the past several years engaged in creating content standards for the professional organizations' content specialty. Such organizations include the National Council of Teachers of English, the National Council of Teachers of Mathematics, the National Center for History in the Schools, and the National Science Teachers Association. Each of these professional organizations has contributed to the creation of standards by which the state, local school districts, and individual schools can compare their curriculums. This comparison is the accepted measurement by which local schools assess the quality of their curriculums. Measurement becomes the baseline for acceptable school instruction and achievement. Utilizing these standards provides for the creation of a curriculum of the highest level.

Most schools establish goals and objectives for teachers and students to achieve, which are measured by some form of paper-and-pencil assessment. These goals are generally broad in nature and focus on the overall intent of the educational process. Goals are nonspecific and do not suggest measurement strategies. On the other hand, objectives stem from goals and describe what students or teachers are supposed to do or accomplish. Both goals and objectives may be stated in conceptual or procedural terms by addressing the questions: What should the student know? and What should the student be able to accomplish (Solomon, Wyatt-Ortiz, and Goldman 1998)?

Standards look like goals but are directed more toward the student's ability to accomplish a specific skill or understand specific knowledge. Thus, standards focus on the student's ability to perform at the level measured by the standard. Standards may appear as a description of self, conceptual, and/or procedural forms and answer the same two questions as do goals and objectives: What should the student know? and What should the student be able to accomplish (Solomon, Wyatt-Ortiz, and Goldman 1998)?

Standards are designed to meet the needs of schools at all levels of academic achievement. Each level, grade, or course has different learning expectations. As students move form one grade level to the next and from one course to the next higher-level course, the standards may remain the same but the expected level of knowledge is increased. For example, the school standard is that students will be good communicators. For sixth graders, the expectations might be communicating thoughts and ideas in writing and for tenth graders an understanding of forms, techniques, and styles of written communication would be expected. Both the sixth and tenth graders focus on the same standard at different levels of sophistication. In the sixth grade, the focus would be on writing good sentences and paragraphs as opposed to the tenth graders who would be writing persuasive essays. Standards are not specific to grade levels or courses but focus on the entire school experience.

When determining where we get our standards, we find two possible sources that attempt to define standards: the national level and the state level. At first blush it appears rather easy to select curriculum standards from the numerous standards documents created by the professional and academic associations. After examination of these various documents, it is apparent that each document was developed in a very different way. Marzano and Kendall (1996) state that documents developed at the national level create the following four problems for the curriculum designers at the local level:

- Multiple iterations of the standards
- Standards with differing definitions
- Multilevel generality
- Complexity of subordination

Multiple iterations of content standards require that the local school consider several standards documents before deciding what level of sophistication it wants to achieve in each content area. Marzano and Kendall (1996) suggest that a school would need to review twelve documents in history, four in mathematics, and twenty-eight in language arts in order to review all of the possible content standards in each content area (21). A great deal of duplication will be found in the various documents, but each one will have specific knowledge requirements that the others do not contain. This single issue makes it almost impossible for an individual school or school district to utilize national standards.

The issue of standards with differing definitions is created by documents that address standards in several different ways. Differing definitions for subject matter content areas creates the possibility that two or more documents are discussing the same content but from a different point of view. Marzano and Kendall (1996) suggest that content and curriculum standards address two different aspects of student learning: that content standards address goals for student achievement and that curriculum standards address supplemental information that leads the student to achieving the goals, thus limiting instructional variety. In this chapter the curriculum standards form the highest level of standards, in fact, they *are* the standards. This difference illustrates the problems schools face as they attempt to resolve the issue of differing definitions.

Multilevel generality in national documents comes about when the document writers decided where specific content should be placed. Some documents are more detailed and others are less specific about the content that makes it exceedingly difficult to match curriculum standards across documents. All of this is to say that the comprehensive nature and the number of standards developed are affected by the detail within the standard (Marzano and Kendall 1996). Standards need to be more general and not as specific as goals and objectives. For example, a curriculum standard should be developed around a global concept such as: understanding the relationship of the art, music, history, and literature of the American Revolution. In drawing a distinction between the level of specificity of two national curriculum documents, one might find a curriculum standard that is very specific such as: students should understand the U.S. Constitution and its effect on people between 1785 and 1800. In reviewing the two examples, it is rather easy to determine that the first is much more global and allows for a multitude of instructional and content options, while the second is quite specific in what is to be taught and the context of the instruction. These examples illustrate the problems created by multilevel generalities.

The final problem created by multiple national curriculum standards is the complexity of subordination. In the problems that Marzano and

Kendall (1996) outline, the term "subordination" refers to the number of levels or subsets of a curriculum standard. Each of the various content standards created by the several professional associations has a different format for outlining a specific standard. For example, the mathematics standards might be configured in the following manner:

Level 1 Topic
Level 2 Standard
Level 3 Understandings
Level 4 Components
Level 5 Examples of student achievement (Marzano and Kendall 1996)

Another professional association might create a document that outlines only the topics included in the curriculum standards. For example, U.S. History would include the following topics.

- American Revolution
- Industrial revolution
- The Great Depression
- World wars and Conflicts
- Age of technology and space exploration

Once again, the problem for the school is deciding how it will integrate the various document formats into a working document that can be used by teachers to guide instruction. Perhaps the key for curriculum design teams ought to be simplicity. Marzano and Kendall (1996) argue that schools and districts should use a two-level curriculum standard outline that uses the term "standard" at the highest level of generality followed by a level entitled benchmark. The benchmark describes the level of expectation for student achievement. In other words, what is it that students are expected to know in terms of information and skills? The benchmark criteria becomes the assessment standard for measuring student growth from one year to the next or one course to the next higher-level course. Many districts have created benchmark assessments for grade levels and courses in order to measure student achievement and instructional success. This entire process goes to the heart of the accountability question for schools, teachers, and principals. Is student growth progressing at the expected rate and if not why? The benchmarking strategy becomes a powerful tool if schools would assess the student's academic gain rather than criteria- or norm-based results.

All fifty states have chosen to become actively involved in the identification of curriculum standards and in some states benchmarking has become the basis for exit-level examinations that determine whether a student graduates from high school. About twenty states have created standards in the core subjects of English, history, mathematics, and science, but only eighteen states have compared their state's standards to those of other industrialized nations. The argument for international comparison of standards is grounded in the need for competition enabling students to compete economically in the international market place. This argument, as lofty as it sounds, may be the least of the reasons to create a standards-based curriculum. Berliner and Biddle in their seminal book *The Manufactured Crisis* (1995) demonstrate that U.S. students have done and will continue to perform quite well in the international academic arena. They go on to argue that much of the hysteria surrounding U.S. students' perceived lack of performance on the international scene is simply not true and in several cases is created by groups with specific political agendas.

As a principal, helping teachers to understand the purpose of having and teaching a standards-based curriculum is in some instances a daunting task. As discussed in chapter 3, change is a difficult task to understand and implement. It requires time and diligence to convince the faculty and staff that it is appropriate to teach to the standards. The common theme from the instructional side is "I don't want to teach the standards because in reality I am teaching the test." Principals must get everyone to understand that teaching the standards is what we should be doing if we want our students to be successful on the local or state exit-level examinations. Teachers and principals want the students in their schools to get their diplomas after twelve or thirteen years of schooling and the way to get that accomplished is to teach students what the standards contain. It makes no sense to teach one concept and measure another concept, teachers would not want to be assessed in that manner and neither should we assess students in that way. Woodfork (1999) cites five challenges facing teachers as they work toward implementation of a standards-based curriculum:

1. Teachers must learn a new instructional planning process.
2. Teachers need staff development in aligning assessment with instruction.

3. Teachers need assistance in identifying data that indicates students have met standards.
4. Teachers need to make sure they are providing equitable learning opportunities for all students.
5. Teachers that understand assessment and alignment will adapt much quicker to the use of standards in the classroom.

Principals that recognize teachers' concerns will have the opportunity to change the curriculum from a collection of stuff to a systematic knowledge base grounded in concepts. Standards provide a systematic curriculum because they are interrelated and in most cases self-correcting. Standards are the targets and achieving anything less short-changes the community, state, nation, and most of all the student.

CURRICULUM ALIGNMENT

According to Leitzel and Vogler (1994), curriculum alignment is composed of a systematic effort toward congruence among the curriculum, instruction, and assessment. Alignment has as its foundation the concept that the instructional plan is derived from subject matter goals with the assurance that instruction and assessment are congruent. Liebling (1997) states that curriculum alignment represents a strategy for developing a logical curriculum. She defines a logical curriculum as one where the district's written curriculum matches the state's curriculum and the district's intended learnings match the written curriculum. Squires (1997) states that curriculum alignment is a process that allows teachers to decide what students need to know in order to coordinate subject matter content among grade levels and courses so that the curriculum contains the knowledge and skills that will allow students to meet the curriculum standards. This process gives teachers the opportunity to assess their ideas in relationship to student needs, instructional strategies, textbooks, content experts, state and district standards, and the objectives measured by standardized tests.

Curriculum alignment helps teachers and the curriculum designers decide what subject matter content students need to be successful on standardized and high-stakes tests. In addition, this process provides the opportunity for teachers to collaborate in making balanced and synchronized curricular decisions. Principals must be aware that subject matter content duplication may be occurring at a much higher rate than suspected and the curriculum alignment process provides the data to answer that question. Duplication of content in and of itself is not detrimental as long as instruction and learning are performed at a higher knowledge. For example, how many times during the elementary years do students have the opportunity to discover the United States through the eyes of Columbus? Perhaps several times in some curriculums and maybe once or twice in others. The historical content surrounding Columbus is not the problem. The problem arises when the content is taught at grades 2–5 with little or no difference in the knowledge and performance expectations of the students. The alignment process allows teachers and principals to know what, how, and where it is being taught.

Aligning the curriculum may be accomplished using several different strategies. Two strategies that are easily understood and implemented are the processes of front-loading and back-loading the intended curriculum. Front-loading the intended curriculum begins by addressing what knowledge students need to know and then creating an assessment to measure student understanding of the intended curriculum. Using this process requires the completion of the curriculum prior to beginning the alignment process and has some advantages and disadvantages.

The advantages of front-loading the intended curriculum are:

- The intended curriculum is not limited.
- The intended curriculum drives process, not the test.
- The concept of local control drives the process.

The disadvantages of front-loading the intended curriculum are:

- The process takes copious amounts of time.
- The process may limit the intended curriculum from addressing national standards.
- The process requires the intended curriculum to be identified prior to beginning the alignment process.
- The process is very costly in terms of human and financial capital (www.tenet.edu/teks).

The back-loading process requires assessment development prior to curriculum development. In this case, the test is the intended curriculum and utilizing this strategy works well to improve student achievement.

The advantages of using the back-loading process for curriculum alignment are:

- The process produces results rapidly.
- The process produces the ultimate assessment.
- The process does not require an entire curriculum to be developed.

The disadvantages for back-loading the intended curriculum are:

- The process limits the curriculum to what can be paper-and-pencil tested.
- The process creates an assessment that is the curriculum.
- The process promotes the teaching of test items, not test objectives (www.tenet.edu/teks).

Either front-loading or back-loading the curriculum is a first step in the
curriculum alignment process. A principal might choose the back-loading
process in order to quickly raise student test scores. In states with high-
stakes testing protocols, moving quickly may be important. This process
also addresses the constant criticism schools receive from the business
community concerning a rapid response to problems. Traditionally,
schools have not been able to react to concerns in a timely manner. Once
the test scores have improved, it might be time to implement the front-
loading process in order to develop an intended curriculum that compares
favorably with national and international standards. Either process will
take the principal and teachers to the next step in curriculum development:
curriculum alignment.

For principals, step one in the curriculum alignment process is to
build a consensus among the faculty to begin the process. Not every faculty member will want to participate, but it is important that the overwhelming majority of the teachers agree. The principal will want to assess the faculty's collaborative coefficient to determine its readiness to
work together for a single purpose. Depending on the results of this assessment, the principal will want to develop a series of staff development activities that address collaboration, working as a team, and interpersonal relationships. Step one may turnout to be the readiness phase
for the process of curriculum alignment, and in other contexts it will be
the first step in the process.

The second step in the process begins by describing the current curriculum. Teachers in the same grade levels or courses meet together to share the specific subject matter they actually teach to students and discuss unit titles and specific time frames for completing the unit. This process works best when teachers one grade level below and one grade level above the target grade level meet to describe what they are teaching. The same would be true for teachers involved in course-specific content areas; one course below and one course above the target course needs to be shared. This step of the process is designed to allow teachers, in an open and collegial manner, to describe what they are teaching without any fear of condemnation or reprisal.

The third step in the process is to determine the overlap in the curriculum that is actually being taught. Most principals would be unable to identify the areas of curricular and instructional overlap in the school that they administer. Teachers from the grade level or course groupings meet to determine where specific subject matter should be placed. This is when teachers agree with one another about the placement of content and it is also the time when teachers make professional pledges about what they will be teaching to students. As a principal, if you discover that a unit about "dinosaurs" is being taught at the third, fourth, and fifth grades and the instructional activities were similar in each grade, you would need to meet with the teachers involved to combine these similar activities in one or two grades. In reality, this discovery should not occur if the curriculum alignment has been done effectively. This step in the curriculum alignment process will reveal the overlaps and provide opportunities for teachers to add subject matter to their grade level or course by eliminating the overlaps. Consolidation of subject matter is an issue that teachers and principals rarely address, but one that needs to be dealt with on a regular scheduled basis. This step of the process should be an ongoing activity that occurs in an informal manner every year and in a formal manner every three years. As a principal, you would want to remember that getting teachers to make deals about positioning of subject matter content is not always easy because many teachers have a lifelong vested interest in specific units and they will not part with them easily. Do you know where the curriculum overlaps are in your school?

Step number four in the curriculum alignment process is aligning the subject matter content that emerges from the description and consolidation phases of the process. Implementing this piece of the alignment puzzle requires teachers and principals to compare the newly created curriculum with local, state, national, and international standards. This is a tedious and time-consuming process of comparing your school's curriculum with each standard to see to what degree your curriculum compares favorably with the standards in question. Keeping accurate records so that there is no misunderstanding by anyone concerning the curriculum to be taught is important.

Once the curriculum is aligned, the fifth step in the process comes into play: assessment. Assessment is the yardstick by which teachers, principals, and the community measure the success of the curriculum alignment process. Squires (1997) argues that curriculum alignment is a "bet" that students will perform better on measures of accountability than they had done previously. Assessment is the mechanism for gathering data about how well students are achieving as measured against the curriculum. The high-stakes testing movement found in various states has generated student assessment. One factor that never emerges from the assessment process is the help it can give teachers in identifying instructional strengths and weaknesses. Analyzing assessment results should provide teachers with information about student understanding of the intended curriculum. If the results are used properly, teachers will be able to make adjustments in their instruction so that future students will be successful on the assessment.

Opponents of high-stakes testing, curriculum alignment, and standards development continue to march to the mantra "this type of curriculum is designed for teachers to teach the test." As a principal, you want your students to be successful and in this case success is measured by student attainment of the assessment's target score. Teachers must teach the objectives that the assessment measures if they expect students to meet the target score. Since the test measures the curriculum, then it is the intended curriculum that must be taught. To do otherwise puts students at a real disadvantage when taking high-stakes tests. Opponents continue to question this process by stating "when using this model you never teach critical thinking skills." First of all, teaching critical thinking skills is an instructional strategy, not part of the intended curriculum. Second, critical thinking skills can be used to teach any concept found in the intended curriculum. Principals and teachers need to observe themselves from a student perspective periodically. Place yourself in the class and ask: Would I want to be tested over subject matter content that I had never been taught? The most obvious answer would be "no" and rightly so. Principals have an obligation, if not moral duty to make sure students in their care are taught with the test in mind.

CURRICULUM ASSESSMENT

Assessment provides feedback to students, parents, and teachers about how well they are performing in relation to the intended learning outcomes, which by definition is the curriculum. Without this feedback, all constituent groups are left wondering how well they did in teaching the curriculum. Schools have for many years measured their success rate with student results from standardized tests. In the 1930s, educators viewed the "college boards" as the test of choice for measuring school success. This college admissions test turned into the only measure of school success for many educators and education policy makers by becoming a national measure of school accountability. Now known as the Scholastic Achievement Tests (SATs), these tests have invaded the world of student achievement to such an extent that most school districts and policy makers stake their reputations on the results. In the 1950s and 1960s, many commercial testing programs were born in an effort to measure school accountability. By the late 1980s and into the 1990s, the call for a national assessment program has been at the top of the political agendas of some policy makers. Policy makers have discovered the political power of state and national assessments as they vie for state and national elected office. Policy makers have gone the extra mile to convince voters that the U.S. economic structure would surely dissolve if our students did not rank higher on international tests of science and mathematics. Even though there is little evidence to support such assertions, test after test is being laid on the alter of these policy wonks. Reviewing the history of assessment and the testing movement brings us to the question: What purpose does all of this testing madness serve? Is all of this assessment done for the good of the students and teachers, a measure of learning? Is assessment a tool of the policy makers seeking an agenda and thus a position of power in the political arena? Is assessment the result of a strong political lobby by test designers and corporations attempting to make a profit at the expense of the unwashed masses? Or is assessment designed to scare teachers and students into working harder to achieve higher levels of achievement? The answers to all of these questions are in the affirmative to a greater or lesser degree, but they depend mostly on the political agenda of the person responding to the questions.

The penultimate question concerning assessment is: Does high-stakes testing motivate teachers and students to higher levels of achievement? The research evidence answering this question is mixed at best, but what seems to be clear is that high-stakes testing is going to remain a priority for most politicians. Stiggens (1999) predicts that high-stakes testing might raise the anxiety levels of parents, student, teachers, and principals without providing the resources to function with the increased anxiety. He further states that educators might respond to this increased tension by:

- Increasing unfocused instructional attention to what would raise test scores
- Becoming defensive and frustrated
- Opposing school improvement activities
- Resigning their positions for more financially lucrative jobs in business
- Leaving the profession because of a perceived and real lack of public support

It is quite clear that these predictions have become reality, as teachers are more frustrated and confrontational than ever in the history of public education. The education profession is graying at a very rapid rate and little evidence exists that replacement personnel are coming into the profession.

High-stakes testing does fulfill the political mantra, but does it fulfill the learning needs of students? If it does not, how might educators meet those student needs? Researchers Black and Wiliam (1998) report that improved classroom instruction and formative assessment activities mean:

- An increase in grade-equivalent scores of three or four grade levels
- An increase of fifteen percentile points on standardized tests
- An increase in ranking on the Third International Mathematics and Science Study

Black and Wiliam (1998) ultimately argue that better formative assessment, that which is administered in the classroom, produces profoundly positive results for low achievers. The entire body of research on formative assessment indicates that students achieve at a much higher level, that it is essential to classroom work, and that developing well-designed assessments help students meet increasing educational standards. In addition, they argue that professional development needs to be implemented because it would help principals and teachers design quality classroom and school assessments.

Principals need to consider an alternative to reducing the pressure on students and teachers that high-stakes testing creates. Teachers, principals, parents, superintendents, and policy makers must remember that success or failure on all types of assessments rests with students and the role of everyone else's job is to find successful ways of motivating students. The pressure of assessment failure appears to lead many students to test anxiety, school dropout, cheating, the pursuit of less challenging courses, and the fear of failure.

A strategy that removes many of the negative consequences created by high-stakes testing is the assessment concept involved in benchmarking. Benchmarking is formative in expectation and summative in substance. Benchmarking provides students, teachers, and parents with specific examples of student learning successes and failures at each administration of the assessment. In addition, the benchmarking assessment strategy provides the student with information concerning his or her progress since the last administration of the assessment. Measuring student gain from one benchmark to the next always shows that students have progressed in relation to the intended learning outcomes. This is a motivating force that encourages students to continue to learn and teaches them to cope with the pressure of tests.

Benchmarks are "statements of information and skill that add definition and detail to the general statements articulated at the standards level" (Marzano and Kendall 1996, 73). These benchmark statements provide the foundation for creating assessment questions that form the benchmark tests. These benchmark tests can be created for grade levels, subject areas, or for specific course content. The benchmark questions are derived from local, state, or national standards.

Generally, there are three formats in which benchmarks may be written: (1) statement of knowledge and skill, (2) as performance tasks, and (3) as performance activities (Marzano and Kendall 1996). The statement of knowledge and skills is written with information for students to comprehend. For example, a benchmark for fourth-grade mathematics might read:

Students can

1. Understand the concept of equations.
2. Apply the concept of decimals.

The first benchmark requires that the student understand information about equations and how they function, while the second benchmark is mostly about mathematics procedures, more specifically, where to put the decimal in the number to convey meaning. As students progress through the grades, the benchmarks change, some in content and some become more sophisticated in what students are expected to understand and apply.

Using benchmarks at the elementary, intermediate, and middle school levels appears to work very well. Teachers in these grades tend to focus more on students and not so much on the content, a flaw detected by some policy makers, and the right direction for most educators. Marzano and Kendall (1996) argue that high school courses do not necessarily proceed in a progressive spiral upward. They argue that some courses are introductory and some are for the advanced student, which does not allow for a continuously more difficult set of intended learning outcomes. This problem can be addressed by creating more than one set of benchmarks for each of the courses, thus addressing the expectation of an introductory course and also the advanced placement course.

Choosing the benchmarking process is by no means the only strategy for assessing the curriculum. As a principal, you might choose to address the assessment issue using program evaluation. Program evaluation should begin with the end in mind. Starting with the end in mind provides the principal with a better understanding of what can be achieved through the evaluation. Eisner and Vallance (1974) discuss the connoisseurship model of program evaluation. This model consists of two basic premises: (1) the connoisseur, and (2) the educational critic. The connoisseur is either an individual or group of experts that understands the intricate details of the content area. The educational critic explains the findings to parents and other interested persons. In this model, the teachers and the connoisseur would observe, survey, and interview the teachers to identify the current status of the program. You would not want to limit the data gathering to only those involved in the program but would search far and wide for information about the program. It is important for the principal to make sure the connoisseur focuses on the positive aspects of the program as well as the negative, a strategy that needs to be addressed at the time the program evaluation process is being developed. Once the connoisseur has gathered the necessary data and the education critic has had time to inform the teacher, parents, and the community about what has been discovered, it is now time for the connoisseur's recommendations, which all members of the school must take very seriously and begin to implement. This model of curriculum assessment provides a rich and detailed analysis of the current state of the curriculum, how it is being implemented, and describes where the intended learning outcome gaps are located. The strength of this model is:

- Gathering of detailed information
- Usage of a large catchment area for information about the program
- A continuous evaluation process
- Flexibility of assessment

Provus (1971) developed a second model for curriculum assessment called the discrepancy model. This model focuses on the discrepancies between standards and actual performance. It defines "program evaluation" as a process for (1) defining program standards; (2) discovering the discrepancy between program performance and professional standards; and (3) using this discrepancy data to change performance (1971).

When performance is compared to the standard, four possible results might occur. The design stage of this model includes objectives, the human resources that must be involved in order for the objectives to be implemented, and the instructional strategies that allow the objectives to be attained (Popham 1993). The next phase of the model determines whether the program as it is implemented is congruent with the implementation process. The question at this point is: When comparing the standards against the program, are discrepancies observed? Curriculum assessors have four possible choices:

- Terminate the program.
- Proceed with the program as it is now functioning.
- Adjust the performance of the program.
- Modify the standards.

The third phase of the model is the process phase and it focuses on the enabling objectives and is similar to what many evaluators describe as formative evaluation, in terms of how the curriculum is doing at this point in time. The fourth phase of the model addresses the question: Has the program met its objectives? This is a measurement of the instruction as compared to the objectives to determine if there are any discrepancies (Worthen and Sanders 1987). The last phase of the discrepancy model is concerned with the cost benefit of the program as compared to other similar programs. Cost-benefit analysis can only be achieved when programs have comparable components. According to Popham (1993), the discrepancy model attempts to put data together in a way that helps decision makers solve problems. The strengths of the discrepancy model are:

- Its simplicity of understanding and ease of implementation
- It causes educators to reflect on what outcomes they want to achieve
- It creates a dialogue with the community about the expectation level for student achievement
- Its measurement practices can be expanded for assessing student achievement

The disadvantages of the discrepancy model are:

- Its evaluative component is relatively weak when comparing student progress
- It focuses exclusively on the objectives, rather than the value of the objectives
- It does not consider the context of the assessment
- It leaves out evidence of program value not covered by the objectives (Worthen and Sanders 1987)

Assessing the curriculum can be accomplished using several different models, all of which provide information for the purposes of curricular decision making. Without these models, it is extremely difficult to measure the relative success of the curriculum. Principals tend to assess the curriculum utilizing an anecdotal model rather than relying on data to support curricular decisions. Anecdotes are useful in some instances, but not for the purpose of deciding which aspects of the curriculum to implement. These anecdotes are sometimes positive about particular aspects of the curriculum but mostly they provide a negative analysis of what is to be taught. In many instances, teachers who neither have the skill nor the desire to teach students the piece of the curriculum being discussed create these anecdotes. It is the principal's responsibility to make sure that each individual student has the opportunity to reach his or her academic potential and the only way to do that is with a diverse and extensive curriculum.

ETHICAL DISCUSSION

Should the Control of Curriculum Remain with the State through Local Districts or Should It Become a National Curriculum?

Control of the curriculum has been a topic of conversation among policy makers and has become a pivotal issue in several presidential elections. Furthermore, it has been hotly debated by parents who believe they should control the curriculum and by state policy makers who believe they have the authority to make curriculum decisions for the children of their state.

The questions that need to be addressed concerning this issue are:

- Is the only way to ensure accountability through a national curriculum?
- Does a national curriculum promote economic competitiveness and provide a better standard of living for the citizens?
- Is a national curriculum necessary in order to allow for geographic mobility and the building of nationalism?
- Will a national curriculum help develop an enlightened electorate and reduce class warfare?
- Schools are supposed to allow each child to experience the best education possible by individualizing instruction. Is this possible with the goal of a uniform curriculum for all students regardless of where they live?
- What dangers abound when state policy makers control the curriculum?
- Who should decide what is important in the curriculum, the professionals or the policy makers?
- Ethical dilemmas are right-versus-right issues. Which side of the curriculum issue do you support and why?

CHAPTER SUMMARY

Curriculum is defined as "intended learning outcomes" or "what is taught to students." Either definition provides the foundation on which to build a useful and vibrant curriculum. Without leaders who are really interested in developing the curriculum to its fullest degree, very little will be done to provide students with a challenging learning environment. Curriculum leadership requires the principal to have a clear vision of curriculum development and knowledge about the use of curriculum development tools. Curriculum development tools, such as the top-down, teacher-to-the-top, and integrated tools, provide principals with the strategies necessary to make significant changes in the schools' intended learning outcomes.

Curriculum leadership emanates from many sources in the school organization, but the central figure is the principal. Principals are in the best position to supervise and direct all aspects of the curriculum development process. The traditional view of school leadership does not fit the context for many schools, thus requiring principals to extend leadership opportunities to others in the school organization. Professional development activities no longer meet teacher's leadership needs. Principals must build each teacher's self-confidence by helping the teacher develop his or her personal leadership character and the skills necessary to provide school-wide leadership.

Curriculum design is influenced by the values and beliefs of the designers. The philosophy of the curriculum designers affects the content that becomes the intended learning outcomes. The Tyler model provides a four-step guide to curriculum design and even though it was developed in 1949 it still has much merit for use by curriculum designers. The conflicting concepts model of curriculum design provides a plethora of options for designers to use as they design intended learning outcomes for students. Comer's balanced curriculum model focuses on describing and aligning the curriculum using teachers as the experts. The "curriculum web" model begins by addressing an "aim," which is similar to what other models call a goal but is more general in nature, holistic in content, and clear in direction. Student experiences form the focus for the intended learning outcomes in this model.

The Tyler, conflicting concepts, balanced, and web curriculum design models contain similar curriculum design parts. In some form, each addresses the needs of students, goals, objectives, and specific subject matter content. Each model has strengths and weaknesses and it is the principal's responsibility to select the model that best fits the school's context.

Standards have become an important aspect of school change ever since the report *A Nation at Risk* became popularized by the dominate media culture. Standards look much like goals but are directed more toward the student's ability to accomplish a specific skill or understand specific knowledge. Standards may answer the same two questions that goals and objectives address: What should the student know? and What should the student be able to accomplish? Standards are created by professional and academic associations and done so in very different ways. Multiple iterations of standards require that the local school consider several documents before deciding what level of sophistication is desired in each content area.

Curriculum alignment is a systematic effort for congruence among the intended learning outcomes, instruction, and assessment. The curriculum alignment concept has as its foundation the principle that the instructional plan is derived from subject matter goals and that a congruence exists between instruction and assessment. This logical curriculum allows teachers to coordinate subject matter content among grade levels and courses. Curriculum alignment can be accomplished by either front-loading or by back-loading the intended curriculum. Advantages and disadvantages exist for both of these alignment strategies. The front-loaded curriculum addresses what students need to know followed by an assessment that measures student understanding of the intended curriculum. Back-loading requires assessment development prior to curriculum development

Curriculum assessment may be accomplished in two very different ways. Benchmarks are statements of information and skill that detail standards. These benchmark statements provide the basis for creating assessment questions that form the benchmark tests. By matching the benchmark statements with the intended learning outcomes, the principal can identify, using a gap analysis, where there are missing intended learning outcomes.

CHAPTER ACTIVITIES AND QUESTIONS

1. Define curriculum leadership as it pertains to your context.
2. Select a curriculum design model and describe how it would be implemented in a school.
3. The curriculum alignment process is designed to provide teachers and administrators with an overall view of what is being taught. How would you implement the curriculum alignment process?

4. Select a curriculum assessment model and outline how you would use the model to improve your school.
5. Where do curriculum standards come from and why should educators be concerned about them?
6. Describe the benchmarking process and discuss how you would implement this strategy in a school.
7. What is the difference between front-loading and back-loading the curriculum? When would you use the front-loading alignment strategy? When would you use the back-loading alignment strategy?
8. Describe the five steps in Tyler's curriculum design model and compare it to Comer's conflicting concepts model by describing similarities and differences.

CASE STUDY ACTIVITIES AND QUESTIONS

1. What structure would work best for Principal Fischbeck as she designed a strategy to move teachers beyond the current satisfaction with student achievement?
2. Which groups should be on the curriculum development committee? Justify your reasons for selecting your groups.
3. What type of background work should Principal Fischbeck pursue in order for the curriculum development process to function smoothly?
4. What type of professional development should Principal Fischbeck provide for the faculty?
5. How could Ms. Fischbeck have avoided the negative comments she received at the faculty meeting? Should principals be concerned about negative faculty comments when attempting to change the curriculum?
6. How could Principal Fischbeck convince Ms. Most that going beyond the state standards was not an unreasonable request?
7. If you were Principal Fischbeck, how would you secure the support of the superintendent and the executive committee of the New Area Road Parent–Teachers Association?
8. Which curriculum development model would you recommend to Principal Fischbeck and why? Make sure you consider the context for the New Area Road Elementary School as you make your recommendation.

REFERENCES

Amuah, I. K. (1988). "A new approach towards curriculum design." School Improvement Coalition Conference (ERIC Document Reproduction Services no. ED 294 750).

Berliner, D. C., and Biddle, B. J. (1995). *The manufactured crisis: Myths, fraud, and the attack on American public schools*. Reading, MA: Addison-Wesley.

Black, P., and Wiliam, D. (1998). "Inside the black box: Raising standards [Monograph]." *Phi Delta Kappan* (October): 139–148.

Brooker, R., Elliott, B., MacPherson, I., Thurlow, G., and Burnett, L. (1997). "Exploring teachers' views of themselves as curriculum leaders." At www.swin.edu.au (accessed November 1, 2001).

Calderhead, J., and Sharrock, S. (1977). *Understanding teacher education*. London: Falmer.

Cohen, S. A. (1987). "Instructional alignment: Searching for a magic bullet." *Educational Researcher* (November): 16–19.

Cunningham, C. (1999). "Curriculum webs: A practical guide to weaving the web into teaching and learning." At cuip.uchicago.edu (accessed November 1, 2001).

Doll, R. C. (1992). *Curriculum improved: Decision making and process*. 8th ed. Boston: Allyn and Bacon.

Eisner, E., and Vallance, E. (1974). *Conflicting conceptions of curriculum*. Berkeley, CA: McCutchan.

Elliot, R., Brooker, R., Thurlow, G, and McInman, I. (1996). "Insights into curriculum leadership: The state of the field." Paper presented as part of the symposium "Theorising Curriculum Leadership for Effective Learning and Teaching: Reporting Progress in an ARC Collaborative Research Project." Singapore, November 25–29, at www.swin.edu.au/aare (accessed November 2, 2001).

Evers, C., and Lakomski, G. (1996). *Exploring educational administration: Coherentist applications and critical debates*. New York: Pergamon.

Fitzharris, L. (1999). "Curriculum development." *Journal of Staff Development* 20 (3): 30–31.

Leitzel, T. C., and Vogler, D. E. (1994). "Curriculum alignment: Theory to practice." (ERIC Document Reproduction Services no. ED 371 812).

Liebling, C. R. (1997). "Achieving standards-based curriculum alignment through mindful teaching." (ERIC Document Reproduction Services no. ED 421 487).

Marzano, R. J., and Kendall, J. S. (1996). *Designing standards-based districts, schools, and classrooms*. Alexandria, VA: Mid-continent Regional Educational Laboratory and Association for Supervision and Curriculum Development.

Popham, W. J. (1993). *Educational evaluation*. Needham Heights, MA: Allyn and Bacon.

Provus, M. (1971). *Discrepancy evaluation*. Berkeley, CA: McCutchan.

Ravitch, D. (1995). *National standards in American education: A citizens guide*. Washington, DC: Brookings Institution.

Rutherford, W. L. (1985). "School principals as effective leaders." *Phi Delta Kappan* 67 (1): 31–34.

Shepard, L. (1993). *Setting performance standards for student achievement*. Stanford, CA: National Academy of Education, Stanford University.

Simpson, R. D. (1999). "Ralph Tyler on curriculum: A voice from the past with a message for the future." *Innovative Higher Education* 24 (2): 85–87.

Solomon, P. G., Wyatt-Ortiz, L., and Goldman, N. (1998). "Designing curriculum that responds to the recent agenda for change: Teachers try the upside down tree." American Educational Research Association (ERIC Document Reproduction Services no. ED 425 528).

Sowell, E. J. (2000). *Curriculum: An integrative introduction*. 2nd ed. Upper Saddle River, NJ: Merrill–Prentice-Hall.

Squires, D. (1998). "Toward a balanced curriculum: Aligning standards, curriculum, and assessments." *ERS Spectrum* 16 (3): 17–24.

———. (1997). "Standards-based curriculum and assessment through curriculum alignment." *Newsline*, at info.med.yale.edu/comer/alignment.html (accessed November 4, 2001).

Stiggens, R. J. (1999). "Assessment, confidence, and school success." *Phi Delta Kappan* 81: 191–198.

Tyler, R. W. (1949). *Basic principles of curriculum and instruction*. Chicago: University of Chicago Press.

Webster's New World Dictionary. Springfield, MA: C & G Merriam.

Woodfork, R. (1999). "When standards fail." *Curriculum Administrator* (August): 31–33.

Worthen, B. R., and Sanders, J. R. (1987). *Educational evaluation: Alternative approaches and practical guidelines*. New York: Longman.

Chapter Six

Principal and Instructional Leadership

*Principal William West of Sierra Middle School had returned to school af-
ter spending five days in an intensive professional development activity
concerned with continuous school improvement sponsored by the state's
middle school principals association. After seven years as a middle school
principal, Mr. West felt he had gotten into an intellectual and professional
crevasse. In his own words, "I have fallen into a deep rut" and he didn't
like the feeling. He knew that student achievement scores had declined
over the past three years, but he attributed that to parental and student in-
difference to learning. Even though he knew he was in a rut, he could not
bring himself to believe that any changes were needed.*

*He had helped supervise the construction and opened Sierra Middle
School and had been its only principal. He had hired all of the teachers
and most of the teachers he had hired seven years ago were still on the
faculty. All of the students knew Mr. West as a caring and kind principal,
but they also knew he was a tough disciplinarian. The school's reputation,
as all of the parents and students would tell you, was a place for learning
with no nonsense being tolerated.*

*Mr. West had the reputation of only hiring teachers that would follow
his orders and tolerated little discussion about how the school would function. He treated the faculty with the greatest amount of professional respect and he always supported what the teachers did in the classroom,
sometimes even when it was clear they had made a mistake. The faculty,
parents, students, and the community trusted Mr. West's judgment on almost all issues about school.*

*For the first time in several years, Mr. West was forced to hire two new sci-
ence teachers. Ms. Philips and Ms. Fuqua had retired after thirty years of*

163

teaching science in the Fort Spirit School District. Principal West had hired Dan Dorfman, a middle school science teacher from a nearby district with five years of teaching experience. For the other science position, he had hired Sally Beth Belkman, a first-year teacher from the regional teacher education institution. Both Ms. Belkman and Mr. Dorfman were very enthusiastic about students learning and had indicated during the interview process that they would do whatever it took to help students achieve. Mr. West was sure he had selected the best possible candidates for his two science positions, nonetheless, he would not feel totally comfortable until he had seen them teach.

Three weeks into the fall semester Mr. West came unannounced into Ms. Belkman's third-period seventh-grade earth science class. She greeted the principal and as the bell rang to begin the class all of the students seemed to be milling around the classroom. Ms. Belkman very quietly asked for the students' attention and they responded by finding a seat near to where they were located. She gave them a few directions about what they were to do for the day and reviewed for about five minutes what they had learned the day before. Ms. Belkman then told them to begin working on their assigned projects. Every student seemed to be working on something, but it was clear to Mr. West that not all of the students were working on the same projects. He continued to watch the students work, talk with one another, write things in their notebooks, and enjoy the day's lesson. Mr. West left the classroom wondering what he had just observed, teaching or chaos. This lesson was certainly not the direct-teach model most all of the faculty at Sierra Middle School employed to instruct students. He was concerned and at the same time he was curious because the students were working and learning, at least it appeared that way. Mr. West was still reflecting on what he had seen in Ms. Belkman's classroom three days after he had observed the class. At lunch, two of the senior members of the faculty asked to speak to Principal West privately in his office after school. Ms. Whilhitt and Mr. Flornoy knocked on the door, came into Mr. West's office, and shut the door. They told him that students taking Ms. Belkman's science class had come into their classroom talking about how much fun they had been having in science class and how they liked her teaching style. Mr. West asked the two teachers for specific problems but they did not have any except to say they did not see how science could be fun. Mr. West assured Ms. Whilhitt and Mr. Flornoy that he would check into the situation.

The next morning, Mr. West asked Ms. Belkman to stop by his office after school. When she arrived, he questioned her about how she was teach-

ing her science classes, because he had some complaints. Ms. Belkman was shocked to hear this news, since she was only doing what she had been taught in her teacher education courses. Mr. West asked her to describe her teaching style and she told him she was using the inquiry model of instruction. Mr. West not knowing what that meant asked Ms. Belkman to explain the inquiry model of instruction in great detail. She responded by talking about discovering the various properties of water by using the scientific method. As she discussed the inquiry model, it seemed to make sense to Mr. West even though he did not really understand how it worked. Mr. West encouraged Ms. Belkman to continue using the inquiry model, after all he had gotten several supportive telephone calls from parents.

As Mr. West was driving home from school, he reflected on the conversation he and Ms. Belkman had just completed. As he thought about what she had said during their meeting, he came to realize that what she was doing was what he had learned at his five-day professional development activity on improving schools, specifically teaching and learning. He reflected on what he had learned and how he might use it to raise student achievement at Sierra Middle School. Principal West went to work the next day with a renewed resolve to change the instructional process for students and vowed he would be the first one to learn a new model for teaching students and would demonstrate an instruction that allowed all children to participate in the teaching and learning process.

In the previous scenario, Mr. West experienced an instructional epiphany. He decided to participate in the instructional development of the entire faculty by leading by example. He wanted to add more instructional strategies to his "instructional tool kit" and at the same time to encourage the faculty to add to their "instructional tool kits." Mr. West had become an instructional leader at Sierra Middle School for the first time in his seven-year tenure as principal.

INSTRUCTIONAL LEADERSHIP DEFINED

The individual who claims to be the instructional leader usually defines the practice of instructional leadership. Principals define instructional leadership from their point of views, seldom examining the teachers' perspectives on instructional leadership. Rarely do principals reflect on the impact their instructional leadership has on teachers. Instructional leadership is something that principals like to believe they are doing on a daily basis but have no evidence to support their beliefs. In reality, instructional leadership may be the single most important attribute that principals possess. The only real way schools change is by improving what happens in the classroom. If principals truly want to become instructional leaders, they must change the manner in which students are taught.

Defining instructional leadership often incorporates the merging of tasks such as evaluation of instruction, professional development, and curriculum development. Glickman (1985) defines instructional leadership in terms of five distinct tasks: working directly with teachers, group improvement, professional development, curriculum improvement, and action research implementation. He further states that all of these attributes brought the teachers' needs and the school goals together. Pajak (1989) formulates a list of instructional leader attributes that mirror many of Glickman's tasks, while adding planning, organizing, creating change opportunities, and motivating teachers. Instructional leadership should be a collaborative activity undertaken in a helpful atmosphere that moves the entire school toward a plan of action (Glickman 1985). Perhaps the most influential instructional leadership strategy at the elementary and secondary levels is the promotion of professional development for teachers (Sheppard 1996).

Researchers Blasé and Blasé (1999b) argue that meeting with teachers in and outside of formal instructional conferences is a lynchpin for successful instructional leadership. Principals need to dialogue with teachers about instructional practice, to encourage them to explore new models of instruction, and to reflect on their current practice. In dialoguing with teachers, principals use the following strategies to encourage teacher reflection:

• Share suggestions
• Provide comment
• Model instructional exemplars
• Use praise
• Solicit advice and respect opinions (Blasé and Blasé 1999b)

Another element of effective instructional leadership that is reported by Blasé and Blasé (1999a) is the teachers' understanding of teaching models and the opportunity to discuss teaching and learning strategies. According to teachers, the most effective instructional leaders use the following strategies to help them grow:

- Reading and studying the teaching and learning process
- Emphasizing collaboration among colleagues
- Encouraging the development of coaching relationships among teachers
- Encouraging the redesign of programs
- Encouraging the use of adult learning strategies for professional development
- Using informed instruction through action research (Blasé and Blasé 1999b)

According to Supovitz (2000), instructional leadership begins when principals talk about being in the classroom and visiting with students about their academic pursuits. The challenge for principals is getting out of their offices into the classrooms, but the key for accomplishment of this challenge is the principal's commitment to instruction. Supovitz (2000) also describes effective habits of instructional focused leaders:

- Visit classrooms and talk with students about their academic work. Active involvement in the classroom sends the signal to teachers and students that teaching and learning are very important.
- Analyze the results of student assessment with faculty members. With this data goals can be developed and strategies for assessing the goals can be created.
- Reduce the mobility of the instructional staff by creating an atmosphere of organizational autonomy.
- Encourage faculty members to exchange instructional strategies, visit each others classrooms, and openly discuss instructional problems.

Spillane, Halverson, and Diamond (1999) argue that principals should move away from the role-based concepts of instructional leadership to one of distributed leadership. In the role-based model, the principal is the evaluator, instructional supervisor, and instructional leader. The distributed instructional leadership model states that all concerned individuals with different areas of expertise fuse their skill and knowledge to accomplish the various roles required of instructional leaders (Elmore 2000). In the distributed instructional leadership environment, principals are shepherds of the process, help others grow into leadership positions, delegate some aspects of instruction to others, and use the expertise and skills of colleagues to accomplish the instructional goals of the school (Supovitz 2000). For the principal, distributed instructional leadership means the opportunity to spend more time in the classroom to increase the teacher's role in instructional improvement and more time to complete the teacher's tasks of improving teaching and learning in their schools.

With all the instructional leadership rhetoric and models found in the professional literature extolling the virtues of collaborative instructional relationships between principals and teachers, the practice of instructional leadership appears to have been limited to assessment, oversight, and evaluation of classroom instruction. Many teachers and some principals describe instructional leadership as fault finding, "snoopervision," protectionism, and instructional "cold war" (Glanz 1995). Sergiovanni (1992) describes principals' and teachers' conversations about classroom teaching as a "nonevent" in which both parties acknowledge strengths and weaknesses but no activities are implemented to correct the weaknesses. Despite the unending pressure on principals to be instructional leaders, there appears to be a scarcity of empirical research that describes attributes of an effective instructional leader or how these attributes influence classroom instruction (Short 1995).

THE PRINCIPAL'S ROLE IN CHANGING INSTRUCTION

Today's principals have a fundamental role in changing instruction, either change instruction or suffer at the hands of high-stakes testing. Given the recent movement by policy makers in almost all fifty states, failing to change instruction may be a fatal flaw. According to Peters (1987), change is fluid, constant, and relentless. As a principal, you either learn to love change or face the consequences of a failed instructional program. Instructional change is challenging, high risk, and more likely than not fraught with uncertainty. Perhaps instructional change is a matter of endurance, of taking the road least traveled by. It is more than doing something in a different way. Instructional change must embrace the concept of continuous instructional improvement.

Utaz (1998) suggests a continuous cycle of diversified supervision as one way of changing instruction. He states that regardless of the school context, the first step in changing instruction begins with a "super vision." This concept is not reverting back to the use of slogans but instead focuses on the core values and beliefs of the members of the organization. It is the principal's untiring task to repeat this vision continuously and passionately. "The vision lives in the intensity of the leader, an intensity that in itself draws in others" (Peters 1987, 406–407). Every hour of every day the principal continues to reinforce the vision by talking to parents, teachers, students, and yes even the superintendent about the vision. Waste no opportunities to bring forth the vision so all will understand your commitment to instruction.

It is important to sustain an environment where teachers and principals feel free to experiment instructionally in the classroom. Encouraging teachers to try new instructional models and strategies is most important. This encouragement takes place when the principal listens to teachers carefully and analyzes what they are saying about their own learning. Encouragement also means giving teachers the freedom to fail and to recognize that failure is part of the learning process. In some instances it is important to allow teachers to try new things, even though, as a principal you have experienced this instructional strategy before and found it to be unproductive. It is possible the teacher will discover the key to making what once was a failure a complete success. Encourage teachers to work together to solve instructional problems even though turmoil is almost certain to occur. Working through the obstacles will provide benefits beyond your wildest dreams. The collegiality that comes from this challenging situation will improve instructional effectiveness and learning will increase.

The principal's participation as a member of a collegial supervision team provides teachers with easy access to an expert in the instructional process (Utaz 1998). The principal takes the opportunity to demonstrate instructional strategies and models for teachers. At this point, the principal has become a participant with the teachers in the instructional process and a player in the instructional improvement process. This team approach to supervision provides the principal with the opportunity to engage in a continuous problem-solving strategy with the teacher team. Utaz (1998) argues that monitoring instruction has two purposes: providing information about new instructional approaches and as a conduit for a comprehensive analysis of instruction.

Instructional approaches that are new for teachers may not be new in terms of when they were created but rather new to the teacher. The principal's role is to provide teachers with the opportunity to know about these instructional models. In some cases the principal should be the expert in demonstrating this new instructional technique and in other situations someone from the instructional staff needs to provide the expert demonstration. Regardless of who becomes the expert provider, the principal is responsible for making sure teachers are exposed and encouraged to use new instructional techniques. The target for the principal in this situation is the improvement of instruction. Most teachers utilize the direct instruction model in most classrooms because they are comfortable and somewhat knowledgeable about how the model works in the teaching and learning process. For example, teachers know, or they should know, that the direct instruction model does not require participation and engagement of students in the learning process. It is the principal's responsibility to provide teachers with the encouragement and skills to use instructional models other then direct teach.

It is also the principal's responsibility to analyze the teacher's instruction. Principals must know what good instruction looks like and be able to diagnose instructional problems, even if they are fortunate enough to have instructional specialists available to help with the diagnosis. Helping teachers improve instructionally is the primary function of being a principal. Diagnosis consists of observing the instruction, identifying the problem areas, and then suggesting strategies that will help correct the problem. The diagnosis process begins with the observation of the student's reaction to the teacher's instruction. Observing the teacher is a small part of the diagnosis process, because students hold the key to what instructional problems exist in the classroom. Identifying the instructional problems in a classroom requires a sound understanding of how students learn. Once the instruction has been analyzed, it is the principal's responsibility to provide strategies that will address the problems. For example, during a fourth-grade mathematics lesson students do not appear to understand the concept of division by two decimals or more. The teacher has demonstrated the placement of the carat to denote the addition of two zeros after the whole number, yet students fail to understand the concept. The principal's roll in this situation is to identify the instructional problem, make suggestions as to how the teacher might address the situation with new instructional techniques, or have the teacher discuss the situation with another teacher that the principal has successfully observed teaching the same concept. The principal may not have the solution to every instructional problem but it is mandatory that the principal know where to get those solutions once the analysis has been made.

INSTRUCTIONAL DELIVERY SYSTEMS

Principals are responsible for student achievement even though they do not actually deliver the instruction to the student. If this premise is accurate, and it is in most situations, how can the principal influence what happens in the classroom? Communication with teachers concerning effective instructional systems is the first step to changing the instructional culture of any school. This communication could begin with the teachers acknowledging what instructional systems they are currently using. The vast majority of teachers would recognize that the instructional system that they employ the vast majority of the time is the direct-teach system. In this system, the teacher lectures, demonstrates, and questions students about what they heard, read, or observed. This system works well for academically at-risk students and should be utilized with those students on a consistent basis. For all other students, the direct-teach system allows them to hide in the classroom and not participate in their own learning. This system allows students to be passive learners and in many situations the students lose focus and are off task for significant parts of the instruction. Once the principal is able to determine the dominant instructional system being used in the school, it is his or her responsibility to encourage, motivate, and in some situations demand that teachers employ other instructional systems so that all children can and will learn.

It is the principal who must make sure that all teachers have more than one instructional system in their "educational tool kit." Joyce and Weil (1986) recommend that teachers have a minimum of five instructional systems that they feel capable of utilizing in addition to the direct-teach system. Teachers who have mastered multiple instructional systems need not rely on only one system to attract the interest of students and to teach the material. Using this variety of instructional systems allows the teacher to meet the needs of all types of learners. This strategy allows the teacher to be an instructional problem solver and decision maker.

The principal must ensure that new approaches to teaching are important to teachers and that they have the opportunity to communicate regularly with their colleagues. The following are concepts that principals must remember if they want teachers to utilize several instructional systems:

- Make the teachers lifelong learners by immersing them in the new systems
- Mentor teachers so they will become instructional systems designers
- Mentor teachers as they implement the new instructional systems in their classroom
- Support teachers' efforts to help each other
- Create networking opportunities for teachers who are implementing new instructional systems (Sage and Thorpe 1997)

Inquiry Instructional System

If the principal will master the following five instructional systems to the point that he or she can demonstrate and critique these systems, then the principal will have taken the first step in becoming a real instructional leader, one with the skills to make a difference in the achievement of students. The first instructional system that principals need to master is the inquiry system. Inquiry is based around the problem-solving strategies that scientists use in finding an answer to questions. This is one of the few instructional systems where the teacher would not begin the class with the lesson objective; in fact, in this system the objective comes at the end of the lesson. The only prerequisite for the inquiry model is that students understand and have the skill to perform scientific research. The level of sophistication for scientific research is dependent on student age, grade level, and intellectual capacity. In other words, the inquiry model can be used with all groups and the only thing that changes is the complexity of the results. According to Suchman (1962), the following seven steps make up the inquiry model:

- Teacher chooses problem.
- Students conduct the research.
- Students collect data.
- Students state a hypothesis and attempt to prove the theory.

- Students outline the rules guided by their theory.
- Teacher and students review the process.
- Teacher and students assess the process.

This instructional system begins by the teacher choosing a problem. The problem can emanate from any of the courses or disciplines taught by the teacher. Choosing an authentic problem with many routes to a successful result are best for students. This process teaches students that there is more than one way to get to the same answer and it is all right to take a different path to the same results. Once the problem has been selected, it is the teacher's responsibility to determine how much information is given to the students at the start of the process. When first using this system, information may need to be front-loaded in order for students to understand the inquiry system and to be successful in arriving at a reasonable solution for a given problem. As the teacher uses the system, the students become more familiar with the process and front-loading may be diminished.

Students conduct the research, record data, and state a hypothesis during the next phase of this strategy. At this point in the system, the teacher is the data source and can answer student questions concerning the problem with only "yes" or "no." Students can continue to ask questions as long as they are answered in the affirmative. Students soon learn to ask questions that really form the root of a hypothesis for solving the problem. Students record data and keep all information so that they can expand on what they know.

Once the data is recorded, the students begin to generate questions that form the basis for their theoretical answer to the problem. In the inquiry system, data relates directly to either proving or disproving the theoretical answer to the problem. Students must determine how they can test their theoretical answer. At this point, students may determine that they have not discovered the answer to the problem because they find they have flaws in their theoretical answer and thus must return to the data gathering phase.

As the teacher and students arrive at this point in this instructional system, students are asked to review the process they utilized to arrive at their solution to the problem. As they review this process, they are encouraged to consider how they could have been more efficient in solving the problem and more effective in their questioning techniques. Evaluation is the final step in this system and it fits together with the review process as they determine their understanding of the system. This can be accomplished by having each student research his or her own problem.

The inquiry system can work as a group or individual project. It may be beneficial for the teacher to teach the system to the students in groups prior to moving to individual problem solving. This makes it much easier for the students since they can learn from each other as well as the teacher. This system requires all students to become involved in their own learning and is more likely to generate total student participation than any form of direct-teach system.

Moving from the classical to the inquiry-based classroom requires a new and different classroom transition for both teachers and students. Both groups need time to transition from conformation type activities and lectures, to the open-ended activities of the inquiry system. The key for principals wanting to make this system part of the instructional system for a school is to remember to change slowly. As the instructional leader, the principal will soon discover that both students and teachers will initially resist inquiry-based instruction, but will grow to like the process and understand its value to the teaching and learning process (Crocker, Bartlett, and Elliott 1976).

Cooperative Instructional System

Perhaps one of the most talked about and least understood of the instructional systems that principals need to understand and be able to demonstrate is the cooperative learning system. Most teachers indicate that they have used the cooperative learning system but when you ask them to describe the various parts of the cooperative learning process what you soon discover is that most of what is called cooperative learning is really some form of group learning. While this process may be pleasing to the teacher, the question arises: How much individual learning is actually taking place? Some conservative groups have initiated an all out assault on the cooperative learning system because teachers have failed to explain the cooperative learning process and to provide for individual assessment of students when using the system. Gunter, Estes, and Schwab (1999) identify five different models of cooperative learning: the jigsaw model; the role-playing model; the graffiti model; team interview; and the think, pair, share model. Each of these cooperative learning models utilizes the concepts of cooperative learning in different ways and principals need to familiarize themselves with the specifics of each.

Johnson, Johnson, and Holubec (1993) state that the elements of cooperative learning are contained in the following five attributes:

- Students feel that they need each other to complete the task
- Students help each other to learn by sharing and encouraging behavior
- Student performance is individually evaluated
- Students need social skills to make the instructional system work effectively
- Students must understand how they achieved their learning goals

Joint rewards, shared resources, and assigned roles make students understand they need each other to solve the problem they have been assigned. Since the goal is the accomplishment of a task, most students are willing to share their thoughts, but the teacher would be well served to teach the students some strategies for allowing each person's ideas in the group to be valued. Perhaps the attribute that gets the least attention from teachers is the idea of individual evaluation, but failing to do this will allow parents the opportunity to attack the process. Teaching students social skills such as respecting others, allowing diversity of opinion, and listening forms the foundation for successful implementation of the cooperative learning system. Students must understand how they arrived at their results so that they might be able to duplicate the process in the future.

In the beginning, the principal needs to understand and be able to demonstrate a generic cooperative learning system. The principal must understand and demonstrate that the teacher's responsibility in the cooperative learning system is to be "the guide on the side, not the sage on the stage," in other words, the teacher is to uncover the material with the students, not cover the material for the students (Johnson, Johnson, and Holubec 1993). Ellis and Whalen (1990) state that starting a cooperative learning lesson should begin by deciding what the student academic and social tasks will be. The academic task might be the solving of a set of math problems. For younger students, the social skill might be learning to share, becoming a better listener, or working together to achieve a common goal. This process should be no different than what the teacher might do using any instructional system.

Planning the lesson for cooperative learning involves the teacher performing the following tasks:

- Establishing the optimum group size
- Deciding where the work will be done
- Deciding what materials are required for the lesson
- Selecting the students who will work together
- Providing the learner with the basic concepts for what is to be learned
- Possibly discovering the need to reteach some basic concepts
- Evaluating individual student learning
- Evaluating the cooperative learning process (Ellis and Whalen 1990)

Group size may be dictated by the number of students in the class, but the smaller the groups the more likely the teacher will be able to determine student participation in the group. Ellis and Whalen (1990) suggest pairing students as the students learn the process of cooperative learning and moving to three or four students in a group when students feel comfortable using this instructional system.

One of the important teacher tasks is assigning students to groups. Heterogeneous grouping appears to work best in most situations. The teacher needs to select these groups keeping in mind the strengths of each of the group members. As the student's comfort level working with all students in the class increases, a random drawing of names may work for assigning groups. Even in the best of situations random assignment of groups is somewhat risky because it may place together the most intelligent students in a group or it might put together the three class clowns. In either case, concern by the teachers is justified.

In this system, principals need to understand that the teacher is responsible for providing the students with the basic concepts of what is to be learned. The teacher provides the foundational learning for each student and this provides each group with a learning point of departure. Making sure the students understand the task is most important and this should be ascertained prior to having students move into their respective groups.

Groups must be monitored and the instructor must be on the alert for anything that might indicate students have not understood the task, are having a difficult time working together, or do not seem to understand their assigned roles. At this point, the instructor must intervene and remedy the problem. This teachable moment requires the instructor to be ever vigilant in monitoring students. Remember, the instructor is a guide not the purveyor of knowledge.

Evaluation of individual student learning is often left out of the cooperative learning system, but it is most important. This can be done in a number of ways such as testing students' understanding of what they learned by asking individual questions. Paper-and-pencil tests are useful in determining student cognitive knowledge. Perhaps the best indicator of student learning is the application of knowledge. Requiring each student to use the information he or she has accumulated is always a great indicator of learning. In this system, it is important to measure individual student learning as well as group learning. Failure to measure individual learning in this system leaves the teacher and the system suspect to challenges by parents and other advocates of the direct instruction system.

Problem-Based Instructional System

The third instructional system that principals must be able to demonstrate and discuss with faculty is problem-based learning. This instructional system has emerged from the cognitive and developmental psychology commonly known today as "constructivist theory." This learning theory states that knowledge is created through a process of reflective abstraction. In the constructivist classroom, the student is presented chances to use prior knowledge and understanding to create new knowledge and cognition from his or her experiences. Teachers take on new roles as collaborators, mentors, and coaches to create an environment that promotes meaningful experiences among students. Problem-based learning is designed to:

- Maximize active student participation in the learning process.
- Foster student problem solving and self-education skills.
- Increase student communication skills.
- Enhance student self-assessment.
- Improve student abilities to access and use information resources. (Seifert and Simmons 1997)

The problem-based learning system involves the use of real problems to create an active, student-centered learning environment. Each problem stimulates small-group discussion among students utilizing basic research techniques. The teacher's role in helping students achieve their goal is to give them direction as they search for solutions to the problem. In addition, they go outside of the school to plan and implement community-based projects, which require parents and community members to share their expertise with the students.

In this system, the teacher serves the student as a guide for learning rather than the primary source for information. The component parts of the problem-based learning system are enumerated by Savoie and Hughes (1994) when they state that the instructor must:

- Identify problems useful to students.
- Place the problem in context for students to make it authentic.
- Structure the subject matter content around the problem.
- Make students responsible for their learning and problem solutions.
- Advance collaboration by creating learning groups.
- Demand all students demonstrate their learning by presenting a product and making a public presentation.

The problem-based learning system can be utilized as an individual or group assignment. Assigning three students to each problem allows the teacher to incorporate some elements of the cooperative learning system in the problem-based system. Groups should be organized based on the teacher's knowledge of each student's academic strengths. After the groups have been formed, it is best to spend time coaching the groups in the process of group learning. Emphasis on creating an equal division of labor and requiring students to put their name on the things they do is an effective way to individualize the assessment process.

Initially, students need to be given a problem-solving strategy. This strategy gives the students a plan for problem formulation and provides the foundation for the entire problem-based learning project. Seifert and Simmons (1997) suggest the following attributes for the problem-solving process:

- Problem formulation
- Data collection
- Brainstorming solutions
- Evaluating and selecting solutions

- Implementing the solution
- Project/product evaluation

The problem formulation strategy is composed of three questions: (1) What do we know? (2) What do we need to know? and (3) What should we do? (Stepien and Gallagher 1993). The answers to these questions form the foundation for solving the problem. At this point, students may want to forge ahead into the problem but good instruction requires them to answer the question: What do we know? This strategy keeps them from solving the problem before they know what the problem really is about.

The data collection aspect of problem-based learning is designed around generally accepted methods of research. At this point in the process, some students will need help with the concept of research especially if they are first-time problem solvers. Data collection methods such as interviewing strategies, survey techniques, library research, and Internet research techniques may need to be demonstrated. In addition, it may be necessary to demonstrate, discuss, and teach students ways of interpreting descriptive statistics such as mean, median, mode, correlation, and standard deviation.

Encourage students to use their imagination as they collect data by:

- Searching places they would not normally search
- Viewing the problem from many perspectives
- Listening carefully and being open to new ideas

As students work the problem-based learning system, ask them to tell you the types and quantity of data they have collected. If students are going to use an interview technique, it would be wise to have them demonstrate their questioning technique prior to the interview.

After data collection is completed, it is now time to brainstorm solutions. All student ideas should be placed on the solution grid regardless of the distance from the final solution. Seifert and Simmons (1997) argue that students be taught to silence the critic in themselves when listening to other's ideas. They state that students must be taught to:

- Immerse themselves in the problem
- Review all possible solutions

- Rearrange the order of the parts
- Share ideas

The key to the brainstorming session is making sure all students feel comfortable submitting their ideas. This may take some work on the part of the teacher but it will pay huge dividends.

Selecting the solution to a problem must be conducted based on the data that has been collected. Only solutions that are supported by the data should be considered by the students. Teach the students to carefully weigh each solution making sure that the final solution is arrived at with all members of the learning team willing to accept the penultimate solution. At this point, students must implement the solution they have selected. Teachers must make students understand that they must be prepared to defend the solution with the data gathered. In some cases, students will need direction in the process of solution presentation and such things as a video demonstration, a class skit, a scale model, or anything else the group might create. This is a presentation to the class and an evening presentation for parents, mentors, interested teachers, and community members. The final product is a written document that is based on the six problem-solving parts and is of such quality that it can be archived in the school library.

Assessing the project/products is based on the utilization of a scoring rubric that the students can help to create. The rubric identifies the requirements of the written project and the presentation aspects of this system. It is important to remember to value what individuals contributed to the process and to measure what they learned about their own project and the work of the other students in the class.

Principals attempting to incorporate the problems-based learning system in their schools should remember that many teachers have great difficulty in understanding how to share control of the learning process in the classroom with students. Teachers helping students make their own decisions conflicts with the teachers' learned behavior as well as their feelings about being in charge. Students who rely heavily on teachers to give them structure, direction, and information will also struggle with the problem-based approach, but they can learn to be more responsible for their own learning. Moving teachers slowly into this instructional system is the key to successful system use.

Concept Attainment Instructional System

Principals who help teachers develop an "instructional tool kit" generally understand that students must develop conceptual thinking modalities in order to be able to use information that they have stored in their brains. Teachers tend to give students large doses of information to be recalled as answers on test items and to be remembered as a demonstration of the students' attention to the teacher. In some limited situations, this information provides students with data that they will need in order to solve future problems or answer future test questions. One way to solve this dilemma of recalling large doses of, in some cases insignificant information, is by teaching concepts instead of unattached information. Teaching students conceptually requires the student to organize and categorize ideas in his or her brain (Wilson 1987). Students give concepts meaning with the attributes they attach to each concept. New ideas are attached to what we already know. These attributes help each person differentiate the various pieces of an idea. Concepts help students develop a notion about the idea or object and in turn are able to infer beyond the idea under consideration. Concept attainment is a technique that extends and refines data captured in our individual brain files (Gunter, Estes, and Schwab 1999). The concept attainment system requires students to identify the characteristics of the concept (Joyce and Weil 1986) and to sort them into categories utilizing their basic characteristics.

The concept attainment instructional system allows the teacher to assess students' prior knowledge and the students to expand their knowledge. Students actively participate in the concept attainment process because they have contributed the ideas and the product is of their making (Gunter, Estes, and Schwab 1999). The following are the essential phases of the concept attainment instructional system:

- List items associated with the subject.
- Group the items with the same characteristics.
- Regroup using individual or group labels.
- Recap the data and form generalizations.
- Evaluate student progress.

The initial phase of the concept attainment instructional system requires all students to list items related to the subject. These items may come from the student's personal experience or they may come from what the student has learned in school. Examples and nonexamples of the concept are collected from the students and written on a chalkboard or newsprint or typed into a program that displays the items on a television screen. Nonexamples of the concept are as important as are the examples and this process allows all student comments to be utilized. Teachers may use actual objects for examples and nonexamples of the concept.

In phase two, the items are grouped because they have similar attributes. This provides the students with some ideas about the relationships among the items and begins the process of building a list of attributes about the concept under investigation. At this point, students begin to regroup the ideas that they contributed to the discussion.

In phase three, the regrouped ideas are given names or labels. Group labels will vary with the age and academic sophistication of the students. The teacher may test the concept attainment of the students at this point by giving the students examples and nonexamples of the concepts by having them label the examples "yes" or "no." Students must be able to support their reasons for labeling each idea an example or nonexample of the concept.

In phase four of this system, students are asked to look at all of the groups and labels and to form a general statement about the concept in one sentence. The teacher may need to provide the students with examples of what generalizations look like and how they are constructed. For example, if the students were studying astronauts, they might say, "Astronauts explore space."

In phase five, the teacher will evaluate students using such things as the sophistication of the created generalizations. In addition, student participation is essential for student learning and the teacher can evaluate this participation by making sure each student contributes to the process. Using a written test to assess the students' knowledge about the concept under discussion is always available for student evaluation. Reflection is another way of assessing student knowledge concerning the concept. The teacher can help the students with reflection by having them answer questions such as:

1. What thinking strategies were helpful in creating examples of the concept?
2. What thinking strategies were helpful in creating nonexamples of the concept?
3. How did you decide on the concept attributes?

4. How did you arrive at your meaning of the term concept?
5. How might you use the concept attainment process in all the courses you take? (Johnson et al. 1992)

For the principal, the development of concepts should be the goal for all instruction. If students are taught conceptually, they are more likely to be able to apply what they have learned. The true test of any instructional system is the ability of the students to apply what they have learned.

Classroom Discussion Instructional System

The classroom discussion instructional system is a system that most teachers will tell you they utilize in their classroom. Perhaps some teachers utilize this instructional system, but most teachers are not looking for opposing points of view from students' responses to their questions. This instructional system is designed to allow students to answer questions and communicate their ideas on a particular subject. The format for this instructional system leads to a richer more advanced level of student and teacher communication. No single answer to any question is absolutely correct, even though some may have advantages over others. So, it is the teacher's responsibility to facilitate the interchange of ideas. Principals must be able to demonstrate the classroom discussion system making sure that teachers understand the difference between what they are calling discussion and what classroom discussion really should look like. The phases of the classroom discussion instructional system are:

1. Question preparation
2. Group the questions
3. The discussion
4. Reflect on the students' discussion

The key to any classroom discussion system is the type of questions that the teacher asks the students, that is, whether the questions are factual, interpretive, or evaluative. Factual questions reflect the words of the literature or text the student has read concerning the topic for discussion. The interpretive questions delve into not only what the author wrote, but also what the reader believes the text means, in this case what the student believes the author was saying. Evaluative questions ask the student to compare what the author has written with his or her own belief system. These three types of questions form the foundation for phase one of this instructional system. Teachers create the type of questions that students will discuss in class and it's the teacher's responsibility to make sure the questions focus on the topic for that day's discussion.

Once the basic questions have been written, it is the teacher's job to categorize the questions and place them in groups according to the content of the readings. The teacher may create follow-up questions if such questions fit the discussion. The sequence of the questions may evolve from the factual to the evaluative in order to get students to participate in the discussion (Gunter, Estes, and Schwab 1999).

Getting students to participate in the discussion is the key to success in this instructional system. The teacher's job is to make sure all students get the opportunity to provide their viewpoint on the topic and not to let a few students dominate the discussion. Encourage students to expand their ideas by asking them to "tell you more" or "could you develop that thought further?" As the moderator of the discussion, make sure that you allow students the "wait time" necessary to answer the questions. Use a chart or a set of tongue depressors with student names pulling out a new name each time a question is asked to make sure all students participate in the discussion. This instructional system is about the process of discussion and not about arriving at one solution (Gunter, Estes, and Schwab 1999).

Reflect on the discussion with the class. Talk about the various ideas that surfaced during the exchange of thoughts and make sure all sides of the issue receive fair treatment. Valuing all student contributions is the key to making this instructional system a success. If the teacher fails to acknowledge and value student contributions, students will not participate the next time the system is employed in the teaching and learning process. Having students write reflection papers about the class discussion is on avenue for evaluating what students learned.

INSTRUCTIONAL COLLABORATION

Instructional collaboration allows teachers and principals to engage in a dialogue concerning the process of instruction. Newton, Fiene, and Wagner

(1999) report that teachers have few opportunities to discuss instruction with the principal. It is unclear why such connections between teachers and the principal fail to occur but it is clear that such dialogue would be helpful to both. Teachers need to understand the principal's definition of what constitutes effective instruction and the principal needs to understand what teachers believe effective instruction entails. Teachers developed their perceptions of the skills needed for nominal instructional leadership by observing the leadership techniques of the principal. Principals appear to have great influence and power, at least from the perspective of most teachers. Principals have the best opportunity to influence the instructional lives of teachers and students, they can make or break a school, and they can either motivate or depress all personnel (Newton, Fiene, and Wagner 1999).

It is the principal's responsibility to create an atmosphere of instructional collaboration between and among the instructional staff. Leading by example is one strategy that appears to provide teachers with the willingness to work together in the teaching and learning process. Principals who take the time and have the skills to dialogue with teachers about effective instruction are more likely to have teachers who are willing to share instructional ideas with each other.

Teacher collaboration has become the watchword for many writers in calling for meaningful school reform. The collaboration called for by many of these reforms extends beyond teachers exchanging and offering instructional ideas to each other. Teachers need to work together to align the curriculum, to create new instructional standards, and to develop an interdisciplinary approach to curriculum. Teacher collaboration can foster collegial relationships among teachers by providing opportunities for exchanging teaching strategies, sharing lesson plans, developing new instructional models, and providing mutual support. Teachers who work together may find improvements in student accomplishment, conduct, and thought. Students may feel the collaborative influence of instruction and thus may feel better about learning and the learning environment. Teachers working together make many of the complex instructional processes more manageable, new ideas are created, and a systemic instructional environment develops. Inger (1993) lists the following benefits of teacher collaboration:

- Removes the isolation of the classroom
- Leads to a more professional attitude

- Relieves the end-of-year burnout
- Simulates enthusiasm for the teacher

Teachers appear to collaborate in more meaningful ways when the principal encourages working together as a means of improving teaching and learning. This encouragement must be more than lip-service by the principal, the encouragement must be very detailed outlining specific steps for teachers to take. Perhaps the most important aspect of collaboration is training. Training teachers to work in group environments is important because most teachers have never had the opportunity to work together. Developing teacher skills in communication, listening, conflict management, and time management is necessary prior to becoming involved in the collaborative process. Time for teachers to work together through the use of common planning periods, regularly scheduled meetings, and financial resources to send teaching teams to professional development conferences is the next piece of the collaboration procedure.

Teacher collaboration is based on the practice of teachers working together daily. Interdependence is the key to collaboration and the joint work will make the time and effort worthwhile. The principal has the responsibility of making collaboration a positive aspect of the teaching and learning process. However, forcing teachers to participate in this type of activity is not in the best interests of the school organization. Teachers must want to work together and if this desire is not present then the prudent principal will not force collaboration. The final judgment concerning the use of collaboration is student achievement. If student achievement is not increased, then one would need to determine the value of collaboration to the organization.

EVALUATION OF INSTRUCTION

Evaluation is almost always a topic of discussion among teachers as they prepare for their classroom observations. The purpose for these observations is twofold: first, to measure the teacher's competence against some standard, and second, it is promoted as a means of determining what professional development on which the teacher should embark. These two purposes represent the ideal for the observation and eventually the evaluation process, but the process generates as many questions from teachers as it does answers. An evaluation process should provide personalized feedback on the instructional needs of teachers. In addition, the process needs to encourage teachers to learn new instructional strategies and receive personal direction from the principal and perhaps colleagues on how he or she might change his or her classroom instruction (Boyd 1989). All evaluators must be specific with teachers concerning the evaluation procedures and standards to which the teacher is going to be held. Standards must:

- Address teaching skills
- Be objective
- Be communicated to the teacher prior to any observation
- Address the teacher's professional development needs (Boyd 1989)

For principals, the task is to understand the standards and be able to convey that understanding to the person being evaluated. It is impossible to evaluate instruction, even with a good instrument, if you don't understand what the individual items on the instrument are trying to measure. It is up to the principal to tell the teachers what each of these items on the instrument means in terms of the teaching and learning process and what the expectation is for meeting the standard in each area observed.

Research about instructional evaluation does not provide any clear evidence to suggest one instructional evaluation model over another. Some researchers argue that nondirective approaches work best with reflective practitioners (Herbert and Tankersley 1993; Nolan and Hillkirk 1991), and better interpersonal relationships create better communication (Blumberg and Jonas 1987). A variety of teaching skills should be addressed by the evaluation. The more sources of information the evaluator can collect the better the opportunity to value the teacher's performance in relation to the evaluation standards. The most common data gathering tool for teacher evaluation is the classroom observation. The observation provides the evaluator with a snapshot of the teacher's instructional capabilities, but only a snapshot in time. Observing a teacher's instruction for thirty, forty-five, or sixty minutes is merely a blink of an eye when considering the amount of time a teacher spends instructing children over the academic year. Gathering enough data about the teacher's instructional ability would take several hours of observation, which is not likely to occur in most schools. Another data gathering device is the lesson plans that teachers develop. Looking for the thoroughness, the objective, and the assessment activities of the lessons provides the evaluator with data about the type of instruction, testing strategies, and experiences the teacher is providing the students. The evaluation strategy that might change the complexion of any observation is the inclusion of more than one observer. Earlier in this chapter, the argument was made for an instructional specialist to help the teacher improve. If one of the goals of evaluation is to promote the teacher's instructional growth, then it seems important that more than one observer must value the teacher's performance. If this is the situation, then the instructional specialist is at the top of the list for helping teachers grow professionally.

Two-Hat Theory of Instructional Evaluation

Principals must serve as the instructional supervisors and at the same time they must function as the school's instructional evaluators. Thus, they wear two hats. One hat is as an evaluator and the other is that of coordinator of instructional improvement. Everyday principals observe instruction, sometimes informally, but more often than not principals enter a classroom with an evaluation instrument that compels them to value the day's instruction. Today, the teacher is being observed for improvement of instruction and for employment purposes, not the best of reasons, but necessary to meet the policy requirements of the board of education and to protect the employment decision makers should the teacher perform in an unacceptable manner. Principals are evaluators of personnel and that's one of the functions that goes with the title principal. To think otherwise is naive. Teacher observations provide data to answer the questions found on the evaluation instrument. Advising teachers of their instructional strengths and weaknesses is consistent with good practice and provides each teacher with a benchmark for comparison against the ideal instruction. How can either party in this evaluation scenario forget the bottom line, that employment is always in the picture? This is the evaluator hat and is never hung on the hat rack, it is always being worn by the principal. Teachers become upset, paranoid, fearful, angry, and political because of the evaluation process.

This leads principals to the second dimension of the two-hat theory: the instructional supervisor. The principal now functions as an instructional helper for the teacher. The observation is viewed as an opportunity for the teacher and principal to work as a team to make sure students get the best education possible. The principal observes the students' reaction to the instruction, not focusing on the teacher but on the students. The principal records observations for the purpose of sharing thoughts and ideas that could help the teacher function instructionally and students achieve at a higher level. Improvement, help, and collaboration are the key concepts the instructional supervisor wants to foster. The wearing of this hat requires principals to have knowledge about what constitutes ideal instruction and to have strategies at their command that will help teachers improve in the classroom. Principals focusing on instructional improvement are the only ones that have an opportunity to change student achievement and thus change the academic culture of the school. Wearing this hat is not an option in the school of the twenty-first century because high-stakes testing and other accountability measures have become incorporated into the mental models of policy makers.

Which hat should principals wear if they really want to be successful principals? The answer appears to be the instructional supervision hat, but they can never take off the evaluator hat. These two hats that principals wear are not mutually exclusive and it is important to remember that many principals wear both hats with some degree of success. However, it is important to note that wearing both hats diminishes the effectiveness of both the evaluation and instructional supervision functions. In the ideal situation, one person would evaluate the instruction and another person would perform the duties of an instructional supervisor. In this ideal situation, the principal would function as the evaluator based on his or her responsibilities for employment. Principals would evaluate the instruction, making note of the strengths and weaknesses of the instruction. The principal would continue to share these observation notes with the teacher but the principal would not provide the help necessary to remedy any observed instructional weakness. An instructional specialist would be responsible for diagnosing and remediating the teacher's observed instructional shortcomings. The principal would observe, once again by wearing the evaluator's hat, the teacher after the instructional specialist had worked with the teacher to change the unacceptable instructional behavior.

Instructional leadership is a two-hat process and in order for it to work effectively it will take two people each wearing only one hat. Providing instructional leadership is a two-headed concept that requires principals to attempt to fulfill both the evaluator and the instructional specialist roles. It is a rare situation where the principal fulfills both roles adequately.

Results-Based Supervision As a Model for Instructional Evaluation

Boyd (1989) suggests that reporting the evaluation results of teachers needs to occur within two to three days of the classroom observation. Evaluators should consider the following strategies when providing feedback to teachers:

- Be positive when talking with teachers about strengths and weaknesses.
- Discuss instructional concerns providing the teacher with strategies that the teacher can perform.
- Attempt to balance the discussion concerning the teacher's strengths and weaknesses.
- Do not overwhelm the teacher with so much data that he or she mentally bails out of the conversation.
- Make sure the feedback conference maintains a professional atmosphere.

The primary responsibility for making sure the teacher understands his or her strengths and weaknesses falls to the evaluator. On far too many occasions, the evaluator fails to convey the level of concern to the teacher about the depth of the instructional problems he or she observed. Principals must be willing and able to explain to teachers what the instructional problems are and how they might go about correcting the problems. When an evaluator observes instruction that is incompatible with instructional standards, it is the evaluator's responsibility to discuss those problem areas with the teacher in a direct manner. Do not dance around the issues and make sure all concerned know the instructional problems. When encountering teachers with multiple instructional problems, it is prudent to focus the teacher on two or three of the most serious of the instructional problems. Trying to remediate eight or ten instructional problems is, in most cases, not possible even for the best instructional specialists.

Instructional remediation may take many forms depending on the instructional needs of the individual teacher. Instructional remediation will take time and patience because changing an individual's instructional behavior is not a simple task. The principal needs to determine the level of energy and the amount of resources that it will take to change the instructional behavior of the teacher. Once the principal determines the human and financial costs of remediation, then and only then should any action be taken to change the teacher's behavior. The decision may be to remediate the teacher with all of the resources the principal can bring to bear on the situation or perhaps the principal might decide to focus his or her energy on counseling the teacher out of the profession. This decision should be contemplated with great care and concern because the decision made today will affect the teacher tomorrow.

From a teacher's perspective, evaluation and observation are not very productive activities when considering instructional improvement. Teachers distrust a system that they do not understand and question its value to themselves, strictly on an individual basis. Boyd describes the following concerns of teachers about the evaluation process:

- Not having input into the development of the evaluation instrument
- Evaluators not spending time to gather enough data to provide useful feedback
- A lack of evaluator training and credibility
- Evaluations are not used for any purpose other than hiring and firing (1989)

Making teacher evaluation a positive and meaningful learning experience for both the teacher and the evaluator is important. Focusing on improvement is the lynchpin to making the evaluation process successful. To be a successful evaluator, teachers must believe that the evaluator is honest and trustworthy, is skilled in knowing what constitutes good teaching and learning, has the analytical skills to diagnose instructional problems, and has the ability to provide instructional help to the teacher.

Most of the evaluation models available to principals come from the body of literature called "supervision of instruction." Supervision implies something other than evaluation; it implies that observation of instruction is concerned with helping teachers improve their instructional skills and indeed most of the models attempt to identify instructional problems and remediate those problems. Most of these supervision models rely on teacher inputs rather then student output. These inputs answer the following questions:

- Did the teacher properly prepare the lesson?
- How does the classroom environment affect learning?
- Did the teacher use a range of instructional strategies?
- Has the teacher completed his or her professional tasks?

The supposition is that these inputs are the key parts in improving instruction and student learning. The supposition is that since the teacher taught the students learned. It is hard to believe that anyone who has anything to do with educating children buys into the equation that teaching equals student learning. Student achievement is but one aspect of the teaching process and other things need to be considered when examining the teacher's culpability for student achievement, so goes the teacher argument. As a principal, if 50 percent of the students in a third-grade class could not read at grade level in any single year or half of the twelfth graders could not write a coherent paragraph, what conclusion would you draw? One question that must be asked is: What responsibility do teachers have in making sure students are successful? Principals and teachers must shoulder some of the responsibility for student success or failure. Without examination of results, little progress can be made toward finding solutions to instructional problems.

Evaluation of instruction in a results-based atmosphere provides the opportunity for principals to focus on those teachers who need the most instructional help. The results-based model of supervision focuses on the use of tests for assessing teacher achievement. In his work on value-added instruction, Sanders (1999) states that the most influential factor in student academic growth is the effectiveness of the teacher. In this model, what the student scores on a paper-and-pencil test is the measure of teacher achievement. Utilizing the pretest–posttest strategy for determining student gain over a 180-day period forms the report card for the teacher. Student gain is the key concept in this results-based model. Hill (2000) reports that Sanders supports this concept when he compares the child's academic success to the child's last performance on standard measures of learning. Measuring the beginning level of academic achievement is important to any teacher because it informs the teacher which concepts the student understands and which concepts the student has yet to grasp. Over time, the student's level of achievement gain is a strong indicator of the instructional ability of the teacher. Some educators would argue that the academic level of the student on entry into the teacher's classroom skews the results, either right or left, and thus the teacher gets credit for instruction he or she did not deserve or loses credit for instruction he or she should have received. If the model called for using only the results of a year-end examination, the argument would be well constructed. However, the results-based model addresses that concern by using achievement gain. Gain is calculated by comparing the results of the test at the beginning of the year with end-of-year test results. For example, third-grade students would take a comprehensive test covering all of the mathematics concepts that were to be taught in the third grade. The results of the test are recorded with the teacher noting which concepts the student did not understand. At the end of the year, the same test would be given and a test score would be calculated. The difference between the two scores is the gain. Could it be a negative gain? Let's hope not for the teacher's sake. Compiling all of the student achievement gains and looking at the median gain score provides the evaluator with evidence about the instructional success of the teacher (see table 6.1).

Table 6.1   Formula for Determining Gain

The formula for determining gain is:				
	Test score 2	minus	Test score 1	=	Gain Score
Student A	85	–	56	=	29
Student B	98	–	85	=	13
Student C	77	–	23	=	54
Student D	65	–	31	=	34
Student E	79	–	45	=	34

In this example, student C has the biggest gain score of all the students studied. A principal could conclude from this example that the teacher is able to match the instruction to the students' needs. In addition, the principal could say with a great deal of certainty that the instruction for these students, as a group, is well conceived, based on the results of the gain score. The principal and teacher might conclude, based on test score 1, that student B already understands the concepts that are going to be taught during that year and should be moved to a more challenging curriculum. The principal might determine from these gain scores that this teacher needs little in the way of observation and evaluation. The data generated by the results-based evaluation model indicates the teacher's instruction had manifested itself in positive student achievement

For the principal, the results-based model provides data that allows the principal to more efficiently use his or her observation and remediation time. Teachers who consistently have strong median achievement gain scores would need to be observed less frequently or perhaps not at all if the median gain scores were consistently strong. This would allow the principal to focus attention on those teachers who need instructional remediation. This model addresses the two-hat theory of supervision by reducing the number of observations and really allows the evaluator to provide instructional help for those teachers who need it.

The results-based model encourages teachers to use instructional models that require active student participation, student interaction, and creative thinking because the instruction is not measured against the common standard of direct teaching. Teachers do not need to worry that the evaluator will misinterpret what is happening in the classroom because the evaluator fails to understand the instructional model being utilized or does not care to discuss the classroom activities with the teacher. The results-based evaluation model encourages instructional risk takers and innovators to try new approaches in the instructional process.

Many teachers argue that you cannot quantify learning and use it as a tool for measuring instructional results. Some make the case that individuals are not all the same, thus, you cannot hold students accountable to one standard. Others assert they hold themselves accountable and evaluation is not necessary. It is paradoxical that teachers quantify student learning everyday by using teacher-made tests, assessing student projects, and by checking students for understanding. Yet, teachers question the use of student assessment as a means of measuring a teacher's instructional success. In no other enterprise do you find a system where the worker chooses what to do, then does the work, decides how to measure that work, and evaluates the results, except in schools. Results-based evaluation is reflected in high-stakes testing and is already informally being utilized by parents to select their child's teacher. In some schools, not only is this model evaluating teachers but principals as well. The job security of some principals currently depends on the instructional results produced by the teachers. In this situation, principals would be well advised to consider results-based evaluation.

Clinical Supervision As a Model for Instructional Evaluation

As an alternative to the results-based instructional evaluation, principals might choose an evaluation model that is more collaborative. Cogan (1973) defines clinical supervision as a cooperative effort between the supervisor and the teacher to explore ways to empower the teacher to improve instruction. Cogan (1973) identifies eight steps and Glickman, Gordon, and Ross-Gordon (1995) identify five steps in the clinical supervision model. Principals using the clinical supervision model will be evaluating not only what they observe in the classroom, but also what the focus of the instruction will be. In addition, this model requires that the principal provide instructional assistance for the teacher, such as demonstration teaching, team teaching, peer coaching, and teacher observation. Assisting the teacher requires that the principal helps the teacher by diagnosing the teacher's instructional strengths and weaknesses. Using the clinical supervision model to evaluate instruction against some standards changes the purpose but not the process of clinical supervision.

Glickman, Gordon, and Ross-Gordon (1995) identify five steps in the clinical supervision model:

1. Conference before the observation
2. Observe the instruction
3. Analyze the data collected during the observation
4. Hold a conference after the observation
5. Reflect and assess the evaluation process

The first step in the clinical supervision model requires the evaluator to meet with the teacher to determine the following: (1) what is the objective for the lesson; (2) what the observer will be looking for during the observation; (3) when the observation will occur; and (4) when will the conference after the observation occur (Jones 1995). The decisions that the teacher and the evaluator make during this first conference guide what will take place during the next three phases of the process. As an example, the objective for the observed class might look like the following: Given a set of thirty slides, each student will identify types of white cells as neutrophils, lymphocytes, monocytes, eosinophils, and basophils by writing the name of the cell on the line corresponding to the slide number. The evaluator would be observing students to see if they understood the various types of white cells and what they would look like under the microscope. The teacher and the evaluator would decide what day and time the observation would take place and when they would meet after the observation to discuss the lesson and to share what was observed by the evaluator.

The observation is structured by time, date, and place with the evaluator observing students and focusing on the learning objective outlined during the conference prior to the observation. The evaluator should focus on what the students are doing, not on the teacher's instructional movements. Are the students on-task and are they understanding what is being taught? The evaluator should write descriptions of what he or she sees happening during the observation by making sure not to value these descriptions. For example, the evaluator might observe a student reading a piece of literature while the teacher is discussing and demonstrating the various white cells found in human blood. In the evaluator's notes the description of who, what, and when allows the evaluator to pinpoint exactly when the student was off-task and what the student was doing.

Once the evaluator finishes the classroom observation, it is time to look at the data collected during the observation. Answering the following questions will help the evaluator make judgments concerning the effectiveness of the observed lesson. Did the teacher fulfill the instructional objective that was agreed on during the conference prior to the observation? If the teacher did not utilize the instructional objective, was there a reason for not doing so? Did the evaluator observe during the classroom visit the activities that were agreed on during the initial conference? Once the evaluator answers these questions and reflects on the lesson, it is the evaluator's responsibility to critique what was observed, both the strengths and weaknesses of the lesson. At this point, the evaluator needs to make a determination about the structure of the postobservation conference.

The postobservation conference will be exciting if the instruction was well done and very few concerns were observed. If the observation has produced several instructional weaknesses, the evaluator must prioritize which of these weaknesses to focus on first. Choose only two or three weaknesses to address immediately because addressing any more is impossible for the teacher to remediate. Provide the teacher with a written copy of the observation and ask the teacher to reflect on the strengths and weaknesses of the lesson. After discussing the observation, the evaluator and the observed teacher should collaboratively create an instructional improvement plan. No matter the quality of the observed lesson, each teacher should leave the conference with a collaboratively created instructional improvement plan; some plans will be more detailed and direct, others will be open-ended and nondirect.

The final step in the clinical supervision model is a reflection by the evaluator about the process. Did the process allow the teacher to improve and did the evaluator diagnose the strengths and weaknesses in an effective manner? Included in this reflection are the evaluator's thoughts about the employment status of the observed teacher. Do the observed instructional problems merit a recommendation of nonrenewal if they are not remedied in a timely manner? What strategies will the evaluator use to help the teacher improve or will this improvement take so much time and energy that it's highly unlikely improvement will occur? The answers to these questions will dictate the renewal or nonrenewal aspects of the contract.

The clinical supervision model provides the teacher and the evaluator with an opportunity to collaborate on instructional improvement. At the same time, the evaluator must be making the decision about the employment status of the observed teacher. The dilemma created by this evaluation process is true of all supervision processes except the results-based instructional evaluation model. Deciding when the role of instructional supervisor and when the role of instructional evaluator is appropriate is the key to this instructional evaluation model.

Democratic Supervision As a Model for Instructional Evaluation

The democratic supervision model mirrors the clinical supervision model utilizing the five steps of the model as its foundation. Jones (1995) states that democratic supervision, while holding many of the same tenets as clinical supervision, is unique in the following four ways:

1. The evaluator serves as a resource for the teacher's development.
2. The evaluator and the teacher negotiate the instructional improvement plan.
3. The five steps of the clinical supervision model are to be utilized in order to provide a systemic structure for this model.
4. This model focuses on instructional growth by the teacher.

In the first step of the democratic supervision model, the evaluator is a resource for the teacher's instructional improvement. The ultimate responsibility for the teacher's professional growth lies with the teacher but the evaluator works collaboratively to help the teacher improve. In this model, the teacher is not required to follow the advice or direction of the evaluator.

Negotiation is the key to the second step in the model as the teacher and evaluator decide what instructional objectives will be observed. In addition, the assessment process must be negotiated in terms of what specifically will be assessed and how it will be assessed. Jones (1995) states that it is the responsibility of both parties to enter into a supervisory relationship, but should this not occur, discontinuing the relationship should take place.

The next step in this model entails the selection of a specific supervisory model. It is at this point that the five steps in the clinical supervision model begin to operate. It is possible that other models of supervision could be employed at this point but the clinical model seems to work nicely with the collaborative philosophy of democratic supervision.

The model is designed to help teachers help themselves become more self-directed and self-reliant. Teachers spend the majority of their working day in isolation from their professional colleagues and it is essential that they effectively diagnose their own instructional problems. No matter how effective teachers become in diagnosing and solving their own instructional problem, the evaluator still makes the final judgment about the teacher's instructional strengths and weaknesses.

A major concern of this evaluation model is the teacher's ability to self-diagnose instructional problems and in some instances to even recognize that a problem exists. The basic tenets of this model provide real possibilities for teachers who are very good at what they do, but if any doubt occurs about the instructional ability of the teacher, closer monitoring of the situation must occur.

INSTRUCTIONAL LEADERSHIP THROUGH
PROFESSIONAL DEVELOPMENT

Everyone agrees that the principal is the key person when assessing the success or failure of a school. Over the past several years the role and expectations for the principal have changed radically. This change has lowered the number of educators interested in pursuing and taking this job. For those currently in the job from an earlier era and for those who will take this position in the future, a planned program of professional development is essential. Richardson (2000) asks the question: What does professional development for the instructional leader look like? She answers this question with ideas from Dennis Sparks, the executive director of the National Staff Development Council, who suggests that the instructional leader's professional development should be: standards-focused, academically demanding, rooted in the job, and continuous. Perhaps the best professional development comes from principals and teachers interacting in the best interest of students. Working together on curriculum, student assessment, instruction, and problem solving in a learning environment provides the best opportunity for principals to develop the knowledge and skills necessary to be an effective leader. An example of a professional development program for the principal that addresses the needs of today's principal is found in Louisville, Kentucky. Principals participate in a four-strand professional development program consisting of:

- A very traditional looking learning institute for both teachers and principals
- Professional development days that address instructional strategies
- A group activity that allows principals to learn with their colleagues who share a similar interest
- Professional development plans that focus on the individual
- A program of peer assessment (Richardson 2000)

While lip-service is paid to professional development programs for instructional leaders, little is done to implement such programs. A professional development program for principals that focuses on instruction is even more rare than professional development for principals in the area of management. Changing times translates into the need for all principals to become instructional specialists, after all, changing instruction is the only activity that improves the academic achievement of students. Quality leadership requires an investment by the organization, which will be returned several times over by effective principals.

Principals who model effective use of professional development in instruction will increase their personal creditability with teachers. Helping teachers become better at their craft of teaching is the most important support that a principal can give to the instructional staff. Many teachers reflect on their last instructional experience and more likely than not it was a college or university classroom where instruction generally took the form of sit-and-get-it. Teachers use this style of instruction because they feel comfortable lecturing to students, after all that's what they experienced. Research studies show that less than 50 percent of teachers use instructional models that promote student involvement in daily classroom instruction. Sparks and Hirsh (2000) report that research is beginning to show a link between achievement and quality of instruction. They discuss the work of William Sanders and David Cohen, which states that teaching effectiveness impacts student learning more than any other single factor and the best way to impact teaching effectiveness is through the use of professional development. Evidence that supports the effectiveness of professional development is generally anecdotal and hard to substantiate. Sparks and Hirsh (2000) cite data from the National Center for Educational Statistics that indicates that almost 66 percent of the teachers involved in extensive professional development focusing on standards developed an interest in learning effective classroom strategies and raising student achievement. The connection between the professional development on standards and the increased interest in learning effective classroom strategies appears to emanate from the teacher's need to help students meet the standards.

Birman et al. (2000) surveyed more than 1,000 teachers in an attempt to discover what professional development approaches were most effective. They found that 79 percent of the teachers participated in a traditional staff development program, 64 percent indicated activities lasted less than a week, and only 20 percent of the teachers were part of an activity that included collective participation. What they discovered was that professional development activities:

- Need to be of a longer duration. By focusing on subject matter content, teachers have more active opportunities to learn. These activities should last a minimum of two hours for each session and be extended over several weeks.
- Need to include collective participation by teachers from the same grade or subject matter area. Collective participation allows teachers the chance to learn from teachers from across the school district and from other districts.

- Need to focus directly on content knowledge. Teachers do not believe generic professional development increases knowledge or skills.
- Need to include activities that require active learning. Active learning includes teachers observing teachers, teaching a lesson, learning new instructional models, presenting a demonstration lesson, or leading a discussion about teaching and learning.

Alford (2000) supports the work of Birman et al. when she reports that 49.6 percent of 595 respondents indicated that professional development had improved them professionally. Sessions with less than twenty participants allowed for dialogue and experiential learning, while large-group activities were considered less than useful. Teachers indicated the closer the professional development activity is linked to the school's goals the more useful it becomes. Teachers also believed that an ongoing seamless professional development plan supported by the principal, with follow-up components, enhanced their sense of success.

Professional development is one strategy that principals can use as instructional leaders. The principal has the power and position authority to influence the type of professional development that brings focus to instructional improvement. As a principal, you have the opportunity to change what's happening in the classrooms in your school and professional development is one way of making sure teachers are on the cutting edge of current thought about teaching and learning.

ETHICAL DISCUSSION

Should Teachers Have Increased Academic Freedom and be Free from Instructional Evaluation?

Teachers are the key to the success or failure of any school. Regardless of the talent of the principal, what happens in the classroom on a daily basis dictates the success or failure of student achievement. Some teachers are zealots and are continually promoting their point of view with students. Tenure laws in some states make it practically impossible for teachers to be terminated, while in other instances they require improvement in teachers' instruction. Teachers need to be treated like professionals and they deserve respect and appreciation for the contribution they make to society. Instructional evaluation can take several forms from the directive to the nondirective depending on the instructional ability of the teacher.

The questions that need to be answered concerning this issue are:

- Should a student's test results be used in a teacher's evaluation? Should these test scores be the only evaluation a teacher receives?
- Should there be any restrictions on what a teacher can cover in class?
- What role should the teacher play in the instructional evaluation process?
- Academic freedom taken to its full potential should allow teachers to discuss any subject they choose. What rights do parents have in dictating classroom curriculum and are they infringing on a teacher's First Amendment right of freedom of speech?
- The principal should be the instructional leader on campus and dictate the instructional models that are utilized on that campus. Agree or disagree and why?
- Ethical dilemmas are right-versus-right issues. Which side of the evaluation–academic freedom debate do you support and why?

CHAPTER SUMMARY

The person who claims the title "instructional leader" most often defines the term, and principals are no different because they define it from their point of view. Principals and teachers have a different view of what instructional leadership ought to entail. Teachers want a principal who can help them grow professionally, personally, and collaboratively, while principals tend to see instructional leadership as assessment, oversight, and evaluation of classroom instruction. Even though instructional leadership appears to be a vital function in the operation of school, there is a scarcity of empirical research that demonstrates a relationship between classroom instruction and effective instructional leadership (Short 1995).

The instructional leader must also be a champion for professional development, because it is in this venue that instructional improvement takes place. Principals who model effective use of professional development increase their personal creditability with teachers. Teachers who participate in a professional development program that focuses on teaching effectiveness are more likely to add to their "instructional tool kit" than those who never participate. Research is beginning to report a relationship between quality of instruction and student achievement.

Principals are responsible for student achievement even though they do not deliver the instruction directly to the student. Principals who understand instructional delivery systems and are able to demonstrate four or five instructional systems have the opportunity to change the instructional culture of the school. It is important for the instructional leader to guide teachers toward making students participate in their own learning. This can be accomplished by making sure teachers have a variety of instructional systems to draw from. It is the principal's role to mentor and support teachers as they begin to move away from their direct-teach mentality. Five instructional systems that change the instructional culture of any school are the inquiry, cooperative, problem-based, concept attainment, and classroom discussion instructional systems. Other systems do exist, but if the principal can demonstrate these systems at a high level of proficiency, teachers will accept the principal as an instructional expert and that is what every principal needs to become.

Today's high-stakes testing has created the need for principals to understand and develop skills in changing the existing instructional paradigm. The direct-teach paradigm no longer meets the needs of students as they prepare to meet the requirements of state-developed assessment instruments. The principal's role is to provide teachers with the opportunity to know about instructional systems that they have never experienced. The school leader needs to be able to diagnose the teacher's instruction and to provide prescriptions for improving what happens in the classroom.

Instructional evaluation is always a hot topic among teachers. Teachers fail to see the value in classroom observation and evaluation of instruction. This phenomenon is created by principals who would not know good instruction even if they experienced it. Evaluation models range from no observation, in the results-based model, to the democratic model, to the observation-heavy clinical evaluation model. Each of these models are structured to value how teachers perform in the classroom.

CHAPTER ACTIVITIES AND QUESTIONS

1. Define instructional leadership from your personal perspective and compare it with the definitions found in this chapter.

2. List the functions that professional development plays in the improvement of instruction and list strategies that the principal uses to motivate teachers to participate in this development.
3. The two-hat theory of instructional supervision describes two roles that a principal plays in the instructional improvement process. Which role fits you the best and does that role have the most impact on classroom instruction?
4. Select one of the instructional delivery systems discussed in this chapter and prepare a lesson demonstrating that system.
5. What are the principal's roles in changing instruction? Develop a plan to change the instructional culture on the campus where you are employed.
6. What is the value of instructional collaboration? Does this collaboration change the quality of the classroom instruction by defending your answer?
7. Select an evaluation model described in this chapter and explain the positive attributes of the model.
8. Find empirical evidence that quality instruction improves student achievement. Anecdotal evidence does not meet this standard.
9. Assess your own instructional intelligence quotient. Write an essay concerning what you know about instruction. Develop a plan you are going to use to fill the void in your understanding of what good instruction looks like.
10. Observe an instructional event in your school and assess its value to student learning.

CASE STUDY ACTIVITIES AND QUESTIONS

1. Describe the process Principal West used to get himself into a deep rut intellectually and professionally.
2. What did Mr. West do that allowed the high-stakes test score to decline on the campus where he was principal?
3. How did Principal West's leadership style affect his instructional evaluation of teachers?
4. Write the first two paragraphs that Mr. West should have said in dealing with Mr. Dorfman and Ms. Belkman that would have created a more positive situation.

5. Mr. West waited three weeks for the initial observation of Ms. Belkman. As her principal, what would you have done with her instructional style?
6. How should the principal have reacted after talking with Ms. Whilhitt and Mr. Flornoy?
7. What should have Mr. West done after observing Ms. Belkman's inquiry instructional model? He clearly did not understand what he saw.
8. Reflect on an instructional problem in your school and analyze it in writing.

REFERENCES

Alford, B. (2000). "Enhancing professional development: Concerns and recommendations." *Insight* 14 (1): 21–23.

Birman, B. F., Desimore, L., Porter, A. C., and Garet, M. S. (2000). "Designing professional development that works." *Educational Leadership* 57 (8): 28–33.

Blasé, J., and Blasé, J. (1999a). "Effective instructional leadership through teachers' eyes." *High School Magazine* 7 (1): 16–21.

———. (1999b). "Principals' instructional leadership and teacher development: Teachers' perspectives." *Educational Administration Quarterly* 35 (3): 349–378.

Blumberg, A., and Jonas, R. S. (1987). "The teacher's control over supervision." *Educational Leadership* 44 (8): 59–62.

Boyd, R. T. C. (1989). "Improving teacher evaluations." *Practical Assessment, Research and Evaluation* 1 (7), at ericae.net (accessed June 2, 2001).

Cogan, M. L. (1973). *Clinical supervision.* Boston, MA: Houghton Mifflin.

Crocker, R. K., Bartlett, K. R., and Elliott, H. G. (1976). "A comparison of structured and instructional modes of teaching science process activities." *Journal of Research in Science Teaching* 13: 267–274.

Ellis, S. S., and Whalen, S. F. (1990). *Cooperative learning: Getting started.* New York: Scholastic.

Elmore, R. F. (2000). *Building a new structure for school leadership.* Washington, DC: Albert Shanker Institute.

Fullan, M. G. (1991). *The new meaning of educational change.* New York: Teachers College Press.

Glanz, J. (1995). "Exploring supervision history: An invitation and agenda." *Journal of Curriculum and Supervision* 10 (2): 95–113.

Glickman, C. D. (1985). *Supervision of instruction: A developmental approach.* Boston: Allyn and Bacon.

Glickman, C. D., Gordon, S. P., and Ross-Gordon, J. M. (1995). *Supervision of instruction: A developmental approach.* 3rd ed. Boston: Allyn and Bacon.

Gunter, M. A., Estes, T. H., and Schwab, J. (1999). *Instruction: A models approach.* 3rd ed. Needham Heights, MA: Allyn and Bacon.

Herbert, J. M., and Tankersley, M. (1993). "More and less effective ways to intervene with classroom teachers." *Journal of Curriculum and Supervision* 9 (1): 24–40.

Hill, D. (2000). "He's got your number." *Education Week* 11 (8): 42–47.

Inger, M. (1993). "Teacher collaboration in urban secondary schools." *ERIC Digests.* ERIC Clearinghouse on Urban Education (ERIC Document Reproduction Services no. ED 363 676).

Johnson, D. W, Johnson, R. T., and Holubec, E. J. (1993). *Cooperation in the classroom.* Edina, MN: Interaction.

Johnson, J., Carlson, S., Kastl, J., and Kastl, R. (1992). "Developing conceptual thinking: The concept attainment model." *The Clearing House* 66 (2): 117–121.

Jones, N. B. (1995). "Professional development through democratic supervision." Paper presented at the annual meeting of the Teachers of English to Speakers of Other Languages, Long Beach, CA (ERIC Document Reproduction Services no. ED 389 209).

Joyce, B., and Weil, M. (1986). *Models of teaching.* 3rd ed. Englewood Cliffs, NJ: Prentice-Hall.

Newton, R. M, Fiene, J., and Wagner, C. (1999). "Teacher perceptions of leadership: How do they emerge?" (ERIC Document Reproduction Services no. ED 436 817).

Nolan, J. F., and Hillkirk, K. (1991). "The effects of a reflective coaching project for veteran teachers." *Journal of Curriculum and Supervision* 7 (1): 62–76.

Pajak, E. (1989). *Identification of supervisory proficiencies project.* Alexandria, VA: Association for Supervision and Curriculum Development.

Peters, T. J. (1987). *Thriving on chaos: Handbook for a management revolution.* New York: Knopf.

Richardson, J. (2000). "Focus principal development on student learning." *Results* (September): 1, 6.

Sage, S. M., and Thorpe, L. T. (1997). "What does it take to become a teacher of problem-based learning." *Journal of Staff Development* 18 (4): 32–36.

Sanders, W. (1999). "Teachers, teachers, teachers!" *Blueprint Magazine,* at www.ndol.org/blueprint/fall/99/solutions4.html (accessed July 3, 2001).

Savoie, J. M., and Hughes, A. S. (1994). "Problem-based learning as classroom solutions." *Educational Leadership* 3: 54–57.

Seifert, E. H., and Simmons, D. (1997). "Learning-centered schools using a problem-based approach." *NASSP Bulletin* 81 (587): 90–98.

Sergiovanni, T. J. (1992). "Moral authority and the regeneration of supervision." In *Supervision in transition: The 1992 ASCD yearbook*, ed. C. D. Glickman. Reston, VA: Association for Supervision and Curriculum Development.

Sheppard, B. (1996). "Exploring the transformational nature of instructional leadership." *Alberta Journal of Educational Research* 42 (4): 325–344.

Short, C. E. (1995). "A review of studies in the first 10 volumes of the *Journal of Curriculum and Supervision*." *Journal of Curriculum and Supervision* 11 (1): 87–105.

Sparks, D., and Hirsh, S. (2000). "Strengthening professional development." *Education Week*, 24 May, 42–45.

Spillane, J. P., Halverson, R., and Diamond, J. (1999). "Distributed leadership: Toward a theory of school leadership practice." Paper presented at the annual meeting of the American Educational Research Association, Montreal.

Stepien, W., and Gallagher, S. (1993). "Problem-based learning: As authentic as it gets." *Educational Leadership* 50 (7): 25–28.

Suchman, J. R. (1962). "The elementary school training program in scientific inquiry." Report to the U.S. Office of Education, Project Title VII. Urbana: University of Illinois Press.

Supovitz, J. A. (2000). "Manage less lead more." *Principal Leadership* 1 (3): 14–19.

Utaz, R. R. J. (1998). "Supervisory behaviors that reflect reality: A diversified supervision model." Paper presented at the annual meeting of the Mid-South Educational Research Association, New Orleans, LA (ERIC Document Reproduction Services no. ED 427 435).

Wilson, J. (1987). *Thinking with concepts*. New York: Cambridge University Press.

Chapter Seven

Student Services and Activities

Dr. Nancy McNew had just left the superintendent's office after a fifty-five-minute conversation with Dr. J. B. Tucker concerning the instructional support services for which she was the director for the district. Judy Boswell, the assistant superintendent for curriculum, was also present for the meeting. Dr. Tucker's tenure with the district had been several years, but he had not made many of the changes that he felt were necessary in terms of supporting the instructional program. He had developed several initiatives that he advocated to Dr. McNew and she felt she needed to evaluate them carefully before beginning the changes he was indicating were necessary.

The issues he advocated include:

- *Development of better coordination among the instructional support services staff, especially in regards to working with students having difficulty in personal adjustment situations. Dr. Tucker believes that many of these students are not being served as well as possible and he feels that their performance on the state exam is impacting the results of the individual schools and the district overall. He asked Dr. McNew and the staff at the schools to develop a better process with the necessary procedures to make a difference for these students.*
- *Establishment of several new positions for school social workers within the district, to be assigned to one or more schools. Dr. Tucker is aware of gang activity that also tends to build within the school framework. This is primarily occurring in the Cameron schools, linked somewhat to the larger minority and disadvantaged student population; however, the influence is also being felt in Bethany due to a degree of this community's*

proximity to Cameron. Dr. Tucker feels that a social worker in the schools can assist in getting a handle on such developments in the student population.

- *A new look at how school discipline is being structured with teachers and administrators. With the growth in the communities involved and its impact on the schools of changes in population, the superintendent is concerned about the structure of school culture and climate that will probably be impacted.*
- *An evaluation of the student activities program for the district's schools is being sought. Dr. Tucker feels that this program has been used without many substantive changes for sometime and wants a fresh look at what is happening to ensure that all students are served and that the program is supportive of progress on instructional fronts—not one that will negate academic efforts of the district.*

The superintendent has charged Dr. McNew and Assistant Superintendent Boswell with involving all principals in these efforts. Their support and involvement will be necessary to coordinate these items in a constructive way with the board, parents, staff members, and students.

Dr. Tucker also called Dr. McNew's attention to a somewhat difficult situation involving Board president Arley Cool's daughter, a junior in high school, who is experiencing personal problems, probably due to her parents' recent divorce. Mr. Cool is not responding, her principal feels, in the girl's or the school's best interests, and needs help in dealing with this sticky situation. Dr. Tucker needs some good recommendations concerning the daughter and how he can support the father—even if the recommendations are not what he would want to hear—under these circumstances. After leaving the superintendent's office, Dr. McNew sought a strategy conference with her supervisor, Judy Boswell.

THE PRINCIPAL AS STUDENT ADVOCATE

Students are what schools are all about. During the process of leading and administering the school and the multitude of programs and people involved with the school, sometimes the vision can become blurred. Principals can become so busy trying to achieve the goals and recognition that are being demanded by politicians, parents, teachers, coaches, and citizens that the student may become somewhat ignored or at least forgotten in the midst of the fog that can seem to hang over the entire operation. It is, in fact, easier for the principal to be responding to the issues and initiatives being levied by the central office or other power brokers and lose the focus on the student concerns; the principal must guard against such a situation. The resulting condition is similar to the saying that the "operation was a success but the patient died" or "they won the battle but lost the war." Schools are first and foremost for students and the ethical principle of making decisions based on that principle must be maintained. Unfortunately, in the environment of high-stakes testing it is a principle that can be lost or at least misplaced in the maelstrom of activity that surrounds the educational setting.

In order to survive the onslaught of demands from the world outside the school and to maintain the right focus on student concerns, the principal must have a centered connection on students and on the instructional program in the school. This also means that the goals of the school must be student-centered. Economic and political forces in the community or state may easily overwhelm the student focus. Principals may find themselves spending all of their time in formal meetings and informal conversation with the central office on matters that involve issues developing from the state's requirements and with legal action from a variety of individuals who are unhappy with their situation. This is not to say these are unimportant, as these issues do help create good and not so good situations for the school's climate. However, the resolution of such issues removes the principal from spending time on the real purposes of the school—educating and developing students. Principals must spend time talking to students and developing programs that help to achieve the growth in students. As part of this task, the principal must also spend time working with teachers who directly interact with students and the learning environment. Only with these types of connections can principals understand and interact with those directly at the focus of the school.

To make such a commitment, a principal must schedule his or her time during the day to plan for such interaction. This connection cannot effectively occur only by happenstance. Blocks of time should be set aside as the week is planned to connect with students and with teachers who also will be establishing these interactions. This activity requires a listening ear on the part of the principal. Oftentimes, notes should be taken as a result of such discussions and then mentally reviewed to stimulate reflection. With these reflections will come new ideas and thoughts of how to meet student needs and better accomplish the purpose of the school. Such blocks of time should be spent visiting and observing student actions in classrooms, visiting with students in the cafeteria during lunch, and interacting with students in forums such as student government or student advisory committees. Of course, the maturation level of students in the school will serve to guide the types of contact to develop. Typically, younger students can interact in instructional settings while older students at the middle school or high school level may be involved in formal meetings such as advisory committees or participating in site-based decision teams. But for some students the formal settings are not functional, and these students can better interact in informal settings between classes, during after school sports activities or in the lunchroom. Through observation in various groups and activities, principals can form judgments that can serve to develop understandings. These understandings, derived from contact, can then help principals to open discussion with faculty and staff to solve problems and stimulate changes to better meet student needs.

Educators often forget that students come to school for different reasons. At an early age in the primary years, students love the interaction with the teachers much more than the older students, although these aged students begin to develop their concept of the greater world through such contact. They learn to get along with others and begin to develop friendships outside their immediate and extended family. School, then, becomes the means for younger students to begin the socialization process, but it also provides an environment where values concerning others continue to develop. As students move into puberty, the school is one of several institutions where students become more independent—although in a more sheltered setting than the outside world; they develop their notions of both dependence and independence. Other such institutions include their religious groups, voluntary associations such as little league, scouting, and other outside interest and culture groups. By the time students are in high school, they have often become much more independent than earlier years and friendships that develop may be the most important reason for attendance at school. The pull of socialization, the need to be with others their own age, and their friendships are much more compelling reasons to be present for the school day than the educational pursuits themselves. Family support oftentimes is less dominant for many of these aged students. The role and the strength of the family has sometimes lessened for these teenagers, and the need or desire for peer acceptance and involvement has become paramount.

The twenty-first-century school must also contend with major developments in society that did not impact schools thirty years ago the way they do today. These include issues such as gangs, drugs, cults, and safety of student environments both inside and outside of school. Schools have had to develop the means to combat these and other developing social problems. Many of these problems, which were once only issues for inner-city urban schools, have and are finding their way into all schools, suburban and rural alike. Gangs have become more violent; drugs are more widespread and have found their way into the elementary age population. Guns and other weapons have necessitated schools taking extraordinary means to control the school environment. Students have greater access to these and other social distracters such as popular music, automobiles, and alcohol due to the level of disposable financial resources available to students as individuals. Each of these areas provides additional stimulation for distracting students from their efforts at learning skills and knowledge that would support their lives in the future.

Two areas of attention are particularly important in dealing with student concerns at school. These are the student instructional support areas and the student activities arena. Both help the principal and the instructional faculty connect with students and meet needs that are more individualized. The student activities program also provides a healthy involvement for students with constructive and educational activities that offer growth and substance for their energies. The third area that focuses primarily on students that must be discussed is that of discipline development within the student and for maintaining the school climate. Each of these arenas are different at the different levels of schools.

INSTRUCTIONAL SUPPORT STAFF

Every school district and oftentimes individual schools have a different mix of the instructional support staff depending on expectations of the parents, the fiscal support available to the school, and the needs of the students and the instructional program. Sometimes these staff members are numerous and other times their availability is somewhat scarce. Not infrequently, part-time staff serve a number of schools and travel between them due to school size and local finances. Such staff include guidance counselors, health services, diagnosticians, psychologists, and social workers. The availability of such staff often relieves teachers to focus more on teaching, but most of all, their presence provides individuals with expertise in specific functions that require advanced study to perform the tasks related to such needs. The goal of such staff members is to provide support to teachers and administrators to enhance the learning process, to deal with individual problems that students bring to school, and to assist in developing a climate of support for student learning.

In dealing with problems in the school, different levels have been classified by the National Association of Social Workers in terms of needs and goals. This classification scheme helps principals, teachers, and the instructional support staff better understand the magnitude and prioritization of the problem. The scheme or classification also considers whether the services are remedial or preventative in nature. Such an understanding provides some structure and definition to thought processes of those responding to such difficult situations. Remedial services focus on the immediacy of the problem—whether a crisis requiring immediacy or a problematic situation needing services to assist the individual(s) in contending with the issue over a more extended time period. Preventative services focus on the compensatory services that can be provided and the development of coping skills to assist in reducing the threat of potential problems.

The delivery of services used to help deal with these varying classifications of problems has become much more integrated than in the past. This model is referred to as school-linked services and works to integrate services provided to children and their families through a collaboration of schools, health care providers, and social service agencies. According to some reformers, there tends to be overprofessionalization, fragmentation, and bureaucratic complexity of these services that keeps them from working together to effectively meet the needs of children and families (Franklin 2000). Still many of these services may be offered by the local school district inside the school and therefore can be integrated to help meet the educational needs of the child. Figure 7.1 depicts such an existence of the services thought of as instructional support that can be integrated to support not only instruction, but also to offer life-changing possibilities in the form of solving problems or other related issues for students and parents.

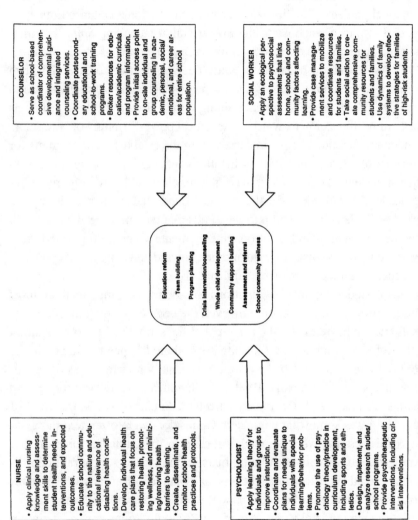

Figure 7.1. Instructional Support Services: The Helping Professionals in Schools

Source: Adapted from National Health Information Center (2002). Washington, DC: U.S. Public Health Services.

NURSE
- Apply clinical nursing knowledge and assessment skills to determine student health needs, interventions, and expected outcomes.
- Educate school community to the nature and educational relevance of disabling health conditions.
- Develop individual health care plans that focus on restoring health, promoting wellness, and minimizing/removing health barriers to learning.
- Create, disseminate, and monitor school health practices and protocols.

PSYCHOLOGIST
- Apply learning theory for individuals and groups to improve instruction.
- Coordinate and evaluate plans for needs unique to individuals with special learning/behavior problems.
- Promote the use of psychology theory/practice in curriculum development, including sports and athletics.
- Design, implement, and analyze research studies/school programs.
- Provide psychotherapeutic interventions, including crisis interventions.

Education reform

Team building

Program planning

Crisis intervention/counseling

Whole child development

Community support building

Assessment and referral

School community wellness

COUNSELOR
- Serve as school-based coordinator of comprehensive developmental guidance and integrated counseling services.
- Coordinate postsecondary educational and school-to-work training programs.
- Broker resources for education/academic curricula and program information.
- Provide initial access point to on-site individual and group counseling in academic, personal, social/emotional, and career areas for entire school population.

SOCIAL WORKER
- Apply an ecological perspective to psychosocial assessments that links home, school, and community factors affecting learning.
- Provide case management services to mobilize and coordinate resources for students and families.
- Take social action to create comprehensive community resources for students and families.
- Use dynamics of family systems to develop effective strategies for families of high-risk students.

GUIDANCE

Although guidance functions have been acknowledged and performed to varying degrees since the beginning of the twentieth century (mostly as a vocational guidance function) in education, the National Defense Education Act of 1958, as a response to the Soviet Union launching *Sputnik*, stimulated and financed the expansion of this area in the public schools (Schmidt 1999). As the nation began to increase development of science and math programs in the public schools, the country recognized that students had to be counseled into more technical training if the existence of these programs was to move the nation forward as a technical power. Training of counselors in guidance functions began in earnest with the establishment of grants for educators to become involved in institutes for training. The result was an expansion of guidance work in the high schools with the major purpose being academic counseling for the college-bound student. It was during the period of the late 1950s and into the 1960s that the guidance function built a momentum that included introducing elementary counseling, standardizing training for counselors, and moving toward developmental guidance that replaced remedial goals for guidance (Baker 1996).

Today, student guidance functions are being accomplished in most schools throughout the nation; however, the degree to which they are successful depends greatly on the principal of the school and the organization of the guidance function by the staff. Also, there has been a change in the preferred name, and today the program is usually referred to as the counseling program. In the early 1980s, as the educational reform movement was taking place with the increased establishment of goals, the field of counseling was somewhat neglected. Counselors were often tending a variety of duties that were somewhat related to the guidance function, but were frequently involved in being quasi-administrators, program coordinators, special and substitute teachers, and planners (Burhans 1999). In responding to the needs of students and the schools as well as to the changes in the education field the American School Counselor Association (ASCA) adopted the National Standards for School Counseling Programs in 1997 that contain essential elements of a quality and effective program. These standards address program content and knowledge, attitudes, and skills that all students should develop through the implementation of school guidance programs (Hogan 1998). A number of states took the lead in developing guidance programs for their schools. The Missouri Comprehensive Guidance Program began in 1984 and continued development for the rest of the decade as it was implemented in the secondary and elementary schools. This model combines the activities of the ASCA national standards into elements that are focused around content, organizational framework, and resources (Gysbers, Lapan, and Blair 1999).

The content element consists of student competencies grouped in three areas of career planning and exploration, knowledge of self and others, and educational and vocational development. The organizational framework element contains the structural components, program components, and the allocation of the time of the counselor. The resources element describes the human, financial, and political resources needed to fully support such a program (see fig. 7.2). Perhaps the most critical aspects of this model for the principal are the content areas and the program components, for only through an understanding of these two areas can a principal give leadership in making guidance functions a reality. The three content areas focus on what students should know and be able to do to achieve academically, to make a successful transition to the world of work, and to provide a foundation for a student's personal and social growth (Hogan 1998). The ASCA's national standards for school counseling programs express these in three areas:

1. Academic Development
   - Acquiring skills, attitudes, and knowledge to learn effectively
   - Employing strategies to achieve success in school
   - Understanding the relationship of academics to the world of work and to life at home and in the community
2. Career Development
   - Strategies to achieve future career success and job satisfaction
   - Fostering an understanding of the relationship between personal qualities, education and training, and the world of work
   - The development of career goals by all students as a result of career awareness and experiential activities
3. Personal/Social Development
   - The acquisition of skills, attitudes, and knowledge that helps students to respect self and others
   - The use of effective interpersonal skills

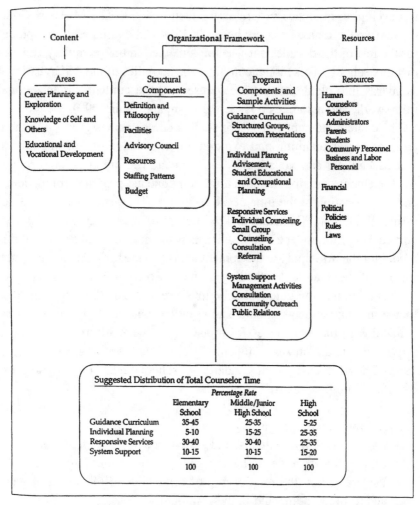

Figure 7.2.   Comprehensive Guidance Program Elements, Missouri. Used by permission of American School Counseling Association from N. C. Gysbers, R. T. Lapan, and M. Blair (1999). "Closing in on the statewide implementation of comprehensive guidance program model." *Professional School Counseling* **2 (5): 357–365.**

- The employment of safety and survival skills
- Understanding the obligation to be a contributing member of our society
- The ability to negotiate successfully and safely in the increasingly complex and diverse world of the twenty-first century (American School Counselor Association 1999–2000)

The content areas in the Missouri model are accomplished through the program components that include the guidance curriculum, individual planning through advisement and occupational planning, responding to individual needs through individual and group counseling, consultation and referrals, and system support for the guidance functions through outreach, public relations, and management.

The principal and other administrators are key to successfully implementing a comprehensive guidance program. Some of the common difficulties with guidance programs include:

- The expectations that counselors perform clerical tasks that keep them from working with students and student goals
- Assigning counselors the task of scheduling teachers and students by building the master schedule for the school and then assigning students to classes like a registrar
- Using counselors as substitute teachers when a regular teacher is absent and a substitute is not readily available
- Dependence on counselors to spend a great deal of time with disciplinary situations involving student behavior
- Placing counselors mostly in a reactive or intervention mode in carrying out their functions as opposed to establishing a balanced program that supports developmental or prevention functions as well as intervention actions (Baker 1996; Burhans 1999; Hogan 1998)

To establish effective use of a counselor's time, the principal must ensure that clerical and administrative tasks are not expected to be part of the guidance function. Clerks or secretaries should be employed to maintain student records maintained by the guidance office. Evaluation of counselors should be developed around the comprehensive guidance program model demonstrating effectiveness of counselors in implementing the model and accomplishing its goals with students. The principal should schedule a time to meet with school counselors to develop open communication and collaborate on problems and their solutions that counselors can respond to in their role. These meetings will help iron out differences in perceptions in areas that have mutual concern such as confidentiality, student advocacy, situational cause and effect, and school climate. Administrators must communicate with others concerning the counselor's role and help establish an understanding with parents and the community of that role and demonstrate support for the guidance program. The principal, as a primary link with the community, should provide counselors with information about community agencies and the overall network that helps support students and teachers. Administrators must respect confidentiality between counselors and students and, unless there is imminent danger for students or others, principals must not expect counselors to violate such ethical expectations. The principal must expect counselors to continue to develop and maintain their expertise though regular professional development. This expectation assumes that the principal employs licensed and credentialed counselors for the school (Hogan 1998).

Expectations for Guidance Programs

At the elementary school, the guidance program and counseling functions are considered to be developmentally oriented. The study of children and adolescents through developmental psychology has shown, in research terms, that intellectual development of a child occurs primarily in the preschool and elementary school years. Developmental studies show that lifelong behavioral patterns are established during the ages of six to ten. Consequently, the time to work with developmental problems of young children is during that period of time. With the change in social and educational patterns that the changing world is experiencing, children of all ages need to be prepared for change in their lives as well as to have a normal development in the growing process by successfully transiting experiences of anxiety, self-doubt, and threats. The counselor at the elementary school works with teachers and parents to assist in providing environments conducive to normal child development. This also includes working individually with children who need assistance to resolve problems. The child needs to mature in self-acceptance and to understand his or her own strengths and developmental areas. Social relationships are being developed, positive self-image needs to be established, and problem-solving and decision-making skills have to be learned. Although much of this can and should go on in the home and the regular classroom, some children need more assistance or structure in these skills and attitudes to develop them at a satisfactory level. The counselor assists teachers and parents to assist their children and, in many cases, the individual student through the maze of problems and opportunities. This is most often done through the programmatic approach, by establishing identified objectives that the school deems important for the student. The work of the counselors is designated to accomplish these objectives with the students in concert with all others in the school. This means that the counselors do not take on tasks that are unrelated to these goals in order to establish program effectiveness.

Middle schools are designed to meet the needs of students who are going through the transition of life's changes, especially those of seeking independence in their personal development, the social and emotional changes associated with transiting puberty, and the mental development and maturation that is associated with their education and moral development. These students need to learn to deal with many pressures of growing up as well as with more sophisticated thought processes in their intellectual development. Thus, a program of developmental or preventive guidance that includes learning emotionally healthy thinking and accepting responsibility for their own action is quite important. Group processes are of value due to their need to belong and be accepted in groups, develop meaningful friendships, and learn to make choices (Schmidt 1999).

High schools are focused on preparing students for the world of work as well as continuing their education in a multitude of postsecondary education opportunities including higher education and technical education. These adolescent students must learn to come to grips with many types of problems they may be facing, but also must often be assisted in actually dealing with intervention needs due to individual challenges such as personal problems, drugs, suicide, alcohol, or truancy. The counselor plays a critical role in developing a student's mental and emotional well-being and collaborates with teachers in a preventative program reflecting a joint effort toward student development and crisis prevention (Hall and Rueth 1999). Counselors usually assist students with information and individual counseling in considering course selection, career opportunities, test results, and higher education choices. Group counseling processes are not as visible at the high school as they are in the middle school (Schmidt 1999).

These expectations are accomplished through the balanced program that contains components: (1) for all students, (2) for students with special needs, and (3) for parents—primarily to assist them in helping and understanding their child.

Counseling Functions

Balanced counseling programs include a number of important functions that are accomplished by the counseling staff to meet stated objectives of the program. These functions include:

- Counseling—usually direct interventions, counseling occurs in individual or group settings and is aimed at helping the student-client make decisions, solve problems, change behaviors, or change environmental circumstances. The counselor gives aid to the student in reaching the goal through verbal interaction and nonverbal techniques such as observation or a combination of both.
- Curriculum programming—counselors are able to provide instructional services similar to regular teachers when they direct instruction for groups of students in making decisions, resolving problems, and changing behaviors and environmental circumstances. This is proactive in nature and tends to be developmental or preventative in its impact. This instruction may be in conjunction with the regular academic program or be created as an independent instructional program. Counselors must develop lesson plans and instructional strategies using media, discussion, and didactical presentations.
- Consulting—in this function, the counselor shares expertise with students, teachers, parents, and the principal in a helping relationship. In many cases, the teacher will then use this help in working with a student such as in dealing with classroom behaviors or in the teacher-advisor relationship to be discussed later.
- Referral and coordination—counselors are both the recipients of referrals from others at the school such as teachers and administrators and they make referrals to other professionals such as psychologists, physicians, social workers, or child welfare agencies. This function requires a knowledge of various sources of help and to make a decision when a referral is appropriate. The counselor may coordinate the results of the referral with other educators involved in providing services to the student. Increasingly, school counseling functions are moving toward short-term counseling and community referral (Kaplan and Evans, 1999).
- Information—students often need information to help in making decisions and resolving problems such as college or career choices as well

as other personal adjustments. Counselors provide this service with their knowledge of sources, acquisition, storage, dissemination, and the process of using such information.

- Transitional enhancement—counselors assist student-clients in making transitions from one level of schooling to another such as elementary to middle school or high school to college and to make the transition to the world of work from school. This should be done from the standpoint of assisting students rather than as agents of employers or educational institutions.
- Assessment—counselors provide assessment services through the use of standardized or nonstandardized measurement instruments such as educational or psychological tests. From such tests generalizations or predictions can be made concerning the individual's behavior or ability. The information obtained is used to assist the student-client in making decisions, changing behaviors, and resolving problems. This function requires a knowledge of such instruments and the ability to administer and interpret the results of the tests.
- Accountability—this function requires that counselor time and efforts be justified by demonstrating how their services are making a difference to student-clients and for the school in general. Such evaluations often use the reactions of student-clients. This function is highlighted by an increased emphasis on the counselor making a difference in students' learning and achievement by working with the whole school and being focused on the whole student. (Baker 1996; Schmidt 1999; Kaplan and Evans 1999)

Counselor–Student Ratios

Counselors are seldom available in numbers that would be most helpful. The standard has often been set at 250 to 350 students per counselor; however, in reality often times the ratio is closer to 500 to 600 students per counselor. The Southern Association of Colleges and Schools presently has the ratio set at 250 to 500 students per counselor (2000). This ratio seems to be most directly impacted by the financial condition of the school district and the perceived value of the guidance program. The need for guidance services is greatest where poverty is most intense and where other family problems are present. In these situations, school failure and dropouts seem to be most prevalent. Historically, children of poverty come from minority groups and from single-parent families, which are increasing dramatically. Poverty, minority status, single-parent families, and two working-parent families tend to be factors requiring additional guidance services. In actuality, high levels of school failure and dropouts should be the determining factors for additional counselors (Baker 1996).

Teacher Advisors

For three decades, the idea of teacher-advisor programs has been periodically advocated by restructuring efforts of schools. Trump (1977) describes this program as one that ensures that every student has an adult specifically interested in his or her individual success. This idea also had some roots in the home room programs that were once a part of junior high school philosophy and now also has a relationship to teaching teams in the middle school philosophy. The program is designed to ensure that all students have a least one adult who knows them well and that all students belong to a small interactive group. In this group, educators seek to promote students' social, emotional, and moral growth while providing personal and academic advisement. The guidance counselor plays an important role in this program by providing services to individual students and small groups, but also to teacher-advisors in establishing work in the small groups. The teacher-advisor does not replace or negate the counselor's professional position work, but seeks to establish a small ratio of advisees to advisors to provide detailed knowledge of these students (Manning and Saddlemire 1998). The small groups meet and discuss advisory topics that students consider relevant such as conflict resolution, peer pressure, anger, delayed gratification, and sexual harassment. High priority is given by advisors to developing interpersonal relationships with students. Also, advisors play an important role in referring students for counseling to the school's counselor (Schmidt 1999).

Principals play an important role in such a program by providing planning time for teams establishing the program, notifying parents of the program and its purposes, training the advisors, developing scope and sequence of the advisement topics, and arranging schedules to permit the small groups to meet and work.

HEALTH SERVICES

The school health services program has been on the educational scene since the late 1800s (Wold 1981); the program began as an extension of public health services, which became important during that period. Many parents and educators are aware of some of the functions of a school nurse, but they do not understand the entire picture of school health services nor do they appreciate the extreme importance of this service for the school as an institution. In order for schools to be able to provide educational services to students, the students must be healthy and able to learn in an environment that is free from health problems. Absenteeism is linked with school failure; students missing more than 11 percent of school days in a semester have trouble remaining at their grade level (Klerman 1988). Health-related risk factors clearly start absenteeism and set the stage for school failure (Lewis and Lewis 1990). The three functions generally ascribed to the school health program include:

• Providing a safe and healthful school environment
• Implementing an ongoing health education curriculum
• Delivering health services to students and staff (Wold 1981)

School nurses today work with a population of students that bring with them a significant number of complex and chronic health needs. The 1990 report *Code Blue: Uniting for Healthier Youth* states: "Never before has one generation of children been less healthy, less cared for, or less prepared for life than their parents were at the same age" (Oda 1991, 29). Today's children and youth bring numerous health and safety issues to school with them including lack of health insurance, child abuse, eating disorders, pregnancy, sexually transmitted diseases, suicide threats and tendencies, the impact of drugs and other controlled substances, the threat of violence and guns on their lives both in and out of school, and increased incarceration rates for juvenile offenses (Hootman 1994; Igoe 1998; Jordan 1992). Chronic illness has been estimated to affect 10 to 15 percent of U.S. children and 5.2 percent have been limited in their usual activities due to chronic illness and impairments (Hootman 1994). Students today are placed in these oftentimes precarious situations due to their risk-related behaviors, the influence of outsiders that impacts their behavior, poor communication and social skills that impact their ability to deflect bad influences, and their lack of skill or ability to refuse temptations (Jordan 1992). As those close to students in daily activity, educators must have the insight and support to assist students in making better choices, which in turn can help them achieve and move ahead educationally.

Students learn to the degree that they are able to adapt to the environment in which they live and study. If the environment is not friendly to the student, then there are many limitations that constrain their educational accomplishments and achievement. The extent to which the health services program of the school can eliminate or help deal with health and health-related problems in the students' environment will help to determine the level that students can perform in their educational activities. The school district often has a director of health services who serves all schools in the district by administering the health services program including the activities of the school nurses located at individual campuses. The nurses work directly with students, parents, faculty, staff, and the principal in providing health services to the school and its students. Nurses provide a helping relationship by performing interventions for student-clients by assessing needs, planning interventions, and evaluating the outcome. This relationship depends on developing rapport and trust with the student-client; in almost every instance, the establishment of such requires a truly helping attitude on the part of the nurse, which is based on a genuineness in personality. School nurses use a systematic process in providing actions that include assessment of the problem, planning of the intervention, and an evaluation of the results.

Six basic responsibilities are enumerated by Wold (1981) that fulfill the components of the health program:

1. Identifying and excluding from the school students and staff with communicable diseases and initiating follow-up to readmit them promptly.
2. Preventing the outbreak and spread of communicable diseases by enforcing laws and policies regarding immunizations for students and personnel.
3. Diagnosing problems as impaired vision, hearing loss, and scoliosis so these potentially chronic problems do not become disabilities to students' learning and functioning. Referrals are made to appropriate community resources for treatment and a follow-up is initiated to ensure that defects are corrected.

4. Minimizing conditions that might interfere with the teaching-learning function such as the elimination of safety hazards, ensuring sanitary food and water supplies, maintenance of adequate heating, ventilation and air conditioning systems, and adequate supervision of recreation and play for students.
5. Providing adequate first aid and emergency care in case of injury or illness at school for students and staff.
6. Developing, implementing, and evaluating the health education curriculum to prepare students to assume responsibility for their own health as a member of the school health team that would include the principal, parents, faculty members, the school psychologist, and the school social worker.

School nurses typically perform a variety of health services that include activities that are direct health services, health counseling, and health education (Newton, Adams, and Maracontel 1997). These services include:

- Evaluating student illness to determine which students are able to return to class, go home, or require medical attention
- Administering emergency care and first aid
- Teaching first aid and CPR to staff who will attend students in the absence of a nurse
- Providing disease control including immunization surveillance and protective measures
- Administering medications prescribed by physicians and dentists and performing special procedures when required by prescribed schedule
- Identifying health problems that may interfere with learning through screenings such as vision and hearing
- Providing physical evaluation of students eligible for Title XIX Early Periodical Screening, Diagnosis, and Treatment Program
- Assessing unique health needs of handicapped students and providing medical procedures where needed
- Serving on admission, retention, and dismissal (ARD) committees in special education to develop individual education programs (IEPs)
- Counseling students regarding potential and identified health problems
- Conferring with teachers and parents in interpreting medical information to make needed adjustments in the school environment

- Providing direct health education information to students and serving as resource person to teachers in conducting health education sessions
- Counseling in the identification and decision making for adolescent parents and helping them to communicate with parents and health professionals
- Conferring with other school professionals as counselors, school resource officers, and social workers

School nurses play important roles in dealing with many problems of school age youth. Nurses administer prescribed medicines such as Ritalin to hyperactive students, which can assist them in focusing on school activities. They may give counseling to students concerning sexual activity, pregnancy, and child care in order to assist such students to complete their education. Nurses almost always serve on the school's crisis team, which can respond to emergencies such as accidents, violence, suicide, or the death of a student on or off campus. Such events have major impact on the school as an institution as well as the school climate. Team response is important to take every necessary precaution and also to react by assessing the event and providing necessary support to students and staff where appropriate.

The Principal and Health Services Program

The effectiveness of the school's health services program depends greatly on the knowledge of the principal and the relationship shared with the school nurse (Pena 1998). Principals need to take time to understand the entire role and potential of the school nurse for school health services. The nurse must be recognized as a professional, just like the counselor and teacher, and be considered as part of the school's team. The nurse's knowledge of educational issues can make a major contribution to the school when these health professionals serve on committees, site-based teams, and the crisis action team and when the communications link with the principal and staff is a productive one. Principals need to have an understanding of what the nurse is permitted to do under the state board of nurse examiners rules and under the laws and policies of the state and district. With these guidelines in mind, the principal must have trust in the school nurse and permit the nurse to do the job and to back the nurse in enforcing statutes such as complying with immunization laws. Also, the principal must be flexible and open to new ideas as the scope of the nurse's skills widens in helping students with new or nonstandard health issues.

Resources are an important factor that impacts the school health program. In some cases, these resources are simply providing adequate space for a scheduled screening program such as vision or hearing. In other cases, it means providing funds and time to attend the state school nurses conference to maintain their professional currency or to learn of newly expected care procedures for special needs students. The need for a computer is especially important for records maintenance and for Internet access to assist students, parents, and teachers in learning about specific health issues and treatments. Records maintenance and confidentiality issues also may necessitate the addition of clerical assistance so the nurse can provide skilled service and not be primarily a records keeper. The principal's time is also a factor so the principal can participate in developing the health plan, coordinate on child abuse procedures, and develop the processes for storage, records maintenance, and administration of medicines to students—especially if the nurse is not present.

SCHOOL SOCIAL WORK

Social work in the school has been in existence since the early part of the twentieth century, however, it became more crystallized as a field of practice in midcentury (Allen-Meares, Washington, and Welsh 2000; Constable 1999). The school social worker (originally referred to as a visiting teacher) is concerned with children whose coping capacity is not as suited for the demands and resources of the school as an institution. Since the school prepares large numbers of students for the future, the school has often gravitated toward a factory model in its operation, frequently because of pressures due to political and economic factors. Many students are not well suited for this model in terms of their vulnerabilities, yet the responsibility is placed on the school and the parent as well as the child to make the system work in fulfilling the child's potential for growth. Also, identifiable characteristics such as gender, race, disability, ethnicity, or socioeconomic class of individual students impacts them due to the messages these characteristics engender for these students by presenting obstacles to their development. The school social worker is there to develop a flexible response to the developmental needs of the student in the institutional environment and the family setting. The goal of social work is to help these students to achieve "appropriate developmental tasks in ways that best respect the values underlying our common human nature, our common human needs and the human potential of each person" (Constable 1999, 4).

Today's schools are confronted with many complex societal and political changes. The school is expected to provide an education to all children despite these changes and the impact that these changes have on the student and on the school. Such changes include the increasing rate of poverty in many parts of the nation; the increasing number of single-parent families, usually headed by a female; increasing violence and acting out of youth; growing multicultural characteristics of the student body of many schools; the increasing requirements of special education being balanced against regular education; the decentralization of authority to make educational decisions; and the development of collaborative linkages between school and other community service agencies (Allen-Meares, Washington, and Welsh 2000).

The social worker focuses attention on problems students are having in the school through a four-phase process (Pincus and Mihahan 1973; Winters and Easton 1983). This process begins with initiating an assessment of the situation using social work skills and then developing a plan for intervention that will be most effective. Normally, the plan focuses on the teacher and the students in the classroom, the parents in the family, and others whose support in the process can bring success in achieving developmental steps for the student. The focus of the plan is referred to as the "unit of attention," that is, the specific place or person for which the intervention is planned. The assessment process may necessitate conferences with the teacher and or the parent as well as observation of the student and the situation (be it in the school or home). Once the assessment process has taken place, consultations with the teacher may be the first response or conferring with the parents may be required. Rapport and trust must be built in these situations. Responses of the student to the planned intervention are implemented and the adaptations of the student are also assessed in the termination phase.

The fundamental zone of social work is where people and their environment are in exchange with each other. It is at this zone where changes in both people and the environment take place and where results in resolving difficulties may be anticipated. Interventions aim to assist individuals in coping and in the adjustment of demands and resources of the environment, so transactions between individuals and the environment may be helpful to both. Garber et al. (1979) stress that it is this duality of focus between people and their environments that distinguishes between social work and other professions (Constable 1999, 15). This is the integration of personal tasks and social tasks. Consequently, the work of the social worker is relational work, taking place in the context of human values (Constable 1999).

Four models of practice have been identified by Alderson (1972) in the field of school social work (see table 7.1). These models help the principal understand the focus of the social worker and the tasks, roles, and the resulting recommendations that are offered to solve difficult issues. These include:

1. The traditional clinical (or casework) model: This model assumes the individual child is having difficulty and seeks to work with the child, parents, and teachers to enable the child to function more effectively.
2. The school change model: This model views everyone involved in the school and seeks to alter dysfunctional school norms, policies, and conditions that have developed to constrict success in the environment of the school.
3. The community school model: This model focuses primarily on deprived or disadvantaged communities and seeks to educate communities to the possibilities of school offerings and the school officials to the dynamics of the community and operant societal factors.
4. The social interaction (or ecological) model: This model emphasizes the reciprocal influences of actions between groups and individuals. It seeks to have the social worker mediate and clarify an understanding between the different parties so they can share common ground and support mutual interests. (Allen-Meares, Washington, and Welsh 2000)

Although much of the school social worker's role is focused toward direct work with students and parents, job studies of tasks have indicated that these tasks fall into five dimensions:

• Relationships with and services to children and families
• Relationships with and services to teachers and school staff

Table 7.1 Alderson's Practice Models for School Social Work

	Traditional Clinical Model	School Change Model	Community School Model	Social Interaction Model
Focus	Pupils identified as having social or emotional difficulties	The milieu of the school (especially school norms and conditions)	Deprived and disadvantaged communities that misunderstand and mistrust the school	Reciprocal interaction between pupils and the school; identify problems in interaction
Goals	Enable the pupil identified as having a school-related social or emotional difficulty to function more effectively	Alter dysfunctional school norms and conditions	Develop community understanding and support; develop school programs to assist pupils who are poverty victims alleviate deprived conditions	Foster development of mutual aid system; remove barriers to reciprocal interaction
Target system	Pupil-clients and their parents	Entire School	Community and school become targets between targets and other systems	Interactional field
View of sources of difficulty	Child's emotional or psychic difficulty, stemming primarily from family, especially Parent–child problems	Dysfunctional school norms and conditions	Poverty and other social conditions; school personnel lack full understanding of cultural differences and effects of poverty	Difficulty of pupil-clients and the various systems within which social interaction occurs to communicate and to mutually assist
Worker tasks and activities	Casework, primarily with pupils and parents; some work with groups and with family as a group; liaison functions between and among pupils, parents, and educational staff, including teachers	Identify school norms and conditions that are dysfunctional; some direct work with pupils, especially group work; consult with teachers and administrators, individually and in groups	Involve self in activities of community; enable community to ask questions and raise issues; assist community in understanding school and vice versa; encourage community-involvement in school Programs	Identify and highlight commonalities; establish mutual goals; improve and assist communication; establish mutual aid system; direct work with individuals, groups, and community
Major workers' roles	Enabling supportive collaboration and consultation	Advocacy, negotiation, consultation, and mediation	Meditation, advocacy, and outreach	Meditation, consultation, and enabling
Conceptual and theoretical base	Psychoanalysis, psychosocial, egopsychology, and casework theory and methodology	Social science theory, especially theories of deviance; organizational theory	Community-school concept, communication theory	Systems theory, social science theory, and communication theory

Source: J. J. Alderson. (1972). "Models of school work practice." In *The School in Community*, ed. R. Sarri and F. Maple. Washington, DC: National Association of Social Workers. Reprinted with permission. All rights reserved.

- Services to other school personnel
- Community services
- Administrative and professional tasks (Nelson 1990)

Four areas of school social work are seen to be very important and are frequently performed in relationship to these dimensions:

- Consultations with others in the school systems and interdisciplinary teamwork
- Assessment applied to direct service, consultation, and program development
- Direct work with children and parents in many forms
- Planning and implementation of school programs (Constable, Kuzmickaitae, and Volkman 1997)

In viewing the areas of concern and concentration for school social workers, a number of issues are typically linked to their work:

- Focusing on school attendance, especially as a part of the compulsory education tradition
- Observing pupil rights and control of behavior in consideration of the legal statutes and decisions of law respecting individual rights
- Coping with violence and crimes within and around schools
- Educating children with disabilities in keeping with the legal concepts and processes
- Assisting children who are vulnerable due to factors such as being disadvantaged, having parents who are migrants, being a student-parent, suffering from or having a family member suffering from AIDS, and many other impacting factors (Allen-Meares, Washington, and Welsh 2000)

Examples of areas of problematic situations that social workers might deal with include:

- Communication difficulties of students speaking languages other than English
- School crisis situations such as the *Challenger* space shuttle explosion that was being watched on television by millions of children

- Resolving difficulties for children with special needs
- Assisting student groups in the transition from self-contained classrooms to departmentalized instruction
- Difficulties of students that may be caused by inappropriate parenting actions—perceived or real
- Mediation of relationships causing fights between various ethnic groups in a school (Constable 1999)

The Principal and the Social Worker

The tasks of the school social worker are very supportive of goals of the school because they seek to find solutions to problems individual students are having. Oftentimes, these solutions are also being contributed to through the efforts by all others in the school community—counselors, nurses, teachers, and administrators. In the assessment and planning phases of social work activity, however, the social worker may come to identify that the school is promulgating policies and procedures that are working against the solutions to these problems. Some of those policies may be handed down by central office staff, the school board, or even the state education policy makers such as education agencies and the legislature. When these issues are identified in problem analysis, the principal must maintain an open mind and seek to understand how power brokers above the school level can be approached in order to eliminate the constraints that serve to exacerbate such problems or block their solution.

SCHOOL PSYCHOLOGIST

The school psychologist is a psychology practitioner who brings a psychological perspective to the school setting. Ultimately, the goal of the psychologist is to apply learning theory to the teaching-learning process and to help teachers improve instruction and students to improve learning. These professionals work with problems of those who live and work in the school, mostly with a perspective of how a student or particular groups of students adjust to the learning process. The school psychologist usually works with particular children as contrasted to the educational psychologist who is more research focused and studies the learning process in general, including such areas as motivation, learning, and human development. School psychologists are also interested in these areas, however, they concentrate on the study of those individuals and groups who have difficulty with the educational process, including both learning and mental health aspects (Fagan and Wise 1994). Training and licensure for school psychologists generally is at the educational specialist or doctoral level; however, a few school psychologists hold only a master's degree. Most school psychologists work for a school district and serve numerous schools within that district according to the needs of the students and schools as identified by educators. Oftentimes, this fact makes them viewed as a guest in the school where they are working, which has important implications to their current role in interventions and consultations. Psychologists, under the collaborative consultation approach, are more often being seen as professional peers and partners with teachers.

School psychologists usually spend about half their time in the psychoeducational assessment area, which includes testing students to help determine what their problems are in relation to learning difficulties. Interventions such as counseling and remediation plans typically take up 20 to 25 percent of their time and consultations another 20 percent. Usually, research and evaluation are rather minor areas of involvement, taking about 1 percent of the time (Fagan and Wise 1994). Traditionally, the school psychologist has been the administrator of tests for students who needed to be evaluated for placement purposes—particularly in special education settings. A corresponding theme has become, however, the nontesting roles such as consultation, therapy, and in-service/staff development education roles. Fagan and Wise (1994) contend that the assessment expertise is the basis of the growth and success of school psychology and that the followup role of intervention at the individual, group, family, and system levels has been a more difficult role to be accorded by the education system. Certainly, the growth and development of the special education field has had much to do with the growth of the education psychologist role in the schools. Today, school psychologists are being trained in very broad areas and have the school climate in which to more greatly involve themselves in interventions. They also have taken a major role in dealing with crisis intervention situations and planning for such events.

School psychologists are involved in a number of issues that have permeated this field for a number of years. Included among these issues are the following:

- Measurement, assessment, and evaluation of psychological and educational constructs that are specially designed or are more widely available for purchase.
- Legislation and court decisions that impact the development of special education programs and the procedures that have been established to implement such programs. School psychologists have major roles as a result of such legal issues.
- Intelligence testing and new developments in this important area have particular significance for school psychologists because of their role in testing and the increased development of gifted and talented education programs.
- Identifying the exceptional child, providing consultant services to teachers, and performing research and evaluation services in relation to this important and growing educational program area. The increased state and federal funding of special education programs have established important roles for the school psychologist.
- The projective techniques for personality assessment and the growing use of such holistic or global techniques in the assessment phases of developing solutions to behavioral and educational problems.
- The increased understanding of brain functions in the educational process and how the neurological assessments conducted by school psychologists may assist in understanding student behaviors.
- Development of future remediation strategies for the individualization of instruction, especially the aptitude-treatment interaction, which operates from the assumption that a single educational intervention cannot be thought of as the "best" treatment even if significant group differences are obtained when this method is used; rather, the characteristics of the learner such as level of intelligence, style of problem solving, degree of anxiety, and need for independence are considered. (Fagan and Wise 1994; Hynd 1983; Jacob-Timm and Hartshorne 1998)

Some school districts have either diagnosticians and/or psychometrists employed as part of the student instructional support team. These professionals have some of the similar duties as psychologists, but are primarily focused on the test administration and assessment phases of the process. Although these staff members are frequently included in the ARD meeting in the special education situations, the intervention decisions and applications are usually completed by parents, teachers, counselors, psychologists, social workers and school health nurses.

The Principal's Role in Relation to the School Psychologist

The principal's role intersects with the school psychologist's work most often in the administration of the ARD committee work in developing IEPs for the special education student. Usually, the principal serves as the chair of this committee in making decisions about the child's educational program. The psychologist serves oftentimes in the consultation role advising this committee about the findings of his or her assessment of the child and the recommendations for the intervention. Of course, the other members of the ARD committee will most often include the parent, counselor, teachers, school nurse, and the social worker. Each of these individuals may have similar recommendations that need to be considered after a thorough discussion of the case. Certainly, the professionals' roles are very important due to their education and experience level with respect to the problem areas. Principals must carefully consider their recommendations and work to establish consensus with the committee members.

Another important involvement with the psychologist is the development of school crisis response and the actual implementation of the response team in case of such an emergency. The psychologist has important advice to offer due to experience and expertise in dealing with individuals oftentimes involved in these crises. The principal's involvement with the psychologist helps to establish the trust and rapport between them that is helpful and necessary to have when such an emergency develops.

STUDENT ACTIVITY PROGRAMS

Student activities have been an important organized part of public education in the United States for nearly one hundred years. Prior to 1900, activities were very informal and were often student initiated and organized. Although the greatest part of these programs are in the middle and

secondary school environment, elementary school students also participate in an increasing number of such programs and events each year.
These programs run the gamut from athletic teams and events to fine arts
to academics to leisure time activities. Schools realize today that these
activities are helping to sustain student interest in continuing in school
and provide many instances where academic learning can find specific
hands-on application opportunities.

Schools, as well as students, benefit from student involvement in these
activities. The benefits of such activities are somewhat broad and will
vary to some degree, depending on the philosophical stance that the
school used in setting up such programs. Students may have a heightened
interest in academic courses, and they may have an environment to practice and develop their leadership and followership skills in greater depth.
Oftentimes, activities provide a setting where students can interact with
faculty members in a different type of setting from the classroom and
thereby learn skills that they would not have the opportunity to learn otherwise. Students frequently receive recognition for activity achievements
that can sustain their interest in school with growth opportunities that are
more to their individual needs and they learn healthy use of leisure time.
Schools benefit from building communication links with students that
otherwise would not be present. Building school spirit and student morale
are benefits that strengthen the climate of the campus. The expansion of
the scope of the classroom activities and the development of feelings of
personal worth both increase the impact on student achievement. The development of social skills and an awareness and appreciation of other ethnic groups and their values help the school meet major goals of human involvement in the twenty-first century (Vornberg 1998). In addition,
elementary schools also see after school programs as an opportunity to
provide students with supervision at a time when antisocial activities
could result, a time when enriching experiences and broadening children's
perspectives can take place and more recently a time when academic
achievement might be improved for students not accomplishing as much
during regular school hours (Fashola 1999).

Today, activities are often classified as extracurricular when they are offered outside class hours and have no direct relationship to regular class
offerings, or as cocurricular when at least part of the activities take place
during class time and/or when they have a direct link to course offerings

or academic credit. The school reform movement of the mid-1980s had at least a slight impact on athletic programs, finances, and administration of student activities in areas such as "no-pass, no play" issues and the amount of time principals had to give attention to these programs. In the elementary school, there is generally considered to be an academic component, a recreational component, and cultural component of after school programs. The academic component may reinforce the classroom activities through enrichment and activities tied to the school curriculum. The recreational component can help solve safety issues in many inner-city communities by providing a location for activities such as little league while the cultural component offers students opportunities to learn skills not taught in the classroom such as hobbies or musical instrument training. At the secondary or middle school, activities include athletics, both intramural and interscholastic; school publications, including newspaper, yearbook, and creative writing; fine arts, such as band, orchestra, chorus, art, and theater; leadership, including student government, class organization, and honor societies; public speaking and forensics; and school spirit activities, including cheer leading and drill teams, social events, clubs, assemblies, and trips/tours (Sybouts and Krepel 1984).

Organizing and developing such programs necessitates the principal to provide structure and supervision. In large schools with many programs, this often requires that a coordinator of student activities be designated to provide daily leadership. Schools of 1,500 students frequently have 50 or more activities occurring. Schools with widely developed athletic programs frequently have a director of these programs to coordinate personnel and fiscal resources in accomplishing their mission. Some schools organize an activities council that provides parent and student input in developing policies and ideas to support these efforts. As programs develop, the financial resources must also be identified to support such goals. Many schools have successfully used booster clubs of parents to assist in these endeavors; however, these support groups must be carefully monitored and coordinated to ensure that efforts do not become controlling factors that eventually work against healthy school goals for the total educational program.

As with any educational endeavor, an annual evaluation of the student activity program must be accomplished to maintain proper focus. This evaluation should be data driven with data being collected from students, parents, and school staff. Such information should include student and parent opinions, the range and balance of activities offered, participation rates and goals achieved in all activities, and support of the school's goals from the program. The evaluation should yield recommendations to strengthen the total program such as identifying new activities and needed policies, changing roles for specific activities, and eliminating activities no longer serving student needs (Joekel 1987; Vornberg 1980).

Implementing program components require the coordinator or administrator to address a number of implementation issues such as participation or attendance in these programs, training for the staff who will provide direction, training volunteers who may be assisting the school with these offerings, aligning the programs with curricular goals, and training the administrator to see the overall scheme of activities in the total school picture (Fashola 1999). Although these issues are present at both the elementary and secondary level, the development and addressing of such problems may take on somewhat different proportions at each of these levels. Elementary programs usually are more closely aligned with specific curriculum goals, while secondary programs have broader educational purposes. Secondary programs usually have greater fiscal implications and often require that large budgets be addressed by participants and school officials.

For activity programs with wide participation, principals should consider the following:

- Designate a coordinator of the program.
- Establish an advisory council with faculty, parents, and students.
- Develop a written statement of philosophy and beliefs concerning the program.
- Establish written policies and procedures for the program that take into consideration the state laws and school board policies.
- Balance the activities in the program so that varied interests of students are considered.
- Ensure that all ethnic and subgroups represented in the school have activities that are of interest or have meaning for them.
- Begin new activities to meet student needs and the school's purpose.
- Designate or establish a purpose for each activity in the program.
- Recruit and appoint qualified advisors and sponsors for activities.

- Offer leadership training for the student leaders in the programs.
- Arrange for staff development training for faculty sponsors.
- Recruit and train parent volunteers where they can assist in appropriate ways.
- Develop budgets and support for the fiscal needs of the activities that follow policies established for fund-raising efforts.
- Schedule activities on a school calendar that include facility reservations.
- Provide means to give recognition and public relations access to activities.
- Develop an activity evaluation process after each event or at the end of the year.
- Conduct an evaluation of the entire student activity program annually.
- Stay apprised of legal precedents that impact student activity programs.

DISCIPLINE, STUDENTS, AND THE SCHOOL

A third area, in addition to instructional support and student activities, must be discussed at this juncture—that of discipline—in order to bring a sense of completing the picture of student services within the school. Student discipline is a prerequisite to almost everything a school has to offer students. If discipline does not exist within the educational institution at any level, almost nothing of major significance will be accomplished as an institution. Discipline is closely linked with both school culture and school climate. In order for a satisfactory climate to exist within a school, a certain level of discipline must exist. Discipline is a very emotionally laden word, which often has unfortunate connotations when used. In the past, the word was often a "trigger term" for punishment. Discipline usually indicates control over actions occurring within the school. If a teacher maintains good discipline, it means that the students' actions are controlled within the classroom and the teaching-learning activity proceeds in a constructive way without negative interruptions by students that block the education process. Discipline must not, however, be thought of as an action that is forced by the teacher on the student. What has to occur is to develop the belief and understanding within the school that discipline is a self-regulated responsibility for all participants in the school community. The method of establishing discipline is, then, very much part of the school culture—the beliefs and attitudes that permeate the values of the school community. Every community member must have responsibility for maintaining control over his or her personal actions. This must be taught in the family and in the school from the time a student first enters this institution. Parents and teachers alike must participate in this value-driven experience. This responsibility is taught more than almost any other manner by the modeling that is present in the child's daily experience.

The school, however, only deals with part of this picture—the part that occurs at school. With a continually expanding diversity in the general population, the values and attitudes that are taught in the home and family are also very diverse. These are then brought to school and may impact what goes on in school in varied ways. In some instances, the school has an opportunity to help impact those family values by teaching the need to support such values to the parents. What must be avoided is to set the school and the family at odds in trying to develop a belief or values system. The best solution, perhaps, is to work from a position of what the family and the school both can agree on, rather than attempt to set up a power struggle between them. Of course, certain expectations will have to be met by students in order to participate in school and learning activities. These normally revolve around behavior of students toward teachers, fellow students, and the school.

As indicated earlier in this discussion, the word "discipline" frequently has become a synonym for control (Slee 1999) or punishment. This is very unfortunate as this confusion sets up a situation that pits self-discipline against freedom to act as one wishes in the school. The idea that the teachers' responsibility is to force control on students in accomplishing educational activities rather than building the belief that all students must learn to be responsible for self-control is reinforced by this confusion. When the teachers' responsibility is to dictate control, their role then becomes one of meting out punishment to maintain that control. The situation then becomes a win-lose situation with external control instead of a win-win situation. The flip side of this scenario is to switch from an "I" to a "we" focus, which means to have internal control occurring with the students taking responsibility. Discipline is not mandated by the teacher but is rather developed with the student and teacher working in a cooperative manner. This occurs best when it starts early in the school experience and is reinforced in the home with the same type of responsibility expected from the child by the parent. To expect to exert control in the educational setting through punishment is to adopt the behaviorism philosophy in managing classrooms and schools. Although it may work on a short-term basis, it does not direct the learning process for long-term success nor promote the values that are required in a democracy. Authoritarian leadership in the classroom places the learner in a position of passivity when considering learning how to think and interact in a problem-solving or inquiry-based classroom (Slee 1999). Classrooms need to change from being teacher-centered to being more "person-centered" to promote democratic citizenship and creative thinking.

Person-centered classrooms can help provide the balance required to advance active participation in cooperative learning environments (Freiberg 1999). They encourage students to think for themselves and help each other. These settings emphasize caring, guidance, cooperation, and building self-discipline. They help students to make choices, manage time, set goals and priorities, and build a sense of order. Teachers provide "the structure, but students have freedom of choice within that structure" (Freiberg 1999, 14). The teacher helps to establish routines for the classroom that enable students to minimize the need for new decisions for each event, thus allowing the students to enable more important events to occur in furthering their education. Instead of the teacher being the sole leader and attempting to control all activities and actions through rules, consequences, and extrinsic rewards, the person-centered classroom involves the idea of shared leadership between the teacher and the students. Discipline is developed so individuals are responsible for their actions; rules are developed in concert between teacher and students. Rewards become mostly intrinsic with students sharing in classroom responsibilities; partnerships are formed with other stakeholders in the school's community.

Freiberg (1999) makes the point that there are three dimensions in such an environment between discipline and instruction: a teacher dimension where the teacher is the source of knowledge and structure; a cooperative dimension where teachers and students work together; and a self-dimension where the student works separately using many sources of assistance. The classroom activities in the teacher-focused dimension include lecture, questioning, and demonstration, while the cooperative dimension uses cooperative groups and guided discovery. The student-focused dimension typically will involve projects of an inquiry nature with self-assessment (see also Rogers and Freiberg 1994, chapter 12).

A Phi Delta Kappa Commission explored characteristics of well-disciplined schools during 1980 and 1981. Some of their findings are very useful in understanding how the school as a unit larger than one classroom can promote the person-centered school. They indicate that schools that make a difference in the educational process have significant school culture bases that are built by principals and faculty members over extended periods. These characteristics include:

- Schools foster good discipline by creating a total school environment conducive to good discipline, rather than adopting isolated practices to deal with problems.
- Educators view their school as a place where staff and students come to work and experience the success of doing something well.
- The schools are student-oriented with programs instituted for the benefit of the students with the staff serving as student advocates.
- When problems arise, the focus is on causes of the problems rather than the symptoms.
- Programs in these schools emphasize positive behaviors and use preventive measures rather than punitive actions to improve discipline.
- Adapting practices to meet their own identified needs and reflecting their own styles of operation rather than adopting any of the widely publicized programs for improving discipline.
- The programs of these schools are often the result of teamwork of the principal and some other dedicated staff member who has the personal leadership qualities that compliment the principal. Often, this is an informal leadership team combining authority of a principal and determination and skills of another staff member or lieutenant.
- The staffs of these schools believe in their school and what its students can do; they expend unusual amounts of energy to realize that belief.
- Teachers in these schools handle all or most of the routine discipline problems without the administrators' involvement.
- Most of these schools have developed stronger-than-average ties with parents and with community agencies.
- These schools are open to critical review and evaluation from a wide variety of school and community sources. (Phi Delta Kappa 1982)

PRINCIPAL'S ROLE IN ESTABLISHING
A PERSON-CENTERED ENVIRONMENT

Perhaps the most important function the principal performs in developing self-discipline in the school is to set the tone of the school culture. The values and beliefs that underlie the philosophy of the educational program are the foundation of both instruction and classroom management. This means that forcing control is not generally good discipline. Self-control is the goal for every student, and self control is best taught in an environment that is orderly, has high standards, and has clear expectations (Blendinger et al. 1993). Setting clear expectations for student behavior, rewarding good behavior, and ensuring that consequences resulting from improper behavior are appropriate, fair, and realistic is a matter of leadership from the principal. Teachers are very much a major factor when good discipline is present and this concept has become an important belief in the culture of the school as an organization. Teachers handle the routine discipline within their own classroom without having to involve the administrators.

To ensure that the necessary expectations are present, the principal must give regular and significant leadership to helping teachers and staff understand and deal with the behavior of students. Translated, this usually means that the principal should conduct regular staff development for faculty and staff in these areas. All faculty must understand the importance of school culture, the function of the philosophy, and how its implementation produces a sound and viable instructional program. Not only do faculty members receive supportive training initially, but the principal revisits this area regularly in faculty meetings, interest group discussions, and anytime instructional and classroom climate concerns are addressed.

One such example of an application of supportive philosophy is called win-win discipline. This system contains five general areas of focus (Blendinger et al. 1993). The first is to *plan* by developing a classroom plan at the beginning of the school year to address rules and consequences and to ensure the classroom plan is in harmony with the schoolwide behavior standards. Next, the teacher *establishes rules* that are clear, stated in positive language that is understood by the students, and compatible with the schoolwide rules. These are in writing and posted where students are reminded of their responsibility. Many advocates of these rules suggest that these be developed with the input and assistance of the students; such development will be an important lesson in democracy and help to win students' responsibility and acceptance. *Consequences* of not following rules is the third step of the process. Students who are not responsible for their own behavior are not so much punished for breaking a rule as being held responsible fairly and consistently for their inappropriate behavior— a choice that they make. Teachers help to establish rapport with students using the fourth step—that of *recognizing success* (good behavior) or what is actually expected of all students in the school. Oftentimes, this takes place through praise of the student by the teacher or by special privileges being earned that are related to the student's school assignments and personal responsibility. The last step is encouraging *parent involvement* through communication. Parents are sent the rules/expectations and their support is solicited. If students have difficulty in being responsible for the rules, then the parents' help is solicited by establishing a contract with the student and parent agreeing to work together to change such activity.

Practicing educators are certainly aware, however, that all students may not respond to the type of environment that is advocated here. In some cases, this is due to past difficulties of the child in his or her educational settings or in his or her home environment. When this is the case, the instructional support personnel of the school may be asked to assist with diagnosing the problem and helping to plan appropriate interventions. In today's environment of mainstreaming special education students, individualized educational programs will address methods and means to assist these students in achieving their educational goals with respect to discipline actions. School social workers, counselors, and school psychologists often assist the teachers and the principal in determining what these means and methods might include.

Today's schools are more and more directed by the action of state agencies such as the legislature or the state board of education, which may direct procedures for local districts and schools to follow involving student problems. Frequently, these procedures include development of a manual that addresses student behavior and responsibilities as well as the appropriate action which is to be taken by the school when the student fails to follow these responsibilities. In cases of punishment (which is definitely an option in these laws or policies), the manual, usually developed by the local board and administrators, defines what sorts of action will be taken by school authorities, such as suspension or expulsion. The state and federal laws address the restrictions of such actions and under what circumstances such actions may be imposed. Although these laws, of both legislature and court origination, are beyond the scope of this chapter, the reader is urged to explore these carefully and understand their implementation so as not to overstep the bounds of authority.

ETHICAL DISCUSSION

What Sorts of Ethical Questions Will Most Likely Surface from the Perspective of Instructional Support Service Professionals When Dealing with Students and Their Concerns?

- When student activities are involving competitive situations between students or teams of students, what ethical principles should be kept at the forefront of the principal's mind in dealing with decisions involving such matters?
- How can administrators and teachers deal with questions of equity in the area of student activities when students make choices of what they want to participate in but yet may not have the resources, money, or time to make any choices they would like?
- How can the principal and other school staff best deal with the accusation that students of different racial or cultural groups are not being treated equally in the disciplinary area? Address this from both a preventative and an after-the-fact situation.
- Ethical dilemmas are right-versus-right issues. Which side of the student equity in the activity program debate do you support and why?

CHAPTER SUMMARY

Principals have a difficult task in maintaining vision on student advocacy in the current situation of the political and economic environment. Constant direction from upper-level policy makers will tend to involve the principals' time and talent in meetings and coordination of activities related to such policy directives. Interaction between the principal and students in the school in a meaningful way is very important and the principal will have to organize his or her time and other resources to maintain interaction with students. Understanding student motivation and also the changes in the culture and society that serve as the student's environment help principals to focus on the needs and responses of students.

The instructional support staff includes the group of specialists that the principal and the faculty rely on to assist in supporting teachers' efforts in reaching students and student efforts in contending with problems encountered at school and in their greater environment. This staff is made up of four specialty areas, each of which helps students and extends the efforts of faculty to best help students. The school counselor is the specialist that is most often experienced by teachers and students chiefly because of the lower student–counselor ratio. This staff member helps students deal with academic and personal decisions and actions within their environment. The school nurse supports the school's efforts to effectively deal with health issues impacting the school and the student's personal life. The school social worker plays a key role linking the school with the family and in dealing with problems students are having due to making adjustments as the result of demands of family, environment, and school difficulties. In some cases, schools are dysfunctional systems when dealing with outside family systems and social workers are involved in offering solutions through interventions. The school psychologist brings a psychologist's perspective to the school setting in applying learning theory to the teaching-learning process. Often, the focus is on assisting the student to adjust to the learning process through the gathering of data with testing efforts. All of these specialist areas seek to develop interventions based on problem identification and assessment techniques. The interventions may deal primarily with student adjustments such as behavior changes or school adjustments such as policy or procedural changes.

Student activity programs provide an important resource for the school in maintaining student interest as well as practical application to many of the school's overarching instructional objectives. Personal benefits to students as well as programmatic benefits to the school are realized when these programs are effectively conceived and well coordinated in the school environment.

The efforts of the school to develop a culture and climate that supports student growth through self-discipline is the philosophy that best teaches long-term adult-like responsibility. This requires the entire school staff to be trained with this belief and supports the best long-term benefits to the greatest number of students and to society. It teaches democracy in actions and also self-control rather than outside control. The philosophy promotes the person-centered environment in the school culture. Where such self-discipline goals do not maintain the environment necessary to conduct educational programs, instructional support staff should enter the response environment on the part of the school to determine the appropriate actions on the school's behalf.

CHAPTER ACTIVITIES AND QUESTIONS

1. Evaluate the student activities program in your school and offer new recommendations for operating these activities.
2. Do a strengths, weaknesses, opportunities, and threats (SWOTs) analysis of the discipline principles used in your school. As a result, what changes would you recommend be implemented?
3. Examine the websites of the professional organizations for counselors (www.schoolcounselor.org), school nurses (www.nasn.org), school psychologists (www.school-psychologist.com), and school social workers (www.sswaa.org). Examine their statements of professional ethics and compare them with each other and what you think should be expectations in this important area.
4. Examine the student rights and responsibilities handbook of several schools or districts and assess these for understandability and completeness. Determine what you think are strengths and weaknesses of each.
5. Develop an outline of what you think a model handbook should include.

CASE STUDY ACTIVITIES AND QUESTIONS

1. Assistant Superintendent Boswell has appointed a task force of Dr. McNew and five principals, yourself included, to address the coordination of the instructional support services staff issue. Develop suggestions, from your perspective, of how to improve the coordination of services task.
2. As principal, what would you do in your individual school to ensure that professional boundaries and conflicts don't interfere with the optimum delivery of services to students by the instructional support staff?

3. Provide direction to your faculty, staff, and assistant principal to get the best results in the school's student activities by offering the principles you think are important in carrying out that program
4. After the district hires two new school social workers, one is assigned to your school, Cameron High School, for the first six months. What would your actions be to best utilize this staff member and to hopefully receive the most benefit to your school and possibly have a permanent position on your school's team?
5. Due to the sensitive nature of Board president Cool's daughter's adjustment, how would you as the daughter's principal orchestrate the staff to assist you in making recommendations to Superintendent Tucker?

REFERENCES

Alderson, J. J. (1972). "Models of school social work practice." In *The school in community*, ed. R. Sarri and F. Maple. Washington, DC: National Association of Social Workers.

Allen-Meares, P., Washington, R. O., and Welsh, B. L. (2000). *Social work services in schools*. Boston: Allyn and Bacon.

American School Counselor Association. (1999–2000). At www.schoolcounselor.org/national.htm (accessed May 21, 2002).

Baker, S. B. (1996). *School counseling for the twenty-first century*. Englewood Cliffs, NJ: Prentice-Hall.

Blendinger, J., Cornelious, L., McGrath, V., and Rose, L. (1993). *Win-win discipline*. Bloomington, IN: Phi Delta Kappa.

Burhans, L. L. (1999). "A fable: Seven counselors and 'the plan'." *Professional School Counseling* 3 (1): 3–4.

Constable, R. (1999). "Theoretical perspectives in school social work." In *School social work: Practice, policy, and research perspectives*, ed. R. Constable, S. McDonald and J. P. Flynn. Chicago: Lyceum.

Constable, R., Kuzmickaitae, D., and Volkman, L. (1997). "The Indiana school social worker: Parameters of an emerging professional role." Paper presented at the annual conference of the Indiana State Association of School Social Workers.

Fagan, T. K., and Wise, P. S. (1994). *School psychology*. New York: Longman.

Fashola, O. S. (1999). "Implementing Effective After School Programs." In *Here's How*. Alexandria, VA: National Association of Elementary School Principals.

Franklin, C. (2000). "The delivery of school social work services." In *Social work services in schools*, ed. P. Allen-Meares, R. O. Washington, and B. L. Welsh. Boston: Allyn and Bacon.

Freiberg, H. J., ed. (1999). *Beyond behaviorism*. Boston: Allyn and Bacon.

Garber, R., Gordon, W. E., Lewis, H., Meyer, C., and Williams, C. (1979). *Specialization in the social work profession*. National Association of Social Workers Document no. 79-3100-08. Washington, DC: National Association of Social Workers.

Gysbers, N. C., Lapan, R. T., and Blair, M. (1999). "Closing in on the statewide implementation of a comprehensive guidance program model." *Professional School Counseling* 2 (5): 357–365.

Hall, S. E., and Rueth, T. W. (1999). "Counselors in the classroom: A developmental approach to student well-being." *NASSP Bulletin* 83 (603): 27–33.

Hogan, C. C. (1998). "Integrate high-school counselors into the learning process." *The Education Digest* 64 (1): 55–58.

Hootman, J. (1994). "Nursing our most valuable natural resource: School age children." *Nursing Forum* 29 (3): 5–17.

Hynd, G. W. (1983). *The school psychologist*. Syracuse, NY: Syracuse University Press.

Igoe, J. B. (1998). "An overview of school health services." *NASSP Bulletin* 82 (601): 14–25

Jacob-Timm, S., and Hartshorne, T. S. (1998). *Ethics and law for school psychologists*. New York: Wiley.

Joekel, R. (1987). "How to evaluate a school's cocurricular activities program." In *Tips for Principals*. Reston, VA: National Association of Secondary School Principals.

Jordan, C. (1992). "School nurses' role in the new health care delivery system." Keynote speaker at Texas Association of School Nurses convention, November.

Kaplan, L. S., and Evans, M. W. (1999). "Hiring the best school counseling candidates to promote students' achievement." *NASSP Bulletin* 83 (603): 34–39.

Klerman, L. (1988). "School absence—A health perspective." *Pediatric Clinics of North America* 6: 1253–1269.

Lewis, C., and Lewis, M. A. (1990). "Consequences of empowering children to care for themselves." *Pediatrician* 17: 63–67.

Manning, M. L., and Saddlemire, R. (1998). "High school advisory programs." *The Clearing House* 71: 239–241.

National Health Information Center (2002). *Instructional support services: The helping professions in schools*. Washington, DC: U.S. Public Health Services.

Nelson, C. (1990). *A job analysis of school social workers*. Princeton, NJ: Educational Testing Service.

Newton, J., Adams, R, and Maracontel, M. (1997). *The new school health handbook*. Paramus, NJ: Prentice-Hall.

Oda, D. (1991). "Is school nursing really the invisible practice?" *Nursing Outlook* 39: 16–29.

Pena, R. A. (1998). "The school nurse: Friend to the school principal, member of the administrative team." *NASSP Bulletin* 82 (601): 84–90.

Phi Delta Kappa. (1982). *Handbook for developing schools with good discipline.* Bloomington, IN: Phi Delta Kappa.

Pincus, A., and Mihahan, A. (1973). *Social work practice: Model and method.* Itasca, IL: Peacock.

Rogers, C., and Freiberg, H. J. (1994). *Freedom to learn*. 3rd ed. Upper Saddle River, NJ: Prentice-Hall.

Schmidt, J. J. (1999). *Counseling in schools*. Boston: Allyn and Bacon.

Slee, R. (1999). "Theorizing discipline—Practical research implications for schools." In *Beyond behaviorism,* ed. A. J. Freiberg. Boston: Allyn and Bacon.

Southern Association of Colleges and Schools. (2000). *Accreditation Standards 2000.* Decatur, GA: Commission on Secondary and Middle Schools.

Sybouts, W., and Krepel, W. J. (1984). *Student activities in the secondary schools.* Westport, CT: Greenwood.

Trump, J. L. (1977). *A School for Everyone*. Reston, VA: National Association of Secondary School Principals.

Vornberg, J. A. (1998). "How to administer student activities programs." In *Tips for Principals*. Reston, VA: National Association of Secondary Principals.

———. (1980). Auditing the student activity program. *NASSP Bulletin* 64 (435) (April): 83–88.

Winters, W. G., and Easton, F. (1983). *The practice of social work in schools: An ecological perspective.* New York: Free Press.

Wold, S. J. (1981). *School nursing: A framework for practice*. North Branch, MN: Sunrise River.

Section III

Campus and Community Collaboration

ISLLC Standard 3

A school administrator is an educational leader who promotes the success of all students by ensuring management of the organization, operations, and resources for a safe, efficient, and effective learning environment. The administrator has knowledge and understanding of:

- Operational procedures at the school and district
- Principles and issues relating to school safety
- Human resource management and development
- Principles and issues relating to fiscal operations and management
- Principles and issues relating to school facilities
- Current technologies that support the management function

Chapter Eight

Mobilizing School and Community Resources

Valrie Watson, in her second year as principal of South Cameron High, had pledged to the superintendent and the school community that she would change the academic standing of South Cameron in three years if she were given sufficient resources. After one year at the high school, she knew she would never be able to change the face of the school if she could not generate additional revenue above and beyond what the central administration was budgeting for the school. On numerous occasions, she had met with Dr. J. B. Tucker and Dr. William Walls, deputy superintendent for finance, about getting additional resources for the school she directed. Both men were more than willing to listen to her requests but they felt they could not provide additional resources for South Cameron High at the expense of all of the other schools in the district. Ms. Watson made the argument that she had the highest teacher/pupil ratio of any of the secondary schools when looking at the core subjects of math, science, social studies, and English. Both Dr. Tucker and Dr. Walls acknowledged that was true and they also agreed that Ms. Watson had the largest percentage of first- and second-year teachers of any of the secondary schools in the district. Ms. Watson continued to pressure Dr. Walls at every opportunity to provide more resources.

South Cameron High School was in need of three more computer labs and technical labs for drafting and architectural drawing. She knew these were big ticket items and the chances of securing district resources were slim, so she wondered how she might purchase the items that South Cameron High needed so badly. She began talking with the teachers and they brainstormed ways to raise the money they needed to meet the needs of high school students in the twenty-first century. Technology was expensive and she knew that maintenance and repair were also costly on the items she

*felt the school needed. As she discussed this situation with the faculty, she
soon realized that she had to reach beyond the faculty to solve her dilemma.*

*Ms. Watson invited the major stakeholders in her attendance zone in-
cluding parents, business leaders, and school supporters to attend a
breakfast to brainstorm fund-raising activities for the school. About
twenty parents and ten business owners came to the meeting. Ms. Watson
made her plea for ideas concerning strategies for securing additional
funding and found the attendees to be most receptive to her idea but they
could shed no additional light on how to raise more resources. After the
meeting, Ms. Watson returned to her office wondering where she could go
to get some help with this problem, since neither Dr. Tucker nor Dr. Wall
were any help. The faculty had worked hard, but it didn't help very much
and all others were of little help in creating more resources. Parents did
suggest they lobby the superintendent and the Fort Spirit School Board
members, but Ms. Watson thought that might do more harm than good. As
she thought further about attaining additional resources, she wondered
what she could do. It also crossed her mind that perhaps this problem was
bigger than she was capable of solving.*

What would you have suggested to Ms. Watson and how would you have
addressed the problem with the central administration? With anger and
frustration, giving up and deciding to accomplish all you could with the
resources currently available, or are there other sources of revenue for a
school? Ms. Watson faces the same problem principals face all across the
United States on a daily basis. The answers are not simple and they require principals to market their school to many stakeholders simultaneously. This chapter is designed to help principals work with the media to
find alternative sources of revenue for their schools utilizing school foundations, grant procurement, gifts, and donations. While schools generally
focus on financial resources, don't forget the human resources in the form
of school volunteers and business-school personnel exchanges.

SCHOOL RELATIONSHIPS WITH THE COMMUNITY

Bradley (1998) states that educators believe that more support and involvement is needed to improve schools academically, but it appears that

there is a growing chasm between the public and the schools. The principal must work to engage the public, which entails working with families, community organizations, and other agencies. Houston and Bryant (1997) scold principals when they state that schools send mixed messages to the public. Schools encourage and welcome the stakeholders to the school and at the same time send them away. Principals want parents involved in their child's school, but not too involved. They want to control the level of involvement and in some situations they want to control which parents are involved. Hopkins and Wendel (1997) note that schools cannot afford to function in isolation from the rest of society and to keep the "public" in public education. Coupled with a rapidly changing society, it is paramount that schools develop real partnerships with all of the stakeholders in the community. The process of developing these coalitions is dependent on the context of the community; the goal remains the same: the building of a stronger school through the external support of the community.

Perhaps the most efficient manner for creating a public conversation is an open forum or town meeting format in order to measure the pulse of the community. Danzberger and Friedman (1997) frame the following three questions that can be used to initiate discussion in the aforementioned formats:

- From your perspective, what are the purposes for public schools?
- What is the effectiveness of the public schools in attaining your purposes?
- What changes would you suggest that would meet your requirements for schools to be effective?

The community forum or town meeting formats should encourage participants to discuss openly their concerns about the school. In addition, these meetings should allow for a diversity of opinion and if the aforementioned questions are utilized the responses should be confined to three or four items.

Parental involvement in schools has become a front-burner issue for many parents and thus a major concern for politicians, policy makers, teachers, and principals. While the politicians and parents see parental involvement as a right of birth, many teachers and principals seem to see the activity as an infringement on the their professional sovereignty. The increase in parental interest about school was generated in part by the Goals

2000: Educate America Act, which stated that by 2000 every school will promote activities that increase parental involvement in all aspects of their child's educational life (Patrikakou and Weissberg, 1999). The Improving America Schools Act, Title I has mandatory language that requires that parents and schools work together to improve student achievement and develop school policies (Black 1998). The academic success of children is dependent on the amount and magnitude of parental involvement in reducing absenteeism, controlling behavior, and developing a positive attitude about completing homework (Epstein 1995; Hara and Burke 1998). This type of involvement helps parents become interested in their child's education and may spur parental learning.

The obstacles to the family–school relationship are grounded in parents who believe that they do not have the expertise to work side by side with teachers. In some schools, the intimidation factor is increased for parents because English is their second language and they do not feel comfortable verbally communicating with teachers or the principal. Other parents believe they lack the academic knowledge to help their children and in some situations parents remember what school was like when they were students, when it was a negative experience, so they avoid working with the school for fear of another negative experience. The key for principals in reducing the fear factor of parents is grounded in mutual trust, respect, and communication. When principals regard their relationship with families as a collaborative venture where the school and home work together to improve student achievement, then and only then will parents feel comfortable and noncombative with the school. This implies a shared responsibility for children's learning among the school, home, and the community.

The family–school partnership provides a plethora of opportunities for participation in the day-to-day operation of the school in terms of school improvement, decision making, and student achievement. It is the principal's responsibility to recruit parents and other community stakeholders to complete school tasks, listen to parent points of view, and create an atmosphere where all teachers and staff develop the necessary skills for working with parents in a successful manner. Very little time is spent educating the faculty about collaborating with families and learning about family dynamics and nontraditional family structures in an attempt to create two-way communication. One strategy for establishing communication between the school and families is to invite school family volunteers to educate teachers and principals about the school's community. Community walks led by these volunteers help teachers to understand the dynamics and social context of their students' neighborhoods (Funkhouser and Gonzales 1997). Funkhouser and Gonzales (1997) emphasize that one size does not fit all schools when they state that appropriate strategies are a matter of context. Nathan and Radcliffe (1994) surveyed 1,823 educators in 29 states and more than 50 percent of the respondents ranked the following strategies as the most important when collaborating with families:

- Meeting with families and conducting conferences
- Working with parents of problem students
- Communicating about student achievement
- Helping parents understand methods of assessment
- Helping parents participate in the curriculum development process

The National PTA has been involved in the development of the National Standards for Parent/Family Involvement Programs in conjunction with the National Coalition for Parent Involvement in Education. The purpose of the standards is to promote meaningful parent and family participation in schools, to make known to all education stakeholders the elements of an effective program, and to create a baseline for schools that want to improve parent–school relationships (National PTA 2001). The standards include:

Standard I—Communication
Standard II—Parenting
Standard III—Student learning
Standard IV—Volunteering
Standard V—School decision making
Standard VI—Collaborating with the community

Communication forms the foundation for developing a partnership between the family and the school. As such, it must be regular, two way, and meaningful. When this communication does occur, it is much easier to solve problems, develop positive parental perceptions about the school, and generally improve student achievement. Two-way communication means that a message is sent to another individual and that individual attaches contextual meaning to the text and understands its implications. Two-way communication demands that all participating parties have the opportunity to clarify the meaning of both written and verbal conversation. Indicators of successful programs include:

- Providing clear information for course expectations, school activities, and student placement
- Mail all student progress reports including end-of-course grades to parents
- Create mechanisms for continuous parent contacts
- Translate documents from English for non-English speakers
- Make positive parent contacts when student behavior and achievement improve
- Provide parents with strategies for effective communication
- Use a variety of communication tools, such as a class newsletter, parent handbooks, parent–teacher conferences, e-mail, fax, teacher homework websites, and telephone (National PTA 2001)

Strategies that create communication opportunities include sponsoring events that allow parents and educators to communicate on an informal basis, developing a document outlining ideas about successful parent–teacher conferences, starting a program of sending "happy grams" by teachers to report positive student behavior or superior citizenship, and adopting a family involvement policy that supports the concepts of the school's desire to work in a partnership relationship with parents, families, and the community.

Principals and teachers need to understand that parents, in most situations, are the most important source of student support. Creating opportunities for parents to develop their skills through school sponsored development programs is a vital role for teachers and the principal. These programs must address issues other than discipline and punishment strategies; they need to inform parents about student sleep, nutrition, learning, and self-esteem needs. Survey parents to find out what types of help they need in helping their child become successful at school and in life. The needs assessment is a commonly used strategy for determining the types of programs that should be presented. The younger the parent the more help he or she will probably need when working through issues of child development and learning. As our society continues to produce children from parents who are children, the more important this standard becomes to the welfare of the children and the school. Indicators of successful parenting programs are:

- Make sure parents understand the value of a solid parent–child relationship
- Provide programs that support parent needs
- Invite all parents to participate in parent development
- Provide a parent resource center that directs individual parents to professionals who can help them solve their child-centered problems
- Make sure all faculty and staff understand and respect the parents' role in raising children (National PTA 2001)

According to Standard III, parents are responsible for playing an important role in student learning. There is evidence that student learning increases when parents are invited into the learning process. It is the responsibility of the principal to foster parents and students working together to create academic success. Generally, parents are willing to help their child if they know what it is they are supposed to do. Making sure parents can help provides an atmosphere that indicates parents value what their child achieves. One of the most often used strategies schools use to implement this standard is the traditional "back to school night," otherwise known as "open house." Most secondary teachers argue that this school event is not successful because the parents of those students they would like to talk with never come to the event. When this type of attendance does occur, it is time to assess the school environment to determine the climate. Bulach and Potter (2000) argue that the key to an open house is the planning that initiates the "open house" concept. Decide who will plan the event: the principal, a committee, or a combination of these two entities. Carefully select a date and check the community calendar to make sure there are no major conflicts. Advertise the open house in all your media outlets, on your website, and through your e-mail list serve. Make sure parents understand the what, when, and who about the event. Emphasize where parents can park, get their child's schedule, where to go when they get to the school, and whether they can bring their child to school with them to the open house.

Prepare faculty and staff by suggesting that they provide parents with displays of instructional materials and student work neatly arranged around the classroom. Make sure faculty and staff understand the format that parents will use in coming to each individual classroom. Remind faculty that they need to greet parents at the classroom door with a smile and a cordial welcome. Be enthusiastic, full of energy, and speak positively about students, colleagues, and the school. It may be prudent to ask teachers to file a lesson plan about how they will spend the time they have with parents. These plans should focus on course objectives, not instructional strategies. Make sure teachers new to the school receive special help in preparing for their first open house (Bulach and Potter 2000).

Standard IV appears to support the concept that parents need to help in the school. Parent volunteers provide services that would cost millions of dollars if schools were required to pay for them. Most volunteers have a greater capacity for the school because they are routinely part of the school's activity. The parent volunteer sends a strong signal to his or her child that he or she cares about what the child is doing at school. In many instances, volunteers bring expertise to the school that could be accessed in no other way. This expertise relieves teachers of some of the academic burden that has been placed on them by the accountability policy makers. Some parents are unable to volunteer during the traditional school day but they can provide help before the school day begins, after school, or by supporting the school in the home. The principal needs to find a person to coordinate and train the parent volunteers. In most cases, this coordinator of volunteers should be someone from the community, not directly tied to the school contractually. It is much easier for this coordinator to inform a parent that his or her services are no longer needed when he or she violates policy created for the management of the volunteer corp. In most situations, volunteering can be enhanced if:

• Parents feel valued and welcomed.
• Parents are offered options to volunteering in the school.
• All parents are contacted about the possibility of volunteering.
• Volunteer projects are useful to the school and meaningful for the volunteer.
• There is a volunteer coordinator, preferably someone from the school community. (North Central Regional Educational Laboratory 2001)

Standard V addresses making parents full partners in decisions that affect their children. This standard includes families as advocates for the school, becoming members of various school councils, and participating as members of school committees. Funkhouser and Gonzales (1997) note that parents and community members can impart ideas and help in the decision-making process related to the budget, teacher and principal hiring, school improvement plans, and parent volunteering activities. Some of the activities simulate the theory of site-based decision making as they directly affect school governance. In most instances, this type of organizational participation enhances the power and authority of the principal by generating community support for the principal. Implementation of this standard provides:

- parents with an understandable structure for accessing and influencing school policy.
- parents with current information about the school's policy and goals.
- parents with the opportunity to be full partners in the vision for the school.
- parents the ability to intervene when addressing academic issues of their own child.
- parents with the ability to understand and interrupt academic data concerning their child and the status of the school. (North Central Regional Educational Laboratory 2001)

Collaborating with the community means that schools must work with the services provided by the community. If schools are to be able to connect social service agencies with families and students, they must provide information and be knowledgeable about the function and criteria for determining eligibility by these agencies. When schools and social service agencies collaborate, families are able to access their resources and students become involved in learning beyond the school walls. Schools connect individuals to the agencies, not agencies to agencies. In addition, this type of collaboration creates an opportunity for students to be part of community service.

Principals are the key to making parent involvement happen. If the principal sets the tone that parent involvement is going to be part of the school, in most cases the teachers will follow. In some instances, teachers believe that parent collaboration will cause the principal and teachers to lose control and thus the authority to operate the school. Without this type of administrative leadership, genuine collaboration will never occur. The critical event for the principal is providing professional development for teachers in the area of parent and family participation in the school, specifically in the areas of communication, interpersonal skills, and respect for all people.

Working with parent, family, and community partnerships is a very useful concept but it is not without its problems. A major concern for teachers is the additional time and work it will take to cooperate and collaborate with parent and community members. In some cases, teachers are mandated to work with parents and are provided no additional time stipend for doing so. In many instances, teachers are never provided with the necessary skills to be effective leaders of parents and community members. The school culture can create an atmosphere that discourages parent and community participation. Inconvenient volunteer times, hostile teachers and staff, poor communication, and the lack of an effective policy are additional indicators of further problems.

THE PRINCIPAL AND MEDIA RELATIONS

When the reporter calls and says "I would like to spend a few minutes talking to you about your zero-tolerance policy," the immediate reaction from you is what's this all about. Waiting for the reporter to arrive in your office is often a very stressful time for any principal. You can conjure up in your mind a hundred different scenarios that fit the telephone discussion and all of them seem to have a terrible outcome for you. The critical element for the principal is preparation. In this situation, knowing all about the zero-tolerance policy and how it functions are the critical attributes of working with the print or electronic media. Hiding behind your office door and refusing to meet with the reporter only makes you look guilty of something that is as benign as discussing the merits of the policy. Avoidance is not the answer, no matter how uncomfortable a principal might feel about meeting the reporter. Loss of public confidence is the end result of a principal who fails to meet the reporter.

As a principal, you may never feel completely at ease around reporters, but meeting with the media is a responsibility that is attached to the job description. Practice makes the experience with reporters much more pleasant and in some cases even tolerable. Prior to ever meeting with any reporter, practice through various scenarios with someone on the faculty or your district's media relations professional. Learn to relax and be yourself and if you absolutely cannot do that then call the superintendent and ask for some help with the situation. Listen to the question from the reporter and answer only the question. Principals get in trouble when they volunteer information that was not part of the questions. Learn to say the right things to the reporter.

Schuman (1998) states that prior to any interview, the principal should keep in mind these four things:

1. Ask for the reporter's name if you do not know or have never dealt with him or her before.
2. Ask what publication or station the reporter represents.
3. Ask about the reporter's topic and deadline.
4. If you are not qualified to address the topic, make sure you stop the conversation. Tell the reporter why you cannot address the issue.

The key to working with any reporter, print or electronic, is making sure the reporter understands and relates to your message. You will want to repeat your message again and again making sure you say the same thing each time. Repeating your message provides the listener with the ideas you want him or her to leave with and it keeps you from providing information that is not being asked. As a principal, your goal is to communicate and garner support for your side of the issue. Getting into a verbal joust with a reporter or intellectual debate generally allows the reporter to focus his or her article or twenty-second television clip on you and not the issue. In most situations where the principal attempts to out smart the reporter, the principal comes off looking rather foolish and condescending. Preparation and practice makes the job of meeting the reporter more comfortable for the principal and the articles created by the reporter are generally more accurate and timely. Anticipate the reporter's questions, step up to the microphone, confidently answer the questions, and you will have turned your fear into an opportunity for your school.

Saying the right thing when talking to reporters is easier when you follow these rules:

- Know you will be asked the who, what, when, why, and how questions. Do not give answers to all of these questions at one time.
- Be honest and always get your positive statements on the record at the beginning of any discussion.
- Listen closely to the question and pause to gather your thoughts before answering.

- Reframe the question when reporters ask leading questions. Avoid answering questions from reporters that begin "Would you say…" and then state an idea for you to react on.
- Always frame your answers in positive terms and never repeat a negative question.
- Avoid one-word responses to reporters. Always view the interview as an opportunity to state your message.
- Talk in sound bites. Short quotable statements that paint a word picture are the work of very experienced principals.
- Repeat your answers and stay on message. When repeating your message, be clear, concise, and likable.
- Anticipate the questions and practice your answers. (Schuman 1998)

No one, especially principals, wants to face reporters when negative news is the topic of discussion. In these situations, the principal must realize that every story will not be positive. In some situations, negative stories about a school's overcrowded conditions can turn out to have a silver lining. It is better to admit the problem exists than to try and cover up the facts. For example, in several states students are required to take grade-level, end-of-course, or exit-level examinations before progressing to the next grade, course, or receive their diploma. On several occasions, teachers and principals have been accused of helping students cheat on the exams. Trying to hide the facts in these situations only causes the public to blame the entire school district rather than the individuals involved. Never talk to a reporter about a negative issue without a plan to solve the problem. Make sure the plan addresses the problem and be prepared to defend your plan. In the cheating situation, the appropriate plan would include making sure the examination materials were secure, teachers proctored students other than their own, and the principal provided examination oversight. Communicate the plan so that everyone can understand the solution to the problem and stay on message.

In delivering negative news to reporters and the public, be prepared to see letters to the editor in the newspaper along with both radio and television segments that embellish the problem. Radio talk shows thrive on other people's problems, so don't be surprised when your school becomes the topic for the day on your local talk radio. Should the principal call the radio station and complain about the discussion? In most cases, it would not be helpful to defend the school on the radio but it might be helpful if the facts were not being accurately portrayed. Calling the station and providing the facts may be the best any principal can hope to do in this situation, but be very careful that you do not violate the privacy of teachers or students while describing the facts. As a school, it would be much better if your school's stakeholders called the radio show and defended the school and their children.

Negative news may generate conflict and some experts would argue that negative news is conflict. As principals engage in interviews with the media about negative news, they must understand that conflict is a process to manage. Conflict in and of itself is neither good nor bad because out of conflict comes solutions to problems. Conflict engages a larger audience thus creating the opportunity for better solutions. If the principal approaches the negative news from this point of view, then negative news soon becomes a direction to a new solution. The end result is in the hands of the principal.

Principals must work to get positive stories about school in print, on the radio, and on television. The single most important aspect of getting the school story told is making sure the information is news worthy. In order to complete the task of getting school stories in the media, it is the principal's responsibility to make sure the media outlets understand why this information is important to readers and viewers. What is news worthy in one community is not in another. For example, in a rural community most newspapers will print any story that the school provides, especially if it is written in final form, while in the larger markets the same story would never be printed. In addition, smaller-market newspapers are more willing to run photos with informational cut lines in order to keep their relationship with the community on firm ground. Knowing the media market will help eliminate story ideas that are nonnews events and reduce the frustration of not getting your story on the air or in the newspaper. Remember, media outlets have slow and busy news days. In most situations, positive school stories are bumped from television, radio, and newspapers for more news worthy stories based on the decisions of producers and editors.

The place for stories that are not marketable to the media could be placed on the school's website. Information of all types is placed on the website and can be changed on a regular basis. This is another means for getting information to all of the school's stakeholders. It is also possible to create an electronic newsletter or school-based publication that provides both students and parents with timely information. Since you control the content of the website, news worthiness is at your discretion. The website also provides the principal with a tool for keeping parents and the community informed about all of the school's activities and problems.

You could use the website to dispel rumors and provide information about specific situations that occurred at school during the day. For example, a student might go home and tell his or her parents that several students had a food fight in the cafeteria during lunch. A wise principal would place the facts concerning the food fight, leaving out specific names, and what he or she planned to do to make sure this did not happen again.

Press releases can be used to tell the school's story for both electronic and print media. This media tool is a strategic way to make sure that communication is understood. The press release should be typed, double spaced, and written in inverted pyramid style. This style of writing places all of the pertinent information in the first paragraph of the release and includes the what, when, where, why, and how for the event or story. In addition, should the editor or producer need to cut the length of the release because of time or space needs, he or she can do so without destroying the important informational aspects of the release. Exhibit 8.1 demonstrates a format that can be used for developing press releases.

PRESS RELEASE   Release Date: **FOR IMMEDIATE RELEASE**
Fort Spirit School District
Bethany High School

TO: Cameron-Bethany Star-Gazette

FROM: Valarie Watson, Principal   Wilma Jones-Johnson English Teacher
                   903-886-5520   903-886-5507
                   Vwatson@fortspiritschools.edu   Wjjones@fortspiritschools.edu

RE: Subject or event

Date: Today's Date

Information should include:

1. Who?
2. What?
3. Where?
4. When?
5. Why
6. How?

-30-
Indicates the end of the story

If you have not answered these questions, you do not have a complete press release.

Exhibit 8.1.   Press Release Format

It is always the best practice to release information in a timely manner. The release date should read "for immediate release," and this is especially important in communities with weekly or biweekly newspapers. Embargoing the release date may provide an advantage for one of the news organizations and that should never be the principal's goal. The information at the top of the release provides the print and electronic media with a contact person for additional information or the selection of a time and date for an interview. At the bottom of the release the number "-30-" indicates that the article has ended.

News conferences should be used sparingly by principals and be attempted by only the most poised and confident individuals. The only reason that a principal would hold a news conference would be to provide information on a breaking story such as student-on-student violence or the need to inform all media simultaneously. A three- to four-hour lead time prior to the news conference should be given to all of the news agencies. In some communities, the local cable television company provides the school with a channel for use during specific times of each day or week and can be used to broadcast news releases to the public. At the beginning of each news conference, provide all reporters with a written copy of your statement. If questions are going to be asked, prepare a list of likely questions and responses to those questions and read your responses. Remember always to stay on message and never provide more information than is requested.

Try to avoid a televised news conference if possible because most principals do not know how to address the camera. If the news conference is to be televised by a local channel or over a cable access channel, always dress appropriately. Avoid white or very light colored blouses and shirts; the best color is light blue. Don't try to be too polished because you may come across as slick. Make sure you avoid repeating hostile questions and don't appear to be defensive. Make sure you build in a cutoff or escape mechanism into an answer so you can end the news conference or plant someone in the audience to provide you with an ending question.

FUND-RAISING, DEVELOPMENT FUNDS, AND GIFTS

In today's educational finance scenario the per pupil cost of educating students is on the rise and the resources are declining. The expectation that tax support alone will provide adequate support for schools may no longer be reasonable given the instability of educational funding (Carlson 1993). A partial answer to this funding problem may be found in the short term by utilizing fund-raising through development foundations that provide a much more stable supply of income. Development funds address long-term projects, are continuous, and evolve from the goals of the school. Development has always been viewed as an activity that colleges and universities use, but, according to a 1990 study more than 1,500 public schools have engaged in this money raising activity (White and Morgan 1990). Most of the time the dollars raised by these development activities were used to supplement school budgets in the areas of personnel retention, student scholarships, and specific programs.

Nonprofit organizations must nurture and build collaboratives with their giving partners rather than just focusing on the money (Savino and Miss 1998). Schools need to position themselves in the development fund environment in order to take advantage of the expected $12 to $18 trillion that baby boomers age thirty-two to fifty will inherit from their parents beginning in the next twenty years. This amounts to about two times the U.S. gross national product and more than fifty times the private savings of U.S. citizens (Savino and Miss 1998). Principals need to reach out and ask people to contribute to schools in ways they have never done before.

Competition for philanthropic dollars is intense and it is essential to have a development fund plan. School excellence and successful students define the direction of the plan, followed closely by showcasing the school's strengths and magnifying student needs. At all times emphasize the advantage these students will gain from use of these dollars. Making the case in human benefit terms is the best way to sell potential donors on the needs you have outlined. If you want a $5 million donation, you must have a plan that will get the school to the target amount (Savino and Miss 1998).

Over the years, fund-raising experts have observed a pattern of donor giving. Using this pattern, it is possible to estimate the size of gifts that will be needed to meet the foundation's revenue goal and the number of donors the foundation should contact. Klein (2001) observes that:

- 60 percent of the school's donated income comes from 10 percent of the donors
- 15 to 25 percent of the school's donated income comes from 20 percent of the donors

• the remaining 15 to 25 percent of the school's donated income comes from 70 percent of the donors.

If Klein is correct, most of the donated income will come from a few donors, but the majority of gifts the school receives will come from small donors. Using Klein's income principle, if the school's revenue goal is $100,000, it will need $60,000 (60 percent of the goal) from major donors, $15,000 to $25,000 (15 percent of the goal) from average donations, and the remaining $15,000 to $25,000 from all of the small donors.

The planning team is the heart and soul of any attempt to establish a development foundation for a school. It requires that team members be selected very carefully and that the team chair or cochairs be community and school leaders. As a principal, you must solicit the help of community leaders in helping determine who should be members of this planning team. Members may include influential business men and women, well-respected teachers, well-known parents, leaders of the parent–teachers association, and others who have special skills that could be used by the team. Team members must be willing donors and support the concept of a development foundation. In addition, they must be willing to call on potential donors just like all of the other volunteers. Potential donors include alumni of the school, current and former teachers staff, corporations, and small community businesses. Typically, more than 80 percent of foundation donations comes from individuals and 20 percent is derived from the business community.

The first step in creating a development foundation is securing permission from the local board of education to undertake such an activity. Have the school district attorney search the education law and school district policies to determine the guidelines that govern fund-raising. It may be necessary to complete official forms in order to hold an event on or off school property. It is also necessary to obtain a tax-exempt number from the Internal Revenue Service and to make sure the school has completed the necessary paperwork to be considered a nonprofit organization, thus allowing donors to deduct their donations as a charitable gift.

The second step in the development foundation process is deciding why the money is being raised. Traditionally, the fund-raising team establishes the reason for the development foundation effort. Schools generally raise money for student scholarships, teacher scholarships, the purchase of specific items, and to support the academic program with additional supplies.

For example, Cameron High School wanted to replace the turf on the competition football field with a synthetic turf at a cost of $1.5 million. It approached the school board about replacing the surface but was denied because the cost was too much and because the school board could not afford to replace the turf at Cameron High School and all of the middle school fields. The district had no development fund prior to this request and at the urging of several members of the Cameron High athletic boosters club the pitch was made to Dr. Tucker to create a development foundation for the single purpose of raising money for synthetic turf. The purpose of any development foundation should be established prior to the implementation of the fund and before money is collected. Dr. Tucker should support the idea of a development foundation but not for the use by special interests.

The next step in creating this fund is the development of a time line, which should include the planning, implementing, and celebration of the project. Creating an organized calendar of events is a must when attempting to raise substantial amounts of money. This organized calendar will help the stakeholders as they call on individuals for donations so that potential donors are not contacted twice. The more detailed the planning the easier it will be to determine the number of volunteers who will be needed to contact potential donors.

Step four in this process is the training of the volunteers who will be contacting the donors. All stakeholders involved in the project need to be trained in telephone etiquette, public speaking, and the purpose for the development fund. It is important that every person involved in the project know all of the details of the project. This requires a thorough and well-constructed process of communication. Two or three special teams should be assigned to contact individuals and businesses for donations in excess of $20,000. The members of these teams will receive training in the process of helping individuals place the school in their wills and management trusts. In addition, donors will be encouraged to donate cash, memorials, insurance, property, and stocks to the foundation.

A face-to-face meeting with potential donors is a frightening event for those volunteers who have never done something like this before. This task is not as ominous as it appears since the potential donor has received a letter or telephone call that a volunteer solicitor will be contacting him or her about a donation. Since the potential donor has agreed to see the volunteer, the solicitor knows the donor has not said "no." The solicitor's job is to move the donor from consideration of giving to "I would very much like to give." This requires the solicitor to be poised, enthusiastic, confident, and prepared to answer any questions the potential donor might ask about the purpose of the foundation and how the donation will be used (Klein 2001).

Each year the development foundation drive should begin with a "kick-off" event that will draw special attention to the project and should receive media coverage, both print and electronic. This event could be a gourmet meal costing $50, $100, or $200 a plate with the profits going to the development fund or the event could be a blind auction were individuals bid on donated products, trips, and memorabilia with the profit deposited in the development foundation. The kick-off event should be something special that does not happen in the community regularly. It is also a time to recognize the planning team members and especially the development chair or cochairs. The purpose of this event is to get all of the volunteers engaged in the process and motivated to go out and make their personal contacts.

The kick-off event is the time to announce the membership of the board of directors. The development fund must have a set of by-laws, generally created with the assistance of an attorney. The members of the board of directors must be separate from the members of the board of education and their function is to direct the operation of the foundation. Traditionally, the principal serves as the executive director of the board of directors and is responsible for all of the budgeting and accounting duties. A chair is selected from the board of directors and this person along with the treasurer of the board have check writing responsibilities. This type of detail is contained in the by-laws.

In creating development foundations, make sure procedures specify how funds are collected, guarded, accounted for, and dispersed. All of these records should be open for public review and be audited yearly. The identity of donors who want anonymity for their contributions should be guarded through development foundation policies. It is clear that students should not be exploited in the process of collecting these funds and they should do so voluntarily and then only if parental consent is gathered in writing. It is the responsibility of the board of education, with recommendations from the school administration, concerning the participation in raising development funds. It is equally important to make sure that development fund donors are not coerced into participation. Make sure the donors are contacted one time only, which requires a coordinated effort by the individuals involved in the fund-raising (Carlson 1993).

The money raised by the foundation must be utilized in the best possible manner. For example, the principal could create a process where teachers develop proposals that enhance classroom instruction. This could be done individually or in teams. A team of teachers could propose to try a new strategy for teaching math facts. One group would try the new strategy and another teacher would continue to use the current method for teaching math facts, the results of both strategies would be assessed to determine which strategy appeared to create the most learning. Providing teachers with the incentive to try a different instructional strategy is a cost benefit for the foundation.

Some individuals are concerned that schools are selling their souls by implementing foundations to generate school revenues. The increased use of selling advertising on school property, school bus advertisement, exclusive contracts with athletic shoe companies, and soft drink manufacturers has caused some individuals to question the entire process of school-generated revenues (Pipho 1997). Some schools have signed contracts between themselves and athletic clothing manufacturers that allow students to purchase athletic clothing at a substantially reduced price. The stakeholders in the community determine the level of revenue that can be generated by this type of activity. It is the school board's responsibility to either approve or disapprove the contracts offered by these requests for advertising and the exclusive use of athletic clothing.

School fund-raising has evolved from the yearly chili supper and candy sale for the benefit of the junior class so it could pay for the junior-senior prom into a major money-raising function. Fund-raising in schools is a big business for the school and for the businesses that provide the various products. In communities where the majority of parents have money, fund-raisers create substantial amounts of money and where the majority of parents do not have extra money to spend on these products and the school's revenue is minimal (Thompson and Wood 1998).

Fund-raising places an additional burden on teachers. They must distribute and logout how much of the product each student was given. As students return with the money from the sale of the product, it is the teacher's responsibility to receipt each student's contribution, count the money, and get a receipt from the school secretary who prepares the school's deposit. In addition, teachers are responsible for obtaining the unsold products and this can be a major consumer of time and energy if students do not cooperate in a timely manner. Neff and Graziano (1998) argue that students would be better served by spending more time on academic pursuits than they do by spending time selling products.

Fund-raising activities almost always impact the parents and other relatives of the students selling the products. In most fund-raising activities, the company that supplies the product gets between 50 and 60 percent of the retail cost of the products sold. For example, a candy bar that sells for $1 generates 40 cents and candles that retail for $4.00 generate $1.60 for the school. Most products sold by schools are not good revenue generators. Soup, spaghetti, bake sales, and chili suppers where most of the ingredients for the food are donated almost always generate a 100 percent profit. School carnivals generate substantial amounts of revenue in communities were the majority of parents have adequate amounts of disposable income.

One of the hottest fund-raisers available for schools today is the sale of scrip. Scrip is the sale of certificates, at a slight discount to the school, which makes its money by reselling them at full value to parents and other school stakeholders. When the parents redeem the scrip for merchandise, the retail outlet provides a discount on each item purchased using scrip. An estimated $600 million to $1 billion in scrip sales allows the purchase of groceries, clothes, household goods, toys, and perhaps even airline tickets (Ellingwood and Hong 2001). At least two companies have gone into the scrip business by buying the certificates at a huge discount and selling them to schools at an increased cost so the school can resell at a higher price and make money as a fund-raiser. Principals who want to use scrip as a fund-raiser need to investigate the rate of return on each certificate sold by students. In some cases, the discount offered by some stores for using the scrip has dwindled to almost zero.

A major concern of school fund-raisers is the need of students to go door-to-door selling the product. Children have been robbed, beaten, and molested as they attempted to sell items the school has asked them to sell. These crimes against children have a long-lasting effect on schools and communities, a pain that never goes away. Some states have banned door-to-door sales by children (Diegmueller 1993). If schools are going to continue to send children door-to-door for the purpose of selling products for cheap prizes, it is the schools' responsibility to provide protection for them. Schools need to create policies that prevent very young children from selling and they need to provide the older students some training about how to remain safe while going door to door. It is also important that schools get media coverage for their fund-raising activities so people in the community know this sale is a school-sponsored activity. In addition, the principal should provide each student with a letter, on school letterhead, announcing what the student is selling and how the money will be used.

Every school needs a procedure to make the fund-raising projects profitable and run smoothly. It is the principal's responsibility to create the procedure and instruct the teachers in the process to be used. The first activity that needs to take place is to determine how many and what type of fund-raisers should be sanctioned. Establish the types of products and events that fit the context of the school. Once the principal, in consultation with teachers, parents, and other community stakeholders, establishes the parameters for what can be sold during the fund-raiser, the several school organizations or grade levels submit proposals to the principal requesting to be placed on the fund-raising calendar. Every principal should construct a fund-raising calendar that displays the organization hosting the fund-raising event and what product is being sold. This calendar should be used to schedule other events such as athletic, music, theater arts, art events, and any other special events. It should be the policy of the principal to not allow more than one fund-raising event during any time frame and no more than two events per month. If you hold to the two-event per month policy, then you could host fourteen fund-raising events by excluding December and May, which are not good months for raising money.

Once all of the fund-raising proposals are presented, the principal must take the time to review each proposal to determine the profit that can be earned, examine the products that are going to be sold, determine the probability that the sale will be successful, and examine which community businesses will suffer because of the fund-raiser. When the principal has reviewed each proposal and determined that the sale of the product meets these criteria, he or she must decide the dates for the fund-raiser. Perhaps some products are time specific, that is, they are only available at certain times of the year. Establishing the calendar makes it possible to spread the fund-raising events across the spectrum of the academic year and it makes sure all of the events have an equal opportunity to have a block time for their sale unimpeded by other school sales. For example, some school organizations sell oranges and grapefruits around Thanksgiving because that's when the product is available while selling magazine subscriptions is not affected by the time of year.

The development and creation of a policy that covers the distribution of a product, the collection of the revenues from sales, and the collection of unsold products must be taught to all of the sponsors who will be working in the fund-raising arena. The more structured this policy is, the fewer the problems. The policy should contain the following:

- A parent-signed fund-raising permission form must be on file for each student participating in the fund-raiser prior to being given any product. The younger the children involved, the more important this document becomes.
- Each sponsor should be instructed to inventory the product before distribution to students.
- Each sponsor should provide receipts to students delineating the number, the dollar value, and the final date for turning in the product or the proceeds from the sale. The student should sign the receipt for the product as an indication that he or she received this product and is expected to return the proceeds from the sale or the product.
- Teachers should be instructed to accept student monies prior to the beginning of the school day only.
- Teachers should not be preoccupied while collecting this money because some student will claim he or she gave the money when he or she did not and the teacher has very little room to prove otherwise.
- Teachers should give each student a receipt for the monies he or she turns in.
- Teachers should be instructed to take this money directly to the school secretary who handles the school's money and they should receive a receipt from the secretary listing the dollar amount submitted. Do not leave this money in a desk or cabinet because you are inviting someone to steal it.
- The fund-raiser sponsors should receive a full account of the dollar amount submitted to the school and the number of products returned. This fund-raising recap should reveal a balance between expected dollar generation and the amount of product received from the wholesaler.

Each year the principal should hold a professional development activity that provides each fund-raising sponsor with the rules and regulations for fund-raising. Almost every practicing principal can relate stories of lost monies through a failure to inventory the product, to keep money secure, and to get students to turn in money from products they were issued. The better the procedures, the more successful the fundraiser will be.

SECURING GRANTS FOR SCHOOL

Since the early 1950s, schools have had the opportunity to secure grants as a form of alternative funding. For many schools securing grant money is seen as a function of higher education or something that the central administration does for the entire district. In a school setting, the principal, or someone who enjoys writing grants, should be provided with the professional development necessary to understand how the grant process works. Schools are familiar with Title I and Title II grants passed through the state to the local school by the federal government. Many state departments of education have opportunities for schools to write grants and in turn get additional revenue for students and teachers.

The first step in grant procurement is developing a school concept about a need that should be met. At this point, the concept should be practical and focused on making the school educationally stronger. Take the concept to faculty members who might have some interest in the concept and discuss with them how this concept could help the students and teachers meet a pressing need. If enough of the faculty believes the concept has merit and it buys-in, then and only then should the principal begin looking for external funding sources.

Locating a funding source is a process of identifying foundations and agencies that historically have funded projects similar to the concept that your school has in mind. Typically, colleges and universities have grant or development offices that can and will usually help find foundations and agencies that fit your concept. If they are unwilling to help you find the proper funding agency, they will point you to some sources that can help you such as the *Chronicle of Higher Education*, the Foundation Center, the Grant Information System, the National Council on Resource Development, and your state education agency.

The sections or parts of any grant proposal may differ from foundation to agency, but the following are features that are found in most grant proposal narratives:

- Statement of the problem
- Review of the literature
- Objectives
- Procedures
- Problem significance
- An evaluation process
- A dissemination process
- Professional qualifications
- Budget (*ERIC Digest* 1981)

The statement of the problem is a description of the concept and a discussion of the school's need for the project. Information about the school provides the background that demonstrates the need for the project. The data from this section can be used for several grant applications of a similar nature and some of the data is useful for all applications. For example, the description of the Fort Spirit School District and South Cameron High School (SCHS) specifically form the background for all grant applications from South Cameron High. The needs of SCHS provide the context for the statement of the problem for a grant proposal.

The review of literature supports the need for the proposal. Finding supporting literature can be time-consuming and often the results of such action fail to discover useful information. One of the first places that investigators should peruse is the Educational Resources Information Center (ERIC) database. The collection of information should provide the investigators with additional sources to support the project. There are several search engines on the Internet that can provide direction for searching the literature on any topic.

Objectives give direction and outline what the project is intended to accomplish. They need to be realistic and achievable and at the same time they must be directly linked to the problem statement. Tied directly to the objectives are the proposal procedures. These procedures include the population being treated and the methodology, and the resulting materials should be discussed in this section of the proposal. These procedures should be so detailed that the methodology cannot be disputed and the results prove that the treatment actually makes a difference. The significance of the problem is the piece of the proposal that describes how the new knowledge created by the treatment adds to the existing knowledge or how it improves the current practice. This section of the narrative emphasizes the importance of the proposal (*ERIC Digest* 1981).

The next section of a typical grant application is the evaluation section. Almost all funding entities require some type of evaluation and it most often requires an external evaluator. The reason for the external evaluation is grounded in finding what is really true about the results generated by the grant. This evaluation should avoid at all costs self-reported data and should include both formative and summative data. In addition, the evaluation process should be described in detail even to the point of naming the external evaluator.

The dissemination section describes how the findings generated by the grant will be distributed to the general population of schools. This dissemination helps describe how other schools might replicate the process and gain similar kinds of student achievement or teacher success depending on the objectives of the proposal. In this dissemination material, a list of professional qualifications for each person participating in the project should be listed. The purpose for this listing is to demonstrate the relevant qualifications of all participants and in addition, this list provides other interested schools with a point of contact should they wish to implement the project.

The final section of any grant is the budget narrative and justification. Most funding agencies specify the budget format and give the investigators directions concerning what they will fund. Mistakes in the budget will eliminate your proposal even if it has substantial merit in all of the other areas. Budget categories that generally appear in a budget format include: personnel costs, benefit costs, equipment costs, office supplies, travel expenses, consultant fees, facility rental and utilities, computer time, publication expense, and indirect costs such as overhead costs (*ERIC Digest* 1981). The overhead costs are those expenses that the school can charge for managing and dispersing the grant dollars and it is typically 48 percent of the personnel costs including fringe benefits. The overhead costs may be negotiated up or down as necessary and in some instances funding agencies will not pay overhead costs. A section in the narrative should justify each item in the budget.

Once the proposal is written, someone outside of the writing team should edit the proposal. The editor searches for inconsistency in the proposal and at the same time attempts to capture one writing style for the proposal. This is necessary when several different writers have contributed pieces to the proposal. After all of the corrections have been made, the proposal is ready for submission to the funding agency. Typically, each funding agency dictates the manner in which the proposal will be transmitted to the agencies' headquarters. Some funding agencies require a letter of transmittal that guarantees that the applicant will fulfill the obligations of the proposal. The superintendent or a designee, generally not the principal, must sign this letter.

Dickinson (1998) interviewed seven experienced grant seekers and developed the following tips for successful grant procurement:

1. Know your own programs.
2. Get to know other grant writers by developing your own network.
3. Get to know the right person at the foundation or agency offering the grant and call that person.
4. Know who will read your proposal and follow the funding agency's guideline.
5. Keep in touch with the funding agency by calling periodically to reinforce the objectives of your proposal.
6. Set ambitious but achievable goals.

Grant procurement is highly competitive and requires an understanding of the grant process, but if successful, it can be extremely beneficial for the school's revenue base. The key to successful grant procurement is the willingness to continue to generate and submit grants when you are not successful. Once you are funded, it is easier to obtain a second and third grant. Many agencies look at what you have done in the past with grant dollars and when you have been successful they may come seeking you.

ETHICAL DECISIONS

Should Students be Allowed to Sell
Products for School Fund-Raisers Door to Door?

Many schools raise money by selling various products door to door every day all across the United States. Generally, the students stay within their own neighborhood calling on relatives and their parents' friends. Principals justify this type of sales by reminding parents that the student is learning the practical aspects of economic theory and business-related concepts of supply and demand. Others motivate students to participate by offering one major prize, such as a bicycle, a boom box, or a television set, and many cheaply constructed minor prizes. Each child, especially those at the elementary school age, believes he or she is going to get the grand prize. In addition, some principals play on the loyalty issue by telling students that they can show their real feelings about the school by selling the product and returning the money to the school for its use. On the other side of the spectrum, are principals willing to send the students door to door with the possibility that they will be robbed, physically assaulted, or molested by older students or other individuals in the community? This is a serious consideration for parents, students, and community stakeholders as they decide how to supplement the school budget. In addition, valuable time is taken out of the instructional day for teachers, not to mention the work teachers must assume in keeping track of money and products.

The questions that need to be answered concerning this issue are:

- Should students engage in fund-raisers that require them to sell products door to door?
- Is the cost-benefit worth the time and effort needed by teachers to collect revenue and dispense products to students?
- What is the principal's responsibility in allowing fund-raisers to be undertaken by students in the school?
- Is the use of prizes for products sold an ethical motivational tool to be used at the discretion of the principal?
- Ethical dilemmas are right-versus-right issues. Which side of the fund-raising debate do you support and why?

CHAPTER SUMMARY

Creating school relationships in the community is more important for today's school than ever in the history of public school education. Principals must work to engage the public in dialogue that will be productive for the school academically. Many principals want parental involvement in the school but not too much involvement. Politicians, policy makers, teachers, and principals all realize education is a front-burner issue that is not likely to shrink from the political limelight any time soon.

The key for engaging parents is the removal of the intimidation factor and it occurs when the principal attempts to accommodate parents by communicating with them in a way all can understand. Principals must remove the fear parents have of school and ground the school in trust, respect, and communication. When principals regard their relationship with parents as a collaborative venture, the school and parents can work together in concert to improve student achievement.

The National PTA has created a set of standards by which the school can measure parent–school relationships. These standards focus on communication, parenting, student achievement, volunteering, parental involvement in school decision making, and collaboration with the community. Each of these standards measures a specific aspect of the relationship and sheds light on what schools need to do to make sure they are parent friendly. The parent–school partnership is vital to the success of students, teachers, and the school in general. Working with parent, family, and community partnerships is very useful, but it is not without its problems. Major concerns include the time teachers must take to work and cooperate with parents, especially when they must perform these activities on their own time and receive no additional salary.

When the reporter puts a microphone in front of the principal and begins asking probing questions, how should the principal react? Being prepared to answer questions about hotly debated topics is an aspect that most principals would like to avoid, but it's not always possible. Knowing what to say when the reporter shows up at your door requires you to be calm and composed. If you know the reporter is coming to talk with you about a sensitive topic, prepare a written statement and stick to the facts you have prepared. Repeat your message over and over until the reporter understands what it is you are saying. Negative news may create conflict but conflict is a process to be managed by you as the principal. Your role in talking to the reporter is to get the school's story in print or on the air.

The school's website can become a valuable window for school-related stories. Information of all types can be placed on the website and can be changed periodically keeping the school stakeholders informed in a very timely manner. This type of information can be used to stop rumors that students pick up at school and take home to parents. Press releases have been the fundamental tool of principals in getting information to print and electronic media outlets. The who, when, why, how, and where information can be written to convince reporters to cover school activities and events.

Foundations form the basis for school development funds. The funds are solicited for use by the school to supplement the school budget. The development of a foundation planning team and a board of directors from outside of the school organizations adds credibility to the process of contacting potential donors and thus receiving donations. The foundation kick-off event should draw attention to the needs of the school and the importance of all stakeholders' participation in generating foundation revenue.

Some individuals deplore the use of foundations and fund-raisers to secure additional school resources because they believe the school is selling its soul by selling advertising on buses, school building roofs, exclusive contracts for athletic gear, and soft drink advertisements on athletic scoreboards, while others disagree as evidenced by the number of advertisements on school property.

Fund-raising affects parents because they usually end up buying most of the products the school is selling. These types of sales are really hidden taxes on parents to help supplement the school's budget. If fund-raisers are to be utilized, then a structured set of procedures must be developed to secure the integrity of the product and the revenue generated. Sponsors of these fund-raisers need to be trained in the procedure to be used every year the school enters into any type of money-raising activity.

The least used strategy for supplementing the school budget is grant procurement. This is a highly competitive process that requires principals to learn a grant-writing format. Using a grant-writing format provides the best opportunity for successful grant procurement. The most important section of any grant is the budget narrative and justification. Most funding agencies specify the budget format and give the grant writer specific directions about what will be funded. Mistakes on the budget narrative will eliminate your proposal even if it has substantial merit. Securing the initial grant may be difficult but once that happens grants tend to get easier to procure.

CHAPTER ACTIVITIES AND QUESTIONS

1. List three strategies that a principal could use to create a positive relationship with parents.
2. Develop a problem topic and structure an open forum for your school to decide how to solve the problem.
3. Take the National PTA standards and measure your school against those standards to see how well you treat your school's parents.
4. Write a press release and get it published by your local media outlet.
5. Set up an interview with a reporter and use the strategies outlined in the chapter to get your message understood.
6. Create an artificial foundation for your school and market it to the school community for further action.
7. Create a fund-raising calendar for your school and implement a fund-raising procedure for the sponsors.
8. Create a grant-writing team on your campus and develop a grant that meets the needs of the school.

CASE STUDY ACTIVITIES AND QUESTIONS

1. Write the introductory paragraph that you would use in trying to convince Drs. Tucker and Walls that your school deserved additional budgeted resources.
2. In outline form, write what you would tell the teachers as they brainstormed ways of raising the money they needed for the building.
3. Write the introduction that you would use to make your case for fund-raising at the breakfast to brainstorm fund-raising activities.
4. Suggest other avenues that Ms. Watson might use in searching for additional resources for South Cameron High School.

5. Write what you would tell parents when a group comes to your office wanting to lobby the superintendent and board of education on behalf of South Cameron High School.
6. If you were sitting in Ms. Watson's chair, would you be willing to create a foundation and if so how would you attain that goal?

REFERENCES

Black, S. (1998). "Parent support." *The American School Board Journal* 185 (4): 50–53.

Bradley, A. (1998). "Public engagement said to hold promise for schools." *Education Week*, 25 March, 10.

Bulach, C., and Potter, L. (2000). "How to host a successful open house." *Principal Leadership*, 81–82.

Carlson, R. (1993). "Developing supplemental funding: Initiatives for rural and small schools." ERIC Clearinghouse on Rural Education and Small Schools (ERIC Document Reproduction Services no. ED 357 910).

Danzberger, J., and Friedman, W. (1997). "Public conversations about public schools: The public agenda/institute for educational leadership town meeting project." *Phi Delta Kappan* 78 (10): 744–748.

Dickinson, M. (1998). "The secrets of their success." At www.tgci.com/publications/98fall/secrettosuccess.html (accessed February 6, 2001).

Diegmueller, K. (1993). "N.Y. to consider ban on charitable fund-raising in schools." At www.edweek.org (accessed February 6, 2001).

Ellingwood, K., and Hong, P. Y. (2001). "Scrambling for scrip." At www.tgci.com (accessed February 6, 2001).

Epstein, J. L. (1995). "School/family/community partnerships: Caring for the children we share." *Phi Delta Kappan* 76 (9): 701–712.

ERIC Digest. (1981). "Proposal writing for two-year colleges." ERIC fact sheet, no. 2 (ERIC Document Reproduction Services no. ED 353 004), at www.ed.gov (accessed February 8, 2001).

Funkhouser, J. E., and Gonzales, M. R. (1997). "Family involvement in children's education: Successful local approaches." At www.ed.gov/pubs/FamInvolve/ (accessed February 8, 2001).

Hara, S. R., and Burke, D. J. (1998). "Parent involvement: The key to improved student achievement." *The School Community Journal* 8 (2): 9–19.

Hopkins, B. J., and Wendel, F. C. (1997). *Creating school-community-business partnerships*. Bloomington, IN: Phi Delta Kappan Educational Foundation.

Houston, P., and Bryant, A. (1997). "The roles of superintendents and school boards in engaging the public with the public schools." *Phi Delta Kappan* 78 (10): 756–759.

Klein, K. (2001). "Getting major gifts. TGI fundraising." At www.tgci.com (accessed February 10, 2001).

Nathan, J. and Radcliffe, B. (1994). *It's apparent: We can and should have more parent/educator partnerships.* Minneapolis: University of Minnesota, Humphrey Institute of Public Affairs, Center for School Change.

National PTA. (2001). "National standards for parent/family involvement programs." At www.pta.org (accessed February 7, 2001).

Neff, M., and Graziano, C. (1998). "Debate: Has student fundraising gone too far?" *NEA Today* 16 (6): 43.

North Central Regional Educational Laboratory. (2001). "Critical school partnerships with families and community groups." At www.ncrel.org (accessed April 10, 2001).

Patrikakou, E. N., and Weissberg, R. P. (1999). "The seven Ps of school–family partnerships." *Education Week*, 3 February, 21.

Pipho, C. (1997). "The selling of public education." *Phi Delta Kappan* 79 (2): 101–102.

Savino, G. H., and Miss, R. E. (1998). "Fundraising." *Momentum* 29 (4): 43–46.

Schuman, P. (1998). "Say the right thing: Winning strategies for talking to the press." *School Library Journal* 44 (9): 110–112.

Thompson, D., and Wood, R. (1998). *Money and schools: A handbook for practitioners.* Larchmont, NY: Eye on Education.

White, G., and Morgan, N. (1990). "Education foundations: The catalyst that mixes corporation and community to support the schools." *School Administrator* 74 (4): 22–24.

Chapter Nine

Principal As Director of Marketing

Dr. J. B. Tucker, superintendent of the Fort Spirit School District, created a unique approach for the delivery of talented and gifted (TAG) services for the intermediate school students in the district. Dr. Tucker had recommended to the board of education a TAG program that resembled a magnet school concept. This program would require that all students eligible and wanting to participate in the TAG program to attend Waldorf Intermediate School. The board of education approved this recommendation by a vote of four to three. Dr. Tucker knew there was not overwhelming support for his TAG idea but he thought it was worth pursuing. He was more concerned about the reaction of the Parents of TAG (PTAG) group that had formed during the past two years than he was about the lack of board support. The PTAG group had lobbied the board of education and Dr. Tucker, and had made a presentation at parent–teachers organization (PTO) meetings throughout the district. This group had pressured Dr. Tucker into doing something to change the instructional landscape for TAG students.

Dr. Tucker approached Principal Micah Maldanado concerning the implementation of the TAG program on the Waldorf campus. After several meetings to discuss the magnet school concept, Principal Maldanado held a faculty meeting to discuss the superintendent's recommendation. The faculty, almost to a person, rejected the idea of a TAG magnet school at the intermediate level. They armed Mr. Maldanado with several reasons for their nonsupport and he set up a meeting with Dr. Tucker to explain the faculty's feelings about the TAG concept. Principal Maldanado explained the reasons for nonsupport to Dr. Tucker and he listened intently. Dr. Tucker very quickly told Mr. Maldanado that he wanted this program, he wanted the program to work, and nothing the teachers said was going to change his mind concerning the implementation of this program. Dr. Tucker went on to tell Mr. Maldanado that he had personally selected Waldorf Intermediate as the sight for this project because he knew Mr. Maldanado would make it successful. Dr. Tucker promised financial support to help get the program started would provide stipends for professional development in TAG education. In addition, Dr. Tucker indicated that he would contract with consultants to help flesh out the magnet TAG concept. He indicated he knew someone at the regional university who could provide structure for this new program. Mr. Maldanado tried to convince Dr. Tucker that several of the other schools were better suited to undertake this project, but Dr. Tucker finally told Mr. Maldanado: "It's yours to create, develop, and make successful, call me if you need further direction."

As Principal Maldanado drove back to his school, he wondered how he was going to explain to the faculty what had just occurred in the superintendent's office. Most faculty would assume he had been in on the plan from the beginning, others would simply believe he had given in to the superintendent, after all that's what normally happens when the superintendent wants something. A few teachers would support what was about to occur and he thought how he might use that small cadre of teachers to operationalize this TAG concept. He also thought about how his colleague principals would react to the creaming effect of students, that is taking the best and brightest from the four other intermediate schools. How was he going to work with the PTAG group and what reaction would he get from parents of non-TAG students? As Mr. Maldanado pictured this new instructional program located in his school, he wondered how he was going to convince his teachers, his colleague principals, and parents on this TAG concept.

"It seems that everyone has to sell themselves these days and schools are no exception" (Wood 1997, 1). In the world of advertisement and marketing, fantastic places provide the viewer with an escape to a make-believe place faraway from reality and the daily angst of life. This tried and true marketing message works in the business world but the education product is not well presented through fantasy. Customer selections about schooling are grounded in their own needs and the needs of their family. Consumerism, the economic environment, community concerns, and competition for educational resources require schools to think about marketing themselves (Wood 1997).

Principals have always been concerned with the public image of their school. The image of most schools is developed through traditions, community gossip, and in some cases print and electronic media are major players in creating this image. In high schools, the activity program drives the school's image. Such activities as athletics, music, art shows, and student theater productions form the image for schools. Middle and elementary school images are created by PTOs and community gossip. The common thread that winds its way through the school image are school patrons verbally discussing the events occurring in the neighborhood school. The principal is the keeper of school traditions and the person most responsible for the school's community image.

As a principal, you may ask: Why is it important to know what the school's image is? That question has many answers and understanding how students, parents, former students, and community members view your school is key to the school's image. Principals must recognize that in today's educational atmosphere charter schools, vouchers, and competition from private education are a real possibility. Even if you assume that other forms of educational delivery are highly remote it seems prudent that marketing the school is a healthy strategy to pursue. If you were the principal of one of the other intermediate schools in the Fort Spirit School District, you should be concerned that all of your best students would be attending Waldorf. Most principals would not take creaming their school lightly. With all of the negative comments concerning schools coming from state and national policy makers, it is imperative that principals become the directors of marketing and customer service for the school.

The *U.S. News and World Report* ("Research reveals" 1999) states that outstanding schools are known by their differences and not by their similarities. It is the responsibility of the campus principal to make sure that his or her school is different than all other schools. It is imperative that schools market:

- High academic standards
- A curriculum that prepares students for college
- Has a strong mentoring program for new teachers
- Develops school–business partnerships
- Reports student attendance rates that indicate students are excited about learning

If the principal will focus on these five aspects, the school's image will improve quickly. These activities are not beyond the reach of any school and not pursuing excellence from these points of view should require the removal of the principal.

WHY MARKET YOUR CAMPUS

The most compelling reason for marketing schools is the reality that competition for students in a climate of high-stakes testing already exists. Schools must be more responsive to the community, parents, business, and to the students themselves. Stokes (1997) states that the purpose of marketing is to create, sustain, and develop customer relationships so that the targets of both groups are met. This concept moves the marketing strategies away from the hard-hitting competitive environment to one of nurturing relationships, especially with existing customers. This marketing strategy is certainly more in line with educators who welcome partnerships with parent customers. Marketing provides a mechanism for identifying the needs of all constituent stakeholders and it helps identify quality services that help satisfy stakeholders over time. Principals need to understand that it costs five times more to get a new customer than it does to maintain a current customer; so keeping your customers satisfied saves resources and improves the image of the school (Wyatt 1999). The goal of each principal assuming the role of director of marketing and customer service is matching the needs of students with the school's curriculum.

Principals can assess the relative strengths of their school in relation to customer service by answering the question: Does your school have a customer service focus? Schools that lack a customer service focus fail to seek the opinions of customers; the faculty and staff force their perception of what works on the customers, and teachers never go beyond minimum service to the customer. Customer-focused schools describe their school in terms of benefits to students, customer needs, complaints taken seriously, and long-term relationships cultivated with all school groups (Vining 2000c). Before principals begin to consider marketing their school, they need to assess the type of school they currently possess.

Marketing schools is a relevant and viable school management strategy and is concerned with people and how they can be persuaded to join the school in reaching its goals. It is about building relationships and using good communication. The essential element in marketing schools is learning to communicate with customers in simple language (Vining 2000c). Principals need to market their schools because there is:

- More uncertainty in the school environment
- More competition
- More deregulation of local and state policy
- More accountability
- Parents view schooling as an investment in their child
- The need for active responsiveness by the school

The school environment is cluttered with uncertainty about the future of vouchers, charter schools, home schooling, and entry into the market of private education. Uncertainty also exists in reference to the number and quality of teachers available for each school. Market forces have played a major role in the quantity and quality of teachers. The more robust the economic picture, the more likely it is that fewer individuals will enter the teaching profession. Teachers are not the only group that is in demand, fewer and fewer individuals are lining up to become building principals. Schools that were attracting fifty to sixty applicants for their principal positions now attract eight to ten and many of these individuals are not qualified to provide leadership.

Competition for quality teachers always has been keen, but competition for certified teachers of any quality is foremost in the minds of many principals. Finding certified teachers is a twelve-month task for most school districts as they go about the process of meeting their personnel needs. Competition is not only in the form of salary and benefits, but also surfaces in the form of facilities and program budgets. Quality teachers can demand program budgets that provide trips for students, instructional technology, and specific equipment. In the past, teachers had very little influence over the program budgets but this is not the case in today's teacher shortage environment. Competition for principals is just as keen as it is for teachers and in some cases principals are able to demand six-figure salaries, bonus programs, annuity packages, and in-district, in-state, and out-of-state travel allowances. Never before has the competition for principals been as ferocious as it has been in the past five years. Teachers and principals are definitely in a seller's market.

Charter schools have created a plethora of deregulation demands by parents as they become more involved in their child's education. Deregulation comes in many forms but the most common form is in noncompliance with state and local requirements. Schools no longer have to meet the strict interpretation of state financial codes, graduation requirements, course requirements, minutes per course, and a whole host of other policy or legal requirements. In most states, the only requirement that must be met is the high-stakes testing for graduation, that is, all students must pass the state's exit-level test.

More accountability is on the horizon as states continue to adopt high-stakes testing programs that require an exit-level examination in order to graduate from high school. In some states, promotion from one grade to the next requires passing an accountability examination. Failure to meet the accountability standards will cause the student to be retained at his or her current grade level. As the accountability examinations become more sophisticated, the probability that more students will fail these assessments increases. At some point in the future, high-stakes testing will reach the point where fewer than 50 percent of the students will be successful on the initial testing.

Principals have the opportunity to market their schools everyday to parents as they come and go from the school site. This untapped market opportunity must be recognized as an opportunity that cannot be wasted, nor should it be. Today's parents are more likely to become involved with the school in a negative way because most parents are not active participants in their child's education. Principals must seize the opportunity to create positive parent contacts and do so on a regular basis. These contacts must go beyond the PTO meetings, activity events, and back to school nights. They must include opportunities to dialogue with parents about their child's education in an atmosphere of mutual trust. Most schools fail to involve parents in constructive learning environments and thus the hostility surfaces when parents are called to school because their child has made some wrong choices. Parents are one of the down stream customers of the school while students are the customers of the school.

The function of any organization, schools included, is to satisfy the needs and wants of the customer, in this case the students and parents. The entire premise behind marketing is that the customer is of the utmost importance to the organization. It is mandatory that the organization understands its customers and sees things from their point of view. In the past, schools have viewed their role as keepers of knowledge and purveyors of information. The flow of information in the school organization is from the top down as depicted in figure 9.1.

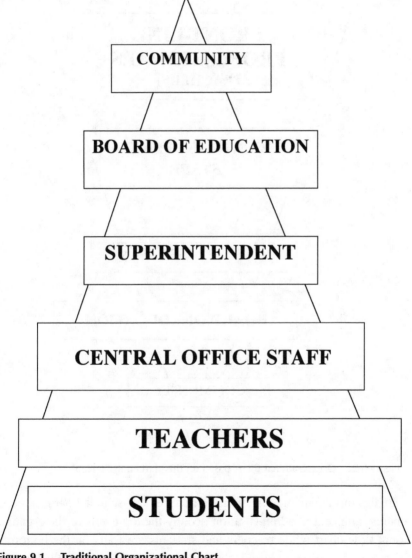

Figure 9.1.   Traditional Organizational Chart

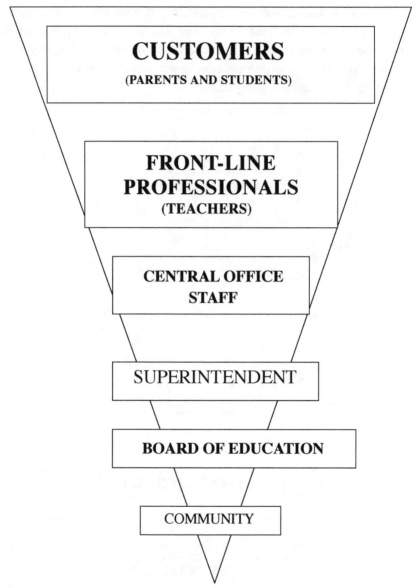

Figure 9.2. Organizational Chart Based on the Marketing Concept

In the top-down organizational structure, the school board, superintendent, and central administration occupy the top levels of the organizational flow chart while teachers and students are found at the bottom of the pyramid. This model sends the message that students are the least important players in the education organization. While some would argue that the organizational chart does not depict how students are viewed, the reality of this chart is its accuracy. Almost everything emanates from the board of education through the superintendent to the building level. Curriculum, professional development, policy, financial resources, human resources, and almost anything else one might consider has its beginning at the very top of the organization.

If the customers were central to the organization, the chart would look very different. Rotate the chart 180 degrees and the customers are at the top of the organizational chart. The organizational chart based on this marketing concept places the focus on students and all the energies of the organization are directed at teaching and learning. The board of education, superintendent, and central administration support the teachers and students by providing the financial resources necessary for the best education possible.

Figure 9.2 provides evidence that placing the students at the top of the organizational chart leads to a much better use of human and financial capital. The central administration staff instructionally supports teachers and provides them with what they need and desire, not what the central staff deems to be important. If this model were used by school districts, building-level principals would be the most important administrators in the school district. Teachers and administrators become the conduit for student learning with little interference from the superintendent, central administrative staff, and the board of education. The organizational chart based on this marketing concept is central to the theme of students first.

A STRATEGIC MARKETING PLAN FOR YOUR SCHOOL

Marketing your school requires that you as the principal make sure you match the curriculum offerings with the student needs. How the principal undertakes this matching process depends on what the school wants to accomplish. The first step in any marketing plan is to assess the economic, social, political, and technological forces that play a role in determining what a principal would use in creating a marketing plan for his or her school. The economic forces that affect schools are directly tied to the financial structure of the state and district in which the school is located.

District wealth and the state legislature have the greatest impact on schools. Social forces affect the curriculum and in some instances the instruction by lobbying board of education members, superintendents, teachers, and principals to accept their point of view. In some cases, these lobbyists use extreme measures to accomplish their goals, including personal and professional attacks. Political forces arrive at the principal's doorstep in the form of pressure to perform a specific task. Most of this pressure comes from board members and central administration staffers who accede to the wishes and desires of political wonks. Technological forces generally appear in the form of requests from parents and in some instances from other constituents who view themselves as technology experts. These individuals may or may not have the knowledge or understanding of the technology needs of the school but they continue to voice their opinions on the topic in a loud voice.

Assessing the economic, social, political, and technological forces in your community will require time and energy, but it is important to understand what people who fall into these categories want to happen in the school. The purpose of this assessment is not about creating strategies to counteract these forces; rather, it is about knowing what people want and need for their children. The data that this assessment provides is essential to matching the needs of the customer with the needs of the organization, in this instance the school. As a principal, how you go about creating this match is the essence of marketing the school.

The matching process that appears in figure 9.3 gives dimension to the concept that school offerings must meet student needs. Matching student needs with school offerings is not always an easy task. The forces mentioned earlier impact what schools are able to offer students. For example, research indicates that there is a real need for sex and sexuality education in most schools of this nation, but political and social forces have demanded that this curriculum be removed or altered. The need may exist but forces outside of the school have poisoned the environment to the point that principals fear for their jobs and in some instances their safety if they do match the needs of students with school offerings. The opposite often occurs, and principals are required by technological forces to implement programs that they neither have the money or the expertise to put into practice. This type of implementation usually ends in failure for both the program and the school. The school offerings and student needs are

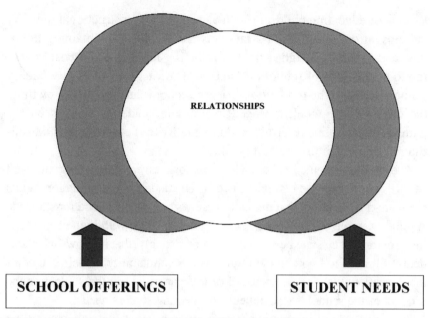

RELATIONSHIPS

| SCHOOL OFFERINGS | STUDENT NEEDS |

Figure 9.3. Marketing as a Process of Building Relationships

brought together through the development of interpersonal relationships. The development of these relationships allows the school to match student needs with a student-driven curriculum.

The second step in this marketing plan determines the market orientation that benefits the school context. This market orientation specifically identifies what line of attack the school has taken in order to communicate its purpose to parents, students, teachers, the superintendent, the board of education, and the community. Hamblin (1999) states that schools fall into four orientation types:

- Production orientation
- Product orientation
- Selling orientation
- Market orientation

Production-oriented schools focus on the idea that their most significant job is to create and deliver educational programs and services as effectively as possible. These schools concentrate on the organizational aspects of educating children, such as scheduling, instructional delivery systems, strong discipline for students and teachers, maintaining facilities, and "running a tight ship." "Producing learners at all cost" is the motto of this type of school orientation. The vast majority of secondary schools appear to be production-oriented schools and are driven by time; the direct-teach model; the need to measure academic success by the number of discipline referrals; and the quality of the heat, light, and ventilation rather than by student need.

The product-oriented school views its task as providing programs and services at the expense of student needs. The underlying assumption in this orientation is the belief that the school knows best what is good for students. A good example of this orientation is found in states with high-stakes testing programs. The state believes, rightly or wrongly, that it knows what students will need to know in the future. The accountability models that color the educational landscape focus all of their attention on the student as the product of the school, at the expense of meeting student needs.

The third school orientation puts forward a belief that schools will be successful if they sell the programs they offer. This orientation focuses on the role as the provider of stimuli in attracting students and parents to existing programs and services. Attracting students to the existing program requires the principal to make a case of why the program meets the needs of students. Selling students and parents is what most schools attempt to do. They focus on what they have to offer, never once attempting to match programmatically what they have with what the students need. In most cases, these types of schools do not know what the students need because they never have asked the customer, the student and his or her parents.

Schools that use the market orientation strategy to create a successful school espouse the belief that the major task of any educational organization is to determine the needs and wants of its students. The implementation of this strategy is to satisfy the customer through the design, consultation, and delivery of desired programs and services. How often have principals and teachers consulted the students to determine what students think they need to be successful in a fluid economic environment? Most teachers and principals would say that students don't know what they need and the bigger question is: Do teachers and principals know what students will need five, ten, fifteen, or twenty years in the future? The answer most assuredly is no, they do not know what students will need in the future, except to say they must know how to learn. Marketing the school requires the principal to consult with the various constituencies to find out what the students need and parents want for their children. This step in the marketing approach is to implement what students need.

The third step in the marketing plan suggests that being customer centered is a very important function. Putting the customer first is vital to any marketing strategy. Principals must remember that students and parents are the customers for the programs and service is what the school offers. Building relationships with various individuals and groups is the cornerstone concept in this step of the marketing plan. Developing relationships requires that principals use the promise concept (Calonius 1988), which includes making promises to customers, thus persuading them to become an active supporter. If the school fails to keep its promises, the customers will become negative talkers in the community and all of the trust relationships will vanish. Relationship marketing forces the school to develop relationships with parents and to focus on the internal segments of the market rather than the external market forces. Failure to develop relationships causes the principal to use anecdotal data to determine school direction, a fundamental mistake many principals make in determining what the school should do to meet the needs of students. The second fatal flaw made by most principals as they assess the needs of students is the assumption that communication is the only marketing tool necessary to be successful in getting the school's story out to the customers.

Principals need to understand and be able to use basic marketing research tools in gathering data concerning the needs and wants of the school customers. Selecting the market research tool, the fourth step in this process, requires that the collection of data can be done in several different ways. Market surveys are one example of a strategy that principals might use in discovering what the customer needs. If the results of this survey are to be used to make decisions about the direction and focus of the school, then it is important to structure the survey so that the answers to the survey provide useful data. It is also important to use appropriate statistical sampling techniques if you plan to generalize the results to the entire school community. Written and telephone surveys can be useful tools if they are done correctly. Focus groups can provide a great deal of data if they are structured appropriately. The first time a principal uses the focus group as a data gathering tool, it might be useful to hire a consultant to structure the activity. Training individuals from the faculty to facilitate focus groups might be very useful in carrying out future focus group activities.

Once the data has been collected, it must be analyzed and conclusions must be drawn. A basic understanding of descriptive statistics might be useful for the principal as the data is analyzed. At this point, step five in the marketing plan for principals is correctly interpreting the data. Make sure the data says what you say it says, because if you misinterpret the information you will be pursuing wrong student needs. After making sure the data has been analyzed correctly, it is time to draw some conclusions. From these conclusions the principal will make decisions about programs and services for the customer.

This marketing plan should answer the following questions.

- Who are the school's customers?
- What do the school's customers want?
- What do the customers value?
- How can the school satisfy its customers and give them what they want?

COMMUNICATION IS THE PRINCIPAL'S LIFELINE

Every school has repute, positive or negative. Every day students, parents, teachers, and staff talk amongst themselves or in the community and that talk is either eroding or building your school image. The more negative the communication in any organization, the wider the audience appeal. As principal, you can attempt to stop the negative talk but more likely than not you will be unsuccessful. The best you can hope to accomplish is to exploit the positive talk about your school. Remind teachers continuously that they are influential members of the community and what they say is taken as the absolute truth. Provide faculty and staff members with positive talking points that need to be shared with community groups. Make sure faculty and staff understand that it is a mortal sin to speak negatively about the school or any of its personnel.

Negative talk not only hurts the school, but in some instances it also damages individuals for the duration of their professional careers. The unfortunate thing about negative talk is it usually begins inside the school and then moves to the community. Negative faculty talk has a powerful influence on parents, students, community members, and other faculty members because it affects the morale and motivation of the faculty and staff.

Vining (2000b) suggests that different types of talk occur in relation to school. She outlines seven types of talk that affect schools:

1. Formal talk—supports the party line and is a powerful voice in creating people's perceptions.
2. Newsletter talk—informs the community about the school. The voice of the newsletter writing is the key to a successful newsletter. Be careful not to use the authoritarian voice in this document.
3. Selling talk—informs the community in the form of brochures, reports, and white papers. These documents project the school's image and should be done in a professional manner.
4. Media talk—is written in a journalistic form and can be very effective if produced on a regular basis.
5. Letter talk—is personal in nature and your writing says a great deal about who you are.
6. Memo talk—internal communication, usually for staff information. Negative talk from the principal can be interpreted in the worst possible way and it usually is interpreted in just that way.
7. Grapevine talk—the informal talk that flows throughout the school from one person to another. As this talk moves from person to person, it is defined by the communication that occurs.

The principal's role requires him or her to talk and communicate with different groups on a daily basis. Positive talk from the principal is the key to making sure communication does occur and all constituent groups feel good about the school. Take advantage of the seven talk types by utilizing them to market your school.

Communication always seems to surface as the reason the program worked or the lack of communication is given as the reason the program failed. Communication by its very nature requires that a message is sent and a message is received. The sender's message must convey the meaning the sender wanted the receiver to understand and in many situations the sender's message does not have the same meaning for the receiver as was intended by the sender. If the sender's message is clear and concise, and it says what it is meant to say, the receiver interprets the message according to his or her experiences and understandings. Verbal messages are more likely to convey the proper meaning to all participants in the communication process because questions can be asked for clarification and misunderstandings can be corrected. Verbal communication is mostly two-way communication. Written communication, which is one-way communication, is much more complex and requires all parties to place meaning on words. Individuals attach different meaning to words and written communication exploits these meanings into misunderstandings and the lack of communication.

Marketing communication requires an outside-in communication process. As a principal, you will want your customer's feedback on the needs and wants. The best way to get customer feedback is to let the customer know that you are really interested in what he or she has to say and you value what he or she thinks. Get customer feedback at least two times per year asking such questions as:

- What do you believe our school does exceptionally well?
- Where would you like to see our school improve?
- Are there any programs or services the school should offer?
- By what means would you prefer we communicate with you? (Marketing Ink 1999)

The most important aspect of marketing communication feedback is what is done with the results of the outside-in communication. You must adapt the school's programs and services to fit the customer's needs and if you fail to do that, why communicate? The more you use the data from the outside-in communication, the better the relationship with the customers.

Your marketing communications plan should include comments from satisfied customers, both students and parents, concerning the programs and services offered by the school. Emphasize the unique qualities of your school by focusing on examples of outstanding student and teacher work. Make sure all of your customers know the benefits your current customers value in the school. Provide customers with steady, but carefully selected information about the changes you have made in the school's programs and services based on what they said and needed. Communicate to the customers what you have accomplished, show them what you have accomplished, and then tell them what you told them.

Internal communication is directed toward students, teachers, and staff. This communication takes the form of newsletters, channel-one television news, daily school bulletins, intercom announcements, faculty meetings, and face-to-face conversations with school personnel. The daily school bulletin is perhaps the least read of all internal communications, because teachers fail to read it to students and teachers are so used to seeing the document they don't even bother to read it. Intercom and channel-one announcements provide a better atmosphere for communication than do daily bulletins but not a great deal more. Teachers use announcement time for a variety of things, but listening is not one of them. Faculty meetings have the potential for internal communication as long as they are not held on a regular basis. Even when faculty meetings are held once every six weeks some teachers spend the time grading papers, drawing basketball plays, or dropping peanuts into their Big Red soda to see if it fizzes. The most useful internal communication strategy is the face-to-face conversation where both parties are involved in trying to understand what the other person is saying. Most principals would find it impossible to have face-to-face conversations with all of their faculty members regularly. Internal communication increases in small groups and a strategy that provides small-group interaction can take place during each teacher's conference period or by utilizing department or grade-level meetings. Principals need to discover what works best internally for themselves and for their faculty.

An internal staff newsletter can be a big boost to morale and internal communication. Perhaps the best way to get the staff to read the newsletter is to have them involved in writing articles, answering staff questions, or creating school trivia contests. The following ideas need to be considered when creating an internal newsletter:

- Make sure the newsletter includes articles by nonadministrators from all areas of the school
- Make sure the school's controversial topics are covered from opposing points of view
- Create contests for the staff that will reward winners with such things as lunch tickets, sports tickets, special parking areas, and so on
- Continuously request feedback from the staff concerning the value of the newsletter

- Make sure the newsletter is published on a consistent basis, monthly, bi-monthly, or quarterly (Marketing Ink 1999)

Newsletters, if they are effective, help prevent rumors and tails of rumors. One of the most damaging aspects of any school organization are the rumors that emanate from the staff. Principals can address those rumors with communication that clarifies the situation.

Communicating with parent customers and other school communities is a much more difficult task than communicating with internal populations. The difficulty with getting information to external populations evolves into no information for this group. While keeping the staff informed is important, informing the external populations is vital to marketing the school. As the principal creates the marketing plan for the external audiences, he or she should consider the following:

- Who are the school's current customer groups: parents, businesses, state and local government agencies, community members, and/or institutions of higher education?
- Define these groups and their needs.
- What avenues do the customers have for communicating with the school?
- What electronic and print media are these customers exposed to?
- What are the school's customer demographics for age, income level, and their personal interests? (Marketing Ink 1999)

Communicating with external customers is not an easy task and it can be a financially costly operation. Some schools use the newsletter concept to inform all district constituents by utilizing bulk mail stamps, some send the newsletter home with students; some put them in the local newspapers as fliers, and some place the newsletters in strategic community locations. Regardless of how the newsletter is distributed, information impact is limited to those who choose to read the communication.

The PTA is a logical venue for communicating with selected customers. The major problem with this venue is, in most instances, the limited numbers of customers who have an opportunity to receive the communication. PTOs lose influence and membership the further one travels up the educational ladder. Still, the PTA can be a beneficial conduit for helping the principal market the school to other customer groups and should be culti-vated as such.

Making presentations at local service clubs and organizations is a strat-egy that places the school in contact with members of the business com-munity. These business customers can be very useful in helping the prin-cipal to communicate with business employees and in some instances they have provided help in creating marketing plans for the school. School–business partnerships have become a much needed source of fi-nancial support for many schools. Other business-related opportunities in-clude displays, school fairs, or continuous loop video presentations housed in shopping malls or town centers.

Technology has changed the face of external communication through the availability of home computers and access to the Internet. Most school districts have their own local area network or are attached to a service provider that supports the district's web page. Principals can communicate and market their school by creating a Web page for the school to post in-formation and receive feedback from its customers. Creating list serves of all customers in the school's catchment area provides the marketing prin-cipal with instant access to many customers. Parental list serves allow the principal to diffuse rumors, provide kudos, and get parent customers in-formation in a timely manner. E-mail provides for a two-way communi-cation between the school and its customers, something that has never been possible except in face-to-face settings. For the principal interested in marketing the school, many positive aspects come from technology but there is a negative side to instantaneous communication. Some customers expect instantaneous replies to their communication and when they do not get them they become angry. Teachers communicating with parents via e-mail should make sure that the parent understands that the teacher will an-swer e-mail communication once a day at a specific time and at no other time during the instructional day.

Complaining customers damage the image of the school and some parents delight in making the school responsible for their child's failure academically or behaviorally. Instead of complaining to the principal about the situation, they voice their concerns in the sphere of public opinion. Market research provides the statistic that 96 percent of cus-tomers never complain to the service provider, but each discontented customer tells six other people about their concern (Vining 2000a). Many of the complaining customers fail to communicate their concerns because they feel nothing will come of the complaint, school personnel get overly defensive, they don't understand the process for making a complaint, or they have memories from their own school days that frighten them (Vining 2000a). Encouraging customers to bring their complaints to you provides you with information that you can get from no other source. Many principals, fearing they will be overwhelmed, avoid encouraging complaints. If you view complaints as a form of communication, you would soon discover that your customers are talking to you and not to everyone else about their problems.

Principals need to develop strategies for handling these complaints and the first strategy is the skill of listening. Most school personnel fail to listen when others talk and as a principal this can escalate the complaint. Listen without interrupting and don't argue, get defensive, or use fighting words. Second, express empathy for the person's plight and attempt to help them solve their concern. Empathy does not mean you are agreeing, but it does mean you are attempting to understand. Third, explain what you can do for the customer, rather than what you can't do. Focusing the conversation on what you can do helps the customer solve his or her problem or in some instances saves face with his or her child. Fourth, thank the customer for bringing this problem into your sphere of influence (Vining 2000a). Make sure the costumer leaves the school feeling like he or she can come back again should the situation warrant such action.

SCHOOL IMAGE ASSESSMENT

As principals contemplate the image of their schools, some may say, "Who cares what people in the community think about the school." Understanding how your school is perceived by students, parents, alumni, colleagues, and other school personnel is important in the marketing and retention of students. Maintaining and attracting the type of students you desire does not happen by chance. In many districts, students have the opportunity to attend any school in the district that is appropriate for their age and grade level. It is important to match student needs with school strengths, because better matches create optimum student and parent satisfaction (Topor 1998). Perceptions provide the context for the school's curriculum development, faculty recruitment, and parental support. Determining what customers think about your organization is another reason for conducting image studies. Image is a powerful tool when used wisely. Topor (1998) argues that the school's actual worth is not as important as is the perceived quality, which in reality, influences parents, students, and the community. At a broader level, image marketing includes a culture of modeling good practice by the faculty and staff. This moves the marketing plan from a single staff member serving as a promotions officer to the entire staff creating an atmosphere of responsibility where staff understand and own the school image.

School image is about welcoming visitors, using good telephone manners, offering assistance to customers, and providing information to those needing it. The principal should test his or her school's telephone image by placing a call to the building to see: how long he or she waits before someone picks up the call, what the recorded message says and how it feels, if he or she is treated courteously, and if his or her inquiry is handled in a business-like manner. When entering your school, do visitors see student work, a clean and tidy facility, and a pleasant atmosphere? If you have a school that values its customers, teachers and staff will greet all visitors quickly, handle complaints in a courteous manner, and provide an environment that is warm and friendly. Too often, customers' first contacts in a school are not friendly and helpful, thereby leaving them with a poor impression of the school and its principal, faculty, and staff.

School image attracts new customers to the school and promoting this image has the capability of attracting new customers. Image also creates the opportunity to celebrate with the community the values the school aspires to attain. This positive image provides parents, teachers, students, and community members with pride and a positive self-esteem (Wood 1997).

The first and most important aspect of any image research is making sure the school does not lose sight of its mission. When attempting to determine the school's image, it can be quite helpful to study your school's mission and how it has evolved over the years of existence. Studying the mission can be very useful in targeting the future because it allows the school to determine its direction in light of the past. The most common problem with image studies is that the results never are acted on and thus change never occurs. It is the principal's responsibility to use the results of an image study to increase the positive aspects of his or her school. Using the results of the study to structure written and verbal communication is one example of image study results. The school should use these results in planning, on its website, in curricular planning, in school–community relations, and in its publications (Topor 1998). Remember, image research data does not have a long shelf life, so image studies need to be conducted on a regular basis.

Topor (1998) suggests the following steps in conducting an image study:

Step 1: Determine the objectives and time line for the study.
Step 2: How will it be governed?
Step 3: How will it be structured?

In any study, one of the things that should be determined first is the study objectives. The study may be grounded around specific concerns that have surfaced in the organization or it may be grounded in a more general context. These objectives are going to drive the study and give direction to the project. Establishing a time line, once the objectives are in place, is an important feature of the image study. The time line gives the group carrying out the study a baseline operational deadline to work toward. For example, one of the objectives for the image study might stipulate what the school should do to prepare students for the world of work. Using a calendar to identify the data gathering and decision points for the research is vital to accomplishing the study as demonstrated in figure 9.4.

The image study needs to have a governance structure that is efficient and allows the organization to reach the objectives outlined in the first step. Whether a committee structure or individual study is utilized, the persons or person need to have some expertise in conducting market research. If a committee structure is to be utilized, the principal may want selected members of the faculty and staff to attend professional development activities that provide training and skill development in image study strategies and data analysis. A committee structure may provide for the involvement of many more constituent groups, but this activity actually slows the process. Training the cadre of committee members is time-consuming and often the members of the cadre become frustrated and less enthusiastic about the project. If the principal wants to use the committee structure for this process, choose wisely.

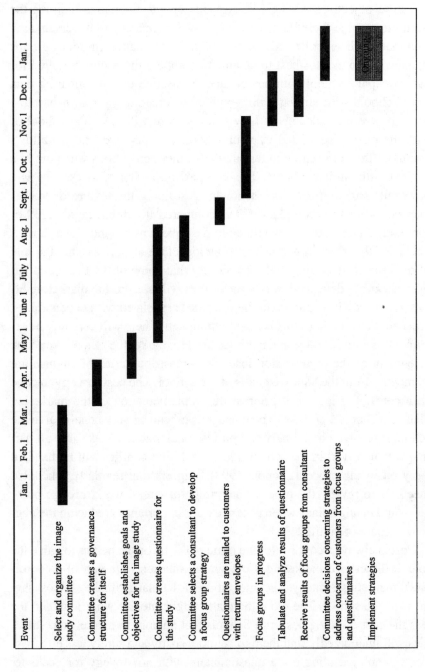

Figure 9.4. Time Line for Completing a Project

The third step involves structuring the study so that the results will address the objectives. Using focus groups or questionnaires requires the committee or the individual conducting the image study to understand the data that has been collected. When analyzing the data from focus groups or questionnaires, it is best to be able to compare the results gathered for the principal's school with benchmark or baseline data. Comparing data from schools with similar demographics or creating your own baseline data gives you an idea about how you compare with a similar school or with the history generated by your school. Comparative analysis allows you to define your school in terms of customer perceptions when put in a context with similar schools. This comparison model of assessment is a powerful structural tool. For example, describing the texture of leather may be easier to accomplish if it is compared to cotton, rayon, silk, or some other fabric, than it would be to describe it as a stand alone fabric.

One of the major concerns that principals face as they assume the role of director of marketing is the possibility that some of the fiscal and human resources delegated to other activities will shift to the marketing effort. Conflict will occur about the priorities associated with expenditures, procedures, and whose turf is being eliminated. There will certainly be arguments about the value and methods used to market the school. Any time a segment of the organization loses resources, loud cries of anguish are trumpeted from the hallowed halls of the school. The best strategy to cope with conflict is to face it prior to the implementation of the marketing plan. Conflict is a process to be managed and can be very beneficial to the school if resolved in a timely and professional manner. Make sure all participants involved in the school understand how conflict will be handled early on in the process. Topor (1998) suggests that regularly scheduled meetings to review the process, determine progress, work through problems, and change plans when necessary are important to reducing the negative impact of conflict.

Cost is always a concern for the principal as he or she begins to value the role of director of marketing. Cost control measures are part of a coordinated marketing strategy. The integration of the plan is the key to cost savings for the school. The more the marketing strategies work together, the less the cost of doing business. Schools that attempt to market solo strategies will undoubtedly find them to be more costly and surely less effective. For example, sending out a questionnaire with no strategy for customer sampling or targeting is a waste of resources. A marketing plan that focuses the questionnaire on target customers and is followed up with a focus group technique provides the school with data at a lower cost per data unit.

The segment of the marketing unit that is most overlooked is the quality of the classroom teachers. This is the most important factor in assessing the school's value to customers. Teachers are most influential when it comes to the perceived strength of the school. Reputation is built around the teachers and what they do in the classroom. Principals need to understand that what happens in the classroom directly affects what happens to the school and the principal. Schools with outstanding instruction can tolerate poor principals, but great principals cannot save schools that have poor instruction without changing members of the teaching staff. Quality teaching produces quality students and this combination is the nucleus for a quality school.

STRATEGIES FOR MARKET RESEARCH

Have you noticed that the makeup of the American family has changed and is still changing? More single-parent families with a male as the single parent, more blended families with children coming together to form one set of siblings, and more two-parent families with both parents working are becoming the norm in the United States. Families have also changed in other ways. For instance, many families have chosen to spend their education dollars on home schooling, private education, or religious education. Increasingly, families have become more demanding in their needs and expectations from the school. These changes in customer needs and wants appear to stem from the parents' need for their child to be successful in school, but even beyond that parents want their child to be able to find a job after schooling that will economically sustain the child for life. Many parents believe that being involved in their child's school will provide them an avenue to influence the school's decision-making process. Parents want the opportunity to serve on site-based school councils, serve on personnel selection committees for principals and other visible school personnel, and be directly involved in the selection of instructional materials and methodologies.

Parents have in the past several years become advocates for specific teaching models and in some cases have gone to court in an attempt to require a specific instructional strategy or to block other instructional strategies they deem inappropriate. In a few situations, state legislatures have enacted laws prohibiting specific instructional models. Specific curriculums have been challenged and none more than sex education, drug education, the phonics versus whole language debate, and the academic value of block scheduling. Parents believe they have not only the right but the duty to use whatever means they have at their disposal to make sure schools adopt their personal educational beliefs.

Parents want and expect the school environment to be safe and secure for their child. They want the school to teach children to manage stress and personal relationships and at the same time they do not want children to experience stress or difficult personal relationships. Single-parent families want the school to provide after school activities, day care, counseling services, and character education without including instruction in values. In addition, all parents want teachers and principals to be role models for their child.

The principal as director of marketing is responsible for the school's quality of service to its customers. The principal is the leader, but every member of the school faculty and staff must be an active participant in the delivery of quality customer service. The principal must provide professional development for all teachers in the area of improving interpersonal interactions and working with customers during times of conflict. Quality must be defined and that definition must be communicated to all school customers not once but on a regular basis. Every time any member of the faculty or staff addresses customers, he or she should redefine quality for those in attendance. Quality is difficult to define and failing to reinforce the concept makes it even more difficult. For many customers, "quality" is a word they use to demonstrate what the school is failing to accomplish. For example, a customer might say, "This is not a quality school because it has no foreign language program for third-grade students." The statement is true if you let the customer define what makes a school a quality learning institution. "Quality" is the word most people add to the discussion when they have no other means of expressing their concern for the actions taking place in the school. As the principal, you define quality for your school based on the needs of all the students/customers.

In order to meet the needs of a changing and fluid school environment, the faculty, staff, and principal must be prepared to meet the needs of single-parent families and customer advocates and address the issue of quality—all in the context of the school setting.

Sampling techniques are the key to gathering accurate data and for making decisions about the operation of a school. It is essential when addressing the ever-changing environment of marketing research and even more compelling when conducting market research for schools. The type and amount of market research that is undertaken depends on the amount of human and financial resources the school has committed to marketing the school. Hamblin (1999) identifies four types of market research strategies:

- Face-to-face surveys
- Telephone surveys
- Focus groups
- Mailed surveys

Using any one of these survey strategies will provide useful data for the school. All of these strategies suffer when the data is not collected in a scientific manner. Interviews must be done correctly and the data recorded properly if the data is to be meaningful.

Face-to-face surveys are normally conducted in an area that is frequented by many patrons of the school, such as the local supermarket, near the post office, or in people's homes. This sampling technique should provide large amounts of data. The advantage of face-to-face surveys is the opportunity for the person asking the questions to clarify the direction of the questions should the respondent fail to understand the question being asked. The key to any survey is developing the right questions to be asked and then asking the right people, in this case the school's customers. Once the questions are asked, the interviewer records the responses accurately.

Face-to-face sampling is done in two ways: either quota or random. Quota sampling requires that a predesigned quota be created with a representative mix of ages, gender, and social class. Most quotas are based on the percentage of age, gender, and social class found in the latest census data. Random sampling of individuals or households eliminates the interviewer's influence on those selected for interviewing. Random sampling removes the chance that the interviewer will select individuals easy to contact. Hamblin (1999) lists the advantages and disadvantages of face-to-face surveys.

Some advantages are:

- Control of the sample provides for more accurate results
- The interviewer can assist with complex questions and more lengthy questions can be asked

Some disadvantages are:

- Costly to conduct
- Sample size reliability is compromised due to the survey costs

Sample size using either the quota or random sample techniques are subject to the accuracy desired, the number of subsamples preferred, and the budget available. Sample size is dependent on the total population of customers. For example, if the population size is 100, the sample size should be 80. If the population size is 500 the sample size should be 217 (Krejcie and Morgan 1970).

Telephone surveys have become the technique most widely utilized in political and product polling. Telephone interview lengths vary according to the respondent's interest in the issue. The attitude about telephone interviewing has changed among social scientists and has become more widely accepted. If done correctly, telephone surveys should provide quality data for the school. Advantages of telephone surveys are that they are cost effective and quick, they produce a high response rate, they provide much more in-depth data, and they are less costly than face to face interviews. A couple of disadvantages surface when discussing telephone interviews: some people do not have a telephone, and some people have unlisted numbers, thus both groups are not part of the telephone sample. It is important that the interviewers record the data accurately and one way to do this is to use a tape recorder to collect the information. If the interview is to be tape recorded, it is vital that the interviewee be told that fact prior to beginning the interview.

Mailed questionnaires are sent to all or a sample of the customers in the school with a cover letter that explains the purpose for the questionnaire and gives the reader the name of a contact person at school. This type of questionnaire requires the recipient to answer the questions and return the document in a prepaid envelope to the school. Mailed questionnaires are a cheap way of collecting data and they provide the best geographic coverage. The most important aspect of mailed questionnaires is that the questions are written clearly and are not ambiguous. The best types of mailed questionnaires are forced-choice response types that cannot be interpreted any way except that which the writer wants them to be understood. Hamblin (1999) describes the following five essentials for a mailed questionnaire:

- Easy to read
- Use only one sheet of paper, preferably on one side only
- An understandable vocabulary is used
- A cover letter that addresses confidentiality
- Respondents should be asked to return the questionnaire within three weeks
- Prepaid return envelope

Using a bulk mail stamp reduces the cost of sending the questionnaire and providing a "business reply" envelope, while being costly on a per piece basis, saves placing postage on each return envelope and saves money in the long run. Schools should provide press releases to both the print and electronic media outlets advertising that the questionnaire will be arriving in the customers' mail in the next several days. The press release should contain information about the purpose and benefits that returning the questionnaire will have for the school and its customers.

The focus group is the fourth type of information collecting tool that schools might use to gather information about the customers' perception of the school. Focus groups are arguably the best way to collect comprehensive attitudinal, insight, and impression information from customers. This technique can be used in combination with mailed or face-to-face interviews as a means of providing detailed information. In addition, the focus group technique can be used to collect information that will be turned into a questionnaire. The limitations of the focus group are the small number of respondents, drawing general conclusions from the data collected, and then making predictions (Hamblin 1999). Focus groups may be randomly selected from the total population, but the results cannot be generalized to the entire school population. Most data collected from focus groups needs to be measured against a larger sample of customers.

When the principal and other members of the marketing committee begin to create a survey or questionnaire, it is important to make sure the questions ask what the group wants to know. Question structure is the key to useful data collection. Using a five-point modified Likert scale will provide useful data and can be scored electronically using a digital scanner. The scale would begin with the highest rating and progress to the lowest rating and would look like this: very satisfied, satisfied, neutral (neither satisfied or dissatisfied), dissatisfied, and very dissatisfied. Other indicators such as strongly agree, agree, and strongly disagree are also useful.

Questions can be structured with either a positive or negative orientation. For some questions a positive response is favorable and for other questions a negative response is favorable. For example, a positive response question would look like this: "Our school provides customer service, one with polite and friendly personnel." A negative response that looks like this: "Our school provides customer service, one that ignores customer suggestions." The ideal response for the first example would be strongly agree and the ideal response for the second question would be strongly disagree. The orientation of the questions is crucial to the desired response.

The following question stems provide ideas for creating face-to-face surveys and mailed questionnaires for marketing a school. For example:

- Direct question: How satisfied are you with the school's customer service?
- Direct request: Please rate our school's customer service.
- Question of frequency: How often does our school exceed your expectations?
- Question of extent: To what extent does our school exceed your expectations?
- Agree or disagree: Our school provides great customer service. (CustomerSat.Com 1999)

Each of the question types approach the same question in a slightly different way. As the principal, you need to decide which of these examples best fits the context of your school. Using the same question type throughout the survey or questionnaire produces the best data.

Earlier in this chapter I discussed school image and how it affects the school. In looking at creating a survey or questionnaire about school image, you could create several statements from the stem "Please rate our school's image" and they might look something like:

1. Our school's image is well respected.
2. Our school's image is one that does not honor its customers.
3. Our school's image has a good reputation.
4. Our school's image is one that misleads our customers.
5. Our school's image is one that uses discriminatory practices.
6. Our school's image is one that supports good causes.
7. Our school's image is one of producing high-quality products.
8. Our school's image is one that gives exceptional service to customers.
9. Our school's image is one that listens to its customers.
10. Our school's image is one where faculty and staff are unwilling to go the extra mile for customers. (CustomerSat.com 1999)

After reading the ten sample statements, decide which ones have a positive orientation and which have a negative orientation. Perhaps principals would never want to include a negatively oriented statement for fear that many respondents might strongly agree with it. If that is the situation, then the principal needs to become the director of marketing for his or her school. Negative statements serve as a check on the respondents to see if they are answering the questions consistently. CustomerSat.com provides over 2,000 sample questions that can be adapted for school surveys and questionnaires.

BUILDING BRIDGES WITH YOUR CUSTOMERS

In a market-driven environment, principals who are able to demonstrate to the school customers that they indeed want to create a quality school will have the best chance to be successful. The principal and the faculty need to concentrate on building bridges with the community and now is the time to begin. Creating an atmosphere of service is essential for success and for many principals and teachers this will be the ultimate struggle. For far too many years schools have operated with little need to pay attention to their customers, and even though some schools still hold on to the time-worn tradition that they always know best, the times have changed.

Perhaps one of the best ways to begin building bridges is to interest the
business leaders in the product your school supplies to them. Elementary
principals might think this is not something that will work for them, but
that would be a major mistake. Businesses and elementary schools form
partnerships all of the time. This partnership pays dividends in the form of
resources, extra teachers, and as a public relations vehicle. Inviting the
business community to a simple breakfast where principals and teachers
inform these leaders about what the school is producing will generate
goodwill and in most cases support.

Principal Bill Free of West Branch High School decided to invite all
of the local business leaders to an early morning breakfast of juice and
pastries to demonstrate the advancements the school had made in teaching students to use technology. Principal Free and the technology faculty
were determined to focus their attention on the needs and wants of the
business leaders, so they titled this meeting "What's in this for you?" All
of the teacher presentations focused on students as active learners and
future employees of the businesses in the community. They told the audience that the futures of their businesses were sitting in the classrooms
of this high school and the surrounding area schools. One of the computer design teachers told the business leaders that many of the elementary students could create an electronic marketing presentation for their
business and would be willing to demonstrate that skill if they were invited to the business. This marketing strategy worked because it personalized what West Branch High School was producing with the business
leaders. Since the early morning breakfast, business leaders have called
on fifteen separate occasions over the past two years to offer students
the chance to participate in technology-related seminars and employment opportunities. Principal Free continues to host these early morning
breakfasts twice a year and the business community has increased its attendance by 50 percent in two years.

The lynchpin of this early morning business breakfast is building relationships with the community leaders, rather than asking for support
for various projects. Create a cadre of friends in the community that
will help market what the school is doing. Follow up the business
breakfast with a letter thanking these leaders for participating and remind them of what was accomplished. Invite these community leaders
to school functions at least four times each academic year, letting them
know each time what great students attend the school. Build bridges

that link your school with the community—that's what Principal Free has done.

School–business partnerships are different depending on how the partnership is structured. Partnerships can be loosely or tightly coupled. In 1988, more than 140,000 school–business partnerships were in operation with about 24 percent of the school population involved and with about four out of every ten partnerships coming from small- and medium-sized businesses (U.S. Department of Education 1988). In the traditional school–business partnerships, the principal and the faculty created these partnerships to foster school–community cooperation. Businesses gained from these partnerships in the form of better media relations and community image (Clark 1992). Originally, schools were the recipients and businesses were the patrons. Schools benefited from the generosity of the business partners by getting equipment, resources for students, and the opportunity to receive business training and skills (Lankard 1995). In some instances, school–school partnerships were created to provide businesses with employees and a consistent workforce. In these types of targeted partnerships, the goal is to meet the needs of each business partner.

School–business partnerships have evolved into relationships that benefit both of the partners. These relationships allow businesses and schools to be full partners, with agreements outlining each partner's responsibilities (Clark 1992). This collaboration creates an atmosphere of mutual trust and working conditions that benefit both partners. These benefits exude energy from one partner to the other, with positive results for customers, businesses, the school, parents, and the community. Some businesses have taken the lead in helping schools do a better job of educating students by mounting a crusade to save public schools (Lankard 1995). In a world where businesses and schools are attached by worker knowledge and skills, it only makes sense that school–business partnerships will thrive.

School–business partnerships are not without their detractors and it is the principal's responsibility to make sure that the school understands the types of involvement it wants to have with the business community. It is imperative that the principal is able to withstand the pressure business leaders place on the school to adopt the goals of the business community. The school must make sure its business partners understand that students are the primary focus of the school, not special interest groups (Baas 1990). Other concerns and controversies may surface if the principal is not vigilant in his or her oversight of the school–business partnership.

ETHICAL DISCUSSION

Should Businesses Have an Increased Influence on Public Schools?

Business leaders, from large and small companies, understand that schools influence the type of employees that are available to them and these business leaders want the public schools to improve. Many of these leaders believe that what's good for the business sector is also good for schools. These same leaders argue that schools fail to prepare students, consume large amounts of tax dollars, and are not accountable to anyone for the learning output. In addition, the use of technology has become a major concern for the business community, as it appraises the technological capability of schools. Many business leaders believe that schools need to improve the teaching of knowledge and attitudes that contribute to society. They believe that the United States is a combination of democracy and capitalism that offers freedom in politics and in the economy without interference from the government. Schools should be in a position to influence the practice of values and ethics in the business community. Business leaders focusing on the "bottom line" are more likely than not to use a single set of criteria to determine each worker's talent. Businesses are also involved in educational reform through the materials and services they generate for reforming schools. The purpose of schools is to prepare students to perpetuate the political system while business leaders view students as employees.

The questions that need to be answered concerning this issue are:

- Should the business community be involved with schools in school–business partnerships?
- Can business leadership provide effective direction in helping schools reform?
- Should schools be dominated by the values of business?
- Is business a good model for schools?
- Should business control schools or should education control business values and practices?
- Ethical dilemmas are right-versus-right issues. Which side of the school–school partnership debate do you support and why?

CHAPTER SUMMARY

Why is it important to know what the school's image is? This question addresses the needs and wants of students, parents, community members, and other interested members of the school. Marketing the school may appear to be outside the purview of the principal, but the principal is the most important person in creating an environment where the teachers and staff understand their roles as service providers. High academic standards, a strong mentoring program for teachers and students, a developing school–business partnership, and a student body that is excited about learning are all items that need to be marketed to the school's customers.

Marketing a school should be an important part of the school's management strategy. Marketing is more about building relationships among people than creating competitive action plans. Competition among schools will continue to increase as school districts adopt plans that allow students to attend any school in the district. In addition, charter schools, voucher plans, and magnet school concepts provide students with the opportunity to attend the school of their choice or their parents' choice. High-stakes testing has created an educational environment that causes school customers to question the quality of the school. Schools have traditionally been organizations that function from the top down, with both policy and resources coming from the board of education eventually reaching the students at the bottom of the organizational pyramid. The ideal organization would require the rotation of the traditional organizational chart 180 degrees, thereby placing students at the top of the chart and the central administration at the bottom. The organizational chart based on the marketing concept is central to the theme students first.

Marketing the school requires that the principal makes sure there is a match between the curriculum being offered and student needs. The first step in the marketing plan is the assessment of economic, social, political, and technological forces that play a role in determining what a principal would use in creating a marketing plan for his or her school. Step two in the marketing plan determines the market orientation that benefits the school context. This orientation defines the marketing plan for communicating its purpose to students, parents, teachers, the superintendent, and the community. The four types of marketing orientations are: production, product, selling, and market.

Step three in the marketing plan identifies relationships as the key to marketing any organization. Putting the customer first is the most important step in the plan. Right behind creating relationships is the ability to communicate with all of the school's customers. Principals need to understand that they cannot stop negative talk but they can create an atmosphere that diminishes the rationale for negative talk.

Communicating internally and externally with the school's customers creates an environment for two-way communication. This communication system provides avenues for customers to exchange ideas, ask questions, and become partners in the operation of the school. Communication occurs using a variety of formats, internal and external newsletters, presentations at organizations, and electronic and print media news releases.

School image assessment addresses the question of how the school is perceived by the school's customers. School image is about welcoming customers, using good telephone manners, and providing information for those needing it. A positive school image attracts new customers and maintains the current cadre of customers. In any study of school image, the first thing that needs to be addressed is the study objectives. Once these objectives have been developed and a time line created, the part of the plan that needs to be developed is how the study will be governed. What type of committee or individual structure will be used to complete the study? The third step in the study structure is the creation of data collection devices that will address the objectives.

Strategies for market research include techniques such as surveys, questionnaires, and focus groups. Surveys can be face to face, written and mailed, or asked over the telephone. The key to successful use of any of these strategies is writing clear and simple questions so that all respondents understand what the questions ask. Using random samples guarantees more useful results and are generalizable to all customers. Questions can be written from a positive or negative orientation depending on what the question writer is attempting to ascertain.

School–business partnerships have evolved into relationships that benefit both of the partners by creating an atmosphere of mutual trust and working conditions. These relationships allow both businesses and schools to be full partners. These benefits exude energy from one partner to the other, with positive results for customers, businesses, the school, parents, and the community. Principals must be careful when entering into a school–business partnership by making sure the partnership meets the needs of the school and customers.

CHAPTER ACTIVITIES AND QUESTIONS

1. What is your school's image and how do you assess it?
2. List the strategies a principal would use to market his or her school.
3. What is the function of any organization, including schools?
4. Compare and contrast the top-down organizational structure with the structure that places students at the top of the organizational chart.
5. Create a marketing plan for your school.
6. Identify and discuss the market orientations that schools assume.
7. What purpose does communication serve in creating a marketing plan?
8. List the tools that can be utilized in the internal and external communications process.
9. Write an essay about the usefulness of school–business partnerships.
10. What is meant by random sampling and why is that strategy considered the most reliable of all sampling techniques?

CASE STUDY ACTIVITIES AND QUESTIONS

1. Create a marketing plan Principal Maldanado can use with the faculty to make sure the new TAG program is successful.
2. Should Principal Maldanado market the TAG program to the customers of Waldorf Intermediate School?
3. Create a marketing plan for Principal Maldanado that assesses the image of Waldorf Intermediate School.
4. Could Principal Maldanado use a school–business partnership to help make the TAG program a success? If so how?
5. What strategies would Principal Maldanado employ to make sure the faculty was using positive talk about the TAG program with the school's customers?
6. List the strategies that Principal Maldanado would use with his colleagues to mitigate the creaming effect of this new program.

7. From Principal Maldanado's point of view, write a memorandum informing the faculty that there was no choice where the TAG program was placed.
8. Which stakeholders should Principal Maldanado attempt to develop and why?
9. Based on this situation, list the communication tools the principal should utilize.
10. How would you characterize the organizational structure of this school district; bottom up or top down? Which of these two structures address customer and student needs?

REFERENCES

Baas, A. (1990). "The role of business in education" (ERIC Document Reproduction Service no. ED 321 344).

Calonius, H (1988). "A buying process model." In *Innovative marketing: A European perspective*, ed. K. Blois and S. Parkinson. Bradford: University of Bradford Press.

Clark, T. A. (1992). "Collaboration to build competence: The urban superintendents' perspective." *ERIC Review* 2 (2): 2–6.

CustomerSat.com. (1999). "2000 sample questions." At www.customersat.com (accessed March 17, 2002).

Hamblin, M. (1999). "Face to face surveys." At www.psopinion.com (accessed March 17, 2002).

Krejcie, R. V., and Morgan, D. W. (1970). "Determining sample size for research activities." *Educational Psychology and Measurement* 30: 607–610.

Lankard, B. A. (1995). "Business/Education partnerships." *ERIC Digest* 156. Eugene, OR: ERIC Clearinghouse on Educational Management (ERIC Document Reproduction Services no. ED 321 344).

Marketing Ink. (1999). "Getting outside-in communication." At www.marketing-ink.com (accessed February 21, 2002).

"Research reveals that outstanding schools share several key traits." (1999). *U.S. News and World Report*, 18 January, 59.

Stokes, D. (1997). "Marketing schools: A case for making relationships work." *Education Marketing Magazine* 11, at www.heist.co.uk (accessed February 21, 2002).

Topor, B. (1998). "Institutional image assessment." At www.marketinged.com (accessed March 1, 2002).

U.S. Department of Education. (1988). *America's schools: Everybody's business.* A report to the president of the United States, Washington, DC (ERIC Document Reproduction Service no. ED 301 973).

Vining, L. (2000a). "Handling parent complaints." At www.edoz.com.au (accessed February 15, 2002).

———. (2000b). "Managing word of mouth." At www.edoz.com.au (accessed February 15, 2002).

———. (2000c). "Why schools need to market themselves." At www.edoz.com.au (accessed February 15, 2002).

Wood, M. (1997). "EQ Australia leadership summer '97." At www.curriculum.edu.au (accessed February 18, 2002).

Wyatt, M. (1999). "Good relations." *Education Marketing Magazine* 16, at www.heist.co.uk (accessed February 18, 2002).

Chapter Ten

Site-Based Decision Making in the Campus Community

Wanda Nugent, principal of Walk-up Road Elementary in Cameron, had recently been discussing problems at the school with Rauel Gomez, president of the parent–teachers organization. Mr. Gomez, representing the parents, had been coming to her with a number of suggestions about the school's operations. These were mostly concerned with how support functions of the school were meeting the needs of students and parents and not instructional issues; however, the new teachers who had been hired for the school recently had approached her about changing some of the instructional features of the school so that the largely Hispanic population would be served better. Ms. Nugent had encountered the site-based decision model at a presentation at the state's principals meeting recently. Although she had discussed this with friends in her administrative education program, she had never worked in a school with a site-based team, nor had she seriously thought about its role at her school before. Now that she was into her third year as principal, she was better able to see where the problems were and how a wider group of teachers and parents could contribute to the solutions to these problems.

She decided to contact Mr. Gomez and several of the experienced teachers to discuss some of her thoughts about a site-based team. She didn't want to jump off into deep water with this idea before she had interacted with some others about it. She was going to the principals' conference later in the month, and decided to explore it with some out-of-district colleagues while she was there. Before a decision could be made—at least in her mind—she would have to open this up for discussion in a faculty meeting and with the assistant superintendent for curriculum.

DECISIONS AND SITE-BASED GOVERNANCE

Site-based decision making, from a literal definition, means that the decision is made at the local campus. From just this term and definition, it is unclear who or what group makes the decision that is being considered. A site-based decision could, then, come from the principal or some other administrator at the school. The primary distinction is that these decisions are made not by the superintendent or central office bureaucracy, but by those at the location where the impact is to be felt. This shift in the location of the decisions has been a part of the decentralization of power from centers such as legislatures, boards, and central offices to where the results are occurring. There is an assumption here that those closest to the activity are the individuals who understand best what is needed to make progress and that they are also those who must implement the decision once it has been made. These individuals have the most vested interests in making the results happen successfully, so they are the educators who should make the decision. The reforms that have been developing in schools for the last ten years have the site-based focus on groups of stakeholders being involved in the site-based decisions—those who see the impact from all directions—not solely from the administrator's vantage point.

IMPETUS FOR SITE-BASED TEAMS

The movement toward site-based decisions received its impetus from the quality movement that has been felt at almost every level of government, business, and private foundation sector operation across this nation and the best-developed industries throughout the world. This movement has become an undertaking, by those leaders involved, to move the decisions made to the location closest to their impact and by those who understand best what is involved. For this reason, the movement became known as Total Quality Management (TQM). The process took hold successfully and made a difference where there was a covenant from the staff to see its decisions through implementation with a great deal of interest and commitment to make them work successfully. The TQM idea has a number of principles that have been discussed in the literature by advocates such as Deming, Crosby, Juran, and others. The term "Total Quality Management" is not as popular now as it was in the early 1990s; however, many of the principles have been adopted and are being used in leading schools today. The site-based team ideas are one of those that have proven to be very helpful.

Site-based management teams are most successful where a principal is present who has a desire to have collaborative decisions with all stakeholders—teachers, staff, parents, and students—involved in the process. These principals are usually competent leaders themselves, who do not feel intimidated by the prospect of having other stakeholders share in the decisions. In that respect, the principals must be risk takers themselves. If a principal feels his or her authority is being usurped or does not wish to share authority with others, and the laws or policies do not dictate otherwise, a principal can manage to keep such a site-based group weak or unable to deal with real issues. This is done by scheduling meetings infrequently, setting agendas that deal with nothing of substance, or otherwise keeping the group's function at a minimal level.

Site-based teams have evolved differently in almost every state or political arrangement that governs schools. In some places, the unionization arrangement has helped to build the site-based teams to their level of impact; in others, the local administrators of the district and school have promoted the concept to bring more stakeholders into a position of sharing responsibility for the schools, instead of only being critics who feel they are left out of the schools. In some states, there has been a legislative mandate that has required the schools to develop site-based councils (Smith 1998). Difficulties in determining responsibilities in some states have reverted to making the teams advisory in nature and ultimately making the principal responsible for the decisions. In Texas, for example, where this is the case, the principal still must work to develop such teams, as there is no climate where a principal can operate independently of the stakeholders; successful principals must encourage well-meaning parents to contribute to the school with their ideas and support. The principal may even be ahead of the advisory team in encouraging change and innovation with their ideas. In Kentucky, the site-based council composition is specified to be three teachers, two parents, and the principal and is endowed with considerable authority in the fiscal and policy areas. The relationship of the site-based team to the principal also varies, with some teams having authority to hire and/or fire the principal or selecting a new one when there is a vacancy. Some directives have the principal as chair of the team and others require that another person be the chair. The charter school movement has created an entire school with a different form of control — that of being de facto site-based managed. Twenty states have created situations where this type of school has developed (David 1995–1996).

In Kentucky, the councils have responsibility of some major policy areas including curriculum, staff assignment, student assignment, school scheduling, instructional practices, discipline, extracurricular activities, and alignment with state standards. The site-based council also has the responsibility of selecting the principal, who is a member of the council (Lindle 1995–1996). Although the legislature requires only six members, schools can choose to elect more, but the proportion of teachers, parents, and administrators must remain the same. Elementary schools usually have six, while some high schools have twelve members for a better representation of diversity. Students in high schools are added, oftentimes in nonvoting capacities.

The goal of site-based decision-making teams also varies, although David (1995–1996) indicates "that all are cloaked in language of increasing student achievement" (5). David cites examples of various reasons for initiating this change:

- At the state level, this type of decision making may be favored to shift the balance of authority between the district, the state, and the school. From this level, there is a larger reform issue of trading school autonomy for that of accountability to the state. In some ways, this is a method of undoing what previous legislatures have put into place, that of shifting the local control of the district to the school itself.
- The shift can be a political reform used to broaden the decision-making base within the school or the community.
- As an administrative reform, this type of management may be more efficient by a move to decentralize or deregulate it. This perhaps is closely linked to the enhancement of student learning by letting the educational professionals closest to the teaching-learning interaction make the important professional decisions.
- Sometimes, there are other complicating factors that have underlying motives such as weakening entrenched and distrusted school boards, creating reforms without investing more fiscal resources, or decreasing

the central district staff and calling it downsizing by shifting responsibilities to the building level, or simply shifting the blame for failure to the school itself.

DEVELOPING THE COMMUNITY'S SITE-BASED TEAM

One of the better scenarios for a shift to these types of school decisions exists when the school's culture values everyone who has a role in the school as a stakeholder. This may include the faculty, the staff of the school, the parents, the students, and the greater community including the business public and the other taxpayers who may not have direct contact with the school, such as senior citizens. If the current climate of the school's community is very antagonistic with parents and other citizens feeling much like outsiders, then prior to a move to site-based decision teams the principal, faculty, and staff should begin a sincere effort to modify this climate and ultimately the culture of the school from a "we-they" type of climate to an "our school" feeling. Fullan and Miles (1991) point out that school improvement initiatives need to do more than focus on structural and organizational changes as these are very limiting. The schools and individuals need to alter their professional perceptions, practices, and beliefs concerning teaching and learning—in short, the school's educators need to alter their professional culture.

Deciding how to improve student learning can be rather difficult. When a new group of parents, teachers, students, and other outside stakeholders get together, they probably have never worked as a group before, may have no experience in collaborative decision making, and many may not have an idea of how to change the school's instructional efforts. David (1995–1996) also points out that some of these stakeholders may have a history of being adversaries to what has been occurring in the school. Also, teachers or others may have the additional relationship factor of being evaluated by another member, usually the principal, in their job. The groups that do manage to function productively may take on issues involving facilities, discipline, or student activities, all of which are high-profile issues that are more easily tackled than instructional changes. Instructional changes require trust and constructive dialogue to have meaningful progress on a function that may be regulated by the state through required examinations.

Although individuals may often be interested in the issues, it is those who have the most expertise and experience in a particular area who need to give leadership on that issue to the council. Uninformed decision-making can be worse than having a decision made by someone who is informed yet is several layers away from the school. What becomes clear, when the process is occurring, is that discussion must take place meaningfully and that teachers, who will shape the implementation, must shape the direction of the change (David 1995–1996). Lindle (1995–1996) points out how significant the prevailing political structure and climate of the community may be impacting the decisions due to family, political, or religious ties and the pecking order within the community. The rituals of the community may, in fact, become those of the council.

Democracy is an important principle in the work of the site-based teams. Conflict is going to be inevitable in discussions and decisions at times, but an important lesson to be learned is that this conflict must be accepted and planned for, as it may not be totally avoided. The focus should be on substantive issues and the group should avoid framing its work in a legalistic manner (Lindle 1995–1996). When the structure gets very formal, there is a tendency to spend too much time on rule making that can guide the body's important work, that of making decisions to improve the school. What tends to occur when structure gets to be too legal or formal is lots of heat and friction about the power struggle and not much light on the purposes to be achieved: that of improving the school's results on student learning. Fullan (1995) concludes that the changes in the governance structures may receive most of the attention rather than the "radical reculturing" of the school and the "basic redesign" of teaching needed to bring about real reform.

A soon realized issue, when site-based teams begin to function, is that principals and teachers have often not been prepared or trained for this participatory arrangement in changing the school (Murphy 1991). There is the need for the principal to understand the changes in the principal's and the teachers' roles. Principals who have been, up to the advent of site-based teams, used to being disseminators of central office directives, now are becoming facilitators of group efforts and extending the leadership role (see chapter 2) to teachers and other site-based team members (Wheeler and Agruso 1996). Both teachers and principals must be prepared to manage in this shared decision environment. For the principal, it means also training teachers to be prepared for their leadership roles. Principals, however, must now become more fluent and knowledgeable in all of the specialized areas that their school is concerned with, such as early childhood, special education, or tech prep. Principals, teachers, parents, and other site-based team members must be prepared to participate in group functions—problem identification, prioritizing, consensus building, cause and effect identification, solution building, communication, and implementation of decisions. To accomplish this latter goal, site-based team members may need to be taught a number of group techniques including processes such as brainstorming, nominal group technique, systems framework technique, small-group roles, developing a cause-and-effect chart, and others (see table 10.1). When skilled in such techniques the group is capable of deciding what tool of this type would be of assistance in accomplishing the task.

Where shared leadership is a process favored by the principal in moving the school forward to achieve increased learning for the students, it will quickly become evident that a site-based committee is going to have a great deal of time and effort committed to consider solutions and make recommendations or decisions for issues needing attention. An important realization will quickly surface—some of these decisions will have to be handed to other subcommittees or task forces to complete. There is not enough time or energy for one group of teachers, parents, and others to consider all of these problems or decisions; therefore, other groups must be formed to carry out some functions. Mohrman and Wohlstetter (1994) indicate that site-based management, merely as a governance change, is constraining. Rather, they see it as a redesign of the school's organization. Within a redesign of the organization, examples of such groups could include:

- A personnel interview committee (this might be focused around the opened position such as a grade-level committee to interview for an opening at that level)
- A budget committee for developing the annual budget (see chapter 12)
- A school facilities committee (probably an ad hoc committee developed to deal with a specific facilities task)
- A staff development committee to set up staff development opportunities to impact school instructional design
- A student activities advisory committee to develop policy and assist in managing the student activities program
- A strategic planning committee to develop a school mission statement and beliefs about learning
- A committee to work on development of a campus improvement plan

Table 10.1   Choosing a Tool to Use with a Team

Purpose to Be Accomplished	*Tool or Technique to Employ*
Decision for selection of problem for focus	Pareto chart Flow chart Brainstorming Nominal group technique
Describing the issue, its definition, extent, and occurance	Pareto chart Check sheet Runs chart Histogram Pie chart
Developing a representation of causes of problem	Check sheet Fishbone diagram Brainstorming Force-field analysis
Developing goals to be achieved	Systems framework Benchmarking
Considering causes of the problem	Check sheet Scatter diagram Pareto chart Brainstorming Nominal group technique
Developing solutions and action plan	Brainstorming Force-field analysis Affinity diagrams PERT charts Pie chart Gantt chart Small group roles
Implementing the solution and assistance in the monitoring process	Pareto chart Gantt chart Histogram Control chart

Mohrman and Wohlstetter (1994) argue that these schools must not limit involvement to only site-based councils; schools need to have other modes of shared involvement, such as indicated in the previous examples.

THE FUNCTIONING TEAM'S OPERATION

Once a team has been established, some method of operation must be selected to function. This could develop from a period of floundering around by the team or, what would be more preferable, the experience of those on the team or the principal involved·can introduce the team to a model that can be used in their deliberations and decisions. To a great degree, the model chosen for this task will also establish the role of the team within the life of the school.

The attitude of administrators toward site-based teams will have a great deal to do with how and to what degree a site-based team can prove useful to the school. If the team is mandated by state policy or statute and the administrator (either superintendent or principal) is not receptive to the team's involvement in the life of the school, then the activity will be mostly superficial and limited to advisory functions. If the administrators welcome the involvement, the activity can prove helpful and may, if conditions are conducive, make the team a part of the school's decision-making network, which can change the attitude of those involved into one of inclusion rather than exclusion.

Three possible models of operation for site-based teams will be discussed. The models are not necessarily totally different, as they have some similarities involved. Each of these models employs a systems approach that Bailey (1991) identifies as the viable means of accomplishing site-based team results. These include the context, input, process, and product (CIPP) model offered by Candoli (1995), the school improvement model developed by the National Study of School Evaluation, and the Monasmith (1997) Empowering Your School Community model.

CONTEXT, INPUT, PROCESS, AND PRODUCT MODEL

The CIPP model is a means of conducting evaluation that was popularized by a Phi Delta Kappa study committee on evaluation in 1966 headed by Stufflebeam. The committee's results were published in 1971 as *Educational Evaluation and Decision Making*. Stufflebeam (1971) focuses on the definition of evaluation as "the process of delineating, obtaining, and providing useful information for judging decision alternatives" (xxv). He identifies evaluation as a continuing activity rather than having a distinct beginning and end.

Educational improvement comes from identifying unmet needs and developing a way or ways of meeting those needs that may not have been available or understood prior to this activity. With this definition and this process of unmet needs becoming understood, the task of a site-based team as an evaluation process becomes more apparent to those preparing to activate such a team. The task for the team then is to utilize the CIPP model to guide its work.

"Defining context" is the task of defining the environment and describing the desired and actual conditions pertaining to the environment that identifies unmet needs and opportunities that have not been used. This helps to diagnosis or identify the problems preventing needs from being realized. Such a diagnosis provides the necessary basis for understanding what can be done to attain the results desired. One of the important tasks in accomplishing context evaluation is to set the boundaries of the system to be evaluated (Candoli 1995). Two modes are involved in context evaluation:

- that of contingency, that searches for opportunities and pressures outside the immediate system to promote improvement within it, and
- that of congruence or comparison of actual and intended system performance, such as consulting a database for information to determine the change of a particular action on another variable.

Through the process of examining the context or environment in which a school or entity finds itself, a site-based team can better determine what needs to be accomplished to make improvements and where those improvements might fit.

"Input evaluation" is used to provide information for determining the utilization of resources for accomplishing program goals. This analyzes various procedural designs in terms of costs and benefits in achieving desired results. Such an analysis helps to understand barriers, alternative designs, and requirements such as staffing, time, and budget requirements. Candoli (1995) points out that five areas of review may be helpful in conducting this part of the model:

- District or board plans from previous years
- District and school budgets from previous years
- District and school plans for the present year
- Reports on effective practices in other districts and schools
- The approach to planning used in the district and school

The data gathered from the context and input evaluation are used then to accomplish the planning—frequently a strategic plan may result, based on the needs as understood by the individuals analyzing the data. This plan may be used to orchestrate the actions of all those working to accomplish the school's goals.

"Process evaluation" gives periodic feedback during the implementation of plans developed by the site-based team. This feedback is used in several ways. By understanding the contextual part of the process, this examination will help to observe problems that would interfere with objective accomplishment. Three aspects make up the focus:

- Monitoring for potential sources of failure for the project, such as interpersonal relationships among the participants, communication complications, logistic problems, resource adequacy such as facilities, or staff and time allocations
- Providing information for preprogrammed decisions by managers of subareas within the project
- Recording main features and activities of the project so that what actually occurred can be reviewed, which will help to identify problems that may have complicated or blocked objective achievement at the conclusion

Candoli (1995) indicates examples of data that could be used for process evaluation. These examples would include progress reports on all parts of the project, accounting reports on the budget for resources, reports on modification of plans as the process ensues, and outside independent assessments of what is occurring. This type of data is very important to determine failure causes and means to change what may have happened during any review of the project.

"Product evaluation" usually occurs at the conclusion of the project to determine success in achieving the projected outcomes. Often referred to as summative evaluation, this is a regular occurrence in any type of systems approach to change. By comparing the designated objectives of the effort to what was accomplished at its conclusion, an analysis may conclude that success was achieved or that shortfalls of the objectives were evident. This will permit major changes (that are usually evident in the process evaluation) to be affected if the project is continued or that the continuation of the project is not recommended. However, if the project is deemed successful from the products, it might be continued or even be widened to other sites for development. Such products are usually indicated by:

- Behaviors of the subjects of the project—that is, students, teachers, or others
- Specific results of student achievement such as measured by exam
- Measurement of some concept change using a developed instrument such as the "school climate"
- A change in the implementation of a policy goal such as racial or cultural integration

The CIPP model is an excellent conceptual model using a systems approach to change. This model can also give a broad picture of applying evaluation concepts to achieving goals that have been initiated by a site-based team.

SCHOOL IMPROVEMENT MODEL

The school improvement model is also a systems type of model that was developed in collaboration with regional school accreditation commissions in the United States by the National Study of School Evaluation (Fitzpatrick 1997). This model has an important strength that other models may not offer, however. This strength lies in the fact that many schools lack the depth of understanding to proceed with a major strategic or long-range plan, yet this model provides materials that assist the site-based team to develop a continuous improvement plan. The model incorporates the tools needed to assess where the school is in its move to strengthen the instructional and organizational aspects of the program, even though the site-based team may not have the sophistication or experience needed to start such an effort. The team will develop the understanding of the steps necessary as the members work their way through the process developed.

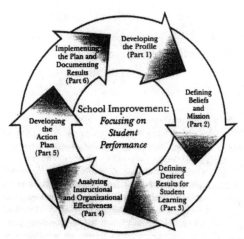

Figure 10.1 School improvement model in Fitzpatrick (1997), *School Improvement: Focusing on Student Performance.* National Study of School Evaluation. Used by permission. All rights reserved.

The model is designed to use a site-based team of stakeholders representing all parts of the school community including teachers, staff, students, administrators, parents, and other community members. The model may be used in the process of developing the school for regional accreditation membership, meeting district or state requirements for site-based teams, planning for the Elementary and Secondary Education Act title programs, or to incorporate the principles of good planning such as might be found in any school for a variety of purposes without any outside requirements. The planning process model has six components designed to assist the site-based team in analyzing the current situation, developing a plan to improve student learning, and implementing a process to assist in making the plan a reality for the school. Although it is prescriptive in its process, the model principally lets the team analyze the situation and develop solutions to the problems identified. The six components are detailed in the guide *School Improvement* (Fitzpatrick 1997) (see fig. 10.1). These are:

- Developing a profile of the school by gathering information on the demographics, student performance, school characteristics, and stakeholder perspectives. The data is analyzed and synthesized to gain an understanding of the school's strengths, limitations, and issues. This is communicated to the stakeholders and used in planning for school improvement.
- Defining the school's beliefs and mission by building a shared vision through a collaborative process. This work ensures that the school has

thought about the instructional beliefs (or philosophy) of those involved and develops a mission statement for the school similar to the one developed for strategic planning in a corporate environment.

- Defining the desired results for student learning by using a process to understand the stakeholders' expectations, the findings of educational research, and current goals of the school, district, state, and national educational expectations and then determining how the students currently are measuring up to these desired results. Once analyzed, this provides a direction to develop measurable student learning goals.

- Analyzing instructional and organizational effectiveness allows the school's current efforts to be explored to understand what types of changes must occur to better meet the student learning goals in the previous component. This component focuses on both the instructional work of the school including instruction, curriculum, and assessment, as well as the organizational work of the support components such as the educational agenda, leadership, culture, and community building.

- Developing an action plan is then accomplished using the analysis and conclusions from each of the previous four components, but heavily influenced from the results for learning and the instructional and organizational effectiveness. This plan details the action steps, a time line, resources needed, and individuals responsible for providing leadership in accomplishing the steps.

- Implementing the plan and documenting results is the component that applies the results of the planning and validates the results by measuring and observing the changes desired. This requires monitoring of the efforts and collecting evidence to verify achievement of goals.

The site-based team, once experienced in this model, will grow in sophistication and application due to the understanding of the team members. Also, individual team members may rotate from the team, yet due to the experience of a core group of the members, the level of maturation of the plans will grow with the continual improvement process concept.

EMPOWERING YOUR SCHOOL COMMUNITY MODEL

Developed by the site-based team led by Monasmith (1997) in a Washington State high school, this model, designed to empower the school community, has the potential to bring students, parents, staff, and citizens together to help solve problems and set priorities. Monasmith describes this model with the understanding that citizens and parents do not have the luxury of attending site-based meetings ad infinitum, therefore, the work the team does must be compressed into a workable schedule without becoming a major burden to these participants.

Membership on the site-based school improvement team consists of four staff members and four faculty members who are elected by their peers, students who are elected as class officers from each grade level at the school, four parents from each grade level, and citizens at large—such as opinion leaders as well as retired citizens who are willing to use their influence in gaining support for the team's efforts. The citizens must be recruited from a pool of individuals who are available and willing to contribute. Senior citizens may often be recruited at senior citizens' centers in the community, where retired but active seniors find activities to devote their time and efforts. Parents are selected by each of the classes and then asked by the students to serve, thereby representing the parents' interests of the class. This is very important for the selected parents, because they are also the supporters and advocates for the students. Elected class officers serve, which actually gives them something to do while they are students, and provides issues to be discussed in class elections. Monasmith (1997) is quick to admit that it is important that some teachers and staff members be elected who understand the big picture at the school, and not be only dissatisfied individuals within the school system. These individuals must be able to present the faculty and staff's view of problems and often have to voice opinions of experienced educators in discussing issues at hand.

This group is quite large if all are present at meetings; however, usually other commitments prevent all of them from attending any one meeting. The principal is present at the meeting, however, he is not the chair; another individual is selected as chair of the team and presides during its meetings. The principal, according to Monasmith (1997), must be present to help discuss aspects of issues and point out constraints on some solutions that might be proposed. Meetings occur bimonthly and last for two hours only. Originally, the teams attempted monthly meetings, but soon learned that recommendations that would be instituted took more than four weeks to get underway.

The team is primarily a problem identification group that brainstorms solutions and formulates consensus recommendations. This may take the biggest part of the meeting. Once a consensus is reached, the team members are responsible for taking the recommendations back to their constituents and gaining their support for the plans developed. If the recommendation needs to be taken before the school board due to the nature of the solution and to get outside approval, then the citizens-at-large are those members who speak to the board concerning the proposal, after the superintendent has been approached by the principal.

Once a proposal has been adopted, the principal is the individual who brings the recommendations to the entire school staff, who then participate in helping to develop the recommendation for application in the school. This is an important step and is necessary to identify additional problems that may not have been recognized earlier by the site-based team that must be dealt with by the faculty and staff. (See figure 10.2.)

The meeting format for the site-based school improvement team is somewhat important due to the length of the meeting and the problem-solving format. The following are included in the meeting:

- Comments about the school's accomplishments (this is important to help set the tone of the meeting; it helps to focus on positive contributions that can be made)
- Follow-up from previous meeting decisions (state of the recommendations now in implementation)
- Problem identification/expectation (begins in small groups; sharing of ideas; and bringing the lists together)
- Priority setting of problems identified (sets priorities on lists developed earlier)
- Group problem-solving activities (brainstorming for ideas that may develop problem solutions)
- Reporting group recommendations (develop a unified solution from ideas)

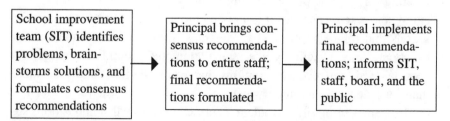

Figure 10.2 Empowering the School—Community Model

- Attaining consensus on recommendations (adoption of consensus following discussion)
- Group sign-off on recommendations (agreement)
- Agenda for the next meeting (thoughts about the next meeting shared)
- Debriefing: How does the group feel? (reflections on the meeting)

This model recognizes the importance of the faculty and staff for implementation of the ideas and the contributions that can be made by all of the other stakeholders in dealing with issues. This is a team effort and it is important that there be cooperation and an attitude of sharing ideas when issues are discussed. Although political agendas and self-serving ideas may arise, the important thing is that the goal of "making students' welfare the benefit of solutions" be kept in the forefront of the team's work.

IMPLEMENTING SITE-BASED DECISION MAKING

Of course, site-based decision making is not a change that ordinarily happens at just the school level. Such changes occur normally within the environment of the school district or sometimes even the state when these changes are promoted by the legislature or a state board of education. Although a principal may utilize the operating models cited earlier within a school on his or her own volition, the real strength of site-based decisions comes from every operating unit being able to adjust its operations for the conditions and individual problems that are being faced by that school. Site-based teams do not usually make major strides toward student improvement overnight. The implementation process is best affected when supported by the district board and administration as this change impacts how the district operates. Many program decisions that may have been made in the past by facilitators or coordinators at the district level may now be decided at the campus level. This requires a reexamination of the roles of these jobs at the district level. Reynolds (1997) projects that it takes a five-year process to fully move through the site-based management change in a school district as the district must also change its operations and beliefs to fully receive the benefits. Reynolds (1997) identifies twenty-five steps to be encountered over a five-year time frame to fully implement and evaluate such changes (171). The time line includes a focus on the central office's role and the principal's and site team's role.

IMPLEMENTING SITE-BASED PLANS

Planning for changes is perhaps the most important step in making such changes happen successfully; however, the actual implementation of the change is a function and part of the role of those closest to the change. A site-based team is made up of stakeholders that includes parents, students, teachers, administrators, and community members. Monasmith (1997) points out in his model that the teachers and staff members of the school are the individuals who must take responsibility for implementing that change. The principal, as leader of the school, must orchestrate the tasks and take charge of the implementation process. Other stakeholders must also support the decision that the site-based team made; however, some of these stakeholders are not present on a regular basis, so the principal must be the leader who coordinates and arranges for the tasks to be performed and the resources to be available.

Implementation is one of twenty-one domains that were identified by the National Policy Board for Educational Administration as major competencies that principals need the skills to carry out. Those tasks required for implementation are just as important for site-based team work as for individual principals. The tasks for nonroutine implementation, as identified by Pankake (1998), include:

- Establishment of a clear purpose for the project
- A view that the project is usable and doable by those doing the implementation
- Arranging for the availability of needed resources
- Training and development of those needing skills and knowledge to make the project happen
- Carry out checks on the continued implementation as it proceeds
- Feedback to the responsible implementers about the progress
- Coaches and cheerleaders who provide support verbally and in other ways

As in most tasks that require the work of many individuals to be successful, training of those involved is critical to the success of the operation. Support of the stakeholders, teachers, and staff who carry out the implementation is also necessary. Sometimes this support is the verbal type that can help the acceptance of the changes to be made; at other times, the support includes specific actions that have to be accomplished. Development of ideas and the continuation of thinking to revise and improve the ongoing changes is also needed. No solution to a problem is perfect; there is always room for improvement and those implementing the change are there to understand what else needs to be developed to make it work. Those additions must be recognized and added to the plans as they progress.

Whenever plans are implemented, there needs to be a monitoring process to complete the cycle. The site-based team initiating a solution should review the implementation as the team continues to meet and discuss other problems or planning issues. Plans should always have a time line developed to assist in understanding the scheduled implementation and also include those who are responsible for implementing specified tasks. The principal would be the logical individual to be the responsible reviewing administrator, or another faculty or staff member providing leadership to those actions can be designated. By monitoring the process while it is occurring, a team may rectify problems, adjust time lines, identify additionally needed resources, and make changes where additional attention to tasks are needed. In many cases, adjustments will be accomplished by the individual responsible for that part of the project and reported to the site-based team. These actions might best be thought of as formative evaluation type changes. After a period of time has elapsed that includes expected realization of the goals or objectives, summative evaluation of the accomplishments should occur. This action will help to verify success and the possible extension of the solution to other sites where similar problems occur. These actions are often referred to as institutionalization of the solution. What must be remembered, however, is that solutions are developed for specific situations, by particular groups. Just because the solution worked in one school or district, it does not mean that it will work equally well in another location. The circumstances and the individuals acting as a group are the key ingredients that make any planned effort successful. When these differ because of location or motivation, then the results will often differ.

ETHICAL DISCUSSION

- How should the feeling that "professionals should lead and manage the school" be dealt with when trying to establish a site-based team?
- What perspective do the parents bring to the discussion table that teachers and administrators fail to understand?
- Why should students be included in a site-based team?

- Develop a mission statement for a school that captures what the site-based movement does for students.
- When the principal disagrees with the site-based team on an issue, who is to have the controlling part of the decision? How can such a standpoint be avoided?
- Ethical dilemmas are right-versus-right issues. Which side of the site-based decision-making debate do you support and why?

CHAPTER SUMMARY

Site-based decision making occurs when decisions are made at the campus level at the site of impact of programs on students. Because those closest to the changes are most likely to understand the students, their needs, and the circumstances that must be dealt with, there is a likelihood that the best decisions will be made there as opposed to those at district or state levels of education.

Site-based teams were heralded by industry and government as solutions to problems not solved in many established bureaucracies. As a result, much of the driving force behind this move has come from those major institutions and the quality movement. The move toward site-based teams is different in every state due to laws and policies—some are a policy requirement and some are at the principal's or other stakeholders' initiative. Although the goal is to increase student achievement, the change is sometimes designed to shift the balance of power, to initiate political or administrative reform, or to make some change in staffing, resources, or blame for failures.

Developing operational site-based teams usually means changing the culture and climate of a school, developing trust among stakeholders, and sharing in the change process. Democracy is an important principle and as a result, some conflict will be encountered. Training for stakeholders and for traditional principals is necessary to alter leadership roles and to develop techniques for addressing problems and choices. One group cannot manage and conduct all the group tasks that are possible; other groups may need to be established. Once established, any site-based group will need to select a model to operate by in order to conduct its systematic analysis and management of change. Examples include the CIPP model and the school improvement model developed by the National Study of School Evaluation. From a district perspective, the implementation of a site-based focus may take several years to adjust and establish workable roles and goals among the stakeholders and the district. Once functioning, the team must not only plan, but also conduct and monitor the implementation process for the reforms, changes, and initiatives that are identified.

CHAPTER ACTIVITIES AND QUESTIONS

1. Discuss the quality movement and principles that help stakeholders and implementers understand the function and need for site-based teams.
2. Read some of Deming's, Crosby's, or Juran's writings and establish some operational goals for the site-based team you would hope to develop in your school.
3. Review the site-based laws and policies that define such an operation in your state and school district.
4. Visit a site-based team meeting in a school of your choosing.
5. Interview a principal who is currently working with a site-based team in his or her school and ask about the team's operation and successes.
6. What principles or rules would you choose to use in developing a site-based team at your school?
7. With a group of educators, study and practice using one or more of the techniques for small-group problem identification, prioritizing, or solving listed in table 10.1.
8. Which of the identified models for conducting a site-based team would you select and why?
9. How would you evaluate the results of a site-based team's accomplishments?
10. With others, develop a list of steps you would use to implement a site-based philosophy at your school.
11. What is the role of the cheerleader in the implementation process after plans are set?
12. What do you see as positive aspects of the site-based team for implementation of changes?

CASE STUDY ACTIVITIES AND QUESTIONS

1. How should Ms. Nugent proceed with her exploration of a site-based management team for her school?

2. What role should the team play? Who should be on the team?
3. What tasks should the team undertake if it came into existence?
4. What support should Ms. Nugent expect from the district if this team is to be a contributing factor for the school?
5. What types of problems might the principal encounter in the establishment of such a team?
6. If you were Ms. Nugent, what type of discussion would you have with district-level administration on this topic if it had never been discussed before?
7. The district has a teachers union that is still a force with which to be reckoned. How should she approach the teachers union representative?

REFERENCES

Bailey, W. J. (1991). *School-site management applied.* Lancaster, PA: Technomic.

Candoli, I. C. (1995). *Site-based management in education: How to make it work in your school.* Lancaster, PA: Technomic.

David, J. L. (1995–1996). "The who, what and why of site-based management." *Educational Leadership* (December–January): 4–9.

Fitzpatrick, K. A. (1997). *School improvement: Focusing on student performance.* Schaumburg, IL: National Study of School Evaluation.

Fullan, M. (1995). "The school as learning organization: Distance dreams." *Theory into Practice* 34 (4): 230–235.

Fullan, M., and Miles, M. (1991). "Getting educational reform right: What works and what doesn't." Unpublished paper. University of Toronto, Center for Policy Research.

Lindle, J. C. (1995–1996). "Lessons from Kentucky about school-based decision making." *Educational Leadership* (December–January): 20–23.

Mohrman, S. A., and Wohlstetter, P. (1994). *School-based management.* San Francisco: Jossey-Bass.

Monasmith, J. (1997). "Empowering your school-community." Paper presented at the symposium for the Meadows Principal Improvement Program at Texas A&M University, Commerce, June.

Murphy, J. (1991). *Restructuring schools: Capturing and assessing the phenomena.* New York: Columbia University Teachers College Press.

Pankake, A. M. (1998). *Implementation: Making things happen.* Larchmont, NY: Eye on Education.

Reynolds, L. J. (1997). *Successful site-based management: A practical guide.* Thousand Oaks, CA: Corwin.

Smith, S. (1998). "School by school." *American School Board Journal* (June): 22–25.

Stufflebeam, D., chair. (1971). *Educational evaluation and decision making.* Itasca, IL: Peacock.

Wheeler, N., and Agruso, R. (1996). "Implementing school centered decision making." Paper presented at the Summit on Education, Nashville, TN, June.

Section IV

Integrity and Ethics
for Campus Leadership

ISLLC Standard 4

A school administrator is an educational leader who promotes the success of all students by collaborating with families and community members, responding to diverse community interests and needs, and mobilizing community resources. The administrator has knowledge and understanding of:

- Emerging issues and trends that potentially impact the school community
- The conditions and dynamics of the diverse school community
- Community resources
- Community relations and marketing strategies and processes
- Successful models of school, family, business, community, government, and higher education partnerships

Chapter Eleven

Ethical Behavior for the Principal

Velma Dietters, principal of South Park Middle School in Cameron, was given a message by her secretary that Mr. Arley Cool wanted to visit with her about his daughter Audra. Mr. Cool indicated that he would visit with Ms. Dietters at Tuesday evening's volleyball game between High Tech Avenue Middle and South Park Middle. She wondered what he wanted to talk about and she could only guess he was upset about the discipline problem with his daughter. She reviewed her procedures and she knew she had done all the right things with this discipline situation. She knew Mr. Cool had, on several occasions, questioned the school district's code of student conduct. He believed that children should be given the opportunity to solve their own behavioral problems and it was the parents' right to decide how the child should be disciplined.

Audra Cool was a seventh grader at South Park and from the first day of school she had let her teachers and Ms. Dietters know that she was the daughter of a school board member. During Friday of the second week of the fall semester, Ms. Smith, a well respected mathematics teacher, sent Audra to the office for refusing to follow a request. Ms. Dietters called Mr. Cool and told him about the discipline problem with Audra and Mr. Cool assured Ms. Dietters that he would have a long talk with Audra about her behavior.

Mr. Cool approached Ms. Dietters during the intermission between the "A" and "B" team volleyball games. He asked Ms. Dietters to step out in to the hall to talk about his daughter and she suggested they go to her office not far down the main hall of the building. After exchanging greetings, Mr. Cool asked Ms. Dietters for a personal favor: He wanted his daughter to be placed in advanced mathematics and English classes and if Ms. Dietters exerted some pressure on the teachers he was sure that his daughter would be a model citizen and that she would be in the proper class. Ms. Dietters was stunned by the request, not suspecting this would be the reason for the discussion. Mr. Cool went on to make the case that Audra's poor behavior was directly tied to her lack of motivation in the regular math and English classes. Ms. Dietters told Mr. Cool that Audra was placed in the regular math and English classes based on her academic performance in the sixth grade. Mr. Cool countered by stating that her grades were below the standard for the advanced classes because of his recent divorce. He went on to say everything in Audra's life was turned upside down and her entire personality changed during the divorce proceedings. Ms. Dietters listened and told Mr. Cool she would investigate the situation.

Ms. Dietters researched Audra's academic history and found out that she had never been in advanced math or English and that her grades actually improved some during the time the divorce proceedings were taking place. She called Mr. Cool and reported what she had found and he became very defensive and angry. He told Ms. Dietters he wanted his daughter in advanced math and English and she was to get her into those classes by the end of the week. Shortly after her conversation with Mr. Cool, the superintendent's secretary called to set up an appointment to talk about Audra Cool.

Superintendent J. B. Tucker listened as Ms. Dietters outlined the situation. When she had finished, Dr. Tucker told her she really needed to consider granting Mr. Cool's request because it would just be easier on everyone concerned. Dr. Tucker went to let Ms. Dietters know the decision was hers and hers alone, and that she should not count on his support in this situation. Ms. Dietters left the building in a state of confusion and frustration. A board of education member wanting special favors for his child, a superintendent not willing to back the principal, and teachers who knew Audra Cool was not an advanced student of any type. What should she do?

The situation that Ms. Dietters found herself in with Mr. Cool is repeated in school districts across this nation on a daily basis. This situation is an example of how a board of education member can get involved in the practice of granting favors to selected individuals in the community, in this case a favor for himself. People in positions of power, such as school board members, choose to abuse that power at the expense of others. This seems to be the situation with Ms. Dietters. Ethical situations can surface where the possibility exists for improper use of power or when the mission of the school district is replaced by personal agendas.

What is ethics? The Markkula Center for Applied Ethics (2000) defines ethics as a well-based standards of right and wrong that direct what people ought to do. Second, ethics is about the study of each person's standards. Ethics is not about religious doctrine, nor is it about following the law, and lastly ethics is not doing whatever society accepts. If ethics focused strictly on religion, then religious people would be the only individuals subject to ethical standards. If being ethical meant doing whatever society accepts, then it would be necessary to find out what the current society accepts.

The National School Boards Association (1997) acknowledges that ethical dilemmas have plagued the country with scandals involving both professional and personal misbehavior at the highest levels of leadership. They state that the most important elements of an ethical life include compassion, fairness, integrity, and moral courage. The question for most educators is: Can you be ethical in your professional life and not in your personal life? It is highly unlikely that a person could be ethical in one phase of his or her life and not in the other. Some individuals would question the roles of teachers and principals in teaching students about ethics, yet education is the very tool that can help students get a clearer sense of right and wrong.

Kidder (1995) defines ethical dilemmas as right-versus-right choices and he calls right-versus-wrong choices moral temptations. Kidder argues most people don't knowingly make wrong or bad choices, but when it comes to the really hard choices people focus on the right-versus-right dilemma. Dilemmas surface when values conflict. These conflicts expand exponentially for principals because of their role in meeting the needs of students, parents, teachers, and the community. As a principal, you will face many right-versus-wrong issues and in general most principals have very little trouble in making the right choice. For example, how many of us have cheated on our income taxes or lied under oath? Clearly a right-versus-wrong dilemma. In schools, principals face choices that affect students, teachers, parents, and even the community. It is the final week for high school football and the team's star player is arrested by the police for driving under the influence of alcohol and also charged for being a minor in possession of a controlled substance. If the football team wins this last game, it will advance to the semifinals of the state football play-offs, something this school has never done. The community, the team, the coach, his parents, and other influentials want this student to participate in the game. Is this a right-versus-right choice or a right-versus-wrong dilemma? The principal must make a choice. If this is a right-versus-wrong issue, a moral dilemma, then the choice seems quite clear. The child has broken school, team, and community rules as well as the law. For most principals the answer is clear, the student does not play in the game. The principal's choice is not always the final disposition of situations like this one, because human beings are willing to sacrifice personal values for the sake of a football victory. This situation is clearly a moral dilemma for some principals, especially those who live in a moral vacuum and for others it is a nonissue, the player does not participate.

Tough choices for principals arrive at the doorstep when right-versus-right issues emerge. For example, in addressing the question: Are school vouchers an appropriate choice mechanism? Both sides of this issue have benefits for students, teachers, parents, and communities. Arguments can be made for the implementation of a voucher system, supported by hard data and educationally sound principles of learning. The arguments that oppose a voucher system are equally defensible and are based on accepted principles of child development and learning. A principal who considers taking a bribe is facing a moral dilemma, while a principal deciding to give scarce resources to a gifted program or an at-risk program faces an ethical dilemma. Right-versus-right dilemmas are the basis for defining ethical dilemmas in this chapter because right-versus-wrong are moral temptations and they address the standards or core values of the individual. Principals without standards and core values that mirror what human beings ought to do surely doom public schools to mediocrity and eventually failure.

Most scholars who study ethics agree that there is no one best way to answer complex questions, but a few have suggested some guiding principles. Starratt (1991) argues that leaders must have and be willing to act on a definite set of ethical standards. He argues that an ethical principal would be concerned about justice, caring about individuals, and critiquing his or her own ethical performance. Kidder (1995) states that dilemmas can be viewed from four perspectives: (1) anticipate the outcomes of each choice and determine how it affects people in the organization; (2) use acceptable moral standards in making choices; (3) use the concept of the Golden Rule, that is, in making choices do you treat people like you would like to be treated?; and (4) is there a third choice that moves away from the either-or thinking, which Kidder calls a trilemma?

ETHICAL CONDUCT AND THE PRINCIPAL

It is the moral duty of the principal to provide moral leadership. This is demonstrated not by what principals say but by what they do. Actions are the key to determining the moral compass of any leader and this applies to the principal as well. Principals as ethical leaders is a must in today's educational venues. In a comprehensive survey of ethics of 8,600 high school students, 71 percent stated they had cheated on an exam at least once, 79 percent cheated two times or more, 78 percent lied to teachers, and 27 percent indicated they would lie to get a job. In this same survey, 92 percent of the respondents stated they lied to their parents, 40 percent had stolen something from a store, and 16 percent stated they had been drunk at school. Even more disturbing was that 68 percent of the students had physically attacked another person, and 47 percent stated they could get a gun if they wanted one (Josephson 2000). Surely, the moral compass is directed toward honesty, courage, stewardship, and trust. These virtues are the moral pointers that give direction to ethical leadership.

Honesty is the moral virtue most admired by students, teachers, and parents (Richardson 1992). Honesty is more than always telling the truth, it encompasses the willingness to act responsibly when things do go wrong in the school. It mandates the principal to treat students and teachers in a fair manner, regardless of their actions against the principal. Honesty is a core value that the individual is unwilling to surrender even in the light of serious personal consequences.

Courage is the willingness to take the blame for what happens in the school. It requires the principal to defend individual faculty members when they have made a mistake with a student or a parent and it requires the principal to disagree with the superintendent and board of education when they have mistakenly made choices that affect students in a negative manner. Courage is the power to withstand personal negative consequences while leading the organization toward its goals. As a virtue, courage is about the ability to do the right thing in the face of social and organizational pressure to select a solution that is divergent from the politically correct solution.

Block (1993) argues that stewardship, the willingness to assume responsibility for school outcomes without attempting to control the outcome, is a moral virtue. He asks leaders to be servant leaders for the people in their organization and for the larger purpose or mission of the organization. In order to be a steward, the principal must be willing to reveal his or her own faults instead of hiding behind the veil of power and authority. Stewardship is mostly about the attitude the principal assumes as he or she works with the various constituencies in the school community, but it is an attitude that is crucial to any organization.

Trust is a virtue that is very hard to get from members of the school organization and once the principal gets this trust it is easily destroyed by one single mistake. Principals develop trust by supporting teachers and students when they are right and when they make mistakes. Trust engenders a feeling of security among the students and faculty, they believe the principal is behind them to pick them up in case they fall. Trust is making sure that all members of the faculty and staff get treated in an equitable manner, not in an equal way. Trust occurs when the principal approaches the superintendent on behalf of teachers who want to attempt a new instructional program, knowing full well that the superintendent isn't likely to approve the program. Trust does not flow only from the principal to the faculty, in fact trust flows in both directions simultaneously.

A principal cannot become an ethical leader until the principal practices daily and makes these virtues a habit. Lashway (1996) states that ethical behavior cannot be held in abeyance until some major crisis occurs—it must be practiced every day. Being an ethical principal is not about following simple guidelines, it is complicated and multifaceted and more about human energy than technical expertise. Answering the following three questions will help the principal each time he or she finds him- or herself in an ethical dilemma:

- Is what I am about to do legal?
- Is what I am about to do going to provide balance and be fair?
- Will my decision affect the way I feel about myself? (National School Boards Association 1997)

Ethical thinking is not an easy task and there are no strategies that will substitute for focusing on what is right. This type of thinking requires self-discipline and an understanding of one's own context.

CORE VALUES AND ETHICAL DECISION MAKING

Values may be defined as principles or standards of behavior in terms of beliefs about good or bad behavior (Frymier et al. 1996). Frymier (1974) believes that "values are close to the center of self" (9). In some instances, values and morals are considered to be similar or the same phenomenon. Weston (2001) defines values as "those things we care about, that matter to us; those goals and ideas we aspire to and measure ourselves or others or our society by" (49). Many individuals in education believe that the teachers and principals are more than a dispenser of knowledge and skills. They argue that all school personnel are moral exemplars who should attempt to behave in a professional, ethical, and moral manner in order to serve as a catalyst for values in children (Beyer 1997; Campbell 1997).

Leadership and ethics are tied together because of the extraordinary relationship between leaders and followers created by the values of the leaders. Principals provide leadership and that leadership is ultimately judged by the values that guide their decisions. Without core values, principals risk heading in the wrong direction and making poor decisions. If principals make decisions without values and beliefs, they diminish their effectiveness and the effectiveness of the school. The following questions provide a basis for making sure we ask ourselves the hard questions and honest answers:

- Are all decisions made in the best interests of students?
- Do you believe that all individuals are responsible for their actions?
- Do you believe in open and honest communication?
- Do you treat others as you would like to be treated?
- What kinds of values could lead someone to think differently than you?

It is important that students are at the top of the academic pyramid and that all decisions concerning the school should focus on what's best for students. Many times decisions are made without consulting the ethical responsibility for students. These types of decisions are not in the best interests of the principal, teachers, or the school and must be eliminated from the list of possibilities. Principals must convey to all school personnel and students that their actions are most important in representing who they are. Most individuals assume that excuses are acceptable reasons for their actions, while principals need to remind everyone that responsible action is the goal.

Open communication is essential to discussions about the ethical basis for decisions that principals face. Ethical situations need to be discussed with teachers and other staff members so that all parties engage in defining problems, addressing ethical implications, and courses of action. Each decision is an opportunity for ethical education to occur. Confronting violations of ethical standards must be exposed and cared for in a very judicious manner. Discussions about values and obligations are not easy because they require introspection by each individual and this is very difficult to do (Brown and Townsend 1997).

Treating others with respect and honor is an important ethical model for principals to demonstrate. It really is about focusing on the "common good." What exactly is the common good? This concept was developed some 2,000 years ago in the writings of Plato, Aristotle, and Cicero and has most recently been defined as specific general conditions that provide equality for all (Markkula Center for Applied Ethics 2000). Perhaps the common good is the social fabric on which we all depend and benefits all people. Treating others with respect and honor fits the term as it benefits all the customers in the organization. Treating others respectfully is not an easy concept to establish because it requires cooperative efforts of many people—just as keeping the school clean depends on students, teachers, custodians, and the principal to pick up the trash in the classrooms and hallways. Treating others with respect and honor challenges each of us to view ourselves as corporate members of the community of humanity.

Professional relationships in the school environment are most basic when working with teachers, parents, and students. Courtesy and cooperation are two of the virtues that principals must be able to utilize if they are going to lead the school in an ethical direction. Very distracting situations can occur from unprofessional relationships especially if one or more of the participants is engaged in personally destructive behavior. Perhaps the most important ethical attribute a principal could possess is the willingness to keep information confidential. This applies to faculty and students alike.

Principals are privy to many private matters about student home life, money problems, personal relationships, health, and academic records. Principals simply cannot share much of this information with teachers, except on a need to know basis and certainly they should never divulge any of this knowledge to other students (Graham and Cline 1997).

Perhaps one of the biggest issues of ethical behavior that confronts a principal is the knowledge that a member of his or her teaching staff works as an exotic dancer at a local bar after the school day concludes. These types of ethical issues depend on the context of the school, in some communities it is not a problem and in others it is not acceptable. As an ethical person and leader, how do you deal with such a situation. Some school districts have policies concerning after hours conduct while others do not, so the legal test may or may not be appropriate. Every good principal needs to develop ethical guidelines personally and be prepared to let others in the organization know what those guidelines look like.

FRAMEWORK FOR ETHICAL DECISION MAKING

Conventional decision making has generally focused on gathering data, interpreting the data, generating solutions, selecting a solution, implementing the solution, and evaluating the results of the solution. Most principals generally skip the evaluating phase of the conventional decision-making model whether it is a success or a failure. No one knows for sure why the implemented decision solved the problem, they just know it worked. The next time a similar problem arises the same solution is implemented, but this time it fails to solve the problem. Once again no one knows why it failed, but the principal does know it did not solve the problem. Many principals would respond to this criticism by stating "I don't have time to analyze or reflect on my decisions," but the discussion should center around the idea that a principal must take the time to analyze or reflect on his or her decisions. Yes, the results of the decision are important but even more important is how he or she arrived at this solution. Keeney (1994) argues that values, not solutions or alternatives, should be the focus in decision making. He expands this concept by describing "value-focused thinking" as the process of using fundamental values as a guide in decision making.

Value-focused thinking allows the principal to generate better solutions for any decision set. The number of solutions identified by decision makers is usually very narrow because ill-defined solutions are avoided in favor of well-defined solutions. The really creative solutions remain hidden and focusing on values helps remove the barriers of the mind (Keeney 1994). Value-focused thinking provides the decision maker with an opportunity to solve the current problem, but at the same time avoid future problems. Viewed from this perspective, solving problems is analogous to problem prevention. Practicing value-focused thinking gets easier the more your practice. Articulating values during less stressful situations prepares you to make the harder decisions easier. Structuring values makes it easier to clarify difficult situations and they will eventually form a coherent pattern (Keeney 1994). Value-focused thinking helps the principal in three ways by:

1. Identifying opportunities for decision making
2. Creating better solutions for solving problems
3. Developing a lasting set of guiding principles (Keeney 1994)

The principal of Berryville High School was notified by the head counselor that all of the parents with children in danger of not meeting the school district's graduation requirement had been contacted by telephone informing them that their child lacked the necessary units of credit to graduate in May. Each December, the counseling staff reviews all potential graduates' transcripts to make sure they are on track to getting their diploma. Graduation day was one week away and the principal had been notified by her secretary that a Ms. Marley Watkins wanted to discuss the reason her child was not being allowed to participate in the graduation ceremonies. The principal investigated the student's situation and it was clear that Ms. Watkins's daughter was lacking three units of credit to meet the required twenty-four units for graduation. The principal informed Ms. Watkins, at their 3 P.M. meeting, of the situation and Ms. Watkins indicated she would appeal to the superintendent. The next day the superintendent called the principal to discuss the Watkins case and quizzed the principal concerning the facts surrounding the situation. As the call was about to end, the superintendent asked the principal to reconsider her decision. The principal knew she had made the right decision based on school policy, fairness to the other eighteen students who were not going to be allowed to participate in graduation, and the fact that historically students had not been allowed to graduate without all of their credits. The day of graduation arrived and the principal was on the athletic field putting the final touches on the graduation set when she was paged to call the superintendent. Once again the superintendent asked her to reconsider her decision on the Watkins child and she refused. At about 1:00 P.M. the superintendent called and asked her to meet at the central administration building. When the principal arrived, she was shocked to see the board of education meeting in an emergency session and the topic of discussion was the Watkins child. The superintendent invited the principal to tell the board of education why she had denied the Watkins child the opportunity to participate in graduation. She went through the entire litany of circumstances surrounding this situation and even gave her rationale for making the decision she made. She left the room and the board voted unanimously to allow the child to participate in the graduation. Needless to say the principal was angry and shocked and wondered why this had happened.

The principal went back to her office to reflect on the situation and to determine her error in judgment. Using value-focused thinking, she began to analyze what had just occurred. She thought she knew the essence of the problem: the Watkins child did not have enough units of credit to graduate and her mother was angry about the child's failure and wanted to blame someone. The principal reviewed the solutions she had considered:

1. Let the child participate in the graduation ceremony without giving her the diploma
2. Do not allow the child to participate in the graduation ceremony
3. Have the child complete summer school and award the diploma when she finishes the units of credit in the summer, but let her participate in the graduation ceremony
4. Create a contract with the child to complete correspondence credit with a local university and if she agrees let her participate in the graduation ceremony

The principal had chosen to not allow the child to participate in the graduation ceremony. Value-focused thinking helped the principal to return to her set of guiding principles, those principles she had been using for the past twelve years as a high school principal. Her guiding principles included fairness: Was it fair to the other eighteen students who did not get to participate in graduation and to allow the Watkins child to do so? She determined the answer to be "no." Was it responsible and reasonable to violate school board policy? Again, the answer was "no." Was she going to break the long-standing tradition of no participation in graduation for those students who did not meet the school district's minimum requirements? She decided that that was not something she wanted on her resume. Based on the value-focused thinking framework, the principal made an ethical decision. These are the type of ethical decisions principals face every day.

The ethical framework outlined by McDonald (2000) for decision making begins by addressing the question: Is there a moral issue involved in this situation and if there is can you identify that issue? The answer to this question triggers a more in-depth investigation of the situation. Using this framework, the principal would need to gather the relevant facts by identifying all of the stakeholders who are directly involved in the situation. During this phase of the decision-making process, the principal should remember to be sensitive to a morally charged situation, should not make quick judgments, should determine what decisions need to be made, and remind him- or herself that there may be more than one decision maker involved in the final outcome (McDonald 2000).

Evaluate the feasible solutions from various moral perspectives. This process entails determining which solution will produce the most good, the least harm, and promote the common good. There also must be an examination of which solution will develop or improve the school. Use the following ethical capital to identify the moral factors in each solution:

- Are ethical principles being violated or supported?
- Are there expectations on the part of others?
- Do no harm.
- Use ethical sources such as school policy, professional expectations, legal precedents, and codes of conduct.
- Use personal judgments supported by thoughts and ideas from close professional colleagues and trusted friends. (McDonald 2000)

Once each of these factors has been considered, it is time to make the decision. Consider your solutions carefully by determining the impact the solution will have on the performance of the stakeholders. Are you making it harder or easier for the stakeholders to do the right thing? Does the solution seem to be the right one and would an ethical person choose this solution? Answering all of these questions brings the principal to his or her decision point. He or she should make the decision, assume responsibility for his or her choice, and live with the results. All decisions are subject to new information and it is possible the wrong choice is made but the objective is always to make a good decision not a perfect one (Markkula Center for Applied Ethics 2000).

Using McDonald's ethical framework to analyze the Berryhill High School situation, begin by answering the fundamental question: Is there a moral issue in this situation and if so what is it? The answer to the first part of the question seems to be "yes." The second part addresses what the moral appears to be and in this situation the issue seems to be the graduation participation by the Watkins child. The two-part question appears to indicate that there is an ethical and moral situation created by the board of education. The principal in this situation gathered the facts and carefully thought about her decision based on the facts she collected. She outlined four solutions for the problem and chose the solution she determined would resolve the situation. She may have failed to realize that there would be more than one decision maker involved in this situation and if she had realized this would her decision have been different?

The principal spent her ethical capital on making sure the student was treated fairly, honestly, and openly. She determined that allowing the student to participate in the graduation ceremony would violate the ethical virtues of honesty and fairness. She also knew that the other eighteen students who failed to meet the graduation requirement would find out about the exception for the Watkins child and she would be inundated with accusations of favoritism and unfair treatment. She felt those eighteen students would have a legitimate concern and perhaps legal recourse. The principal felt very strongly that she should do no harm to those eighteen students because they had accepted responsibility for not meeting the graduation standard, even though most of them were disappointed and unhappy. She addressed the question of ethical sources by referring to the school district's policy on graduation requirements and the historical documentation that no student had ever graduated from Berryhill High School lacking course credits. The principal contacted professional colleagues

and discussed the situation with her professional mentor prior to render-
ing her decision. One of her trusted friends told her not to fight this battle; it just wasn't worth the time, trouble, and energy, but she chose to stick
with her decision.

This analysis of the Berryhill High School situation reaches the same
conclusion as did the value-focused thinking model but in a slightly different way. The target for the principal was to solve the situation in an ethical manner choosing not to focus on the situation but instead to utilize the
ethical guidelines she had created for herself to solve the problem.

The utilitarian model of ethics is defined as taking the morally right
course of action. The morally right course of action would be one that
creates a balance of benefits over harm for all stakeholders. As long as
the individual's choice creates maximum benefits for all concerned,
utilitarian ethics cares little if the results are produced by lies, manipu-
lation, or coercion (Velasquez et al. 2000). In essence, this ethical
model is a means-end model meaning that the ends justify the means.
It's not important how you get to your target, it's just important that you
do get to the target.

The utilitarian model uses a simple paradigm for arriving at the
morally and ethically right action to employ. The first step in utilizing
this model is to identify the various solutions that could be performed.
Step two requires that benefits and harms be analyzed for each of the
solutions. In step three, the decision maker chooses the solution that
provides maximum benefits at the lowest cost to the organization. Utilitarianism is currently popular with politicians, business leaders, and
superintendents, and any person relying on this model for his or her
sole method of ethical decision making may experience problems determining the cost-benefit values that result from his or her actions
(Markkula Center for Applied Ethics 2000). The biggest problem with
this model is the failure to account for the virtue of justice. Most principals could envision a scenario where specific action would create
benefits for the school and be clearly unjust. It is clear that many people involved in school leadership are participants in the utilitarian
mantra of "self-interest" and those individuals need to remind themselves ethics requires us to look beyond self to the common good. Mill
(1863), a utilitarian, writes: "The happiness which forms the utilitarian
standard of what is right and in conduct, is not . . . one's own happi-

ness, but that of all concerned. As between his own happiness and that of others, utilitarianism requires him to be strictly impartial as a disinterested and benevolent spectator" (15).

Mill focuses on his concern that all of the stakeholders be considered as the decision maker weighs the benefits. In today's society, it appears that Mill's concern has come full circle as decision makers focus on the benefits to themselves or small groups of politically powerful individuals and at the same time disenfranchising large segments of the populous.

If the Berryhill High School principal had used the utilitarian model to make her decision about the Watkins situation, how would the results have been different? In this model, the first step is to identify the solutions that could be used. The principal outlined four specific actions she could take. The next step makes the decision maker view the solutions in terms of benefits and harms.

In table 11.1, the principal has described the benefits and harms of the solutions she has developed for the school. There are benefits and harms for the individual child and her parents depending on which of the solutions is enacted. The utilitarian decision maker at this point must weigh the benefits and harms for all of the students, teachers, and community stakeholders. In this situation, the principal could choose to allow the child to participate in the graduation by manipulating the child's transcript, by simply ignoring the school district's policy, or by viewing the parents as influentials in the community. Theoretically, she could have lied to the faculty and other students by denying that the Watkins child lacked the necessary credits to graduate. In this situation, the principal must assume that the end justifies the means. Perhaps this ethical new age is appealing to individuals who believe they have the ability to change your perceptions about any problem and some principals are quite skilled at shading the truth. As a principal, if you are going to engage in this type of ethical behavior be aware of its limits and where it fails.

Kidder (1995) in his book *How Good People Make Tough Choices* identifies three principles for addressing ethical dilemmas: (1) ends-based thinking, which is Kidder's description for utilitarianism; (2) rule-based thinking, which is defined by laws and policy statements: and (3) care-based thinking, which is a reflection of the Golden Rule: do unto others as you would have them do unto you. He uses these three principles for

Table 11.1   Utilitarian Solutions: Benifits versus Harms

Solutions	Benefits	Harms
1. Let the child participate in the graduation ceremony without giving her the diploma.	The child gets to participate in the graduation ceremony with her friends. The Watkins family does not have to tell its friends why its child did not graduate. The principal does not have to defend her actions to the board of education.	Eighteen other students are treated in an unfair manner. The principal is not following school policy so her job may be in jeopardy. The principal might face legal action for discriminating against the eighteen who did not get to participate.
2. Do not allow the child to participate in the graduation ceremony.	It is the fair solution for all of the students, both current and future. It upholds the school district's policy on graduation requirements. It supports the long-standing quality traditions of the high school.	Does not let the child graduate with her class and causes embarrassment for her. The child's parents are going to push this issue to the top decision makers and take it out of the hands of the principal.
3. Have the child complete summer school and award the diploma when she finishes the units of credit in the summer, but let her participate in the graduation ceremony.	The child meets the school district's requirements and gets to participate with her class. The child's parents do not take the issue to the board of education. No negative publicity for Berryhill High School.	The principal loses control of the graduation requirements. Other students see this as an opportunity to pressure the principal on other issues. The principal is not following her ethical guidelines.

Table 11.1   (Continued) Utilitarian Solutions: Benifits versus Harms

Solutions	Benefits	Harms
4. Create a contract with the child to complete credit through a local university correspondence course and if she agrees let her participate in the graduation ceremony.	The child gets to participate in the graduation ceremony with her friends. The Watkins family does not have to tell its friends why its child did not graduate. The principal does not have to defend her actions to the board of education. No negative publicity for Berryhill High School.	Eighteen other students are treated in an unfair manner. The principal is not following school policy so her job may be in jeopardy. The principal might face legal action for discriminating against the eighteen who did not get to participate. The principal would be jeopardizing her relationship with the faculty, staff, students, and community stakeholders.

the purpose of making decisions in his nine-step paradigm for addressing ethical dilemmas:

- Acknowledge a moral issue is present
- Who owns the issue?
- Collect the pertinent facts
- Examine the issue as a moral dilemma
- Examine the issue as an ethical dilemma
- Apply the three principles for addressing ethical dilemmas
- Is there a trilemma choice available?
- Decision time
- Reflect on the decision (Kidder 1995)

If the principal uses Kidder's paradigm to analyze the Berryhill High School situation, she must first acknowledge that a moral dilemma is present. From her perspective, she must decide if the issue of the Watkins child's participation in graduation ceremonies is a moral question. When making this decision, the principal must determine if the situation is about moral issues or conflicting values, which is not always easy for a principal to determine. In the Berryhill situation, the principal made the determination that this situation was indeed an ethical issue.

Who owns the ethical issue? Is it mine or does it belong to someone else? The test that answers this question is one of responsibility, mine or someone else's. In the Berryhill situation, the principal is morally obligated to do something about the situation. It is her responsibility to determine how she wants to handle the parental request based on ethical principles or guidelines. If the principal is morally responsible for doing something about the situation, then she must act.

Gathering pertinent facts is the key to any good decision-making process ethical or otherwise. Pertinent means locating the facts that control the essence of the situation. The details give rise to the motivation behind why people act the way they act in specific situations. In the Berryhill High School situation, the facts seem fairly straightforward: the Watkins child did not have enough credits to graduate, the principal denied the student's participation in the graduation ceremony, the parents protested the decision and appealed it to the board of education, and the board overturned the principal's decision. Are these the pertinent facts? Perhaps we need to add that the school district's policy on requirements for graduation was the foundation that the principal used in making her decision. How then can a board of education violate its own policy? Legally, ethically, and morally it cannot, but in this situation no one challenges its decision.

There is one question that any principal should ask: Is there any wrong doing in this situation? The tests for this question include the answer to the aforementioned question and the answer is "yes." The second test is the legal test and the answer to the question "is this a violation of law" is "no." Are school district policies law or do they carry the weight of law? They probably do not, but operationally they are the guidelines by which the school functions and in this sense they are quasi legal. Kidder (1995) adds the stench, front-page, and the "mom" test to determine right-versus-wrong issues. The stench test says if something smells bad it probably is bad. In reality, this test is about the principal's gut-feeling about the situation. The front-page test asks the question: How would you feel if this situation landed on the front-page of the nation's newspapers? The third test is the mom test, which asks the principal to consider how he or she would tell his mother about the situation and how his or her mom would handle this situation. In the Berryhill High School situation, the principal knew that she had the legal test on her side, that her gut-feeling was to deny the student request, that the situation could become a front-page story in the local community, that she felt comfortable about how that might read, and lastly that her mom would have made the same decision she had made.

If the situation passes the right-versus-wrong test, it surely must be an ethical dilemma. In the Berryhill case, it appears that perhaps the situation is a moral dilemma. The moral dilemma for the principal doesn't appear to be the case, but it may be the situation for the board of education. Perhaps the board of education needs to decide how it should handle the issue of district policy or parental pressure.

If the principal applies Kidder's (1995) resolution principles for ethical decisions, then clearer choices might emerge. The ends-based or utilitarian principle guides the principal in making a means-end decision where the decision is based on what's best for the most. In the Berryhill situation, it appears that the principal believes that eliminating the Watkins child from the ceremony is what's best for most of the students. If the principle applies the rule-based principle, it would seem that the school district's policy becomes the guiding principle and supports the principal's decision. The care-based principle asks the decision maker to choose a solution that the decision maker would make if he or she were in this same situation. The Berryhill principal would have to assume if it were her child that she would come to the same conclusion and in this instance that appears to be the case.

Is there an alternative to the solution that moves to the middle ground? Kidder (1995) states that in some situations this does exist and he calls this the "trilemma." The Berryhill principal could have found common ground by allowing the Watkins child to participate in the graduation ceremony, but at what costs to the faculty, other students, and the community? Sometimes the rigidity of both sides can be modified so that all participants can go along with the solution.

Make the decision and go forward with the solution. The solution chosen by the principal seems to be an ethical decision using the Kidder framework. Choosing not to decide is more damaging to the organization than any one single act of deciding. The more the people in the organization see the leader failing to lead, the more likely they are to take advantage of the situation themselves and pursue activities they know are unethical. Along with decision making comes the act of reflection on those decisions. As the principal of Berryhill High School reflected on the Watkins situation, she thought about how the entire dilemma could have been avoided. As she pondered the child's fate and the board of education's actions, she wondered whether her stand on the issue was worth the personal capital she had expended. Two weeks after the graduation ceremony, the Berryhill High School principal resigned to pursue her career in higher education. She knew she had made the correct choice on the Watkins child and she also knew the board of education was not going to forget her stand on principle. It was the very stand on principle that propelled her to a new career, one where she could influence others to make the ethical decision.

Can principals be taught ethics or is it part of a person's mental capacity at birth? Some 2,500 years ago Socrates debated this question and came to the conclusion that ethics was about knowing what ought to be done. He stated, without reservation, that ethical knowledge could be taught. Research indicates that behavior is influenced by moral perception and judgment (Markkula Center for Applied Ethics 2000). It appears that ethical behavior can be taught to those individuals willing to utilize ethical frameworks for decision making. Learning to be ethical is neither easy nor quick, but the payoffs for decision makers is manyfold.

You now have a set of ethical models from which to function in an ethical manner and what you need now is a "tool kit" that will allow you to put what you have learned into action. Weston (2001) argues that the following four goals will provide a schema for putting ethics into action:

- Always explore the issue
- Find ways to get past the sticking points in any issue
- Take one side of the issue and make your case
- Take a stand on the issue after deciding what that stand should be

Table 11.2.   Putting Ethics into Action

GOALS	TOOLS		PITFALLS
	Main move	Follow-up	
Explore an issue	Pay attention to values	Pay attention to factual issues and terms	Don't stop too soon, that is, expect diversity; look in depth
To get unstuck	Multiply options, shift problems	Pay attention to values to open up new possibilities for integrating values	Don't slight the other sides—don't just be creative with your values
To make a case	Make the key values explicit	Defend/define key factual claims and terms	Don't overlook better options
		Consider key objections such as other theories and key inferences	Be sure to judge like cases alike
To decide for yourself	Prioritize or integrate the key values	Seek new and creative options	Don't close your mind, maybe the question is not settled for good
		Check facts and inferences	

Source: From A. Weston. (2001). *A 21st century ethical toolbox.* New York: Oxford University Press. Used by permission of Oxford University Press, Inc.

Table 11.2 outlines the process for putting ethics into action. Always take time to explore the issue because your goal is to find out as much as possible about the issue. You are attempting to establish your position on the issue. Be open minded and look at both sides of the issue. Put yourself in a position to help your group get past the sticking points that emerge in any debate over an issue of ethical proportions. Get unstuck by reframing issues and adding information to the discussion. Make your case in the most eloquent way possible by demonstrating the value-laden course of action you have taken. Decide for yourself by choosing where you stand on the issue.

ETHICAL LEADERSHIP

Principals who are real leaders focus their attention on doing the right thing and not on doing things right. Greenfield (1991) argues that principals face moral and ethical dilemmas every day they come to work. They have obligations to the school, the community, other professionals, the board of education, parents, and students, and many times they are unable to discern what is right or wrong in ethical or moral terms. Most principals have had little or no opportunity to work through these types of issues in preparation programs (Beck and Murphy 1994). The ethical leader is required to meet the same moral and ethical standards whether the issues are the day-to-day ethical dilemmas or the more mundane decisions that have the hidden potential for ethical implications. The principal must be the role model for the school, if he or she is to create an ethical institution. The stakeholders involved with the school organization must believe that the principal is modeling values that they can sustain. Some research indicates that loyalty to superordinates can affect ethical decision making. Kirby, Pardise, and Protti (1990) ask principals how a "typical colleague" would react to a series of dilemmas surrounding the relationship between subordinates and superordinates. The principals indicated most often that their colleagues would take the path of least resistance by deferring to their superiors or hiding behind policy. Is the Kirby, Pardise, and Protti research indicative of the behaviors of most principals? This question can only be valued as it is applied to the individual principal, but most principals would agree it is the behavioral norm.

Ethical leaders create ethical institutions by providing faculty and staff the opportunity to discuss ethical issues. This means providing time, space, and motivation to participate in right-versus-right discussions about issues of great importance to the faculty and staff. The principal might appoint an ethics committee to raise faculty and staff awareness of ethical issues that find their way into the school. Sergiovanni (1992) argues that the most effective organizations have an articulated set of core values and it is the leader's job to make sure the core values are followed and enforced. When these core values are not followed, it is up to the principal to "lead by outrage."

Thomas and Davis (1998) argue that being an effective leader is not the criterion to be used in ethical leadership. Al Capone, William J. Clinton, and Josef Stalin were considered effective leaders, but ultimately leaders are judged by their actions in relation to basic social morality. All leaders are governed by legal, ethical, and historical principles. Principals must have strong core values that provide the foundation for public education and those values include equality of access to an equitable education for all children. According to Thomas and Davis, ethical educational leadership occurs when the following core values appear as part of the principal's day-to-day actions:

- The principal uses laws, rules, policies, and the principles of democracy to operate the school.
- The principal supports and encourages the best professional practices available.
- The principal provides the faculty and staff with ethical guidelines and decision-making tools.
- The principal models moral behavior and expects the same from faculty, staff, and students. (Thomas and Davis 1998)

Laws, rules, and policies enforced in a fair and equitable manner is one strategy that allows the principal to operate the school ethically. The key is fair and equitable treatment, which does not mean everyone gets treated in the same way. Cutting-edge professional practice becomes the conduit for successful teaching and learning, but the ethical application of these practices by teachers and principals is key to creating successful adults. It is the principal's responsibility to provide faculty with ethical guidelines; without these principles, the school organization has no direction. Utilizing these guidelines, along with an ethical decision-making tool, assures parents, students, and community stakeholders that the school will do no harm, but in fact will develop model citizens for the community. Principals who expect to lead must model a moral behavior that is beyond reproach. Questions about the principal's character and behavior undermine the integrity of the principal and leaves him or her without the moral compass and leverage to make the necessary changes to make the school continuously improve.

Most professional organizations have ethical standards that provide the framework for the ethical behavior of their members. These codes of ethics provide the foundation on which standards of practice are outlined for the members of the organization. The following examples demonstrate principles that should guide ethical leadership:

- Do not use hearsay evidence to harm others.
- Do not financially profit from your position in the organization.
- Respect the principle of confidentiality with students and teachers.
- Principals must guard financial accounts, which must be open to public scrutiny and operated using the best business practices.
- Principals must not use school or district equipment or personnel for personal matters.

These ethical guidelines are examples and are not intended to cover the gamete of possibilities or address any professional codes of ethics, but they do clarify the level of concern ethical principals must achieve in order to provide ethical leadership for the school.

A PERSONAL APPROACH TO ETHICS

Rebore (2001) contends that an individual's conscience is the driving force behind ethical decisions. He defines the individual's conscience as an instinct that guides the actions of human beings in specific situations, or as a skill that is learned through experience and is used to make decisions. Principals face decisions of conscience daily as they evaluate the fate of teachers, students, staff, and programs. Every principal has or will face the dilemma of whether to ask a teacher for his or her resignation or to proceed through the process of termination. How does a principal make the decision to allow a teacher of many years to complete just one more year in order to receive a full retirement benefit, when that principal knows the teacher is no longer effective in the classroom? Sometimes, teachers at the end of their careers are not as effective as they once were, but members of the board of education still see that teacher as they did when they were in his or her classroom. The principal must have a process for making these ethical decisions so that his or her judgments are consistent and fair.

An ethical principal takes responsibility for his or her actions. Principals make free choices, even though board of education policies, superintendent pressure, and community influence must be considered when making decisions. According to Rebore (2001), the choices are free because the principal is not outside of the role of the principalship of a given building. Each decision the principal makes affects the principal in some form and the only way to avoid being tied to the decision is by resigning from the position, which in reality is a decision.

The ethical principal attempts to find meaning in what he or she accomplishes daily. The question that principals must answer for themselves is: Has my career made a difference? For many principals, the daily routine of keeping students, teachers, and staff safe is a task that makes it impossible to focus on the real objective of education, that being teaching and learning. Most educators, either directly or indirectly, want to make a difference in students' lives and to discover that very little has been accomplished is demoralizing.

The search for meaning in one's life is an important aspect of creating a personal approach to ethical leadership. To begin to address the issue of searching for meaning, the principal must address his or her view of society in relation to how human beings ought to treat each other. The view must be presented to all of the school's stakeholders daily. The principal must be willing to share his or her personal approach to ethical leadership with all the school's stakeholders and the principal cannot be a minimalist in making this known to all.

Principals work in schools that have diverse students and faculty, not only ethnically, but also culturally and economically. People contend that diversity in school is valued as a means of teaching students and teachers to appreciate individual differences. It is the principal's role in this diverse school to model ethical virtues of equity, equality, honesty, truthfulness, and caring for all students. It is the principal's responsibility to make sure that all students are treated with these virtues as demonstrated by stakeholder behavior. Students and teachers who do not believe a diverse setting is best for teaching and learning will not change their behavior through feeble attempts at diversity training. Little evidence exists that diversity training changes behavior or minds. Evidence does exist that ethical treatment of students and teachers creates an atmosphere where all groups appreciate and work together for the common good.

The principal can develop his or her personal approach around one of the models of ethical decision making outlined in this chapter. These frameworks provide the structure for creating decisions in ethical and moral ways. To do less is a violation of the principal's code of conduct as outlined by the American Association of School Administrators (1998). The educational administrator:

1. Makes the well-being of students the fundamental value of all decision making and actions
2. Fulfills professional responsibilities with honesty and integrity
3. Supports the principle of due process and protects the civil and human rights of all individuals
4. Obeys local, state, and national laws and does not knowingly join or support organizations that advocate, directly or indirectly, the overthrow of the government
5. Implements the governing board of education's policies and administrative rules and regulations
6. Pursues appropriate measures to correct those laws, policies, and regulations that are not consistent with sound educational goals
7. Avoids using positions for personal gain through political, social, religious, economic, or other influence
8. Accepts academic degrees or professional certification only from duly accredited institutions
9. Maintains the standards and seeks to improve the effectiveness of the profession through research and continuing professional development
10. Honors all contracts until fulfillment or release

Principals in the day-to-day operation of the school organization should use these guiding principles as the foundation for operating the school. Without these guiding principles, the school organization would be twisting in the wind with a mindless ethical direction. Operating a school without principle is a sure formula for creating moral and ethical dilemmas. This code of conduct provides teachers, parents, and students with an understanding of what the principal expects of each and every stakeholder associated with the school organization. The principal is also responsible for making sure that teachers know and understand their code of conduct. Every state has a code of conduct for educators and it is paramount that all teachers and principals know what the code says and what it means. Most state codes of conduct address such things as:

- Teachers shall help students reach their full academic potential
- Teachers shall make sure students have the opportunity to acquire knowledge and understanding
- Teachers shall not stifle students' acquisition of differing points of view
- Teachers shall create a diverse classroom atmosphere
- Teachers shall establish a pattern of excellence in instruction that supports the trust that is given to them by the public
- Teachers shall protect the privacy rights of children and their colleagues

These codes of conduct guidelines for teachers are essential if principals and teachers expect to regain any of the respect from the state and national policy makers they have lost over the past two decades. Principals must encourage and model ethical behavior as the foundation for creating an ethically driven school. It is this inspiration that will drive the conduct of any organization.

ETHICAL DISCUSSION

Can "Character Education" Reverse Moral Decline?

Is the purpose of schools to teach students a moral code of conduct and can students be taught virtues? Should value-laden issues be discussed in the public school classrooms and can schools avoid representing a "middle-class morality" that does not represent the diversity of public schools? The current belief being perpetuated by national, state, and local policy makers is that schools are a dismal failure and the moral condition of U.S. society is in need of reevaluation at a minimum and a total reconstruction at a maximum, all based on the observation that today's young people are void of any character. Substantial arguments can be made on both sides of the character education question. Those supporting the idea have identified three causes for the need for "character education":

- A decline in the family unit, which has been the child's primary moral educator
- Trends that suggest young people lack proper parenting and adult role models
- The discovery that society is in a moral decline

On the opposite side of this issue, character education denotes a specific type of moral education, one that reflects particular values and codes of conduct. Some would argue that character education is mostly about trying to get children to work harder academically and to obey specific commands. This type of education is similar to indoctrination and has little to do with values or fairness and leaves little time for reflection and critical thinking.

The questions that need to be answered concerning this issue are:

- What is the purpose for character education, indoctrination or society building?
- At what levels are the questions of morals and virtues addressed?
- Whose values should be taught and how is this decision made?
- Can schools overcome the political and theological issues that surround character development?
- Should character education be a curriculum that stands alone or should it be integrated into the existing curriculum?
- Ethical dilemmas are right-versus-right issues. Which side of the character education debate do you support and why?

CHAPTER SUMMARY

Ethics is defined as standards of right and wrong, as well as dilemmas of right-versus-right issues. Principals face increasingly difficult choices as schools become more complex and externally driven. The key to providing an ethical learning and working environment is the establishment of a specific set of ethical standards. This set of standards can be established but they are only as useful as the principal makes them on a daily basis. These standards are directed by the moral compass that the principal utilizes in making decisions for the school. This moral compass is guided by the virtues of honesty, courage, stewardship, and trust.

Core values frame the ethical decisions of the leader and these values come from self, the inner core of the individual's belief system. It is important that all stakeholders involved in the school understand and embrace the educational core values of the principal. Without this relationship it is very difficult for the principal to lead the organization. Treating others with respect is the most important principle of any ethical model and is the central premise of Aristotle, Plato, and Cicero when they focused on the common good some 2,000 years ago. This is the social fabric that all individuals depend on.

Ethical decision making can be accomplished in a variety of ways from a value-focused framework, McDonald ethical framework, utilitarian framework, and the Kidder decision-making framework. The value-focused framework provides the decision maker with an opportunity to solve the current problem and at the same time avoid future problems. McDonald's ethical framework addresses the question: Is there a moral issue involved in the situation and if there is can you identify the issue? Using this framework requires the principal to gather all of the relevant facts involved in the situation and to create solutions to solve the problem based on the facts. The utilitarian framework focuses on the benefits and harms created by the decision as a disinterested and benevolent spectator. A maximum benefit at the lowest cost to the organization is the test for the principal. The Kidder framework values the right-versus-right dilemmas, rather than the moral dilemmas created by right-versus-wrong situations. Using any of these frameworks, the principal places him- or herself in the position to use guidelines to create an ethical decision.

A personal approach to ethics is important for the principal to contemplate in order to make sure the school organization has an ethical role model to follow. Principals must provide all stakeholders with the ethical principles necessary to function in society for the common good.

CHAPTER ACTIVITIES AND QUESTIONS

1. Use the Kidder framework for ethical decision making by contrasting the right-versus-right situation and the right-versus-wrong situation with an ethical situation in your school district.
2. List ethical virtues you as a principal or potential principal hold closest to your core values?

3. List your core values and how you will implement them in the school you administer.
4. What process should a principal use in making his or her decision?
5. Describe the common good concept and where it originated.
6. Outline the major concepts of value-focused thinking and describe how you might apply the concept in your school setting.
7. Describe McDonald's ethical framework?
8. What are the concepts outlined in the utilitarian framework and how would you apply them in a school situation?
9. Create an ethical foundation for yourself and describe the guidelines that support this foundation.
10. Describe the relationship between the ethics and the law. Which of these two concepts is most important to a school principal?

CASE STUDY ACTIVITIES AND QUESTIONS

1. Outline the strategies found in this chapter that would help Ms. Dietters meet with Mr. Cool about his daughter.
2. Describe the ethical obligation Mr. Cool has as he discusses his daughter's discipline problem.
3. Ms. Dietters uses the utilitarian ethical model by agreeing to help Mr. Cool by moving his daughter into advanced mathematics and English. Write a short essay defending Ms. Dietters's use of the utilitarian model.
4. Utilizing Kidder's ethical model, what should Ms. Dietters infer from her conversation with Superintendent Tucker?
5. If you were in Ms. Dietters position, which ethical model would you use and why?
6. Ethically, should Ms. Dietters consider the marital situation of Mr. Cool in her decision about Audra?
7. Describe a school board member's special ethical privileges or constraints when talking to the principal as a parent. What privileges and constraints should this board member employ?
8. Outline the ethical behavior that is expected from a school board member. How should Mr. Cool display this type of behavior?
9. Reflecting on the models of ethical behavior found in this chapter, what type of support should Ms. Dietters expect from Superintendent Tucker? In two paragraphs, write the type of behavior you would expect.

10. Looking at the situation from an ethical point of view, what obligation does the child have in this situation: no obligation or some obligation?

REFERENCES

American Association of School Administrators. (1998). "Code of ethics for school administrators." At csep.nt.edu/codes/coe/aasa-a.htm (accessed October 25, 2001).

Beck, L. G., and Murphy, J. (1994). *Ethics in educational leadership programs: An expanding role*. Thousand Oaks, CA: Corwin.

Beyer, L. E. (1997). "The moral contours of teaching education." *Journal of Teacher Education* 48: 245–254.

Block, P. M. (1993). *Stewardship: Choosing service over self-interest*. San Francisco, CA: Berrett-Koehler.

Brown, J, and Townsend, R. (1997). "Developing an ethical framework." *Thrust for Educational Leadership* 27: 12–14.

Campbell, E. (1997). "Connecting the ethics of teaching and moral education." *Journal of Teacher Education* 48: 255–263.

Frymier, J. (1974). *Motivation and learning in school*. Bloomington, IN: Phi Delta Kappa.

Frymier, J., Cunningham, L., Duckett, W., Gansneder, B., Link, F., Rimmer, J., and Scholz, J. (1996). *A study of core values and the schools*. Bloomington, IN: Phi Delta Kappa.

Graham, P. T., and Cline, P. C. (1997). "The ethical behavior of teachers in an ever-changing American social system" (ERIC Document Reproduction Services no. ED 411 234).

Greenfield, W. B. (1991). "Rationale and methods to articulate ethics and administrator training." Paper presented at the annual meeting of the American Educational Research Association (ERIC Document Reproduction Services no. ED 332 379).

Josephson, M. (2000). "Report card on ethics of American youth." Josephson Institute of Ethics and Character Counts, at www.josephsoninstitute.org (accessed June 11, 2001).

Keeney, R. L. (1994). "Creativity in decision making with value-focused thinking." *Sloan Management Review* 48: 33–41.

Kidder, R. M. (1995). *How good people make tough choices*. New York: Simon and Schuster.

Kirby, P. C., Pardise, L. V., and Protti, R. (1990). "The ethical reasoning of school administrators: The principled principal." Paper presented at the annual meeting of the American Educational Research Association (ERIC Document Reproduction Services no. ED 320 253).

Lashway, L. (1996). "Ethical leadership." *ERIC Digest* 107, at eric.uoregon.edu (accessed June 11, 2001).

Markkula Center for Applied Ethics. (2000). "What is ethics?" *Ethics Connection*, at www.scu.edu/SCU/Centers/Ethics (accessed February 18, 2002).

McDonald, M. (2000). "A framework for ethical decision making: Version 4." Centre for Applied Ethics, at www.ethics.ubc.ca/mcdonald (accessed July 12, 2001).

Mill, J. S. (1863). "Utilitarianism." At www.utilitarianism.com (accessed July 12, 2001).

National School Boards Association. (1997). "Ethical schools administration." *Updating School Board Policies* 28 (2): 3–7 (ERIC Document Reproduction Services no. ED 407 722).

Rebore, R. W. (2001). *The ethics of educational leadership*. Upper Saddle River, NJ: Merrill–Prentice-Hall.

Richardson, M. D. (1992). "Teacher perception of principal behavior—A study." Paper presented at the annual meeting of the Mid-south Educational Research Association, Knoxville, TN (ERIC Document Reproduction Services no. ED 352 710).

Sergiovanni, T. J. (1992). *Moral leadership: Getting to the heart of school leadership*. San Francisco, CA: Josey-Bass.

Starratt, R. J. (1991). "Building an ethical school: A theory for practice in educational leadership." *Educational Administration Quarterly* 27 (2): 185–202.

Thomas, M. D., and Davis, E. E. (1998). "Legal and ethical bases for educational leadership." *Phi Delta Kappa Fastbacks* (426), at firstsearch.oclc.org (accessed June 6, 2001).

Velasquez, M., Andre, C., Shanks, T., and Meyer, M. J. (2000). "Thinking ethically: A framework for moral decision making." At www.scu.edu (accessed June 6, 2001).

Weston, A. (2001). *A 21st century ethical tool box*. New York: Oxford University Press.

Section V

Organizational Management and Operations

ISLLC Standard 5

A school administrator is an educational leader who promotes the success of all students by acting with integrity, fairness, and in an ethical manner. The administrator has knowledge and understanding of:

- The purpose of education and the role of leadership in a modern society
- Various ethical frameworks and perspectives on ethics
- A professional code of ethics

Chapter Twelve

Budgeting within the School's Community

William Walls, the assistant superintendent for finance, had brought the high school principals together for a strategy meeting to begin planning the next fiscal year's budget. He and Dr. J. B. Tucker had discussed the need for streamlining some of the activities for all schools in order to get better results from the finances that were being utilized. The previous superintendent had relied heavily on incremental budgeting as the method of building budgets for the recent few years. There had been little effort to examine what the schools had been doing from a programmatic standpoint to achieve any measure of improved accountability from a fiscal standpoint. Teachers and department heads had been sending their purchase requests to the principal who had built the budget requests based on a percentage increase each year without much examination as to what was working to produce success. Actually success in many of the programs was satisfactory, except for the dropout rates. Students were graduating and going on to college or entering the workforce in the industrial and computer industries in the area without much difficulty. However, this was a conservative district and several board members wanted better results for the money being spent. The best way of looking at this was to find out from those closest to the activity what could be done to be more efficient and effective. Superintendent Tucker had experienced site-based budgeting in the district where he had moved from with somewhat mixed results, but he was confident more time was needed and it would be better. So he asked Mr. Walls to introduce the concept and train the principals in development of this budgeting philosophy to hopefully become more productive, at least from a fiscal standpoint.

After an introduction of site-based budget, lasting about forty-five min-
utes, Manny Flores, principal of Cameron High School, expressed doubts
as to the successful implementation of such an effort to the entire group,
primarily because individual teachers will not admit there might be a bet-
ter way of accomplishing instruction. They would be reticent to change
their ideas as teachers would have to work harder to implement anything
that would save dollars. After a lot of discussion and reaction from the
other principals present, Mr. Walls asked the three principals to develop a
plan that could be utilized to try the site-based budget with one area of the
budget in each of their schools for this budgeting cycle.

UNDERSTANDING BUDGETING

The fiscal operations of a school are very basic to everything that occurs
within the campus; yet at the level of many who participate in school activities, these fiscal functions may be almost invisible. Teachers and staff
members do realize that supplies and other goods and services are pro-
cured with financial resources, but their involvement in this process on
many campuses may be almost nonexistent or at most very limited.

Budgeting is actually a planning function for every activity that is taking place in a school. While many teachers and sometimes parents may be
involved in program or curriculum planning for the school, the allocation
of financial resources is often not a direct part of many of these decisions.
Such involvement is carried out with the assumption that the decisions or
changes to the program will be implemented with the staff and other resources already available. Time will be reallocated so it is used differently
or students will be reorganized into a different configuration as the program proceeds. This assumption, when considered carefully, is usually not
appropriate. Somehow, money enters the picture and additional or different supplies or materials are necessary. Perhaps new staff members need
to be added or personnel assignments must be changed. Each of these adjustments actually involves budget decisions.

As a planning function, budgeting should be part of most decisions involving program changes. Because budgeting is an extended process taking, at the building level, usually six months or longer, many substantive
changes to programs, curriculum design, instructional modifications, and

other decisions impacting how a school accomplishes its goals must be considered long before they can actually be implemented. In addition to the time frame of developing budgets, administrators, teachers, and other stakeholders involved must keep in mind that the school budgets are also part of a larger plan of allocating resources for the total school district. When the school's stakeholders make programmatic decisions, they do so as part of a greater context—that of the entire program that prepares their students from the time they enter school until they graduate.

Then, too, the district's work on a fiscal plan is circumscribed by a number of other factors and groups who make decisions. These usually begin with the state legislature that develops the overall funding plan for all school districts in the state. Another important governmental body includes the courts that make decisions concerning the equity and quality of educational resources as set by the legislature. Finally, the school board of the local district typically approves the budget that is developed in conjunction with the local administrators and district committees that have been organized to assist. Additionally, in some states the voters must be rallied to approve the tax levy that is needed to fund the budget. With the number of additional bodies necessary to move these plans forward, it becomes easy to understand that these decisions are very much impacted by political considerations. Board interests, local business desires, the local control movement that has developed across the nation, and also the total resources that are necessary to operate the other local government entities such as cities, counties, water and hospital districts, and other educational districts such as community colleges all impact these decisions. These influences are also impacted by the rapidly growing populations and the demographic changes, such as age and ethnicity that are occurring in many parts of the nation.

Competition for the resources that are available becomes very fierce, particularly when the increase in student expectations is considered. The taxpayer revolt against additional tax resources coupled with the accountability movement and the court decisions requiring equity for all has served to intensify the problem. The administrator and those participating in the budgeting process must comprehend that the philosophy of education drives the program; the program drives the budget requirements; and the budget requirements drive the revenues that must be raised in order for a planned educational program to occur (see fig. 12.1).

Educational Philosophy/Goals → Educational Program → Budgets → Revenues

Figure 12.1.   Forces that Drive the Fiscal Processes for Schools

However, stakeholders must also realize that the total revenue available for all public programs has a limit and schools are only part of the complete picture when it comes to allocating revenues for all public as well as education needs. Education is an intangible product and competing needs for public resources are sometimes more visible such as roads, power supplies, water supplies, and hospital availability.

BUDGETING MODELS

Budgeting has undergone developmental changes over the last fifty years that have attempted to better justify allocation requests and institute new procedures in the decision-making process. The models that are identified and discussed briefly in this chapter are used to produce a planned document for achieving goals of the school or district. Most districts guide the budget development process from a central office perspective as ultimately the budget document must represent the entire school district and be approved by the local board of education. In developing the district's budget, each school makes recommendations as to what resources are needed to offer the programs for achieving the educational goals for that building. Progressive schools use input from a range of stakeholders at that campus to drive the decisions to request funds. An examination of the various models explained will help to understand the openness or closed considerations for budget requests.

INCREMENTAL BUDGETING

The incremental model of budgeting assumes that the costs for the next budget cycle will continue for each area, and usually will be raised by an incremental amount based, to a degree, on the inflation costs or on the percentage of increase that the entire budget is raised. If new expenditures for added programs are needed, then the total increase must also allow for that unless some other past expenditures are eliminated. This allows for changes to be tracked or examined easily. Proposed budgets often show one or more past years' allocations and percentage of increases for each item listed, allowing for an analysis of trends. This type of budgeting is easily accomplished without knowing what changes will actually be made. It also assumes that what is supported by last year's budget is the best way to accomplish next year's goals, unless some other factors are examined. It fails to take into consideration major shifts in technology or how goals may be accomplished differently. A shift in technology that could actually reduce expenses over a period may go by without being considered.

LINE-ITEM BUDGETING

This model gathers like costs together in displaying how allocations will be made and are usually grouped as objects of expense like salaries, supplies, and insurance or may be grouped in functional classifications as administration, instruction, health service, transportation, food service, operations, fixed charges, and others of traditional groupings recommended by the U.S. Department of Education. Within each functional classification, allocations may be broken down into lines toward which specific amounts are allocated. Such a budget structure may be required by the state, even though a district may utilize other more aggressive methods of control.

PLANNING, PROGRAMMING, AND BUDGETING SYSTEM

The Planning, Programming, and Budgeting System (PPBS) is a planning method designed to group expenses into programs that are developed around goals that are to be achieved by the school's efforts. For example, reading program expenses may be linked together into one program, so when changes to a program are considered, the goals that are desired are the standards, which are the focus when considering alternative methods of achieving desired results. This method tends to link unlike expenses into programs, such as combining instructional salaries with instructional materials, textbook costs, the use of technology for the program, and even the costs of classroom space and operation. Such decision packages also enable the start-up costs for new programs for areas such as equipment to be prorated costs over a period of years when making decisions of efficiency and effectiveness. As the program is implemented, the achievement of goals or objectives may be evaluated and judgments considered. This may allow for changes in procedures or possibly the elimination of programs that are ineffective or the choice of a new alternative for meeting the established goals. The term "evaluation" is also added to the PPBS to make it the Planning, Programming, Budgeting, and Evaluation System when the evaluation aspect is paramount. This model is difficult and consumes more time to implement. Oftentimes, once the budget is built using PPBS procedures, the final budget document may be restructured into a line-item budget for board discussion and voting.

ZERO-BASED BUDGETING

The zero-based budgeting (ZBB) model is primarily a process used to assess each decision and to justify all expenditures annually. As such, it is the antithesis of incremental budgeting. Every allocation for the next budget must be assessed and the decision made to continue funding or to make changes by elimination or continuation of that cost in the program. In completing this process, the expenditures are defined as program packages and identified as decision units. The program packages are then ranked as to their importance and allocations are established. The ZBB process was originally established in governmental circles to eliminate waste and consider eliminating unneeded expense. Although the idea has merit, the internal strife that is caused in its implementation made ZBB difficult to implement. There is a tendency to micromanage from the policy level and it could be considered a waste of manpower to have to justify basic programs in the educational setting.

SITE-BASED BUDGETING

With the development of the site-based management concept, decentralization of decision making made its way into the management of schools. The philosophy undergirding this concept is that better decisions are made when the decision makers are closest to the activity being managed. These individuals understand the problems that are being faced by teachers and students and can act to change conditions to better achieve success. This means that all stakeholders usually have a role in the process—the principal, the teachers, the staff, and the patrons of that school. This model also recognizes the importance of resource decisions at the point of utilization when the focus of the decision is the fiscal resources. This is known as school-based budgeting or site-based budgeting (SBB).

Typically, the school board or district makes a decision of how available funds will be allocated to each of the schools within its purview. Most often this is done by the number of students served, the types of programs being offered and the grade-level distribution of the students. Once the allocation has been determined for the school, the budgeting committee or SBB team begins the process of developing the budget for the following year. The exact range of authority of this group has been determined in advance, but this usually covers salaries, supplies, capital outlay purchases, and program-linked decisions such as athletics and student activities. The decisions must be made without violating any policies or statutes such as federal regulations or statutes, state mandated requirements, collective bargaining agreements, and policies such as school calendar or hours of instruction (Thompson, Wood, and Honeyman 1994). There are hidden problems, however, including the training necessary to understand the fiscal planning aspects, the technical side of budgeting, the collaboration necessary to complete the job, and the development of a nonthreatening environment. There are legal and ethical questions that may be raised, especially with the authority of determining salary decisions. However, the rewards for the school are great if these bridges can be crossed successfully. The school will be more responsible for its success or failure and decisions about other aspects of the program will be taken more seriously by the faculty and other stakeholders. This model is usually adopted as part of a comprehensive school-based management plan. The purpose is to improve productivity by changing authority relationships (Peterson 1991). Even so, a study of four large urban school districts found that in only two of the cases were school-based planning and school-based budgeting procedurally linked (Goertz and Hess 1998).

THE BUDGETING PROCESS

The budget process is complicated when observing it from a district perspective. Many functions that are part of the planning document come together. Each budgeted activity must be planned and the costs projected. At some point, these are all integrated together in a plan for the entire district. Each school is one component of the plan and each activity in every school must be part of the plan. As a result of the massive planning effort that is necessary, several areas must be considered: the calendar for budgeting, the organization for budgeting, the data collection, guidelines, and the form of the budget documents.

BUDGET CALENDAR

For the district to be able to develop the budget in a timely manner, a calendar needs to be established that lists the activities and the time needed for each as well as dates for the initiation and completion of each task. These normally include planning and preliminary steps to organize the development process; the budget development including student projections, school and department expenditure requests, revenue estimates, and preparation of the document; and review and approval at the district and board level (Hartman 1988). The individual school is involved in generating the estimates for its requests and submitting them appropriately and on time. At the building level this will mean, assuming an SBB model is followed, that the budgeting committee must be selected, oriented, and organized to receive requests from each of the departments or teaching teams and the support activities, which are part of the school. Typically, these tasks are completed in midwinter and requests are submitted in January for the following fiscal year (assuming a September to August fiscal year).

SBB ORGANIZATION

Two broad types of SBB are possible: one where the principal is the center of decisions and ultimately makes them with advice from teachers (termed "centralized") and the other where a site-based team assembles the requests and develops the budget that will be submitted with advice from the principal (termed "decentralized"). Both the superintendent and the local board's philosophy would have a bearing on which is selected within the district and certainly the principal's ability to share the decisions would have implications for the school's arrangements for SBB. If the building principal is one who can delegate responsibility, has an open leadership style, trusts the staff members, and is able to welcome debate on issues, the decentralized arrangements can empower the staff and make them collaborative. The power of the purse is the power of making program decisions possible; consequently, if the staff is highly participative in program development, then it makes it feasible for this group to have decision-making power in budget matters. One other matter is important, that of the fiscal health of the school district in situations where SBB is the norm. If the district is struggling under financial pressure due to control of shortfall in revenues, then the ability for budgeting teams to have leeway is limited greatly (Hartman 1988).

DEVELOPING THE BUDGETING TEAM

Going about the process of establishing a budgeting team can be precarious for the principal and other teachers in the school. There must be some trust among teachers for this to work. But where to start can be a difficult question. The principal will have to be the individual to make such a budgeting team work by establishing the tasks to be completed, how the committee will be selected, and how and what input will be expected from the remainder of the faculty and staff. The process cannot be learned overnight and so the work of such a team is continually developing along with its experience, success, and the insight members have in the process.

Monasmith (1997) suggests that the budgeting committee be made up of five to seven individuals who are elected and empowered by the faculty and classified staff in the school. This group is called the budget allocation team (BAT). The principal is an "ex-officio member" and acts as the resource to the team to answer questions and to also ask questions that might not be considered in the process. The team members are elected for multiple-year terms that are staggered in starting. This enables the members to learn the processes in the first year and serve to provide leadership in the decision-making processes in subsequent years.

TEAM PROCESSES

A goal or objective that becomes the team's guiding principle needs to be established. An example might be to reduce costs wherever and whenever possible in order to make additional resources available for curriculum, instruction, staff development, or other identified staff priorities. The process would proceed in a fashion as follows:

- The total allocation by the district to the school is identified and established.
- The BAT presents to the total staff a list of categories that must be dealt with for the budget. The staff arrives at a consensus on ranking these categories in the order of priority to examine and consider each category.
- Each of the categories are considered by the staff over the next few weeks so that the staff has an opportunity to discuss every category and provide input on its thinking, how the resources will move the students and school toward achieving learning goals, or other determined criteria.
- An example: "Fixed costs" may be ranked first to "come off the top" before other categories are considered. The BAT presents a list of the fixed-cost items to the staff with an allocation estimate for each. The staff and principal brainstorm to reduce these "fixed costs" so more dollars might be allocated to other instructional areas.
- The BAT team then develops and presents the first draft of the campus budget funding plans and priorities to the faculty and staff.

The staff responds to the newly proposed budget by including:

- What it liked about the proposed budget
- What it thinks needs to be improved
- Its recommendations for improvement
- The BAT makes revisions based on this input and presents the second proposed budget
- The process is then repeated until a final budget, including contingency funds for emergencies, has been presented by the BAT for faculty/staff consensus.
- When the consensus is attained, the budget goes to the district for approval and inclusion in the district budget

Important features that must be included in the process include:

1. Nothing is sacred in terms of being considered.
2. Everything goes on the table for discussion. Information is made available on all items discussed.

3. Everyone on faculty and staff has input.
4. The principal also submits his or her requests to the team for consideration.
5. Alternative or creative methods of meeting needs are often discovered that can provide hidden or extra resources.

The BAT's work continues during the year with written monthly summary updates of actual expenditures at faculty/staff meetings so everyone on the staff understands where the money goes. Any existing budget surplus is brought to the staff for its input on how the surplus should be allocated.

DEVELOPING THE BUDGET

The actual development of the budget for the school usually hinges, to a great degree, on the projected pupil enrollment for the school. Although the enrollment figures may help to project the number of teachers, administrators, and support staff to be employed, another important aspect is the special programs that are located in the school, usually determined by the special needs of students enrolled. Oftentimes, these programs are supported by supplemental appropriations or funds from federal sources, state sources, or private or public grants-in-aid that have been awarded to the school or district due to application for such funds. Most revenues that support the school come from state support combined with district-generated local tax funds. These typically make up what is called the foundation program, which is the amount of money needed by a school district to support the needed education of each student served. Each state has a formula or plan by which these funds are generated for schools. The formula provides for a basic education for every child. Usually, state and local funds combine to provide about 90 percent or more of the funds for a school. Federal program funds, often referred to as categorical aid, provide 6 to 8 percent of the district's budget; however, some schools actually receive a larger percentage of their total budget from federal categorical funds due to larger numbers of students enrolled from the targeted programs such as English for Speakers of Other Languages (comprised of Bilingual and English as a

Second Language programs), students from low income families, and vocational education. Programs for students with handicaps are also funded with additional finances due to the low teacher–pupil ratios and special services needed.

Personnel needs are estimated from the enrollments and the funds for salaries and fringe benefits. Similar expenses are then estimated for the budget (Hartman 1988). One area that must be considered is the hiring of temporary employees and substitute teachers. Expenditures for the programs are then developed. In these areas, the work of the instructional and support staff in projecting needs for instructional materials and support of all other services such as counselors, health programs, athletics, custodial services, instructional support of aides and clerks, and administrative support of the office must be developed. Additionally, funds for maintenance of the building such as replacement of equipment, painting, or other redecoration of facilities must be projected. The utilities for the building support must be projected as these funds come from the regular budget.

Also, new equipment must be justified and estimated. Large items such as computer or other technology systems or additions of rooms to a facility are usually part of capital improvement budgets. The funds for these expenses may be paid for from long-term loans that extend over the life of the purchases. These items require special approval by boards of education and sometimes voters to be approved for long-term payback from bonds that the district sold.

Computer technology is an ongoing cost for schools; the purchase of the hardware is only a beginning. As the number of computers grows so do the necessary costs for infrastructure like rewiring for electrical power and connectedness for local and wide area networks. Internet connections may also add considerable expense, which then adds expense for Internet filters to prevent access to sexually explicit material. As computers age, they are unable to carry the latest in software and peripheral costs mount as more and more students begin using them for their projects and retrieval of research information. Costs for paper and ink cartridges for printers continue to grow as the use of this tool becomes more integrated with the curriculum. Computer technology must be added to the school through a strategic plan that promotes a fiscal strategy known as total cost of ownership (Stover 1999). This strategy incorporates all future support costs to determine the true fiscal impact of ownership. Also included is the cost of training teachers to use this asset so the school and students receive the expected benefits from this acquisition.

After all of the expenses are projected, these figures are then compared to the estimated support from the revenues to be allocated to the school. The most difficult decisions come when expenses exceed the support, as choices must be made, or additional income must be located or obtained. These are the types of decisions that school budgeting committees can assist with; however, federal, state, and local guidelines must be considered in doing this and where employee agreements are negotiated on a long-term basis, these agreements must be included in the decision process.

An example breakdown of a school's budget might look similar to the estimates in exhibit 12.1.

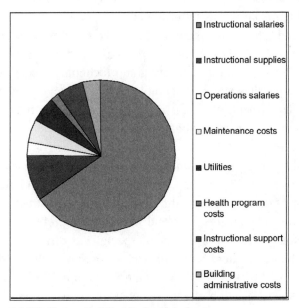

**Exhibit 12.1a   Building budget breakout
(line-item budget)**

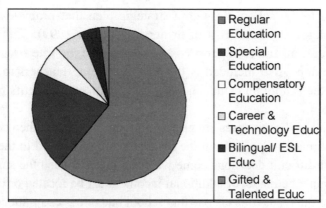

Exhibit 12.1b   Building budget breakout
(Programmatic budget)

ADMINISTERING THE BUDGET

Once the budget has been developed and approved, it becomes the plan used to allocate resources to various programs and activities. The greatest portion of the resources, as indicated earlier, are allocated to salaries of employees and other fringe benefits that have been established. Instructional supplies and materials, library purchases, administrative supplies, travel costs, health program expenses, and technology expenses usually require that a purchase order be completed and approved and sent to the purchasing department of the district. This sets into motion the department that administers the purchasing procedures and encumbers funds from the budget to pay for these costs once the supplies or services are delivered. Utility costs are encumbered also and paid for each month as these are consumed. Capital improvements must also be administered as purchases or as contracts, depending on the items. Construction costs, of course, require other inspections and monitoring before these are paid; these are usually the responsibility of specialized offices at the district level. In each case, as items are approved for purchase, the funds must be checked to verify that allocations remain in the applicable budget item. This requires classification of each expense and verification of availability of funds. Most schools assign this task to a financial secretary at the building level; these decisions are again checked at the district fiscal office where distributions are handled.

GRANT AWARDS

More often in today's environment, schools are depending on grants from government, private foundations, or businesses to support innovative programs or ideas to assist with difficult or unusual problems. To obtain these funds, staff members or administrators must identify a potential source of funding from a request for proposal or other announcement or go out and convince a funding agency about the value of their idea to solve a problem. After writing a grant proposal and submitting it to the funding agency, the school would hope for success. The success in obtaining grants to fund such ideas means that staff members should take advantage of workshops or other training in developing such proposals and their identification of possible funding agencies. Faculty and staff must be encouraged and assisted in developing such proposals through the offering of training and the encouragement of the principal and other administrators.

ACTIVITY FUNDS

Funds that are generated from sources other than appropriations or grants are an important part of funding school programs or that utilize locally controlled sources. These are also referred to as student activity funds if they are generated for student programs. In some cases, these funds are generated by sales of soft drinks, snacks in vending machines, or student supplies in a school store, the profits which can support activities that are not otherwise funded. These moneys are a source of difficulty for school campus administrators since the actual cash that changes hands must be protected and accounted for properly. Generally, these funds become public or school funds once collected and are subject to the laws, regulations, and policies governing such funds for that state or that school district. In some states, these must be deposited in district accounts and accessed by purchase orders just like appropriated funds. Other states allow more direct control and the principal or other administrator may sign checks and make distributions directly from a school bank account set up for this purpose. In the case of the latter scenario, there is more latitude for problems to occur due to less stringent safeguards than in district accounts.

Funds for such accounts frequently come from sales in school, sales away from campus designed to raise money for activities, dues, trip fees, admission charges, and other sources. Most schools have procedures to approve fund-raising activities such as sales or ticketed events. There are guidelines recommended by the Association of School Business Officials designed to protect all those handling money in these types of accounts. These procedures include:

- Receipts should be for all money collected with prenumbered receipts or tickets.
- Deposits should be made daily and a receipt issued to those making the deposit.
- Money should not be stored overnight in a desk or in the school.
- Purchases should be preapproved by a purchase order, properly invoiced, and paid by a mailed check.
- Two individuals should sign checks on the local bank.
- No loans or accommodation for an employee or nonstudent should be made from these student activity funds.
- Budgets should be developed and approved for the activities generating and using these funds (e.g., see exhibit 12.2).
- The records and accounts should be audited periodically, both internally and externally.
- Reports should be made on the funds to the principal and the business office of the district.

A study of more than 1,000 high school principals (Gonzalez and Bogotch 1999) and their fiscal management practices of discretionary, school-generated funds indicated that more than 75 percent of the schools studied generated more than $100,000 per year. Approximately 11 percent generated more than $1 million each year. In 86 percent of the cases, the principals were authorized to sign checks at their schools. Ninety-two percent could carry funds over for the next year and of that number 69 percent had the authority to invest these funds in interest bearing accounts.

Sources of learning for these principals in the fiscal area focused most heavily on learning and advice from other principals or colleagues, collaborative decision making with teachers, their assistant principalship experience, professional reading, and site-based management. Suburban and rural high

Fort Spirit School District Clubs and Organizations—Budget and Activity Report

Organization_____Year_____
School_____ Number of Students served_____

The Purpose or Goals of this Club or Activity:

EXPENDITURES

Proposed Service Activities	Estimated Cost	Actual Cost

(Helping others)

First Semester_____
_____

Second Semester_____
_____

Proposed Curricular and/or Extracurricular Activities (banquets, proms, conventions,
activity contests, competitions, awards, dues, pictures, misc. costs)

_____
_____
_____
_____
_____

INCOME

Proposed sources	Estimated	Actual

First Semester_____
_____

Second Semester_____
_____

Totals   _____

Beginning Balance _____Actual Income _____ Actual costs _____

Proposed social activities (costs must be borne by students)
First Semester_____
_____

Second Semester_____
_____

Sponsor_____
Principal_____

Exhibit 12.2.   Plans for an Organizational Budget and Applicable Purposes and Events

school principals used more sources of learning than did urban high schools; and larger schools were more affected by educational trends and less likely compliant with hierarchical authority. These principals of districts larger than 20,000 students were more creatively insubordinate (i.e., finding ways around rules or guidelines that thwarted their innovative ideas) than those of smaller districts in trying to get the most from their resources. In looking toward situational problem decisions, the choice was always to follow state policies; however, the content of the scenario often had them collaborating with site-team members or consulting with district-level administrators.

ETHICAL DISCUSSION

- The school board has been discussing the possibility of an exclusive contract with one of the soft drink companies. If it could be agreed on and signed, only one soft drink company's products would be sold at the school district's facilities. In return for a fifteen-year contract of this type, the district would receive several million dollars. Should this be approved? If so, what should the money received by the district be used for?
- Another company, a name-brand athletic shoe manufacturer, has approached the board about installing advertising signs on the school buses for a sizable fee. What are the implications of this type of decision?
- What should be the role of a parent booster club in providing funding for established activities at the school?
- What type of ethical guidelines should be established when a school staff enters the school or site-based budgeting process?
- Discuss assumptions that the use of zero-based budgeting entails.
- Ethical dilemmas are right-versus-right issues. Which side of the revenue generation debate do you support and why?

CHAPTER SUMMARY

Budgeting within the school is a planning function that eventually helps to direct many other decisions. Budgets are circumscribed by state laws that direct the financial resources for schools. The courts also impact the equity and quality of educational resources by their decisions. Educational philosophy and goals provide direction for educational programs that then determine the budget estimates for these programs to be implemented. These estimates eventually help to decide what tax levels must exist in order to fund the budget required for ensuring a successful program.

A number of budgeting models have evolved to offer methods or philosophies of developing estimates in the budgeting process. Traditionally, line-item budgets were developed using incremental budgeting based on the previous year's budget. The Planning, Programming, and Budgeting System and zero-based budgeting concepts were developed to help control costs through an examination of the results and determine how useful the plan would be to attain these results. School-based or site-based budgeting is the process of depending on those closest to the teaching process—the teachers—to evaluate other options in achieving results and to make the decision on how to best plan financially for programs.

The budgeting process requires that a calendar be developed to complete the various phases of planning in order to meet time requirements. The decentralized method of providing teacher and staff input for the budget is now in favor, as opposed to the principal developing the plan without much input. Monasmith describes the process of developing a budgeting team and accomplishing the budget tasks to develop a budget for the school that will incorporate the staff's best effort to achieve success while reallocating funds to meet needs otherwise unmet due to shortfalls. The budget process includes estimating personnel costs, program expenditures including support functions, and funds for utilities, equipment, and other fixed costs. Once all expenses are estimated, these must be balanced with the revenues available.

Administration of student activity funds is another important fiscal function for the school. This task requires that careful policies and procedures be developed to protect those handling the finances.

CHAPTER ACTIVITIES AND QUESTIONS

1. Examine and compare budgets from a secondary and elementary school.
2. Compare budgets from several schools of the same level—that is, elementary or secondary.

3. Discuss and decide what the strengths and weaknesses of SBB, PPBS, and incremental budgeting are and how they would affect the implementation of each.
4. Interview a principal on how he or she develops or encourages others to help develop the school budget.
5. Develop a budget calendar for the budgeting functions in your school.
6. What are the variables in projecting costs for the many parts of the school's budget?
7. Explain how equipment might be purchased with the maintenance budget allocation.
8. Examine a request for proposal and reflect on what types of actions would be necessary to fulfill the intent of the request.
9. Generate a list of policies or procedures that you would need to administer the student activities fund in your school.
10. Why should a budget be developed for each student activity in the school? Why should this document be approved?

CASE STUDY ACTIVITIES AND QUESTIONS

1. What sorts of ideas should principals develop to implement SBB processes?
2. What type of leadership will principals have to demonstrate for SBB to be successful?
3. How could SBB also benefit from incorporating ZBB or PPBS?
4. How would the budget calendar change if SBB was used instead of incremental budgeting?
5. How long should SBB take to implement in a school district?

REFERENCES

Goertz, M. E., and Hess, G. A. (1998). "Processes and power in school budgeting across four large urban school districts." *Journal of Educational Finance* 23 (Spring): 490–506.

Gonzalez, K., and Bogotch, I. (1999). "Fiscal practices of high school principals: Managing discretionary school funds." *NASSP Bulletin* 83 (610) (November): 37–48.

Hartman, W. T. (1988). *School district budgeting*. Englewood Cliffs, NJ: Prentice-Hall.

Monasmith, J. (1997). "Site-based budgeting processes." Paper presented at the symposium for the Meadows Principal Improvement Program at Texas A&M University, Commerce, June.

Peterson, D. (1991). "School-based budgeting." *ERIC Digest* 64 (October) (ERIC Document Reproduction Services no. ED 336 865).

Stover, D. (1999). "School boards need to plan for the hidden costs of technology." *School Board News*, 19 March, 8, at www.NSBA.org/sbn/1999/030999-all.htm#story8 (accessed May 21, 2002).

Thompson, D. C., Wood, R. C., and Honeyman, D. S. (1994). *Fiscal leadership for schools*. White Plains, NY: Longman.

Chapter Thirteen

Leadership in Managing Human Resources

Harry Boggess, Manny Flores, Harley Fugua, and Darva Morgan had been organized into a district task force by Dr. Jane Thomas, executive director for human resources. As principals of schools representing all levels in the district, Dr. Thomas requested the benefit of their thinking to develop a plan for stabilizing the teaching staff of the district. For the last two years the district had to recruit and hire 200 new teachers to fill classroom requirements each year. "The turnover seems too high to me," Dr. Thomas stated, "to satisfactorily move our student population forward on the state accountability exam. Every time a new teacher is hired, we must spend a great deal of resources in time and money to prepare them to deal with the state's objectives and the exam, not to mention traditional teaching roles. Of our new hires, 82 to 86 percent have been new teachers each of those years. Our principals are anticipating a drop in scores this next year, due to the rising standard the state board has set and now with 35 percent of the teachers in the district having less than 2 years experience, our efforts are very vulnerable to a major dip in satisfactory scores. The upswing in business activity in Bethany has also created opportunities for young teachers who hope to do better financially to leave the schools for higher salaries in some of the technical areas. Bethany parents are particularly concerned about the level of performance of their sons and daughters, as several schools had decreasing scores last year."

Harley Fugua spoke first. "At my school we had a particularly difficult time last year selecting satisfactory new hires. The applicants seemed less enthusiastic and more focused on areas of interest outside of school. They performed satisfactorily on the teacher evaluation instrument, but were not stars by any sense of the imagination. This year we seemed to have even less to choose from in terms of applicants." Darva Morgan supported some of Harley's observations, but said she was "also concerned about the lack of interest of her teachers in pursuing a master's degree. Some of them have been here for eight years, yet have made no effort to retool their educational thinking except for our local in-service offerings."

"Yes, we do have problems at Bethany High School," stated Mr. Rabbit. "Our teachers are seeing students from our computer program move into the private sector and begin making as much as they have after more than eight years as an educator. What a morale dip that is for them! It's not only the money, however. It's also the prestige and recognition that seems to be missing at times in Fort Spirit School District." Manny Flores spoke finally. "I am truly at a loss to make progress with less motivated teachers. Many are doing quite well, particularly those in the math and science academy. However, the basic education teachers of literature and reading and ninth grade math are somewhat jealous of the equipment and materials that the grant purchased for the academy. It is easy to see how morale sags for them."

Dr. Thomas spoke again. "Well it seems to be a general feeling that personnel factors are not where we would like them. Where do you think we should start and how shall we structure our ideas?"

In the already famous book series by J. K. Rowling about Harry Potter, the young wizard who is attending school to learn the arts of wizarding, Harry and his fellow students attend a class on the "Care of Magical Creatures." In the eyes of young students, teachers are sometimes seen as magical creatures as they lead their students through new experiences and their interaction with new and different ideas. Yet principals do not attend a course or staff development in the "Care of Magical Creatures—the Teachers." Perhaps they should.

The most critical job of the principal is working with the staff of the school—both faculty and instructional support staff—in order to deliver the best possible instructional program for students. This effort by those who support and deliver first hand the instructional activities, the love and care of their students, and open the door to new thinking and ideas must be stimulated and encouraged by those who provide leadership. First and foremost, that individual is the school's principal. Over the years, schools and districts have frequently been besieged with problems of an economic or political nature that have thrown the schools or districts into chaos for a period of time. Yet, the instructional program has continued to have an impact of no less importance on the students, despite the problems. Success of students in the classroom often continues to occur because good teachers do not let problems outside the classroom overwhelm the school's purpose. The importance of selecting good teachers and supporting their development in a variety of ways is paramount for the school's effectiveness.

Leading and managing the school's human resource function is shared by both district and campus administrators. District administrators accomplish many support duties for human resource management. These vary with each school district, but usually include planning, recruitment, selection, development, evaluation, and benefits/rewards. Certain parts of each of these functions are also accomplished at the campus or site-based level, for which the principal is the responsible administrator. The district's board of education/trustees sets the policies that surround the human resource functions and the district's human resource management administrators coordinate those policies from the district level, enabling the principal to function at the campus level. The communication between the school system level and the school site level is critical while implementing the policies. Although the school campus is usually seen as the site of accomplishment of school district goals of educating children, the district's support in accomplishing this can thwart or support such goal achievement. Consequently, the coordination of these functions between the district level and the principal is paramount. Although the district-level functions impact the teacher in important ways such as policies, pay levels, benefits, and financial support of induction programs and staff development, the building faculty and staff are most directly impacted by the selection of fellow teachers, teacher assignment, induction and staff development planning and implementation, evaluation of teaching, and the intangible rewards that principals control.

Thus, the principal's role in human resource processes is of extreme importance to school and student success. Burnett's (1998) model of personnel acquisition and retention processes is helpful in understanding the relationship of the principal to the district level of human resource functions (see fig. 13.1)

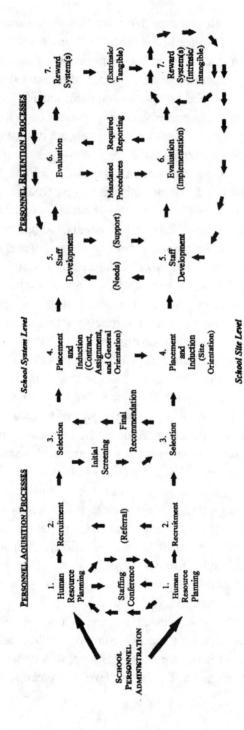

Figure 13.1.

Source: I.E. Burnett Jr.(1998). "A paradigm for teaching basic functions of school personnel administration." A Paper presented at National Council of Professors of Educational Administration, University of Alaska Southeast, Juneau, August 8. Used by Permission.

PLANNING FOR HUMAN RESOURCES

The principal is responsible for certain planning tasks in conjunction with the district administrators. Typically, the principal requests additional personnel to add to the staff based on additional student enrollment or, in a best case scenario, based on the enrollment projections for the coming year(s). Districts often project enrollments based on historical data, anticipated changes in the economic factors, and projected development of the community. This data coupled with changes in curriculum and instructional needs serve to identify anticipated personnel needs. Of course, enrollment increases or decreases are not the only factors that impact such needs. The languages spoken by the enrolled students is an example of a factor that may impact the skills needed by the faculty and staff. Bilingual and English as a Second Language teachers may be needed due to a changing population in the district. The increased use of new technology will also create technological instruction skills that all teachers may not have. Examples of factors that can impact the programmatic needs of a school include:

- Examination of the district's strategic plan and the school's vision and mission statement
- Addition of preschool enrollments in the school's program
- Addition of limited English-speaking population
- Changes in state laws or policies
- Acquisition of new technology for the instructional program
- Changes in graduation requirements or subjects to be taught
- Projection of budget resources for the following year
- Anticipated retirements of faculty or staff members
- Anticipated special needs students
- Impact of state-required testing programs and the school's success
- Projected loss of faculty or staff due to school transfers, relocation, or exit due to spousal transfers, family leaves, or extended disability

Following the identification of instructional needs for the school, the inventory of current personnel and their skills can be used to examine the range and depth of personnel and skills now available. Such an inventory should include what current teachers' personal preferences for assignment are. This type of data can be made accessible by building a computerized database that includes certifications, interests, computer/technology skills, desired assignments, extracurricular assignments, and possibly projected goals for their own professional future.

With this data in hand, the principal does an analysis of needed skills and staff for the future. From the projected needs, the current skills inventory is used to determine what new personnel should be employed and what skills they should have. This resulting data is communicated to the district administration that in turn must develop staff projections for the district and ultimately needed budget projections. The principal may also determine what new skill training might be included in staff development ideas for the future and may also offer opportunities for desiring teachers to retrain for different assignments.

RECRUITMENT AND SELECTION
OF SCHOOL PERSONNEL

The actual task of recruitment is to build a pool of interested individuals for selecting new faculty and staff members. Oftentimes, the district human resource office takes responsibility for the primary accomplishment of this task; however, the principal of each school is certainly responsible for continuing this process of recruitment as individuals are interviewed by the school's personnel—administrators, team leaders, or perhaps site-based teams including teachers or parents. Recruitment also includes building an individual's interest in taking a position if offered by the school or district.

Teacher recruitment often begins at the teacher preparation institution by attracting newly prepared teachers for the school or district. Participation in the college of education programs by hosting teacher candidates for student teaching is perhaps the most beneficial way of attracting these candidates to a position. Such participation requires dedicated teachers and administrators who are responsive to teachers'-in-training needs and situations. Other sources of new teachers can be encountered at professional association meetings and conferences and with alternative teacher certification programs, which today are completing the preparation of 30 to 40 percent of new teachers. Contact with corporations and industry will also ensure that newly arriving employees with teacher-spouses are invited to apply for positions. Frequently, current teachers at the school will be in contact with other fellow professionals seeking changes and such contact can stimulate new applicants for position openings. Programs that help paraprofessionals transition to regular teachers and teacher cadet programs that "grow your own" faculty members by interesting high school students in choosing a teaching career have proven helpful (Association for Supervision and Curriculum Development 1999). Every faculty and staff member can actually be a recruiting resource if he or she understands how a simple contact with other professionals can promote the school. Although financial benefits may be helpful in attracting applicants, the best enticement is a good school climate and culture in which to pursue an education career. Treating current staff members fairly and being concerned about their professional development are the ways to build a school's reputation as a good place to work.

Selection of new personnel is, perhaps, the most critical job of the building administrator. This action can be a major turning point for the school in changing various aspects of the program from instructional issues to school climate. In a time when teaching personnel are somewhat scarce as a result of alternative employment opportunities, districts must take advantage of all means to develop a good school climate and culture so the school is a desirable place to work. One of the ways this can be done is to involve faculty members through site-based decision making in selecting new teachers who will work with the current staff in delivering the educational program. Sound educational experiences are delivered to students by teams of teachers who coordinate what will be taught and how the concepts will be integrated between subjects and teachers. This organization requires teamwork and cooperation as well as collaboration. Teacher input is often helpful, if not required, to make such a team come together.

School districts with multiple schools at each level—elementary, middle, and high schools—usually have a district human resources officer who begins the recruitment and screening process for new personnel. Applications and related documentation are gathered and categorized as to teaching levels and subjects; these are then referred to principals as openings develop. Often, an initial interview is accomplished at the district level to determine if the candidate would meet minimal qualifications before applications are referred to the school level. Once the referral has been accomplished, it is often the principal's decision as to which candidate is offered the position.

When examining the applications and documentation on candidates, it is often difficult to establish who is the best-suited individual. Professional human resource managers and consultants have developed many methods of evaluating these documents—oftentimes with scientific methodology used to establish validity and reliability. Experts (Castetter and Young 2000; Harris and Monk 1992) usually recommend that "job content" be established for the position—these refer to the tasks that the position will be expected to perform on the job. "Job criteria" are also determined to identify the knowledge base and the skills the individual should have who will fill the position. Lastly, "job predictors" are measures or indicators that those selecting individuals use to decide if the candidates have the knowledge and skill criteria to be successful at filling the position. The process of deciding what composes these three areas is called "job analysis."

Prior to the busy season of recruiting and selecting new staff, the principal could ask faculty members of the school what traits that all teachers who are hired in the future should have. Working in small groups, faculty members can develop ideas that are very worthy criteria—some being attitudes, some beliefs, and some behaviors. By pooling these ideas, the entire faculty can help develop what all good educators who are employed should emulate. This list can be the start of job criteria that all teachers are expected to exhibit. Such results may vary when done, but the task of working together to determine these criteria can also be important to help current teachers meet such standards (for an example of such a result, see table 13.1).

Table 13.1.   Faculty and Staff Traits

Traits expected of all faculty and staff

- Genuinely likes kids
- A belief that all kids can learn, if taught properly
- Positive, enthusiastic, and caring—toward everyone at school
- Establishes high expectations for self and students
- Flexible team player who is a good listener and problem solver

Teachers and others who serve on screening committees can use this list of criteria to begin their task. In addition, job criteria and job content aimed at specific positions with respect to teaching assignments are important. The principal, department heads, team leaders, and other staff who participate should identify these criteria before beginning the search. Haberman (1998) states that over the years, educators have learned to identify abilities that help discriminate between star teachers and failures who might enter the teaching ranks, if employed. He specifically points out the problem of working with low-income children of diverse ethnic backgrounds as a paramount quality that must be identified in new teachers, because of the great number of children who enter schools from such backgrounds (Haberman's list of qualities needed for star teachers, see table 13.2).

Once the documents of appropriate applicants have been identified, the principal and selected staff members should screen these for indications of job predictors—that is, how well the individual will meet the criteria. This is a more difficult task than it first would seem. The documents frequently include applications, résumés, letters of reference, transcripts, certificates, testing results, previous teaching evaluations, teaching tapes, and portfolios. Unless the district requires only a certain amount of these documents to be included with the application and prohibits extras, such documentation may not include the same predictors. Finally, the interviews may be scheduled for those the principal and/or the committee considered as the best applicants.

Although interviews are often the deciding factor in the selection process, the principal should be cognizant that an interview does not tell how an individual actually performs on the job. To help judge the candidate's suitability for the job, some schools invite the candidate to spend the entire day at the school working with the instructional team. This may provide an opportunity for some instructional observation of an informal nature. Interviews generally help judge the candidate's interest, philosophy, personality, and thought processes. If team leaders and members are part of the interview process, those who will be working closely with new individuals can help to evaluate how such persons may fit into collaborative processes. In these cases, a series of questions for use in the interview should be developed to ask all candidates and probing, listening, observing, rating, and recording are important functions of the interview team.

Table 13.2.   Qualities of a Star Teacher

1. Star teachers persist in continuous generation and maintenance of student interest.

2. Star teachers protect learners and learning by learning themselves and involve their students in transcending the curriculum in their learning also.

3. Star teachers apply ideas to practice by generating practical, specific applications of the ideas and theories presented to their students; these teachers understand what those many activities add up to in terms of principles and goals to be learned.

4. Star teachers accept responsibility for reaching at-risk students regardless of the students' life conditions. They have a sense of efficacy in their work with students.

5. Star teachers have a personal orientation to students by caring and having respect and concern for them. They do not have to be loved to function as a teacher, nor do they instill guilt to maintain order.

6. Star teachers protect themselves from burnout by stress, the system, or bureaucracy. They develop networks, teams, or kindred spirits as a source of emotional sustenance.

7. Star teachers know they are fallible and understand that students will make mistakes also.

8. Star teachers are organized and understand what is happening at all times with their students, their work, and the materials. They can manage students, time, resources, and content simultaneously.

9. Star teachers have physical and emotional stamina to maintain an incredible pace, reassure their students, deal with stress of many decisions, and live with tension in their lives.

10. Star teachers coach their students and make them understand they are on the same side or team.

11. Star teachers tell their students that effort leads to success and that ability is not the determining factor for winning.

12. Star teachers have good rapport with their students by indicating that this is their classroom, their learning, and their activities that define success. "We are here for your benefit and participation is the way we succeed together."

13. Star teachers work from students' current level of achievement and don't declare them not ready if they don't have certain knowledge. They understand there is wide variation in achievement.

14. Star teachers want to turn their students on to learning. That is the most important goal—to show that one can learn him- or herself and interest and persistence lead to achieving anything one wants to achieve.

Source: M. Haberman. (1998). "Star Teachers." *Instructional Leader* 11 (2). All rights reserved. Used by permission, Texas Elementary Principals and Supervisors Association.

This process assumes that the interview team participants are willing and thoughtful partners and share goals of the principal. The principal must provide some training to these team members in beginning such a process, not only to detail the task, but to also protect the interviewee and the school from improper questions being asked that may violate individual rights. If the principal finds it necessary to make major changes in the personnel of the school or to impact the culture of the school in a developmental way, such screening teams will have to be selected from faculty who understand and share the need for changes. Whether or not an interview team is used, the principal is responsible for the selection process. If the committee is used, the principal must indicate exactly what form the recommendation of the screening committee will take and how it will ultimately be factored into the final decision. Before the final selection is completed, the principal should verify by personal conversation, the references of the applicant. In this day of litigious procedures, such personal information from other employers may not be easily obtained. Once a job offer is accepted, there is no easy way to correct major mistakes that may have been identified if a contact had been made prior to the offer.

After the judgment to hire has been made, the candidate should be invited back to be informed of the decision and offered the job. At this point, the hiring principal should go over how pleased he or she is to offer the candidate the job, but in accepting the job, the principal expects the teacher to agree to live up to certain norms and values. If he or she cannot or will not agree to these, then the job offer should be turned down. At that point, the principal discusses goals of having a world-class school, responsibility for all students, expectation of teacher improvement, communication between teams and individuals, adherence to rules and programs, and other items of importance to the principal and district (Slosson 1999). After an affirmative response, the principal welcomes the new teacher to the team.

NEW TEACHER INDUCTION

Career Stages

Teachers are theorized to go through career stages similar to and in conjunction with life's development. The anticipatory career stage occurs as the newly certified teacher is hired or returns after a significant break in teacher employment. This stage is characterized as one of idealism, energetic, open to new ideas, creative, and ready for growth orientation. As experience grows and the job match is satisfactory to both the school and the teacher, the individual grows into an expert or master teacher over a period of time.

Here, the teacher is characterized as being in control, self-actualized, focused on the students and school, and yet is still evolving by accommodating new growth opportunities and challenges. As challenges are mastered, lulls in career development may ensue and individuals may go back into a renewal stage that indicates reactivation and interest, focused growth, acquiring new skills, and becoming less independent of others within the school. In some cases, however, this transition results in a withdrawal stage in the career cycle and is characterized by low energy, fatigue, weariness, and frequent illness. Individuals may become depressed, dependent on alcohol or chemicals, have negative attitudes, and become pessimistic. If this develops into an unresponsive obstructionist or into psychosocial problems, the principal may need to encourage reevaluating the teacher's career choices or respond with dismissal procedures. In other cases, however, a once dynamic teacher may go into a renewal stage and become the productive and helpful individual he or she had been previously. A career exit stage is also an option for those who have a commitment shift, become judgmental, and realize that their personal priorities are better met doing another type of work.

Induction Programs

For the newly hired teacher who has never taught before, new teacher induction programs have been found to make them more successful first-year teachers and help socialize them to the profession and to the school or district. This type of induction is a structured series of events usually beginning in the summer before the school year starts, and continuing on through the first and possibly the second year of teaching. There has been frequent and extensive development of induction programs by researchers, state agency staff, and local district staff developers, and principals. These programs often incorporate a teacher mentor arrangement as part of or in addition to the induction program.

The National Association of Secondary School Principals developed an induction program that had many of the attributes identified today in such successful programs (Hunt 1969). The program began as soon as the new teacher was hired, sometimes in the spring of a senior year in college or in the summer. A day-long visit to the school by the teachers where they were to begin work helped them to understand the challenges they would face, meet individuals who they would be working with, and obtain curriculum and instructional materials such as texts, curriculum documents, goals, and other helpful information. During the period before school began, a coordinator of the induction program such as a staff development team member met with the new teachers to discuss the school's demographic characteristics and their meaning to the school's programs. This time offered an opportunity for new teachers to become familiar with the school's clientele and also the community, especially if they had relocated from another area to take the position. Social opportunities for these individuals to meet other teachers and to interact with other new faculty were offered. A community tour and introduction to community resources, for both personal and professional needs, was a welcomed activity for those who had relocated for the job. The week before the school year began, the school comprised a fairly comprehensive look at the curriculum, instructional support resources, handling daily routines such as attendance, grade books, and organizing classrooms and disciplinary procedures. This week was primarily devoted to the immediate concerns of new teachers. As the year progressed, new teachers met regularly to discuss a variety of instructional topics. During the first semester, these focused on daily instructional concerns; the second semester focused more on long-term issues such as curriculum development and addressing more extended problems such as difficult students.

During the first year, new teachers typically experience a series of phases as the year progresses and their development as a professional teacher moves forward. Moir (1996) describes the five phases:

- An anticipation phase begins as they start the first year in which they are excited yet anxious. They are somewhat idealistic and very much want to make a difference.
- The survival phase sets in as they are attacking the variety of problems that are not anticipated and they become inundated by the amount of work required in developing a routine, understanding what works for them, and dealing with the many demands.
- A disillusionment phase starts as they begin questioning their commitment and competence, usually encountered about November as a variety of obligations and challenges are stressful. Illness may be a response to this phase for some.

- The rejuvenation phase arrives after the winter break when rest and re-organization help the new teachers' attitudes rise and they have a better understanding of the job.
- A reflection phase occurs as the year is coming to a close and the new teachers review their work and teaching strategies, thinking about how they will apply what they learned for the next year.

As beginning teachers pass through these phases, the teacher induction program offers information and practices in seminars and workshops that can help them navigate the new experiences that typically are prominent in each of these phases. Both induction programs and mentor relationships can assist new teachers to maneuver through the periods of stress and self-doubt and help them to understand the nuances and pitfalls along the way.

Mentors

Most of the induction programs currently in place also rely on a mentor for new teachers; in fact, some place the bulk of the interaction and cul-turalization process on the mentor (Ganser 1996). These programs are de-signed to give moral support as well as guide good instruction and keep worthy teachers in the classroom. Such a mentor relationship helps new teachers not feel isolated in their assignment (Telzlaff and Wagastaff 1999). How a mentor is selected varies; usually someone such as the principal or a coordinator matches the beginning teacher with a mentor. Some schools or districts may arrange for the new teacher to select a mentor from those with whom they may have formed a bond. In both situations, mentors must be willing to serve and assume a caring and helping stance toward the new teacher. Oftentimes, mentor training is offered to those who take on this role. Matching the mentor to the new teacher is often difficult and if an assignment does not appear to be working, a process for terminating the arrangement with dignity should be available.

Mentoring roles are quite varied with one study describing 285 roles, indicating that the process is complex and multifaceted (Ganser 1993). The ten most frequently cited roles were:

- Provide support and encouragement.
- Inform about policies, procedures, and paperwork.
- Inform about school culture, expectations, and staff.

- Help with lesson plans and materials.
- Help with discipline and classroom management.
- Provide link to other personnel.
- Inform about job, benefits, and activities.
- Help with teaching skills and grading practices.
- Meet with beginning teacher regularly.
- Provide information about special education.

Fewer than half of the mentors, however, cited meetings with protégés or classroom observations as important roles. Although mentors should not be used to perform summative evaluations, coaching following an instructional observation could certainly be worthwhile. Because the mentors' role is not clearly defined, they tended to make their contacts somewhat intuitive and safe. Conflicting schedules and lack of classroom coverage for released time were obstacles preventing better assistance. Mentors' assistance focused on helping beginning teachers survive rather than helping them develop instructional strategies (Ganser 1996).

An important point about teacher induction programs is that they take time and fiscal resources to develop and maintain. Some individual must coordinate the activities, train mentors in their roles, and establish communications between all of the participants. The principal should play a significant role in this process. Yet, this function is one of many roles in which he or she needs to be active; consequently, other professionals must also be involved in coordinating the processes. The success of such an induction is to help new teachers have a successful beginning, navigate the initial year without being a casualty, as well as educate their students in a professional manner. It costs several thousand dollars to recruit and select a new teacher. Currently, fifty percent of new teachers leave their profession within five years of starting (as cited in Association for Supervision and Curriculum Development 1999). If induction helps to make a good teacher satisfied and successful, the school avoids the increased costs of recruiting and the turnover in faculty that can be difficult for a school to adjust to each year.

TEACHER ASSIGNMENT

The purpose of teacher assignment is to staff the school's positions in the best way possible. At the elementary level, this refers usually to assigning grade levels to each teacher for the ensuing year. For the secondary school or possibly the elementary school where teaching is more specialized by subject matter, it would also include the scheduling of courses for each teacher. Assignment to teaching teams in the elementary or middle school would be part of this task. Annual assignment is an opportunity to make changes that may alter the way individuals have operated in their teaching for many years. This opportunity is a powerful one for the school and for the principal's understanding of the need for changes. New assignments can oftentimes mean growth of the individual teacher in this process, but also can risk antagonizing well-established teachers toward the principal. Assignments should take into consideration a number of factors including teaching load, such as the number of preparations, class sizes, extracurricular assignments, administrative responsibilities, teaching styles, and teacher strengths, weaknesses, and preferences. Above all, the teacher's professional preparation program and subject specialties (certification) are critical. The support that is offered by the existence of teacher aides, parental volunteers, and instructional support personnel are factors involved when looking at a teaching load. When teaching teams are a part of the assignment, individual personalities of the team members also must be weighed. A teacher's seniority within the school should be a factor; however, the long-tenured teachers should not necessarily receive all of the most desirable classes or the easiest grade level. In many cases, the teacher with considerable experience is best able to teach and deal with students needing the most help. Also, teachers who have taught the same assignment for long periods may benefit from reassignment in order to avoid burnout or stress.

Assignments should consider the individual, the job to be accomplished, and the situation in which it is to be accomplished. These factors have been referred to as "the man, the job, and the situation." As the end of each year draws to a close, some teachers will be requesting transfers to other grades or course assignments and possibly to other schools. All returning teachers should be asked to fill out a "desires" list to be considered in making assignments. Where subject level or team chairs are involved in a school's decision making, these leaders should confer with the principal. In any case, individuals should be made aware of their assignments at the earliest possible time in order to prepare for changes mentally as well as from an instructional standpoint.

STAFF DEVELOPMENT

Today's environment is one of change and certainly education is on the forefront of having to respond to this environment. The effort to improve the school and its impact on student achievement calls for reevaluation of how instruction is delivered and how the curriculum is structured. The effort also reminds principals to see the school as a system that has many aspects affecting students and learning. The entire system must be studied and considered in making changes in order to determine the right mix of such adjustments.

Sparks and Hirsh (1997) point toward three important shifts in thinking about schools that principals must consider in looking to the future of education. These include:

- The shift to results-driven education and judging success by what the student actually knows and can do as a result of time in school. This focus is to start with desired results and structure the knowledge, skills, and plans around these goals.
- The view of educational change as a system with many factors interrelated rather than one that is causing change to occur, "the system is always in a state of flux" and changes may not become evident without extended time frames.
- The development of constructivism as an educational idea that today is driving the shift of how students are educated. Knowledge is not just transmitted from teacher to learner, but is constructed in the mind of the student by his or her reflection. That construct will be different for every student.

For teachers to effectively respond to this environment of change in the educational setting, growth on their part must also occur. Educators in every position have become and must continue to be lifelong learners. There is no stopping of education when a formal degree or a certificate to teach is completed. The school must be a part of this movement in order to make constructive changes occur. The school's role is to make staff development a major growth happening in the lives of all faculty and staff. The test of good staff development is to improve teaching and to effect better and improved learning.

Staff development has undergone a major change in the recent past and is closely linked to school improvement (Sparks 1992). No longer is this growth referred to as in-service training. Such development is much more than what in-service infers. It takes place in many forms and at diverse times during and after the normal school day. Staff development should not only be led by the district efforts at improving staff members, but also by the efforts of the building principal by defining where changes need to occur within the school, the instruction, and the curriculum. Consequently, staff development is needs driven through the efforts of the principal and teachers in a team determining what changes need to occur at the building and in its environment. This is goal setting and should be tied in to any campus improvement plan that is developed. Creative design for such goal achievement is the plan for effecting changes. Such designs should impact the school as a unit and also individual teachers and staff members. Individuals should make personal staff development plans as part of this creative design.

To better design a staff development program, the principal must understand that the design process has three major guiding attributes. First is the context of the effort. This context is very much like the factors that compose the environment in which it will be developed including the policies, the mission and goals of the district or school, and the school's culture, beliefs, values, and such things as the needs that are recognized or unrecognized that would include both planned and unplanned agendas. The second attribute is the process that is chosen to deliver the development effort. This could include the large- or small-group training environment or could involve the individualized personal effort of faculty. Third is the attribute of content, that which is to be internalized or learned by the participants—also referred to as "what is taught." In working the design of a staff development plan, the context is usually the factor that decides what changes should be targeted for achievement by the institution. The content is then identified to understand what information, skills, or attitudes should be conveyed to the subject faculty; lastly, the process is determined by identifying what is the most effective manner to impact the staff in delivering this information or skill (Sparks 1983). This has been referred to as a "nested process" with the content being delivered by the process within the context of an environment of policy and support (see fig. 13.2).

Examples:

Context:
School culture
School mission, vision, and goals
Policies/support of the board
Fiscal support for development

Process:
Scheduling of activities
Types of activities
Direct presentation
Small group/committee effort
Coaching
Reflection on practice

Goals/Content:
Understanding use of learning styles
Supporting student growth in solving
 problems
Classroom management practices
Developing student character
Harnessing technology for teaching
reference

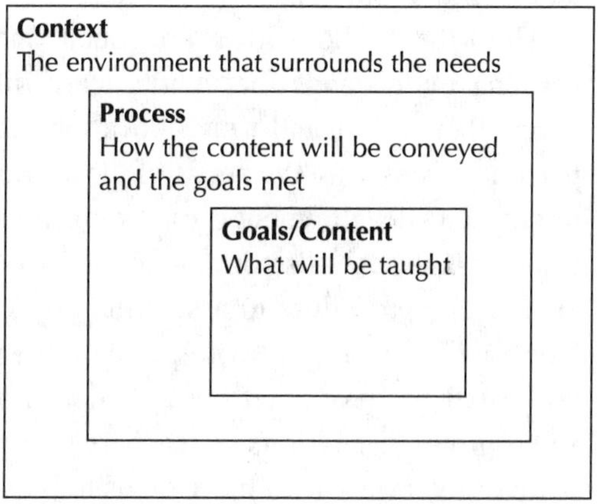

Context
The environment that surrounds the needs

Process
How the content will be conveyed
and the goals met

Goals/Content
What will be taught

Figure 13.2.   The Nested Process of Staff Development

All staff development does not occur through group training, although that is certainly a focused method to introduce a specific topic to a large group of faculty and staff (Sparks 1992). Multiple models can be included in promoting development. Individually, staff members may attend conferences with specific topics needing attention or they might visit other classrooms while activities are occurring to better understand the application of new strategies or ideas. Committee work with groups of teachers may assess and plan for an improvement process or develop a new curriculum construct for application. One or more teachers may conduct an inquiry into new methodology or assess the school climate in an action research project to assess efforts to change. Work with professional associations can also offer ideas and innovation through the association with other professionals from different educational organizations. Likewise, acting as a mentor or cooperating teacher to teacher interns (student teachers) can offer connections to teacher preparation institutions that can provide new insights as well as offer opportunities to recruit soon-to-be teachers. Some of the most powerful activities occur in what is referred to as "job embedded learning"—which "links learning to the immediate and real-life problems faced by teachers and administrators" (Sparks and

Hirsh 1997, 52). This type of learning occurs in response to current challenges and encourages immediate application, experimentation, and adaptation on the job.

All of the previous ideas are couched in terms of adult learning. Adult learning understands that adults learn differently than children and respects their effort and time allocations in an adult way, balancing their personal needs with the needs of the school's program. Finally, evaluation of any staff development effort is made in terms of the results it hopes to achieve. The school's committee on staff development should develop an appropriate procedure to assess the impact that staff development efforts have on the school as a whole and on the individual teachers. This evaluation will be developed by a group effort, but could include reflective small-group discussions of teachers or a gathering of data by a questionnaire or interview with individuals to better understand how teachers perceive such efforts (see fig. 13.3).

Fort Spirit School District

Respondents should read each item and assign a rating from 1 to 5 as indicated:
1 = statement does not represent the staff development program of the school
2 = statement seldom represents the staff development program of the school
3 = statement sometimes represents the staff development program of the school
4 = statement frequently represents the staff development program of the school
5 = statement consistently or always represents the staff development program of the school

1. There is regular opportunity to have input concerning teachers' needs in the development of the staff development programs.   1 2 3 4 5

2. Staff development program topics are identified through a process that involves teachers' ideas, administrator/district concerns, the state's priorities, and students' weaknesses.   1 2 3 4 5

3. Staff development programs impact instructional knowledge and skills of both teachers and administrators.   1 2 3 4 5

4. Teacher and administrator attitudes are impacted positively by staff development efforts.   1 2 3 4 5

5. Staff development is viewed from a systems perspective so that these efforts are designed as they dynamically interact with all parts of the school's program.   1 2 3 4 5

6. The staff development program is planned and developed in a way that the faculty and administration achieves intended results.   1 2 3 4 5

7. Staff development programs help teachers create their own knowledge structures rather than merely receive them from others.   1 2 3 4 5

8. Building administrators support staff development programs through planning efforts and personal participation.   1 2 3 4 5

9. The staff development program is school-focused rather than district-focused.

1 2 3 4 5

10. The staff development program is driven by a clear, coherent strategic plan that reflects the needs of the school and the learning outcomes of students.　　1 2 3 4 5

11. Staff development includes multiple forms of job-embedded learning.　　1 2 3 4 5

12. Staff developers provide consultation, planning, and facilitation services in addition to training.　　1 2 3 4 5

13. Staff development is seen as a critical function and major responsibility of all principals and teacher leaders.　　1 2 3 4 5

14. Staff development is treated as a significant building tool in the instructional improvement process rather than a frill that can be cut when resources are scarce.

1 2 3 4 5

15. Staff development is focused toward continuous improvement in performance for everyone who affects student learning.　　1 2 3 4 5

16. Staff development efforts are planned and impacted by teachers and other staff who participate in the programs.　　1 2 3 4 5

17. Staff development efforts are evaluated regularly by all participants.　　1 2 3 4 5

18. Staff development efforts have structured follow-up support that enables desired changes to be realized in student instruction.　　1 2 3 4 5

19. Staff development includes both content-specific learning as well as generic approaches to learning.　　1 2 3 4 5

Figure 13.3.　Teachers on Staff Development
Source: ©1998 James Vornberg, used with permission, all rights reserved.

SUPERVISION AND EVALUATION OF TEACHING

The supervision role of the principal has changed immensely from that of an inspector of teachers and teaching to one of encouragement and assisting in bringing about change in improving instruction. Today, there is a human relations emphasis on the relationship between the principal and teachers. The principal must maintain his or her skill in understanding the dynamics of instruction in order to be successful and respected as an instructional leader. He or she must set high expectations for staff and students and model appropriate teaching behavior in interactions with both teachers and students. Principals should spend considerable time working with teachers and visiting classrooms; this is the route to be both respected by teachers and to stay informed about the educational processes in the school.

Supervisory functions include helping to set goals and objectives with site-based leadership teams and working closely with instructional changes and curriculum development efforts. Major insights about the school come from assessing staff utilization decisions and considering helpful changes. These efforts can affect staff morale and school climate and establish the principal as a leader. When the principal recognizes that processes are not supporting teachers in their instructional efforts or that resources are not adequate for achieving educational goals, he or she has the opportunity to bring about change. This change can be either through decisions about initiatives and resources the principal controls or by approaching others who influence such decisions that are outside those of his or her authority.

Perhaps the most feared part of supervision is that of evaluating teachers. It is feared by teachers because they want to be viewed as successful and the evaluation process will probably point out that they have areas that are not perfect or at least need to be worked on through a developmental process. Evaluation is feared by principals as it is time consuming and breaks into all the other activities that present themselves to be dealt with by the principal. Principals also must be skilled instructional observers if they are to interact with teachers in a meaningful way about their teaching skills. This latter skill is demanding and perhaps can be as threatening to the principal as the evaluation process is to the teacher. If teacher evaluation is going to be helpful to the school and to the teacher, it must be seen by all participants as a journey that is taken regularly and that the journey will provide some ideas for teacher growth.

The most recognized process for evaluation of teachers is the clinical supervision model. This process is designed to build a level of rapport between the teacher and principal so that a professional atmosphere that is friendly and helpful can exist. This model, developed by Morris Cogan and others (Wiles and Bondi 2000), follows a five-step process that focuses the principal's and the teacher's attention on the teaching-learning process:

1. A preconference with the teacher to discuss what is planned in the lesson and to select a specific skill, technique, or approach that the teacher would like to have observed.
2. Observation of the lesson discussed in the preconference. The principal scripts verbatim the lesson as much as possible and observes the full lesson.
3. An analysis of the lesson is made by the principal focused on the lesson's objective, its appropriateness, and the achievement of the objec-

tive. The analysis should yield a growth and a reinforcement objective to be discussed in the postconference.

4. A teacher–supervisor conference is held that is designed to be on a positive note and in a teacher friendly location. The conference should be a lesson in itself, discussing the analysis questions and selecting a growth and or a reinforcement objective for the teacher to work on in the future. An action plan might be developed at this point.

5. A postconference analysis is accomplished by the principal to critique conference skills and to see if the teacher can identify the objectives discussed.

There are many other philosophies of evaluation that have modified or extended the clinical supervision model such as those developed by Madeline Hunter and Carl Glickman. Other models such as the Teacher Expectations and Student Achievement model are designed to teach specific behaviors to teachers for use with interacting with low-achieving students. The Flander's model of Interaction Analysis lets the teacher review the types of interaction going on between student and teacher and then make healthy decisions on what to alter or continue. The cognitive coaching model uses a fellow teacher to become one's coach in observing and selecting growth areas followed up with a conference with the principal. Allan Glatthorn advocates a model of differentiated supervision, which recognizes that not all teachers benefit from clinical supervision and other alternatives can be used for those teachers where a high level of growth is already in place. Most of these supervision models are couched in terms of giving assistance to developing/practicing teachers. This, of course, is known as formative evaluation. Try as educators have, most teachers realize it is very difficult for the principal to separate formative evaluation—that of assisting a teacher to make changes—from summative evaluation—that of making organization decisions concerning individual teachers' reemployment and promotion.

Marginal Teachers

In today's work environment with an increasing student population and somewhat limited teacher resources, principals must strive to make every teacher successful in the classroom. The current environment of increased accountability requires principals to rely on "capacity building" within the schools. To build the school's capacity to meet the challenge, administrators must do everything possible to retain, assist, retrain, and support all teachers and staff who are capable of helping move toward the school's goal of achieving high standards. Any individual who is struggling as a teacher would be such a staff member. Expert opinion and empirical research indicate that 5 to 15 percent of public school teachers perform at incompetent levels—meaning there is a lack of relevant content knowledge and/or skill in instruction and classroom management (Tucker 2001; Hendersson-Sparks, Ehrgott, and Sparks 1995). This lack of competency can be observed as nonachievement of performance goals with students in the teacher's classroom.

Principals, through the supervision process, can usually diagnose initially that a teacher is having difficulty in his or her classroom. This indication can come from direct observation of teaching, indications of problems from the numbers of students referred to the office for discipline, or from parental complaints concerning the teacher's handling of instruction, homework, or other issues. One problem, however, is that the principal or assistants sometimes do not carefully call attention to marginal demonstrations of effectiveness in their observation work. Sweeney and Manatt (1984) offer a team approach for such situations in assisting change. Frase (1992) offers a four-phase process for managing activities in dealing with the teacher having difficulty. Through this process, the principal must take detailed notes of efforts to assist the teacher and whenever such contact is made between the teacher and supervisor(s).

Initially, legal and ethical considerations must be considered, such as is this teacher tenured or on continuing contract, and what are the implications under state law or policy? Once that determination is made, the question must be answered as to the cause of the deficiency: Is the performance due to lack of skill (training) or motivation/effort (attitude)? Another possible cause is a personal problem outside the school, which the teacher must recognize or address (Fuhr 1993; Hendersson-Sparks, Ehrgott, and Sparks 1995). This determination will help to explain the problem to the teacher and identify specifically what the deficiency is. It is important to identify the problem to the teacher and offer assistance in ways that are helpful, such as suggesting topics to get assistance, conferences or workshops to attend, and observations to learn methods of teaching. This supervision is offered in the most helpful way possible and, if deemed feasible in relation to the deficiency, a mentor teacher might be arranged to assist. Regular contact by the principal should be maintained and an honest assessment of progress made is analyzed. If the deficiency is corrected or sufficient progress made, then the process may end at this point with normal supervision being the only follow-up. If progress does not prove satisfactory, then consideration should be given as to the realistic probability of improvement with further assistance. If this is not realistic and the teacher is untenured, then a decision to nonrenew a contract may be made at this point, depending on state law.

The formal plan phase is begun at this time if assistance continues after conferring with district and legal advisors. Here, the formal plan is developed with the assistance of the supervisor with activities specified to focus on alleviating the deficiencies now set out in writing. The plan should align the objectives, the activities, and the evaluation methods. Although the supervisor assists in developing the plan, the teacher is responsible for improving. Both the teacher and administrator should sign the plan. A mentor teacher may be designated for assistance to the teacher. Walk through visits to the classroom should be more frequent. An outside evaluator may also be used to validate progress or lack thereof; however, the principal is the responsible administrator for decisions. Once the plan has been carried out, the evaluation for this phase is conducted after adequate time. If sufficient improvement is not made, then phase three begins.

The official corrective action is indicative that the teacher, tenured or probationary, is in a difficult position. The corrective action plan, now developed as a second plan with the teacher, must indicate satisfactory progress by a specified date. Without such progress, the teacher will be dismissed or nonrenewed at the end of the contract. This third phase is often required by the district teaching contract with the teachers' professional organization or union. This third-phase communication with the teacher is in writing and contains a statement of specific deficiencies, corrections required, criteria and instruments to be used in judging performance, and the improvement plan and time line with deadlines. After the implementation of the plan, judgment must be made concerning progress meeting the criteria. Assuming adequate progress is not made, then the last phase begins.

The termination process begins with the teacher being informed that he or she will not be rehired the following school year. Many states require hearings for teachers with tenure to demonstrate that the teacher has not met certain policy standards. During this phase, the documentation is prepared for the hearing with all legal requirements being demonstrated, such as adequate notice to the teacher concerning the deficiencies, a plan, and time frame for remediation of the deficiencies. For cases involving probationary teachers, hearings may not be required, depending on state laws. In any case, the school district's legal counsel should review all documents and will probably demonstrate the district's case to the board, panel, or group designated as hearing body. The principal will be most likely the official to testify for the hearing on the problems encountered by the teacher and the process used to attempt correction of the deficiencies.

Following the previous process completely is not what any principal would desire for a teacher, inexperienced or experienced. Successful change at the initial step or through regular supervision is the goal of caring and resourceful principals. To help effect such a change, the principal should start by being honest with the teacher in question and convey that he or she understands the teacher's difficulty and will do everything possible to assist in making the teacher successful; however, the teacher must make progress in handling the classroom changes. Trust must be built between the teacher and the principal, recognizing that the teacher is in a difficult position (Frase 1992). The principal must indicate to the teacher what a satisfactory classroom situation would look like in terms of acceptable performance of the teacher and acceptable behaviors of the students in response to the teacher. From this point, the principal assists the teacher in developing a plan of activities to promote change in the teacher to which students will respond differently. This experience should be characterized by high expectations for all staff with direct support and feedback by the principal; teachers will then view this offer with greater trust (Tucker 2001). In today's environment, the expectation is not only positive student rapport, but effective levels of collaborative effort with other teachers, effective use of technology, and successful achievement of knowledge and skill goals on the part of the students.

The plan of activities to assist the teacher in making changes can be viewed as a series of intervention strategies. These strategies should be designed to first focus on the area with the most difficulty. No one can handle a lengthy laundry list of problems at once; the focused areas should be prioritized and then activities designed or selected to meet specific goals. Examples can include formal course work or workshops, asking a mentor to assist by giving feedback after observations in the class, video-taping, teaching for analysis, visiting other master teachers' classes for ideas, and better integration of resource and reference materials (Tucker 2001). In some cases, assignments in urban schools have teachers with lit-tle background in working with and teaching ethnic or racial minority stu-dents doing just this. These teachers have to adjust their perceptions of these students without any formal training or experience in their teaching backgrounds. Such teachers should be linked with mentors who have em-pathy for people of other cultures, are free of ethnocentrism, use multi-cultural materials, and are able to describe a student's behavior without judging it. The goal for the teacher being helped is to instill student pride with the students' native culture and to recognize and accept both the lan-guage spoken in the home and the standard language in working with these students (Leake and Leake 1995).

Dismissal of a Faculty or Staff Member

Like it or not, everyone who enters the education field as a career choice is not destined to be a credit to the calling. Generally, there are two routes to dismissal: dismissal for a specific action that is not acceptable under the law or education policies for a teacher working at a school, and dismissal or termination for incompetence as a teacher or staff member.

Most, if not all positions that are noncertified or classified positions are at-will employees. These employees do not have tenure rights to their po-sitions; however, they may have legal recourse to bring court action if they are dismissed for what might be considered trivial or inappropriate reasons. If they are incapable of performing the tasks of the job or have been inappropriate in their actions, then the school and district have the duty to protect the best interests of the citizens and dismiss the employee.

Dismissal of certified or professional employees is generally done un-der the state's education code or statutes. The law usually lists specific reasons that dismissal is accomplished such as immoral conduct, dishon-esty, unprofessional conduct, violation or refusal to obey school laws, al-coholism or drug abuse, or conviction of a felony (McGrath 1993). In many of these cases, dismissal can be accomplished by the principal and district officials after verifying or establishing that, in fact, the conduct or behavior was committed. In the case of professional employees who are in a tenured or protected status, a hearing may be required to effect the dismissal. During the hearing, the teacher has the right to understand the charges, be represented by counsel, to be heard and present evidence that refutes the charges, and have the decision made by an officer or panel (such as the board of education) in an open-minded and fair way. In many instances of gross or willful misconduct where the evidence is clear and unmitigated, the individual will resign or accept the proposed dismissal rather than go through the hearing process. If the employee is a union member, that organization may furnish an attorney and fight the recommendation for dismissal, even if it is clear to most individuals that the employee's behavior or actions are not acceptable.

In cases of incompetency as a teacher or professional employee, the process is more difficult and lengthy to complete. This requires the steps to be completed under the marginal teacher situation process described earlier. The principal's accomplishment of the documentation will be critical in these instances, in order to verify that every action was taken in the best interests of sound education and that the employee received assistance in performing the teaching tasks as expected. A hearing with evidence and legal representation may be needed to complete the process. When the decision is made to nonrenew the teacher's contract, their employment ends at the completion of the school year. In cases where harm is possibly being done to students or their educational experience including the school's organization culture, the school should normally move the teacher to another assignment and employ a replacement teacher to complete the year. In extreme cases, it may be possible to dismiss the teacher following the hearing and not complete the instructional year as an employee. In the case of probationary teachers who do not yet have tenure or some type of protected status under the law, nonrenewal may be possible without the necessity of a hearing. Every state has unique statutes regarding these processes that must be followed by the district and school administrators. Legal counsel is always advised in navigating these processes.

Often, the dismissal process is a difficult one to endure for the principal. However, to avoid it when it is necessary in the cases of incompetence is to invite poor performance on the part of all students and teachers. Teacher morale will be lowered and the culture of the school as an educational institution will be weakened. Parents will learn of the problems and eventually the effectiveness of the principal and all other teachers will be impacted. When this occurs, the only way out eventually may be to find a new principal for the school.

ETHICAL DISCUSSION

- Is it ethical for teachers to assist in making staffing decisions for the school rather than having the responsible administrator or principal make these decisions?
- What is the ethical action to take for a teacher who is not performing well for a particular school's program? Should the district's human resource department transfer the teacher to another school where he or she might be more suited?
- A student has made hints about a teacher's possible romantic interest in herself to a friend who shared these with the school's counselor. What should the response be on the part of the counselor? On the part of the principal? Should this information be conveyed to him or her?
- What should the role of a mentor teacher to a beginning teacher be with respect to evaluating the new teacher's performance in the classroom?
- The principal has made staff development decisions for a two-day in-service for the faculty. Members of the faculty do not understand the rationale for the presentations. What should be done?
- Ethical dilemmas are right-versus-right issues. Which side of the teacher selection debate do you support and why?

CHAPTER SUMMARY

The school's principal is the leader impacting the teaching-learning process in every classroom when decisions are made and initiatives are launched for improving the school's human resources. These tasks are not done alone but with support from the district level administration. Both levels of administration have functions that they are responsible for accomplishing; yet, these tasks also mesh within the district's framework and the school's system of teaching. Communication and

sharing are important between the two levels as are the tasks of planning, recruiting candidates, selecting teachers and staff members,
preparing them to be a part of the educational system, supervising and
improving their work, and assisting them when they have problems as
teachers.

Planning requires that the needs for the future be prognosticated
through projection of enrollments and the needs of the programs from a
teacher skills standpoint. By also inventorying the current human resource
skills, it is then possible to determine the future needs for staff/faculty
numbers and skills acquisition. This process also offers staff development
needs for the current and new staff.

Recruitment and selection processes offer opportunities for teacher or
site-based team involvement in doing a job analysis to define specific
skills needed and examining the predictors that are revealed in the
screening and interview tasks. This team involvement requires training
for the staff involved in order for it to recognize qualities needed or desired in outstanding teachers as it assists with the interview and ensuing
evaluative discussion. Once the decision has been made, the principal
should inform the newly selected teacher and also share his or her expectations and goals for the school to be considered in the decision to
accept the position.

As new teachers enter the profession, they begin a period of adjustment to new expectations and demands. Because of the critical nature
of teaching and student interaction, beginning teachers often find this
period a difficult one so outstanding schools offer an induction program to assist these new faculty members through the first year. Structured events including training and mentoring by experienced, caring
veteran teachers can assist beginning teachers through the stressful
events and tasks as well as being socialized into a profession with many
demands.

Other major human resource tasks for the principal include assigning
faculty to specific teaching assignments, organizing and managing the
staff development program, supervising and evaluating teachers and staff,
and working with marginal teachers who are struggling in their work with
classroom management and instruction. Each of these is closely aligned
with success in helping students learn and require planning and intense effort on the principal's part. In a few instances, it may be necessary for the

principal to hurdle the detailed processes of terminating a teaching employee. This latter step requires detailed work in making an effort to assist the teacher and in documentation.

CHAPTER ACTIVITIES AND QUESTIONS

1. Outline a plan to train a team of teachers in the interview and selection process to hire new teachers.
2. What questions would you ask teachers to supply data in your effort to understand their requests or preferences for assignments?
3. It is often said that the secretary of the school runs the place. Outline what qualities and skills you would look for in employing a secretary.
4. Do you support the notion of teacher mentors for new teachers? What do you see as problems and benefits to this effort?
5. Working with others, develop an annual plan for your school for staff development efforts. Include how the principal should set up for faculty input, participation, evaluation, and decisions.
6. Explain the purpose of teacher evaluation and the major components of at least one process developed to assist the principal in evaluating teachers.
7. Reflect on your experiences or philosophy of assisting a teacher who is struggling with his or her teaching activities and class organization. How would you set up such a program to assist this teacher?
8. What guidelines are important to include in any efforts to dismiss a teacher from the school?
9. How could a principal develop a role for the site-based team for human resource functions in the school yet still provide the level of leadership and decision making with which he or she was comfortable?
10. What data would you gather or questions would you ask of teachers in order to build an inventory of skills to begin planning for the future needs of the human resources in your school?
11. Select a position, either instructional or support function, and develop job content tasks and job criteria that relate to those tasks that could be used in helping to identify what candidate might best fit the position. How would you propose evaluating the candidates and their credentials in terms of job predictors?

CASE STUDY ACTIVITIES AND QUESTIONS

1. What sort of plan for impacting human resources in the school might be appropriate for this group of principals?
2. How would you deal with morale when considering human resources? Is this a district-level activity or is it primarily a school-level concern?
3. Reflect on ways to create recruiting processes to better impact the supply of teacher applicants.
4. What actions might be taken to reduce the threat of low scores simply due to faculty turnover?
5. Create a process that reduces teacher turnover and stabilizes your faculty.

REFERENCES

Association for Supervision and Curriculum Development. (1999). "Preparing two million: How districts and states attract and retain teachers." Education Update 41 (1): 1, 7–8.

Burnett, I. E., Jr. (1998). "A paradigm for teaching basic functions of school personnel administration." Paper presented at the National Council of Professors of Educational Administration, University of Alaska Southeast, Juneau, August 8.

Castetter, W. B., and Young, I. P. (2000). *The Human resource function in education*. Upper Saddle River, NJ: Merrill.

Frase, L. E. (1992). *Maximizing people power in schools*. Newberry Park, CA: Corwin.

Fuhr, D. L. (1993). "Managing mediocrity in the classroom." *The School Administrator* (April): 26–29.

Ganser, T. (1996). "Mentoring beginning teachers." Streamlined Seminar NAESP 15 (1).

———. (1993). "How mentors describe and characterize their ideas about mentor roles, benefits of mentoring and obstacles to mentoring" (ERIC Document Reproduction Services no. ED 354 237).

Haberman, M. (1998). "Star teachers." *Instructional Leader* 11 (2): 1–9.

Harris, B. M., and Monk, B. J. (1992). *Personnel administration in education*. Boston: Allyn and Bacon.

Hendersson-Sparks, J. C., Ehrgott, R. H., and Sparks, R. K. (1995). "Managing your marginal teachers." *Principal* 79 (March): 32–35.

Hunt, D. (1969). "Guidelines for cooperating teachers." Project on the Induction of Beginning Teachers, National Association of Secondary School Principals. Washington, DC.

Leake, B. H., and Leake, D. O. (1995). "Mentoring the marginal urban school teacher." *Education and Urban Society* 28 (1): 90–102.

McGrath, M. J. (1993). "When it's time to dismiss an incompetent teacher." *School Administrator* (April), 30–33.

Moir, E. (1996). "Phases of new teacher growth." In *A Guide to Prepare Support Providers for Work with Beginning Teachers*. Sacramento: California Department of Education.

Slosson, J. (1999). "Hiring the right people." *High School Magazine* 7 (2): 26–30

Sparks, D. (1992). "The keys to effective staff development." *Principal* 71 (5) (January): 43–44.

Sparks, D., and Hirsh, S. (1997). *A new vision for staff development*. Alexandria, VA: Association for Supervision and Curriculum Development.

Sparks, G. M. (1983). "Synthesis of research on staff development for effective teaching." *Instructional Leadership* 4 (3): 65–72.

Sweeney, J., and Manatt, D. (1984). "A team approach to supervision the marginal teacher." *Educational Leadership* 41 (7): 25–27.

Telzlaff, J. A., and Wagastaff, I. (1999). "Mentoring new teachers." *Teaching and Change* 6 (3): 284–295.

Tucker, P. (2001). "Helping struggling teachers." *Educational Leadership* 58 (5) (February): 52–55.

Wiles, J., and Bondi, J. (2000). *Supervision: A guide to practice*. Upper Saddle River, NJ: Merrill.

Chapter Fourteen

Creating Safe Schools

Zelda Zimmerman, principal of High Tech Avenue Elementary, was meeting with her administrative staff discussing the spring faculty evaluation cycle when Ms. Steinmiller, the school secretary, knocked on the door to interrupt the meeting and barged into the office, saying that the school's weather scanner had just come on with a warning about severe thunderstorms, lighting, hail up to one inch in diameter, and a warning that tornados were reported on the ground in the Bethany area. A second weather warning was broadcast from the NOAA weather radio as Ms. Zimmerman and her two assistant principals emerged from her office into the reception area. This tornado warning stated that a tornado was on the ground in the vicinity of State Highway 972 and High Tech Avenue moving east northeast at twenty miles per hour. Ms. Zimmerman realized that the tornado was on a collision path with the school and it was only minutes from impact.

Ms. Zimmerman told Ms. Steinmiller to sound the tornado signal on the intercom system. Zelda and the two assistants proceeded to their duty stations, one principal in each of the three main corridors. Students and teachers were coming out of their classrooms and kneeling face first against the hall walls covering their heads with books. Most of the teachers thought this was another weather-related drill until they saw the look on the administrators' faces. Approximately two minutes after the tornado signal was sounded, Ms. Zimmerman could hear what she knew was the sound of a tornado coming and she thought that the building was going to take a direct hit from the monster wind. The sound of the tornado was deafening and she could see that some of the children were beginning to understand the gravity of the situation as they began to cry and move closer to one another. At impact, the building shook and in a split second the entire roof disappeared

and rain began pouring into the exposed structure. As Ms. Zimmerman re-
gained her composure, she realized that children and teachers in her hall
were crying and two of the teachers had panicked and left their children.
She moved to see what was happening in the other two halls of the building
and discovered that the roof was still intact in those two wings. She returned
to her hall with one of the assistant principals and began moving the teach-
ers and children to the part of the building that was still under the roof.
While doing this, they quickly discovered that one group of second graders
and their teacher were trapped in the hall by falling debris and an arching
electrical panel. One of the students was trying to clear a path through the
rubble when it began to shift and pinned a child under a steel rafter. A sec-
ond student told Ms. Zimmerman that four members of the class were bleed-
ing and the teacher was unconscious.

The second assistant principal came running down the hallway and in-
dicated to Ms. Zimmerman that she could smell natural gas. Ms. Zimmer-
man told the two assistants to move all of the students out of the building
to the park across the street making sure they surveyed the path for elec-
trical and other types of harmful debris. As the students moved to the park,
Ms. Zimmerman stayed with the trapped class trying to figure out how
they were going to get the students to safety and medical treatment. She
could hear emergency vehicle sirens and she wanted them to be coming
toward the school. The emergency first responders on the scene were
Bethany Pumper Engine 7 from the fire station about three miles away.
Students had visited that fire station on several occasions and she knew
some of the firemen personally. The firemen entered the building and
found Ms. Zimmerman trying to tell students to not move and that the fire-
men would be getting them out soon. The firemen called for back-up help
along with orders to contact the electrical and gas companies to turn off
the utilities.

This situation came to a happy ending as all of the trapped children
were freed and those children needing medical attention were trans-
ported to the hospital along with the unconscious teacher. Teachers ac-
counted for all of their children and most went home that evening with a
weather-related crisis as part of their life's experiences. Ms. Zimmerman
went to the hospital to check on those children who needed medical care
and found them all doing well. The teacher had regained consciousness
and appeared to be resting comfortably.

The building would need significant repair and all the children, teachers, and staff were free from harm. Ms. Zimmerman knew she was indeed fortunate that no one was killed. A week later, Ms. Zimmerman and the assistant principals sat in their new office in one of the community churches reflecting on the tornado experience. Ms. Zimmerman knew that the children, teachers, and assistant principals were not as prepared as they should have been for this disaster. As this administrative team began to dissect the activities of the tornado attack, it began to think how it might have done things in a different way and it knew one sure thing: the team needed to practice emergency drills more often.

As principals ponder the safety of students, it is important to keep in mind that practice and preparation for crisis events are the only way to make sure teachers, students, and administrators react in a proactive manner in stressful situations. Most of the focus on school safety has been generated by the media's attraction to students' use of guns at school. The proliferation of twenty-four-hour television news channels competing with one another and airtime to fill has changed the way news is delivered to the public. Within minutes, television pictures of school shootings are live on millions of television screens around the world. In most of these situations, the media focuses on the perpetrators and not the victims. Beginning with the February 1996 incident in Moses Lake, Washington, where a fourteen-year-old boy wearing a trench coat and carrying a hunting rifle walked into his algebra class and killed his teacher and two students, and culminating with the media's attraction to the Columbine massacre, more than nineteen incidents of students wounding or murdering fellow students or teachers have been recorded. After Columbine came the Heritage High School incident in Conyers, Georgia, where a fifteen-year-old male shot fellow students, and in March 2000 a six-year-old murdered another six year old. At about the same time, a sixth grader threatened to shoot fellow students before the teacher talked him in to giving her the gun. Schools reflect the environment where they reside. In December 2000, the U.S. Justice Department reported a six-year decline of 68 percent in the juvenile homicide rate in the 1993–1999 time frame and the Federal Bureau of Investigation reported a 36 percent decrease in juvenile violent crimes (Knutson 2001). Currently, about twenty states require safe school plans and twelve states keep track of school violence.

Violence in schools is a major concern for students, parents, teachers, and principals. In the Northwestern National Life Study (1993), 93 percent of the adults responding indicated violence against students and teachers in elementary and secondary schools was a concern and 70 percent of these respondents stated they were very concerned. The magnitude of concern about school violence is demonstrated by survey results stating that 91 percent of school violence is a bigger concern than concerns over academic standards. Today's parents are concerned their children are no longer safe, afraid their child might become the next victim of school violence.

The Safe Schools Survey 1998 (1998) revealed that students experience school violence far too often. Sixty percent of the respondents reported observing violence between one and five times during the school year, 60 percent revealed being verbally insulted, 39 percent had property stolen from them, and 19 percent were kicked, bitten, or hit. One of the most disturbing aspects of this Safe Schools Survey indicated that 59 percent of the respondents had been victims of violent acts and failed to report these facts to the principal, teacher, or any other adult associated with the school.

The question remains: Is school violence increasing or decreasing? The evidence seems to be mixed. Volokh and Snell (1998) cite the National Center for Education Statistics' report *Violence and School Discipline Problems in U.S. Public Schools: 1996–97*, which states that about 1,000 crimes per 100,000 students occurred in public schools. As one would expect, crime was more prevalent in high schools, 103 crimes per 100,000 students, as compared to elementary schools with 13 crimes per 100,000 students. Perhaps the increase or decrease in overall school violence is subject to debate depending on the data collection strategies.

In a 1999 survey of Texas high school principals, 88.1 percent of the respondents indicated they had been threatened verbally or physically by parents and 53.3 percent indicated that parents had directed vulgar language toward the principal. In this same survey, 58 percent of the respondents indicated that students had verbally or physically threatened them. While these numbers are not staggering, one would have to believe that many principals never report the actual number of threats they receive for fear of being considered weak or unable to control their respective schools (Seifert 2000).

The types and amount of school violence is directly related to what students are experiencing at home, on the street, in their religious communities, and with their peers. Many principals are wondering "where will it happen next?" Most principals will never struggle with school violence of this magnitude but you could. More likely than not, every principal will face the prospects of dealing with students, parents, or teachers who die in automobile accidents and weather-related disasters, from catastrophic illnesses, and from committing suicide. Safety of students can be measured by how well prepared the school is when one of these less-than-media-friendly incidents occurs. Crisis by its very nature is unpredictable, thereby making practice and preparation the key to successful resolution of these incidents in the school setting.

How prepared was Ms. Zimmerman to meet the tornado disaster? It is possible that a principal will make appropriate decisions and protect the welfare of students, teachers, and staff even without a plan. It is dangerous to bank on good fortune. Even if outcomes are positive, the process of facing a crisis unprepared may take its toll on the principal (Seifert 2000).

SCHOOL SAFETY PLANNING TASK FORCE

The school safety planning task force has the responsibility of addressing policy issues concerning student and teacher safety. This group is charged with creating an environment for students and teachers free from fear, which promotes the development of children. Community involvement in the development of the school safety plan must include a wide variety of key individuals from the community. Members of the safety planning team could include the superintendent of schools, parents, judges, city manager, church leaders, representatives of civic organizations, police chief, fire chief, and representatives from the medical community including emergency medical technicians. Choosing the leader of the school safety team is a very important task and the person chosen must have the time and expertise to guide a large and diverse task force.

According to Stephens (2001), the steps in creating a safe schools planning task force include:

1. Selecting team members who represent and are influential in the community
2. Making sure all safe school team members attend the open forum

3. Holding an open forum on school safety and inviting all stakeholders to participate in the discussion
4. Making sure the invitation for the community meeting is sent out well in advance of the meeting date
5. Including all first responder agencies to participate in the community open forum
6. Either audiotaping the comments of the forum attendees or enlisting two or three individuals to take copious notes
7. Making sure all stakeholders have the time line for creating the safe schools plan
8. Informing all stakeholders of the meeting times and dates of the safe school planning team

Creating a safe schools plan is not a cookie cutter process because of community politics and the differing opinions held by community members. Some members of the safe schools planning task force will be opposed to practicing the plan because it will scare the students and others will demand the latest electronic surveillance equipment at all schools regardless of cost. Stephens (2001) declares that the biggest problem in creating the plan will be the egos and strained relationships that come from activities outside of the school setting. It is the responsibility of the task force chair to make sure the group works in the best interests of the school and its students and that each member leaves his or her personal dislikes outside the meeting room.

Each safe schools planning task force needs to review the school's mission statement and demand that a reference to school safety be included in the statement. By placing the safe school concept in the mission statement, the message is projected to all stakeholders that student safety is of paramount importance. A school mission statement containing a reference to school safety might look like the following: "Foster Middle School will provide students with an equal opportunity to obtain a quality education. With parental support and student involvement in the learning process, the school's mission is for students to achieve academic and social success in a safe environment. Students are being prepared to be productive members in a diverse and changing society."

A major responsibility of the school safety planning task force is the creation and development of policy that addresses student and teacher safety while at school.

SAFE SCHOOLS PLAN

Planning for the safety of children is a daunting task when viewed through the responsibility lens of a principal. The principal is responsible for the well-being of students while in school and the best way to do that is to develop a comprehensive school safety plan that covers every imaginable crisis. The first hour of a severe crisis is the worst time and by its very nature it will be chaotic and fluid (Poland and McCormick 1999). In any severe crisis, the principal will experience three waves of response and emotion. The first response will come from the first responders such as police and fire and medical personnel, followed by a surge of media, and the crush of parents (Peterson and Straub 1992). In order to minimize these three emotional events, Rettig (1999) outlines a seven-step school safety plan:

1. Create a school safety team.
2. Conduct a yearly school safety audit.
3. Develop policies and procedures for imaginable crises.
4. Provide all stakeholders with training and behavior management strategies.
5. Teach students to share information and help each other.
6. Educate students about violent actions.
7. Create contingencies for each crisis.

While a district safety plan is necessary from a policy perspective, even more important is the campus plan. Almost all school safety issues occur on a single campus rather than directly affecting an entire district. It is important to develop the school safety plan utilizing all the school's stakeholders, including parents, teachers, staff, and community agencies. Even before the plan is developed, the following topics should be considered:

• Community stakeholders, including first responder agencies, in conjunction with the school's faculty and staff, need to discuss the various types of safety issues that might occur on the campus.
• Once the safety issues are determined, a team of teachers, first responder agencies, and administrators must develop a plan to address each issue when it occurs.
• The safety plan must be shared with all community and school stakeholders.

- The ethical and legal aspects of protecting students, parents, teachers, staff, and administrators when a school crisis occurs should be addressed by the legal community prior to finalizing any safety plan and should be incorporated in the plan.
- Stakeholder training in implementation and utilization of the safety plan must be part of the district's policy.

The creation of the school safety team should be of utmost importance to the building principal, for it is this group that will be responsible for carrying out the safety plan should a crisis occur. It is the responsibility of the principal to select the members of the school safety team. Many faculty and staff members feel uncomfortable working through crisis situations. This is particularly true when they must work with situations such as student or teacher suicide, automobile accidents, catastrophic medical situations, and violence against children. For these reasons, it is very important that principals choose very calm and emotionally stable faculty to be members of the school safety team. In addition, safety team members must be good communicators, listeners, and negotiators.

The members of the school safety team should receive the majority of the staff development time that is devoted to the school safety plan, but all faculty and staff should be instructed in some aspects of school safety. This staff development should be done yearly, especially for those teachers and staff members new to the school. The key to implementing the plan is practice, practice, practice.

The school safety team should be composed of the following members:

- Safety team leader
- Police/fire/medical coordinator
- First-aid responders
- Site coordinators
- Sweep team coordinators
- Media spokesperson
- Parent coordinator (Stephens 2001)

The safety team leader is generally the building administrator and in most instances will be the principal. This person coordinates all emergency response efforts, remains in the command center, and manages all of the activities prior to the first responders arrival. The safety team leader will remain in control of all media interaction and the release of student, teacher, or staff names.

The police/fire/medical coordinator will meet all first responder and emergency personnel and direct them to the scene of the crisis. After directing the emergency personnel, this person returns to direct the media, parents, and central office personnel to their appropriate locations. This coordinator is not directly involved in the activities of the police/fire/medical personnel on the site and need not have special training in any of these areas; he or she simply provides directions and a map to the scene.

The first-aid responders are teachers, staff, and other administrators who are certified first-aid givers. Many times, the physical educators and coaches are required to be certified first-aid givers and they can be assigned that task during a time of crisis. The first-aid responders provide emergency aid until medical assistance arrives. If you do not have certified first-aid givers on your campus, it is your responsibility as the principal to provide training for teachers and staff members to become certified.

Site coordinators are responsible for going to the emergency site and controlling access to the site. If a crime has been committed, it is the responsibility of the site coordinators to preserve the crime scene until the police arrive and assume control. Site coordinators should never put themselves or anyone else in harm's way to protect the crime scene, only after all of the action has ceased do the site coordinators begin their assigned duties.

Sweep team coordinators are responsible for checking rest rooms, hallways, and other nonclassroom areas for students. Their job is to make sure the building is clear of all personnel and they will be the last people to leave the building. The sweep team members never put themselves or anyone else in harm's way to complete the building sweep, safety is the key for this group of teachers and staff.

The media coordinator works directly with the safety team leader and is responsible for meeting and briefing all types of media, print and electronic. This person meets the media and arranges for their needs. The media coordinator, in most instances, should be located off-site, in order to help control the media's urge to get into the middle of the crisis. The media coordinator helps prepare press releases and arranges for interviews.

In addition, this person must be well versed in the ethical and legal release of personal information about students and teachers.

The parent coordinator is responsible for working with parents who may arrive at the school. This person must be prepared to advise parents of the situation and is responsible for telling parents if their child is involved in the crisis. The parent coordinator needs to be housed off-site and parents should be directed to go to that off-site building for information. The parent coordinator must be able to understand the emotional distress brought by parents and at the same time this person must remain calm.

The school safety team must be prepared to function as a unit regardless of the magnitude of the crisis. A student killed in an automobile accident will create almost as much concern in the community as does some student bringing a gun to school. The only way to prepare for a crisis situation is to practice your safety plan using simulations that include emergency responders such as firemen, police, SWAT team, and emergency medical personnel. All members of the campus safety team will carry credit card–sized directions that tell them exactly what they are to do should a crisis occur. Exhibit 14.1 provides two examples of what crisis information cards might look like.

These cards remind each member of the safety team of his or her responsibilities during a crisis. Using the cards helps each person remember exactly what he or she needs to do and provides the secure telephone and pager numbers for all team members. Often, individuals forget what it is they are supposed to do during highly emotional and chaotic times; these cards provide direction and remove some of the uncertainty of the moment.

The yearly school safety audit can be the most valuable tool that the principal has at his or her disposal. The purpose of the audit is to examine the building and the safety procedures to determine where problems might occur. A team of experts composed of local law enforcement and school security professionals can perform the audit or school district personnel can complete it. The school safety audit addresses such things as:

- Design and location of rest rooms—ease of supervision and use of entrance and exit doors or lack of doors.
- Windows—windows should be limited depending on the type of construction.

Safety Team Leader – Zelda Zimmerman
Emergency Tel. 886-8888   Emergency Fax No. 886-8807
Pager Numbers: 886-8889, 886-8887, 886-8886, 886-8885
Safety Team Leader: Pager No. 886-8884

1. Declare a crisis and activate the crisis-response team
2. Notify community agencies, as appropriate
3. Notify the central administration
4. Collect facts for information dissemination
5. Notify first responders, as necessary
6. Arrange for the media spokesperson
7. Arrange for faculty and staff information
8. Stay calm and keep emotions under control
9. Remain in the emergency command center

Parent Coordinator – Betsy Bliss
Emergency Tel. 886-8888   Emergency Fax No. 886-8807
Pager Numbers: 886-8889, 886-8887, 886-8886, 886-8885
Safety Team Leader: Pager No. 886-8884

1. Move to the place where parents will be directed
2. Direct parents to the area where they will be
   informed of their child's involvement in the crisis
3. Calm parents if possible and be empathetic
4. Report any problems to the safety team leader
5. Advise parents of the current situation
6. Advise parents of their child's involvement in the crisis
7. Stay at the post until the safety team leader declares
   the crisis over

Exhibit 14.1.   Emergency Cards

- Control the entrance to the building—access to the building should be limited with video cameras at each entrance. Entrance should be electronically controlled, the doors should have panic bars not chains, and they should be locked at all times. Outside doors should be solid metal and contain no glass.
- Use of lighting—make sure the outside perimeter of the building and school campus is adequately lighted. This makes it much more difficult for vandals and other destructive individuals to go undetected. While trees and shrubs look nice around the building, it is prudent to limit trees and shrubs around the building, especially if it has a lot of windows. At the end of the day, the principal needs to walk the outside perimeter of the building looking for anything unusual. A night custodian should be

assigned to walk the perimeter of the campus prior to leaving, reporting anything out of the ordinary to the night supervisor or law enforcement.

- Identification of low traffic areas—low traffic areas invite outsiders to remain in the building unnoticed. Always have some faculty or staff members observing these low traffic areas during lunch, passing periods, and before and after school.
- Surveillance capabilities—the use of twenty-four-hour surveillance cameras both inside and outside the building may provide valuable information about any activities taking place on the campus. The cameras coupled with good lighting help secure the building at night and on weekends.
- Identification of school personnel and students—adult and student identification (ID) badges are useful if they are displayed. Many schools provide students with ID badges but never require the students to wear them, thus, they are of very little use to anyone. The key to successful use of badges is consistency by all persons in the school.
- Areas inhabited by certain groups of students—while some would argue targeting students for surveillance is not an activity that should be undertaken, it may be the very activity that keeps these students from engaging in creating a school crisis or at a minimum trouble.
- Class schedules that result in large concentrations of students coming together—make sure adequate supervision is placed in areas where large concentrations of students gather, such as the cafeteria, gymnasiums, athletic stadiums, and auditoriums. Visible supervision keeps students from attempting to create chaos.
- Structurally unsafe rooms in the building during violent weather—utilize structural engineers to provide data on where the structural problems in the building are located.
- Flaws in the campus evacuation plan—observe evacuation activities as students and teachers evacuate the building, making sure the evacuation avenues provide the quickest way out of the building for all students and teachers
- Law enforcement videos the internal and external elevations of the building—take the time, in conjunction with the local police department, to video the entire school, making sure the video shows all of the hidden areas inside and outside the building.

For example, a safety audit might require a structural engineer's analysis of the structural integrity of the roof of a gymnasium. Without this analysis, the safety plan might allow students to be housed in the gym during a violent wind storm. With this analysis, the plan would require removal of students during such a weather-related crisis. The structural analysis would provide information about the best places to house students during a crisis that involves a tornado, high winds, or an accumulation of snow on the building roof. In addition, the structural analysis would inform the safety planners about placement of students during a crisis should someone begin shooting from the exterior of the building or from the hallways.

The safety audit should include the collection of community and school data such as community crime data. This data reflects the types and magnitude of crimes committed in the community. In addition, data should be collected for the school district and this can be collected from the work orders generated for vandalism. Other indicators of school crime are the presence of gang activity and the number of students with ten discipline referrals or more.

The audit should reveal flaws in the safety plan such as where students go during a building evacuation. Many plans call for the students to move to the athletic field or stadium, others evacuate to the playground or parking lot. All of these places are logical but they all carry a significant level of danger for students. The evacuation plan must provide for movement to various evacuation sights in order to avoid perpetrators placing explosive devices in the predetermined evacuation area. School faculty and staff must be trained in evacuating students to several different areas.

The safety audit should address the types of communication devices that are available during a crisis. Each classroom and office must have an in-house talk-back intercom system that can be accessed easily by students and teachers. The intercom system needs to be accessible from more than one central location. Perhaps even better than an intercom system is an in-house telephone system that places a telephone in each classroom, office, gymnasium, locker room, on the athletic fields, and play areas. Many administrators use two-way radios to communicate because of the ease of operation and maneuverability. These radios work well in a crisis situation by allowing the principal to secure help or notify emergency responders where they need to go in the building.

One of the areas that appear to create the most concern in a building audit is the number of keys that have been distributed to faculty and staff. If you remember, one of the discoveries of the Columbine High School incident was the fact that one of the teachers gave his or her keys to one of the perpetrators to go get something during class. It is realistic to believe that when a teacher gives a student his or her keys, the possibility exists that the student can copy the key. In most cases, far too many faculty and staff have exterior door keys. Most faculty and staff would like you to believe that they come to the school on weekends to work and plan their lessons, but very few actually do. The best way to control the exterior key problem is to install smart card–controlled electronic locks. An additional advantage to this type of locking system is the identification of each person entering the building and when they entered and exited, thus, a record of who actually was in the building is kept and may prove to be very useful in the aftermath of a crisis.

Each safety plan requires the development of policies and procedures that address almost every imaginable crisis. Policies and procedures need to address potential problems at the school level (Schwartz 1997). These policies need to include violence prevention, a zero tolerance for drugs, drug paraphernalia, and weapons, a dress code, and an unknown persons policy (Rettig 1999). In addition, policies and procedures should address medical emergencies, student runaways, student and teacher death, and bomb threats. Weather-related and facility disasters such as gas leaks, explosions, and power outages must be addressed. Once the policies and procedures are completed, each and every school member should know what they are to do in any given crisis. Once again, the key to successful implementation of these policies is practice. Practice the procedure often so that you can prepare all participants for a real crisis

Perhaps the most often overlooked area of crisis policy and procedure is postcrisis planning. Planning and creating an aftercare safety team is often a forgotten element in preparing for student safety. The aftercare team is designed to work with students, teachers, and parents in a counseling or mental health environment. Once this crisis has been stabilized, it is time to bring in qualified mental health workers, counselors, and perhaps clergy depending on your context. It is absolutely essential that all of the aforementioned individuals hold state or national licensure in their specific mental health specialty. It is mandatory that principals contact these mental health workers at the beginning of each school year to see if they would be available should a crisis occur. You cannot wait for a crisis to occur to secure the services of these mental health workers because by the time you locate and secure their services it's too late to help students and teachers.

The composition of the aftercare team is dependent on the context of the school and size of the district. In small- to medium-sized districts, the aftercare team will be composed of some counselors and mental health workers who are external to the school district. In larger districts, the team members may all come from the district to the school with the crisis. The team should be composed of the following:

- Team leader—in this case, the team leader is a principal from another campus. The team leader performs the daily duties of the campus principal, allowing that person to deal with the crisis rather than worrying about the daily operation of the campus.
- Counselors with training in grief counseling—these counselors have been trained in how to work through issues of death and dying. Every school should have one counselor who has this skill. If it is not practical for the district to have its own cadre of grief counselors, a person with these skills should be contacted and asked to be on call for this type of crisis.
- Social workers—the social worker can provide the contact between the school and the home of the deceased student or teacher. This person is the intermediary between the family and the principal, teachers, and student body. He or she brings the wishes from the family to the school and provides assistance to the family. In a district that has no access to a social worker, a teacher should be selected to provide these same services.

The aftercare of students provided by the school can be accomplished in several different ways. After the death of a student or teacher, the aftercare team can provide counseling and mental health support for both students and faculty members as they grieve the loss. Providing grief counseling can be useful for the school as it attempts to return to its daily operation. For example, after the death of a well-known student the district aftercare team went to the campus and provided support for the students, faculty, and administration by creating a dedicated space called "a safe room" where the counselors and mental health workers talked with students and teachers about the recent tragedy. Students were allowed to come to the safe room by their teacher if the teacher thought the grief demonstrated by the student was distracting to the student's learning. The safe room was furnished with small stuffed animals, beanbag chairs, snacks, and blankets for students to use for sitting on the floor. Students would come and go from the safe room in an orderly and mature manner after talking together or with one of the counselors. This room provided the opportunity for students to grieve the loss of their friend in a safe and protected environment.

The lynchpin for school safety planning is the amount of training and practice that teachers and staff receive. Every year all faculty must participate in a simulation of an active crisis. The simulation should be as realistic as possible and all aspects of the crisis plan should be tested (Harper 1989). It is important the principal provides several opportunities for all school stakeholders to become proficient in first-aid and CPR administration. Not all but most of the teachers in a school should be proficient in lifesaving skills (Rettig 1999). Teachers and staff should be able to help students who have cut themselves, received a puncture wound, are having seizures, or are choking.

Steps five and six in the school safety plan are to educate students about violent actions. Dwyer, Osher, and Warger (1998) suggest that students knew that violent activities were going to occur prior to the violent act, but failed to tell a teacher, principal, or parent. In many instances, students harbor blind loyalty to fellow students even though they know the impending activities are destructive to the perpetrator and/or other fellow students. Students can help create safe schools by:

- Listening to their friends and seeking help for them if troubling feelings surface in daily conversations
- Joining student support organizations such as Students against Destructive Decisions
- Participating in peer mediation and conflict resolution programs and using the skills they have learned
- Working with all school stakeholders to create a safe process for reporting threats, weapons, drugs, gang activity, and vandalism
- Mentoring younger students to settle arguments with words not fists or weapons
- Supporting their school's code of conduct with their actions and words
- Serving as positive role models by getting involved to make their school a safer and better place

- Getting help from parents and other trusted adults (Dwyer, Osher, and Warger 1998)

An additional strategy that helps students to participate in their own safety are activity programs before and after school. Given the proper leadership these after school programs can pay dividends not only in the safety area but in the academic arena as well.

Step seven in creating a school safety plan is the need to create crisis contingencies. Given the worst scene scenario, how could communication occur should electricity be cutoff from the building? Are there battery backups for the intercom system and is there emergency lighting in the halls? As the principal, are you sure all of the batteries are viable and in good working condition? Contingency plans for school evacuations are in place, but where will parent's pick up their children? Who will make the necessary calls and take charge if the safety team leader is away from the school. Is there an assistant safety team leader to take the place of the missing leader? Should each member of the safety team have a colleague or partner who can take over the duties should the team member be absent during the crisis? Taking the time to brainstorm improbable crisis scenarios will pay off over time and help create plans that will help prevent or reduce the results of any school crisis.

Implementation of the seven-step school safety plan requires some specific equipment that schools may already have in their possession, but if they do not it is the responsibility of the principal to find resources to purchase the following items:

- Each school should have a private telephone line that can only be accessed by the members of the school safety team.
- Each principal should be issued a cellular telephone to be used only in crisis situations. These cell phone numbers are printed on the emergency cards each safety team member receives.
- Fax machines should be placed in the room that will most likely be used as the safety team command post. Messages can be sent to the media and central administration and may be more secure than cell phones.
- Bullhorns should be issued to all principals in case of a power outage and for use during the chaos that may occur during a crisis.
- Two-way radios are effective communication devices, but cell phones provide a much more secure means of communication.

These pieces of equipment are the minimum that any principal should have at his or her disposal during any type of crisis, large or small. More sophisticated equipment such as palm pilots that can transmit written messages from one person to another wirelessly are available and could be used in lieu of two-way radios or cellular telephones. Technology is constantly changing and the proactive principal is aware of these changes that will create the best paths of communication possible among the safety team.

In addition to this equipment, each school needs to create a "Go Bag" that is available to the safety team leader. This bag contains all of the items necessary to function during a crisis. The Go Bag should contain:

- A cellular telephone
- Architectural drawings of the building floor plan, including marked electrical, gas, and water cutoffs
- All student and teacher rosters in case a teacher fails to take his or her student roster during an evacuation
- A list of safety team telephone numbers
- Safety team assignments
- A small first-aid kit

These items provide the safety team leader the materials he or she needs to advise the first responders and guide them to the crisis site. There is so much chaos during a crisis that it is impossible for the safety team leader to remember all aspects of the building, all of the students, all of the faculty, and still complete his or her tasks as the safety team leader. The Go Bag provides backup information for the person leading the safety team.

MEDIA RELATIONS DURING A CRISIS

A component of the school safety plan must be the development of a strategy for working with the electronic and print media during and after the crisis is contained. Each school should have a well-thought-out media policy in place. Some larger districts have only one person who speaks for the district, while others rely on the school principal to serve in that capacity. In a crisis situation, the principal will be functioning as the safety team leader and will not have the time to address the media regularly. If the school has no district media person, it will be necessary for someone on the faulty or staff to be trained in school-media relations and serve as the school media representative as part of the school safety team.

The first activity in any school safety plan is to contain the print and electronic media. This task may be a major problem, especially if members of the national television and newsmagazine reporters are involved. These reporters are much more likely to portray the situation in the worst possible way, as opposed to local media reporters who are more likely to avoid gratuitous pictures of destruction, injured students, or distraught parents. In order to contain reporters, your school's safety team member working with the media should:

- Not allow media access to the school while the crisis is in progress
- Hold media briefings away from the crisis site
- Never reveal the names of student and teacher victims until after next of kin have been notified
- Never allow the media to attend faculty/family/community meetings held to discuss the crisis
- Never reveal the names of the perpetrators, regardless of their school affiliation
- Not provide the names of witnesses to any crisis situation
- Not provide background information about students, teachers, or the crisis situation
- Shield students from the media by providing safe pathways to buses and automobiles
- Students, teachers, and family members should be cautioned about talking with the media, especially about student or teacher victims (Poland and McCormick 1999; Kelly, Stimeling, and Kachur 1989)

These suggestions about media containment are not meant to stifle the story but to make sure the story is told accurately and to limit the opportunity for reporters to sensationalize the facts. The media spokesperson must not allow the reporters to pressure him or her into making statements off of the record. This is why it is important that a teacher spokesperson be well trained in working with the media. It takes skill to answer leading questions in an honest manner and not reveal specific facts and most principals lack the skills to work with the electronic media.

The school media representative must understand the legal implications of releasing student and faculty names prior to notifying next of kin and must be willing to only respond to questions in a factual manner, never dealing in speculation. The mantra of this person must be: "I will never lie to the media about any activities or actions the safety team implements." Honesty and a sense of calmness helps create an atmosphere of mutual respect and tones down the rhetoric on both sides of the issue. The school media representative must not be afraid to say "I don't know" and at the same time assure the reporters that the answer to the question will be provided as quickly as possible. Never spend time arguing with a reporter, he or she will always win the debate on the air or in the paper. Remember, print reporters buy their ink by the barrel and electronic media get even in twenty-second sound bites. Make sure all media outlets get the same information at the same time even though you might prefer one outlet to another.

The school media representative should never "go off the record" with any reporter, even if he or she knows the reporter personally (Hughes and Hooper 2000). Remember, everything that is said is on the record and the media spokesperson must learn to choose his or her words well. Honesty is important but in some instances it is wiser to leave some things unsaid. The safety team leader may withhold information from the media spokesperson in order to make sure he or she cannot lie. In order to stay on message, the media spokesperson should always read and answer questions from written copy prepared by the safety team leader and the media spokesperson. Never answer questions that are not addressed by the written copy. If questions surface that the spokesperson is not prepared to answer, he or she should respond by promising to get the answer in a timely manner and keep that promise.

The school media representative should normally avoid the "no comment" statement to media questions because it is generally interpreted to be a lie or negative response. Perhaps the only time this statement is appropriate is when the school media representative is not cleared to speak on behalf of the school, is angry, or does not know how the facts affect the school district or the community. Using the "no comment" statement should be used as a last resort answer because of the trust factor generated by the statement. Perhaps it is better to respond to the media with "I can't release that information now."

Prior to any contact with the media, the school media representative in conjunction with the safety team leader should anticipate the questions that reporters will ask. Creating a list of questions and responses helps the school media representative prepare for future reporter contact, whether it be a formal news conference or an interview setting. For the inexperienced school media representative, all responses to the media should be written and read to the reporters. Listed below are questions that Jones (1983) anticipates would be asked by reporters:

- Where and when did this event occur?
- Who was injured and what were the extent of their injuries?
- Is the situation under control or has it been terminated?
- What is the possibility of visiting with the principal, teachers, and students?
- Can we view the area where the event occurred?
- Can you please give us the names of the injured?

It is the responsibility of the school media representative to keep the various school stakeholder groups informed concerning the events of any school crisis, large or small. The reason for making public school crisis events public information, regardless of the magnitude, is to control the rumors that will circulate among parents, students, and eventually find their way to the media. The first group that should be informed in any crisis event is the faculty and staff. Informing faculty and staff allows them time to adjust emotionally as they prepare to meet students, parents, and colleagues. The information that is given to faculty and staff should be done in a face-to-face meeting not via the intercom or in a written memorandum. A general faculty meeting, grade level or department meetings, or one-on-one meetings are the best conduits for making sure everyone understands the facts. It would be prudent to provide each faculty and staff member with written answers to questions so that the same message is communicated to the general public. The meeting will provide faculty and staff the opportunity to work through their own grief and to take care of others should the crisis be a catastrophic event. Also, the safety team leader and the school media representative can inform the faculty and staff of how students and the community will be informed of the crisis event. Depending on the magnitude of the crisis event, these meetings can provide the principal with the opportunity to inform the faculty and staff of the schedule for the remainder of the day and/or the schedule for the next several days.

Informing students of a crisis event is troubling when required to tell teenagers or children that one of their fellow students has been hurt or has died. Powers (1987) suggests some guidelines for accomplishing this activity:

- Teachers or principals should inform students of catastrophic events that happen to other students and teachers. The best way to accomplish this task is by preparing a factually written statement that is read to students by their classroom teacher. This strategy gives all the students the same information at the same time and reduces rumors. Providing students this information in small groups allows students to grieve and share feelings in a more intimate setting and allows the teacher to answer questions within the structure of the written statement and to help quiet unsubstantiated rumors.
- If the crisis event affects a single student, it may be helpful to invite a counselor or close student friend to be present at the time of the information. This would be especially true if the teacher or principal is the person who tells the student that one of his or her parents has been hurt or has died and making sure the discussion occurs in a secluded office area.
- Students should be informed in a straightforward nonemotional manner sparing unnecessary details.
- If the teacher is the informant, he or she should be prepared for a variety of student reactions. These reactions may include crying, screaming, the need to flee the room, and perhaps even no reaction.
- Student silence is normal and should not be unexpected.
- If the crisis is the result of a catastrophic student event, it is very important that the student teacher or teachers be informed immediately. It is also necessary for the principal and teachers to inform the injured or deceased student's brothers and sisters at the same school or other schools in the district.

Three examples of written statements that would be read by teachers to students in their classes are included in exhibit 14.2. Each of the statements can be altered to meet the needs of any context or situation.

In-Classroom Statement
about the Death of a Parent

As you know, Steve is absent from school today because his mother and father were killed in a vehicle accident. Steve will not be returning to class for several more days, but when he does return to our class he will feel very sad. As members of this class and Steve's friend, what can we do to help him when he returns?

In-Classroom Statement
about a Catastrophic Illness of a
Student

Many of you know that Samantha has been very sick and I have been told by her parents that she is very sick and will not be back at school for several more weeks. Samantha is being treated for her illness at Seven Seas Hospital in Cameron and will be at the hospital for the next several days. Please think of some things that we can do to help Samantha feel better, so that she can return to our class as soon as possible. Please share your ideas with me.

In-Classroom Statement
about a Schoolwide Loss of a Teacher

Our Principal Dr. Bill Smith has been very sick the past six months. We have been told by his wife that his illness took his life at Seven Seas Hospital last night. As a tribute to Dr. Smith and all of the students he touched and to the community he served for twenty-five years, we will celebrate his life next Wednesday morning with a gathering at the school's flagpole. Students please think about how your class might participate in this celebration. Share your ideas with me and your classmates.

Exhibit 14.2

The school media representative and/or the principal must be open and honest about the events surrounding any school-related tragedy. Implementing this policy will ensure a level of trust with parents and students that cannot be achieved any other way and it helps begin the healing process. Informing parents of a school crisis is of the utmost importance so that they can participate in their child's grieving and to help begin the healing process. This information can be transmitted using several different mediums. Schools can utilize a variety of information tools to get information to parents by sending home letters with students with the appropriate information, using newspapers and radio and television newscasts, and posting on the school or campus website. In addition, and each school may have a list of student e-mail addresses located on a computer list serve that provides instant information to all parents who are connected to the Internet. Whatever tool is used to send information to parents, it must communicate that that personal counseling services are available for students and how that counseling can be accessed.

VIOLENT EVENTS AND THE
THREATS OF VIOLENT EVENTS

In the past several years, principals have experienced bombs in school, students being shot by fellow students, students held as hostages, teachers being killed in front of their students, and administrators gunned down in their offices. O'Toole (2000) points out that teenage violence and homicides have decreased since 1993, but the very public shootings have gotten more attention than less extreme acts of violence. She states that media representations of violent perpetrators are wrong. Among these unverified or wrong impressions are:

- School violence is at epidemic proportions
- All student shooters are psychologically the same
- Student shooters never have friends
- All student shooting is reprisal motivated
- Access to guns is the single most important factor in student shooting
- Unusual hobbies and behaviors are keys to violent students

While some of these impressions may be useful in identifying potential violent students, they are only true when placed in context with several other student behaviors. The major problem facing schools when violent events do occur is the public's need for immediate security precautions, stricter laws, and more sophisticated surveillance equipment (O'Toole 2000).

In assessing the threat of violent events in school, the National Threat Assessment Center of the U.S. Secret Service convened a symposium to determine the characteristics that surround the student shooter. The following characteristics for shooters are:

- Incidents of shooting are rarely impulsive; they are almost always well planned.

- The student shooter always told someone else he or she was going to commit the violent act.
- There is no accurate way to profile student shooters.
- Student shooters used guns prior to the violent activity.
- Most school shootings never involve law enforcement and are over in less than twenty minutes.
- Student bullies play a key role in motivating student shooters to act. Sometimes, the bully is the shooter and sometimes the shooter is the victim of the bully.
- Most student shooters contemplate suicide at some point prior to committing a violent act. (Stephens 2001)

While the student shooter was the focus of the Secret Service symposium, it is very clear that the school must be ever vigilant in order to avoid such actions. Students must be encouraged to inform teachers and the principal when they hear about possible violence and teachers must be more interested in assessing changing student behavior in order to reduce the chance of student violence.

Many schools employ school resource officers (SROs) on campus on a daily basis to prevent violent activity. The SRO is a permanently assigned certified law enforcement officer with the responsibility to perform the roles of:

- Law enforcement officer whose purpose is to "keep the peace" in schools so that learning takes place
- Law-related counselor who provides students guidance on law-related issues and provides a link between student services inside and outside the school
- Law-related education teachers who provide schools with law expertise (Center for the Prevention of School Violence 1998)

These roles are vital to the success of the SRO program, as is the officer serving as a role model for many students. The officer may be the only positive role model many students ever observe and the SRO must send a strong message that violence is unacceptable. In addition, the SRO addresses both the prevention and intervention aspects of law enforcement and helps the school focus its resources on school safety and security.

In a survey completed by the Center for the Prevention of School Violence (1998), the data indicated that 38 percent of the SRO respondents worked in high schools, 23 percent in middle schools, 3 percent in elementary schools, and the remaining 36 percent cover combinations of schools. Ninety percent of the respondents indicated that they had attended training specifically designed for an SRC, and 93 percent indicated they wanted to work in a school. When asked what percentage of their time was spent on specific roles, they indicated 50 percent of their time was spent on law enforcement activities, 33 percent as a law-related counselor, and 17 percent in law-related education. SROs also referred students to social services, public health organizations, legal aid, and private services.

The SRO is the first line of defense in any school safety prevention and intervention program. The magnitude to which this officer is inculcated in the culture of the school depends on the faculty, staff, and principal's acceptance of the office. It is vitally important that all school stakeholders embrace the SRO as an important member of the educational team. SRO participation in campus activities, student organizations, and athletic events helps develop rapport with students and increases the probability that students will share information about violent activities prior to them happening.

It is clear that the SRO program provides knowledge and the ability to respond to violent events that principals are neither trained, experienced, or psychologically prepared to handle. In addition, the SRO becomes the school's liaison among all emergency first responders including police, fire, and emergency medical agencies. Schools must develop and cultivate positive relationships among all first responder agencies and the school SRO is the key to making this relationship work.

In responding to violent events, the school safety plan should include a system that will notify the faculty and staff of a violent event in progress and the action they should take to protect students. Voice commands or bell signals can be used to inform faculty exactly what event is in progress. Exhibit 14.3 demonstrates the use of voice commands to activate specific action.

When hearing the voice command "code yellow," the teacher automatically instructs the students to get on the floor and move to the outside wall of the classroom; in a room with no outside wall, they should move to the wall that joins the next classroom. Pull all window shades down, including the small shade in most doors. The outside wall of the building affords the most protection against bullets penetrating the building. In the

Voice Command Code/ Bell Code	Action
Code Yellow	Total lockdown—Lock all doors, windows, and pull down all window shades, including those covering door windows. The indication for the teacher is an unauthorized person is in the building and may have a weapon. Instruct the students to move to the prescribed place in the room quickly. 3 LONG BELLS
Code Blue	Illness or severe accident—A person in one of the school corridors is experiencing a catastrophic medical event such as stroke or heart attack, is choking, or was hurt in an accident. Do not send students into the corridors; instead, hold them in the classroom until it is time for a passing period or the all clear is sounded. 4 LONG BELLS
Code Red	Weather—Weather-related events such as a tornado, blizzard conditions, and severe thunderstorms. Instruct the students to move to the prescribed area in a quick but calm manner. 5 LONG BELLS

Exhibit 14.3.   Faculty Warning, Voice Command/Bell System

case of an outside classroom with ground floor windows, moving against the outside wall helps shield the students from someone looking in. Placing the students against a corridor wall in a code yellow event generally exposes students to being hit by bullets penetrating the structurally less protective materials. Buildings with interior walls constructed of concrete blocks would provide more protection than sheet rock products, but when bullets hit the concrete blocks they splinter and become smaller pieces of shrapnel. The key to keeping students safe in a code yellow event is placing them in the room where they are afforded the most protection. The room risk assessment is conducted during the school safety audit and each teacher is informed of the primary safety area for each type of crisis event.

"Code blue" indicates that someone in a corridor of the building is experiencing a catastrophic medical event. When teachers hear this voice command, they will know to ignore any student, passing bells, or time sequences where they take their students to some other part of the building. Keeping the corridors clear for emergency medical personnel, keeping students from surrounding the situation as observers, and keeping small children isolated from this trauma is important. During a code blue event, a designated person should be stationed in each major corridor to remind teachers and students to remain in the classrooms and other specific areas until the "code green" all clear is sounded.

A "code red" command requires teachers to move quickly since weather-related events happen very quickly in many cases. Tornados are the most unpredictable of all severe weather events that affect schools and it is mandatory that schools have a plan to protect students to the greatest extent that is possible. The plan should include moving students to the nearest structurally safe part of the building. In many buildings, this safe area would be the corridor adjacent to the classroom and would be near the interior corridor walls. Have the students move quietly to the corridor and kneel down facing the wall, covering their head with their arms and hands. In most situations, it would be prudent to have students bring their biggest book with them to the corridor and to hold the book over their head for protection. Students may become very frightened and in these situations it is the teacher's responsibility to get the student into the safety position. In situations where no warning is given, instruct the students to get away from the windows and under their desks. Tornados generate flying debris and glass from windows should be a major concern for student safety, which means staying away from windows and doors.

In several states the major weather related events are attached to severe snow and ice storms. In some instances the snow accumulates at such a rapid rate that students are required to stay at the school because the school buses and their parents are unable to get through the snow. In these areas, the school safety plan should include the storing of blankets, food, and heating devices should the students be trapped at the school. Provisions for a three- or four-day period should be stored that will meet the needs of students, teacher, and staff. It is better to be safe in the building than stranded on a school bus with limited resources.

Every school should be equipped with a NOAA weather radio that sounds an alarm in the case of severe weather and in some situations the county sheriff's department provides weather-related warnings over special radios they provide to schools. In any event, it is the school's responsibility to arm itself with equipment that will give it as much advanced warning as possible concerning weather-related events. It is also prudent for each principal to keep the telephone numbers of the police, sheriff, local radio and television stations, and the nearest office of the National Weather Service at his or her finger tips in case they are needed. The national 911 service is always available in emergency situations. Don't forget your Go Bag because it has cell telephones, first-aid equipment, a bullhorn, student and teacher rosters, and other equipment that may be useful in any one of these crisis events (Seifert 2000).

SAFE SCHOOLS CREATE PREVENTION PLANS

The key to safe schools is the creation of plans that address both crisis management and prevention. It is now time to focus on activities that help prevent student-on-student and student-on-teacher violence, and teacher and student suicide. The prevention plan is designed to help students, teachers, and the community in identifying emotional and behavioral signs of troubled students. A safe environment for all students is the goal of any prevention plan. Dwyer, Osher, and Warger (1998) describe the following five parts of a prevention plan:

- Descriptive characteristics of violent behavior and a process for identifying students with these characteristics
- Descriptive strategies for intervention with troubled students
- Interventions strategies that have worked in other communities
- A safe schools plan that provides for immediate intervention for students exhibiting these identified behaviors
- Technological solutions for school safety

The plan must be consistent with local, state, and federal law, as well as school district policy and procedure. It is the responsibility of the principal to provide training for faculty and staff in prevention strategies.

Prevention training should include strategies for identifying student behavior that can be destructive or dangerous. The U.S. Department of Education outlines several early warning signs that suggest that students might possess aggressive or violent behavior. These signs include:

- Students withdraw from their social group
- Extreme feelings of rejection that are manifested in negative ways
- Feelings of being picked on and victimized may cause students to withdraw socially before they act out in a violent manner

- Poor grades and a lack of interest in school is important when students' academic behavior changes radically or becomes chronic
- Violent drawings and writing over a prolonged period of time may indicate emotional problems that lead to violent behavior
- School discipline problems that include uncontrolled anger, bullying, intimidation, and hitting
- Drug and alcohol abuse
- Affiliation with gangs that support violence and antisocial behavior (Dwyer, Osher, and Warger 1998)

Any one of these signs taken individually is not sufficient for predicting violent behavior and it is inappropriate to use these warning signs as a checklist to measure individual children's violence quotient. While no single warning sign is significant, imminent warning signs such as fighting with peers or family, severe rage, threats of violence, and possession of weapons should be taken seriously and parents should be notified immediately (Dwyer, Osher, and Warger 1998). The answer to understanding these warning signs is training and practice identifying these characteristics in conjunction with a principal who encourages teachers and staff to report their concerns to administrators.

The principal may choose to create a safe schools prevention team that has as its responsibility the collection and dissemination of information concerning students or teachers that display changes in their behavior. This team would receive referrals from teachers, staff, and students making sure all information is kept confidential. The team would review the information and create a plan of action to help the student or teacher. The caution for the prevention team is acting on only one symptom of any observed behavior, yet it is far superior to overreact to a potential problem student than it is to ignore the situation. This is why the team should be composed of licensed professional counselors, psychologists, mental health workers, and teachers. The prevention plan must bring together the person with the observed problem and someone who can help the person begin to solve his or her issues. This help could be provided by a teacher, counselor, coach, nurse, custodian, or a professional from the community who possesses the skills to help the person.

At some point in this intervention process, the person's parents or in the case of teachers a spouse must be informed of the concerns of the prevention team. This information must be delivered in a way that will generate help for the person not antagonism. All parents and community stakeholders should be invited to attend an evening staff development session that discusses detection of depression, suicide, alcohol abuse, and drug abuse and how the referrals to the prevention team should be handled. The more the community stakeholders know about crisis prevention, the easier it will be to implement the prevention program.

Another prevention idea is that of using students, called peer counselors or peer mediators, to work with students who appear to be depressed or have demonstrated behavioral problems. Peer counselors and mediators require many hours of training and must understand their limitations. Peer counseling and mediation will not work if all of the students serving in the counseling or mediation role are perceived to be the "good kids" in the school. Peer counselors and mediators should come from all segments of the school population (Seifert 2000). A prevention strategy that helps meet individual student needs is a "buddy system" that provides students with peer support. Utilizing this idea, students who need additional support could be assigned a buddy to share problems and concerns with school and home problems.

Develop a crime prevention program similar to the Crimestoppers programs found in most communities. This type of program provides financial incentives for those reporting potential and perpetrated crime. Along with pay for information, programs recruit student-led clubs and organizations to help with minor school maintenance and beautification projects. It is important to remove graffiti from school building walls as quickly as it appears. One strategy for dealing with graffiti is to contract with someone who will come to the school early in the morning to power wash walls where the graffiti is placed. If a custodian will walk or drive the perimeter of the school each morning when he or she comes to work at 5:30 to 6:00 A.M. searching for graffiti and if some is found calls the removal contractor immediately and the removal is done prior to students arriving at the school, then the graffiti is less likely to occur in the future. It is also important to video or photograph the graffiti to document it for law enforcement. Many law enforcement communities keep photographs of prior graffiti in a systematic file and they can tell by looking at the symbols who might have created the graffiti.

The principal needs to decide the amount of safety technology that he or she believes is necessary to keep the school safe. Cost, security problems,

and the level of invasiveness into the school life are the three major considerations when deciding which safety technology to use, such as: (1) smart
cards, (2) metal detectors, (3) alarm systems, and (4) surveillance cameras.
Control of the entrance to the building has become a common problem, especially on weekends, as keys issued to faculty and staff find themselves in
the wrong hands. The smart card is integrated with the computer system as
a means of tracking whom and at what time the individual entered the building. For example, each card is specifically coded to meet the needs of the
individual; the custodian needs to arrive at the building by 5:30 A.M. each
morning to open doors, finish cleaning, and to set up the cafeteria for an
awards program; while a cook might need early access to the kitchen, but
not to any other part of the building. One major advantage to the smart card
is the ability to instantly cancel the card if it is lost or stolen, thereby making it useless. The cost of the smart card system initially costs more to install than to rekey locks, but the security options outweigh the cost.

According to Schneider (2001), metal detectors are hard to justify in a
low-crime school and may even undermine the integrity of the school. The
context of the school is important when measuring the cost benefit of purchasing metal-detector wands, which are inexpensive, or detection portals
that individuals must walk through which are very costly. Schneider argues that the effectiveness of metal detectors is mixed at best because of
the numerous entry points for weapon insertion such as open windows and
doors, the time consumed, and the personnel needed to operate the equipment. Even if free-standing metal-detection portals are utilized where
building entrance cannot be accomplished, if metal is detected someone
must monitor the intercom and the closed circuit monitor for the device.

Surveillance equipment may be a worthwhile investment because documentation and identification of individuals are important. Closed circuit
television cameras allow the identification of individuals after the event
has occurred. Cameras can be placed in areas that are visually remote, all
corridors, the parking lot, the perimeter of the building, and in specific
classrooms where behaviorally challenged students reside. Many schools
that employ surveillance equipment still use the videotaped recording format, but the most recent use of digital video recording (DVR) allows the
system to record up to 100,000 hours of information and send alarms to the
security staff that the perimeter has been breached (Schneider 2001).

Before investing in any security equipment, identify the problem, measure the cost benefit with school needs, and address the issue of student fear

generated by the equipment. The hidden costs of equipment are the costs of repair on the equipment and finding a company or individual who can be trusted to make those repairs. Make sure you understand the possibility of system upgrades and expansion before purchasing security equipment.

EVALUATING THE SCHOOL SAFETY PLAN

Evaluating the school safety plan is critical to its function. Evaluation is about making continuous improvement and subtle changes in the plan as students, teachers, and the facility change. In the absence of a real crisis, and hopefully there is an absence, the best way to evaluate the plan is through a simulation. It is important to bring in individuals outside of the school to evaluate the effectiveness of the plan. First responder agencies should participate in the simulation so it is important to use community members and individuals from nearby communities to critique how well the plan functioned. The school safety plan should be evaluated yearly and each time the school safety team is activated the actions of the team should be evaluated. The following questions may form the bases for creating an evaluation instrument that can be used yearly to evaluate how well the plan is implemented:

- What was the nature of the crisis?
- What steps did the school safety team put into action?
- What other steps could the school safety team put into action?
- Did the school safety plan work as it was designed to work? If not, where did it fail? (Seifert 2000)

The time spent on the evaluation of the school safety plan and its function is well worth the time and a change in some aspect of the plan may save a life the next time it is implemented. Once again, the key to any successful evaluation of the school safety plan is the time spent practicing the plan. In reviewing any school safety plan, the evaluator must make sure the plan includes the following:

- Strategies for detecting early signs of violence
- Strategies for getting help for students demonstrating behavioral or emotional problems

- Strategies for intervening should a crisis occur
- Strategies for helping students cope after a crisis
- Strategies for evaluating the actions of the school safety team

It will be impossible to prevent all types of school crises since some crises happen away from the school site and out of the control of the school safety team. The best that can be hoped for is a good plan, people to implement the plan, and a good evaluation process so that the same mistakes are not made twice.

ETHICAL DISCUSSION

Is School Violence a School or Societal Responsibility?

The behavior of students is directly related to the society from which they come. If the society is violent, then it is expected that schools will be violent because students emulate what they see at home and on the streets of their community. Violence increasingly affects the lives of children. The United States is a violent nation and it has been so for many years. Television and movies provide students with role models for violence. Violence takes many forms in school: student-on-student, student-on-teacher, and in some situations teacher-on-student. Most teachers feel they are safe from student or parental assault, but in some cases that is not the situation. Children do not come to school the first day of kindergarten as mindless robots ready to be filled with knowledge; rather, they come with the what the environment has given them for the past five or so years. Parents have etched into their brains certain patterns of behavior, some socially acceptable and in some instances behavior that is unacceptable. These children are victims of poor parenting or perhaps no parenting. Children raising children manifest the problem of no parenting. Teenage parents would rather be out with their friends than home taking care of their child.

The questions that need to be answered concerning this issue are:

- Should schools remove students that demonstrate unacceptable behavior?

- What should be done with troubled students?
- Should schools move away from the child-centered curriculum that many educators believe is responsible for decreases in academic standards and the erosion of school discipline?
- Is it the responsibility of the schools to curb or prevent school violence? If so, how should that be accomplished?
- What is the role of society and parents in helping schools be safe harbors for students?
- Which side of the violence debate do you support and why?
- Ethical dilemmas are right-versus-right. Should schools focus less on the problem students and more on the well-mannered students?

CHAPTER SUMMARY

The facts that surround school safety are magnified by the print and electronic media to the point that many people in American society believe that schools are not safer. Parents keep their children home from school based on the most benign rumor or hearsay evidence. The question of whether school violence is increasing or decreasing depends on who you believe. The evidence is mixed at best, but certainly the types and amounts of school violence and societal violence is more observable than it has been in the past. The real focus for the principal should be on non-violent types of school safety issues such as weather, automobile accidents, catastrophic illnesses, and teacher and student suicides. Principals are much more likely to face one of these events than they are to see a student shooter.

The key to any school safety plan is the creation of a planning task force to create and develop a school safety plan. The members of the planning task force should come from a wide variety of backgrounds from outside and inside the school. Beginning with the school mission statement, every aspect of the school's daily operation should be taken into consideration when creating the safety plan.

Perhaps the most important piece of the school safety plan is the formation of the school safety team. What individuals need to be part of this team and how much training they receive is key to any successful application of the school safety plan. The school safety audit can and should provide much needed information about the structure of the building, the least observable locations, and building design. The safety audit needs to address vandalism and maintenance records for the school and the community. These indicators provide direction for the school safety team in suggesting and implementing new strategies for prevention of threats of all types.

Policies and procedures that surround the safety plan should address almost every imaginable crisis, from gun-related events to illness events and everything in between. These polices need to address violence prevention, dress code, drugs, and unknown persons violations. Perhaps the most overlooked area of policy development is postcrisis planning. The aftercare or postcrisis team is the group that works with the traumatized students, teachers, and in some cases parents. It is important that only licensed professional health care workers be allowed to work with students and teachers.

The most important aspect of any school safety plan is the type and amount of practice the safety team members receive. Simulations provide the best type of training and practice for the team outside of an actual crisis, in which no one wants to participate. It is important that all safety team members become proficient in first-aid and CPR techniques. Knowing lifesaving skills is the responsibility of all teachers and staff.

Making sure students feel comfortable in providing information to teachers and staff is the first step toward eliminating student-on-student and student-on-teacher violence. Removing the blind loyalty students feel for one another is not an easy task and requires repeated assurances that it is the right thing to do. This requires that all stakeholders in the school model the highest level of moral and ethical behavior.

The school safety plan requires pieces of equipment that perhaps every school does not have on its current inventory but should have if it is safety conscious. Private telephone lines, cellular telephones, fax machines, bullhorns, and two-way radios are minimum pieces of equipment necessary to work all types of crises. The most essential piece of equipment is the Go Bag that is entrusted to the safety team leader. This bag contains the essentials that any safety team might need as it faces a crisis event.

Media relations during any crisis event are a major undertaking. Without a seasoned media relations representative available it becomes very important that someone on the faculty be trained to work with the media. The key to working with the media is honesty and truthfulness. The school media representative must understand the legal implications of releasing student and teacher names prior to notification of next of kin and at the same time he or she must be able to tell reporters, "I don't know, but I will get back to you concerning that question." Remember, nothing is "off of the record"—anything that is said is on the record. Avoid at all costs the "no comment" statement because those two words cause people to think you are being less than truthful. The school media representative should always work from written copy and should never answer questions for which they do not have written responses. It is the responsibility of the media relations person to keep all stakeholders informed in a systematic and responsible manner.

Student threat prevention has been addressed by the U.S. Secret Service and the Federal Bureau of Investigation and they have supplied schools with some threat assessment characteristics, such as a student shooter is rarely impulsive, always tells someone what he or she is going to do, and is either a bully or has been bullied. These events almost never involve law enforcement. According to these two agencies, it is almost impossible to profile student shooters. The best way to prevent student shooters is student information to school personnel. Other prevention strategies include the employment of an SRO at a school to help keep the peace, serve as a law-related officer, and to provide students with law-related expertise. The SRO is the first line of defense in any school safety prevention and intervention program. The more this officer is integrated into the main stream of school operation, the more effective the officer will become.

The creation of a safe schools prevention program addresses several aspects of working with troubled students by providing them with an opportunity to work with counselors, teachers, peer counselors, and other mental health workers. Early warning signs for aggressive or violent behavior helps all stakeholders prepare to meet the challenges of helping students in distress. Creating a safe school prevention team will allow the funneling of information concerning troubled students to one group that will analyze the data and send it forward to individuals who can provide services for the person in question.

Evaluation of the school safety plan is critical to an effective and efficient plan. Answering specific questions about the nature of the crisis and action to be taken provides the school safety team with an assessment of how well the plan worked during a simulation or actual crisis. Evaluation of the plan should be completed by a source outside of the school and district, with area police, fire, and emergency medical agencies as the best candidates for reviewing the plan.

CHAPTER ACTIVITIES AND QUESTIONS

1. List the people who should be asked to participate in the safe schools planning task force and why.
2. The school mission statement should include a reference to safe schools. Write a mission statement for your school including a reference to safe schools for students.
3. Document the essential elements of a safe schools plan.
4. The school safety team should be composed of what types of individuals? Outline the roles of the individual members of the team.
5. Discuss your relationship with first responder agencies and describe the role they play in creating a safe schools plan.
6. Conduct a school safety audit in your building and report the results.
7. Create an aftercare safety team and define the role of each member.
8. Create the role for the school media representative and describe the types of information that this person should have at his or her disposal.
9. Develop strategies for preventing school violence.
10. Design a voice command or bell system for your campus focusing on the types of emergency equipment at your disposal.

CASE STUDY ACTIVITIES AND QUESTIONS

1. Write down what Ms. Zimmerman should tell the assistant principals prior to leaving for their assigned posts during this crisis.
2. What would be your first action once you discovered that the rubble from the building trapped a group of students?
3. List the type of equipment Ms. Zimmerman should take with her as she leaves the office suite.
4. Write Ms. Zimmerman's one-page report to the media after the tornado.
5. If you were evaluating Ms. Zimmerman's actions during the crisis, what would you say she did well and what needs to be improved?

6. Survey your building and decide the areas you should avoid placing students during a violent weather event.
7. Develop a five-question survey to be administered to the faculty and staff about the way the crisis situation was handled.
8. What action should Ms. Zimmerman employ to help the wounded children and the unconscious teacher? Who should have gone to the students' and teacher's aid?
9. Ms. Zimmerman received a telephone call at 5:30 A.M. on Saturday (the day after the tornado) from a parent of one of your students advising her that one of the PTO mothers and her two daughters, both students in her building, were killed in an automobile accident. The parent tells her that the preliminary details indicated that alcohol and excessive speed were factors in the incident. What would be the first thing that Ms. Zimmerman should do, the second thing, the third thing, and so on?

REFERENCES

Center for the Prevention of School Violence. (1998). "The school on 'the beat': Law enforcement officers in school." At www.NCSU.edu/cpsu/Research_Bulletin_National.htm (accessed February 1, 2001).

Dwyer, K., Osher, D., and Warger, C. (1998). *Early warning, timely response: A guide to safe schools*. Washington, DC: U.S. Department of Education.

Harper, S. (1989). *School crisis prevention and response*. Malibu, CA: National School Safety Center (ERIC Document Reproduction Services no. ED 311 600).

Hughes, L. W., and Hooper, D. W. (2000). *Public relations for school leaders*. Needham Heights, MA: Allyn and Bacon.

Jones, J. V. (1983). "Crisis management and media relations." *NSPRA Journal* 21 (2): 36–40.

Kelly, D. G., Stimeling, W. E., and Kachur, D. S. (1989). "Before worst comes to worst, have your crisis plan ready." *Executive Educator* 11 (1): 22–23.

Knutson, L. L. (2001). "Clinton says hotline, site to help teens resolve disputes." *Fort Worth Star-Telegram*, 14 January, 23A.

Northwestern National Life Study. (1993). "Combating work force violence." At www.state.il.us/isp (accessed February 1, 2001).

O'Toole, M. E. (2000). "The school shooter: A threat assessment perspective." Federal Bureau of Investigation. Washington, DC: National Center for the Analysis of Violent Crime.

Peterson, S., and Straub, R. (1992). *School crisis survival guide*. West Nyack, NY: Center for Applied Research in Education.

Poland, S., and McCormick, J. S. (1999). *Coping with crisis: Lessons learned*. Longmont, CO: Sopris West.

Powers, H. L. (1987). "Death and grief: A plan for principals to deal with tragedy affecting the school community." *ERS Spectrum* 5 (4): 24–26.

Rettig, M. A. (1999). "Seven steps to school wide safety." *Principal* 71 (9): 10–13.

Safe Schools Survey 1998. (1998). "Safe schools." At www.ag.state.mn.us (accessed March 2, 2001).

Schneider, T. (2001). "Newer technologies for school security." ERIC Clearinghouse on Educational Management, at eric.uoregon.edu./publications/digests/digest145.html (accessed March 2, 2001).

Schwartz, W. (1997). "An overview of strategies to reduce school violence." ERIC Clearinghouse on Urban Education, at eric-web.tc.columbia.edu/digests/dig115.html (accessed February 1, 2001).

Seifert, E. H. (2000). "Responding to crisis." In *Public relations in schools*, ed. T. J. Kowalski. 2nd ed. Englewood Cliffs, NJ: Merrill–Prentice-Hall.

Stephens, R. D. (2001). "Safe school planning." Paper presented at the meeting of the Meadows Principal Improvement Center, Mesquite, TX, January 25.

Volokh, A., and Snell, L. (1998). "School violence prevention: Strategies to keep schools safe." Reason Public Policy Institute, at www.rppi.org/ps234.html (accessed February 2, 2001).

Chapter Fifteen

Facilities Leadership

Betty Bones, principal of Reagan Intermediate School in Bethany, had been a very organized and thematic type educator while she was a classroom teacher at the elementary level. She had developed numerous themes that she had used over some fifteen years in the classroom, integrating many of the curriculum concepts from cross-subject areas. One of her favorite combinations was to integrate social studies concepts with science and technology instruction.

After taking a course in school facilities and attending several instructional conferences where she participated in discussion groups and presentations on facilities as an important component of learning, she became more and more interested in developing her school by making the classrooms themselves better factors in the learning process. But since she was no longer in the classroom, she felt she could only be an expediter of these ideas. She found that Pat Hernandez, one of her assistant principals, also had an interest in this idea, so they began to plan how to introduce this idea of making the classroom more of a teaching asset than it had been in their school. They began to read more on the subject and felt they would introduce some of these principles to the faculty in a regular faculty meeting. They would determine who had enthusiasm for the ideas presented and would organize a study group that could begin to implement some of the concepts to make the classroom a more teaching friendly environment. They hoped this might take off, after some successes were realized, and other teachers would join their effort. However, they still had a lot of planning to generate and teachers to interest in the concept. They spent three afternoons brainstorming and decided they could introduce it in two weeks at the staff meeting after school.

THE FACILITY AS PART OF THE LEARNING SYSTEM

School facilities are one of the major building blocks supporting the educational program. The building itself is the first thing that a student and a teacher encounter when they arrive in the morning and the last thing that is experienced as they leave for the day. If the building offers an attractive and helpful environment, then the educational climate tends to be satisfying and inviting. If the building is cold in appearance and unattractive to the psyche, then the climate of the school has a negative component. Students, teachers, and staff need to have a warm, inviting atmosphere for learning and working if the best possible results are to occur. Facilities can be negative or positive in contributing to the system of learning and experiencing that students encounter.

Buildings are just one part of the total educational environment that makes up the school climate. Other parts include the instructional equipment, the values and beliefs that are considered important, the individual feelings of the students and teachers, the noise levels that are encountered, and the satisfaction that the students or employees feel during their experience. These are components of the learning system that make up the whole or gestalt (Kowalski 1983). The facility part or subsystem of the learning system includes the space, the sonic (sound), the visual experience, the thermal experience, the safety and hygiene, the equipment, the support experiences, and the structural components. These subsystem components come together to achieve outputs of the facility subsystem that in turn supports the educational experience. These outputs include:

- Flexibility—the ability to serve changing purposes
- Adaptability—the ability to serve varying purposes of the educational experience
- Expansibility—the option of serving larger numbers by adding to the facility
- Functionality—the ability to accommodate teaching and learning activities
- Efficiency—the ability to serve these needs in a fiscally manageable way (i.e. energy constraints)
- Adequacy—the degree to which the facility meets the needs of teachers and students
- Suitability—the appropriateness of the environment for learning

- Economy—the cost-benefit results to achieve good value
- Aesthetics—the artistic qualities of design that meet site constraints and the educational goals
- Identity—the ability to identify the place as one for learning (Kowalski 1983)

The School Facility As a Teaching Tool

This facility subsystem either supports or constrains the learning system. The extent to which it is a plus for the learning experience is often determined by not only how it is designed to provide the needed support, but also by how well it is maintained to offer continuing service. The principal of the school can influence both of these factors; therefore, the principal's role is influential in just how much support the building or facility can offer to the educational program.

Every building and every component of the school facility makes assumptions concerning the educational program that is being supported by the facility. As educators, there is a compelling need to ask if the assumptions that are made by the components or the building are congruent with the program that is being offered in that facility. Should there be little or no congruency, then there is a mandate to reassess the facility and components to make them supportive of the program that is being housed within that facility. The school, then, is a tool for teaching. It makes an important contribution to the learning philosophy and to the teaching efforts of the faculty. The facility supports the learning goals that the students are trying to master. If this does not happen in a suitable or appropriate way, then the principal should do all within his power and influence to change this situation.

An example of such action might be illustrated by a school where the social studies program values lots of exchange and discussion between small groups of students. This discussion will assist the students to become fluent in analyzing data and events and assessing the impact of these on the historical past or perhaps understand how these may continue to influence coming events of a political nature. If the facility where such discussion takes place offers only desks that are fixed to the floor of a room more suited for lecture or demonstrations, then it is not very conducive to promoting these types of valued activities. The principal may either reassign another room for such experiences to take place or might decide to modify the room in order to make it more supportive to the program activities. The former is a less costly way of meeting the needs as compared to the latter, which would be a more permanent way of supporting this program. Such changes take into consideration the instructional philosophy of the teacher and such concepts as constructivism, the belief that students learn from assembling their own meaning to the events being studied.

Taylor, Aldrich, and Valastos (1988) believe that school environments are largely untapped as active contributors to the learning process. They propose that classrooms be thought of as containing zones, each contributing to encouraging learning. These include the entry zone to welcome students, the work zone of aesthetically pleasing interaction with the environment and the surroundings, storage and display zones, a "living things" zone, a research and library zone, a soft zone with a living room ambiance, a graphic arts zone on a wall area for visual learning, a teacher zone, and a technology zone. These types of environments demand a trust relationship between teachers and students and they help to make the students more responsible and independent as learners and citizens, creating respect for each other.

Over the last fifteen years educators have begun to include the ideas of learning styles in their teaching efforts. This concept helps educators to understand the individualized nature of learning from one student to the next and then use this knowledge in assisting the student to learn new material by the choice of activities and assignments for that student. Different researchers have established different models for identifying the components of different students' styles. The Dunn and Dunn (1978) model focuses on five stimuli strands: those of environment, emotional, sociological, physical, and psychological. Some of these strands are influenced heavily by facility components that may assist the students in having a better chance to learn the material or skills that are the objects of the learning. These include the environmental and sociological strands. The environmental strand includes sound, light, temperature, and design of the room and components. To illustrate, some students may focus better when they listen to appropriate music as they read an assignment. Such music may be "white noise" to lessen the other distractions or may actually change the student's proclivity to read and think by softening their attitude. If appropriate music is made available through headphones or overhead speakers for those who request it, their success in completing the work and understanding its meaning may be better. Similarly, bright light may be preferred by some students, while others read or study better with low light. By arranging room lighting to students' preferences, such differences in settings may help individuals read better. Some students like a cool environment while others prefer a warmer place to work. Allowing jackets to be worn by those who like a warmer study location may make them more comfortable in a room that might be considered cool. A relaxed design in the environment may be more suitable for studying for some while others like a formal or structured setting. Often, teachers have arranged for pillows or a carpet for a reading center for those who like such a casual environment while other students read at their desks. Sociologically, some students like working in small groups, while others are independent learners and some others benefit most from formal large-group lectures or presentations. Such differences call for varied environments to be available for study and interaction between students.

Perhaps closely associated with learning styles is the brain-based research that also can provide insights even into the design of buildings and grounds (Chan and Petrie 1998). Schools are often designed without considering to any great degree the extent of the environment of learning. The use of art can challenge the brain in nonthreatening ways; physical activity is essential in promoting growth of mental functions, and color and light increase muscular tension, respiration rate, pulse, blood pressure, and brain activity. Insufficient lighting causes visual fatigue as do distracting color combinations that contribute to confusion and slow reactions.

Although many of the principles identified by educational psychology seem very academic, such principles may be used in applied ways to enhance learning. Many of these principles have implications for designing or arranging learning environments (Castaldi 1987). Such principles include active student involvement in learning; the fact that children's attention span varies with age; task complexity and activity becomes a factor in student involvement; learners differ in their rates of learning; readiness for learning varies with individuals; the social need to belong, for security, and peer status; and the multistimuli effect on learning retention. Each of these principles has some feature that can be utilized in arranging or designing facilities. Often, diverse settings for teaching are indicated, but also frequently the varied use of equipment and activities are indicated by the principles. The instructional leader's knowledge of these ideas is supportive for arranging of such instructional support by the facility's components.

The field of environmental psychology (Heyman 1978) also offers ideas that influence educators' understanding and use of the facility. Environmental psychology assesses the influence of space on attitudes, emotions, and behaviors. As a result, such study has indicated that the symbolic meaning of spaces and the arrangement of furniture are important. Furniture placement may connote one's status or rank, the welcoming of discussion, and the availability of the teacher for communication. Placement of components makes a barrier for setting up territoriality by laying claim to an area or controlling space. Also, privacy may be arranged by setting up barriers to sight or sound. Chair or desk arrangement may easily depict the learning philosophy by indicating the level of availability of the teacher. From such studies, educators understand the individual differences with which people interact and their need for order or disorder. Individuals are very sensitive to their environment; therefore, seating arrangements, open spaces, office arrangement, and the decorations in classrooms all can have an impact of student attitudes and learning.

The building or the facility itself can be a learning experience for the student when educators and architects work together for such an arrangement. Lessons of a practical nature can be taught with the inclusion of glass walls so the heating, ventilating, and air conditioning (HVAC) equipment may be observed, studied, and understood. Outdoor environmental gardens may be used for class field trips; a marsh or pond on the school site can be the center of science experiments; and the inclusion of an outdoor challenge course can be used to build confidence and teamwork among students. Lessons in establishing cooperation may be the focus of many levels of students in varied subjects with diverse goals. An outdoor classroom can add a special opportunity that teachers can utilize to maintain students' interest in numerous subjects, sometimes for no more reason than to provide an alternative location for class; in other situations, it may offer specific advantages for lessons in science, biology, or the arts.

The school reform movement itself also has created a number of ideas in trying to reinvent education in U.S. schools that have important implications for school facilities (Fiske 1992). Systemic reform has created or reinforced a variety of ideas that attempt to make major changes to educational practices that have ceased to serve children in the best manner possible. As school reform attempts to move education away from the "factory" model, centralization has given way to decentralization, standardization to diversity, time on task has taken a back seat to academic performance as a basis for organizing instruction, and from a focus process to a focus on results. National standards have begun to be developed not only in industry, but also for the education of students. The roles of teachers and students have been altered to one degree or another, going from a teacher focus to a student focus in doing the work accomplished and with the teacher as coach and the student as worker. In making these changes, more realistic for accomplishment, the architecture may best change to alter the environment so smaller and more personal learning units may be the norm. Teachers, as professionals, must be provided with space to engage in professional activities and students will need different types of spaces so they may accomplish their role in personal working space as opposed to the public space of the past. In order to move the school toward more personal units for study, schools may be reorganized in houses of smaller learning environments with their own faculty and resources.

Renovation of the School Facility

School facilities seldom go very long without some modifications to the classrooms or the support systems that help to maintain good programs. Even new schools often have modifications to accommodate more students or to change features that might better serve to accommodate teaching-learning functions in just a short period. All buildings age from the time they enter service. With hundreds or even thousands of students entering and leaving a facility on a daily basis, wear and tear on the building's components can be great in a relatively short period of time. Even with all of the new school construction over the past decade, there are still many schools in urban centers that have not been updated and maintained to the extent that they need to be. When these schools were enhanced with new wings or had major modifications to accommodate some changes, they still did not keep pace with the technological changes that have become available recently. As a result, there will probably always be a need to renovate or modify facilities. The national studies by the U.S. General Services Administration have indicated that there are billions of dollars in backlogged maintenance updating that needs to be completed just to keep the buildings functional. The principal of the school is the administrator and planner who is closest to the need; consequently, the principal needs to be aware of the trends and changes in building technology that can make the facility more suitable as a learning tool and as a site of educational significance to students and teachers. When the facility does not adequately support the educational goals and program, the principal should begin to request changes to the school building to make it more adequate. Certainly, the requirements of section 504 of the Rehabilitation Act of 1973 and the Americans with Disabilities Act of 1990 both place a major duty on schools to serve those with handicaps and to support educational goals for all. These needed changes typically enter the picture when budgets are being built by the district. Oftentimes, a seed must be planted in the minds of those in politically important positions so they, too, can understand what is missing in the educational setting. Major renovations are complicated and must consider not only the building itself, but also the site's adequacy, financial considerations, and the political and emotional issues that come from spending large amounts of fiscal resources (Earthman 1994). In the case of very inadequate facilities, it may be necessary to build a new facility rather than to renovate. Today's environment often makes it fiscally sound to find the resources to build new rather than renovate. Such decisions ultimately are made by the board of education after (1) a structural and support systems evaluation of the old facility by the architect and engineers is conducted and (2) a projection of the adequacy of continued use of the facility for the education objectives if the building was renovated is made. If these two indicators are acceptable, the decision ultimately boils down to a combination of money and political acceptability of the choice—to build new or to renovate—which is favored.

Health and Safety

In today's mode of reducing HVAC expenses due to rising utilities, many school facilities have been either built with tighter building envelopes or been renovated to reduce outside air flow to help conserve energy. This effort, coupled with moisture that has entered the school environment, can reduce the indoor air quality by the development of microorganisms inside air ducts or on surfaces. In these buildings, the indoor air stream contains dominant organisms that do not resemble the outdoor air. These microorganisms include fungi, bacteria, and viruses (Straus and Kirihara 1996). Nonspecific symptoms, as eye, nose, and throat irritation, headaches, and fatigue are usually associated with what is known as Sick-Building Syndrome. The exact causes are not known, but it is likely that microorganisms and their by-products or those organisms in combination with particulate matter and chemicals are primary contributors. When more specific symptoms cause disease that is traceable to specific causes and oftentimes stays with an individual after they leave the building, the ailment is referred to as Building-Related Illness (BRI). Examples of BRI include Legionnaires' Disease, hypersensitivity pneumonitis, and humidifier fever.

Health problems occur for some occupants of buildings that suffer from some or all of these problems. Testing for indoor air quality to see if the profile of this air is similar to the outside air is the first step in combating possible problems. If higher levels or microorganisms are present in the indoor air, then fertile conditions for problems may be identified and corrected. This may be done by a decontamination procedure to remove the organisms, but first the conditions that allow for the problems to develop must be changed. This may mean reducing moisture intrusion into the environment by building barriers and controlling humidity and by responding quickly to any flood or roof leak to eliminate favorable conditions for the microorganisms.

Another health and safety problem that schools have been dealing with for more than two decades is the use of asbestos as a building material. Schools built in the 1940s until 1978 had a great deal of asbestos used in a variety of products in the building process, prior to its acknowledged health threat. The material was relatively inexpensive, strong, resisted corrosion, would not burn, and insulated well. A mineral-type substance, asbestos is made of small fibers 1,200 times smaller than a human hair. As a building material, it was used in insulation, floor and ceiling tiles, cement pipe, corrugated paper pipe wrap, acoustical and decorative insulation, pipe and boiler insulation, spray applied fireproofing, roofing felt, patching and taping compound, and reinforcement for concrete sheets. The problem developed as the material aged and started to decompose—it became "friable," which allows the fibers to float in the air for hours and days because they are so light. In the friable state, the substance can enter the lungs by breathing it and disrupt normal lung functioning, causing asbestosis, lung cancer, and mesothelioma. Federal law requires that schools must be inspected for the use of asbestos and where asbestos is suspected, samples must be taken and analyzed. If, in fact, asbestos is present, an exposure assessment is mandated and corrective action taken. Parents of school children must be notified and employees working in the environment also must be apprised of the situation. Corrective action is quite an involved process and often enclosure or encapsulation of the material is used; however, the most preferred method is removal of the product under controlled conditions so it cannot contaminate the environment. The process requires a trained technician to oversee all asbestos activities, a management plan, and regular comprehensive inspection for any changes or deterioration of the material. Principals must be knowledgeable of such possibilities and take the necessary action when asbestos is a threat.

SCHOOL OPERATIONS

Operations within the school are normally the responsibility of the principal. From a facilities standpoint, this means making the school building operate on a daily basis in the best way possible to support the educational program (Vornberg and Vornberg 2002). Operation functions in the facility usually are considered to include:

- Housekeeping services
- Grounds upkeep
- Security of the building
- Safety monitoring
- HVAC operations
- Equipment servicing
- Electrical plant operations (including utilities)
- Simple repairs
- Assistance to the staff

To successfully operate the building, numerous employees assist in various ways. The custodial services are perhaps the most visible task at the building with custodians usually present on a full-time basis. An administrator at the building often supervises the custodial staff or possibly only a head custodian who in turn directs other staff, if the building size warrants a larger crew. During the school day custodial staff usually clean heavily used areas and react to emergencies and problems. The principal should work closely with the operations staff to maintain adequate standards and complete all housekeeping jobs required. Evening custodial staff members clean classrooms and help maintain building security. Custodians may also be designated to monitor equipment such as HVAC and electrical utilities. Ground crews are usually specialized in maintaining lawns and outdoor grooming of the site.

Building security is considered an operations function and many schools have some type of security officer present. School districts frequently have specialists who develop security plans to best protect the building and students. With school resource officers assigned to the school, who are often local police officers, security is combined with a law enforcement officer who can develop communications with students, teachers, and outside agencies of the community. Principals in such situations have a ready ally when difficulties arise with students or with outside individuals entering the school (see chapter 14 on safety and security). Security has become a very important aspect of operating a school due to the vandalism, drugs, gang warfare, and most recently the lone student who has difficulties operating within a very structured system that responds to him or her in what he or she perceives as unsupportive ways. An undetected psychosocial maladjustment may also add to this student's list of difficulties. These types of difficulties mean that everyone in the school, students and staff alike, need to be aware of students who have problems that may take them out of the field of reality. Referrals to adequate assistance must be the response in such situations for the individual, immediately after securing the school environment.

Most recently, another aspect of facilities security has been developed—that of Crime Prevention through Environmental Design (CPTED) (Schneider, Walker, and Sprague 2000). CPTED focuses on the student behavior that is desired and attempts to identify problems in the physical and social environment and then to craft facility modifications to reinforce positive behavior. Examples of such changes would be the greater use of windows to enhance visibility and reduce isolation, student art displays to build a sense of pride, changing seating arrangements to encourage supportive group interaction, or altering scheduling with the use of space to avoid conflicts. Elements of CPTED include natural surveillance (keeping an eye on the whole environment without extraordinary measures), natural access control (setting up obstacles to control unlocked doors), and territoriality (establishing recognized authority and control over the environment, such as defining borders of the site). To implement such a concept, an analysis is conducted, usually by an outside consultant, and once problems are identified changes are developed and implemented. In the best of scenarios, CPTED is integrated into new planning of school sites and facilities.

MAINTENANCE OF THE FACILITY

"Building maintenance" is a term sometimes confused with "custodial services of the building." Maintenance refers to the upkeep or repair of facilities within the site, building, or equipment that keeps these accommodations restored, as nearly as possible, to their original condition or efficiency. Such upkeep means that the repairs or replacement will take place in order to continue to support the learning activities and programs. Craftspeople and technicians from outside the school usually do the work in order to meet this goal. The principal or other building administrator normally reports by phone, online, or in writing problems to a central maintenance office for the school district when repair or work orders are needed. The necessary skilled workers or technicians are sent from a central maintenance shop or a contracted company is sent to complete the repairs. As older equipment has ceased to function properly, new replacement equipment is purchased and installed if necessary, to continue to do the tasks required. Examples of replacement would include replacing HVAC equipment, furnishings such as desks and chairs, or technology equipment that had ceased to perform as required. Principals should be aware that there is a difference in replacement from the maintenance budget and an upgrade of equipment from the new equipment budget, which in many cases may be considered a capital outlay item requiring or necessitating a long-term purchase supported by bonded indebtedness.

Annually at budget preparation time, the principal should complete an inventory of the building needs to determine what scheduled maintenance needs to be anticipated for the next year. Such things as painting portions of the building, replacing fixtures and carpeting, and repairing parking lots and playgrounds must be anticipated and budgeted for in the fiscal needs of the school. When budgets become strained and some needs go unfunded, there has often been a tendency to reduce the maintenance budget of the school district. This decision creates deferred maintenance items that should be completed and now will go unattended. This is usually false economy as breakdowns will have a major impact on the program and often will actually increase costs when repairs are no longer possible on some components and replacement is required.

Maintenance is usually classified with the following designations:

- Preventative maintenance involves an ongoing process of inspection and servicing of components to reduce or eliminate mechanical, physical, or structural breakdown to prevent more costly repairs or replacements and protects against disrupting programs during unanticipated failures.
- Emergency maintenance is unexpected and requires immediate response to continue to use the facility or have the support of the specific component. A high incidence of emergency maintenance may be related to poor management of the facilities.
- Scheduled maintenance is the result of good practices that permit changes to equipment or repair of facilities to be done when it least disrupts normal activities of the school.
- Replacement maintenance is conducted when components of the facility are changed out as opposed to repair of the present unit. A good preventative maintenance program can determine replacement cycles and avoid negatively impacting the educational program.
- Routine maintenance refers primarily to demand maintenance conducted as the need arises but not of an emergency nature. Building administrators report the routine maintenance requests to the maintenance department, which then schedules the task.
- Contract maintenance includes those maintenance tasks that require an outside person to complete the job. This requirement is necessitated by the infrequency of the type of job to be done, its specialized nature, and the district's size. (Vornberg and Vornberg 2002, 414–15)

Large school districts that are providing maintenance to many school facilities typically have skilled craftspeople and trained technicians who can provide very specialized services for the large amount of equipment throughout the district. Smaller districts, however, may perform only the very routine work with their employees and send the more specialized jobs to be completed to outside contractors. In either case, larger jobs needing completion will need to have estimates done to anticipate costs as budgets are completed for the next year. Unanticipated emergency maintenance may require that the school or district budget for contingencies, when the problem involves required equipment to continue operating the school; such an example would include an HVAC equipment item that had been destroyed from a fire in the school damaging classrooms or other required space.

EQUIPMENT FOR SCHOOL SAFETY AND SECURITY

The school of this era has tremendous resources available to accommodate safety and security considerations. These help to protect the buildings' occupants by providing communications, free egress, controlled access, surveillance, notification, and automatic response to catastrophic events such as fire. As new schools are built, there should be a careful analysis of the types of equipment that are available and the advantages that each offers in developing plans. Older facilities need to consider how such equipment might be added during a renovation activity to bring these schools into compliance with codes as well as to add the protective services and conveniences they have to offer. Any type of system can only accomplish the stated goals if people utilize it properly and do not circumvent it. The most sophisticated building access system is useless if someone props the back door open, and an elaborate media retrieval system and library of information sources is of no value if the instructor is hesitant to learn to use the system. Consequently, all stakeholders must be involved in determining the needs, the costs associated with these goals, and agree to participate in staff training and support for the new systems as well as the associated policy and procedural changes. All involved must help establish their proper use and avoid the natural resistance to change and new ideas. Some of the potential advantages will be discussed next.

Telephone Systems

Telephone systems are often installed so every classroom has direct access to an intrabuilding communications systems that can provide quick assistance when it is warranted by connecting to the office, technical support personnel, other classrooms, and to emergency facilities. Outside communications is also facilitated for teachers to contact parents for conferences and other assistance. In some cases, these systems also help supply the infrastructure to other communications services such as media retrieval system hook ups to the library/media center that can send and control the media signal to the classroom for viewing. Two major system types are currently available: Direct Inward Dial (DID) and Automated Attendant (AA). With DID each room or station is assigned its own number and a direct line. With AA there is one number for the school or district and an automated attendant answers and the local extension must be dialed. The AA system is owned by the school and requires only one number for everyone. The equipment is owned by the school and requires less total expense on a monthly basis as well as less clerical time to answer the calls.

In some cases, the classroom telephone can be integrated with other devices such as a digital intercom system or the master clock and class change tone system. Usually outside incoming calls can be restricted by the use of a "do not disturb" signal. The use of a personal identification number can be utilized to access outside lines. Also voice mail may be included.

Building Access Systems

Controlling access to the school building is very important in this time of security consciousness. Although schools are public institutions that normally have open invitations at the front door during and after school hours, access through other doors is usually controlled to keep strangers or unauthorized individuals from entering. Control of who may enter is provided only at a controlled entry door that is fitted with an electric strike, an electric latch, or a magnetic lock. A reader, which is actuated by a magnetic card or a similar device, is installed to allow entry to those authorized by the use of proximity cards, tokens, or magnetic cards. A central processing unit or computer is used to maintain a database of users and to update the system. A field processor unit operates the locks independently of the central unit, which enables operation without the main central processing unit in case of a breakdown. Such a system can provide the capability of disabling lost or revoked cards from entering the facilities; however, all students and staff must make a concerted effort to keep uncontrolled entry doors locked and not to allow others to use their cards or to let people in uncontrolled doors locked from outside entry.

Fire Alarm Systems

Current technology has two primary types of alarm systems for fires: conventional zoned alarms and addressable device panels. In addition to signaling a fire emergency to the building inhabitants and the fire monitoring personnel at an off-site location, the system can provide information to fire fighters on their arrival about the location, size, and spread of the fire. The conventional zoned system has numerous devices on each zone and it is not possible to tell which device is alarmed without an inspection of each device. The devices may include manual pull stations for an occupant to report a fire and automatic smoke and/or heat detectors. Once alarm activation occurs, the zone must be reset before additional devices will alarm. With addressable systems, each initiating device has a distinct digital address and an alarm signal can be located on the monitoring panel as to its location. Under normal conditions, each device is scanned every four seconds and sends a signal to the alarm panel if actuated by a fire.

An alarm, in addition to notification of personnel, can also shut down HVAC blowers, close smoke fire dampers, and release fire door holders. In some cases, a waterflow alarm condition can be indicated on the panel when an automatic building sprinkler system is monitored, which gives the indication that in addition to fire, the building is subject to water damage. In most cases, the more expensive addressable system is the standard for the industry, except in the case of small buildings where the conventional zone system may be selected.

Surveillance Systems

Video surveillance systems generally consist of several cameras: a switching device, a recorder, and a video monitor. Such cameras would be set up in critical areas such as entrances and major gathering points to record activities. Basic systems have up to four black and white, low-resolution, fixed-focus analog cameras, a quad multiplexer, and a time lapse video recorder. All four cameras use the same recorder and with time lapse, recording on the tapes may run for twelve to twenty-four hours before being changed. Other systems are also available that offer more cameras, split image screens, color systems, and digital or digital/analog hybrid systems. Such systems usually make it easier to identify the activities and individuals on the recordings. Where digital recorders are used, there are no tapes to change or heads to clean, and the defects often seen in videotape playback are eliminated.

ROLE OF COMMUNITY MEMBERS IN FACILITIES

Within the school community there are numerous contributions that can be made in enhancing the facilities at the school and in making them more pleasant for work and study. The contributions in this area are very important as these add to the school culture and the school's climate when these are of a positive nature. Often, the site-based committee of the school can be involved in offering inputs, but it is not uncommon for the entire faculty or student groups that are providing a service to the school to be involved by identifying a project that would be suitable and carrying out efforts to make it a reality. Such examples might include the purchase of equipment needed for a specialized function or decorating an area of the school with art or a logo to help build the esprit de corps of the student body. Planning functions of broader nature are also important ways that such groups can contribute. These would include long-range planning, building issues, and educational specifications.

Long-Range Planning

Long-range planning is a function of the district or the school that numerous individuals, citizens and school employees alike, can play a role. In terms of school facilities, long-range plans are usually developed as a follow-on to strategic planning efforts. Strategic planning focuses on developing a mission and vision for the school that is more detailed in design by goals and strategies refined to reach those goals. Long-range plans usually are more specifically aimed at identified functions that play a certain role in meeting the school's mission. Examples would include plans for curriculum revisions, human resource development, or school facilities development.

At the building site, a planning committee could examine the building's resources and determine how these could be enhanced to better meet the instructional needs for the programs being offered. These plans could focus on what expectations are anticipated in the future such as additional students, new programs to be offered, or the technological additions that would be needed to maintain pace with the world. Although the principal would have the ultimate responsibility to make recommendations to the superintendent for major additions or changes, the assistance of knowledgeable faculty would be important to gather a wider range of thinking. When visionary ideas are included in discussions by faculty, these should be much more accurate than when only the principal is offering thoughts for such development.

Building Issues and Problems

Another area less involved than long-range planning is the identification of issues or problems that are related to the facility that can be solved through team thinking and action. Rather than the principal being the only person trying to orchestrate solutions to facility problems, the entire faculty or a site-based committee can meet to identify problem areas. Some of these issues can be irritations to teachers or students, but some could be major difficulties that disrupt instruction. With a group of teachers brainstorming such a matter, a number of issues can be tentatively identified. Priorities are then set to choose issues to work on and the group proposes ways of solving the issues selected. Again, brainstorming can offer numerous solutions that can be studied and finally a plan is put in place to correct the problem. The plan may be something that everyone involved will be required to participate in making work, or it may be one that the principal must work with district-level administrators or board members to resolve the problem. The important thing is that those concerned are part of the solution and that everyone takes a part in making it happen. It is not only the principal's responsibility to implement such a solution; all those participating in the school community can and should make contributions.

Planning for a New or Renovated Facility

The process of planning for a new facility or making major modifications to an older facility offers the opportunity for cooperation from the administrators, teachers, and other stakeholders who will be housed in the new facility. These professionals should be consulted during the process of developing educational specifications and documents that the school district gives to the architectural firm that will be designing the facility. Educational specifications describe the educational programs that will be offered in the new facility or the areas to be modified in a retrofitted or renovated facility. This description includes the educational activities that will be taking place in the newly designed components, the numbers of students to be served, the support functions that must take place, the technology that will be required, as well as environmental characteristics that are necessary for supporting these programs. One assumption that must be met for this to work in the best interests of the school is that the program is based on a fully defined curriculum that has been recently examined by the educational staff for currency. The architects use these descriptions to compile "programming requirements" and then to state an "architectural problem" to which the firm employed then develops an architectural solution. Some architectural firms actually do this design on site at the school now in use. As their ideas develop from the specifications, the future users of the new facility may actually observe the process and offer their reactions as the design is developed on paper by the designers. At the end of the process, the new building has had extensive input from those who will be teaching and operating in the facility.

TECHNOLOGY IN THE EDUCATIONAL ENVIRONMENT

Technology in the school may be one of the fastest moving concepts in education. The possibilities for technological changes in education are enormous, yet the changes are mind-boggling to most educators. Principals are not usually experts in the technology area, yet they must be able to offer leadership and vision in the area of technology use and be able to communicate this vision to all the stakeholders in a school. This will mean that with their leadership, the school's community will develop a long-range and systemic technology plan that will guide the school in reaching its vision. To be able to do this, the principal will have to maintain cohesion and momentum, foster responsible risk taking that promotes innovation, use data to drive leadership decisions, and advocate research-based best practices (International Society of Technology in Education 2001). The

International Society for Technology in Education recently issued its list of tech standards for school leaders, in which the above is advocated.

Planning for Instructional Technology and for Technology Education

Society and technology are interconnected in today's world. As technology becomes more developed, the rate of change continues to speed up the demands on individuals and on the institutions that make up society today. As the technological changes continue, they impact society through the social, political, and economic arrangements that are altered. These societal changes then impact the value systems that have been much slower to change, which then affect the personal and environmental welfare of the nation and the world. Because of the extreme impact of technology on society, students in today's schools need to experience technology education. This, of course, is different from educational technology. The latter is understanding how to use technology in the educational process, while the former is understanding how technology impacts the world, how to make value judgments involving technology, and how to use it for sound development.

As schools plan for educational technology, the stakeholders must make judgments about the needs of students in learning, the desired outcomes, the costs involved, and the changes that leadership decisions will have on the students, their ethical and moral education, and how the use of educational technology will impact their view of technology in society. This calls for value judgments to be made, the result of which can only be speculated on much of the time. To achieve this goal, stakeholders must develop a technology plan or strategies to guide their tactical actions and decisions. Developing a technology plan means being able to look to the future while harnessing the technology presently available for educating students.

The goal of educational technology plans seems to be the education of students to use technology:

- as an essential tool in their education,
- to be equipped with the best technological tools for later employment,
- to use the skills developed in association with academic subjects, and

- to be equipped with the competencies needed to understand recent technological hardware, software, and programming. (Lowe and Vespestad 1999)

Boiled down, this means to be technologically literate and to integrate that literacy with growth in other fields (Marcoux 1999).

Technology has a number of important advantages. It allows for quick access to information for both educators and students. It assists in managing the information that is available or that has been developed into databases that may be assembled by others, the school organization, or by oneself. Moreover, it enables those involved to communicate with others in a variety of ways (Hermond 1999).

The computer is the primary piece of equipment that has made most of these advantages available to educators and students. The hardware is the basic vehicle that makes this possible. When linked with the software designed to provide the tools to manipulate the data or perform the tasks, the advantages mentioned by Hermond become possible.

To provide such equipment and the software for a school means much planning has to be done. Among the issues that must be resolved are those of access, connectivity, flexibility, and integration. Access requires the necessary hardware and appropriate software for students to use in the right locations within the school or, in some cases, outside the school. This means that funds have to be identified and acquired such as through grants, gifts, and regular school budgets or through capital outlay arrangements such as bonded indebtedness. In many cases, Technology Infrastructure Fund grants through state departments of education can help acquire these resources. In some cases, schools have gone so far as to supply laptop computers to individual students who may take them home or connect into the school's area network through stations throughout the school. Such a resource provides students with at least part of the equation for technology to make a difference in their studies. This brings forth the second issue—that of connectivity. To best utilize this technology resource for access to information, it is necessary to become connected to the information through a network. This infers connection through the Internet or some local or wide area network that is also connected to the information. In today's world, anyone can supply information to the Internet, so it becomes both a fantastic resource to get information and also a mediocre source of poor or harmful information to the student if the student chooses to use it in an improper way. Connectivity means acquiring the resources to take advantage of the Internet and the many Web pages available or to have access to resources through library databases and online materials. This means wiring the school facility for computer connections and making the connections necessary for Internet access from such a system.

The third issue is flexibility. Because computers are constantly being upgraded with new tools, faster speeds, and larger memories and the fact that new technology is constantly changing the connectivity channels, the school must keep in mind how improvements can be made when the newer solutions are available. This may mean more resources are required or it may mean building facilities so they can later accommodate newer solutions to access and connectivity issues. Integration is the fourth issue; this refers to the need to integrate the use of the technology with the curriculum and into the classroom. Computers are not the subject studied in most classrooms; the computer is the means to better achieve information and to understand how to better understand the subject matter with which it is integrated. The instructor should play an important role in this process by being trained in the use of technology in teaching. The instructor must know what tool to use when performing a teaching task for the student to best acquire the knowledge or skill. So the selection of the technology means for learning becomes important for the teacher. This model of technology integration is the Seamless Technology Integration (Izat and Mize 2002). This means for a particular educational task there is a technological tool that will best help to teach the skill through the process of creative problem solutions. The teacher's job is not only to help the student understand the use of the technological tool, but also how to select the best tool for the solution process when problems are encountered.

Developing Plans and Assessing Needs

Therefore, developing new plans means to assess needs from an instructional standpoint and to select the technological tools that best help to solve the problems encountered in the teaching-learning process. As outside problems are encountered, then new solutions must be developed.

Such an example is the problem of screening out improper Internet sites for use by the students. This would require content filters in the Internet connection process and can create more difficulties such as freedom of information issues or protection of students from harmful people who use Internet and "chat rooms" for improper purposes.

USES OF TECHNOLOGY

The technological tools that are now available to schools can impact the education of students as both an instructional tool as discussed earlier and a management tool to assist in determining where the student is in understanding the material. These also may be used as management and communications tools in operating the school, by both storing and analyzing data to help make decisions, and in communicating with teachers, other administrators, as well as parents throughout the school or the district about concerns such as instructional issues or behavior management.

EDUCATIONAL OPPORTUNITY

Technology has made possible new designs in teaching students through the use of distance education over televised, real-time instruction with students in different locations. This provides an important option for schools that do not have the necessary numbers of students to be able to offer courses with fewer students than might be possible otherwise. Web-based instruction makes possible course offerings that are scheduled at the student's convenience. Each of these options requires additional hardware and software that can support such instructional programs. These each make possible some different protocols than high school or elementary students have been accustomed to in the past. Also, it demands that the student be better motivated and focused on task in order to complete the work that is required.

Programmed learning is another type of computer assisted instruction that has been available for some time. These types of instruction are normally used to reinforce standard classroom material, but in a more basic way than collaborative or cognitive learning. The material is explained via voice and/or screen, to which the student responds to questions that are asked by the computer. If the student understands the material, then he or she moves on to the next sequence. If understanding is not present, then the student receives more instruction until successful. When the computer makes decisions as to the student's mastery of the material, the sequence is usually called Computer Managed Instruction. This is normally centered on the behaviorist instructional philosophy as contrasted to the constructivist philosophy now being considered more appropriate for higher-order thinking.

In today's environment, the constructivist philosophy is apparent from applying research on human learning to issues of education by "making meaningful learning: real-world contexts for learning connecting to outside experts; visualization and analysis tools; scaffolds for problem solving; and opportunities for feedback, reflection and revision" (Means 2001, 58). Examples of such opportunities include the:

- Global Learning and Observations to Benefit the Environment program that helps elementary and secondary students learn science by involving them in real scientific investigation
- Hands-On Universe program of University of California, Berkeley, which gives students the opportunity to use image processing software to investigate images from a network of automated telescopes
- Knowledge Forum that provides a communal database that can help students exercise collaboration skills while sharing information and feedback in accumulating knowledge over time with teacher support
- TinkerTools software that helps middle school students learn about velocity and acceleration through "scaffolded inquiry activities" that help students understand motion and direction culminating in learning Newtonian mechanics

Unfortunately, such examples of outstanding learning opportunities, although available, are not representative of mainstream practice today. Most teachers and instruction are still dealing with word processing, research from the Internet or CD-ROMs, and assignments of games and software drills. But the advances in technology will also make available other low-cost learning appliances like wireless personal hand-held devices that would be lower cost than today's computers, yet light weight and portable. These may be tailored for specific applications and may be able to exchange information with a teacher workstation (Means 2001).

Despite all the advancements that will become available, teachers will continue to guide students and the application of these new tools for education will be dependent on teachers being able to be prepared and to improve through their training—both preservice and staff development. Teachers must be prepared to do this; however, data gathered by the National Center for Educational Statistics indicates that only one-third of the teachers responding felt well prepared to use computers and the Internet for instructional purposes (Jones 2001). Furthermore, less experienced teachers were more likely to use computers and the Internet in planning lessons. Despite the indication that three-quarters of the teachers had some professional development activities in technology, most did not feel they had the training necessary to incorporate technology use in their classroom. To help meet this challenge, the principal will have to offer leadership in teachers acquiring necessary skills. Beavers (2001) offers three major solutions to this challenge involving the teachers themselves as solutions through peer coaching, study group organization, and the use of thematic curriculum in integrating technology with instruction.

DESIGNING A NEW ENVIRONMENT FOR LEARNING

Not every principal has the opportunity to plan a new school facility. In fact, often the principal to be has very little, if any, input into a new or replacement facility design or planning efforts. These tasks are the responsibility of the district level due to the size of the district or political factors of the community and the board of education. The purpose of this discussion is not to go into detailed planning processes. There are many specialized volumes that can assist the principal and other planners in doing this; however, the purpose here is to familiarize the principal with some major concepts of planning that should be considered when the opportunity is offered to participate in these tasks.

Planning Processes and Tasks

Perhaps the most important function of the principal and staff at a school that will have a new facility built is to build a school profile and project the needs of the students and staff in designing the school's program. Programs change in schools (see chapter 10) as the population changes, the instructional philosophy is developed or matures to a different level, or the needs are altered by changes in the broader society. In many sections of the nation, the needs of the students served are being altered as the demographics of the population have changed due to immigration. More and more in large cities and in many rural areas there is a greater need to teach students who do not have English language as their primary or family language. The intensity of language instruction may be greater in such situations where this segment of the population is growing. The technological developments in society have changed the need for instructional topics in this area to be much more focused in order for students to have skills that can support their continued study in higher learning or their employment in developing industries. And instructional philosophies have been altered in recent years by learning theories moving from a behavioral approach to a cognitivist approach to a constructivist approach. This development in learning theories has had a major impact on how learning activities have changed in the classroom, which in turn makes classroom design a task needing teacher input. To build a school profile, a careful study of the current school population should be compared to the recent past in terms of demographic changes, learning successes, and desires and needs of the community that is being served. The expectations for graduates of the school become more diverse in the high school than in the elementary school. So building a profile of what the school's population will look like in the near future and how the needs of these students will be the same or different from those served now will have important implications for those planning a new facility.

The information in the school's profile will provide the basis for the work on the educational specifications. This document is the projection of what is needed in the facility, the activities that will occur, and the extent to which these are needed—numbers to be served, size of rooms, and specialized equipment. These specifications will then serve the architects in completing the design tasks (see the section on planning a new or renovated facility).

Design Innovations in New Facilities

New or renovated facilities for which interiors and furnishings are being selected should involve careful work with those taking a leadership role in the instructional program. Today's instructional activities have moved from the behaviorist mode of learning theory toward the constructivist mode. What this means is learning activities are most apt to be in smaller groups with problems being solved and that facts are used to foster new learning in individuals by constructing meaning from how they fit together with what they already know. Brooks and Brooks (1993) indicate that students construct understanding that is meaningful to them and teachers ask students to look at other questions rather than just questions asked by the teachers. The learner needs a responsive environment in which consideration is given to the learner's individual style as an active, self-regulating, reflective learner (Jonassen 1991). Battista (1999) clears the notion that this is not a pedagogical stance that entails nonrigorous intellectual anarchy, allowing for students to pursue whatever interests them, whether it is relevant learning or not. He indicates that to develop powerful thinking in students, instruction must focus on and support their personal construction of ideas. This type of instruction encourages students to invent, test, and refine their ideas rather than blindly following procedures and information given them by others. The type of environment to promote such activity must be one that allows for discussion, individual and small-group activity, and interaction with ideas. The design of furnishings for such a setting may differ greatly from the rows of desks that have been used for several hundred years in U.S. classrooms and calls for tables and moveable equipment, various designs for layout, and décor of the environment.

Sustainability

Sustainable design reflects the idea that schools must not compromise the ability of future generations in order to meet their own needs. Sustainable thinking is being environmentally sensitive to the implications of planning and building in today's world and to link all of the strategies available to meet the student's needs today with the needs of tomorrow's students. Examples of components of sustainable design might include:

- Protecting existing landscaping and natural features in the site planning and landscape design as to protect from erosion, retaining water, Xeriscape landscaping, maximizing solar access, and natural lighting
- Develop strategies to provide daylight inside, minimizing use of artificial light
- Utilize solar systems to reduce peak electrical demands and incorporate this into the instructional program
- Collect rainwater for site irrigation and gray water for toilet flushing. Use low-flow and water-conserving fixtures
- Develop systems to enable recycling to occur
- Maximize use of recycled and environmentally friendly products to reduce the pollutant effects of construction
- Use energy efficient lighting, electrical, and mechanical and HVAC systems
- Design the school as a teaching tool and incorporate this feature into the educational program

MOVING INTO A NEW FACILITY

Whenever a faculty and students move into a newly built school, there should be an orientation program offered by the designers and those involved in the planning processes. Assuming at least some of those closely involved with the planning are from the school's staff, these individuals should play a major role in this orientation, helping to explain how the facility's design was developed to accommodate the programs and activities in the specifications. Technical training may be necessary for specified individuals who are responsible for particular equipment such as HVAC, alarm systems, communications systems, water controls, lighting timers, security systems, learning technology, bell systems, keys, and circuit breakers (Lane and Betz 1987). Since several years generally elapse from the time a building is envisioned and the physical facility becomes a reality, this orientation is important as the personnel entering the school have oftentimes changed from the beginning of the project until the moving in date.

ETHICAL DISCUSSION

- What should be the response of the principal when the output of *economy* interferes with the output of *adequacy* in dealing with the school as a learning tool?
- The need for safety of students in the school may collide with the rights of others in terms of controlling access to the school or the use or introduction of certain types of personal belongings. How should the school or principal handle these types of conflicts of personal behavior? Does surveillance of the school by video or closed circuit television carry this need too far?
- Maintenance tasks on facilities are often delayed for one or more years due to budget constraints. In the meantime, health and safety of students or faculty might be at risk. Is this a question that requires reconsideration? Why or why not?
- The use of site-based committees in facility decision making may slow down the decision processes or spread the responsibility too much in some individuals' observation. How can society justify this use of such groups in facility decisions?
- The introduction of computer filters will tend to control student access to certain Internet websites. Is it justifiable, in the name of education, to restrict student access to these sites?
- Ethical dilemmas are right-versus-right issues. Which side of the student surveillance debate do you support and why?

CHAPTER SUMMARY

The school facility has much to offer as part of the learning system. As such, it can be a warm and supporting atmosphere or a cold and foreboding environment for teaching and learning. The environment offers the sight and sound environment that can be made more supportive by teachers and administrators. The building and the classrooms offer components that can be congruent with the program and methods of instruction or at odds and ill-supportive of these efforts or the instructional philosophy. Learning can be encouraged by the facility or hindered by it. Students can be made to feel more responsible for their actions or made to feel this is not a place they want to be. Different concepts are involved in these efforts: learning styles, environmental psychology, educational psychology, brain research principles, and systemic reform as a factor that can assist in making changes in today's roles of teachers and students.

As the administrator responsible for the school, the management of the facility becomes an important aspect of that role. In almost all instances, renovations or changes to the facility are made, usually within a few years, even when the building is newly built. As programs change in a school, facilities need to be made more supportive of new ideas in instruction. Handicapped modifications often must be made on older facilities. In all instances, principals must be advocates for supporting these changes and work with the district's administrators and board of education for supporting these financially.

Health and safety issues are also entering the school facility picture in a big way, due to poor air quality from contaminates. Asbestos still remains an issue in older facilities and in some areas radon gas has proven a problem.

The principal is also directly responsible for managing operations within the building, including housekeeping, security, HVAC, and utilities. Maintenance is also a key role, at least in terms of reporting problems and making sure students and facility are not at risk due to problems before repairs are made. Closely related to these functions are the safety and security equipment, including communications, building access, fire alarm systems, and surveillance systems.

Faculty councils or site-based management committees can aid the principal in contributing in a positive manner to the management and/or the input concerning the school facility. Areas of assistance could include developing long-range planning needs for the site or facility, identifying issues and problems that can be solved relating to the facility, and developing educational specifications for building additions or a new facility that is planned.

Technology applications in the school are perhaps the paradigm change that has impacted education the most of all types of changes in the educational setting. There are two distinct parts to the picture—that of technology education and also educational technology. One is the education focus; the other is the use of technology as a tool for advancing education. Hardware and software are the technical pieces to this puzzle.

To get the most from technology use, there must be access, connectivity, flexibility, and integration of these possibilities to the curriculum program and to the users who gain by its availability. To make technology function to the school's advantage, there must be an assessment of needs and plans to solve the issues identified. Such a tool offers many possibilities for educational development and use by the widening of educational opportunity to the development of instruction, communication, and management possibilities.

In addition to technology, other major facility developments impacting both new and renovations of schools include interior design innovations and the integration of sustainability concepts in designing schools and conservation measures for school resources.

CHAPTER ACTIVITIES AND QUESTIONS

1. Select a learning philosophy that you personally prefer or appreciate and reflect on how changes in a school or classroom might better support that philosophy.
2. How could a school adapt the facility to promote the sociological configurations of small-group, large-group, and individualized learning to best achieve the instructional goals?
3. Evaluate a classroom set up or arrangement for supporting instruction. Make recommendations for change.
4. Walk through a school facility and develop a list of recommendations for modification or renovation that would enhance the educational support given by the facility or classrooms.
5. Locate a school that you feel might potentially have indoor air quality problems. Interview the principal, the school nurse, and a teacher concerning this problem.
6. Develop a daily plan for the custodian to accomplish the needed tasks. Interview a principal concerning supervision of the custodial staff.
7. Interview the director of maintenance of a school district concerning the scheduling and follow-up on maintenance tasks.
8. After examining the safety equipment in a school, make a prioritized list of changes needed and explain why these were prioritized as they were.

9. Discuss building needs and long-range planning for these with a principal. Make a list of principles you think were important from this discussion.
10. What is the difference in technology education and educational technology? Is one more important than the other? If yes, what type of educational environment is this true in?
11. Discuss how your school resolves the issues of access, connectivity, flexibility, and integration in the use of technology.
12. Visit a school that uses technology heavily in its program. After discussing the program with teachers, students, and the principal, reflect on what you learned and how it fits into your vision of a progressive education program.
13. Visit a facility that incorporated sustainable architecture and planning in its development. How does such a facility meet the educational needs of today's youth?

CASE STUDY ACTIVITIES AND QUESTIONS

1. If you were Ms. Bones, how would you introduce the concept of making the facility more friendly toward the curriculum and instructional efforts of the school?
2. How can you make a classroom more conducive to the introduction of learning styles to support teaching-learning efforts?
3. Discuss aesthetics as an output of the facility development process that would promote learning in the school or classroom.
4. Develop a plan to set up or arrange a classroom to facilitate learning at a selected grade level or subject area of the curriculum.
5. What reforms of the current reform movement might be supported by facility modifications?

REFERENCES

Battista, M. (1999). "The mathematical miseducation of America's youth." *Phi Delta Kappa* 80: 424–433.
Beavers, D. (2001). "Outside the workshop box." *Principal Leadership* 1 (9) (May–June): 43–46.

Brooks, J., and Brooks, M. (1993). *In search of understanding: The case for constructivist classrooms*. Alexandria, VA: Association for Supervision and Curriculum Development.

Castaldi, B. (1987). *Educational Facilities*. Newton, MA: Allyn and Bacon.

Chan, T. C., and Petrie, G. F. (1998). "The brain learns better in well-designed school environments." *Classroom Leadership On Line* 2 (3), at www.ascd.org/readingroom/classlead;9811/2nov98.html (accessed October 25, 2000).

Dunn, R., and Dunn, K. (1978). *Teaching students through their individual learning styles: A practitioner approach*. Reston, VA: Reston.

Earthman, G. I. (1994). *School renovation handbook*. Lancaster, PA: Technomic.

Fiske, E. B. (1992). "Systemic school reform: Implications for architecture." In *Designing places for learning*, ed. Anne Meek. Alexandria, VA: Association for Supervision and Curriculum Development.

Hermond, D. S. (1999). Leadership and technology. In *The principal as leader*, ed. L. W. Hughes. Upper Saddle River, NJ: Merrill.

Heyman, M. (1978). *Places and spaces: Environmental psychology in education*. Bloomington, IN: Phi Delta Kappa Educational Foundation, Fastback 112.

International Society of Technology in Education. (2001). "Technology Standards for School Administrators." At www.eschoolnews.org/showstory.cfm?ArticleID=2343 (accessed May 24, 2002).

Izat, J. G., and Mize, C. D. (2002). "Texas schools, technology integration, and the twenty-first century." In *Texas public school organization and administration: 2002*, ed. J. A. Vornberg. Dubuque, IA: Kendall/Hunt.

Jonassen, D. (1991). "Objectivism vs. constructivism." *Educational Technology, Research and Development* 39: 5–13.

Jones, C. A. (2001). "Preparing teachers to use technology." *Principal Leadership* 1 (9) (May–June): 35–39.

Kowalski, T. J. (1983). *Solving educational facility problems*. Muncie, IN: Accelerated Development.

Lane, K. E., and Betz, L. E. (1987). "The principal new to a school—What questions to ask about a facility." *NASSP Bulletin* 71 (502): 125.

Lowe, M. J., and Vespestad, K. M. (1999). "Using technology as a tool to enhance teaching and learning." *NASSP Bulletin* 83 (607): 30–36.

Marcoux, B. (1999). "Developing the national information literacy standards for student learning." *NASSP Bulletin* 83 (605): 13–19.

Means, B. (2001). "Technology use in tomorrow's schools." *Educational Leadership* 58 (4): 57–61.

Schneider, T., Walker, H., and Sprague, J. (2000). *Safe school design: A handbook for educational leaders*. Eugene, OR: University of Oregon, ERIC.

Straus, D. C., and Kirihara, J. (1996). "The indoor microbiological garden." *Building Operating Management* (August): 78–84.

Taylor, A., Aldrich, R. A., and Valastos, G. (1988). "Architecture can teach." *Context* 18: 31.

Vornberg, M. E., and Vornberg, J. A. (2002). "Planning and management of educational facilities." In *Texas public school organization and administration: 2002*, ed. J. A. Vornberg. Dubuque, IA: Kendall/Hunt.

Section VI

The Politics of the Educational Environment

ISLLC Standard 6

A school administrator is an educational leader who promotes the success of all students by understanding, responding to, and influencing the larger political, social, economic, legal, and cultural context. The administrator has knowledge and understanding of:

- The role of public education in developing and renewing a democratic society and an economically productive nation
- The political, social, cultural, and economic system and processes that impact schools
- Models and strategies of change and conflict resolution as applied to the larger political, social, cultural, and economic contexts of schooling
- The dynamics of policy development and advocacy under our democratic political system

Chapter Sixteen

Politics for the Principal

Mary J. Mills, the principal at Forsythe Elementary, had engaged the entire faculty in researching the advantages and disadvantages of whole language reading versus phonics-based reading. She began this discussion trying to find out what the research indicated about each approach. She had several teachers developing "white papers" on the topic. Ms. Mills knew that the whole language–phonics issue was very controversial, depending on who was speaking. The day for the big debate came and went with both sides making valid points on behalf of their reading philosophy. Approximately two weeks after the debate, the faculty was to meet and decide which reading philosophy was to be adopted by the faculty at Forsythe Elementary.

At the faculty meeting, both sides had the opportunity to remind the entire faculty of the instructional benefits to teachers and the added learning that students would achieve if their philosophy were to be adopted. Ms. Mills asked if the group could come to a consensus, meaning that some teachers would be willing to suspend their feelings for their side of the issue, in order to select a reading philosophy. After about forty-five minutes of discussion, the group representing the phonics philosophy agreed to suspend their stance on the position and to work, in principle, with the entire faculty to make the whole language reading philosophy productive for students and teachers. Ms. Mills left the faculty meeting feeling that the entire process had worked well and that the school was on its way to developing a program that would benefit students.

Three weeks later, Ms. Mills received a telephone call from the chair of the Forsythe Elementary parent–teachers organization (PTO). She indicated that she was at a social function on Saturday evening and overheard one of the veteran Forsythe teachers telling a parent about the decision to use the whole language concept in reading. She went on to explain to the principal that the teacher (Ms. Ima Right) and the parent were planning to begin a grassroots movement among the school's stakeholders to force the teachers to abandon the whole language concept and to replace it with a phonics program. Ms. Mills thanked the parent for the information and decided to confront Ms. Right about the conversation she had with the PTO president. She specifically remembered Ms. Right agreeing to support the faculty consensus, but she also knew Ms. Right was a very influential member of the Cameron community. Her father had been a long-time mayor of Cameron and her husband was the chief executive officer of a big Cameron–Bethany automobile dealership. Mr. Right was a very personable and effective member of the business community and he had been a business partner with Forsythe Elementary for the past ten years.

Ms. Mill knew she needed to approach Ms. Right about the situation in order to find out what the situation was all about. She arranged for an after school meeting and she met Ms. Right in the conference room to discuss what she had been told. After explaining the situation and declaring that she (Ms. Mills) was sure this was a misunderstanding, Ms. Right declared that what Ms. Mills had heard was indeed true. Ms. Right went on to explain that her friend Shelly Soccermom was adamant about the use of phonics and she was going to help Ms. Soccermom mount a grassroots campaign to make sure Forsythe Elementary used the phonics concept. As Ms. Mills probed further, she discovered that Ms. Right never had any intention of using whole language with her students and had agreed in the faculty meeting only to avoid peer pressure. Ms. Mills reminded Ms. Right that her decision to perpetuate a hoax on her colleagues was less than professional and perhaps bordered on being unethical. Ms. Right made sure the principal knew that this was a free country and she would support whomever she thought was correct. The conversation ended with both individuals very upset by the other's statements.

Ms. Mills decided that she needed to inform Superintendent J. B. Tucker of the situation because she knew Ms. Right and Ms. Soccermom would be contacting the central administration and perhaps the members of the board of education. She explained the process she had used in coming to the whole language decision and Dr. Tucker appeared to be comfortable and indicated that she had used the correct process. Ms.

Mills felt she had the superintendent and board's support for the decision that had been developed.

Two days prior to the April meeting of the Forsythe Elementary PTO, a full-page advertisement appeared in the Cameron News Observer outlining negative aspects of the whole language concepts and listing the positive attributes of the phonics reading philosophy. The advertisement quoted Ms. Right as opposing the whole language philosophy and listed twenty influential school stakeholders agreeing that phonics was the most effective concept in teaching children to read. Ms. Mills was very upset with the advertisement and she knew she had a political fight on her hands if she were going to maintain the integrity of the faculty's decision-making process.

The day of the PTO meeting several teachers approached Ms. Mills and offered to help her develop a strategy to counteract the Soccermom/Right assault on the school curriculum. They agreed to meet the next morning to begin developing a plan to market their plan to the community stakeholders. Ms. Mills knew this would be a battle and the opposition would disparage her name, but this was a fight she needed to wage in order to protect her teachers and students.

More and more principals are caught in events created by community pressure and politics. Everyday, principals are required to communicate and engage community stakeholders who affect the school. It is important to be able to work with a wide variety of people, events, and pressures that are represented by factions and special interest groups that advocate issues and solutions to issues that are juxtaposed to the philosophical foundations of the school. These individuals and groups need to bring pressure on the school, the principal, and the teachers in order to force their beliefs on the school and its stakeholders. As a principal, you cannot ignore these individuals and groups. Howe and Townsend (2000) state that the crosscurrents blowing around the schoolyard can be creative, energizing, disgusting, and challenging. They state that the principals must confront and resolve these issues, and they must do so in a timely manner. The principal's effective quotient is measured by his or her ability to:

- Create a strategy for dealing with these challenges.
- Analyze an event quickly based on the information available.

- Develop strategies to work with groups and issues.
- In making decisions, focus on the analysis of the problem and the impact on the present and future.
- Be empathetic when communicating his or her final decision.

In these days of volatile school politics, principals must establish a set of core beliefs and educational values. His or her values may be diametrically opposed to the community's beliefs about parental rights, student rights, consensus building, and accommodation of religious and social issues. The challenges that face the principal are not the issues in and of themselves but the legal consequences that evolve from a stakeholder's interest in litigation.

CONCEPTS OF POLITICS

"Politics" as it is defined in this chapter is a form of social conflict grounded in differences among groups about values subsidized by public resources to meet individual needs (Wirt and Kirst 1997a). This predictable disagreement between and among groups with different values leads to social conflict. In some cases, individuals work through the conflict privately; if you don't like the prices at the grocery store or your next door neighbor, you can choose to shop at another store, move, or ignore your neighbor. Easton (1965) argues that the political system governs conflict by directing the allocation of values and resources. Politics is the result of value differences among diverse groups as they affect the governance system. These group leaders attempt to secure the values they hold sacred by using the political system to create public policy. In the case of schools, the object is to influence campus or district policy in a way that is compatible with the values of the group. Schools are political systems because they allocate resources and values to children, teachers, and community stakeholders in the same fashion, as does the U.S. Congress, state legislatures, and local boards of education. For example, various groups want specific issues addressed by the principal. When the principal is required to select only a few of these issues due to financial constraints and when a gap exists between the groups' wants and the school's resources, social and political pressure emerges.

The political model is an accurate description of organizational decision making. Elements of the political model include:

- Stakeholders attempt to influence school decisions at all levels of the organization.
- The foundation of this model is based on the decision maker. All decision makers, whether individual or group, work with the same set of community stakeholders: superordinates, subordinates, peers, customers, and the values, goals, and motivations of the decision maker.
- Stakeholders make demands on decision makers when appropriate.
- Decision makers with power over stakeholders make decisions autonomously.
- When power resides in the chain of command, the power resides with the decision maker's superordinate.
- Organizational direction is developed by the cumulative effect of all decisions.

Power is the ability to exert influence over others even when those others resist. Power can be hierarchical or influential. Hierarchical power comes with the position in an organization and is generally attached to the position. A principal has hierarchical power over students, custodians, teachers, and staff by the position he or she holds and by the ability to influence his or her superordinate. School policy provides the tools for this type of power.

Influential power comes from outside the organization and is grounded in community longevity, wealth, or family relationships. Principals must understand that influential power is outside of their control and they have very little opportunity to influence the holders of this power. Neither school policy nor position authority affect influential power.

Are schools political because they are part of the state or national governments or are they political in and of themselves? Perhaps schools are miniature political systems. Regardless, the vast majority of teachers and parents would like to view schools as "apolitical," meaning they have nothing to do with politics. By definition what happens on the school campus is highly political and is becoming more political as the state government, the national government, and parents attempt to influence curriculum, academic standards, and extracurricular programs. In the not so distance past principals were rather isolated from the political pressures that were associated with the superintendent. However, with time comes change, and now one would discover very quickly that principals face the same political pressures as do superintendents. While the political issues may be different, the reality is the same. It is not uncommon for parents to develop grassroots initiatives concerning curricular issues that they hold in high regard. Some of these issues are faith based and some are values based but the bottom line suggests that these parents are a force that principals must take the time to address.

Figure 16.1 outlines the flow of political influence operating in the school's political organization. These events represent the challenges that schools face and the process that concludes in operationalizing the events through administrator decision making.

Wirt and Kirst (1997b) argue that the framework outline in figure 16.1 is more than a single allocated process, that it represents the larger issue of how many events exist. State and national events affect the demands on schools created by several single-issue groups. These inputs are processed through the school's political system and emerge as outputs. Outputs arrive in the form of state legislation, school board policy, voter decision, and superintendent directives. The outputs are implemented and the results are returned to the political system in the form of outcomes. These outcomes will receive the scrutiny of time and evaluation with some of these issues returning to the school's political system in the form of demands. This fluid political scheme is ongoing and self-correcting, which by definition makes it a system.

According to Wirt and Kirst (1997a), parents became more than participants in the school as they became more educated. In 1960, one in twelve parents had a college degree, but by 1993 one in five parents had earned a bachelor's degree. At the turn of the twenty-first century, parents are more knowledgeable and feel empowered to question their child's academic direction. At the same time, taxpayers are attempting to redistribute school wealth as a means of reducing school taxes. The 1973 U.S. Supreme Court ruled in the *Rodriguez* case that school district wealth in relation to student expenditure was not unconstitutional, but pressure to redistribute school resources has been under constant pressure from antitax groups. While the antitax leagues have gone underground, they still

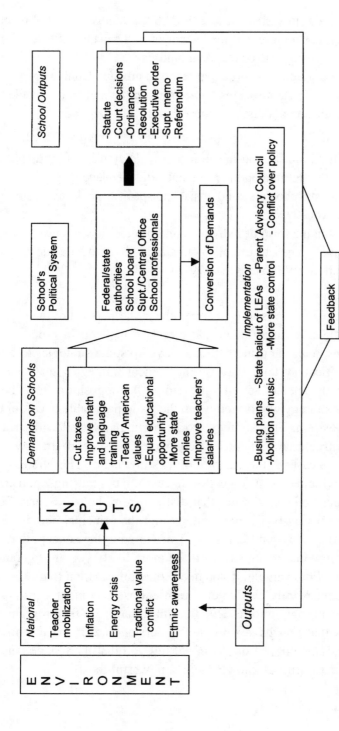

Figure 16.1.   The Flow of Influences and Policy Consequences in School's Political System.
Source: F. M. Wirt and M. W. Kirst. (1997). *Schools in conflict: The politics of education*. Richmond, CA: McCutchan. Copyright © 1997 by McCutchan Publishing Corporation, Richmond, CA 94806. Used by permission of the publisher.

have the potential to surface at any time. Both college educated parents and antitax groups represent a small segment of the many political groups that attempt to change the educational landscape.

In the political arena, the principal receives pressure from many groups and individuals. These pressures come from within and from outside the school's organizations. Pressures come from:

- The central administration in the form of policy directives, rules, and procedures that intrude on the principal's independence
- Community stakeholders who insist on specific goals and reinforce their wants vocally
- The faculty in the form of individual and professional interests
- The principal's need to establish standards for academic success and student welfare (Wirt and Kirst 1997a)

The principal's role is to influence others and make sure the organization functions in an efficient and effective manner. In order to accomplish this goal, the principal must develop some strategies to manage the political system. One of the typical strategies that can be employed is the ancient activity of dividing the opposition. The divide and conquer strategy works well when the principal is able to co-opt the weaker opposition. This strategy works particularly well with groups that are unstructured and loosely connected. A second strategy that works in some cases is the creation of a "straw man." This strategy requires the principal to change the discussion by causing opposition groups to focus on straw issues that distract from the real issues. Controlling information is another strategy that the principal could use in working through any political issue. This supports the concept that the more you know in a given situation the more likely you are to control that situation. For example, if you need some information to make a report that is not readily available, you might ask a computer programmer to write a program to retrieve that information. If the programmer understands that you have a limited understanding of the machinery and the program code, he or she might tell you that there is no way to get that data. Control of knowledge is a powerful tool.

POLITICAL IMPLICATIONS FOR PRINCIPALS

The principal who can identify and accurately monitor the potential competitors of the school creates a big advantage for the political life of the school organization. The principal can identify the competitors by asking the question: Who would oppose the school if we wanted to increase our instructional budget? In answering this question, the list that develops seems to be endless but just consider the government entities that compete for tax revenues:

- City government
- Other schools
- Police departments
- Fire departments
- Public hospitals
- Senior citizen programs
- Public libraries

This list could be expanded manyfold and in your community the list of competing government agencies would be different. One way to monitor these agencies to find out what they are interested in accomplishing is to read the local newspaper and listen to local radio and television. In addition, principals need to establish and nurture a network of community leaders. Participating in community service organizations, such as chambers of commerce, Lions, Kiwanis, or Rotary Clubs, is a good way to stay attuned to the community "grapevine." Members of these organizations often know several months ahead of stories that might be read in the newspaper. Principals must never forget that politics is more about resources and values than any other issue. Principals competing for resources need all of the information they can secure.

Principals need to understand that political success is most often about timing. Finding the "window of opportunity" when community groups and businesses are willing to listen to issues and ideas is essential to the success of any change in resources or values. Recognizing when the window is open is of primary importance for political success because it is at this time that the principal must be ready to move to implement the policy or value change in the school. The window of opportunity is most predictably open when a new superintendent begins to take control of the school district (Fowler 2000). This happens because the new incumbent to the superintendent's office is more willing and able to implement politically difficult changes. In some cases, this situation is referred to as the "superintendent's honeymoon" and is generally considered to last anywhere from six months to a year.

Skills need to be developed that allow principals to be successful and at the same time reduce the negative effects of problems. In some instances, all of the skill and training a principal has accumulated might not be enough to solve a problem. With the beginning of parental involvement, school politics has become volatile and most unpredictable, thereby requiring that principals must have closely held beliefs and core values. Problem analysis, judgment, and creativity form the framework for working with political issues effectively.

Principals must be informed about the issues that will divide the community. This is especially true when trying to understand the beliefs and values of special interest groups and how they affect the school. A principal who understands his or her community will know the strategies and influences that extremist groups bring to the political arena. However, the best principal and the most astute political observer cannot solve all of the political issues that face the school. A formula does not exist for deciding how to handle the political "hot potato," but the principal can affect the outcome of problems by increasing the number of positive resolutions (Howe and Townsend 2000). Principals can choose to react to situations in many different ways, some more positive and some less positive than others. Exhibit 16.1 lists twenty-five statements that principals can use to judge their personal strategy for creating positive or negative consequences for themselves and their school. No right or wrong answers exist to these questions, but they do reveal the political skills the responder possesses.

Answering these questions provides you the opportunity to assess your ability to handle political conflict and community concerns. Reflecting on your responses should provide you with information about the type of community that fits your leadership style.

Answer the following questions by reading and selecting how you would react to each statement by marking 1, 2, 3, 4, 5 where 1 indicates "I never do this" and 5 indicates "I always do this." Select the position along the 5-point scale that best fits where you reside. Assess yourself accurately because there are no right or wrong answers.

	Never 1	2	3	4	5 Always
1. I encourage those with differing opinions to express those opinions to me.	1	2	3	4	5
2. I understand the agendas of the groups that interact with the school.	1	2	3	4	5
3. I encourage faculty, support staff, and community input as I work to resolve problems.	1	2	3	4	5
4. I find time to handle a problem thoroughly.	1	2	3	4	5
5. I take notes when people express their concerns to me.	1	2	3	4	5
6. I know when a problem is serious enough to call my superior.	1	2	3	4	5
7. I know when to call legal counsel.	1	2	3	4	5
8. I think of alternative ways to solve problems.	1	2	3	4	5
9. I test each of the solutions for possible outcomes.	1	2	3	4	5
10. I respond to requests in a timely manner.	1	2	3	4	5
11. I ask colleagues or superiors for feedback on my ideas.	1	2	3	4	5
12. I seek feedback about the possible consequences of my ideas.	1	2	3	4	5
13. I avoid making emotional decisions.	1	2	3	4	5
14. I treat people fairly.	1	2	3	4	5
15. I discuss with my superior my concerns over ethical decisions made at the district level.	1	2	3	4	5
16. I refuse parental requests that have negative implications for students.	1	2	3	4	5
17. I reflect on how my decision for one student/parent/group could affect others.	1	2	3	4	5
18. I tell those affected by a decision what the decision is.	1	2	3	4	5
19. I tell those affected by a decision the reasons for my decision.	1	2	3	4	5
20. I make my final decision based on doing the right thing.	1	2	3	4	5
21. I spend time reflecting on the quality of my decisions.	1	2	3	4	5
22. I avoid letting stereotyping or prejudices influence my decisions.	1	2	3	4	5
23. I deal with the individual apart from the group to which he or she belongs.	1	2	3	4	5
24. I look for points of agreement even with disagreeable people.	1	2	3	4	5
25. I visit the community to see where my students live, play, and worship.	1	2	3	4	5

Exhibit 16.1. Principal Political Awareness Inventory

Source: M.L. Howe and R. Townsend. (2000). "The Principal as politcal leader." *High School Magazine*, 7 (6). Reprinted by permission.

POLITICAL CULTURE

The political culture of any school is subsumed by the expression "that's the way we do things in this school." It is a collective way of describing the political process for a school. Over the life of a principal and certainly from the dedication of a school overtime to the present, the political culture is created. The development of fund-raisers, school open houses, athletic events, and spelling bees crystallize into the culture of the organization and soon become part of the political culture. Fowler (2000) states that political scientists have categorized political cultures into the following three concepts: traditionalistic, moralistic, and individualistic. The interesting part of these three concepts is that they represent, in a very general way, specific sections of the United States.

Traditional political culture is the dominant political philosophy in the south. The characteristics of this political culture support the concepts of an established elite and concern for commercial trade (Fowler 2000). The idea of the "good ole boy" system in one context and in another context the highly educated elite are all tied together by family and social relationships directed toward maintaining the status quo. The traditional political culture surfaces in the schools in the form of family connections and personal relationships. Working in a school with a traditional political culture requires the principal to develop strong personal relationships, recognize social connections, and understand the power of the family. If Forsythe Elementary School were located in an area composed of a politically traditional culture, Ms. Mills would need to understand the relationship between Ms. Right and Ms. Soccermom. Is this relationship bounded by family ties, social connections, or personal relationships? Since Ms. Mills knows that the relationship was spawned at a social gathering, she would be persuaded that the political connection was social and probably educationally elite. It is important for Ms. Mills to identify the social elite because they will be active participants or have close relationships with those who are active. Ms. Mills must understand that it is essential that Ms. Right and Ms. Soccermom keep the support of this group. In addition, Ms. Mills should have made an attempt to find out what the local education traditions were and to never surprise the elite, but instead use the social network to create new policies and programs.

The dominant political culture for the northeast, selected states in the western Rocky Mountains, and a few Midwestern states is the moralistic political culture. This political philosophy surrounds itself with concepts that remind us that politics is a public activity, for the public good, and in the public interest. These concepts motivate people to participate in government and on boards of education and to actively debate issues of common interest (Fowler 2000). Individuals who subscribe to this political culture expect to be involved in the governance of the school. A principal leading a school in this context must be willing to communicate openly with all community stakeholders using newsletters, open meetings, reports, and electronic information. Principals need to identify their educational principles and values; they should be able and willing to defend these principles and values with data supported from reputable research literature (Fowler 2000).

If the Forsythe Elementary School context was politically moralistic, Ms. Mills failed to recognize the need to communicate to all community stakeholders the wishes of the faculty concerning the whole language/phonics debate. Had she recognized the political context of the school, she could have published information in newsletters, placed information on the school website, written a series of articles for the local newspaper, and perhaps appeared on local radio and television explaining the educational reasoning that supported the decision. Instead, Ms. Mills created the impression that the school was trying to implement the whole language concept behind closed doors. In this situation, was Ms. Mills trying to hide information from the community? On the one hand, perhaps she knew how controversial this reading debate had become on the state and national scene and was trying to avoid a community dialogue, and on the other hand, perhaps she did not take the time to understand the politics of the local community. Either way, it appears that the debate will take place in the political arena.

The individualistic political philosophy is grounded in the utilitarian concept of government nonintervention and it supports the idea of non-ideological politics (Elazar 1984). This culture is grounded in the concept of mutual obligation and loyalty in the strictest since. An example of mutual obligation would entail the school providing several rooms for meetings of the city council at no cost and in return the city council would grant the school exclusive rights to the use of a city park for the schools play days at no cost. The priority for a principal working in this political culture is an efficient, effective, business-like operation and if individuals abuse the concept it can become corrupt (Fowler 2000). The caution for principals engaging in political activity in this culture type is the possibility of corruption, so it is important to work behind the scenes. If the dominant political culture in the Forsythe Elementary School area was grounded in the individualistic culture, how could Ms. Mills have avoided the eminent political debate? Utilizing the attributes of the individualistic culture, Ms. Mills would have known that she needed to work with members of the community by supporting their issues so that she would have retained their support for the whole language reading decision. Ms. Mills needed to engage Ms. Soccermom and Ms. Right in discussions so that the mutual obligation benefit meets all of the parties' needs. Ms. Mills must be careful about what favors she

---

For each of the following categories, "yes" answers suggest the presence of a given culture; the more "yes" answers in each category, the more dominant the culture.

Traditionalistic Political Culture
1. Is political participation viewed as a privilege for an elite few?
2. Do most political leaders belong to an elite group based on kinship or social ties?
3. Are government bureaucracy and civil service systems viewed negatively?
4. Are most political conflicts played out within a single dominant party?
5. Is government's major role seen as maintaining the existing status quo?

Moralistic Political Culture
1. Is widespread political participation valued?
2. Are issues and principles important, especially in political conflicts?
3. Are government bureaucracy and civil service systems viewed positively, as a way to have impartial government?
4. Do two parties exist with different ideological platforms, supplemented by occasional third-party activity?
5. Is government's role seen as advancing the common good?

Individualistic Political Culture
1. Is politics viewed as a "dirty" marketplace best left to the few professionals?
2. Do two political parties exist that are business-like organizations, characterized by a high level of cohesiveness and competition between themselves?
3. Is remembering one's political debts and paying them off in an appropriate manner important?
4. Are government bureaucracy and civil service systems viewed ambivalently— efficient but too restrictive of the system of mutual favors?
5. Is government's major role seen as favoring economic development?

Exhibit 16.2. A Framework for Analyzing the School's Political Culture
Source: F.C. Fowler. (2000). Policy studies for educational leaders. Upper Saddle River, NJ: Merrill. Reprinted by permission of Pearson Education, Inc. Upper Saddle River, NJ 07458

agrees to accommodate and she would be wise to work behind the scenes, through third parties, or utilize back channels to gain support.

Principals must analyze the community culture if they are going to be successful in the political life of the community. Fowler provides a list of questions that help the principal assess the culture. Exhibit 16.2 provides a framework to be used to analyze the school's political culture.

Using the questions in exhibit 16.2, a principal could use this tool to decide how to advance the political needs of the school. Principals need to understand both the political culture and the political structure in the context where they work. This is a complex task that needs continuous reflection in order to avoid the pitfalls that may surface in any political context. It is certainly better for the principal to work within the political context than to work against it.

POLITICS OF SPECIAL INTEREST GROUPS

According to Lowi (1979), most political systems are based on the relationship between special interest groups, politicians, and government administrators. One of the big three political special interest groups at the national level are foundations that support the creation and dissemination of information. For example, the Carnegie Corporation of New York and the Rockefeller Foundation have been very active in providing resources for projects and philosophies that fit their political agendas.

The second of the big three special interest groups are the teachers unions and professional associations. Since the early 1970s, the National Education Association and the American Federation of Teachers have been involved in the teacher power and governance movement (Spring 1993). This activity moved these groups out of the boardroom onto the political stage at the local, state, and national levels where they participated in the development of state and national legislation that supported their governance agenda. Most of the time, these teacher associations would like everyone to believe that they are interested in high academic achievement and student welfare, but principals need to understand these groups are first and foremost interested in securing new members and leading the charge for increased teacher power and authority.

The third member of the big three special interest groups is the business sector. Since the early 1980s through the 1990s and now into the twenty-first century, businesses have successfully influenced education policy (Spring 1993). Businesses have never wavered from the concept that increased profits is their target. While many individuals would agree that the free enterprise system is founded on the aforementioned premise, it is nonetheless important to recognize that low wages and taxes are the profit attributes of successful business. Spring (1993) makes the connection between business and education when he points out businesses:

- Want schools to create well-educated workers at a low tax cost per unit
- Want schools to create a reduction in the cost of labor by developing an oversupply of workers
- Want schools to focus the curriculum on the skills needed by the employers
- Want schools to create compliant workers
- Want schools to teach a business mentality that focuses on business profitability

While principals must understand the big three special interest groups, they also must recognize that special interest groups are not always tied to a state or national issue. For example, the local parent–teachers organization, athletic booster clubs, band booster clubs, and academic booster clubs would be considered special interest groups, albeit generally friendly school groups. The principal must recognize the purpose for these groups and make every attempt to know the group's leadership. The principal's role is not to control these groups but to manage their activities in such a way that will allow the groups' activities to reflect a positive light on the school. If the principal is going to accomplish the task of working with these groups, he or she must understand the issues each group supports; develop strategies for responding to requests of individuals or subgroups of the whole; understand the positive and negative aspects that each group has on him or her, faculty, and the stakeholder community; understand the kinds of challenges that the special interest group brings to the table; and understand the skills needed to respond to requests in an empathetic manner (Howe and Townsend 2000).

Perhaps the most influential special interest group is the teacher cohort. Most principals would not consider teachers in the same vein as they do other groups that lobby the school. The reality facing today's principal is that teachers are a powerful special interest group. In several states site-based decision making has become the mantra of teacher groups as they attempt to govern schools. Over the past several years it has become evident that principals have bought into the idea that site-based decision making is a better way of governing the school. Much has been written and discussed about the concept of collaboration in terms of teacher–principal working relationships. The concept of site-based decision making is mostly about governance of school; in simpler terms, who is in charge of the school, teachers or the principal? The fundamental question that must be addressed is: What evidence exists that demonstrates that students achieve at a higher level in a school governed by a site-based decision making or collaborative governance model? Greenblatt, Cooper, and Muth (1983) discover that the relationship between teacher participation and student-perceived teaching quality is curvilinear rather than direct. They deduce that the best teaching quality occurs where teachers think of themselves as consultants to students rather than knowledge purveyors. Instructional quality is lower in authoritative and high participatory school settings. Weiss (1993) discovers that teachers in site-based decision-making settings feel more professional but these feelings do not translate into increased teaching. While this may be good for teachers, it's not a great deal for students. While the teacher groups try to make the connection between achievement and governance by saying that happy and empowered teachers do a better job in the classroom, the empirical evidence indicates that such is not the case. The empirical relationship between site-based decision making and student achievement does not exist. Teacher groups have sold and principals have purchased the idea of collaboration and site-based decision making as tools to increase student achievement. The truth seems to indicate that the aforementioned concepts are mostly about who is in charge of the school organization. Teachers are involved in lobbying groups through their professional associations and they have done a stellar job of selling a straw house. Principals must respect teachers for what they do with children in the classrooms but they also must recognize the fact that teachers are one of the strongest special interest groups with which principals must work. Conway and Calzi (1996) argue that involving teachers in management decisions might lead to serious problems. The test for any educational concept is how does it affect students in the teaching and learning process? Perhaps the answer is right in front of us but the blinders of political influence and special interest have dimmed our view of the truth.

One of the biggest challenges that face principals is getting beyond the idea that all teachers are in teaching for the right reasons, that is, to do what is in the best interests of the children in school. No principal likes to deal with negative staff members, but good principals do this routinely. The goal for principals in dealing with negative teachers is improving in the way they work with students, colleagues, and the community. This does not mean they will turn into the best teachers, but they need to stop being our worst. Whitaker (1999) argues that the best advice he ever got was "You don't have to prove who's in charge" when referring to working with difficult teachers. The politics of working with these difficult teachers is not giving them power because too often principals make decisions based on the faculty troublemakers. For example, when considering a new program or teaching assignments how often do you consider the teacher who complains the most? The fact remains teachers with strong personalities will take advantage, through intimidation, of other faculty members and in many situations the principal is intimidated as well. These individuals can almost always be spotted sitting near the door, in the back of any meeting, and always together.

Whitaker (1999) suggests the following strategies for working with the politically difficult faculty.

- Reverse the arrangement of the meeting room so that the back is now the front and vice versa
- Remove all the extra chairs in the room so that as much physical closeness as possible is created
- Have your assistant principal come into the meeting last and sit by the difficult faculty members
- Remove the chairs from around the back tables and use them as places to put snacks for the meeting

The goal for any principal dealing with politically influential faculty is reducing their power so that the best faculty members have a chance to change and grow the school. It is the principal's responsibility to make sure that students are receiving the best possible education and one way to make sure this is happening is to render the politically powerful ineffective.

When the principal has identified a special interest group that is in opposition to the school's position, he or she needs to assess the group's political strength, its leadership, and its willingness to meet privately. Communication with the leadership helps clarify the opposition's positions on the issue. This communication also helps the principal discover early on what the group wants done (Hughes and Hooper 2000). The decision the principal needs to make in relation to the special interest group is compromise or fight. If the choice is to compromise, it must be done prior to any public discussion of the issue. It is almost impossible for any group to change its position on an issue once the position becomes public information because ego and pride become the major points of concern, not the original disagreement.

If the principal values the issue and feels it is in the best interests of students and teachers, it is time to fight. President Harry Truman used the following five steps when issues became confrontational:

- Inventory your resources—who can you rely on and to what level.
- Calculate approximately the resources of the enemy.
- Define the goals you want to attain, define the outcomes you desire, and develop a plan.
- Implement your plan.
- Sell your plan to leaders and mass your forces to attack.
- Attack, attack, and attack. (Hughes and Hooper 2000)

Most principals would rather compromise than fight even when they know they are supporting the right issue for the right reasons. In most situations, the special interest group plans for you to compromise because that is how it gets what it wants. It might fit your needs to compromise because you neither have the support or energy to carry out the fight, but far too many schools lose control when they compromise. Schools lose when they compromise because issues are never divided straight down the middle—one side or the other manages the superior position.

LOCAL SCHOOL POLITICS

The politics at the local level has changed since the early 1990s when two patterns of political control emerged: (1) state centralization in the form of high-stakes testing, and (2) site-based decision making. Site-based decision making is controlled by the requirements created by state legislatures and high-stakes testing. If national tests are developed, the content and control of the curriculum will take precedence over anything the state might wish to require.

In local politics, the type of community dictates the type of school board and the type of superintendent that is hired to operate the district. Spring (1993) suggests that four types of community power structure exist:

- Dominated
- Factional
- Pluralistic
- Inert

The community's rich control the dominated community. This may be a group of wealthy individuals or in some communities one person controls the local politics. You might discover that these wealthy individuals all come from the same religious, ethnic, or political affiliations. This type of political power would most likely be found in a small town or an urban area where one industry dominates the community's economy. In this type of community, you would never find much opposition to the wishes of the wealthy political leaders. The school board in this type of community almost always shares the values and beliefs of the wealthy elite (Spring 1993). In some instances, the power structure operates behind the scenes and directs the control of the superintendent. Seldom will candidates for the board be opposed in the election process. The board almost always supports the values established by the wealthy and very seldom does the majority on the board ever swing to any group not represented by the economic elite (McCarthy and Ramsey 1971).

The superintendent hired by a dominated school board will reflect the values and act in the interests of the controlling political belief. This person is in no position to be creative with the school policies. In this political model, the superintendent carries out the policies of the board, never questioning the value of the policies. What effect does the dominated political structure have on the principal? If the superintendent is receiving his or her orders from the school board and in some cases from a power group outside the board, the principal is going to experience the same pressures, as does the superintendent. Whatever the superintendent values, the principal will value in his or her manner. In this type of community, principals are going to receive special requests for children of the politically wealthy and if the principal chooses to ignore the request he or she will surely hear that same request in the form of an order from the superintendent. Principals working in a dominated community need to understand where the political power lies. This means knowing and using the values of the political elite to the advantage of the school.

The factional community is dominated by conflict. Various political factions that reside in the community generate this conflict. These factions may be based on race, religion, ethnicity, school taxes, and in some college communities the town people at odds with the college community. According to Spring (1993), religion is a frequent cause of factionalism. Religious arguments over the teaching of evolution or creationism, birth control, abortion, and sex education create a political explosion. In some contexts, school taxes are opposed by groups of people because they oppose all forms of government taxation. In many cases, school board elections are hotly contested with factions campaigning for their candidates. Factional school boards are dominated by individuals who are, in most cases, single-issue political radicals. Each time this school board attempts to hire a superintendent, each faction attempts to influence the hire toward an individual who supports its values. This makes the employment of any individual extremely tenuous since the majority on the school board could change at the next election. A superintendent attempting to work in this environment must, as a political strategist, show no favoritism, attempt to balance the factions, use board committees, and maintain a community silence on issues of great conflict.

The principal working in a factional school must make every attempt to make sure both sides feel he or she is working for their side. Principals should always use large committees composed of a real cross section of community members to study issues that affect the majority of the community stakeholders. Any negative feeling about the direction of the school created by the committee's decision can be directed back to the committee and not the principal. Large committees provide a sounding board for all types of ideas and in some instances the committee reports can reduce the conflict and the emotions that are tied to the issue. In this type of environment, the principal must understand and be able to utilize several political strategies, including silence, remaining neutral, and using committees liberally.

The pluralistic political community has gone through the dominated and factional phases of politics to a time when groups tended to not form lasting coalitions (Spring 1993). This type of community is usually willing to listen to the facts before making any type of decision and board members represent a wide variety of groups (McCarthy and Ramsey 1971). Committees are used to investigate and report to the school board and the superintendent. Boards in the pluralistic community are generally interested in getting the facts and creating good policy for the children of the district. Board members, in the pluralistic community, are almost always elected because they represent some special interest group. If possible, this community would prefer to use a caucus to select individuals to run for the board of education. In the pluralistic community, the superintendent serves as an advisor to the school board and moves slowly in creating change in the school system. The superintendent should study each board member to determine what the board values. The best way for the superintendent to accomplish the role of adviser is to surround him- or herself with competent advisers. The role of the superintendent moves from adviser to decision maker depending on the attitude of the board.

A principal working in a pluralistic community must understand the various roles of the superintendent and be prepared to assume some of those roles at the school. In some instances, the principal will be a decision maker and in other instances the principal will be an adviser to the superintendent. The secret to being a successful principal in the pluralistic community is knowing when to function in the various roles and what strategies to utilize in each of the roles. One strategy that a principal must be able to use is that of providing expert advise to the superintendent, the board, and to the community stakeholders. This strategy requires the ability to communicate in a two-way conversation with those community members interested in any issue. Having the community understand the issue and the facts tied to that issue is of the utmost importance.

The inert political community is homogeneous with little diversity in thought, ethnicity, religion, or race. Special interest groups are a part of the community but maintain little or no power (Spring 1993). Most members in this community are proud individualists wanting nothing more than to be left alone to live life. Board members represent themselves and are hardly ever influenced by special interest groups. In this political structure, the superintendent has a great deal of influence and power—influence over who will get elected to the school board and the power to be the sole decision maker for the district. In this context, the superintendent controls the type and amount of information the school board receives, utilizes the back channel to work with board members, and avoids conflict at all costs. In this political community, board members rely on the administrative team for leadership and almost always support the recommendations of the administration.

The principal in this situation relies heavily on the superintendent for power and direction. On all school-related issues, the principal will attempt to influence the community stakeholders by working behind the scenes to generate support for any issue. In most situations, the principal will be given credit for his or her knowledge and the community will support the values established by the principal. In order to work behind the scenes of any school, the principal must know the influential members of the community.

All of the administrators in each of the political types described must fit that community's political culture and maintain its values. Perhaps the first activity that any applicant for a principalship should undertake is that of determining the political type of the school and community to assess the "goodness of fit" for him- or herself. The goodness of fit concept is most important when applying and accepting any principalship. Measuring your strengths against the needs and political landscape of the school should be well thought out. It makes little since for a person who wants to avoid conflict to work in a factional community and likewise a person who wants to be the constant and only decision maker should avoid the dominated community unless his or her values are in direct alignment with the economic elite of the community.

In analyzing the Forsythe Elementary situation, Ms. Mills probably should have analyzed the political type of the Fort Spirit School District prior to making a decision about the reading program. Which one of the political types outlined earlier comes closest to fitting the Forsythe situation? Not knowing a great deal about the school district, the pluralistic political type appears to fit the school and the district. There does not appear to be a factional board of education, nor do we see a dominant political structure. We do see a superintendent who appears to give direction to the board and does not always support principals when their values are not compatible with his own and perhaps those of the board members. If you were to analyze your school and district, what would you discover?

Once the principal determines the community and board type, it is time to find out who holds the power and influences community decisions. Three of the more widely known techniques used to study power and influence are the:

- Reputational model
- Event analysis model
- Demographic studies model (Hughes and Hooper 2000)

The reputational model (Hughes and Hooper 2000) requires individuals involved in civic affairs to be asked who the influential members of the community might include. The list of names is generated, a select panel of community leaders is brought together, and the list is reduced to a final list. The third step in this process is to interview each member on the final list to determine his or her thoughts about how the community makes decisions about specific issues. After the interviews are concluded, the data that has been gathered should provide the principal with a list of the powerful and influential members of the community. Could the principal use this model in his or her community? Perhaps not with the current state of resources in most school districts. Perhaps step one, asking people in the community who the influentials are in the community, might be doable and even part of step two might be accomplished.

The event analysis model (Dahl 1961) requires that several community activities be identified, such as education, welfare, and business development. After identifying the activities, individuals involved in these activities are asked to select the most significant event in their area in the past few years. Once these events are selected, data is collected from newspaper, board minutes, and interviews in an attempt to reconstruct the activities that led up to the decision. The last step is analyzing the data generated by the community power structure. This model suggests that different community activities have different influentials and power brokers. Once again, the entire structure of this model would be impossible for the principal to undertake, but it seems possible to review current board of education minutes for clues about the district and how the various issues have been treated over the last two or three years.

The demographic model (Hughes and Hooper 2000) costs the least and it may be the most unreliable of the three models discussed. Collecting data on housing starts, telephone hookups, census tracts, and community drive-arounds provides some information about the community. From this data it may be possible to generate a general picture of the community. Making judgments about community power and influence based on demographic data is probably misleading at a minimum and dangerous if taken as fact. Principals need to be very careful that they do not get drawn into accepting this type of data as fact.

COMMUNICATION AND POLITICS

Communication is essential for an organization to be effective and schools are no different. Communication is affected by the perceptions of the groups involved. The symbols and messages that permeate the school organization can be altered and manipulated by the electronic and print media. The media impact on schools, according to Kirst and Wirt (1996), influences the policy-making function of schools by setting the schools' public agendas. If indeed the media influences schools' political agendas and the evidence to date, limited as it may be, supports the concept, how can principals change the perception of the community stakeholders? The answer seems to be communication.

The simple model of communication identifies a sender and a receiver with messages that are understood. The key to this model is the piece that says both the sender and the receiver understand the message. Senders are the sources for the messages and receivers are the ones to whom the messages are directed (Ellsworth and Stahnke 1976). Communication occurs when the original sender becomes a receiver. This feedback allows all of the participants to process what is being said from their own perspective. All communication is processed from the receiver's frame of reference, which is utilized to determine reliability and usefulness. In essence, each receiver practices selective perception by placing meaning on what is seen and heard. For example, a principal chooses to place either more or less significance on what a teacher would say based on the principal's perception of the teacher's ability in the classroom. If the principal sees the teacher as a competent, hard-working, and talented professional, more attention is given to the messages sent by the teacher. Selective attention and perception are the necessary prerequisites to selective retention. All of us remember concepts and ideas that fit our frame of reference and political communication is no different.

The key to political communication espoused by Ellsworth and Stahnke (1976) is the unification of ideological symbols that communicate meaning to divergent groups. Most politicians attempt to use words that fit the frames of reference for members of all groups. The lesson for principals is that they too must send their messages to receivers in words that fit the frame of reference of their schools' stakeholders, students, and teachers. For example, the three aforementioned groups can be persuaded to agree on a policy that identifies the level of attainment necessary to be promoted from one grade to the next when the contextual form is communicated in words that are understood and have an attached meaning.

With any communication comes the possibility that it will be misunderstood. The best way to avoid a communication glitch is to make sure you observe the following:

- Be concise by speaking and writing in short sentences.
- Make sure your purpose is clear.
- Know with whom you are communicating.
- Use action verbs to make your points.
- Use common-sense communication. (Bates 1978)

Most principals can learn to communicate utilizing the aforementioned concepts. It is not that principals don't know how to effectively get their messages out, it is more likely that they don't plan ahead and are communicating under pressure. Pressure situations generally change how people act, write, and speak. Principals need to take the opportunity to address their community stakeholders for two reasons: (1) to practice the art of oral communication, and (2) to get their message to the community.

Political communication is the link between the political system and the context of the school. It is communication that allows leaders to influence the community, students, and teachers. The inability to communicate with all groups hampers the sending and receiving of messages, thus, it is impossible to influence any issues. To be truly effective, political communicators administrators must be able to satisfactorily perform both orally and in writing. This means that the communication must be understood by all of the audiences and it must influence their behavior. This cannot be accomplished orally or in writing when the principal chooses to be eloquent, esoteric, or multisyllabic. At best, communication can be misunderstood. Principals must develop their oral and written communication skills if they hope to be a player in the world of politics.

ETHICAL DECISIONS

Should Principals Become Active Participants in the Politics of the School and Community?

Politics is a contact sport and principals need to know that when they get involved in political issues in a community. It is possible that they might find themselves on the losing end of a power struggle between two very aggressive groups. This political loss can and often does carry over to the principal in his or her school. The winning group on any issue will exert its power over people and attempt to influence issues outside of its original agenda. Principals need to understand that politics is an activity that should not be entered into as a secondary thought. Engaging in political conflict can become very personal and divisive and it will cost the losing side something.

On the other side of the issue, influencing issues that affect the school and students is part of the job description of a principal. If individuals are trying to influence the community stakeholders in a direction that is detrimental to students or teachers, it is the principal's obligation to communicate the harm or destructive aspects of this influence. By definition, this action requires the principal to become a politician as he or she attempts to ensure the record is accurate.

The questions that need to be answered concerning this issue are:

- How can the principal provide active political direction and at the same time remain somewhat neutral on issues that do not affect the school? The answer to this question is: The principal must choose only those issues that affect the school directly. Over time, the principal may create a power base for his or her position providing he or she is willing to use communication channels that are not of the public variety.
- Principals need to be aware of the political type of the community in which they work. Not knowing may play havoc with their position longevity and make them less effective in operating the school.

CHAPTER SUMMARY

The principalship has evolved from an "apolitical" position to one of being a central figure in the political life of a school. More than twenty-five years ago the district superintendent was considered the only educator to be affected by educational politics, but in the recent past principals have become the target of social pressures. Principals understand that specific groups attempt to force their beliefs on the school and its stakeholders. The effective principal demonstrates the ability to deal with challenges, analyze events, develop strategies, and be empathetic when making decisions.

Politics is defined as a form of social conflict grounded in differences among groups about values. This disagreement leads to social conflict. Schools are political systems because they allocate resources and values to children, teachers, and community stakeholders in the same fashion as does Congress, state legislatures, and local boards of education. This political model focuses on influence and power over other groups and individuals. The flow of political influence begins at the national, state, and local levels and surfaces in demands on schools and is converted to policy and court decisions.

Parents became players on the school's political radar when more parents became better educated. In 1960, 8.3 percent of parents had a college degree and in 1993 more than 20 percent of parents had a degree. This change has empowered parents to question their child's academic direction and almost every other school action. At the same time principals are receiving parental pressure. The central administration, community stakeholders, faculty, and the need to establish standards are also pressuring them.

Principals must develop strategies to manage the political system. One strategy that seems to allow the principals to manage the system is the concept of divide and conquer. If the principal can co-opt the opposition's values and principles, the principal will be successful in winning the battle. A second strategy is the creation of a straw man where the principal is successful in changing the discussion by causing opposition groups to focus on straw issues that distract from the real issue. Control of information is a strategy that any principal could use with any political issue. The more you know about any issue the more likely you are able to control the situation. For example, if you are not knowledgeable about the operation of computers and the code that makes them run, you are less likely to get the information you want from the machine.

Various groups in the community compete for all types of resources—financial, human, facilities, and influence. Political success against these various groups may be based on the window of opportunity when the community is willing to listen to your ideas. Principals must be informed about the issues that will divide the community and take steps to keep from getting involved in those issues.

The political culture of the school organization can be demonstrated by three concepts: traditionalistic, moralistic, and individualistic. These concepts describe the political cultures of boards of education and the types of superintendents and principals they would employ. Principals can analyze the community culture for their school by answering questions about each culture. It is very important for the principal to know the community political culture if he or she wants to be successful.

The big three special interest groups are foundations, teachers associations and unions, and business groups. These three groups attempt to press their educational agendas on the school and community. In addition, special interest groups can be found at the grassroots level created by single issues such as gender, ethnicity, and religion. Principals must understand how these groups attempt to get their agendas put in place, sometimes at all costs to the school and community. Many principals would rather compromise than fight even when they know they are right. Most of the time special interest groups plan for you to compromise because that's how they get what they want. Principals should compromise when they neither have the support nor energy to carry out the fight, but when they compromise they will lose control. Principals lose when they compromise because issues are never divided straight down the middle and one side manages the superior position.

The four types of political culture are dominated, factional, pluralistic, and inert. Each type has specific characteristics that provide information about the community, school board, and superintendent. Communities elect board members who in turn hire superintendents to carry out the policies and political wishes of the school board. Principals must be able to determine the political culture in the community if they are going to be successful in providing leadership to a school.

The principal in this situation relies heavily on the superintendent for power and direction. On all school-related issues, the principal will attempt to influence the community stakeholders by working behind the scenes to generate support for any issue. In most situations, the principal will be given credit for his or her knowledge and the community will support the values established by the principal. In order to work behind the scenes of any school, the principal must know the influential members of the community.

Communication is the lynchpin for any organization that wants to be effective and schools are no different. Communication is based on the perceptions of the groups involved. These symbols and messages that permeate the school organization may be altered and manipulated by the media, community stakeholders, and the professional staff. The principal must keep the messages simple and consistent so that real understanding can take place. The simple model of communication identifies a sender and a receiver with messages that are understood. The key to this model is the piece that says both the sender and receiver understand the message. The lesson for principals is that they, too, must send their messages to receivers in words that fit the frame of reference of their schools' stakeholders, students, and teachers.

CHAPTER ACTIVITIES AND QUESTIONS

1. Politics as it is defined in this chapter is concerned with social conflict. In your school, identify the teachers who influence the school's agenda and define the issue that these influentials attempt to control.
2. Is your school a political organization? If you would agree most schools are political organizations, then why do teachers and principals view themselves as "apolitical"?
3. Using an issue of major concern to you, use figure 16.1 to analyze your issue.
4. Political pressure on the principal comes from many sources, including the central administration through policy directives, rules, and procedures. What strategies should the principal use if he or she deems these directives counterproductive to the students and teachers?
5. What groups in your community compete for additional resources with the school?
6. Select an issue that you believe would divide your community and develop a plan to keep the issue from becoming a political nightmare for your school.

7. Select one of the three political cultures described in this chapter and determine which culture best fits your community. Write a two-page white paper on your analysis and discuss your thinking with the superintendent in an attempt to determine his or her analysis of the community.

8. Answer the questions on the Principal Political Awareness Inventory and reflect on your responses with another member of your administrative team to determine their perception of your accuracy in answering the questions.

9. Special interest groups attempt to influence school policy. Select a special interest group in your community and attempt to find out the group's leadership, major issues, and its strategy for influencing the community.

10. What type of community and school board does your district enjoy: dominated, factional, pluralistic, or inert? What factors influenced your decision and why?

CASE STUDY ACTIVITIES AND QUESTIONS

1. In analyzing the Forsythe Elementary situation, construct a plan that would keep the political activity of the community from dividing the faculty.

2. What clues existed that indicated that those opposing the whole language reading program would make a political issue of this curriculum change?

3. Write what you would have said to Ms. Right when you met with her, prior to her admission that she was supporting Ms. Soccermom and after she stated that she was indeed going to help her friend fight this battle.

4. Should Ms. Mills have anticipated the attack advertisement in the local newspaper and what could she have done to counter the ad?

5. Outline a strategy or "battle plan" that you would use to fight this political conflict if it were in your school.

6. Based on what you know about Superintendent Tucker, what strategies would you use in getting and maintaining his support throughout this conflict?

7. Which community stakeholders would you select to help you develop your campaign for the whole language concept?

8. Would you sanction Ms. Right through the school's evaluation process for unprofessional activity?
9. Draft an opinion piece for the local newspaper concerning whole language versus phonics reading. Should the process Ms. Mills used be part of this piece?

REFERENCES

Bates, J. D. (1978). *Writing with precision*. Washington, DC: Colortone Press Creative Graphics.

Conway, J. A., and Calzi, F. (1996). "The dark side of shared decision making." *Educational Leadership* 95 (7): 45–49.

Dahl, R. (1961). *Who governs*. New Haven, CT: Yale University Press.

Easton, D. (1965). *A framework for political analysis*. Englewood Cliffs, NJ: Prentice-Hall.

Elazar, D. J. (1984). *American federalism*. 3rd ed. New York: Harper and Row.

Ellsworth, J. W., and Stahnke, A. A. (1976). *Politics and political systems: An introduction to political science*. New York: McGraw-Hill.

Fowler, F. C. (2000). *Policy studies for educational leaders*. Upper Saddle River, NJ: Merrill.

Greenblatt, R. B., Cooper, B. S., and Muth, R. (1983). "School management and effectiveness: Finding the best style." Paper presented at the American Educational Research Association Conference, Montreal, Canada.

Howe, M. L., and Townsend, R. (2000). "The principal as political leader." *High School Magazine* 7 (6): 10–16.

Hughes, L. W., and Hooper, D. W. (2000). *Public relations for school leaders*. Needham Heights, MA: Allyn and Bacon.

Kirst, M. W., and Wirt, F. M. (1996). "Unexplored dimensions of 'political' in the politics of education field." Paper presented at the annual meeting of the American Educational Research Association (ERIC Reproduction Document Services no. ED 396 411).

Lowi, T. J. (1979). *The end of liberalism: The second republic of the United States*. New York: Norton.

McCarthy, D., and Ramsey, C. (1971). *The school managers: Power and conflict in American public education*. Westport, CT: Greenwood.

Spring, J. (1993). *Conflict of interests*. 2nd ed. White Plains, NY: Longman.

Weiss, C. H. (1993). "Shared decision-making about what? A comparison of schools with and without teacher participation." *Teachers College Record* 95 (1): 69–92.

Whitaker, T. (1999). "Seizing power from the most difficult teachers." *High School Magazine* 7 (2): 36–39.

Wirt, F. M., and Kirst, M. W. (1997a). *The political dynamics of American education*. Berkeley, CA: McCutchan.

———. (1997b). *Schools in Conflict: The Politics of Education*. Richmond, CA: McCutchan.

Chapter Seventeen

Economic and Policy Implications for the Principal

Manny Flores, principal of Cameron High School for the past ten years, was facing some pressure from the local business community to produce well-educated, low-cost workers for the community. Mr. Flores had never thought about the economic impact of the graduating seniors on the community and he was not concerned about the long-range effect of schooling on students. He was not aware that almost 30 percent of the families in his attendance area were headed by a single mother with no husband in the house and more than 32 percent of all family groups with children were single-parent groups.

Mr. Flores was not concerned with marketing his high school and did not see the need to prepare students to do anything except go on to college. Over the ten years that he had been principal at Cameron High School, the number of students who were attending colleges, universities, and further education had risen from 15 percent to 65 percent of the graduating student population. Even with this increase, community leaders were complaining about the number of quality workers Cameron High School was producing. Mr. Flores met with the Cameron Chamber of Commerce Leadership Council to figure out what the business community wanted from the high school.

The council appeared to want more students to become technically trained so that they could go to work right out of high school. The members of this chamber group acknowledged that Mr. Flores had increased the number of students going to college and getting further education, but they also wanted the high school to provide some school-to-work experiences for students.

The following morning Mr. Flores met with Superintendent J. B. Tucker to discuss a couple of student expulsions that were coming before the Fort Spirit Board of Education at Monday's meeting. Superintendent Tucker wanted to make sure Mr. Flores and his assistant principals had followed the proper policies and procedures in requesting the expulsions. Superintendent Tucker reviewed the procedures that were used and was satisfied that Mr. Flores had indeed followed the school district's due process policy for expulsions. Mr. Flores then told Dr. Tucker of his meeting with the chamber of commerce leadership and informed him about their discussions. Dr. Tucker listened intently but said nothing after Mr. Flores concluded his story.

Mr. Flores went back to his campus and discussed the conversation with the teachers at a faculty meeting on Thursday. Some teachers seemed concerned, but the vast majority had little interest in what the community stakeholders wanted from the high school. Ms. Watkins, a first-year teacher, approached Mr. Flores after the faculty meeting to express an interest in studying the economics and demographics of Cameron High School's attendance zone. She wanted to research this information for the school and thought it would make several good projects for her economics classes.

Ms. Watkins had her students research the number of new building permits issued by the city for their attendance zone and compared it with the number of building permits issued for the entire county to determine the increase or decrease in economic activity for the Cameron High School attendance zone. She and some of the students met with the staff of the chamber of commerce to see what kinds of economic data the chamber had accumulated. They found some labor force data, housing information, and the number of water and telephone hookups that had been documented in the last year. The students compiled an economic report that forecasted the economic future for the entire community and the Cameron High School attendance zone in particular. The students titled their report "Cameron High School's Best Guess for the Economic Future." Mr. Flores read the report and was impressed that Ms. Watkins had gotten the students to predict the economic future of Cameron.

As Mr. Flores began to read the report more closely, he discovered that this document would be useful in predicting the student population for Cameron High School for the next six to seven years. As he read some of the census data that the students had collected, he realized that the information before him contained data that could predict the number of children who might come from the families in his attendance zone. According to the numbers, it would not be very long before Cameron High School would grow from 1,700 students to 2,700 students over the next six- to seven-year period. He made an appointment to talk with Dr. Tucker about what he had discovered.

As Mr. Flores talked with Dr. Tucker, he quickly realized that the superintendent was not impressed with his predictions, even though he had the students' data and some information he had discovered himself using the census information. The conversation ended with Dr. Tucker thanking Mr. Flores for his work but assured him his predictions were not very close to reality. Mr. Flores was surprised at the reaction he had received from Dr. Tucker so he took his information to the Cameron Chamber of Commerce Leadership Council and shared what he had discovered. The council was impressed with the students' work and welcomed the report as part of its meeting minutes. Some members of the council were concerned with the information and some seemed skeptical about what it said. After the meeting, the chair of the leadership council pulled Mr. Flores aside to discuss the report further, indicating that perhaps he should not share this report with the school board or community since it might frighten some people into believing that a school bond issue would be needed to handle the rising enrollment at Cameron High School.

Mr. Flores was really confused because he thought that was what the leadership council was looking for when he first met with the group. Mr. Flores thought this report would help direct the programs of the future for Cameron High School. Confused by the reaction of the chamber and the superintendent, Mr. Flores began to ponder what he should do with the report: share it widely or put it in the vault? As he reflected on this situation, he began to realize how the economic implications of education affected the principal. In his situation, the implications were profound but no one wanted to listen. How could he make the policy makers at school and in the community understand what was about to happen to Cameron High School and the surrounding area?

More and more principals are seeing the need to monitor national demographics and collect local demographic data in order to predict what the future holds for their schools. Principals who take the time to analyze this data will be better equipped to structure their educational programs to meet the needs of students. Many principals are unaware of the demographic data, found in the federal census data, that can provide them with a good look at the future. City zoning boards are another place to look for information about the future of school attendance zones by viewing plans that tell the principal where single-family and multifamily housing will be constructed.

The school's role in the community's economic development is much more important than most principals would believe. The creation, attraction, expansion, and retention of jobs and income in the community are directly related to the quality of schools in the community. More than any single factor, the availability of a skilled labor force affects the attraction and retention of businesses, thus the attachment to schools.

The local economic development committee needs to work in conjunction with the school to gain widespread support for new business and industry. Community leaders from all facets of the community should staff this committee. Schools should be major players on this committee and principals must be part of the school contingent. This committee should:

- Investigate the advantages and disadvantages of attracting new business and industry for the community.
- Seek out businesses that would be beneficial to the community.
- Market the community to potential businesses.
- Conduct all recruiting of business and industry.
- Be the clearinghouse for all local resources in the recruiting process. (Sloggett and Woods 2001)

While most principals would not consider participation in this community activity, it is vital that they participate in order to understand the wants and needs of the community.

The economy is growing in the service sector much more rapidly than in the manufacturing sector. The implications for this change are the type of workforce that is needed to staff these enterprises. The service sector demands skilled and trainable productive labor. This is the value-added effect of a quality school and education. Principals have a community responsibility to make sure students are being prepared to academically and financially support themselves after graduation.

THE ECONOMICS OF SCHOOL ADVERTISING

Over the past several years, schools have considered the use of advertisement on building roofs, on school buses, and at various places on athletic fields. Most schools have attempted to avoid these advertisements but those that have enjoyed the economic benefits of advertising seem to have avoided any community repercussions. The economic benefits appear to be the major reason for allowing advertising on school district property. With decreasing budgets, schools have been supporting their revenue stream with dollars generated by the advertisers. If schools were fully funded, it would be unlikely that any of these initiatives would surface (National Association of State Directors of Pupil Transportation Services 2001).

Principals might want to consider advertisements on buildings and athletic fields, providing the board of education is willing to support the concept. A few court cases have addressed the issue of advertising on school property. In *San Diego Committee against Registration and the Draft v. The Governing Board of Grossmont Union High School District* (1986), the court ruled that the school did not have to take advertisements, but if it did it was open to the public. This decision was based on the right of a citizen to place an advertisement in a student newspaper and the school refused the ad (National Association of State Directors of Pupil Transportation Services 2001). The decision in this case appears to send a clear message that if you are going to accept advertisements for buses, buildings, and fields, you cannot limit it to selected specific advertisements. Supporters of advertisements argue that schools should establish committees of community stakeholders to create guidelines for the appropriateness of advertising. Criteria of this type could avoid the emptiness for a court case.

Moving from buses, buildings, and fields, some school districts have negotiated exclusive contracts for athletic wear. This means that all school athletic uniforms would contain the uniform provider's logo. In most situations, the school receives the athletic wear at a significantly reduced cost and student athletes can receive substantial discounts on athletic wear they purchase. Generally, schools solicit competitive bids for athletic equipment with the lowest bidder receiving the bid. The aforementioned advertisements on uniforms changes the outcomes of the bid process as athletic wear vendors reduce the costs and student athletes become walking advertisements. Colleges and universities have been signing exclusive contracts with major athletic vendors for several years and it is beginning to affect K–12 schools.

In schools across this country, advertising has invaded school libraries. Advertisements on computer search engines, Channel One, and book covers emerge as companies attempt to create brand recognition. Does a dichotomy exist between advertising in schools and intellectual freedom? Those who suggest that library advertising chips away at the students' ability to think critically would certainly oppose this form of intellectual intervention. Penner (2001) argues that advertising turns students into mindless slaves and makes us believe happiness is buying more things. She posits that library and school advertising is intrusive because the student cannot avoid viewing the marketing of the product or service. If you view the world through Penner's eyes, one might assume that *Blues Clues* might sponsor first-grade reading.

The reason that schools choose to advertise on buildings, buses, fields, and athletic wear is for the revenue it generates. The decision for the principals in deciding whether to allow this type of advertising is directed by school policy. In the absence of school policy, principals need to weigh the cost benefit of the generation of revenue. Does the benefit of additional dollars outweigh the political cost of implementing advertising and its effect on students? The case for advertising in school is mixed at best and is controversial in most contexts. If you are planning to implement advertising on school property, it would behoove you to make sure the issue is thoroughly discussed by all school stakeholders with a sense of support surfacing.

PREPARING THE COMMUNITY WORKFORCE

One of the issues that principals must face is the concept that the local schools are responsible for providing the community with workers for the business community. Some principals would not support the thought that student learning would be translated into a community workforce. The question becomes: Should the local schools be involved in developing programs that meet the needs of the local business community as well as preparing students for higher education? The context of the community may dictate the type of school-to-work programs the district provides, but all districts need to meet the needs of all students. In your community, you will find students who are talented in ways other than academically and you have a responsibility to provide programs that meet the needs of these students.

For many years, the term "apprentice" has been associated with various trades and not necessarily with high-paying jobs. According to Hashberger (2001), this entire concept is changing as apprenticeships begin to fill the void between jobs and the skills necessary to do these jobs. Apprenticeship programs that provide students with salable skills are more in demand than ever before. These programs provide careers for students in addition to the ever-present two- or four-year degree programs. This combination of on-the-job training and attached instruction provides students with skills that the normal educational program cannot and will not provide. For example, the student who wants to be an automotive technician can no longer expect to have the same skills as the traditional auto mechanic. The ability to read and understand highly sophisticated, computer-driven diagnostic equipment is mandatory if the automobile is to be repaired. The modern school may teach the theory of the internal combustion engine to students, but in most situations the school cannot afford the diagnostic equipment necessary to continue to teach students to be automobile technicians. The average auto tech can earn in excess of $100,000 a year. This is one example of many, including such occupations as HVAC and machine maintenance operators, robotics engineers, animal trainers, glass blowers, nurses, secretaries, bakers, machinists, and so on. The future for many students will be found in the service industries, rather than with a traditional bachelor's degree.

If you are one of those principals who believes that apprenticeship programs are for students who are academically challenged, think again. The apprenticeship programs provide full-time jobs and academic courses at the local community college at night. The apprenticeship programs require dedicated and ambitious students who are willing to make sacrifices in order to earn the training and knowledge they need to be successful. Principals need to understand that the apprenticeship programs help retain students in the community workforce. The apprenticeship program is an agreement between an employer and a person who wants to earn money while learning a skill (James 2001).

Principals must support the concept that a skilled labor force affects the community by determining which businesses stay in the community. They also must have working knowledge of what it takes to work smarter and more effectively for the community. Principals need to be directly involved in the communities' "one-stop" service centers that keep home-grown talent from slipping away. Principals know these students and have the power to persuade them to become part of the community (Nordenberg 1999).

Principals must be cognizant of the economy in their community and the surrounding areas. They attain this information from both the print and electronic media, including Web-based sources. Principals must know when new houses are being constructed in their attendance zones and what those houses cost. Fowler (2000) suggests a set of questions for analyzing the economics of the community:

- Is business increasing or decreasing?
- Are the businesses growing?
- Is shopping brisk or do businesses appear deserted?
- Is new construction underway?
- Are new houses selling rapidly?
- Is the food service industry on the rise?

Answers to these questions help provide the principal with information about the economy of the community and in turn help the decision-making process about educational programs.

The business cycle has implications for the funding level that schools will be able to attain. Guthrie and Koppich (1987) analyze the economy that surrounded four national reform movements: (1) the National Defense Education Act enacted after *Sputnik*; (2) the Elementary and Secondary Education Act during the Johnson administration; (3) Public Law 94-142 of the Education for Handicapped Children Act; and (4) the student accountability movement of the 1980s. When they compare these four reform movements with nine variables, only two emerge across all four reforms. What they discover is that each reform was supported by a specific activity such as *Sputnik* or the release of a commission report and that a surging economy provided the foundation for all four reforms. The conclusion that is drawn and the message for principals is that reform movements almost always happen when the economy is strong. Principals need to lay the groundwork for changes during slow economic times and implement these changes during robust periods in the economy. For example, the U.S. economy expanded at sustained rates never before seen from the mid-1990s through 2000. At the same time, the state and national policy makers increased the call for more educational reform. If principals are able to use the economic news to time their changes, they have a greater opportunity to enjoy a successful implementation. The message for all administrators is to pay attention to the business cycle.

The economic impact on education is found in two diametrically opposed concepts: "do more with less" or "do a lot more with a little more." Those who subscribe to the "do more with less" money concept believe that schools already have more money than they need to operate in an efficient manner. William Bennett, the secretary of education during the Reagan presidency, stated in a 1988 speech: "Money doesn't cure school problems" (Baker 1991, 628). Bennett's beliefs were structured around the ideas espoused by Hanushek, who studies the correlation between school district expenditure and student achievement. Hanushek (1994a) argues that the incentive structure in education needs to be changed, not the amount of money. The need to change the incentive structure has led to vouchers, charters, and other school choice models, all with one single concept: competition (Fowler 2000). Schools get better or go out of business.

The "do a lot more with a little more" crowd is willing to increase the resources for schools if the money is spent as it sees fit. Clune (1994) argues that schools should get more resources in order to bring all children to a specified minimum academic level with targeted schools receiving even more dollars. He believes that additional resources should be used to cultivate:

- Outcome-based learning
- Authentic assessment
- Integrated school services
- Higher-order thinking skills in students
- Professional development of teacher and administrators

Fowler (2000) believes that most current school finance models focus on educational productivity that imposes program and performance criteria. Educational productivity can be measured in many ways, but the most important aspect of productivity is student achievement.

EDUCATION IS AN INVESTMENT

State and local governments spend public money on education in order to satisfy their belief that education benefits the state and local community. In addition, the state and local governments suggest that the benefits of an education exceed the costs of having an uneducated workforce. An education is the state's way of making sure that students will have the necessary knowledge and skills to compete for good paying jobs and in turn will help the state economically (Hy 2000). The concept that an educated populace will reduce the social infirmities that have plagued countries where educating children is not held in high regard is important in the overall scheme of U.S. education. Policy makers value and support public education because they believe that an educated society leads to economic development (Fox, Murray, and Murray 1990). More than thirty years ago research found that personal income increases with education and it is still true today, among both men and women.

Increased expenditures for schools has had both a positive and negative effect on the economy. The assessment of financial success is dependent on how the money is spent. Spending money on educating children at higher and higher levels will not lead to increased personal income and tax revenues. State and local subsidy of education is necessary but only in proportion to achieved results. It is the responsibility of the principal to make sure that the cost-benefit factors of educating children are assessed. The principal is accountable to the public for making sure that the educational funds made available to the school are used to purchase a quality education for children.

Connecting the school inputs and outputs is a challenging task for the principal and certainly there is a mixed review when using input and output measures to assess the quality of student learning. Kazel-Thresher (1993) argues that early studies indicated a strong relationship between inputs, such as teacher quality, class size, and per pupil expenditure, while others did not. More recent studies have indicated a strong relationship between the quality of schooling and reading scores. Hanushek (1994b) finds that good teachers and incentive programs for students are two variables that increase student achievement. The Committee on Economic Development (CED) (1994) argues that principals must create a school organization that effectively promotes student achievement by ensuring that financial resources improve teaching. The CED states:

- Schools must allocate money more efficiently within current spending levels.
- Each school should have total control of these resources.
- Increase of dollars should be tied to the successful attainment of academic learning targets.

• Needs of students must be considered when taking resources into consideration.

Local policy makers need to provide principals with the authority and responsibility to manage and appropriate the resources that are allocated to the school. Stringent local finance policies make it very difficult for the principal to work with parents, teachers, and students in utilizing these resources.

Traditionally, the financing of public school has focused on the distribution of resources. In the past seven years, the focus has changed from the equitable distribution of resources to the issue of productivity. Productivity is measured by the efficient use of the resources in relationship to student achievement (Picus 2000). Over the past sixty years, the percentage of dollars spent on instruction has declined and the percentage spent on operations has increased. Picus (2000) cites statistics that in the 1990s instructional expenditures ranged from a low of 60.5 percent in 1991 to a high of 61.7 percent in 1995. He also states that 10 percent of the resources were used for student and instructional support, 3 percent for administration, 10 percent for operations, and 10 percent for other school and student needs.

The vast majority of school resources is allocated to personnel costs. These costs approach 80 percent of the budget in most school districts. When a principal looks at the school budget, the majority of the expenditures are allocated for faculty salary and benefits. When principals are asked why more of the budget doesn't go for instruction, the answer is that almost one-third of the budget goes for building maintenance and repair. According to Picus (2000), the percentage of teachers decreased by 33 percent since 1950, mostly in the form of instructional aides and pupil support personnel.

The argument continues to rage about the impact of additional dollars on schools. While the research is mixed about the results of increased spending on schooling, it is clear that money spent in an effective manner does increase student performance, especially in those instructional models that lower class size. Miles (1995) finds that if all those classified as teachers actually taught children, the average class size would be reduced from twenty-two students per class to thirteen students per class. The principal's role in allocating money is to get the most out of each dollar that he or she has available for expenditure. Dramatic results can be achieved in average class size and student achievement if the principal is willing to allocate resources for instruction in a creative manner. The key to this allocation is the analysis of staffing patterns and a less traditional way of delivering instruction.

SCHOOLS' DEMAND FOR SERVICES

Schools not only produce workers for community businesses, they also create a demand for services. These services come in the form of transportation, custodial, food, nursing, office supplies, and construction services. These services are vital to the daily operation of the school and the students. Without these local services, the school could not function in a productive and efficient manner.

Should the school use local vendors for its various needs if the product or service can be purchased at a lower price from vendors outside of the community? Some school districts purchase goods and services from local dealers regardless of the cost and in some cases local venders take advantage of the good will of the school by increasing the cost to the school. Principals need to be aware of the costs of goods and service and make every attempt to get the most good or service for the dollar spent.

The programs used to educate students control the school's demand for services. If the school utilizes the apprenticeship program, the community becomes a supplier of goods and services. These goods and services are returned to the community in the form of workers. This concept is very visible at the secondary level and less visible in the elementary schools. Elementary schools, while not directly involved with the development of workers for the community, vicariously provide the academic foundation for all workers in the community.

ECONOMIC IMPACT OF CLASS SCHEDULES

The development of a class schedule appears to have little to do with the economic impact that schools might have on a community. In many communities throughout the United States, the school district is by far the biggest employer and in many situations pays the highest salaries. For example, the school secretary may be the highest paid secretary in the community and may be a position of prestige and power. The bigger issue for most schools is the number of teachers, instructional aides, and special programs they implement. Reducing the average class size is always something that principals should attempt to incorporate in planning the class schedule. At the high school level, the debate continues to rage over the use of a block schedule versus the traditional six- or seven-period day schedule. Economically, the accelerated block schedule provides the smallest classes and the most teacher instructional time for the dollars spent. Calculate the number of teaching sections created by the accelerated block and compare that to the traditional six- or seven-period day over the course of an entire school and you will discover that more sections will be taught if teacher planning time is equal. Moving away from an accelerated block schedule would increase the need for additional teachers in almost every academic area, thus increasing financial costs for the district.

At the elementary level, the cost of instruction once again is subject to the type of scheduling that is done. The most expensive model is the self-contained classroom structure that most schools use. It would be much more cost effective to infuse a continuous progress learning environment where teachers work with similar types of learners and as they progress through the learning curve they move to another teacher. The use of instructional support personnel would be utilized to tutor students at each stage of learning, thus reducing the need for a total cadre of teachers. The teachers in this model are the experts and provide the direct instruction with instructional support helping students to master the intended learning. This model provides the most cost effective way of educating students and at the same time ensures a productive learning environment.

Schedules that utilize large amounts of human capital place an economic strain on the community. Infusing special programs into the learning environment increases the financial cost of student learning by a factor of two. Most schools escalate the cost of scheduling when they add special programs. This does not occur only in terms of increased personnel costs, it also increases the costs in terms of special equipment and classrooms. The difficulty in creating an elementary schedule is compounded by the number of pullout and special programs the school utilizes. These pullout programs require students to leave the regular instructional setting to go to a more specialized instructional, thus reducing the on-task learning time of one content area for another, which decreases the impact of both content areas.

It is highly unlikely that schools will assess the economic impact of their schedules any time soon. With a downward economic pressure on school budgets and an increase in costs, schools are going to need to assess how they educate their students. With the increased demands on state and local governments for increased funding for all their agencies, it appears that schools will continue to struggle financially. State and local policy makers give lip-service to increasing school resources but in reality very little is done to change the financial landscape.

POLICY IMPLICATIONS FOR THE PRINCIPAL

Schools are agencies of the state, just like the motor vehicle and health departments are state agencies (Alexander and Alexander 1998). Education policy has changed over the past several years due to the economic environment and its changes. Early in the 1980s, many states created new policy initiatives based on several national reports and the change in passing the economic burden on to the states. Keeping this in mind, principals are part of the organizational structure that develops rules and regulations. Principals need to understand that state departments of education establish broad-based rules and regulations, which are further refined by local boards of education, but it is the principal who operationalizes these rules and regulations. For this reason, it is the principal's responsibility to understand the policy process. For example, if the principal perceives that students and faculty are not driving at a safe speed in the school parking lots and several auto accidents have occurred in the parking area, understanding the policy-making process will help direct the course of action that the principal undertakes. If this policy discussion is just beginning, it would be wise for the principal to define the problem and to appoint a committee of students, teachers, and parents to create several alternative solutions prior to the implementation of a formal policy. In this particular situation, the principal needs to shepherd the policy recommendation through the process in the event that unintended consequences change the structure of the policy. In this case, the board of education might add content to the policy that would make the policy unenforceable.

The unintended consequences that policies generate can be both harmful and destructive for the principal. Policy creates change and change is always difficult especially if the new policy is unpopular with teachers, parents, or students. Principals implementing policy changes in stressful situations are more likely to make mistakes than they otherwise might make. In order to avoid these mistakes, the prudent principal will reflect on previous issues of policy implementation, ferreting out problems that occurred in the past. This helps reduce the stress and concerns of policy implementation. Concerning the parking lot problem, the principal put together a solution that required students to register their vehicle for a nominal fee with the school. This fee was to be used to maintain the parking lots and to build several speed bumps along the extended part of the school's driveway. The board of education added to the policy by stating that all individuals parking on the school's lot should be charged a parking fee. The policy was implemented and the teachers association immediately protested. This became an item in the district's collective bargaining agreement. An unintended consequence of policy development is an issue that all principals must consider when creating new policy.

Principals need to be aware of hot-button issues at the state and national levels. State legislatures are more involved in education policy than ever before in the history of schooling. Principals need to be aware of what is happening in their state legislature and in some cases at the federal level, especially in the social and economic environment. Some of these discussions will eventually become policy issues for the principal to implement.

Principals are in a position to influence policy decisions at the state and federal levels if they are willing to become involved. Influence can be optimized with face-to-face conversations with specific state and federal policy decision makers. Making personal contacts with legislative aides, state department of education personnel, and executive directors of professional associations provide the most efficient use of time in influencing policy makers. Principals need to attach themselves to professional organizations that help influence state and federal policies. Principals have a very different role than they once had. They need to be more aggressive in providing leadership, and if they fail to provide this leadership they will be more likely to be surprised about policy changes than they would be if they were participants in the policy dialogue.

Mazzoni (1991) develops a framework to explain policy implementation and development. He defines an "arena" as "the political interactions characterizing particular decisions sites through which power is exercised to initiate, formulate, and enact public policy" (116). He identifies four policy arenas:

- Subsystem
- Commission
- Leadership
- Macro

The arena where the policy is developed is important since it identifies the people, resources, and politics that will be developed and implemented. The subsystem arena is made up of legislators and influential educators working in concert to establish educational policy. The subsystem is long-standing and not likely to disappear.

The commission arena is the place where new policy is created using unique and interesting strategies for policy development. This arena goes beyond the minor tinkering that legislators attempt to do every time they meet. Most legislators fail to address the real issues in terms of policy; they mostly focus on making sure they support their specific parties' agenda.

The leadership arena may create innovative policy, if the members of the leadership are on the same policy page. In addition, these leaders generally will move forward on changes as long as the political pressure remains low. When the political pressure becomes substantial, these leaders abandon the change. As long as the special interest groups remain on the sideline, these leaders remain in the game.

In the macro arena, more people are involved in the policy development with wide-ranging agendas with politics becoming the overriding factor. The macro arena takes into consideration public opinion, the media, increased resources, and increased leadership. As the politics of policy development increases, the usefulness of policies decreases.

Policy develops in all of the arenas. The commission and leadership arenas work together as politicians and educational leaders select members to serve on local and state commissions. At the subsystem arena smaller and less visible committees are used by the leaders to develop and refine policy (Mazzoni 1991).

In the scenario at the beginning of this chapter, Mr. Flores was totally confused by the agenda outlined by the local chamber of commerce. If Mr. Flores would use the Mazzoni policy model, he would discover that the subsystem of legislators and influential educators was supporting the ideas outlined by the chamber. Perhaps the local chamber of commerce was operating in the commission arena as it attempted to change the direction of Cameron High School. Moving from the traditional college-bound agenda to one that promotes the education of students in a way that meets the new technologies utilized by businesses is important to the local economy. The macro arena certainly lends itself to the diversity of any chamber of commerce and the varying opinions that exist in a group of this type.

Most principals have experienced pressure to change and have observed arena shifts occurring at the state and local levels. These arena shifts may or may not lead to policy changes (Freedman and Hughes 1998). Most of the time, major policy changes require additional resources that never trickle down to the student. It is the principal's responsibility to make sure these policy makers understand the impact the proposed changes have on students.

If policy is to be an instrument of leadership for the principal, it must be seen by the school's stakeholders as an instrument of leadership. The principal's use of policy must get the teachers, students, and parents to move to action according to the principal's purpose (Gardner 1986). To accomplish this task, the principal should focus policy toward the following:

- Policy should focus on the long term
- Policy should influence stakeholders
- Policy should bring all constituent groups together for one common purpose
- Policy should focus on the principal's vision for the school
- Policy creation should be a process that adapts to the needs of the organization
- Policy should direct the school's expectations (Van Alfan 1993)

As the principal involves him- or herself in policy creation, he or she is most certainly becoming involved in school leadership. The principal must understand that in order to develop this leadership policy statements must create expectations in the stakeholders. As these stakeholders focus on specific areas of change, the stronger their bond becomes and the greater the opportunity they have to get their policy implemented. As the process of policy development becomes more routinized, the opportunity for the principal to become a leader is greater.

Policies should reflect the "big picture" rather than the small segments of individual wants and needs. Policies might be seen as global goals with direction. These statements should not contain specific skills or commands but rather an overall direction. Principals must make sure that policies are directed at the best interests of students and their achievement. Without this direction, policies can and will become weights around the necks of the students, teachers, parents, and the principal.

ETHICAL DISCUSSION

Should the School Allow Advertising on Buildings, Buses, and Athletic Fields?

The school's role in the community's economic development is much more important than most principals would believe. The economic expansion of a community is directly tied to the quality of schools in the community. The programs that schools deliver affect the attraction and retention of businesses. Principals might want to consider advertising on buildings and athletic fields as additional sources of revenue. These sources of revenue help defray the costs of student and teacher materials, thus keeping school taxes from escalating.

Other stakeholders believe that public property should not be used by businesses for advertising goods and services. They believe that the benefit of additional dollars does not outweigh the political cost of implementing advertising and its effect on students. The decision by this group of stakeholders in based on what, in their opinion, is best for students.

The questions that need to be asked are:

- Should the principal assume the responsibility for determining whether the school uses advertising?
- Is the use of advertising on school property unethical? Why or why not?

- Should students be subjected to daily advertising in the school building and at athletic events?
- Students using computers in the school library are subjected to advertising as they use computer search engines. Should students be restricted from using these computer search engines as they complete class assignments?
- Does advertising affect student behavior in a negative manner? If so, how?
- Should parents be involved in the decision to use advertisements on school property?
- Does the cost benefit of school advertising outweigh any negative aspects of school advertising?
- Ethical dilemmas are right-versus-right issues. Which side of the advertising debate do you support and why?

CHAPTER SUMMARY

The school's role in the local economy and its economic development is much more important than most principals would believe. The development of jobs and income in the community sustains the schools and in turn quality schools sustain the local workforce. Principals need to work with the local economic development committee to make sure educational programs meet the needs of the community's businesses.

School advertising provides an additional revenue stream for each school and can be used to supplement school budgets. The use of advertisements on buildings, athletic fields, and school buses is common practice in school districts. Advertising has gone beyond these facilities when students go to the library to conduct research using computers, on printed book covers, and via television. Students are subjected to advertising in many forms and they also benefit from reduced costs for athletic wear when the school agrees to use specific brands of athletic equipment. The case for advertising is mixed at best and is controversial in most contexts.

Schools are responsible for supplying the community with workers for the various businesses. While some would argue that supplying the workforce is not the role of the school, it is impossible to believe that these individuals would argue that the community is required to supply operating dollars while not getting anything in return.

Apprenticeships appear to meet the needs of both the school and the community. The apprenticeship provides the student with a saleable skill, reduces the educational costs of the school, and provides community workforce. The combination of on-the-job training and attached instruction provide students with skills that the normal educational program cannot and will not provide. For individuals who believe that apprenticeship programs are not for the academically talented, reconsider the following: The apprenticeship program requires dedicated and ambitious students who are willing to make sacrifices in order to earn the training and knowledge they need to be successful.

The economic impact on schools is found in ways to "do more with less" or "do a lot more with a little more." For those who subscribe to the "do more with less" money concept, they believe that money does not cure the problems of educating children. The "do a lot more with a little more" crowd is willing to increase the resources if the money is spent as it sees fit. This becomes a targeted increase for schools that may not need what money is designed to improve.

State and local governments spend public money on education in order to satisfy their belief that education benefits the state and local communities. Education is the state's way of making sure that students are knowledgeable and have the necessary skills to compete for good paying jobs and at the same time keeping students off of the streets and out of prison.

Increasing school expenditures has both a positive and negative effect on the economy. The determination of success or failure is dependent on how the money is spent. The argument continues to rage about the impact of additional dollars on schools. The principal is accountable to the public for making sure that the educational funds made available to the school are used to purchase a quality education for children. Connecting school inputs and outputs is a task for the principal and certainly there is a mixed review when using input and output measures to assess the quality of student learning.

The economic impact of class schedules is based on the number of teachers the schedule would require to staff the schedule. Reducing class size increases the cost of the schedule and enlarging class size reduces the cost. For example, moving from the accelerated block schedule to any other scheduling format increases the cost because it would increase the number of teachers needed to staff the schedule. At the elementary level, the most expensive scheduling model is the self-contained classroom model. For example, the continuous progress learning schedule reduces the cost of personnel by about 20 percent. This is accomplished by staffing at various salary levels within the school structure.

The unintended consequences that policies create can be both harmful and destructive for the principal. Principals implementing policy changes in a stressful situation are more likely to make mistakes than they otherwise might make. Avoiding these mistakes is based on the principal's ability to ferret our prior mistakes and take corrective action. In order to avoid mistakes, principals must be aware of hot-button issues at the state and local levels. In addition, the principal must be influential at the state and local levels.

Policy is an instrument of leadership for the principal and must be used to influence teachers, students, parents, and community stakeholders. Being involved in policy creation is a stepping stone to community leadership for the principal. Policies should reflect the "big picture" of what the community stakeholders want and need. These policies become global goals for the school.

CHAPTER ACTIVITIES AND QUESTIONS

1. Investigate your community's economic development committee and discuss with your colleagues how you could become part of the committee.
2. Create a five-minute speech supporting the use of advertising on school property.
3. Write a white paper defending the use of computer advertising in the school library.
4. In conjunction with a business in your community, develop an apprenticeship program that benefits the school, the business, and the student.
5. Create a marketing plan to help sell the apprenticeship program you have created.
6 What effect does the local economy have on your school?
7. How can schools "do more with less" or "do a lot more with a little more"?

8. The funding of schools has traditionally focused on the distribution of resources. How has this changed from equitable distribution to productivity?
9. Describe the impact of changing your school's present schedule in terms of cost to the district.
10. Describe the unintended consequences of a policy that was implemented in your district.
11. Describe the process you would use in creating a policy for your campus.
12. Policies should reflect the "big picture" of the organization. How would you make sure this was happening with the policies you are creating?

CASE STUDY ACTIVITIES AND QUESTIONS

1. How could you as principal of Cameron High School make sure you are aware of the economic needs of the community?
2. What strategies should Mr. Flores use with the chamber of commerce to ensure its support for Cameron High School?
3. If you were principal of Cameron High School, how would you find out about the economy and demographics of the area?
4. Would you support the work of Ms. Watkins and if so how much credence would you place on the work?
5. If you were Mr. Flores, would you share the report with the community? Support your decision in writing.
6. How would you attempt to convince people that the projections from the report were accurate?

REFERENCES

Alexander, K., and Alexander, M. D. (1998). *American public school law*. 4th ed. Belmont, CA: Wadsworth.

Baker, K. (1991). "Yes, throw money at schools." *Phi Delta Kappan* 72: 628–631.

Clune, W. H. (1994). "The shift from equity to adequacy in school finance." *Educational Policy* 8: 376–394.

Committee for Economic Development. (1994). *Putting learning first: Governing and managing the schools for high achievement.* A Statement by the Research and Policy Committee of the CED. New York: Committee for Economic Development.

Fowler, F. C. (2000). *Policy studies for educational leaders.* Upper Saddle River, NJ: Prentice-Hall.

Fox, W., Murray, W., and Murray, M. (1990). "Local politics and interregional business development." *Southern Economic Journal* 57: 413.

Freedman, H. E., and Hughes, A. L. (1998). "The development of educational policy in Connecticut." Paper presented at the annual meeting of the American Educational Research Association (ERIC Document Reproduction Services no. ED 422 649).

Gardner, J. W. (1986). *The tasks of leadership.* Washington, DC: Independent Sector.

Guthrie, J. W., and Koppich, J. (1987). "Exploring the political economy of national education reform." In *The politics of excellence and choice in education,* ed. W. L. Boyd and C. T. Kerchner. London: Falmer.

Hanushek, E. A. (1994a). "A jaundiced view of 'adequacy' in school finance reform." *Educational Policy* 8: 460–469.

———. (1994b). *Making schools work: Improving performance and controlling costs.* Washington, DC: Brookings Institute.

Hashberger, K. (2001). "Apprenticeships are still preparing workers." *Blue Ridge Business Journal,* at www.wc.cc.va.us/ (accessed February 18, 2002).

Hy, R. J. (2000). "Education is an investment: A case study." *Journal of Educational Finance* 26 (2): 209–218.

James, R. (2001). "Apprenticeship gives employer, student a boost." *Blue Ridge Business Journal,* at www.wc.cc.va.us/ (accessed January 15, 2002).

Kazel-Thresher, D. M. (1993). "Educational expenditures and school achievement: When and how money can make a difference." *Educational Researcher* (March): 30–32.

Mazzoni, T. L. (1991). "Analyzing state school policymaking: An arena model." *Educational Evaluation and Policy Analysis* 13 (2): 115–138.

Miles, K. H. (1995). "Freeing resources for improving schools: A case study of teacher allocation in Boston public schools." *Educational Evaluation and Policy Analysis* 17 (4): 476–493.

National Association of State Directors of Pupil Transportation Service. (2001). "Advertising on school buses." At www.nasdpts.org (accessed January 15, 2002).

Nordenberg, M. A. (1999). "Preparing workers for jobs of the future." *Case Studies,* at www.accdpel.org (accessed January 15, 2002).

Penner, C. (2001). "Does advertising have a place at library school?" At www.gslis.mcgill.ca/ (accessed January 15, 2002).

Picus, L. O. (2000). "How schools allocate and use their resources." Clearing-house on Educational Management, at eric.uoregon.edu (accessed January 15, 2002).

San Diego Committee against Registration and the Draft v. The Governing Board of Grossmont Union High School District, 790 F. 2d 1471 (9th Cir. 1986).

Sloggett, G., and Woods, M. D. (2001). "Critical factors in attracting new business and industry to Oklahoma." Oklahoma Extension Facts, F-862, at ag-web.okstate.edu/pearl/ (accessed February 2, 2002).

Van Alfan, C. (1993). "School board policy as an instrument of empowering leadership in America." Paper presented at the annual conference on Creating Quality Schools (ERIC Document Reproduction Services no. ED 358 518).

Fort Spirit School District
Background and Information Data

The information and data is provided as a source to help solve the various case situations attached to each chapter. This fictitious nature of this school district in no way resembles any past, present, or future school district.

Elementary Mathematics Scores by Campus on the State Accountability Examination

School	African American	Hispanic	White	Asian Pac. Is.	Male	Female	Econ. Disadv.	Spec. Educ.
Bethany	89.9%	88.9%	92.1%	94./6%	90.1%	92.1%	89.2%	66.8%
Bethany Springs	90.2%	92.0%	94.6%	98.4%	92.1%	94.5%	90.2%	83.7%
Cameron	56.7%	60.2%	64.8%	89.1%	62.1%	65.1%	61.0%	39.8%
City Line Road	92.1%	91.2%	92.0%	97.2%	90.1%	92.4%	90.2%	67.8%
East	79.8%	71.4%	92.8%	93.7%	82.3%	83.8%	69.7%	61.5%
Falcon	84.6%	69.8%	90.8%	99.8%	82.9%	82.1%	67.7%	76.9%
Forsythe	86.9%	87.1%	90.2%	94.6%	88.1%	90.3%	87.3%	55.8%
High Tech Avenue	60.0%	62.9%	91.5%	**	92.9%	88.1%	76.5%	55.6%
Logan	85.4%	86.3%	89.8%	**	88.4%	88.7%	85.2%	54.7%
New Area Road	94.7%	94.2%	95.1%	**	92.8%	95.6%	79.8%	77.7%
Northwest	90.1%	91.2%	98.1%	**	92.1%	94.3%	81.7%	76.2%
Old Cameron Road	89.3%	84.3%	92.2%	**	88.2%	89.2%	82.6%	56.1%
Tractor Plant Road	81.3%	87.2%	90.2%	87.4%	86.2%	89.3%	82.1%	41.7%
Walk-up Road	87.7%	87.8%	87.9%	92.7%	86.1%	88.3%	87.0%	79.2%

**No Students in this Category

Elementary Reading Scores by Campus on the State Accountability Examination

School	African American	Hispanic	White	Asian Pac. Is.	Male	Female	Econ. Disadv.	Spec. Educ.
Bethany	85.1%	91.5%	93.8%	93.8%	92.0%	94.7%	87.1%	56.3%
Bethany Springs	95.1%	90.2%	98.3%	93.2%	90.4%	96.2%	89.7%	65.8%
Cameron	70.1%	72.4%	82.8%	78.8%	76.5%	80.2%	74.5%	45.7%
City Line Road	91.2%	90.1%	97.2%	89.3%	91.2%	95.4%	**	87.3%
East	78.4%	83.8%	94.8%	75.4%	87.2%	91.7%	82.2%	69.4%
Falcon	81.1%	88.5%	97.0%	71.7%	93.5%	96.3%	89.3%	100.0%
Forsythe	87.2%	65.8%	93.8%	77.6%	85.1%	89.8%	77.1%	51.4%
High Tech Avenue	81.3%	80.0%	95.6%	**	98.0%	92.9%	93.3%	60.0%
Logan	79.1%	81.4%	90.2%	**	89.1%	91.2%	86.7%	57.1%
New Area Road	88.8%	87.2%	94.7%	**	89.9%	94.3%	90.7%	79.2%
Northwest	82.4%	81.2%	89.7%	**	80.4%	87.6%	77.3%	51.0%
Old Cameron Road	89.1%	91.3%	90.1%	**	89.2%	92.1%	85.4%	63.7%
Tractor Plant Road	57.6%	87.2%	88.4%	90.2%	85.8%	91.7%	82.8%	77.1%
Walk-up Road	92.1%	92.4%	90.7%	94.5%	89.7%	93.1%	89.8%	72.4%

**No Students in this Category

Elementary Writing Scores by Campus on the State Accountability Examination

School	African American	Hispanic	White	Asian Pac. Is.	Male	Female	Econ. Disadv.	Spec. Educ.
Bethany	91.2%	90.1%	95.8%	96.8%	93.1%	96.1%	90.0%	84.5%
Bethany Springs	92.7%	91.8%	98.5%	97.6%	94.1%	97.0%	91.3%	88.1%
Cameron	78.7%	76.8%	84.1%	78.9%	76.2%	78.8%	72.1%	42.3%
City Line Road	90.2%	89.9%	94.7%	91.1%	90.2%	93.2%	89.5%	87.6%
East	81.7%	79.1%	95.7%	81.7%	85.7%	90.1%	79.5%	72.2%
Falcon	78.8%	74.6%	91.8%	98.4%	86.4%	82.3%	74.2%	76.9%
Forsythe	81.6%	82.5%	90.3%	85.3%	83.7%	85.6%	76.4%	31.4%
High Tech Avenue	80.0%	80.0%	96.6%	**	98.0%	95.0%	84.6%	56.7%
Logan	87.1%	87.7%	89.9%	**	87.1%	89.4%	86.2%	29.3%
New Area Road	93.6%	93.1%	94.1%	**	93.2%	94.8%	86.7%	88.1%
Northwest	89.1%	83.2%	88.2%	**	84.1%	86.2%	86.1%	73.3%
Old Cameron Road	76.1%	74.2%	78.9%	**	75.1%	76.3%	72.2%	40.1%
Tractor Plant Road	89.1%	90.2%	93.4%	79.6%	89.7%	94.7%	90.2%	76.8%
Walk-up Road	90.1%	87.1%	90.0%	97.4%	90.0%	92.2%	90.1%	77.8%

**No Students in this Category

Intermediate and Secondary Mathematics Scores by Campus on the State Accountability Examination

School	African American	Hispanic	White	Asian Pac. Is.	Male	Female	Econ. Disadv.	Spec. Educ.
Bethany H.S.	83.3%	80.0%	93.3%	100.0%	93.1%	92.6%	92.3%	72.0%
Cameron H.S.	50.0%	76.2%	95.3%	90.2%	86.2%	90.3%	66.0%	65.2%
Deleon Inter.	87.6%	83.5%	91.7%	100.0%	86.5%	88.3%	81.7%	67.1%
Foster M.S.	90.1%	88.9%	92.6%	**	89.7%	88.1%	88.5%	37.6%
High Tech Avenue M.S.	**	**	94.6%	88.9%	92.3%	95.6%	77.8%	60.0%
Kennedy Inter.	95.1%	94.9%	96.1%	97.2%	95.4%	96.9%	89.3%	79.6%
Mary Motley H.S.	84.6%	81.2%	80.1%	81.2%	80.3%	82.1%	81.2%	**
Moss Inter.	86.8%	88.4%	91.2%	**	88.2%	90.1%	82.3%	68.4%
New Directions H.S.	82.4%	86.2%	85.4%	92.1%	86.3%	87.3%	84.2%	**
Reagan Inter.	**	91.2%	96.2%	97.4%	95.6%	95.1%	**	**
Sierra M.S.	60.0%	75.0%	92.8%	86.3%	84.6%	85.3%	75.7%	33.3%
South Cameron H.S.	80.1%	81.1%	87.3%	89.4%	83.2%	85.3%	82.0%	52.2%
South Park M.S.	66.7%	68.8%	88.5%	**	68.2%	72.3%	65.7%	41.2%
Waldorf Inter.	89.2%	87.1%	91.7%	93.7%	88.7%	89.3%	78.2%	65.8%

**No Students in this Category

Intermediate and Secondary Reading Scores by Campus on the State Accountability Examination

School	African American	Hispanic	White	Asian Pac. Is.	Male	Female	Econ. Disadv.	Spec. Educ.
Bethany H.S.	83.3%	93.3%	97.6%	100.0%	97.3%	97.2%	97.2%	77.3%
Cameron H.S.	66.7%	78.4%	95.7%	87.2%	86.7%	91.9%	76.9%	61.5%
Deleon Inter.	83.7%	81.6%	90.7%	85.4%	83.1%	88.4%	87.3%	57.8%
Foster M.S.	87.8%	74.9%	92.4%	**	69.0%	79.1%	73.9%	51.0%
High Tech Avenue M.S.	**	**	93.6%	100.0%	90.6%	97.3%	85.0%	50.0%
Kennedy Inter.	97.4%	96.3%	98.1%	100.0%	94.8%	97.9%	89.1%	87.3%
Mary Motley H.S.	82.1%	83.2%	81.2%	82.1%	82.0%	83.0%	89.7%	**
Moss Inter.	87.8%	88.4%	90.2%	**	89.1%	90.2%	83.2%	45.7%
New Directions H.S.	86.2%	88.3%	87.2%	95.0%	87.1%	88.3%	85.1%	**
Reagan Inter.	**	93.4%	97.6%	98.4%	94.3%	96.9%	**	**
Sierra M.S.	80.0%	79.0%	93.3%	86.8%	86.4%	88.4%	79.3%	58.7%
South Cameron H.S.	81.1%	82.1%	89.7%	90.4%	83.2%	85.3%	82.1%	57.6%
South Park M.S.	66.7%	76.8%	90.8%	**	75.5%	82.8%	74.0%	55.0%
Waldorf Inter.	90.1%	89.7%	93.8%	92.7%	90.1%	92.9%	80.1%	67.8%

**No Students in this Category

Intermediate and Secondary Writing Scores by Campus on the State Accountability Examination

School	African American	Hispanic	White	Asian Pac. Is.	Male	Female	Econ. Disadv.	Spec. Educ.
Bethany H.S.	100.0%	93.3%	97.1%	100.0%	94.2%	99.5%	100.0%	77.9%
Cameron H.S.	100.0%	90.4%	96.5%	87.2%	91.0%	97.4%	88.9%	60.9%
Deleon Inter.	84.8%	83.7%	92.7%	86.3%	84.2%	88.4%	86.2%	59.8%
Foster M.S.	87.9%	83.2%	90.7%	**	81.5%	85.5%	82.4%	46.3%
High Tech Avenue M.S.	**	**	91.7%	77.8%	86.7%	95.8%	70.6%	64.7%
Kennedy Inter.	98.4%	96.3%	97.9%	100.0%	94.8%	96.9%	87.1%	86.1%
Mary Motley H.S.	81.2%	82.1%	80.1%	81.1%	82.0%	83.0%	84.6%	**
Moss Inter.	87.6%	89.4%	92.3%	**	89.9%	90.4%	82.1%	42.8%
New Directions H.S.	85.3%	86.2%	85.3%	93.7%	85.2%	87.3%	83.9%	**
Reagan Inter.	**	95.7%	99.0%	98.9%	96.2%	97.8%	**	**
Sierra M.S.	80.0%	81.5%	91.8%	88.2%	86.1%	88.7%	83.4%	53.8%
South Cameron H.S.	82.9%	83.8%	90.4%	91.4%	83.2%	86.2%	80.1%	58.1%
South Park M.S.	80.0%	80.1%	93.5%	**	79.5%	84.6%	78.2%	50.0%
Waldorf Inter.	92.1%	91.8%	95.8%	95.7%	91.1%	94.7%	82.2%	70.8%

**No Students in this Category

Elementary Certified And Support Staff by Campus

Campus	Num. Teachers	Num. Students	Num. Asst. Prin.	Couns	Librarian	Vocal Music	Phys. Educ.	Nurse	G&T Teach/ Coord.	Spec. Educ.
Bethany	43	903	3	2	1	1	2	1	2	2
Bethany Springs	38	798	2	3	1	1	2	1	6	3
Cameron	25	500	0	1	1	½	½	1	1	1
City Line Road	25	525	0	2	1	1	2	1	4	3
East	18	345	0	1	1	½	½	½	1	1
Falcon	17	357	0	1	1	½	½	½	1	1
Forsythe	22	455	0	1	1	½	½	½	1	1
High Tech Avenue	37	756	2	1	1	1	1½	1	5	2
Logan	19	395	0	1	1	½	½	½	1	1
New Area Road	30	630	1	1	1	1	1½	1	4	2
Northwest	16	336	0	1	1	½	½	½	1	1
Old Cameron Road	18	378	0	1	1	½	½	½	1	1
Tractor Plant Road	19	387	0	1	1	½	½	½	1	1
Walk-up Road	20	420	0	1	1	½	½	½	1	1

Elementary School Student and Teacher Ethnicity by Campus

Campus	Students				Teacher/Administrator			
	African American	Hispanic	White	Asian/ Pac. Is.	African American	Hispanic	White	Asian/ Pac. Is
Bethany	1.0%	—	98.0%	1.0%	0.5%	—	99.5%	—
Bethany Springs	1.5%	1.5%	96.0%	1.0%	2.0%	1.0%	94.3%	2.7%
Cameron	26.2%	19.8%	51.3%	2.7%	3.2%	2.5%	94.5%	—
City Line Road	19.0%	20.1%	56.9%	3.0%	—	—	97.3%	2.7%
East	58.1%	23.5%	10.4%	9.4%	0.5%	1.3%	98.2%	—
Falcon	24.6%	25.8%	49.1%	0.3%	—	2.7%	96.1%	1.2%
Forsythe	33.1%	8.3%	56.5%	2.1%	—	0.8%	94.1%	5.1%
High Tech Avenue	—	—	99.7%	0.3%	—	1.3%	98.7%	—
Logan	12.5%	8.9%	78.6%	—	1.2%	5.1%	93.7%	—
New Area Road	0.7%	23.9%	85.4%	—	—	—	99.5%	0.5%
Northwest	14.2%	38.1%	47.7%	—	—	—	100.0%	—
Old Cameron Road	51.8%	1.2%	47.0%	—	12.5%	—	87.5%	—
Tractor Plant Road	1.7%	53.5%	35.3%	1.2%	1.5%	2.9%	95.6%	—
Walk-up Road	5.7%	43.6%	40.4%	10.3%	0.5%	13.2%	84.8%	1.4%

Secondary Certified And Support Staff by Campus

Campus	Num. Teachers	Num. Students	Num. Asst. Prin.	Couns	Librarian	Vocal Music	Instrum Music Educ.	Spec.	Nurse
Bethany H.S.	120	251	3	8	1	2	4	1	1
Cameron H. S.	97	1,660	2	6	1	2	3	4	1
Deleon Inter.	32	789	1	2	1	1	1	3	1
Foster M.S.	28	710	1	3	1	1	2	3	1
High Tech Ave. M.S.	47	1,352	2	5	1	2	2	2	1
Kennedy Inter.	52	1,306	3	4	1	2	2	5	1
Mary Motley H.S.	8	75	0	2	0	0	0	0	0
Moss Inter.	27	605	1	2	1	1	0	3	1
New Directions H.S.	12	120	0	2	0	0	0	0	0
Reagan Inter.	48	1,199	3	4	1	1	1	1	1
Sierra M.S.	31	820	1	3	1	1	2	2	1
South Cameron H.S.	89	1,513	2	6	1	2	3	1	1
South Park M.S.	27	701	1	3	1	1	2	1	1
Waldorf Inter.	37	903	3	3	1	1	1	3	1

Secondary School Student and Teacher Ethnicity by Campus

Campus	Students				Teacher/Administrator			
	African American	Hispanic	White	Asian/ Pac. Is.	African American	Hispanic	White	Asian/ Pac. Is
Bethany H.S.	1.0%	1.0	93.0%	5.0%	—	1.0%	98.0%	1.0%
Cameron H.S.	19.1%	20.2%	58.4%	1.9%	3.1%	1.0%	95.9%	—
Deleon H.S.	21.4%	43.7%	34.0%	0.9%	1.0%	3.1%	95.9%	—
Foster M.S.	19.8%	11.2%	69.0%	—	2.7%	3.2%	94.1%	—
High Tech Ave. M.S.	—	—	97.1%	2.9%	1.0%	—	98.6%	0.4%
Kennedy Inter.	1.1%	1.4%	96.3%	1.2%	—	—	100.0%	—
Mary Motley H.S.	37.0%	33.0%	28.0%	2.0%	—	—	100.0%	—
Moss Inter.	14.5%	15.1%	70.4%	—	—	1.5%	98.5%	—
New Directions H.S.	30.0%	35.0%	30.0%	5.0	25.0%	50.0%	25.0%	—
Reagan Inter.	—	2.1%	94.7%	3.2	—	—	97.1%	2.9%
Sierra M.S.	10.1%	47.6%	40.1%	2.2	1.8%	3.1	94.1%	1.0%
South Cameron H.S.	10.3%	9.8%	77.8%	2.1	1.0%	—	95.6%	3.4
South Park M.S.	0.8%	14.1%	85.1%	—	—	1.0%	99.0%	—
Waldorf Inter.	15.6%	15.4%	68.1%	1.9%	2.4%	5.7%	90.8%	1.1%

Index

About the Authors

Edward H. Seifert has spent the past thirty-five years serving as a school superintendent, high school principal, assistant principal, university faculty member, university department chair, and assistant dean in two colleges of education. He has written and published more than one hundred journal articles, book chapters, and books and has made numerous presentations on the leadership and management functions of the principalship. Dr. Seifert has worked with state and national professional committees and organizations as they attempted to change the focus of the principalship.

Dr. Seifert is currently working on a change process that requires principals to understand, analyze, and develop prescriptions for changing instruction. This process is predicated on his belief that the only way to change schools is to change the way instruction is delivered to students. One element of this process is discussed in chapter 6 of this book when he makes the case for student gain in learning as the essential measurement of school quality and success. His Ed.D. degree is from Oklahoma State University.

James Vornberg is a lifelong educator with twenty-nine years of service teaching in higher education. He is presently professor and department head of educational administration at Texas A&M University, Commerce. For the past seventeen years, he has been the director of the Principals Center, which serves principals with staff development programs. He has also been a public school teacher and an administrator.

Dr. Vornberg's academic career has been focused primarily on the principalship where he has taught more than 1,600 graduate students in his principalship classes over the years. A member of both the National Elementary and Secondary Principals Associations, he has worked closely with practicing principals in consulting roles. He is the author of more than fifty journal articles and monographs as well as the editor of a textbook in administration that is now in its eighth edition: Texas Public School Organization and Administration. More than sixty doctoral students have completed their dissertations under his guidance. His master's and doctorate are from the University of Arizona.